THE LIFE AND SELECTED WRITINGS OF THOMAS JEFFERSON

THE LIFE AND SELECTED WRITINGS OF

THOMAS JEFFERSON

EDITED AND WITH AN INTRODUCTION BY
ADRIENNE KOCH AND WILLIAM PEDEN

THE MODERN LIBRARY
NEW YORK

1998 Modern Library Paperback Edition

LIBRARY OF CONGRESS CATALOGING-IN-PUBLICATION DATA
Jefferson, Thomas, 1743–1826.
[Selections. 1998]
The life and selected writings of Thomas Jefferson/edited and with an introduction
by Adrienne Koch and William Peden.—Modern Library paperback ed.
p.   cm.
Includes index.
ISBN 0-375-75218-8
1. Jefferson, Thomas, 1743–1826. 2. United States—Politics and government—
1775–1783—Sources. 3. United States—Politics and government—1783–1809—Sources.
4. Presidents—United States—Biography. I. Koch, Adrienne, 1912–1971.
II. Peden, William Harwood, 1913–   . III. Title.
[E302.J442   1998b]
973.4'6'092—dc21   [b]   98-21092

Modern Library website address: www.modernlibrary.com

Printed in the United States of America

6   8   9   7

Preface

This selection from the writings of Thomas Jefferson is planned to be a comprehensive presentation of his thought. The greatest amount of space has been allotted to his letters, in the belief that they are of primary importance in revealing the man and his intellect. Jefferson's two original full-length works, the *Notes on Virginia* and the *Autobiography*, are given virtually complete. Along with his best-known public papers, selections from his minor writings are also included. Together, all these serve to depict the man who more aptly than any of his countrymen might be called the American Leonardo.

Despite its limitations, the Memorial Edition (Andrew A. Lipscomb and Albert Ellery Bergh, eds., *The Writings of Thomas Jefferson*, 20 vols., The Thomas Jefferson Memorial Association, Washington, D. C., 1905) has been used as the basis of the text. The Ford Edition, though better edited, does not offer the quantity and variety of the Memorial Edition. Whenever the Memorial Edition is not the source, we have cited the editor or author, or the manuscript collection from which an item is taken.

We wish to thank the staffs of the Alderman Library of the University of Virginia and of the Library of Congress for their generous co-operation.

Contents

INTRODUCTION   xvii

I   AUTOBIOGRAPHY   3
Including The Declaration of Independence

II   THE ANAS   105

III   TRAVEL JOURNALS   123

IV   ESSAY ON ANGLO-SAXON   141

V   BIOGRAPHICAL SKETCHES   159

VI   NOTES ON VIRGINIA   173

VII   PUBLIC PAPERS   269

A Summary View of the Rights of British America, 1774   273
An Act for Establishing Religious Freedom, 1779   289
Report of Government for the Western Territory, 1784   291
Opinion of Secretary of State, July 15, 1790   293
Opinion of Secretary of State, March 18, 1792   293
Opinion of Secretary of State, April 28, 1793   294
Opinion of Secretary of State, December 16, 1793   296
Inaugural Address, March 4, 1801   297
First Annual Message, December 8, 1801   301
Reply to Danbury Baptist Association, January 1, 1802   307
Indian Address, January 7, 1802   308
Second Annual Message, December 15, 1802   308
Third Annual Message, October 17, 1803   309
Fourth Annual Message, November 8, 1804   313
Second Inaugural Address, March 4, 1805   313
To the General Assembly of North Carolina,
    January 10, 1808   318
To the Society of Tammany, February 29, 1808   319
Eighth Annual Message, November 8, 1808   320

VIII LETTERS   323

To: John Harvie, Jan. 14, 1760   327
    John Page, Dec. 25, 1762   327
    John Page, July 15, 1763   331
    John Page, Oct. 7, 1763   331
    Robert Skipwith, Aug. 3, 1771   332
    Dr. William Small, May 7, 1775   334
    John Randolph, Esq., Nov. 29, 1775   335
    Francis Eppes, July 15, 1776   336
    John Fabroni, June 8, 1778   338
    Col. James Monroe, May 20, 1782   339
    François Jean, Chevalier de Chastellux, Nov. 26, 1782   340
    Martha Jefferson, Dec. 22, 1783   341
    Col. Monroe, June 17, 1785   341
    Dr. Price, Aug. 7, 1785   342
    The Count de Vergennes, Aug. 15, 1785   343
    Mrs. Trist, Aug. 18, 1785   346
    Peter Carr, Aug. 19, 1785   347
    John Jay, Aug. 23, 1785   351
    Baron Geismer, Sept. 6, 1785   352
    James Madison, Sept. 20, 1785   353
    Mr. Bellini, Sept. 30, 1785   355
    Hogendorp, Oct. 13, 1785   356
    J. Banister, Jr., Oct. 15, 1785   358
    Rev. James Madison, Oct. 28, 1785   360
    A. Stuart, Esq., Jan. 25, 1786   362
    James Madison, Feb. 8, 1786   364
    John Page, May 4, 1786   364
    Mr. Wythe, Aug. 13, 1786   366
    Mrs. Cosway, Oct. 12, 1786   367
    James Madison, Dec. 16, 1786   377
    John Jay, Jan. 9, 1787   379
    Monsieur de Creve-coeur, Jan. 15, 1787   379
    Col. Edward Carrington, Jan. 16, 1787   381
    James Madison, Jan. 30, 1787   382
    Madame la Comtesse de Tessé, March 20, 1787   384
    Martha Jefferson, March 28, 1787   386

To: Martha Jefferson, April 7, 1787 388
   The Marquis de Lafayette, April 11, 1787 389
   James Madison, June 20, 1787 391
   T. M. Randolph, Jr., July 6, 1787 393
   Edward Carrington, Aug. 4, 1787 395
   Col. Monroe, Aug. 5, 1787 396
   Peter Carr, Aug. 10, 1787 397
   John Adams, Aug. 30, 1787 401
   John Adams, Nov. 13, 1787 402
   Col. Smith, Nov. 13, 1787 403
   James Madison, Dec. 20, 1787 403
   E. Carrington, Dec. 21, 1787 408
   Mr. A. Donald, Feb. 7, 1788 408
   The Count de Moustier, May 17, 1788 410
   William Carmichael, May 27, 1788 411
   Col. Carrington, May 27, 1788 412
   Mr. Izard, July 17, 1788 413
   E. Rutledge, July 18, 1788 414
   Mr. Cutting, July 24, 1788 415
   James Madison, July 31, 1788 416
   James Madison, Nov. 18, 1788 417
   Dr. Price, Jan. 8, 1789 418
   John Jay, Jan. 11, 1789 422
   Francis Hopkinson, March 13, 1789 424
   James Madison, March 15, 1789 426
   Col. Humphreys, March 18, 1789 428
   Dr. Willard, March 24, 1789 430
   General Washington, May 10, 1789 431
   Monsieur de St. Etienne, June 3, 1789 432
   John Jay, June 24, 1789 434
   John Jay, June 29, 1789 438
   Thomas Paine, July 11, 1789 440
   John Jay, July 19, 1789 442
   James Madison, Sept. 6, 1789 448
   William Hunter, Esq., Mayor of Alexandria,
      March 11, 1790 453
   The Marquis de Lafayette, April 2, 1790 454

To: Maria Jefferson, April 11, 1790   455
Mr. Thomas Mann Randolph, May 30, 1790   456
John Garland Jefferson, June 11, 1790   457
Maria Jefferson, June 13, 1790   459
Count de Moustier, Dec. 13, 1790   460
Martha Jefferson Randolph, Dec. 23, 1790   461
Mr. Hazard, Feb. 18, 1791   461
Major L'Enfant, April 10, 1791   462
Thomas Mann Randolph, June 5, 1791   463
T. M. Randolph, July 3, 1791   464
John Adams, July 17, 1791   465
William Short, July 28, 1791   466
Benjamin Banneker, Aug. 30, 1791   467
Martha Jefferson Randolph, Jan. 15, 1792   468
The President of the United States, May 23, 1792   468
Thomas Paine, June 19, 1792   474
The President of the United States, Sept. 9, 1792   474
William Short, Jan. 3, 1793   478
James Madison, June 9, 1793   479
The President of the United States, July 31, 1793   482
Eli Whitney, Nov. 16, 1793   483
John Adams, April 25, 1794   483
Tench Coxe, May 1, 1794   484
James Madison, Dec. 28, 1794   485
Monsieur d'Ivernois, Feb. 6, 1795   486
M. de Meusnier, April 29, 1795   488
Mann Page, Aug. 30, 1795   489
George Wythe, Jan. 16, 1796   490
Philip Mazzei, April 24, 1796   492
John Adams, Dec. 28, 1796   493
James Madison, Jan. 1, 1797   494
Elbridge Gerry, May 13, 1797   495
Edward Rutledge, June 24, 1797   498
Elbridge Gerry, Jan. 26, 1799   499
Edmund Pendleton, Jan. 29, 1799   501
Maria Jefferson Eppes, Feb. 7, 1799   502
Edmund Randolph, Aug. 18, 1799   503

To: Dr. Joseph Priestley, Jan. 18, 1800 506
Dr. Joseph Priestley, Jan. 27, 1800 507
Dr. William Bache, Feb. 2, 1800 509
Samuel Adams, Feb. 26, 1800 509
Dr. Benjamin Rush, Sept. 23, 1800 510
Martha Jefferson Randolph, Jan. 26, 1801 511
T. M. Randolph, Feb. 19, 1801 512
John Dickinson, March 6, 1801 513
Dr. Joseph Priestley, March 21, 1801 514
Samuel Adams, March 29, 1801 516
Robert R. Livingston, Sept. 9, 1801 517
The Secretary of the Treasury (Albert Gallatin),
    April 1, 1802 518
Dr. Benjamin Rush, April 21, 1803 519
General Horatio Gates, July 11, 1803 523
Monsieur Cabanis, July 12, 1803 524
Wilson C. Nicholas, Sept. 7, 1803 524
Jean Baptiste Say, Feb. 1, 1804 526
Judge John Tyler, June 28, 1804 527
C. F. C. de Volney, Feb. 8, 1805 528
The Chiefs of the Cherokee Nation, Jan. 10, 1806 529
The Reverend Doctor G. C. Jenner, May 14, 1806 531
John Norvell, June 11, 1807 532
Governor James Sullivan, June 19, 1807 533
Dr. Casper Wistar, June 21, 1807 534
Monsieur DúPont de Nemours, July 14, 1807 536
Charles Pinckney, March 30, 1808 537
The Prince Regent of Portugal, May 5, 1808 538
Monsieur Lasteyrie, July 15, 1808 539
Thomas Jefferson Randolph, Nov. 24, 1808 540
Thomas Leiper, Jan. 21, 1809 543
John Hollins, Feb. 19, 1809 544
M. Henri Grégoire, Évêque et Sénateur à Paris, Feb. 25, 1809 544
Monsieur DuPont de Nemours, March 2, 1809 545
The Inhabitants of Albemarle County, in Virginia,
    April 3, 1809 546
John Wyche, May 19, 1809 547

To: Dr. B. S. Barton, Sept. 21, 1809 548
Rev. Samuel Knox, Feb. 12, 1810 549
General Thaddeus Kosciusko, Feb. 26, 1810 550
Governor John Langdon, March 5, 1810 553
Governor John Tyler, May 26, 1810 554
Colonel William Duane, Aug. 12, 1810 555
J. B. Colvin, Sept. 20, 1810 556
Dr. Benjamin Rush, Jan. 16, 1811 556
Colonel William Duane, March 28, 1811 561
Dr. Benjamin Rush, Aug. 17, 1811 562
John Adams, Jan. 21, 1812 564
F. A. Van der Kemp, March 22, 1812 566
James Maury, April 25, 1812 567
John Melish, Jan. 13, 1813 568
Colonel William Duane, Jan. 22, 1813 572
Colonel William Duane, April 4, 1813 573
John Adams, May 27, 1813 573
John Adams, June 27, 1813 574
Dr. Samuel Brown, July 14, 1813 575
Isaac McPherson, Aug. 13, 1813 576
John Adams, Oct. 13, 1813 577
John Adams, Oct. 28, 1813 579
Dr. Thomas Cooper, Jan. 16, 1814 580
Monsieur N. G. Dufief, April 19, 1814 581
Thomas Law, Esq., June 13, 1814 582
John Adams, July 5, 1814 586
Edward Coles, Aug. 25, 1814 586
Peter Carr, Sept. 7, 1814 588
Dr. Thomas Cooper, Sept. 10, 1814 594
Samuel H. Smith, Esq., Sept. 21, 1814 594
William Short, Esq., Nov. 28, 1814 596
The Marquis de Lafayette, Feb. 14, 1815 598
James Maury, June 15, 1815 599
Albert Gallatin, October 16, 1815 600
Colonel Charles Yancey, Jan. 6, 1816 601
Charles Thomson, Jan. 9, 1816 603
Joseph C. Cabell, Feb. 2, 1816 603

To: Joseph Milligan, April 6, 1816   605
   John Adams, April 8, 1816   609
   John Taylor, May 28, 1816   611
   Samuel Kercheval, July 12, 1816   615
   John Adams, Aug. 1, 1816   618
   Mrs. Abigail Adams, Jan. 11, 1817   618
   Charles Thomson, Jan. 29, 1817   620
   Joseph Delaplaine, April 12, 1817   620
   Baron Alexander Von Humboldt, June 13, 1817   622
   Monsieur Barbé de Marbois, June 14, 1817   622
   George Ticknor, Nov. 25, 1817   624
   John Trumbull, Jan. 8, 1818   624
   Count Dugnani, Feb. 14, 1818   625
   Dr. Benjamin Waterhouse, March 3, 1818   626
   Nathaniel Burwell, Esq., March 14, 1818   628
   John Adams, Nov. 13, 1818   630
   Dr. Vine Utley, March 21, 1819   630
   Mr. Laporte, June 4, 1819   632
   William Short, Oct. 31, 1819   633
   Dr. Thomas Cooper, March 13, 1820   636
   John Holmes, April 22, 1820   637
   William Short, Aug. 4, 1820   638
   John Adams, Aug. 15, 1820   639
   William Roscoe, Dec. 27, 1820   640
   John Adams, Sept. 12, 1821   641
   James Smith, Dec. 8, 1822   642
   Robert Walsh, April 5, 1823   643
   John Adams, April 11, 1823   644
   General Samuel Smith, May 3, 1823   646
   The President of the United States (James Monroe),
     Oct. 24, 1823   646
   Monsieur A. Coray, Oct. 31, 1823   649
   The Marquis de Lafayette, Nov. 4, 1823   650
   Mr. David Harding, President of the Jefferson Debating
     Society of Hingham, April 20, 1824   651
   Major John Cartwright, June 5, 1824   651
   Henry Lee, August 10, 1824   652

To: Charles Sigourney, Aug. 15, 1824   653
    John Adams, Jan. 8, 1825   654
    Thomas Jefferson Smith, Feb. 21, 1825   655
    Henry Lee, May 8, 1825   656
    Ellen W. Coolidge, August 27, 1825   657
    Dr. James Mease, Sept. 26, 1825   659
    George Washington Lewis, Oct. 25, 1825   660
    James Madison, Feb. 17, 1826   663
    Roger C. Weightman, June 24, 1826   665

Introduction

by Adrienne Koch and William Peden

----------------------------- ✍ -----------------------------

The writings of Thomas Jefferson are today more meaningful than ever before in America's history. No better record of the social principles which are the heart of the American democratic "experiment" exists than these letters and documents. Those who are eager to know the varied and subtle character of the *man* will find in them another, not inconsiderable, reward. No leader in the period of the American Enlightenment was as articulate, as wise, as conscious of the implications and consequences of free society as he. To Jefferson, therefore, we must go for fresh contacts with the commanding personalities and events of those days, and for the fullest expression of government through consent, through reason, through law, and through energetic and progressive change.

Thomas Jefferson was born on April 13 (April 2, Old Style), 1743, at Shadwell, the most important of the tobacco plantations owned by his father Peter Jefferson, in the Virginia upcountry. A vigorous and intelligent man, although uneducated, Peter Jefferson became a successful surveyor, prosperous landowner, and member of the Virginia House of Burgesses from Albemarle County. His wife Jane Randolph, a member of one of the most distinguished Virginia families, could trace her pedigree far back in English and Scottish annals. Concerning this, Jefferson, late in life, laconically remarked, "To which let every one ascribe the faith and merit he chooses."

Perhaps the young Jefferson might not have made such a statement. Certainly as a child he enjoyed to the full the numerous advantages accompanying his family's substantial position: the books, the horses, the good life of the "Big Houses" at Tuckahoe and Shadwell. And when Peter Jefferson died he left his fourteen-year-old son not only valuable lands and property—the base and measure of Virginia wealth at that time—but sound and loving advice. Denied a formal education himself, he was careful to direct that his son be given complete classical training. Years later, Thomas Jefferson often referred to the effect the classical moralists, philosophers, poets, and dramatists had had upon him. Quite honestly he could say, in 1800, "I thank on my knees, Him who directed my early education, for having put into my possession this rich source of delight; and I would not exchange it for anything which I could then have acquired. . . . " No matter how scientific and progressive Jefferson became in his outlook, the moral and political wisdom of Greece and Rome continued to give depth and flavor to his thought.

As his father had stipulated, Thomas studied at Reverend Mr. Maury's school, just a few miles from Shadwell. After two years' coaching by this "correct classical scholar," in the spring of 1760 he left his native Albemarle to attend William and Mary College.

During these early years in Williamsburg, colonial capital of Virginia, Jefferson gives every evidence of enjoying to the full the parties, the music, the dancing, the flirtations, the versifying, the punch-drinking—in short, the good society of the sparkling young Virginians who were his friends. Fond of cotillions, the theatre, and races, he is far from unhappy in these frivolous surroundings. No Beau Brummel, the tall gangling redhead possessed humor, warmth, and intelligence which won him many close friends. Apparently more successful in gaining the boon companionship of friends like John Page than in capturing the hearts of the Williamsburg belles, he occasionally luxuriates in the despondent mood of a romantic failure. Jefferson's letters devoted to this theme, sometimes gay, sometimes gloomy, but always dashed off in the extreme and impetuous language of youth, are a good corrective to the serious picture painted of him by keepers of the public faith.

But indications of discipline and earnestness are present as solidly as rocks in a swirl of water. Jefferson's passion for rationalization, as well as his pose of stoic detachment, is well illustrated in his "love affair" with Rebecca Burwell. In the midst of a dance in the Apollo Room of the Raleigh Tavern, later the scene of momentous political stratagems, Jefferson blurted a stumbling marriage proposal to his "Belinda." Subjecting even this action to his habit of deliberation, shortly thereafter he confessed to Page careful plans for his travel and further education abroad. Meanwhile "Belinda," one surmises, must patiently await his return, schooling herself in the duties necessary for a Virginia house-wife and manager. Jefferson alone was surprised, and even he did not claim to be morally injured, when the spirited girl announced her engagement to a less phlegmatic and more immediate suitor.

Jefferson had already matured intellectually more than the average diligent student. He became a favorite of the social and intellectual leaders of Williamsburg, including Dr. William Small, his learned professor of mathematics and moral philosophy; George Wythe, foremost legal mind in Virginia; and Governor Fauquier, finished gentleman and patron of the arts. Respected for his abundant intellectual curiosity and his modest but sympathetic nature, Jefferson was a welcome fourth at the dinner parties in the Governor's Palace, where the group engaged in spirited discussions of ideas, politics, literature, and music. Jefferson was a good conversationalist—not in the sense of being a self-conscious perfectionist, but rather because of his almost organic interest in ideas, and his tireless curiosity about human nature, history, and science. His letters suggest the kind of talk he was capable of: courteous, deferential, mild; completely honest and sincere; steeped in the flavor of philosophy yet integrated with specific data drawn from his own experience and wide reading.

After graduating from William and Mary in the spring of 1762, Jefferson studied law five years under George Wythe. His attitude toward the law is in itself a good index to his sense of values. Knowledge of the law, an essential prerequisite to an understanding of governmental procedure, he respected. He recognized the fact that good government depended upon law as the stabilizer of national will. Realizing the terminological hair-splitting of lawyers as a group and aware of the crushing weight of precedent in law, he regarded it merely as an instrument of the people's service and protection rather than as their master. It was fitting, then, that he become a successful practicing lawyer, but even more fitting that he should forsake the single practice of law as a career.

Jefferson was just turning thirty when he began his political career in earnest. In January of 1772 he had married the much courted and girlish widow, Martha Wayles Skelton. With her, he had established residence in his still incompleted Monticello, not far from his old home Shadwell, which had been destroyed by fire in 1770. By the time of his marriage, he already possessed some political experience. As a law student in Williamsburg, he had been impressed by Patrick Henry's "splendid display" of oratory in the Virginia House of Burgesses debates concerning the Anti-Stamp Act Resolutions of 1765. He had been a member of the Virginia House of Burgesses from 1769, where his first action was an unsuccessful bill allowing owners to free their slaves.

The impending crisis in British-Colonial relations, however, soon overshadowed routine affairs of legislature. In 1772 public indignation against George the Third's political and economic tyranny had culminated in the burning of the British revenue cutter *Gaspee*. When the Crown threatened to transport to England the "traitors" suspected of the deed, a small group of Virginia patriots, including Jefferson and Patrick Henry, decided that colonial committees of correspondence were needed as protection against further British encroachments.

Inevitably, inter-colonial bonds were cemented by such actions. In 1774, for example, the first of the "Intolerable Acts" closed the port of Boston until Massachusetts should pay for the Boston Tea Party of the preceding year. When this news reached Williamsburg, Jefferson and other younger members of the Virginia Assembly, now in control of formulating Virginia policy, ordained a day of fasting and prayer to demonstrate their sympathy with Massachusetts. Thereupon, Virginia's Royal Governor Dunmore once again dissolved the Assembly. Meeting, as usual, in the Apollo Room of the Raleigh Tavern, the members then planned to call together an inter-colonial congress.

The machinery for this dynamic national action having been set up, Jefferson began writing resolutions which were more radical and better written than those from other counties and colonies. He rehearsed some arguments against British tyranny in his "Resolves for Albemarle County." This was soon followed by Jefferson's impassioned tract on natural rights and limited privileges, "A Summary View of the Rights of British America." Read at the Virginia convention in Williamsburg (August, 1774), these resolutions were considered too revolutionary and not adopted. They were printed, however, and widely circulated. Thenceforth, important writing assignments almost automatically were entrusted to Jefferson.

When Jefferson arrived in Philadelphia in June, 1775, as a Virginia delegate to the Second Continental Congress, he already possessed, as John Adams remarked, "a reputation for literature, science, and a happy talent of composition." It was inevitable that the Congress make full use of this happy talent, and almost immediately Jefferson's pen was enlisted in the cause of independence. When he returned to the Congress the following year, he was appointed to the five-man committee, including Benjamin Franklin and John Adams, which was charged with the most momentous assignment ever given in the history of America: the drafting of a formal declaration of independence from Great Britain. On Jefferson alone was placed the responsibility of preparing the draft. The confidence placed in him as a man to make and weigh judgments, to reason cogently in legal, historical, and political affairs, and to write with feeling and technical mastery was strikingly justified. The document, after heated debate, was finally approved by Congress on July 4, 1776. Cut and occasionally altered by Adams, or Franklin, or the Congress itself, the Declaration is almost completely Jefferson's, and is undoubtedly the triumph and culmination of his early career. Jefferson was not unaware of the importance of this document. It, along with his "Statute of Virginia for Religious Freedom," and his work in founding the University of Virginia, is one of the three things he wished remembered in his epitaph.

By the age of thirty-three, his reputation as a master of the art of government by committee was great. Had he chosen political leadership it is logical to believe he could have attained it. Instead, he made the choice which shows instantly the kind of man he was and would always prefer to be. His absence had been felt at home by his wife, who was in poor health. His estate needed his management. He preferred to return to Mrs. Jefferson and Monticello, and to give his public service to Virginia.

Three years of hard work and little glory followed this choice. Returning to the Virginia House of Delegates in October, 1776, Jefferson at once set to work on a carefully planned reform of the laws of Virginia, a reform aimed, in effect, at the realization of the "inalienable rights" of man embodied in the Declaration of Independence.

He lost no time in successfully introducing a bill to reorganize the courts of justice, and another, still more important, to abolish primogeniture and entails, thereby terminating an antiquated patrician pattern of society. Then, along with George Wythe and Edmund Pendleton, he devoted his energies to a thorough revision of the laws of Virginia. This revision was completed in 1779; the majority of its bills, however, were not enacted until 1785 or later. Herein, Jefferson made the most of his opportunity to modernize and to prune from the body of the law some of its flagrant redundancies. Further, he surveyed the whole field of education, and proposed a systematic plan of statewide education. And, as his crowning effort, he attempted to write religious toleration into the laws of Virginia by separating Church and State; when the "Bill for Establishing Religious Freedom" was finally passed in 1785, he considered it a major contribution to American society.

In addition to leading this social revolution in Virginia, Jefferson found time to enjoy the companionship of his wife and children, to study nature and delight in its wonders, to cultivate his lands and manage his private affairs, to ride and read and write vigorous letters to his many friends and acquaintances. It was not long, however, before public life again claimed him.

In June of 1779, Jefferson was elected Governor of Virginia. He commenced his career as a public executive, sanguine, confident of his abilities, assured of the respect and almost the affection of his commonwealth. Any other years, however, would have been less fraught with pitfalls for the head of a state. Jefferson took up his duties at a time when the British were raiding Virginia; in control of the sea, they could send forth plundering parties to capture food and ammunition, and destroy property. Indian warfare on Virginia's western border was a perpetual source of worry and unrest. The treasury funds were at their lowest ebb in Virginia's history. General Washington needed support from Virginia in the north. Men and supplies were required to support the new nation on battlefields in the Carolinas. By 1781 the Governor found himself in the plight of watching, with hands almost tied, the British sweep through his state, burning and ravaging as they advanced. Jefferson petitioned General Washington to dispatch troops to meet the threat of Cornwallis's invasion, but Washington, hard pressed in the north and short of men, could do nothing. Consequently the burden of Virginia's defense fell upon an untrained and insufficient militia. Jefferson himself narrowly escaped capture at the hands of troops dispatched by Colonel Tarleton. The legislators, at considerable loss of face, were forced to flee their new capital city of Richmond. Jefferson, as head of the state, was inevitably singled out for criticism and abuse.

No evidence has ever shown that Jefferson failed in his attempts to provide a suitable defense for Virginia. Later material indeed, including his letters to Generals Washington and Greene, shows him to have been an extraordinarily conscientious Governor, diligent, zealous, careful of the welfare of his fellow-citizens. Perhaps a dictator was wanted. This Jefferson would not and could not be. The crisis over and his second term at an end, he influenced his friends to support a military governor and announced his retirement.

Washington's complete approval of Jefferson's actions as Governor is in marked contrast to the heated charges of dereliction of duty made by certain members of the legislature. When the war fever subsided, the same legislature shamefacedly passed a resolution officially clearing Jefferson of all such charges. These experiences would have been cruel for any public figure; for Jefferson, with his whole-souled attitude toward public service and his extreme sensitivity to hostility of any kind, his last months as Governor had been crushing ones. Nevertheless, politically and intellectually he was a tougher man from that point onward; he had developed a realism which was to stand him in good stead in later years.

Home at Monticello, Jefferson buried himself in writing. In June of 1781 he had injured his wrist and was unable to ride for some time. During this period of enforced idleness, he wrote careful replies to a series of questions about Virginia put him by the Marquis de Marbois, Secretary of the French Legation at Philadelphia. The careful observations Jefferson had been making for years about the surrounding country, its climate, its natural beauties, its fauna and flora, minerals, waterways, agriculture, and its government somehow added up to an impressive total. The manuscript was later the *Notes on Virginia*. This remarkable book, as rich in its minute analysis of the details of external nature as in its clarification of moral political, and social issues, was read by savants and scientists of two continents for years to come.

The intellectual exhilaration and comfort Jefferson derived from these months of writing was soon submerged by the greatest personal tragedy he had ever borne. His wife, ill since the birth of their last daughter in May, 1782, died early in September of the same year. Jefferson kept to his room for three weeks thereafter, pacing, in the words of his daughter Martha, "almost incessantly night and day, only lying down occasionally, when nature was completely exhausted." A man of extreme reserve, he rarely mentioned his wife in his letters. Yet it was well known among his intimates that he never forgot this woman he had lived with and loved for ten years. Many, many, years later, when Lafayette lost his own wife, he wrote to Jefferson as the one man who could best understand the peculiar depth of sorrow he was then enduring.

In the months following Mrs. Jefferson's death, Monticello lost much of its normal charm for the lonely refugee from politics. Previously he had steadily declined numerous appointments. But the day came when he was in a mood to accept an offer from Congress to go to Europe to negotiate peace. His mission, however, was cancelled when it was learned that preliminary negotiations had already been engineered. Shortly thereafter (in June, 1783), the General Assembly of Virginia elected Jefferson a delegate to the Confederation Congress where he again headed important committees and drafted many reports and official papers. Here, he criticized the proposed currency system and provided, in his "Notes on the Establishment of a Money Unit," a sound coinage system to take its place. He drew up a draft for temporary government of the Western Territory (the original of his better-known "Ordinance of the Northwestern Territory"), stressing the importance of equality between the original and the new states, and attempting to exclude slavery from all the territories He advocated the necessity of more favorable international commercial relations, and compiled, in April and May of 1784, instructions for ministers negotiating commercial treaties with European nations.

Finally, on May 7, 1784, Jefferson was appointed Minister Plenipotentiary of the United States to assist Benjamin Franklin and John Adams, both of whom had preceded him to Europe to arrange commercial agreements. Thus, through the medium of commerce, Jefferson entered the European stage where diplomacy and society, arts and sciences, revolution and love were to provide him the richest years of his life.

In one sense, Jefferson was experienced and highly civilized before he set out for Paris. In another, his real understanding of men and ideas matured in Europe. That complex pattern of habits which had characterized Jefferson up to this time—his curiosity, his patient observation, his learning, his attention to the manners, the personalities and the needs of the people around him—was crystallized during his five-year residence abroad. He listened attentively to foreign philosophers, to foreign writers, to foreign politicians and statesmen of all creeds, doctrines, and dogmas. He bought books, many of them, wandering by the hour among the second-hand bookstalls on the Quai, "hand-picking" his volumes, gathering the treasures of classical learning, of humanism and the Renaissance, of the advanced, rational European age in which he was then so active. He met the leaders of French society. He became a favored *habitué* of the most intellectual and powerful salons in Paris. In 1785, on Franklin's departure for America, Jefferson was made Minister Plenipotentiary to the Court of France. He was regarded favorably as a symbol of rational, republican America, Virginia-gentleman style—not, as he had so gracefully commented, "replacing" Franklin, but "succeeding" him admirably.

Lafayette proved to be an invaluable friend. He coached Jefferson in the intricacies of European royal politics; his friends and acquaintances were made accessible to the American Minister when he needed information or contacts. Jefferson, in his turn, advised the impetuous nobleman and patriot. His experience as a fighter for a free democratic republic was inestimably valued by Lafayette, who consulted Jefferson more and more as the forces of revolution began to make themselves felt throughout France. He brought his numerous political friends to listen to the talk of Jefferson and the men gathered at his table. Jefferson at this time believed that, through discussion of the people's needs and the King's privileges, compromise was possible. He thought that a limited monarchy, capable of solving the pressing national problems, could be achieved without bloodshed. He proposed that a charter of rights be offered by the King to the people, and went so far as to write a draft of the charter which he sent to Lafayette.

That Jefferson should speak his mind concerning matters of fundamental political principle was inevitable. Occasionally, disturbed at his violation of that neutrality which tends to make ciphers of visiting diplomats, he withdrew into the shell of his reserve, and maintained the proprieties, keeping silent even when he knew what was happening and knew what was needed to direct or avert it. One meeting, at Lafayette's request, took place at Jefferson's residence, where eight leading members of the "Patriot" (Reform) Party spent several hours projecting a constitution in behalf of the Assembly. Jefferson later justified his conduct by explaining that he had sat by in complete silence while their "chaste eloquence" reigned. The next morning he called on Count Montmorin, the Foreign Minister, to explain why his house had been pressed into such service, and to offer apologies. Montmorin, who already knew what had taken place, strongly urged Jefferson's assistance in all such future meetings, knowing, he said, that Jefferson would throw his weight only on the side of "wholesome and practicable reformation."

These were happy, as well as politically stirring and intellectually stimulating, years for Jefferson. Martha, his oldest daughter, had accompanied her father from the beginning; a year and a half later, little Mary arrived in Paris to reside under the watchful eye of her adoring papa. And in the summer of 1786 he met Maria Cosway, one of the most beautiful and gifted women in the French or British capitals. The wife of a fashionable English painter, charming, talented, warmly feminine, Maria Cosway affected Jefferson as no other woman ever would again. When the Cosways left Paris in the fall of 1786, Jefferson was desolate and wrote her the longest letter of his life, the impassioned "Dialogue between the Head and the Heart," in which his restraint makes the head win, but so unconvincingly that both writer and lady must have been wretched with the logic of the argument. On his subsequent trips through Southern France and Italy, and later, Jefferson wrote to her again, more intimately than before. That Maria Cosway returned his affection is unquestionable. While Jefferson, in succeeding years, urges Maria to come to Paris without the great following of friends and admirers who manage to steal her from him, she reproaches him for not writing enough, for not coming to London to visit for a long time, for not, in truth, allowing his heart to triumph over his head.

Enjoying the fulness of his life in Paris, only the most urgent duties could have persuaded Jefferson to leave the Continent. He wished his daughters to grow up in the world in which they would have to marry and live; he believed it was necessary to renew personal contact, for a short time, with his own people and government. For these reasons, he thought it best to return to America. Just before leaving he wrote a brief farewell note to Maria Cosway in London, more affectionate than usual and full of references to a speedy return. It was late in October of 1789 when he sailed for America from Cowes. He never went back.

Almost unconsciously, little by little, his European experiences had increased the range and power of Jefferson's political understanding. Although he was the first to insist on loyalty to America and things American, his view of history and government was so broad that he had no respect for the cultural isolationists whose ignorance of European affairs was being converted into a fetishistic patriotism. He returned, bringing to his countrymen a knowledge of comparative statecraft almost unparalleled at that time. He had grown wise in the ways of the commercial and financial world through his role as promoter of American commerce abroad, and by his efforts to pull American credit out of the slump into which it had fallen in the banking houses and bourses of Europe. He had traveled through France, Italy, Holland, Germany; he had visited England; and every place he went he was not only the American diplomat, but the student of the useful sciences. He showed tireless interest in local methods and improvements, jotting down notes on variations in making wine and cheese, planting and harvesting crops, and raising livestock. His keen eye had missed no single detail of wages for workers, the kind and quantity of food they normally consumed, the degree to which they were satisfied or oppressed by their economic opportunities. He sent home information on the culture of rice and capers, of figs and olive trees, and forwarded to America the actual seeds of a variety of grasses not native to America, olive plants, and Italian rice. Nor did he ever miss a nightingale's song, or fail to record the color of the soil and sky.

Returning to America, Jefferson had not only grown inwardly: it seemed to be universal opinion that he had achieved an outstanding success as American Ambassador to France. Even the critical *Edinburgh Review* admitted that "The skill and knowledge with which he argued the different questions of national interest that arose during his residence will not suffer even in comparison with Franklin's diplomatic talents."

American problems proved to be more demanding and just as compelling as those of republican France. The Constitution, which had been adopted during Jefferson's absence and about which he had written critical letters from Paris, was now being launched in earnest. No sooner had Jefferson's ship docked at Norfolk than he saw in a newspaper that President Washington, busy forming his first Cabinet, wished him as Secretary of State. A few days later, in November, he received Washington's letter confirming the news. Jefferson's reply was reluctant, stating his desire to return to France, and his hesitation at undertaking an office at once so important and so confining. The President's courteous but firmly repeated invitation was the next step. A little personal pressure from Madison followed, and the deed was done. There were only a few months left to spend at Monticello, reminiscing about his friends in France, taking leave of them by letter, and preparing himself for the American political world, vibrant with personalities and issues, which he was to enter.

Jefferson was shocked, after arriving in New York in March of 1790, to contrast the political temper and sentiment of French revolutionary patriots with old-guard American loyalists who were the leaders of New York society. The preliminary battle for democratic reliance on the sense and responsibility of "the people" had not been won in these quarters. Jefferson found them hankering after the very system whose corruption and decline he had witnessed in Europe—a system of aristocratic privilege, headed by a King in deed if not in name. These antidemocrats, with their fawning admiration for the British scheme of government, constituted, Jefferson believed, a mountainous obstacle in the path of progress. Earlier, Jefferson had objected vigorously to party membership, stating, "If I could not go to heaven but with a party, I would not go there at all." Despite this attitude, his general support of the Constitution, and his belief in its usefulness in binding together the people and their local governments, had brought him closer to the Federalists than to the anti-Federalists. Now that the Constitution, supplemented by the Bill of Rights, was the unquestioned charter of the democratic system in the United States, there were no existing political parties. Inevitably, however, as conflicts born of clashing political beliefs arose, political parties developed.

Alexander Hamilton, Washington's brilliant and ambitious Secretary of the Treasury, had proved himself a man to be reckoned with even before Jefferson commenced his official duties as Secretary of State. His plan for funding at par the national debt already passed, Hamilton was busy sponsoring his Assumption Bill, which he represented to Jefferson as the only practical method of securing the credit of the United States, particularly abroad. Jefferson, knowing that sharpers and speculators had been buying up the "worthless" paper money from innocent citizens in anticipation of some such national measure, was distrustful of this plan in which the States' debts were to be taken over by the national government. But Hamilton, shrewdly understanding Jefferson's desire to locate the capital city in the South, won Jefferson's support of the Assumption Bill in exchange for northern support of a national capital on the Potomac after a ten-year period in Philadelphia. When Hamilton followed his successful Assumption Bill with chartering the Bank of the United States, and then passing the Excise Bills, Jefferson realized how adroitly he had been duped. The "general principles" which he felt were at issue between Hamilton and himself were fundamentally and irrevocably opposed. All of Hamilton's acts, Jefferson thought, were dominated by one controlling purpose: to establish government by and for a privileged few. Actually Hamilton wanted more than this. He wanted, and vigorously fought for, a king, titles, rule by a central executive and aristocratic aides rather than by representatives of the people.

Jefferson repeatedly thought of retiring from the vexations of a cabinet post in which he was constantly pitted against the most power-hungry man in the capital. The bitter political contest was no longer a matter confined to the comparative quiet of cabinet meetings. Conducted publicly largely through the medium of two partisan newspapers—John Fenno's *United States Gazette,* the mouthpiece of the Hamiltonians, and Philip Freneau's belligerently Jeffersonian *National Gazette*—the issues became, in the heat of conflict, exaggerated or distorted. Groups forming around Madison and Jefferson began to think of themselves as democratic Republicans. Those who sympathized with Hamilton's ideas of centralization of power and approved of his

taxation policy, his encouragement of commerce, and his banking and
credit schemes, became the nucleus of the new Federalist Party.

Only Washington's repeated requests that he remain in office, and
the disturbing developments in French-American relations known to
the world as the "Affair of Citizen Genet" kept Jefferson from returning to Monticello. Citizen Genet had arrived in America in April,
1793, with a revolutionary conception of the role which a French minister abroad could play. His newly established republic was badly in
need of funds to finance the war which had broken out, in February
of 1793, between France and Great Britain. Genet was determined to
get these funds, and to stir up trouble for Great Britain. Jefferson, as
Secretary of State, found himself in a difficult position. He believed
sincerely that France deserved the loyalty and co-operation of the
States. The American people, too, were so enthusiastic in their desire
to support Republican France that war with England was imminent.
Jefferson had to argue with Hamilton and his pro-English supporters
that our treaties with France were still valid, and made it state policy
to honor our debts to France. On the other hand, he was faced with
the problem of moderating the mounting excitement of the American
people and rebuking the increasingly undisciplined Genet who had
ignored Washington's declaration of neutrality (April 22, 1793).
When Genet found that the American advance on the debt to France
was to be less than he had expected, he spoke of going over President
Washington's head and of carrying the issue directly to the people.
Jefferson, despite his sympathy with the French cause, was heartily
disgusted with the French minister—"hot headed, all imagination,
passionate, disrespectful"; in August, his request that Genet be
recalled was acceded to, although Genet remained in this country as
a private citizen.

Jefferson could now see his way to retirement. He had performed
well the difficult task of negotiating his country's foreign affairs. The
President was loathe to see him depart. Even John Marshall, relaxing
momentarily his customary antagonism toward Jefferson, admitted that
"this gentleman withdrew from political station at a moment when he
stood particularly high in the esteem of his own countrymen." More
important to Jefferson, back at Monticello by the middle of January
of 1794, were the rewards of being once more a private citizen, a free

man able to read, to write, to hear music, to talk at leisure with his friends and family, and to express opinions without entering into the daily battle of the capital. He rejoiced in the thought that he had said farewell forever to public life. He felt tired. In his own opinion he was, at fifty, already an old man.

After the first months of his retirement Jefferson recovered his customary energy. He supervised the farming of his estates and designed a plow which revolutionized agriculture; he started a nailery in one of his workshops; he tended his library like a garden; he changed the architectural plans for Monticello, and supervised the construction; he entertained his neighbors and men of good will from all Europe, including a radical French republican and a liberal French ex-nobleman. And inevitably, despite his once firm desire not to meddle with contemporary political problems, he began to write letters of policy to old friends like Madison—letters about avoiding war with Britain, and on the growing power of the "Anglican, monarchical, aristocratical party," the Federalists, who, he felt, were perverting republican principles of government.

After three rather active years of "retirement," Jefferson felt refreshed and encouraged. He evinced renewed interest in politics. When, therefore, the Republican Party drafted him in 1796 to run for President (doing so in face of his express wish that Madison be the party candidate), he dubiously accepted. Jefferson seemed genuinely moved by his Party's preference, yet hesitant to undertake a task of such magnitude. He wrote his objections, however, not as a weary Odysseus but as one mindful of having been one.

So Jefferson ran for President, not against Hamilton, as he might have thought, but against John Adams. The contest was close, with Jefferson finally trailing his Federalist opponent by three votes, which, under the prevailing system, meant being elected Vice President. Jefferson was quite happy to serve under the older Adams, with whom he had worked amicably in Europe and who, he felt, might be induced to abandon some of his Federalist persuasions and serve as an effective barrier against Hamilton. Of all the political positions which Jefferson might have held, that of Vice President seems to have been, at this time, most attractive to him. In March of 1797, Jefferson again returned to Philadelphia, where he could witness the ensuing political drama and have a hand in legislative affairs, without the wearing passions and responsibilities so certain to be the President's.

Jefferson soon realized that the pronounced Hamiltonian tendencies of Adams' cabinet made political compromise impossible. Subsequent events confirmed his impressions. Foreign affairs still constituted the crucible of political conviction for the American people; Anglophiles fought Francophiles until Jefferson sternly recommended a "divorce from both nations." He strove to make the Republicans consciously a peace party. Although the Jay treaty had for the time averted the threat of war with Britain, the decrees of the French Directory against neutral commerce had caused American war sentiment to flare up against France. Jefferson, closely scrutinizing events in Europe, was dismayed by the news that the American peace mission—Gerry, Pinckney, and Marshall—had been flagrantly insulted by Talleyrand's brokers, the men subsequently designated "X. Y. Z." The country at large was aroused by the attempt to obtain a bribe from the American envoys, and a united Federalist-Republican chorus of revenge burst upon the Administration.

The next move was as ill-fated as it was unexpected. The Administration turned upon its political opponents, using the popular hysteria of the war fever of 1798 for its own purposes. In rapid succession it passed the Alien Act, to deport foreign radicals and liberals, propagandists and agitators, and the Sedition Act, to curb the "licentiousness" of the press. The Sedition Act in practice was particularly formidable, empowering the Administration so to fine, imprison, and legally prosecute any opposition writer that the Republicans were virtually muzzled in the remaining years of Adams' administration.

Such was the setting for Jefferson's famous Kentucky Resolution. The Kentucky Resolution, along with Madison's Virginia Resolution, declared the illegality of the Alien and Sedition Laws because of their violation of the Constitution, and were skillfully devised to check the partisan encroachment of the Chief Executive. Just as Jefferson feared a large standing army, and held its presence in France responsible for the emergence of the dictator Bonaparte, so he saw in these Federalist measures, which were eating away the basic guarantees of individual liberty, the re-introduction of despotism. Technically, the issue had to be stated in terms of basic constitutional law, States' Rights, and limited powers of the Chief Executive. Therefore, Jefferson tried to make the existing states serve as barriers against an Administration which was assuming the character of an Inquisition—Jefferson called it a "witch-hunt." Devised primarily as expedients in this particular situation, the underlying principle of the Resolutions is as firm as any article in Jefferson's political creed: that of ensuring freedom of person, of thought and action, of property, to the free citizens of America.

The Republicans were quick to take advantage of the split ensuing in Federalist ranks when President Adams, having listened to suggestions of peace reliably attributed to a chastened Talleyrand, opened negotiations with France. Prior to the presidential election, Adams dismissed his Hamiltonian Secretaries of War and State; Hamilton lost his temper, wrote a pamphlet attacking Adams, and tried to manipulate his erstwhile chief out of the Federalist candidacy, but failed. Clearly, it was the Republican's day, with Jefferson running for President and Aaron Burr for Vice President.

The electoral vote, in marked contrast to the popular vote, resulted in a tie between Jefferson and Burr. The last desperate device of the Federalists, whose campaign against Jefferson had scraped the muddiest bottom of political trickery and libel known at that time, was the Machiavellian ruse of using this deadlock as a lever to extract concessions from Jefferson before he assumed office. Should Jefferson refuse to bargain, they threatened that Burr would be made President in the re-vote. Jefferson stood firm, made no promises, and waited without noticeable loss of composure through the really dangerous week of balloting when rumors throughout the capital whispered of a bill to cede the Administration to the Federalists. He at last triumphed when the Federalists gave way before his obvious merits and the people's obvious choice.

Mindful of Adams and Marshall's unseemly effort to sew up the incoming administration by packing American courts with Federal judgeships, lawyers, and clerks; recalling the feverish days when fundamental American rights had been revoked in the very home of the "great experiment"; remembering the defiant, fantastic schemes for South American exploitation projected by Hamilton; still smarting from the slander, the unclean epithets picturing him as infidel, atheist, and apostle of the "race-track and the cock-pit," Jefferson wrote his

Inaugural Address. In the light of such events, Jefferson's feeling that the triumph of the people and of the Republican Party was a revolution comparable to that of 1776 is understandable. America, he felt, had been plunged into terrifying depths of political intrigue and corruption, yet had managed to recover. The Inaugural Address of March 4, 1801, in accents of unfeigned piety, rejoiced that the democratic experiment had been given a new lease on life.

As President, Jefferson's first project was to eradicate the intolerance which had recently infected America, and to do it quickly before it became a permanent part of the national heritage. Sounding the keynote of his administration with the words "We are all Republicans—we are all Federalists," and taking advantage of the lack of affection many of the Federalists now entertained for their party leaders, Jefferson offered them ungrudging union with the Republicans. For the most part, they accepted. Much of the rancor and party strife of the preceding decade was obliterated during Jefferson's first months as President. His policy of general reconciliation and reform and his success in freeing the victims of the Alien and Sedition laws were generally supported by a favorable Congress. He was aided greatly in his Presidential duties by a sympathetic and capable Cabinet headed by the ever-reliable Madison as Secretary of State, and including the Swiss economic expert Albert Gallatin who, as Secretary of the Treasury, saw eye to eye with Jefferson on questions of reduced taxation, government frugality, and a minimum public debt. Although his simple manners as President in the newly established capital city of Washington irked and bewildered some people who thought his very avoidance of ceremony ostentatious, Jefferson's popularity as a public figure was greater during his first term as President than at any other time in his entire career. Even the depredations of the Barbary pirates had been swiftly crushed and Jefferson could remark to a friend that things were noiseless, "unattractive of notice"—a sure sign that society was happy.

Such noiselessness and happiness were soon disturbed, however, by the menacing news that Spain by the secret treaty of San Ildefonso (1800) had transferred to France its rights over the mouth of the Mississippi, the port of New Orleans, and the great stretch of land constituting the province of Louisiana. Western farmers and merchants depended upon the outlet of New Orleans for their shipping; Jefferson, even during his career as Secretary of State, had been aware of the strategic importance of Louisiana. Louisiana in the strong hands of the French rather than the weak hands of Spain placed an almost insurmountable obstacle in the path of American growth and prosperity. It was essential that America acquire the Louisiana territory—either through peaceful negotiation or by war. When the French dictator Napoleon, fearing the renewal of war with Great Britain, suddenly offered to sell for $15,000,000 not only the port of New Orleans but the entire fabulous slice of land from the Mississippi to the Rockies, Jefferson was confronted with perhaps the most momentous problem of his career.

For years Jefferson had been the guardian of democratic rights for the individual, small local units, and the states. He had taken his stand on the "strict construction" interpretation of the Constitution. Now he was faced with a decision in which quick—and unauthorized—executive action would guarantee doubling America's territory and increasing the chance of maintaining the self-government and independence for which American blood had already been spilled. Was he to take Napoleon's offer and violate a cherished principle, or should he wait upon a Constitutional amendment authorizing such an act and possibly lose the very territory so vital to national existence and well-being? In very genuine distress, he wrote to his friends Thomas Paine, John Breckenridge, and Wilson Cary Nicholas, soliciting their opinions. Eventually, of course, after tremendous moral strain, Jefferson authorized the purchase, the treaty being signed on May 2, 1803. Although he was reluctant to do so, he was fortified largely by the consideration that his dictatorial use of power was in this case the lesser evil.

The subtleties of principle underlying this purchase were of small concern to Americans in general. The financial bigwigs of New York and New England still feared and opposed him; nor had reactionary and orthodox churchmen completely abandoned their habit of tongue-lashing the "Atheist." But without question Jefferson's first term closed in a blaze of glory when the people, united in their national good fortune, almost unanimously sent their President back for a second term.

Busy as he had been during these momentous years, Jefferson had found time to follow his favorite intellectual pursuits. He had not only aided in establishing a National Library, but had made many valuable additions to his own private collection. He had pondered the morality of early Christianity with liberal thinkers like Priestley and Rush. He had found time to enlarge his extensive collection of primitive Indian vocabularies. His interest in science and agriculture had remained as keen as ever. In short, these were rich and productive years, marred solely by the death of Maria (Jefferson) Eppes, his younger daughter, a blow comparable only to the loss suffered years before upon the death of his wife.

As his second term began, Jefferson was plunged into difficulties against which his ingenuity or wisdom could make little headway. The national and international strife which characterized his second administration is in marked contrast to the comparative tranquility of the earlier years of the century.

The exact boundaries of the territory retroceded from Spain to France, and thereafter sold to America, had never been accurately established. Jefferson's knowledge of American maps and geography together with research in his valuable collection of Americana at Monticello, convinced him that the land of Western Florida was included in the Louisiana Purchase. He was avowedly eager to possess not only Western Florida but Eastern Florida and Texas as well, as all were essential to a solid American coastline on the Gulf of Mexico. He directed negotiations for this purpose through his envoys in Spain and through the Spanish Minister in Washington. In 1805, when a state of war existed between England and Spain, he considered a "provisional alliance" between America and her old enemy England, as a possible means of achieving the expansion of America. Still later, he tried to purchase the territory. Although frustrated in all these attempts, his policy bore fruit in later years when all the disputed territory finally came into the possession of the United States.

The problems of rounding out America's natural boundaries were minor, however, compared with the deluge of European interference with our shipping. Powerful British mercantile interests had long been worried by America's emergence as a maritime power. In April, 1806, England culminated her blows against American shipping in a blockade of the Continental coast. In November of the same year, Napoleon retaliated with decrees blockading Britain. The practical effect of such blockades on a neutral country like America was severe impairment of its European import and export trade, amounting virtually to ultimate economic annihilation.

Further, as seizure of American ships by the belligerents mounted and as impressment of seamen on American vessels grew more frequent, American prestige was seriously threatened. Jefferson had proclaimed that "peace was his passion," and there is every reason to believe that it was. He also had judgment to back his passion, in this case, since America could gain nothing at this time by war with powerful England or France. For these reasons, Jefferson judged it essential to fight a delaying action. The Non-Intercourse Act of 1806 and the much discussed Embargo terminating all foreign commerce of the United States (1807) were measures promulgated in this spirit. Jefferson described the Embargo as "the last card we have to play short of war"; and he was determined that it *be* played. Although it meant tying up our trade and shipping until either England or France yielded on the question of the rights of neutral nations to the freedom of the seas, Jefferson saw no equally practical and honorable alternative. It is noteworthy, too, that however much his Embargo was criticized, no workable suggestions were proposed to replace it.

To make still heavier the load of his second term, the domestic front was racked with defections and desertions. Impatient John Randolph of Roanoke had been outraged by Jefferson's conciliatory methods of dealing with the Federalists. Rejecting Jefferson's policy involving territorial controversies with Spain, he led a small but troublesome faction of anti-Administration Republicans in the House of Representatives.

Much more sensational was the Burr conspiracy to lead a revolution in the Western States, and, after welding them into an empire with Mexico, to become their resplendent dictator. John Marshall, presiding over the Circuit Court, used the ensuing treason trial as an opportunity for political warfare against his old enemy Jefferson who, for his part, had betrayed his strong desire for Burr's conviction. The country had not yet forgotten Burr's duel with Hamilton, and never before was a legal case followed by the American public with such intensity. Despite the strength of public opinion against Burr, and many evidences of guilt adduced, he was acquitted by the jury.

As Jefferson's second term drew to a close, the peaceful instrument he had devised to stave off bloodshed was subjected to unrelenting attack. The Embargo had not been able to effect a repeal of the British or French decrees. At home all that big New England shippers and merchants, together with Southern and Western planters and farmers, could see was the stagnation of their export trade before their very eyes. Jefferson himself faced this prospect, and, as a matter of fact, stood to lose as much financially by the Embargo as other landowners did. Ever since the British attack upon the *Chesapeake,* Jefferson had believed that war was the only honorable solution for America. He had also been deeply depressed by John Quincy Adams' news of violent New England opposition to the Embargo which threatened to culminate in secession. In addition, since it had proved impossible to enforce the Embargo, particularly in New York and New England, Jefferson was thoroughly disappointed in the ineffectual measure. Not wishing, however, to set a definite policy for the incoming President to follow, he left the final disposition of the Embargo to the Congress. The Embargo was repealed and replaced with the weaker Non-Intercourse with Great Britain and France Act, a result more of confusion and Republican timidity than a serious step toward the solution of a critical problem. When his Presidential term expired on March 3, 1809, and he was free at last to turn over the reins of government to his trusted successor Madison, Jefferson was surfeited with "politics." The "hated occupation" had absorbed some forty years, and no fields ever looked greener than those which led away from power to the peace and freedom of private life.

Jefferson's real nobility of mind and spirit deepened when he finally returned to Monticello. He was sixty-six when he was at last permitted to live in that intimate, less troubled world where, as he had so often said, his deepest satisfactions were centered. There are men whose political ambitions and prejudices are their chief sources of vital enjoyment. For them, the end of a political career is like the end of life itself. Not so Jefferson, who regarded the realm of knowledge, friendship, and love as ideal and the only one for which he would willingly suffer.

Jefferson's old age is a remarkable proof of the observation made by his daughter Martha that her father had never forsaken a friend or a principle. Jefferson kept alive his acquaintance with friends of Revolutionary days; he wrote to the men and women he had known in France; he continued his spirited contacts with distinguished thinkers and scientists, American and European. He wrote, as always, to Madison and Monroe, to Lafayette and Kosciusko. With Joseph Priestley, Thomas Cooper, Benjamin Waterhouse, and William Short he exchanged searching philosophic opinions. He and John Adams, their earlier political differences reconciled, wrote many letters—provocative, stimulating, probing the mystery of what the human mind had solved in their day, and what it had thus far failed to solve. Jefferson frequently complained about the time consumed in maintaining his ever-increasing correspondence but he could not resist an intellectual challenge or turn down an appeal for his opinion, advice, or help, and continued to discuss with frankness, thoroughness, and a brilliant clarity such diverse subjects as anthropology and political theory, religion and zoology.

There was so much at Monticello to absorb his time and engage his affections that the days never seemed long enough. Over the years his family had gained many new members: by 1811 he was a great-grandfather. Much of the same love and affection he had lavished on his two daughters flourished anew for his grandchildren who, in turn, revered him and cherished his memory for their lifetimes. His estates were in need of personal overseeing. Almost until his death Jefferson went on daily rides over his many acres. Monticello, not yet quite perfect in his eyes, always needed a little altering here or some additional building there. Guests, some of them friends whom Jefferson was delighted to entertain, others mere acquaintances or friends of acquaintances, made their claim upon his time. Occasionally he was forced to flee to Poplar Forest, his estate near Lynchburg, where he could read much in the blessed quiet of his brick cottage, and work on some project which then engrossed him.

In a large sense, Jefferson's major concern during these last years was education and educational philosophy. Personally, Jefferson considered knowledge not only a means to an end, but an end in itself, enjoyed for its own sake. Socially, he felt, it was the key to virtue as it was to happiness. It was the basic necessity for self-government. Free government could exist only by its grace and through its habitual action. Jefferson had safeguarded men's liberties in earlier days on the well-founded belief that only in an environment where men are free from religious dictation, political tyranny, and personal oppression, could the mind be free to advance knowledge and foster the arts and sciences. Political experience had served only to reinforce this belief, and to show more clearly the pitfalls existing where fear and prejudice thrive. Educational facilities, general and specialized, equally open to all whose aptitudes rendered them fit, became crucial requirements for a flourishing and well-organized society. It was with some sense of urgency, therefore, that Jefferson reopened his campaign for a system of general education in Virginia, his "bantling of forty years' growth and nursing," the apex of which was to be a State University for Virginia. Jefferson was convinced that this single institution could be the greatest achievement in a lifetime dedicated to the belief that truth makes men free.

The "little academical village" which was born of Jefferson's anxious motherhood, fatherhood, and midwifery was not only the first great University of the South, but the first American University to be free of official church connection. The University of Virginia was Jefferson's daily concern during his last seven years. He sent abroad a special emissary to select the most distinguished faculty available. He chose the books for the college library, drew up the curriculum, designed the buildings, and supervised their construction. Even the ordering of the bell which was to ring out upon the Charlottesville air could not be left to a casual and possible unconscientious hand!

How characteristic was this constant busy-ness! The University, unquestionably first in his interests and duties, finally opened in 1825—the winter before Jefferson's death. Despite this preoccupation, however, Jefferson continued to pursue a multitude of other tasks. In his eightieth year, for example, he wrote with singular energy on politics, sending President Monroe long expositions later known to the world in Monroe's version as the Monroe Doctrine.

Amidst these interests there was one intrusion on his time and thought which caused Jefferson endless mortifications. His finances, often strained before and in recent years growing more shaky and unreliable with every adverse national financial upheaval, at last collapsed. Jefferson had frequently advanced money to friends who fancied themselves more hard-pressed than he, and occasionally had been forced to make good on their notes when they found it impossible to do so. He had spent money lavishly on his libraries and the arts, on Monticello, on his guests, on his children's education. He had undertaken so many projects for the advancement of a neighbor or friend, a worthy paper, book, or cause, that, carefully as he kept his accounts, his expenses still ran high. His passion for architecture, it has been remarked, cost him a small fortune. His unwillingness to overwork his overseers, hired people, and slaves was another notorious drain on his pocketbook. At the final stage of his financial distress, Jefferson petitioned the Virginia legislature to grant him permission to dispose of Monticello and its farms by lottery. The almost immediate response of private citizens, in New York, Philadelphia, and Baltimore, on hearing this news was to subscribe a sum of over $16,000 to aid the leader who had devoted his industry and resourcefulness to all America for half a century. The sting of being thus "helped" was almost dissolved in Jefferson's recognition that the subscription had been spontaneous, the citizens' "pure and unsolicited offering of love."

So there was hardly time to waste even in the last years, months, and days of his long and good life. Less than two weeks before he died, Jefferson sat down at his much-used writing desk to reply to an invitation to attend the celebration of the fiftieth anniversary of American independence. He was conscious of the significance of the coming ceremony as was no one else in America. His life had been rich and deep, astonishing in its complexity, rewarding to his family, his friends, his countrymen, and, in a very real sense, to the civilized European world. Not politics, but the image of that moral freedom and peace which had animated democracy for the Greeks, Republicanism for the Romans, the Eternal City for the Middle Ages, Scientific Utopia for the tyrant-ridden Renaissance, and modern representative democracy for eighteenth-century America and France—this was still, as it had always been, his cherished ideal.

He therefore wrote, expressing his real disappointment that he was old and ill and would be unable to celebrate the day on which the choice was made which had revolutionized a world. Ten days before the Fourth of July, 1826, ten days before he died, Jefferson wrote of America's day with that moving honesty characteristic of the many letters which help form the record of his life:

May it be to the world, what I believe it will be (to some parts sooner, to others later, but finally to all), the signal of arousing men to burst the chains under which monkish ignorance and superstition had persuaded them to bind themselves, and to assume the blessings and security of self-government. That form which we have substituted, restores the free right to the unbounded exercise of reason and freedom of opinion. All eyes are opened, or opening, to the rights of man. The general spread of the light of science has already laid open to every view the palpable truth, that the mass of mankind has not been born with saddles on their backs, nor a favored few, booted and spurred, ready to ride them legitimately, by the Grace of God. These are grounds of hope for others. For ourselves, let the annual return of this day forever refresh our recollections of these rights, and an undiminished devotion to them.

War, disillusionment, corruption, betrayal, inequality have since found old outlets and new formulas. As Jefferson foresaw, the favored few, booted and spurred, have ridden far and ridden hard—and will ride again. The "blessings and security of self-government" are not easily won. But in America, North and South, in Europe, in Africa, and in Asia, those who love the ideas for which Jefferson struggled may some day perfect the mechanisms which can best promote their realization.

THE LIFE AND SELECTED WRITINGS OF THOMAS JEFFERSON

Autobiography

Introduction

Thomas Jefferson's *Autobiography*, which he began at the advanced age of seventy-seven, was composed for his "more ready reference" and for the information of his family. This work furnishes an honest, revealing, and usually interesting account of Jefferson's career and the epoch-making times in which he lived, from his birth until March, 1790, when he became George Washington's Secretary of State. Compiled from notes and memoranda taken in some cases almost half a century earlier, reminiscences, letters, and similar sources of information, the *Autobiography* contains occasional inconsistencies or misstatements of fact. For example, in 1787 Jefferson said that John Adams had been elected Vice President of the United States while in Europe. Actually, Adams had returned to America before his election. Despite such limitations, the *Autobiography* contributes to the understanding of a great American and one of the most significant periods of American history.

With the exception of minor deletions of footnotes or illustrative material, the *Autobiography* is printed in its entirety.

The Autobiography of Thomas Jefferson

January 6, 1821

At the age of 77, I begin to make some memoranda, and state some recollections of dates and facts concerning myself, for my own more ready reference, and for the information of my family.

The tradition in my father's family was, that their ancestor came to this country from Wales, and from near the mountain of Snowdon, the highest in Great Britain. I noted once a case from Wales, in the law reports, where a person of our name was either plaintiff or defendant; and one of the same name was secretary to the Virginia Company. These are the only instances in which I have met with the name in that country. I have found it in our early records; but the first particular information I have of any ancestor was of my grandfather, who lived at the place in Chesterfield called Ozborne's, and owned the lands afterwards the glebe of the parish. He had three sons; Thomas who died young, Field who settled on the waters of Roanoke and left numerous descendants, and Peter, my father, who settled on the lands I still own, called Shadwell, adjoining my present residence. He was born February 29, 1707–8, and intermarried 1739, with Jane Randolph, of the age of 19, daughter of Isham Randolph, one of the seven sons of that name and family, settled at Dungeoness in Goochland. They trace their pedigree far back in England and Scotland, to which let every one ascribe the faith and merit he chooses.

My father's education had been quite neglected; but being of a strong mind, sound judgment, and eager after information, he read much and improved himself, insomuch that he was chosen, with Joshua Fry, Professor of Mathematics in William and Mary college,

7

to continue the boundary line between Virginia and North Carolina, which had been begun by Colonel Byrd; and was afterwards employed with the same Mr. Fry, to make the first map of Virginia which had ever been made, that of Captain Smith being merely a conjectural sketch. They possessed excellent materials for so much of the country as is below the Blue Ridge; little being then known beyond that ridge. He was the third or fourth settler, about the year 1737, of the part of the country in which I live. He died, August 17th, 1757, leaving my mother a widow, who lived till 1776, with six daughters and two sons, myself the elder. To my younger brother he left his estate on James River, called Snowdon, after the supposed birth-place of the family: to myself, the lands on which I was born and live.

He placed me at the English school at five years of age; and at the Latin at nine, where I continued until his death. My teacher, Mr. Douglas, a clergyman from Scotland, with the rudiments of the Latin and Greek languages, taught me the French; and on the death of my father, I went to the Reverend Mr. Maury, a correct classical scholar, with whom I continued two years; and then, to wit, in the spring of 1760, went to William and Mary college, where I continued two years. It was my great good fortune, and what probably fixed the destinies of my life, that Dr. William Small of Scotland, was then Professor of Mathematics, a man profound in most of the useful branches of science, with a happy talent of communication, correct and gentlemanly manners, and an enlarged and liberal mind. He, most happily for me, became soon attached to me, and made me his daily companion when not engaged in the school; and from his conversation I got my first views of the expansion of science, and of the system of things in which we are placed. Fortunately, the philosophical chair became vacant soon after my arrival at college, and he was appointed to fill it *per interim*: and he was the first who ever gave, in that college, regular lectures in Ethics, Rhetoric and Belles Lettres. He returned to Europe in 1762, having previously filled up the measure of his goodness to me, by procuring for me, from his most intimate friend, George Wythe, a reception as a student of law, under his direction, and introduced me to the acquaintance and familiar table of Governor Fauquier, the ablest man who had ever filled that office. With him, and at his table, Dr. Small and Mr.

Wythe, his *amici omnium horarum*,[1] and myself, formed a *partie quarée*, and to the habitual conversations on these occasions I owed much instruction. Mr. Wythe continued to be my faithful and beloved mentor in youth, and my most affectionate friend through life. In 1767, he led me into the practice of the law at the bar of the General court, at which I continued until the Revolution shut up the courts of justice.

In 1769, I became a member of the legislature by the choice of the county in which I live, and so continued until it was closed by the Revolution. I made one effort in that body for the permission of the emancipation of slaves, which was rejected: and indeed, during the regal government, nothing liberal could expect success. Our minds were circumscribed within narrow limits, by an habitual belief that it was our duty to be subordinate to the mother country in all matters of government, to direct all our labors in subservience to her interests, and even to observe a bigoted intolerance for all religions but hers. The difficulties with our representatives were of habit and despair, not of reflection and conviction. Experience soon proved that they could bring their minds to rights, on the first summons of their attention. But the King's Council, which acted as another house of legislature, held their places at will, and were in most humble obedience to that will: the Governor too, who had a negative on our laws, held by the same tenure, and with still greater devotedness to it: and, last of all, the Royal negative closed the last door to every hope of amelioration.

On the 1st of January, 1772, I was married to Martha Skelton, widow of Bathurst Skelton, and daughter of John Wayles, then twenty-three years old. Mr. Wayles was a lawyer of much practice, to which he was introduced more by his great industry, punctuality, and practical readiness, than by eminence in the science of his profession. He was a most agreeable companion, full of pleasantry and good humor, and welcomed in every society. He acquired a handsome fortune, and died in May, 1773, leaving three daughters: the portion which came on that event to Mrs. Jefferson, after the debts should be paid, which were very considerable, was about equal to my own patrimony, and consequently doubled the ease of our circumstances.

[1]Friends of all the hours.

When the famous Resolutions of 1765, against the Stamp-act, were proposed, I was yet a student of law in Williamsburg. I attended the debate, however, at the door of the lobby of the House of Burgesses, and heard the splendid display of Mr. Henry's talents as a popular orator. They were great indeed; such as I have never heard from any other man. He appeared to me to speak as Homer wrote. Mr. Johnson, a lawyer, and member from the Northern Neck, seconded the resolutions, and by him the learning and the logic of the case were chiefly maintained. My recollections of these transactions may be seen on page 60 of the life of Patrick Henry, by Wirt, to whom I furnished them.

In May, 1769, a meeting of the General Assembly was called by the Governor, Lord Botetourt. I had then become a member; and to that meeting became known the joint resolutions and address of the Lords and Commons, of 1768–9, on the proceedings in Massachusetts. Counter-resolutions, and an address to the King by the House of Burgesses, were agreed to with little opposition, and a spirit manifestly displayed itself of considering the cause of Massachusetts as a common one. The Governor dissolved us: but we met the next day in the Apollo [public room] of the Raleigh tavern, formed ourselves into a voluntary convention, drew up articles of association against the use of any merchandise imported from Great Britain, signed and recommended them to the people, repaired to our several counties, and were re-elected without any other exception than of the very few who had declined assent to our proceedings.

Nothing of particular excitement occurring for a considerable time, our countrymen seemed to fall into a state of insensibility to our situation; the duty on tea, not yet repealed, and the declaratory act of a right in the British Parliament to bind us by their laws in all cases whatsoever still suspended over us. But a court of inquiry held in Rhode Island in 1762, with a power to send persons to England to be tried for offences committed here, was considered, at our session of the spring of 1773, as demanding attention. Not thinking our old and leading members up to the point of forwardness and zeal which the times required, Mr. Henry, Richard Henry Lee, Francis L. Lee, Mr. Carr and myself agreed to meet in the evening, in a private room of the Raleigh, to consult on the state of things. There may have been a member or two more whom I do not recollect. We were all sensible that the most urgent of all measures was that of coming to an understanding with all the other colonies, to consider the British claims as a common cause to all, and to produce a unity of action: and, for this purpose, that a committee of correspondence in each colony would be the best instrument of intercommunication: and that their first measure would probably be, to propose a meeting of deputies from every colony, at some central place, who should be charged with the direction of the measures which should be taken by all. We, therefore, drew up the resolutions which may be seen in Wirt, page 87. The consulting members proposed to me to move them, but I urged that it should be done by Mr. Carr, my friend and brother-in-law, then a new member, to whom I wished an opportunity should be given of making known to the house his great worth and talents. It was so agreed; he moved them, they were agreed to *nem. con.,*[1] and a committee of correspondence appointed, of whom Peyton Randolph, the speaker, was chairman. The Governor (then Lord Dunmore) dissolved us, but the committee met the next day, prepared a circular letter to the speakers of the other colonies, inclosing to each a copy of the resolutions, and left it in charge with their chairman to forward them by expresses.

The origination of these committees of correspondence between the colonies has been since claimed for Massachusetts, and Marshall has given into this error,[2] although the very note of his appendix to which he refers, shows that their establishment was confined to their own towns. This matter will be seen clearly stated in a letter of Samuel Adams Wells to me of April 2nd, 1819, and my answer of May 12th. I was corrected by the letter of Mr. Wells in the information I had given Mr. Wirt, as stated in his note, page 87, that the messengers of Massachusetts and Virginia crossed each other on the way, bearing similar propositions; for Mr. Wells shows that Massachusetts did not adopt the measure, but on the receipt of our proposition, delivered at their next session. Their message, therefore, which passed ours, must have related to something else, for I well remember Peyton Randolph's informing me of the crossing of our messengers.

The next event which excited our sympathies for Massachusetts,

[1]Unanimously.

[2]Jefferson is referring to John Marshall's *Life of Washington*.

was the Boston port bill, by which that port was to be shut up on the 1st of June, 1774. This arrived while we were in session in the spring of that year. The lead in the House, on these subjects, being no longer left to the old members, Mr. Henry R. H. Lee, Fr. L. Lee, three or four other members, whom I do not recollect, and myself, agreeing that we must boldly take an unequivocal stand in the line with Massachusetts, determined to meet and consult on the proper measures, in the council-chamber, for the benefit of the library in that room. We were under conviction of the necessity of arousing our people from the lethargy into which they had fallen, as to passing events; and thought that the appointment of a day of general fasting and prayer would be most likely to call up and alarm their attention. No example of such a solemnity had existed since the days of our distresses in the war of '55, since which a new generation had grown up. With the help, therefore, of Rushworth, whom we rummaged over for the revolutionary precedents and forms of the Puritans of that day, preserved by him, we cooked up a resolution, somewhat modernizing their phrases, for appointing the 1st day of June, on which the portbill was to commence, for a day of fasting, humiliation, and prayer, to implore Heaven to avert from us the evils of civil war, to inspire us with firmness in support of our rights, and to turn the hearts of the King and Parliament to moderation and justice. To give greater emphasis to our proposition, we agreed to wait the next morning on Mr. Nicholas, whose grave and religious character was more in unison with the tone of our resolution, and to solicit him to move it. We accordingly went to him in the morning. He moved it the same day; the 1st of June was proposed; and it passed without opposition. The Governor dissolved us, as usual. We retired to the Apollo, as before, agreed to an association, and instructed the committee of correspondence to propose to the corresponding committees of the other colonies, to appoint deputies to meet in Congress at such place, *annually*, as should be convenient, to direct, from time to time, the measures required by the general interest: and we declared that an attack on any one colony, should be considered as an attack on the whole. This was in May. We further recommended to the several counties to elect deputies to meet at Williamsburg, the 1st of August ensuing, to consider the state of the colony, and particularly to appoint delegates to a general Congress, should that measure be acceded to by the committees of correspondence generally. It was acceded to; Philadelphia was appointed for the place, and the 5th of September for the time of meeting. We returned home, and in our several counties invited the clergy to meet assemblies of the people on the 1st of June, to perform the ceremonies of the day, and to address to them discourses suited to the occasion. The people met generally, with anxiety and alarm in their countenances, and the effect of the day, through the whole colony, was like a shock of electricity, arousing every man, and placing him erect and solidly on his centre. They chose, universally, delegates for the convention. Being elected one for my own county, I prepared a draught of instructions to be given to the delegates whom we should send to the Congress, which I meant to propose at our meeting. In this I took the ground that, from the beginning, I had thought the only one orthodox or tenable, which was, that the relation between Great Britain and these colonies was exactly the same as that of England and Scotland, after the accession of James, and until the union, and the same as her present relations with Hanover, having the same executive chief, but no other necessary political connection; and that our emigration from England to this country gave her no more rights over us, than the emigrations of the Danes and Saxons gave to the present authorities of the mother country, over England. In this doctrine, however, I had never been able to get any one to agree with me but Mr. Wythe. He concurred in it from the first dawn of the question, What was the political relation between us and England? Our other patriots, Randolph, the Lees, Nicholas, Pendleton, stopped at the half-way house of John Dickinson, who admitted that England has a right to regulate our commerce, and to lay duties on it for the purposes of regulation, but not of raising revenue. But for this ground there was no foundation in compact, in any acknowledged principles of colonization, nor in reason: expatriation being a natural right, and acted on as such, by all nations, in all ages. I set out for Williamsburg some days before that appointed for our meeting, but was taken ill of a dysentery on the road, and was unable to proceed. I sent on, therefore, to Williamsburg, two copies of my draught, the one under cover to Peyton Randolph, who I knew would be in the chair of the convention, the other to Patrick Henry. Whether Mr. Henry disapproved the ground taken, or was too lazy to read it (for he was the laziest man in reading I ever knew) I never learned: but he communicated it to nobody. Peyton Randolph informed the convention he had received such a paper from a member, prevented by sickness from offering it in his place, and he laid it on the table for perusal. It was read generally by the members, approved by many, though thought too bold for the present state of things; but they printed it in pamphlet form, under the title of "A Summary View of the Rights of British America." It found its way to England, was taken up by the opposition, interpolated a little by Mr. Burke so as to make it answer opposition purposes, and in that form ran rapidly through several editions. This information I had from Parson Hurt, who happened at the time to be in London, whither he had gone to receive clerical orders; and I was informed afterwards by Peyton Randolph, that it had procured me the honor of having my name inserted in a long list of proscriptions, enrolled in a bill of attainder commenced in one of the Houses of Parliament, but suppressed in embryo by the hasty step of events, which warned them to be a little cautious. Montague, agent of the House of Burgesses in England, made extracts from the bill, copied the names, and sent them to Peyton Randolph. The names, I think, were about twenty, which he repeated to me, but I recollect those only of Hancock, the two Adamses, Peyton Randolph himself and myself. The convention met on the 1st of August, renewed their association, appointed delegates to the Congress, gave them instructions very temperately and properly expressed, both as to style and matter; and they repaired to Philadelphia at the time appointed. The splendid proceedings of that Congress, at their first session, belong to general history, are known to every one, and need not therefore be noted here. They terminated their session on the 26th of October, to meet again on the 10th of May ensuing. The convention, at their ensuing session of March, '75, approved of the proceedings of Congress, thanked their delegates, and reappointed the same persons to represent the colony at the meeting to be held in May: and foreseeing the probability that Peyton Randolph, their president, and speaker also of the House of Burgesses, might be called off, they added me, in that event, to the delegation.

Mr. Randolph was, according to expectation, obliged to leave the chair of Congress, to attend the General Assembly summoned by

Lord Dunmore, to meet on the 1st day of June, 1775. Lord North's conciliatory propositions, as they were called, had been received by the Governor, and furnished the subject for which this assembly was convened. Mr. Randolph accordingly attended, and the tenor of these propositions being generally known, as having been addressed to all the governors, he was anxious that the answer of our Assembly, likely to be the first, should harmonize with what he knew to be the sentiments and wishes of the body he had recently left. He feared that Mr. Nicholas, whose mind was not yet up to the mark of the times, would undertake the answer, and therefore pressed me to prepare it. I did so, and, with his aid, carried it through the House, with long and doubtful scruples from Mr. Nicholas and James Mercer, and a dash of cold water on it here and there, enfeebling it somewhat, but finally with unanimity, or a vote approaching it. This being passed, I repaired immediately to Philadelphia, and conveyed to Congress the first notice they had of it. It was entirely approved there. I took my seat with them on the 21st of June. On the 24th, a committee which had been appointed to prepare a declaration of the causes of taking up arms, brought in their report (drawn I believe by J. Rutledge) which, not being liked, the House recommitted it, on the 26th, and added Mr. Dickinson and myself to the committee. On the rising of the House, the committee having not yet met, I happened to find myself near Governor W. Livingston, and proposed to him to draw the paper. He excused himself and proposed that I should draw it. On my pressing him with urgency, "We are as yet but new acquaintances, sir," said he; "why are you so earnest for my doing it?" "Because," said I, "I have been informed that you drew the Address to the people of Great Britain, a production, certainly, of the finest pen in America." "On that," says he, "perhaps, sir, you may not have been correctly informed." I had received the information in Virginia from Colonel Harrison on his return from that Congress. Lee, Livingston, and Jay had been the committee for that draught. The first, prepared by Lee, had been disapproved and recommitted. The second was drawn by Jay, but being presented by Governor Livingston, had led Colonel Harrison into the error. The next morning, walking in the hall of Congress, many members being assembled, but the House not yet formed, I observed Mr. Jay speaking to R. H. Lee, and leading him by the button of his coat to me. "I understand, sir," said he to me, "that this gentleman informed you, that Governor Livingston drew the Address to the people of Great Britain." I assured him, at once, that I had not received that in formation from Mr. Lee, and that not a word had ever passed on the subject between Mr. Lee and myself; and after some explanations the subject was dropped. These gentlemen had had some sparrings in debate before, and continued ever very hostile to each other.

I prepared a draught of the declaration committed to us. It was too strong for Mr. Dickinson. He still retained the hope of reconciliation with the mother country, and was unwilling it should be lessened by offensive statements. He was so honest a man, and so able a one, that he was greatly indulged even by those who could not feel his scruples. We therefore requested him to take the paper, and put it into a form he could approve. He did so, preparing an entire new statement, and preserving of the former only the last four paragraphs and half of the preceding one. We approved and reported it to Congress, who accepted it. Congress gave a signal proof of their indulgence to Mr. Dickinson, and of their great desire not to go too fast for any respectable part of our body, in permitting him to draw their second petition to the King according to his own ideas, and passing it with scarcely any amendment. The disgust against this humility was general; and Mr. Dickinson s delight at its passage was the only circumstance which reconciled them to it. The vote being passed, although further observation on it was out of order, he could not refrain from rising and expressing his satisfaction, and concluded by saying, "There is but one word, Mr. President, in the paper which I disapprove, and that is the word *Congress*"; on which Ben Harrison rose and said, "There is but one word in the paper, Mr. President, of which I approve, and that is the word *Congress.*"

On the 22d of July, Dr. Franklin, Mr. Adams, R. H. Lee, and myself, were appointed a committee to consider and report on Lord North's conciliatory resolution. The answer of the Virginia Assembly on that subject having been approved, I was requested by the committee to prepare this report, which will account for the similiarity of feature in the two instruments.

On the 15th of May, 1776, the convention of Virginia instructed their delegates in Congress, to propose to that body to declare the colonies independent of Great Britain, and appoint a committee to prepare a declaration of rights and plan of government.

In Congress, Friday, June 7, 1776.

The delegates from Virginia moved, in obedience to instructions from their constituents, that the Congress should declare that these United colonies are, and of right ought to be, free and independent states, that they are absolved from all allegiance to the British crown, and that all political connection between them and the state of Great Britain is, and ought to be, totally dissolved; that measures should be immediately taken for procuring the assistance of foreign powers, and a Confederation be formed to bind the colonies more closely together.

The House being obliged to attend at that time to some other business, the proposition was referred to the next day, when the members were ordered to attend punctually at ten o'clock.

Saturday, June 8. They proceeded to take it into consideration, and referred it to a committee of the whole, into which they immediately resolved themselves, and passed that day and Monday, the 10th, in debating on the subject.

It was argued by Wilson, Robert R. Livingston, E. Rutledge, Dickinson, and others—

That, though they were friends to the measures themselves, and saw the impossibility that we should ever again be united with Great Britain, yet they were against adopting them at this time:

That the conduct we had formerly observed was wise and proper now, of deferring to take any capital step till the voice of the people drove us into it:

That they were our power, and without them our declarations could not be carried into effect:

That the people of the middle colonies (Maryland, Delaware, Pennsylvania, the Jerseys and New York) were not yet ripe for bidding adieu to British connection, but that they were fast ripening, and, in a short time, would join in the general voice of America:

That the resolution, entered into by this House on the 15th of May, for suppressing the exercise of all powers derived from the crown, had shown, by the ferment into which it had thrown these middle colonies, that they had not yet accommodated their minds to a separation from the mother country:

That some of them had expressly forbidden their delegates to consent to such a declaration, and others had given no instructions, and consequently no powers to give such consent:

That if the delegates of any particular colony had no power to declare such colony independent, certain they were, the others could not declare it for them; the colonies being as yet perfectly independent of each other:

That the assembly of Pennsylvania was now sitting above stairs, their convention would sit within a few days, the convention of New York was now sitting, and those of the Jerseys and Delaware counties would meet on the Monday following, and it was probable these bodies would take up the question of Independence, and would declare to their delegates the voice of their state:

That if such a declaration should now be agreed to, these delegates must retire, and possibly their colonies might secede from the Union:

That such a secession would weaken us more than could be compensated by any foreign alliance:

That in the event of such a division, foreign powers would either refuse to join themselves to our fortunes, or, having us so much in their power as that desperate declaration would place us, they would insist on terms proportionably more hard and prejudicial:

That we had little reason to expect an alliance with those to whom alone, as yet, we had cast our eyes:

That France and Spain had reason to be jealous of that rising power, which would one day certainly strip them of all their American possessions:

That it was more likely they should form a connection with the British court, who, if they should find themselves unable otherwise to extricate themselves from their difficulties, would agree to a partition of our territories, restoring Canada to France, and the Floridas to Spain, to accomplish for themselves a recovery of these colonies:

That it would not be long before we should receive certain information of the disposition of the French court, from the agent whom we had sent to Paris for that purpose:

That if this disposition should be favorable, by waiting the event of the present campaign, which we all hoped would be successful, we should have reason to expect an alliance on better terms:

That this would in fact work no delay of any effectual aid from such ally, as, from the advance of the season and distance of our situation, it was impossible we could receive any assistance during this campaign:

That it was prudent to fix among ourselves the terms on which we should form alliance, before we declared we would form one at all events:

And that if these were agreed on, and our Declaration of Independence ready by the time our Ambassador should be prepared to sail, it would be as well as to go into that Declaration at this day.

On the other side, it was urged by J. Adams, Lee, Wythe, and others, that no gentleman had argued against the policy or the right of separation from Britain, nor had supposed it possible we should ever renew our connection; that they had only opposed its being now declared:

That the question was not whether, by a Declaration of Independence, we should make ourselves what we are not; but whether we should declare a fact which already exists:

That, as to the people or parliament of England, we had always been independent of them, their restraints on our trade deriving efficacy from our acquiescence only, and not from any rights they possessed of imposing them, and that so far, our connection had been federal only, and was now dissolved by the commencement of hostilities:

That, as to the King, we had been bound to him by allegiance, but that this bond was now dissolved by his assent to the last act of Parliament, by which he declares us out of his protection, and by his levying war on us, a fact which had long ago proved us out of his protection; it being a certain position in law, that allegiance and protection are reciprocal, the one ceasing when the other is withdrawn:

That James the Second never declared the people of England out of his protection, yet his actions proved it, and the Parliament declared it:

No delegates then can be denied, or ever want, a power of declaring an existing truth:

That the delegates from the Delaware counties having declared their constituents ready to join, there are only two colonies, Pennsylvania and Maryland, whose delegates are absolutely tied up, and that these

had, by their instructions, only reserved a right of confirming or rejecting the measure:

That the instructions from Pennsylvania might be accounted for
from the times in which they were drawn, near a twelve-month ago,
since which the face of affairs has totally changed:

That within that time, it had become apparent that Britain was
determined to accept nothing less than a *carte-blanche*, and that the
King's answer to the Lord Mayor, Aldermen and Common Council
of London, which had come to hand four days ago, must have satisfied
every one of this point:

That the people wait for us to lead the way:

That *they* are in favor of the measure, though the instructions given
by some of their *representatives* are not:

That the voice of the representatives is not always consonant with
the voice of the people, and that this is remarkably the case in these
middle colonies:

That the effect of the resolution of the 15th of May has proved this,
which, raising the murmurs of some in the colonies of Pennsylvania
and Maryland, called forth the opposing voice of the freer part of the
people, and proved them to be the majority even in these colonies:

That the backwardness of these two colonies might be ascribed,
partly to the influence of proprietary power and connections, and
partly, to their having not yet been attacked by the enemy:

That these causes were not likely to be soon removed, as there
seemed no probability that the enemy would make either of these the
seat of this summer's war:

That it would be vain to wait either weeks or months for perfect
unanimity, since it was impossible that all men should ever become
of one sentiment on any question:

That the conduct of some colonies, from the beginning of this contest, had given reason to suspect it was their settled policy to keep in
the rear of the confederacy, that their particular prospect might be better, even in the worst event:

That, therefore, it was necessary for those colonies who had thrown
themselves forward and hazarded all from the beginning, to come forward now also, and put all again to their own hazard:

That the history of the Dutch Revolution, of whom three states only confederated at first, proved that a secession of some colonies would not be so dangerous as some apprehended:

That a Declaration of Independence alone could render it consistent with European delicacy, for European powers to treat with us, or even to receive an Ambassador from us:

That till this, they would not receive our vessels into their ports, nor acknowledge the adjudications of our courts of admiralty to be legitimate, in cases of capture of British vessels:

That though France and Spain may be jealous of our rising power, they must think it will be much more formidable with the addition of Great Britain; and will therefore see it their interest to prevent a coalition; but should they refuse, we shall be but where we are; whereas without trying, we shall never know whether they will aid us or not:

That the present campaign may be unsuccessful, and therefore we had better propose an alliance while our affairs wear a hopeful aspect:

That to wait the event of this campaign will certainly work delay, because, during the summer, France may assist us effectually, by cutting off those supplies of provisions from England and Ireland, on which the enemy's armies here are to depend; or by setting in motion the great power they have collected in the West Indies, and calling our enemy to the defence of the possessions they have there:

That it would be idle to lose time in settling the terms of alliance, till we had first determined we would enter into alliance:

That it is necessary to lose no time in opening a trade for our people, who will want clothes, and will want money too, for the payment of taxes:

And that the only misfortune is, that we did not enter into alliance with France six months sooner, as, besides opening her ports for the vent of our last year's produce, she might have marched an army into Germany, and prevented the petty princes there, from selling their unhappy subjects to subdue us.

It appearing in the course of these debates, that the colonies of New York, New Jersey, Pennsylvania, Delaware, Maryland, and South Carolina were not yet matured for falling from the parent stem, but that they were fast advancing to that state, it was thought most prudent to wait a while for them, and to postpone the final decision to July 1st; but, that this might occasion as little delay as possible, a committee was appointed to prepare a Declaration of Independence. The committee were John Adams, Dr. Franklin, Roger Sherman, Robert R. Livingston, and myself. Committees were also appointed, at the same time, to prepare a plan of confederation for the colonies, and to state the terms proper to be proposed for foreign alliance. The committee for drawing the Declaration of Independence, desired me to do it. It was accordingly done, and being approved by them, I reported it to the House on Friday, the 28th of June, when it was read, and ordered to lie on the table. On Monday, the 1st of July, the House resolved itself into a committee of the whole, and resumed the consideration of the original motion made by the delegates of Virginia, which, being again debated through the day, was carried in the affirmative by the votes of New Hampshire, Connecticut, Massachusetts, Rhode Island, New Jersey, Maryland, Virginia, North Carolina and Georgia. South Carolina and Pennsylvania voted against it. Delaware had but two members present, and they were divided. The delegates from New York declared they were for it themselves, and were assured their constituents were for it; but that their instructions having been drawn near a twelve-month before, when reconciliation was still the general object, they were enjoined by them to do nothing which should impede that object. They, therefore, thought themselves not justifiable in voting on either side, and asked leave to withdraw from the question; which was given them. The committee rose and reported their resolution to the House. Mr. Edward Rutledge, of South Carolina, then requested the determination might be put off to the next day, as he believed his colleagues, though they disapproved of the resolution, would then join in it for the sake of unanimity. The ultimate question, whether the House would agree to the resolution of the committee, was accordingly postponed to the next day, when it was again moved, and South Carolina concurred in voting for it. In the meantime, a third member had come post from the Delaware counties, and turned the vote of that colony in favor of the resolution. Members of a different sentiment attending that morning from Pennsylvania also, her vote was changed, so that the whole twelve colonies who were authorized to vote at all, gave their voices for it; and, within a few days, the convention of New York approved of it, and thus supplied the void occasioned by the withdrawing of her delegates from the vote.

Congress proceeded the same day to consider the Declaration of Independence, which had been reported and lain on the table the Friday preceding, and on Monday referred to a committee of the whole. The pusillanimous idea that we had friends in England worth keeping terms with, still haunted the minds of many. For this reason, those passages which conveyed censures on the people of England were struck out, lest they should give them offence. The clause too, reprobating the enslaving the inhabitants of Africa, was struck out in complaisance to South Carolina and Georgia, who had never attempted to restrain the importation of slaves, and who, on the contrary, still wished to continue it. Our northern brethren also, I believe, felt a little tender under those censures; for though their people had very few slaves themselves, yet they had been pretty considerable carriers of them to others. The debates, having taken up the greater parts of the 2d, 3d, and 4th days of July, were, on the evening of the last, closed; the Declaration was reported by the committee, agreed to by the House and signed by every member present, except Mr. Dickinson. As the sentiments of men are known not only by what they receive, but what they reject also, I will state the form of the Declaration as originally reported. The parts struck out by Congress shall be distinguished by a black line drawn under them;[1] and those inserted by them shall be placed in the margin, or in a concurrent column.[2]

A DECLARATION BY THE REPRESENTATIVES OF THE UNITED STATES OF AMERICA, IN *GENERAL* CONGRESS ASSEMBLED

When, in the course of human events, it becomes necessary for one people to dissolve the political bands which have connected them with another, and to assume among the powers of the earth the separate and equal station to which the laws of nature and of nature's God entitle them, a decent respect to the opinions of mankind requires that they should declare the causes which impel them to the separation.

[1]The editors have substituted the device of italicizing and enclosing in brackets the parts struck out by Congress.

[2]These insertions are printed in capitals.

We hold these truths to be self evident: that all men are created equal; that they are endowed by their Creator with CERTAIN [*inherent and*] inalienable rights; that among these are life, liberty, and the pursuit of happiness; that to secure these rights, governments are instituted among men, deriving their just powers from the consent of the governed; that whenever any form of government becomes destructive of these ends, it is the right of the people to alter or to abolish it, and to institute new government, laying its foundation on such principles, and organizing its powers in such form, as to them shall seem most likely to effect their safety and happiness. Prudence, indeed, will dictate that governments long established should not be changed for light and transient causes; and accordingly all experience hath shown that mankind are more disposed to suffer while evils are sufferable, than to right themselves by abolishing the forms to which they are accustomed. But when a long train of abuses and usurpations, [*begun at a distinguished period and*] pursuing invariably the same object, evinces a design to reduce them under absolute despotism, it is their right, it is their duty to throw off such government, and to provide new guards for their future security. Such has been the patient sufferance of these colonies; and such is now the necessity which constrains them to ALTER [*expunge*] their former systems of government. The history of the present king of Great Britain is a history of REPEATED [*unremitting*] injuries and usurpations, ALL HAVING [*among which appears no solitary fact to contradict the uniform tenor of the rest, but all have*] in direct object the establishment of an absolute tyranny over these states. To prove this, let facts be submitted to a candid world [*for the truth of which we pledge a faith yet unsullied by falsehood*].

He has refused his assent to laws the most wholesome and necessary for the public good.

He has forbidden his governors to pass laws of immediate and pressing importance, unless suspended in their operation till his assent should be obtained; and, when so suspended, he has utterly neglected to attend to them.

He has refused to pass other laws for the accommodation of large districts of people, unless those people would relinquish the right of representation in the legislature, a right inestimable to them, and formidable to tyrants only.

He has called together legislative bodies at places unusual, uncomfortable, and distant from the depository of their public records, for the sole purpose of fatiguing them into compliance with his measures.

He has dissolved representative houses repeatedly [*and continually*] for opposing with manly firmness his invasions on the rights of the people.

He has refused for a long time after such dissolutions to cause others to be elected, whereby the legislative powers, incapable of annihilation, have returned to the people at large for their exercise, the state remaining, in the meantime, exposed to all the dangers of invasion from without and convulsions within.

He has endeavored to prevent the population of these states; for that purpose obstructing the laws for naturalization of foreigners, refusing to pass others to encourage their migrations hither, and raising the conditions of new appropriations of lands.

He has OBSTRUCTED [*suffered*] the administration of justice BY [*totally to cease in some of these states*] refusing his assent to laws for establishing judiciary powers.

He has made [*our*] judges dependent on his will alone for the tenure of their offices, and the amount and payment of their salaries.

He has erected a multitude of new offices, [*by a self-assumed power*] and sent hither swarms of new officers to harass our people and eat out their substance.

He has kept among us in times of peace standing armies [*and ships of war*] without the consent of our legislatures.

He has affected to render the military independent of, and superior to, the civil power.

He has combined with others to subject us to a jurisdiction foreign to our constitutions and unacknowledged by our laws, giving his assent to their acts of pretended legislation for quartering large bodies of armed troops among us; for protecting them by a mock trial from punishment for any murders which they should commit on the inhabitants of these states; for cutting off our trade with all parts of the world; for imposing taxes on us without our consent; for depriving us IN MANY CASES of the benefits of trial by jury; for transporting us beyond seas to be tried for pretended offences; for abolishing the free system of English laws in a neighboring province, establishing therein an arbitrary government, and enlarging its boundaries, so as to render it at once an example and fit instrument for introducing the same absolute rule into these COLONIES [*states*]; for taking away our charters, abolishing our most valuable laws, and altering fundamentally the forms of our governments; for suspending our own legislatures, and declaring themselves invested with power to legislate for us in all cases whatsoever.

He has abdicated government here BY DECLARING US OUT OF HIS PROTECTION, AND WAGING WAR AGAINST US [*withdrawing his governors and declaring us out of his allegiance and protection*].

He has plundered our seas, ravaged our coasts, burnt our towns, and destroyed the lives of our people.

He is at this time transporting large armies of foreign mercenaries to complete the works of death, desolation and tyranny already begun with circumstances of cruelty and perfidy SCARCELY PARALLELED IN THE MOST BARBAROUS AGES, AND TOTALLY unworthy the head of a civilized nation.

He has constrained our fellow citizens taken captive on the high seas, to bear arms against their country, to become the executioners of their friends and brethren, or to fall themselves by their hands.

He has EXCITED DOMESTIC INSURRECTION AMONG US, AND HAS endeavored to bring on the inhabitants of our frontiers, the merciless Indian savages, whose known rule of warfare is an undistinguished destruction of all ages, sexes and conditions [*of existence*].

[*He has incited treasonable insurrections of our fellow citizens, with the allurements of forfeiture and confiscation of our property.*

He has waged cruel war against human nature itself, violating its most sacred rights of life and liberty in the persons of a distant people who never offended him, captivating and carrying them into slavery in another hemisphere, or to incur miserable death in their transportation hither. This piratical warfare, the opprobrium of INFIDEL powers, is the warfare of the CHRISTIAN king of Great Britain. Determined to keep open a market where MEN should be bought and sold, he has prostituted his negative for suppressing every legislative attempt to prohibit or to restrain this execrable commerce. And that this assemblage of horrors might want no fact of distinguished die, he is now exciting those very people to rise in arms among us, and to purchase that liberty of which he has deprived them, by murdering the people on whom he also obtruded them: thus paying off former crimes committed against the LIBERTIES of one people, with crimes which he urges them to commit against the LIVES of another.]

In every stage of these oppressions we have petitioned for redress in the most humble terms: our repeated petitions have been answered only by repeated injuries.

A prince whose character is thus marked by every act which may define a tyrant is unfit to be the ruler of a FREE people [*who mean to be free. Future ages will scarcely believe that the hardiness of one man adventured, within the short compass of twelve years only, to lay a foundation so broad and so undisguised for tyranny over a people fostered and fixed in principles of freedom.*]

Nor have we been wanting in attentions to our British brethren. We have warned them from time to time of attempts by their legislature to extend AN UNWARRANTABLE [*a*] jurisdiction over US [*these our states*]. We have reminded them of the circumstances of our emigration and settlement here, [*no one of which could warrant so strange a pretension: that these were effected at the expense of our own blood and treasure, unassisted by the wealth or the strength of Great Britain: that in constituting indeed our several forms of government, we had adopted one common king, thereby laying a foundation for perpetual league and amity with them: but that submission to their parliament was no part of our constitution, nor ever in idea, if history may be credited: and,*] we HAVE appealed to their native justice and magnanimity AND WE HAVE CONJURED THEM BY [*as well as to*] the ties of our common kindred to disavow these usurpations which WOULD INEVITABLY [*were likely to*] interrupt our connection and correspondence. They too have been deaf to the voice of justice and of consanguinity. WE MUST THEREFORE [*and when occasions have been given them, by the regular course of their laws, of removing from their councils the disturbers of our harmony, they have, by their free election, re-established them in power. At this very time too, they are permitting their chief magistrate to send over not only soldiers of our common blood, but Scotch and foreign mercenaries to invade and destroy us. These facts have given the last stab to agonizing affection, and manly spirit bids us to renounce forever these unfeeling brethren. We must endeavor to forget our former love for them, and hold them as we hold the rest of mankind, enemies in war, in peace friends. We might have a free and a great people together; but a communication of grandeur and of freedom, it seems, is below their dignity. Be it so, since they will have it. The road to happiness and to glory is open to us, too. We will tread it apart from them, and]* acquiesce in the necessity which denounces our [*eternal*] separation AND HOLD THEM AS WE HOLD THE REST OF MANKIND, ENEMIES IN WAR, IN PEACE FRIENDS!

[1]We therefore the representatives of the United States of America in General Congress assembled, do in the name, and by the authority of the good people of these [*states reject and renounce all allegiance and subjection to the kings of Great Britain and all others who may hereafter claim by, through or under them; we utterly dissolve all political connection which may heretofore have subsisted between us and the people or parliament of Great Britain: and finally we do assert and declare these colonies to be free and independent states,*] and that as free and independent states, they have full power to levy war, conclude peace, contract alliances, establish commerce, and to do all other acts and things which independent states may of right do.

And for the support of this declaration, we mutually pledge

We, therefore, the representatives of the United States of America in General Congress assembled, appealing to the supreme judge of the world for the rectitude of our intentions, do in the name, and by the authority of the good people of these colonies, solemnly publish and declare, that these united colonies are, and of right ought to be free and independent states; that they are absolved from all allegiance to the British crown and that all political connection between them and the state of Great Britain is, and ought to be, totally dissolved; and that as free and independent states, they have full power to levy war, conclude peace, contract alliances, establish commerce, and to do all other acts and things which independent states may of right do.

And for the support of this

---

[1]In this closing section, where additions and deletions have been lengthy, the editors follow Jefferson's device of printing his version in the left column, and the final adopted text in the right column.

each other our lives, our fortunes, and our sacred honor.

declaration, with a firm reliance on the protection of divine providence, we mutually pledge to each other our lives, our fortunes, and our sacred honor.

The Declaration thus signed on the 4th, on paper, was engrossed on parchment, and signed again on the 2d of August.

[Some erroneous statements of the proceedings on the Declaration of Independence having got before the public in later times, Mr. Samuel A. Wells asked explanations of me, which are given in my letter to him of May 12, '19, before and now again referred to. I took notes in my place while these things were going on, and at their close wrote them out in form and with correctness, and from 1 to 7 of the two preceding sheets, are the originals then written; as the two following are of earlier debates on the Confederation, which I took in like manner.][1]

On Friday, July 12, the committee appointed to draw the articles of Confederation reported them, and, on the 22d, the House resolved themselves into a committee to take them into consideration. On the 30th and 31st of that month, and 1st of the ensuing, those articles were debated which determined the proportion, or quota, of money which each state should furnish to the common treasury, and the manner of voting in Congress. The first of these articles was expressed in the original draught in these words. "Art. XI. All charges of war and all other expenses that shall be incurred for the common defence, or general welfare, and allowed by the United States assembled, shall be defrayed out of a common treasury, which shall be supplied by the several colonies in proportion to the number of inhabitants of every age, sex, and quality, except Indians not paying taxes, in each colony, a true account of which, distinguishing the white inhabitants, shall be triennally taken and transmitted to the Assembly of the United States."

Mr. Chase moved that the quotas should be fixed, not by the number of inhabitants of every condition, but by that of the "white inhabitants." He admitted that taxation should be always in proportion to

[1]In this case, the remarks in brackets are Jefferson's.

property, that this was, in theory, the true rule; but that, from a variety of difficulties, it was a rule which could never be adopted in practice. The value of the property in every State, could never be estimated justly and equally. Some other measure for the wealth of the State must therefore be devised, some standard referred to, which would be more simple. He considered the number of inhabitants as a tolerably good criterion of property, and that this might always be obtained. He therefore thought it the best mode which we could adopt, with one exception only: he observed that negroes are property, and as such, cannot be distinguished from the lands or personalities held in those States where there are few slaves; the surplus of profit which a Northern farmer is able to lay by, he invests in cattle, horses, &c., whereas a Southern farmer lays out the same surplus in slaves. There is no more reason, therefore, for taxing the Southern States on the farmer's head, and on his slave's head, than the Northern ones on their farmer's heads and the heads of their cattle; that the method proposed would, therefore, tax the Southern States according to their numbers and their wealth conjunctly, while the Northern would be taxes on numbers only: that negroes, in fact, should not be considered as members of the State, more than cattle, and that they have no more interest in it.

Mr. John Adams observed, that the numbers of people were taken by this article, as an index of the wealth of the State, and not as subjects of taxation; that, as to this matter, it was of no consequence by what name you called your people, whether by that of freemen or of slaves; that in some countries the laboring poor were called freemen, in others they were called slaves; but that the difference as to the state was imaginary only. What matters it whether a landlord, employing ten laborers on his farm, gives them annually as much money as will buy them the necessaries of life, or gives them those necessaries at short hand? The ten laborers add as much wealth annually to the State, increase its exports as much in the one case as the other. Certainly five hundred freemen produce no more profits, no greater surplus for the payment of taxes, than five hundred slaves. Therefore, the State in which are the laborers called freemen, should be taxed no more than that in which are those called slaves. Suppose, by an extraordinary operation of nature or of law, one-half the laborers of a State could in the course of one night be transformed into slaves; would the State be made the poorer or the less able to pay taxes? That the condition of the laboring poor in most countries, that of the fishermen particularly of the Northern States, is as abject as that of slaves. It is the number of laborers which produces the surplus for taxation, and numbers, therefore, indiscriminately, are the fair index of wealth; that it is the use of the word "property" here, and its application to some of the people of the State, which produces the fallacy. How does the Southern farmer procure slaves? Either by importation or by purchase from his neighbor. If he imports a slave, he adds one to the number of laborers in his country, and proportionably to its profits and abilities to pay taxes; if he buys from his neighbor, it is only a transfer of a laborer from one farm to another, which does not change the annual produce of the State, and therefore, should not change its tax: that if a Northern farmer works ten laborers on his farm, he can, it is true, invest the surplus of ten men's labor in cattle; but so may the Southern farmer, working ten slaves; that a State of one hundred thousand freemen can maintain no more cattle, than one of one hundred thousand slaves. Therefore, they have no more of that kind of property; that a slave may indeed, from the custom of speech, be more properly called the wealth of his master, than the free laborer might be called the wealth of his employer; but as to the State, both were equally its wealth, and should, therefore, equally add to the quota of its tax.

Mr. Harrison proposed, as a compromise, that two slaves should be counted as one freeman. He affirmed that slaves did not do as much work as freemen, and doubted if two effected more than one; that this was proved by the price of labor; the hire of a laborer in the Southern colonies being from £8 to £12, while in the Northern it was generally £24.

Mr. Wilson said, that if this amendment should take place, the Southern colonies would have all the benefit of slaves, whilst the Northern ones would bear the burthen: the slaves increase the profits of a State, which the Southern States mean to take to themselves; that they also increase the burthen of defence, which would of course fall so much the heavier on the Northern: that slaves occupy the places of freemen, and eat their food. Dismiss your slaves, and freemen will take their places. It is our duty to lay every discouragement on the importation of slaves; but this amendment would give the *jus trium liberorum*[1] to him who would import slaves: that other kinds of property were pretty equally distributed through all the colonies: there were as many cattle, horses and sheep, in the North as the South, and South as the North; but not so as to slaves: that experience has shown that those colonies have been always able to pay most, which have the most inhabitants, whether they be black or white; and the practice of the Southern colonies has always been to make every farmer pay poll taxes upon all his laborers, whether black or white. He acknowledges, indeed, that freemen work the most; but they consume the most also. They do not produce a greater surplus for taxation. The slave is neither fed nor clothed so expensively as a freeman. Again, white women are exempted from labor generally, but negro women are not. In this, then, the Southern States have an advantage as the article now stands. It has sometimes been said, that slavery is necessary, because the commodities they raise would be too dear for market if cultivated by freemen; but now it is said that the labor of the slave is the dearest.

Mr. Payne urged the original resolution of Congress, to proportion the quotas of the States to the number of souls.

Dr. Witherspoon was of opinion, that the value of lands and houses was the best estimate of the wealth of a nation, and that it was practicable to obtain such a valuation. This is the true barometer of wealth. The one now proposed is imperfect in itself, and unequal between the States. It has been objected that negroes eat the food of freemen, and, therefore, should be taxed; horses also eat the food of freemen; therefore they also should be taxed. It has been said too, that in carrying slaves into the estimate of the taxes the State is to pay, we do no more than those States themselves do, who always take slaves into the estimate of the taxes the individual is to pay. But the cases are not parallel. In the Southern colonies slaves pervade the whole colony; but they do not pervade the whole continent. That as to the original resolution of Congress, to proportion the quotas according to the souls, it was temporary only, and related to the moneys heretofore emitted: whereas we are now entering into a new compact, and therefore stand on original ground.

[1]Right of three freemen.

August 1. The question being put, the amendment proposed was rejected by the votes of New Hampshire, Massachusetts, Rhode Island, Connecticut, New York, New Jersey, and Pennsylvania, against those of Delaware, Maryland, Virginia, North and South Carolina. Georgia was divided.

The other article was in these words. "Art. XVII. In determining questions, each colony shall have one vote."

July 30, 31, August 1. Present forty-one members. Mr. Chase observed this article was the most likely to divide us, of any one proposed in the draught then under consideration: that the larger colonies had threatened they would not confederate at all, if their weight in Congress should not be equal to the numbers of people they added to the confederacy; while the smaller ones declared against a union, if they did not retain an equal vote for the protection of their rights. That it was of the utmost consequence to bring the parties together, as, should we sever from each other, either no foreign power will ally with us at all, or the different States will form different alliances, and thus increase the horrors of those scenes of civil war and bloodshed, which in such a state of separation and independence, would render us a miserable people. That our importance, our interests, our peace required that we should confederate, and that mutual sacrifices should be made to effect a compromise of this difficult question. He was of opinion, the smaller colonies would lose their rights, if they were not in some instances allowed an equal vote; and, therefore, that a discrimination should take place among the questions which would come before Congress. That the smaller States should be secured in all questions concerning life or liberty, and the greater ones, in all respecting property. He, therefore, proposed, that in votes relating to money, the voice of each colony should be proportioned to the number of its inhabitants.

Dr. Franklin thought, that the votes should be so proportioned in all cases. He took notice that the Delaware counties had bound up their delegates to disagree to this article. He thought it a very extraordinary language to be held by any State, that they would not confederate with us, unless we would let them dispose of our money. Certainly, if we vote equally, we ought to pay equally; but the smaller States will hardly purchase the privilege at this price. That had he lived in a State where the representation, originally equal, had become unequal by time and accident, he might have submitted rather than disturb government; but that we should be very wrong to set out in this practice, when it is in our power to establish what is right. That at the time of the Union between England and Scotland, the latter had made the objection which the smaller States now do; but experience had proved that no unfairness had ever been shown them: that their advocates had prognosticated that it would again happen, as in times of old, that the whale would swallow Jonas [sic], but he thought the prediction reversed in event, and that Jonas had swallowed the whale; for the Scotch had in fact got possession of the government, and gave laws to the English. He reprobated the original agreement of Congress to vote by colonies, and, therefore, was for their voting, in all cases, according to the number of taxables.

Dr. Witherspoon opposed every alteration of the article. All men admit that a confederacy is necessary. Should the idea get abroad that there is likely to be no union among us, it will damp the minds of the people, diminish the glory of our struggle, and lessen its importance; because it will open to our view future prospects of war and dissension among ourselves. If an equal vote be refused, the smaller States will become vassals to the larger; and all experience has shown that the vassals and subjects of free States are the most enslaved. He instanced the Helots of Sparta, and the provinces of Rome. He observed that foreign powers, discovering this blemish, would make it a handle for disengaging the smaller States from so unequal a confederacy. That the colonies should in fact be considered as individuals; and that, as such, in all disputes, they should have an equal vote; that they are now collected as individuals making a bargain with each other, and, of course, had a right to vote as individuals. That in the East India Company they voted by persons, and not by their proportion of stock. That the Belgic confederacy voted by provinces. That in questions of war the smaller States were as much interested as the larger, and, therefore, should vote equally; and indeed, that the larger States were more likely to bring war on the confederacy, in proportion as their frontier was more extensive. He admitted that equality of representation was an excellent principle, but then it must be of things which are co-ordinate; that is, of things similar, and of the same nature: that nothing relating to individuals could ever come before Congress; nothing but what would respect colonies. He distinguished between an incorporating and a federal union. The union of England was an incorporating one; yet Scotland had suffered by that union; for that its inhabitants were drawn from it by the hopes of places and employments: nor was it an instance of equality of representation; because, while Scotland was allowed nearly a thirteenth of representation they were to pay only one-fortieth of the land tax. He expressed his hopes, that in the present enlightened state of men's minds, we might expect. a lasting confederacy, if it was founded on fair principles.

John Adams advocated the voting in proportion to numbers. He said that we stand here as the representatives of the people: that in some States the people are many, in others they are few; that therefore, their vote here should be proportioned to the numbers from whom it comes. Reason, justice and equity never had weight enough on the face of the earth, to govern the councils of men. It is interest alone which does it, and it is interest alone which can be trusted: that therefore the interests within doors, should be the mathematical representatives of the interests without doors: that the individuality of the colonies is a mere sound. Does the individuality of a colony increase its wealth or numbers? If it does, pay equally. If it does not add weight in the scale of the confederacy, it cannot add to their rights, nor weigh in argument. A. has £50, B. £500, C. £1000 in partnership. Is it just they should equally dispose of the moneys of the partnership? It has been said, we are independent individuals making a bargain together. The question is not what we are now, but what we ought to be when our bargain shall be made. The confederacy is to make us one individual only; it is to form us like separate parcels of metal, into one common mass. We shall no longer retain our separate individuality, but become a single individual as to all questions submitted to the confederacy. Therefore, all those reasons, which prove the justice and expediency of equal representation in other assemblies, hold good here. It has been objected that a proportional vote will endanger the smaller States. We answer that an equal vote will endanger the larger. Virginia, Pennsylvania, and Massachusetts, are the three greater colonies. Consider their distance, their difference of produce, of interests, and of manners, and it is apparent they can never have an interest or inclination to combine for the oppression of the smaller: that the smaller will naturally divide on all questions with the larger. Rhode Island, from its relation, similarity and intercourse, will generally pursue the same objects with Massachusetts; Jersey, Delaware, and Maryland, with Pennsylvania.

Dr. Rush took notice, that the decay of the liberties of the Dutch republic proceeded from three causes. 1. The perfect unanimity requisite on all occasions. 2. Their obligation to consult their constituents. 3. Their voting by provinces. This last destroyed the equality of representation, and the liberties of Great Britain also are sinking from the same defect. That a part of our rights is deposited in the hands of our legislatures. There, it was admitted, there should be an equality of representation. Another part of our rights is deposited in the hands of Congress: why is it not equally necessary there should be an equal representation there? Were it possible to collect the whole body of the people together, they would determine the questions submitted to them by their majority. Why should not the same majority decide when voting here, by their representatives? The larger colonies are so providentially divided in situation, as to render every fear of their combining visionary. Their interests are different, and their circumstances dissimilar. It is more probable they will become rivals, and leave it in the power of the smaller States to give preponderance to any scale they please. The voting by the number of free inhabitants, will have one excellent effect, that of inducing the colonies to discourage slavery, and to encourage the increase of their free inhabitants.

Mr. Hopkins observed, there were four larger, four smaller, and four middle-sized colonies. That the four largest would contain more than half the inhabitants of the confederated States and therefore, would govern the others as they should please. That history affords no instance of such a thing as equal representation. The Germanic body votes by States. The Helvetic body does the same; and so does the Belgic confederacy. That too little is known of the ancient confederations, to say what was their practice.

Mr. Wilson thought, that taxation should be in proportion to wealth, but that representation should accord with the number of freemen. That government is a collection or result of the will of all: that if any government could speak the will of all, it would be perfect; and that, so far as it departs from this, it becomes imperfect. It has been said that Congress is a representation of States, not of individuals. I say, that the objects of its care are all the individuals of the States. It is strange that annexing the name of "State" to ten thousand men, should give them an equal right with forty thousand. This must be the effect of magic, not of reason. As to those matters which are referred to Congress, we are not so many States; we are one large State. We lay aside our individuality, whenever we come here. The Germanic body is a burlesque on government; and their practice, on any point, is a sufficient authority and proof that it is wrong. The greatest imperfection in the constitution of the Belgic confederacy is their voting by provinces. The interest of the whole is constantly sacrificed to that of the small States. The history of the war in the reign of Queen Anne sufficiently proves this. It is asked, shall nine colonies put it into the power of four to govern them as they please? I invert the question, and ask, shall two millions of people put it in the power of one million to govern them as they please? It is pretended, too, that the smaller colonies will be in danger from the greater. Speak in honest language and say, the minority will be in danger from the majority. And is there an assembly on earth, where this danger may not be equally pretended? The truth is, that our proceedings will then be consentaneous with the interests of the majority, and so they ought to be. The probability is much greater, that the larger States will disagree, than that they will combine. I defy the wit of man to invent a possible case, or to suggest any one thing on earth, which shall be for the interests of Virginia, Pennsylvania and Massachusetts, and which will not also be for the interest of the other states.

These articles, reported July 12, '76, were debated from day to day, and time to time, for two years, were ratified July 9 '78, by ten States, by New Jersey on the 26th of November of the same year, and by Delaware on the 23d of February following. Maryland alone held off two years more, acceding to them March 1, '81, and thus closing the obligation.

Our delegation had been renewed for the ensuing year, commencing August 11; but the new government was now organized, a meeting of the legislature was to be held in October, and I had been elected a member by my county. I knew that our legislation, under the regal government, had many very vicious points which urgently required reformation, and I thought I could be of more use in forwarding that work. I therefore retired from my seat in Congress on the 2d of September, resigned it, and took my place in the legislature of my State, on the 7th of October.

On the 11th, I moved for leave to bring in a bill for the establishment of courts of justice, the organization of which was of importance. I drew the bill; it was approved by the committee, reported and passed, after going through its due course.

On the 12th, I obtained leave to bring in a bill declaring tenants in tail to hold their lands in fee simple. In the earlier times of the colony, when lands were to be obtained for little or nothing, some provident individuals procured large grants; and, desirous of founding great families for themselves, settled them on their descendants in fee tail. The transmission of this property from generation to generation, in the same name, raised up a distinct set of families, who, being privileged by law in the perpetuation of their wealth, were thus formed into a Patrician order, distinguished by the splendor and luxury of their establishments. From this order, too, the king habitually selected his counsellors of State; the hope of which distinction devoted the whole corps to the interests and will of the crown. To annul this privilege, and instead of an aristocracy of wealth, of more harm and danger, than benefit, to society, to make an opening for the aristocracy of virtue and talent, which nature has wisely provided for the direction of the interests of society, and scattered with equal hand through all its conditions, was deemed essential to a well-ordered republic.—To effect it, no violence was necessary, no deprivation of natural right, but rather an enlargement of it by a repeal of the law. For this would authorize the present holder to divide the property among his children equally, as his affections were divided; and would place them, by natural generation, on the level of their fellow citizens. But this repeal was strongly opposed by Mr. Pendleton, who was zealously attached to ancient establishments; and who, taken all in all, was the ablest man in debate I have ever met with. He had not indeed the poetical fancy of Mr. Henry, his sublime imagination, his lofty and overwhelming diction; but he was cool, smooth and persuasive; his language flowing, chaste and embellished; his conceptions quick, acute and full of resource; never vanquished: for if he lost the main battle, he returned upon you, and regained so much of it as to make it a drawn one, by dexterous manoeuvres, skirmishes in detail, and the recovery of small advantages which, little singly, were important all together. You never knew when you were clear of him, but were harassed by his perseverance, until the patience was worn down of all who had less of it than himself. Add to this, that he was one of the most virtuous and benevolent of men, the kindest friend, the most amiable and pleasant of companions, which ensured a favorable reception to whatever came from him. Finding that the general principle of entails could not be maintained, he took his stand on an amendment which he proposed, instead of an absolute abolition, to permit the tenant in tail to convey in fee simple, if he chose it; and he was within a few votes of saving so much of the old law. But the bill passed finally for entire abolition.

In that one of the bills for organizing our judiciary system, which proposed a court of Chancery, I had provided for a trial by jury of all matters of fact, in that as well as in the courts of law. He defeated it by the introduction of four words only, *"if either party choose."* The consequence has been, that as no suitor will say to his judge, "Sir, I distrust you, give me a jury," juries are rarely, I might say, perhaps, never, seen in that court, but when called for by the Chancellor of his own accord.

The first establishment in Virginia which became permanent, was made in 1607. I have found no mention of negroes in the colony until about 1650. The first brought here as slaves were by a Dutch ship; after which the English commenced the trade, and continued it until the revolutionary war. That suspended, *ipso facto*, their further importation for the present, and the business of the war pressing constantly on the legislature, this subject was not acted on finally until the year '78, when I brought in a bill to prevent their further importation. This passed without opposition, and stopped the increase of the evil by importation. leaving to future efforts its final eradication.

The first settlers of this colony were Englishmen, loyal subjects to their king and church, and the grant to Sir Walter Raleigh contained an express proviso that their laws "should not be against the true Christian faith, now professed in the church of England." As soon as the state of the colony admitted, it was divided into parishes, in each of which was established a minister of the Anglican church, endowed with a fixed salary, in tobacco, a glebe house and land with the other necessary appendages. To meet these expenses, all the inhabitants of the parishes were assessed, whether they were or not, members of the established church. Towards Quakers who came here, they were most cruelly intolerant, driving them from the colony by the severest penalties. In process of time, however, other sectarisms were introduced, chiefly of the Presbyterian family; and the established clergy, secure for life in their glebes and salaries, adding to these, generally, the emoluments of a classical school, found employment enough, in their farms and schoolrooms, for the rest of the week, and devoted Sunday only to the edification of their flock, by service, and a sermon at their parish church. Their other pastoral functions were little attended to. Against this inactivity, the zeal and industry of sectarian preachers had an open and undisputed field; and by the time of the revolution, a majority of the inhabitants had become dissenters from the established church, but were still obliged to pay contributions to support the pastors of the minority. This unrighteous compulsion, to maintain teachers of what they deemed religious errors, was grievously felt during the regal government, and without a hope of relief. But the first republican legislature, which met in '76, was crowded with petitions to abolish this spiritual tyranny. These brought on the severest contests in which I have ever been engaged. Our great opponents were Mr. Pendleton and Robert Carter Nicholas; honest men, but zealous churchmen. The petitions were referred to the committee of the whole house on the state of the country; and, after desperate contests in that committee, almost daily from the 11th of October to the 5th of December, we prevailed so far only, as to repeal the laws which rendered criminal the maintenance of any religious opinions, the forbearance of repairing to church, or the exercise of any mode of worship; and further, to exempt dissenters from contributions to the support of the established church; and to suspend, only until the next session, levies on the members of that church for the salaries of their own incumbents. For although the majority of our citizens were dissenters, as has been observed, a majority of the legislature were churchmen. Among these, however, were some reasonable and liberal men, who enabled us, on some points, to obtain feeble majorities. But our opponents carried, in the general resolutions of the committee of November 19, a declaration that religious assemblies ought to be regulated, and that provision ought to be made for continuing the succession of the clergy, and superintending their conduct. And, in the bill now passed, was inserted an express reservation of the question, Whether a general assessment should not be established by law, on every one, to the support of the pastor of his choice; or whether all should be left to voluntary contributions; and on this question, debated at every session, from '76 to '79, (some of our dissenting allies, having now secured their particular object, going over to the advocates of a general assessment,) we could only obtain a suspension from session to session until '79, when the question against a general assessment was finally carried, and the establishment of the Anglican church entirely put down. In justice to the two honest but zealous opponents who have been named, I must add, that although, from their natural temperaments, they were more disposed generally to acquiesce in things as they are, than to risk innovations, yet whenever the public will had once decided, none were more faithful or exact in their obedience to it.

The seat of our government had originally been fixed in the peninsula of Jamestown, the first settlement of the colonists; and had been afterwards removed a few miles inland to Williamsburg. But this was at a time when our settlements had not extended beyond the tide waters. Now they had crossed the Alleghany; and the centre of population was very far removed from what it had been. Yet Williamsburg was still the depository of our archives, the habitual residence of the Governor and many other of the public functionaries, the established place for the sessions of the legislature, and the magazine of our military stores; and its situation was so exposed that it might be taken at any time in war, and, at this time particularly, an enemy might in the night run up either of the rivers, between which it lies, land a force above, and take possession of the place, without the possibility of saving either persons or things. I had proposed its removal so early as October, '76; but it did not prevail until the session of May, '79.

Early in the session of May, '79, I prepared, and obtained leave to bring in a bill, declaring who should be deemed citizens, asserting the natural right of expatriation, and prescribing the mode of exercising it. This, when I withdrew from the House, on the 1st of June following, I left in the hands of George Mason, and it was passed on the 26th of that month.

In giving this account of the laws of which I was myself the mover and draughtsman, I, by no means, mean to claim to myself the merit of obtaining their passage. I had many occasional and strenuous coadjutors in debate, and one, most steadfast, able and zealous; who was himself a host. This was George Mason, a man of the first order of wisdom among those who acted on the theatre of the revolution, of expansive mind, profound judgment, cogent in argument, learned in the lore of our former constitution, and earnest for the republican change on democratic principles. His elocution was neither flowing nor smooth; but his language was strong, his manner most impressive, and strengthened by a dash of biting cynicism, when provocation made it seasonable.

Mr. Wythe, while speaker in the two sessions of 1777, between his return from Congress and his appointment to the Chancery, was an able and constant associate in whatever was before a committee of the whole. His pure integrity, judgment and reasoning powers, gave him great weight. . . .

Mr. Madison came into the House in 1776, a new member and young; which circumstances, concurring with his extreme modesty, prevented his venturing himself in debate before his removal to the Council of State, in November, '77. From thence he went to Congress, then consisting of few members. Trained in these successive schools, he acquired a habit of self-possession, which placed at ready command the rich resources of his luminous and discriminating mind, and of his extensive information, and rendered him the first of every assembly afterwards, of which he became a member. Never wandering from his subject into vain declamation, but pursuing it closely, in language pure, classical and copious, soothing always the feelings of his adversaries by civilities and softness of expression, he rose to the eminent station which he held in the great National Convention of 1787; and in that of Virginia which followed, he sustained the new constitution in all its parts, bearing off the palm against the logic of George Mason, and the fervid declamation of Mr. Henry. With these consummate powers, were united a pure and spotless virtue, which no calumny has ever attempted to sully. Of the powers and polish of his pen, and of the wisdom of his administration in the highest office of the nation, I need say nothing. They have spoken, and will forever speak for themselves.

So far we were proceeding in the details of reformation only; selecting points of legislation, prominent in character and principle, urgent, and indicative of the strength of the general pulse of reformation. When I left Congress, in '76, it was in the persuasion that our whole code must be reviewed, adapted to our republican form of government; and, now that we had no negatives of Councils, Governors, and Kings to restrain us from doing right, it should be corrected, in all its parts, with a single eye to reason, and the good of those for whose government it was framed. Early, therefore, in the session of '76, to which I returned, I moved and presented a bill for the revision of the laws, which was passed on the 24th of October; and on the 5th of November, Mr. Pendleton, Mr. Wythe, George Mason, Thomas L. Lee, and myself, were appointed a committee to execute the work. We agreed to meet at Fredericksburg to settle the plan of operation, and to distribute the work. We met there accordingly, on the 13th of January, 1777. The first question was, whether we should propose to abolish the whole existing system of laws, and prepare a new and complete Institute, or preserve the general system, and only modify it to the present state of things. Mr. Pendleton, contrary to his usual disposition in favor of ancient things, was for the former proposition, in which he was joined by Mr. Lee. To this it was objected, that to abrogate our whole system would be a bold measure, and probably far beyond the views of the legislature; that they had been in the practice of revising, from time to time, the laws of the colony, omitting the expired, the repealed, and the obsolete, amending only those retained, and probably meant we should now do the same, only including the British statutes as well as our own: that to compose a new Institute, like those of Justinian and Bracton, or that of Blackstone, which was the model proposed by Mr. Pendleton, would be an arduous undertaking, of vast research, of great consideration and judgment; and when reduced to a text, every word of that text, from the imperfection of human language, and its incompetence to express distinctly every shade of idea, would become a subject of question and chicanery, until settled by repeated adjudications; and this would involve us for ages in litigation, and render property

uncertain, until, like the statutes of old, every word had been tried and
settled by numerous decisions, and by new volumes of reports and
commentaries; and that no one of us, probably, would undertake such
a work, which to be systematical, must be the work of one hand. This
last was the opinion of Mr. Wythe, Mr. Mason, and myself. When
we proceeded to the distribution of the work, Mr. Mason excused himself, as, being no lawyer, he felt himself unqualified for the work, and
he resigned soon after. Mr. Lee excused himself on the same ground,
and died, indeed, in a short time. The other two gentlemen therefore,
and myself divided the work among us. The common law and statutes
to the 4 James I. (when our separate legislature was established) were
assigned to me; the British statutes, from that period to the present
day, to Mr. Wythe; and the Virginia laws to Mr. Pendleton. As the
law of Descents, and the criminal law fell of course within my portion, I wished the committee to settle the leading principles of these, as
a guide for me in framing them; and, with respect to the first, I proposed to abolish the law of primogeniture, and to make real estate
descendible in parcenary to the next of kin, as personal property is,
by the statute of distribution. Mr. Pendleton wished to preserve the
right of primogeniture, but seeing at once that that could not prevail,
he proposed we should adopt the Hebrew principle, and give a double portion to the elder son. I observed, that if the eldest son could
eat twice as much, or do double work, it might be a natural evidence of
his right to a double portion; but being on a par in his powers and
wants, with his brothers and sisters, he should be on a par also in the
partition of the patrimony; and such was the decision of the other
members.

On the subject of the Criminal law, all were agreed, that the punishment of death should be abolished, except for treason and murder;
and that, for other felonies, should be substituted hard labor in the public works, and in some cases, the *Lex talionis*.[1] How this last revolting
principle came to obtain our approbation, I do not remember. There
remained, indeed, in our laws, a vestige of it in a single case of a slave;
it was the English law, in the time of the Anglo-Saxons, copied probably from the Hebrew law of "an eye for an eye, a tooth for a tooth," and

---

[1]The law of retaliation.

it was the law of several ancient people; but the modern mind had left it far in the rear of its advances. These points, however, being settled, we repaired to our respective homes for the preparation of the work.

In the execution of my part, I thought it material not to vary the diction of the ancient statutes by modernizing it, nor to give rise to new questions by new expressions. The text of these statutes had been so fully explained and defined, by numerous adjudications, as scarcely ever now to produce a question in our courts. I thought it would be useful, also, in all new draughts, to reform the style of the later British statutes, and of our own acts of Assembly; which, from their verbosity, their endless tautologies, their involutions of case within case, and parenthesis within parenthesis, and their multiplied efforts at certainty, by *saids* and *aforesaids*, by *ors* and by *ands*, to make them more plain, are really rendered more perplexed and incomprehensible, not only to common readers, but to the lawyers themselves. We were employed in this work from that time to February, 1779, when we met at Williamsburg, that is to say, Mr. Pendleton, Mr. Wythe and myself; and meeting day by day, we examined critically our several parts, sentence by sentence, scrutinizing and amending, until we had agreed on the whole. We then returned home, had fair copies made of our several parts, which were reported to the General Assembly, June 18, 1779, by Mr. Wythe and myself, Mr. Pendleton's residence being distant, and he having authorized us by letter to declare his approbation. We had, in this work, brought so much of the Common law as it was thought necessary to alter, all the British statutes from *Magna Charta* to the present day, and all the laws of Virginia, from the establishment of our legislature, in the 4th Jac. I. to the present time, which we thought should be retained, within the compass of one hundred and twenty-six bills, making a printed folio of ninety pages only. Some bills were taken out, occasionally, from time to time, and passed; but the main body of the work was not entered on by the legislature until after the general peace, in 1785, when, by the unwearied exertions of Mr. Madison, in opposition to the endless quibbles, chicaneries, perversions, vexations and delays of lawyers and demi-lawyers, most of the bills were passed by the legislature, with little alteration.

The bill for establishing religious freedom, the principles of which had, to a certain degree, been enacted before, I had drawn in all the latitude of reason and right. It still met with opposition; but, with some mutilations in the preamble, it was finally passed; and a singular proposition proved that its protection of opinion was meant to be universal. Where the preamble declares, that coercion is a departure from the plan of the holy author of our religion, an amendment was proposed, by inserting the word "Jesus Christ," so that it should read, "a departure from the plan of Jesus Christ, the holy author of our religion;" the insertion was rejected by a great majority, in proof that they meant to comprehend, within the mantle of its protection, the Jew and the Gentile, the Christian and Mahometan, the Hindoo, and Infidel of every denomination.

Beccaria, and other writers on crimes and punishments, had satisfied the reasonable world of the unrightfulness and inefficacy of the punishment of crimes by death; and hard labor on roads, canals and other public works, had been suggested as a proper substitute. The Revisors had adopted these opinions; but the general idea of our country had not yet advanced to that point. The bill, therefore, for proportioning crimes and punishments, was lost in the House of Delegates by a majority of a single vote. I learned afterwards, that the substitute of hard labor in public, was tried (I believe it was in Pennsylvania) without success. Exhibited as a public spectacle, with shaved heads and mean clothing, working on the high roads, produced in the criminals such a prostration of character, such an abandonment of self-respect, as, instead of reforming, plunged them into the most desperate and hardened depravity of morals and character. To pursue the subject of this law.—I was written to in 1785 (being then in Paris) by directors appointed to superintend the building of a Capitol in Richmond, to advise them as to a plan, and to add to it one of a Prison. Thinking it a favorable opportunity of introducing into the State an example of architecture, in the classic style of antiquity, and the Maison Quarrée of Nismes, an ancient Roman temple, being considered as the most perfect model existing of what may be called Cubic architecture, I applied to M. Clerissault, who had published drawings of the Antiquities of Nismes, to have me a model of the building made in stucco, only changing the order from Corinthian to Ionic, on account of the difficulty of the Corinthian capitals. I yielded, with reluctance, to the taste of Clerissault, in his preference of the modern capital of Scamozzi to the more noble capital of antiquity. This was executed by the artist whom Choiseul Gouffier had carried with him to Constantinople, and employed, while Ambassador there, in making those beautiful models of the remains of Grecian architecture which are to be seen at Paris. To adapt the exterior to our use, I drew a plan for the interior, with the apartments necessary for legislative, executive, and judiciary purposes; and accommodated in their size and distribution to the form and dimensions of the building. These were forwarded to the Directors, in 1786, and were carried into execution, with some variations, not for the better, the most important of which, however, admit of future correction. With respect to the plan of a Prison, requested at the same time, I had heard of a benevolent society, in England, which had been indulged by the government, in an experiment of the effect of labor, in *solitary confinement,* on some of their criminals; which experiment had succeeded beyond expectation. The same idea had been suggested in France, and an Architect of Lyons had proposed a plan of a well-contrived edifice, on the principle of solitary confinement. I procured a copy, and as it was too large for our purposes, I drew one on a scale less extensive, but susceptible of additions as they should be wanting. This I sent to the Directors, instead of a plan of a common prison, in the hope that it would suggest the idea of labor in solitary confinement, instead of that on the public works, which we had adopted in our Revised Code. Its principle, accordingly, but not its exact form, was adopted by Latrobe in carrying the plan into execution, by the erection of what is now called the Penitentiary, built under his direction. In the meanwhile, the public opinion was ripening, by time, by reflection, and by the example of Pennsylvania, where labor on the highways had been tried, without approbation, from 1786 to '89, and had been followed by their Penitentiary system on the principle of confinement and labor, which was proceeding auspiciously. In 1796, our legislature resumed the subject, and passed the law for amending the Penal laws of the commonwealth. They adopted solitary, instead of public, labor, established a gradation in the duration of the confinement, approximated the style of the law more to the modern usage, and, instead of the settled distinctions of murder and manslaughter, preserved in my bill, they introduced the new terms of murder in the first and second degree. Whether these have produced more or fewer questions of definition, I am not sufficiently informed of our judiciary transactions to say. . . .

The acts of Assembly concerning the College of William and Mary, were properly within Mr. Pendleton's portion of our work; but these related chiefly to its revenue, while its constitution, organization and scope of science, were derived from its charter. We thought that on this subject, a systematical plan of general education should be proposed, and I was requested to undertake it. I accordingly prepared three bills for the Revisal, proposing three distinct grades of education, reaching all classes. 1st. Elementary schools, for all children generally, rich and poor. 2d. Colleges, for a middle degree of instruction, calculated for the common purposes of life, and such as would be desirable for all who were in easy circumstances. And, 3d, an ultimate grade for teaching the sciences generally, and in their highest degree. The first bill proposed to lay off every county into Hundreds, or Wards, of a proper size and population for a school, in which reading, writing, and common arithmetic should be taught; and that the whole State should be divided into twenty-four districts, in each of which should be a school for classical learning, grammar, geography, and the higher branches of numerical arithmetic. The second bill proposed to amend the constitution of William and Mary college, to enlarge its sphere of science, and to make it in fact a University. The third was for the establishment of a library. These bills were not acted on until the same year, '96, and then only so much of the first as provided for elementary schools. The College of William and Mary was an establishment purely of the Church of England; the Visitors were required to be all of that Church; the Professors to subscribe its thirty-nine Articles; its Students to learn its Catechism; and one of its fundamental objects was declared to be, to raise up Ministers for that church. The religious jealousies, therefore, of all the dissenters, took alarm lest this might give an ascendancy to the Anglican sect, and refused acting on that bill. Its local eccentricity, too, and unhealthy autumnal climate, lessened the general inclination towards it. And in the Elementary bill, they inserted a provision which completely defeated it; for they left it to the court of each county to determine for itself, when this act should be carried into execution, within their county. One provision of the bill was, that the expenses of these schools should be borne by the inhabitants of the county, every one in proportion to his general tax rate. This would throw on wealth the education of the poor; and the justices, being generally of the more wealthy class, were unwilling to incur that burden, and I believe it was not suffered to commence in a single county. I shall recur again to this subject, towards the close of my story, if I should have life and resolution enough to reach that term; for I am already tired of talking about myself.

The bill on the subject of slaves, was a mere digest of the existing laws respecting them, without any intimation of a plan for a future and general emancipation. It was thought better that this should be kept back, and attempted only by way of amendment, whenever the bill should be brought on. The principles of the amendment, however, were agreed on, that is to say, the freedom of all born after a certain day, and deportation at a proper age. But it was found that the public mind would not yet bear the proposition, nor will it bear it even at this day. Yet the day is not distant when it must bear and adopt it, or worse will follow. Nothing is more certainly written in the book of fate, than that these people are to be free; nor is it less certain that the two races, equally free, cannot live in the same government. Nature, habit, opinion have drawn indelible lines of distinction between them. It is still in our power to direct the process of emancipation and deportation, peaceably, and in such slow degree, as that the evil will wear off insensibly, and their place be, *pari passu,*[1] filled up by free white laborers. If, on the contrary, it is left to force itself on, human nature must shudder at the prospect held up. We should in vain look for an example in the Spanish deportation or deletion of the Moors. This precedent would fall far short of our case.

I consider four of these bills, passed or reported, as forming a system by which every fibre would be eradicated of ancient or future aristocracy; and a foundation laid for a government truly republican. The repeal of the laws of entail would prevent the accumulation and perpetuation of wealth, in select families, and preserve the soil of the country from being daily more and more absorbed in mortmain. The abolition of primogeniture, and equal partition of inheritances,

---

[1] On an equal basis.

removed the feudal and unnatural distinctions which made one member of every family rich, and all the rest poor, substituting equal partition, the best of all Agrarian laws. The restoration of the rights of conscience relieved the people from taxation for the support of a religion not theirs; for the establishment was truly of the religion of the rich, the dissenting sects being entirely composed of the less wealthy people; and these, by the bill for a general education, would be qualified to understand their rights, to maintain them, and to exercise with intelligence their parts in self-government; and all this would be effected, without the violation of a single natural right of any one individual citizen. To these, too, might be added, as a further security, the introduction of the trial by jury, into the Chancery courts, which have already ingulfed, and continue to ingulf, so great a proportion of the jurisdiction over our property.

On the 1st of June, 1779, I was appointed Governor of the Commonwealth, and retired from the legislature. Being elected, also, one of the Visitors of William and Mary college, a self-electing body, I effected, during my residence in Williamsburg that year, a change in the organization of that institution, by abolishing the Grammar school, and the two professorships of Divinity and Oriental languages, and substituting a professorship of Law and Police, one of Anatomy, Medicine and Chemistry, and one of Modern languages; and the charter confining us to six professorships, we added the Law of Nature and Nations, and the Fine Arts to the duties of the Moral professor, and Natural History to those of the professor of Mathematics and Natural Philosophy.

Being now, as it were, identified with the Commonwealth itself, to write my own history, during the two years of my administration, would be to write the public history of that portion of the revolution within this State. This has been done by others, and particularly by Mr. Girardin, who wrote his Continuation of Burke's History of Virginia, while at Milton, in this neighborhood, had free access to all my papers while composing it, and has given as faithful an account as I could myself. For this portion, therefore, of my own life, I refer altogether to his history. From a belief that, under the pressure of the invasion under which we were then laboring, the public would have more confidence in a Military chief, and that the Military commander, being invested with the Civil power also, both might be wielded with more energy, promptitude and effect for the defence of the State, I resigned the administration at the end of my second year, and General Nelson was appointed to succeed me.

Soon after my leaving Congress, in September, '76, to wit, on the last day of that month, I had been appointed, with Dr. Franklin, to go to France, as a Commissioner, to negotiate treaties of alliance and commerce with that government. Silas Deane, then in France, acting as agent for procuring military stores, was joined with us in commission. But such was the state of my family that I could not leave it, nor could I expose it to the dangers of the sea, and of capture by the British ships, then covering the ocean. I saw, too, that the laboring oar was really at home, where much was to be done, of the most permanent interest, in new modeling our governments, and much to defend our fanes and fire-sides from the desolations of an invading enemy, pressing on our country in every point. I declined, therefore, and Mr. Lee was appointed in my place. On the 15th of June, 1781, I had been appointed, with Mr. Adams, Mr. Franklin, Mr. Jay, and Mr. Laurence, a Minister Plenipotentiary for negotiating peace, then expected to be effected through the mediation of the Empress of Russia. The same reasons obliged me still to decline; and the negotiation was in fact never entered on. But, in the autumn of the next year, 1782, Congress receiving assurances that a general peace would be concluded in the winter and spring, they renewed my appointment on the 13th of November of that year. I had, two months before that, lost the cherished companion of my life, in whose affections, unabated on both sides, I had lived the last ten years in unchequered happiness.[1] With the public interests, the state of my mind concurred in recommending the change of scene proposed; and I accepted the appointment, and left Monticello on the 19th of December, 1782, for Philadelphia, where I arrived on the 27th. The Minister of France, Luzerne, offered me a passage in the Romulus frigate, which I accepted; but she was then lying a few miles below Baltimore, blocked up in the ice. I remained, therefore, a month in Philadelphia, looking over the papers in the office of State, in order to possess myself of the general state of our foreign

[1]Jefferson is, of course, referring to the death of Mrs. Jefferson.

relations, and then went to Baltimore, to await the liberation of the frigate from the ice. After waiting there nearly a month, we received information that a Provisional treaty of peace had been signed by our Commissioners on the 3d of September, 1782, to become absolute, on the conclusion of peace between France and Great Britain. Considering my proceeding to Europe as now of no utility to the public, I returned immediately to Philadelphia, to take the orders of Congress, and was excused by them from further proceeding. I, therefore, returned home, where I arrived on the 15th of May, 1783.

On the 6th of the following month, I was appointed by the legislature a delegate to Congress, the appointment to take place on the 1st of November ensuing, when that of the existing delegation would expire. I, accordingly, left home on the 16th of October, arrived at Trenton, where Congress was sitting, on the 3rd day of November, and took my seat on the 4th, on which day Congress adjourned, to meet at Annapolis on the 26th.

Congress had now become a very small body, and the members very remiss in their attendance on its duties, insomuch, that a majority of the States, necessary by the Confederation to constitute a House even for minor business, did not assemble until the 13th of December.

They, as early as January 7, 1782, had turned their attention to the moneys current in the several States, and had directed the Financier, Robert Morris, to report to them a table of rates, at which the foreign coins should be received at the treasury. That officer, or rather his assistant, Gouverneur Morris, answered them on the 15th, in an able and elaborate statement of the denominations of money current in the several States, and of the comparative value of the foreign coins chiefly in circulation with us. He went into the consideration of the necessity of establishing a standard of value with us, and of the adoption of a money Unit. He proposed for that Unit, such a fraction of pure silver as would be a common measure of the penny of every State, without leaving a fraction. This common divisor he found to be 1–1440 of a dollar, or 1–1600 of the crown sterling. The value of a dollar was, therefore, to be expressed by 1,440 units, and of a crown by 1,600; each Unit containing a quarter of a grain of fine silver. Congress turning again their attention to this subject the following year, the Financier, by a letter of April 30, 1783, further explained and urged the Unit he had proposed; but nothing more was done in it until the ensuing year, when it was again taken up, and referred to a committee, of which I was a member. The general views of the Financier were sound, and the principle was ingenious on which he proposed to found his Unit; but it was too minute for ordinary use, too laborious for computation either by the head or in figures. The price of a loaf of bread, 1–20 of a dollar, would be 72 units.

A pound of butter, 1–5 of a dollar, 288 units.

A horse or bullock, of eighty dollars value, would require a notation of six figures, to wit, 115,200, and the public debt, suppose of eighty millions, would require twelve figures, to wit, 115,200,000,000 units. Such a system of money-arithmetic would be entirely unmanageable for the common purposes of society. I proposed, therefore, instead of this, to adopt the Dollar as our Unit of account and payment, and that its divisions and sub-divisions should be in the decimal ratio. I wrote some notes on the subject, which I submitted to the consideration of the Financier. I received his answer and adherence to his general system, only agreeing to take for his Unit one hundred of those he first proposed, so that a Dollar should be 14 40–100, and a crown 16 units. I replied to this, and printed my notes and reply on a flying sheet, which I put into the hands of the members of Congress for consideration, and the Committee agreed to report on my principle. This was adopted the ensuing year, and is the system which now prevails. I insert, here, the Notes and Reply, as showing the different views on which the adoption of our money system hung.[1] The divisions into dimes, cents, and mills is now so well understood, that it would be easy of introduction into the kindred branches of weights and measures. I use when I travel, an Odometer of Clark's invention, which divides the mile into cents, and I find every one comprehends a distance readily, when stated to him in miles and cents; so he would in feet and cents, pounds and cents, &c.

The remissness of Congress, and their permanent session, began to be a subject of uneasiness; and even some of the legislatures had recommended to them intermissions, and periodical sessions. As the Confederation had made no provision for a visible head of the government,

[1]The appendix is not included in this volume.

during vacations of Congress, and such a one was necessary to superintend the executive business, to receive and communicate with foreign ministers and nations, and to assemble Congress on sudden and extraordinary emergencies, I proposed, early in April, the appointment of a committee, to be called the "Committee of the States," to consist of a member from each State, who should remain in session during the recess of Congress: that the functions of Congress should be divided into executive and legislative, the latter to be reserved, and the former, by a general resolution, to be delegated to that Committee. This proposition was afterwards agreed to; a Committee appointed, who entered on duty on the subsequent adjournment of Congress, quarreled very soon, split into two parties, abandoned their post, and left the government without any visible head, until the next meeting in Congress. We have since seen the same thing take place in the Directory of France; and I believe it will forever take place in any Executive consisting of a plurality. Our plan, best, I believe, combines wisdom and practicability, by providing a plurality of Counsellors, but a single Arbiter for ultimate decision. I was in France when we heard of this schism, and separation of our Committee, and, speaking with Dr. Franklin of this singular disposition of men to quarrel, and divide into parties, he gave his sentiments, as usual, by way of Apologue. He mentioned the Eddystone lighthouse, in the British channel, as being built on a rock, in the mid-channel, totally inaccessible in winter, from the boisterous character of that sea, in that season; that, therefore, for the two keepers employed to keep up the lights, all provision for the winter were necessarily carried to them in autumn, as they could never be visited again till the return of the milder season; that, on the first practicable day in the spring, a boat put off to them with fresh supplies. The boatman met at the door one of the keepers, and accosted him with a "How goes it, friend? Very well. How is your companion? I do not know. Don't know? Is not he here? I can't tell. Have not you seen him to-day? No. When did you see him? Not since last fall. You have killed him? Not I, indeed." They were about to lay hold of him, as having certainly murdered his companion; but he desired them to go up stairs and examine for themselves. They went up, and there found the other keeper. They had quarrelled, it seems, soon after being left there, had divided into two parties, assigned the cares below to one, and those above to the other, and had never spoken to, or seen, one another since.

But to return to our Congress at Annapolis. The definitive treaty of peace which had been signed at Paris on the 3d of September, 1783, and received here, could not be ratified without a House of nine States. On the 23d of December, therefore, we addressed letters to the several Governors, stating the receipt of the definitive treaty; that seven States only were in attendance, while nine were necessary to its ratification; and urging them to press on their delegates the necessity of their immediate attendance. And on the 26th, to save time, I moved that the Agent of Marine (Robert Morris) should be instructed to have ready a vessel at this place, at New York, and at some Eastern port, to carry over the ratification of the treaty when agreed to. It met the general sense of the House, but was opposed by Dr. Lee, on the ground of expense, which it would authorize the Agent to incur for us; and, he said, it would be better to ratify at once, and send on the ratification. Some members had before suggested, that seven States were competent to the ratification. My motion was therefore postponed, and another brought forward by Mr. Read, of South Carolina, for an immediate ratification. This was debated the 26th and 27th. Read, Lee, Williamson and Jeremiah Chase, urged that ratification was a mere matter of form, that the treaty was conclusive from the moment it was signed by the ministers; that, although the Confederation requires the assent of *nine States* to *enter into* a treaty, yet, that its conclusion could not be called *entrance into it;* that supposing nine States requisite, it would be in the power of five States to keep us always at war; that nine States had virtually authorized the ratification, having ratified the provisional treaty, and instructed their ministers to agree to a definitive one in the same terms, and the present one was, in fact, substantially, and almost verbatim, the same; that there now remain but sixty-seven days for the ratification, for its passage across the Atlantic, and its exchange; that there was no hope of our soon having nine States present; in fact, that this was the ultimate point of time to which we could venture to wait; that if the ratification was not in Paris by the time stipulated, the treaty would become void; that if ratified by seven States, it would go under our seal, without its being known to Great Britain that only seven had concurred; that it was a question of which they had not right to take cognizance, and we were only answerable for it to our constituents; that it was like the ratification which Great Britain had received from the Dutch, by the negotiations of Sir William Temple.

On the contrary, it was argued by Monroe, Gerry, Howel, Ellery and myself, that by the modern usage of Europe, the ratification was considered as the act which gave validity to a treaty, until which, it was not obligatory.[1] That the commission to the ministers reserved the ratification to Congress; that the treaty itself stipulated that it should be ratified; that it became a second question, who were competent to the ratification? That the Confederation expressly required nine States to enter into any treaty; that, by this, that instrument must have intended, that the assent of nine States should be necessary, as well to the *completion* as to the *commencement* of the treaty, its object having been to guard the rights of the Union in all those important cases where nine States are called for; that by the contrary construction, seven States, containing less than one-third of our whole citizens, might rivet on us a treaty, commenced indeed under commission and instructions from nine States, but formed by the minister in express contradiction to such instructions, and in direct sacrifice of the interests of so great a majority; that the definitive treaty was admitted not to be a verbal copy of the provisional one, and whether the departures from it were of substance, or not, was a question on which nine States alone were competent to decide; that the circumstances of the ratification of the provisional articles by nine States, the instructions to our ministers to form a definitive one by them, and their actual agreement in substance, do not render us competent to ratify in the present instance; if these circumstances are in themselves a ratification, nothing further is requisite than to give attested copies of them, in exchange for the British ratification; if they are not, we remain where we were, without a ratification by nine States, and incompetent ourselves to ratify; that it was but four days since the seven States, now present, unanimously concurred in a resolution, to be forwarded to the Governors of the absent States, in which they stated as a cause for urging on their delegates, that nine States were necessary to ratify the treaty; that in the case of

[1] Jefferson's footnote omitted here.

the Dutch ratification, Great Britain had courted it, and therefore was glad to accept it as it was; that they knew our Constitution, and would object to a ratification by seven; that, if that circumstance was kept back, it would be known hereafter, and would give them ground to deny the validity of a ratification, into which they should have been surprised and cheated, and it would be a dishonorable prostitution of our seal; that there is a hope of nine States; that if the treaty would become null, if not ratified in time, it would not be saved by an imperfect ratification; but that, in fact, it would not be null, and would be placed on better ground, going in unexceptionable form, though a few days too late, and rested on the small importance of this circumstance, and the physical impossibilities which had prevented a punctual compliance in point of time; that this would be approved by all nations, and by Great Britain herself, if not determined to renew the war, and if so determined, she would never want excuses, were this out of the way. Mr. Read gave notice, he should call for the yeas and nays; whereon those in opposition, prepared a resolution, expressing pointedly the reasons of their dissent from his motion. It appearing, however, that his proposition could not be carried, it was thought better to make no entry at all. Massachusetts alone would have been for it; Rhode Island, Pennsylvania and Virginia against it, Delaware, Maryland and North Carolina, would have been divided.

Our body was little numerous, but very contentious. Day after day was wasted on the most unimportant questions. A member, one of those afflicted with the morbid rage of debate, of an ardent mind, prompt imagination, and copious flow of words, who heard with impatience any logic which was not his own, sitting near me on some occasion of a trifling but wordy debate, asked me how I could sit in silence, hearing so much false reasoning, which a word should refute? I observed to him, that to refute indeed was easy, but to silence was impossible; that in measures brought forward by myself, I took the laboring oar, as was incumbent on me; but that in general, I was willing to listen; that if every sound argument or objection was used by some one or other of the numerous debaters, it was enough; if not, I thought it sufficient to suggest the omission, without going into a repetition of what had been already said by others: that this was a waste and abuse of the time and patience of the House, which could not be justified And I believe, that if the members of deliberate bodies were to observe this course generally, they would do in a day, what takes them a week; and it is really more questionable, than may at first be thought, whether Bonaparte's dumb legislature, which said nothing, and did much, may not be preferable to one which talks much, and does nothing. I served with General Washington in the legislature of Virginia, before the revolution, and during it, with Dr. Franklin in Congress. I never heard either of them speak ten minutes at a time, nor to any but the main point, which was to decide the question. They laid their shoulders to the great points, knowing that the little ones would follow of themselves. If the present Congress errs in too much talking, how can it be otherwise, in a body to which the people send one hundred and fifty lawyers, whose trade it is to question everything, yield nothing, and talk by the hour? That one hundred and fifty lawyers should do business together, ought not to be expected. But to return again to our subject.

Those who thought seven States competent to the ratification, being very restless under the loss of their motion, I proposed, on the third of January, to meet them on middle ground, and therefore moved a resolution, which premised, that there were but seven States present, who were unanimous for the ratification, but that they differed in opinion on the question of competency; that those however in the negative were unwilling that any powers which it might be supposed they possessed, should remain unexercised for the restoration of peace, provided it could be done, saving their good faith, and without importing any opinion of Congress, that seven States were competent, and resolving that the treaty be ratified so far as they had power; that it should be transmitted to our ministers, with instructions to keep it uncommunicated; to endeavor to obtain three months longer for exchange of ratifications; that they should be informed, that so soon as nine States shall be present, a ratification by nine shall be sent them: if this should get to them before the ultimate point of time for exchange, they were to use it, and not the other; if not, they were to offer the act of the seven States in exchange, informing them the treaty had come to hand while Congress was not in session; that but seven States were as yet assembled, and these had unanimously concurred in the ratification. This was debated on the third and fourth;

and on the fifth, a vessel being to sail for England, from this port (Annapolis), the House directed the President to write to our ministers accordingly.

January 14. Delegates from Connecticut having attended yesterday, and another from South Carolina coming in this day, the treaty was ratified without a dissenting voice; and three instruments of ratification were ordered to be made out, one of which was sent by Colonel Harmer, another by Colonel Franks, and the third transmitted to the Agent of Marine, to be forwarded by any good opportunity.

Congress soon took up the consideration of their foreign relations. They deemed it necessary to get their commerce placed with every nation, on a footing as favorable as that of other nations; and for this purpose, to propose to each a distinct treaty of commerce. This act too would amount to an acknowledgment, by each, of our independence, and of our reception into the fraternity of nations; which, although as possessing our station of right, and in fact we would not condescend to ask, we were not unwilling to furnish opportunities for receiving their friendly salutations and welcome. With France, the United Netherlands, and Sweden, we had already treaties of commerce; but commissions were given for those countries also, should any amendments be thought necessary. The other States to which treaties were to be proposed, were England, Hamburg, Saxony, Prussia, Denmark, Russia, Austria, Venice, Rome, Naples, Tuscany, Sardinia, Genoa, Spain, Portugal, the Porte, Algiers, Tripoli, Tunis, and Morocco.

On the 7th of May Congress resolved that a Minister Plenipotentiary should be appointed, in addition to Mr. Adams and Dr. Franklin, for negotiating treaties of commerce with foreign nations, and I was elected to that duty. I accordingly left Annapolis on the 11th, took with me my eldest daughter, then at Philadelphia (the two others being too young for the voyage), and proceeded to Boston, in quest of a passage. While passing through the different States, I made a point of informing myself of the state of the commerce of each; went on to New Hampshire with the same view, and returned to Boston. Thence I sailed on the 5th of July, in the Ceres, a merchant ship of Mr. Nathenial Tracey, bound to Cowes. He was himself a passenger, and, after a pleasant voyage of nineteen days, from land to land, we arrived at Cowes on the 26th. I was detained there a few days by the indisposition of my daughter. On the 30th, we embarked for Havre, arrived there on the 31st, left it on the 3d of August, and arrived at Paris on the 6th. I called immediately on Dr. Franklin, at Passy, communicated to him our charge, and we wrote to Mr. Adams, then at the Hague, to join us at Paris.

Before I had left America, that is to say, in the year 1781, I had received a letter from M. de Marbois, of the French legation in Philadelphia, informing me, he had been instructed by his government to obtain such statistical accounts of the different States of our Union, as might be useful for their information; and addressing to me a number of queries relative to the State of Virginia. I had always made it a practice, whenever an opportunity occurred of obtaining any information of our country, which might be of use to me in any station, public or private, to commit it to writing. These memoranda were on loose papers, bundled up without order, and difficult of recurrence, when I had occasion for a particular one. I thought this a good occasion to embody their substance, which I did in the order of Mr. Marbois' queries, so as to answer his wish, and to arrange them for my own use. Some friends, to whom they were occasionally communicated, wished for copies; but their volume rendering this too laborious by hand, I proposed to get a few printed, for their gratification. I was asked such a price, however, as exceeded the importance of the object. On my arrival at Paris, I found it could be done for a fourth of what I had been asked here. I therefore corrected and enlarged them and had two hundred copies printed, under the title of "Notes on Virginia." I gave a very few copies to some particular friends in Europe, and sent the rest to my friends in America. A European copy, by the death of the owner, got into the hands of a bookseller, who engaged its translation, and when ready for the press, communicated his intentions and manuscript to me, suggesting that I should correct it, without asking any other permission for the publication. I never had seen so wretched an attempt at translation. Introverted, abridged, mutilated, and often reversing the sense of the original, I found it a blotch of errors, from beginning to end. I corrected some of the most material, and, in that form, it was printed in French. A London bookseller, on seeing the translation, requested me to permit him to print the English original. I thought it best to do so, to let the world see that it was not really so bad as the French translation had made it appear. And this is the true history of that publication.

Mr. Adams soon joined us at Paris, and our first employment was to prepare a general form, to be proposed to such nations as were disposed to treat with us. During the negotiations for peace with the British Commissioner, David Hartley, our Commissioners had proposed, on the suggestion of Dr. Franklin, to insert an article, exempting from capture by the public or private armed ships, of either belligerent, when at war, all merchant vessels and their cargoes, employed merely in carrying on the commerce between nations. It was refused by England, and unwisely, in my opinion For, in the case of a war with us, their superior commerce places infinitely more at hazard on the ocean, than ours; and, as hawks abound in proportion to game, so our privateers would swarm, in proportion to the wealth exposed to their prize, while theirs would be few, for want of subjects of capture. We inserted this article in our form, with a provision against the molestation of fishermen, husbandmen, citizens unarmed, and following their occupations in unfortified places, for the humane treatment of prisoners of war, the abolition of contraband of war, which exposes merchant vessels to such vexatious and ruinous detentions and abuses; and for the principle of free bottoms, free goods.

In conference with the Count de Vergennes, it was thought better to leave to legislative regulation, on both sides, such modifications of our commercial intercourse, as would voluntarily flow from amicable dispositions. Without urging, we sounded the ministers of the several European nations, at the court of Versailles, on their dispositions towards mutual commerce, and the expediency of encouraging it by the protection of a treaty. Old Frederic, of Prussia, met us cordially, and without hesitation, and appointing the Baron de Thulemeyer, his minister at the Hague, to negotiate with us, we communicated to him our Projét, which, with little alteration by the King, was soon concluded. Denmark and Tuscany, entered also into negotiations with us. Other powers appearing indifferent; we did not think it proper to press them. They seemed, in fact, to know little about us, but as rebels, who had been successful in throwing off the yoke of the mother country. They were ignorant of our commerce, which had been always monopolized by England, and of the exchange of articles it might offer advantageously to both parties. They were inclined, therefore, to stand aloof, until they could see better what relations might be usefully instituted with us. The negotiations, therefore, begun with Denmark and Tuscany, we protracted designedly, until our powers had expired; and abstained from making new propositions to others having no colonies; because our commerce being an exchange of raw for wrought materials, is a competent price for admission into the colonies of those possessing them; but were we to give it, without price, to others, all would claim it, without price, on the ordinary ground of *gentis amicissimae*.[1]

Mr. Adams being appointed Minister Plenipotentiary of the United States, to London, left us in June, and in July, 1785, Dr. Franklin returned to America, and I was appointed his successor at Paris. In February, 1786, Mr. Adams wrote to me, pressingly, to join him in London immediately, as he thought he discovered there some symptoms of better disposition towards us. Colonel Smith, his secretary of legation, was the bearer of his urgencies for my immediate attendance. I, accordingly, left Paris on the 1st of March, and, on my arrival in London, we agreed on a very summary form of treaty, proposing an exchange of citizenship for our citizens, our ships, and our productions generally, except as to office. On my presentation, as usual, to the King and Queen, at their levees, it was impossible for anything to be more ungracious, than their notice of Mr. Adams and myself. I saw, at once, that the ulcerations of mind in that quarter, left nothing to be expected on the subject of my attendance; and, on the first conference with the Marquis of Caermarthen, the Minister for foreign affairs, the distance and disinclination which he betrayed in his conversation, the vagueness and evasions of his answers to us, confirmed me in the belief of their aversion to have anything to do with us. We delivered him, however, our Projét, Mr. Adams not despairing as much as I did, of its effect. We afterwards, by one or more notes, requested his appointment of an interview and conference, which, without directly declining, he evaded, by pretences of other pressing occupations for the moment. After staying there seven weeks, till within a few days of the expiration of our commission, I informed the minister, by note, that my duties at Paris required my return to that place, and that I should, with plea-

[1]Most favored nation.

sure, be the bearer of any commands to his Ambassador there. He answered, that he had none, and, wishing me a pleasant journey, I left London the 26th, and arrived at Paris the 30th of April.

While in London, we entered into negotiations with the Chevalier Pinto, Ambassador of Portugal, at that place. The only article of difficulty between us was, a stipulation that our bread stuff should be received in Portugal, in the form of flour as well as of grain. He approved of it himself, but observed that several Nobles, of great influence at their court, were the owners of wind-mills in the neighborhood of Lisbon, which depended much for their profits on manufacturing our wheat, and that this stipulation would endanger the whole treaty. He signed it, however, and its fate was what he had candidly portended.

My duties, at Paris, were confined to a few objects; the receipt of our whale-oils, salted fish, and salted meats, on favorable terms; the admission of our rice on equal terms with that of Piedmont, Egypt and the Levant; a mitigation of the monopolies of our tobacco by the Farmers-general, and a free admission of our productions into their islands, were the principal commercial objects which required attention; and, on these occasions, I was powerfully aided by all the influence and the energies of the Marquis de La Fayette, who proved himself equally zealous for the friendship and welfare of both nations; and, in justice, I must also say, that I found the government entirely disposed to befriend us on all occasions, and to yield us every indulgence, not absolutely injurious to themselves. The Count de Vergennes had the reputation, with the diplomatic corps, of being wary and slippery in his diplomatic intercourse; and so he might be with those whom he knew to be slippery, and doublefaced themselves. As he saw that I had no indirect views, practised no subtleties, meddled in no intrigues, pursued no concealed objects, I found him as frank, as honorable, as easy of access to reason, as any man with whom I had ever done business; and I must say the same for his successor, Montmorin, one of the most honest and worthy of human beings.

Our commerce, in the Mediterranean, was placed under early alarm, by the capture of two of our vessels and crews by the Barbary cruisers. I was very unwilling that we should acquiesce in the European humiliation, of paying a tribute to those lawless pirates, and endeavored to form an association of the powers subject to habitual depredations from them. I accordingly prepared, and proposed to their Ministers at Paris, for consultation with their governments, articles of a special confederation, in the following form:

"Proposals for concerted operation among the powers at war with the piratical States of Barbary.

1. "It is proposed, that the several powers at war with the piratical States of Barbary, or any two or more of them who shall be willing, shall enter into a convention to carry on their operations against those States, in concert, beginning with the Algerines.

2. "This convention shall remain open to any other powers, who shall, at any future time, wish to accede to it; the parties reserving the right to prescribe the conditions of such accession, according to the circumstances existing at the time it shall be proposed.

3. "The object of the convention shall be, to compel the piratical States to perpetual peace, without price, and to guarantee that peace to each other.

4. "The operations for obtaining this peace shall be constant cruises on their coast, with a naval force now to be agreed on. It is not proposed that this force shall be so considerable as to be inconvenient to any party. It is believed that half a dozen frigates, with as many Tenders or Xebecs, one half of which shall be in cruise, while the other half is at rest, will suffice.

5. "The force agreed to be necessary, shall be furnished by the parties, in certain quotas, now to be fixed; it being expected, that each will be willing to contribute, in such proportion as circumstances may render reasonable.

6. "As miscarriages often proceed from the want of harmony among officers of different nations, the parties shall now consider and decide, whether it will not be better to contribute their quotas in money, to be employed in fitting out and keeping on duty, a single fleet of the force agreed on.

7. "The difficulties and delays, too, which will attend the management of these operations, if conducted by the parties themselves separately, distant as their courts may be from one another, and incapable of meeting in consultation, suggest a question, whether it will not be better for them to give full powers, for that purpose, to their Ambas-

sadors, or other Ministers resident at some one court of Europe, who shall form a Committee, or Council, for carrying this convention into effect; wherein, the vote of each member shall be computed in proportion to the quota of his sovereign, and the majority so computed, shall prevail in all questions within the view of this convention. The court of Versailles is proposed, on account of its neighborhood to the Mediterranean, and because all those powers are represented there, who are likely to become parties to this convention.

8. "To save to that Council the embarrassment of personal solicitations for office, and to assure the parties that their contributions will be applied solely to the object for which they are destined, there shall be no establishment of officers for the said Council, such as Commissioners, Secretaries, or any other kind, with either salaries or perquisites, nor any other lucrative appointments but such whose functions are to be exercised on board the said vessels.

9. "Should war arise between any two of the parties to this convention, it shall not extend to this enterprise, nor interrupt it; but as to this they shall be reputed at peace.

10. "When Algiers shall be reduced to peace, the other piratical States, if they refuse to discontinue their piracies, shall become the objects of this convention, either successively or together, as shall seem best.

11. "Where this convention would interfere with treaties actually existing between any of the parties and the States of Barbary, the treaty shall prevail, and such party shall be allowed to withdraw from the operations against that State."

Spain had just concluded a treaty with Algiers, at the expense of three millions of dollars, and did not like to relinquish the benefit of that, until the other party should fail in their observance of it. Portugal, Naples, the two Sicilies, Venice, Malta, Denmark and Sweden, were favorably disposed to such an association; but their representatives at Paris expressed apprehensions that France would interfere, and, either openly or secretly, support the Barbary powers; and they required, that I should ascertain the dispositions of the Count de Vergennes on the subject. I had before taken occasion to inform him of what we were proposing, and, therefore, did not think it proper to insinuate any doubt of the fair conduct of his government; but, stating our propositions, I mentioned the apprehensions entertained by us, that England would interfere in behalf of those piratical governments. "She dares not do it," said he. I pressed it no further. The other Agents were satisfied with this indication of his sentiments, and nothing was now wanting to bring it into direct and formal consideration, but the assent of our government, and their authority to make the formal proposition. I communicated to them the favorable prospect of protecting our commerce from the Barbary depredations, and for such a continuance of time, as, by an exclusion of them from the sea, to change their habits and characters, from a predatory to an agricultural people: toward which, however, it was expected they would contribute a frigate, and its expenses, to be in constant cruise. But they were in no condition to make any such engagement. Their recommendatory powers for obtaining contributions, were so openly neglected by the several States, that they declined an engagement which they were conscious they could not fulfill with punctuality; and so it fell through.

In 1786, while at Paris, I became acquainted with John Ledyard, of Connecticut, a man of genius, of some science, and of fearless courage and enterprise. He had accompanied Captain Cook in his voyage to the Pacific, had distinguished himself on several occasions by an unrivalled intrepidity, and published an account of that voyage, with details unfavorable to Cook's deportment towards the savages, and lessening our regrets at his fate. Ledyard had come to Paris, in the hope of forming a company to engage in the fur trade of the Western coast of America. He was disappointed in this, and, being out of business, and of a roaming, restless character, I suggested to him the enterprise of exploring the Western part of our continent, by passing through St. Petersburg to Kamschatka, and procuring a passage thence in some of the Russian vessels to Nootka Sound, whence he might make his way across the continent to the United States; and I undertook to have the permission of the Empress of Russia solicited. He eagerly embraced the proposition, and M. de Sémoulin, the Russian Ambassador, and more particularly Baron Grimm, the special correspondent of the Empress, solicited her permission for him to pass through her dominions, to the Western coast of America. And here I must correct a material error, which I have committed in another place, to the prejudice of the Empress. In writing some notes of the life of

Captain Lewis, prefixed to his "Expedition to the Pacific," I stated that the Empress gave the permission asked, and afterwards retracted it. This idea, after a lapse of twenty-six years, had so insinuated itself into my mind, that I committed it to paper, without the least suspicion of error. Yet I find, on recurring to my letters of that date, that the Empress refused permission at once, considering the enterprise as entirely chimerical. But Ledyard would not relinquish it, persuading himself that, by proceeding to St. Petersburg, he could satisfy the Empress of its practicability, and obtain her permission. He went accordingly, but she was absent on a visit to some distant part of her dominions, and he pursued his course to within two hundred miles of Kamschatka, where he was overtaken by an arrest from the Empress, brought back to Poland, and there dismissed. I must therefore, in justice, acquit the Empress of ever having for a moment countenanced even by the indulgence of an innocent passage through her territories, this interesting enterprise.

The pecuniary distresses of France produced this year measure of which there had been no example for nearly two centuries, and the consequences of which, good and evil, are not yet calculable. For its remote causes, we must go a little back.

Celebrated writers of France and England had already sketched good principles on the subject of government; yet the American Revolution seems first to have awakened the thinking part of the French nation in general, from the sleep of despotism in which they were sunk. The officers too, who had been to America, were mostly young men, less shackled by habit and prejudice, and more ready to assent to the suggestions of common sense, and feeling of common rights, than others. They came back with new ideas and impressions. The press, notwithstanding its shackles, began to disseminate them; conversation assumed new freedoms; Politics became the theme of all societies, male and female, and a very extensive and zealous party was formed, which acquired the appellation of the Patriotic party, who, sensible of the abusive government under which they lived, sighed for occasions of reforming it. This party comprehended all the honesty of the kingdom, sufficiently at leisure to think, the men of letters, the easy Bourgeois, the young nobility, partly from reflection, partly from mode; for these sentiments became matter of mode, and as such, united most of the young women to the party. Happily for the nation, it happened, at the same moment, that the dissipations of the Queen and court, the abuses of the pension-list, and dilapidations in the administration of every branch of the finances, had exhausted the treasures and credit of the nation, insomuch that its most necessary functions were paralyzed. To reform these abuses would have overset the Minister; to impose new taxes by the authority of the King, was known to be impossible, from the determined opposition of the Parliament to their enregistry. No resource remained then, but to appeal to the nation. He advised, therefore, the call of an Assembly of the most distinguished characters of the nation, in the hope that, by promises of various and valuable improvements in the organization and regimen of the government, they would be induced to authorize new taxes, to control the opposition of the Parliament, and to raise the annual revenue to the level of expenditures. An Assembly of Notables therefore, about one hundred and fifty in number, named by the King, convened on the 22d of February. The Minister (Calonne) stated to them, that the annual excess of expenses beyond the revenue, when Louis XVI. came to the throne, was thirty-seven millions of livres; that four hundred and forty millions had been borrowed to re-establish the navy; that the American war had cost them fourteen hundred and forty millions (two hundred and fifty-six millions of dollars), and that the interest of these sums, with other increased expenses, had added forty millions more to the annual deficit. (But a subsequent and more candid estimate made it fifty-six millions.) He proffered them a universal redress of grievances, laid open those grievances fully, pointed out sound remedies, and, covering his canvas with objects of this magnitude, the deficit dwindled to a little accessory, scarcely attracting attention. The persons chosen were the most able and independent characters in the kingdom, and their support, if it could be obtained, would be enough for him. They improved the occasion for redressing their grievances, and agreed that the public wants should be relieved; but went into an examination of the causes of them. It was supposed that Calonne was conscious that his accounts could not bear examination; and it was said, and believed, that he asked of the King, to send four members to the Bastile, of whom the Marquis de La Fayette was one, to banish twenty others, and two of his Ministers. The King found it shorter to banish him. His successor went on in full concert with the Assembly. The result was an augmentation of the revenue, a promise of economies in its expenditure, of an annual settlement of the public accounts before a council, which the Comptroller, having been heretofore obliged to settle only with the King in person, of course never settled at all; an acknowledgment that the King could not lay a new tax, a reformation of the Criminal laws, abolition of torture, suppression of corvees, reformation of the gabelles, removal of the interior Custom Houses, free commerce of grain, internal and external, and the establishment of Provincial Assemblies; which, altogether, constituted a great mass of improvement in the condition of the nation. The establishment of the Provincial Assemblies was, in itself, a fundamental improvement. They would be of the choice of the people, one-third renewed every year, in those provinces where there are no States, that is to say, over about three-fourths of the kingdom. They would be partly an Executive themselves, and partly an Executive Council to the Intendant, to whom the Executive power, in his province, had been heretofore entirely delegated. Chosen by the people, they would soften the execution of hard laws, and, having a right of representation to the King, they would censure bad laws, suggest good ones, expose abuses, and their representations, when united, would command respect. To the other advantages, might be added the precedent itself of calling the Assemblée des Notables, which would perhaps grow into habit. The hope was, that the improvements thus promised would be carried into effect; that they would be maintained during the present reign, and that that would be long enough for them to take some root in the constitution, so that they might come to be considered as a part of that, and be protected by time, and the attachment of the nation.

The Count de Vergennes had died a few days before the meeting of the Assembly, and the Count de Montmorin had been named Minister of Foreign Affairs, in his place. Villedeuil succeeded Calonne, as Comptroller General, and Lomenie de Bryenne, Archbishop of Thoulouse, afterwards of Sens, and ultimately Cardinal Lomenie, was named Minister principal, with whom the other Ministers were to transact the business of their departments, heretofore done with the King in person; and the Duke de Nivernois, and M. de Malesherbes, were called to the Council. On the nomination of the Minister principal, the Marshals de Segur and de Castries retired from the departments of War and Marine, unwilling to act subordinately, or to share the blame of proceedings taken out of their direction. They were succeeded by the Count de Brienne, brother of the Prime Minister, and the Marquis de La Luzerne, brother to him who had been Minister in the United States

A dislocated wrist, unsuccessfully set, occasioned advice from my surgeon, to try the mineral waters of Aix, in Provence, as a corroborant. I left Paris for that place therefore, on the 28th of February, and proceeded up the Seine, through Champagne and Burgundy, and down the Rhone through the Beaujolais by Lyons, Avignon, Nismes to Aix; where, finding on trial no benefit from the waters, I concluded to visit the rice country of Piedmont, to see if anything might be learned there, to benefit the rivalship of our Carolina rice with that, and thence to make a tour of the seaport towns of France, along its Southern and Western coast, to inform myself, if anything could be done to favor our commerce with them. From Aix, therefore, I took my route by Marseilles, Toulon, Hieres, Nice, across the Col de Tende, by Coni, Turin, Vercelli, Novara, Milan, Pavia, Novi, Genoa. Thence, returning along the coast of Savona, Noli, Albenga, Oneglia, Monaco, Nice, Antibes, Frejus, Aix, Marseilles, Avignon, Nismes, Montpellier, Frontignan, Cette, Agde, and along the canal of Languedoc, by Bezieres, Narbonne, Cascassonne, Castelnaudari, through the Souterrain of St. Feriol, and back by Castelnaudari, to Toulouse; thence to Montauban, and down the Garonne by Langon to Bordeaux. Thence to Rochefort, la Rochelle, Nantes, L'Orient; then back by Rennes to Nantes, and up the Loire by Angers, Tours, Amboise, Blois to Orleans, thence direct to Paris, where I arrived on the 10th of June. Soon after my return from this journey, to wit, about the latter part of July, I received my younger daughter, Maria, from Virginia, by the way of London, the youngest having died some time before.

The treasonable perfidy of the Prince of Orange, Stadtholder and Captain General of the United Netherlands, in the war which England waged against them, for entering into a treaty of commerce with the United States, is known to all. As their Executive officer, charged with the conduct of the war, he contrived to baffle all the measures of the States General, to dislocate all their military plans and played false into the hands of England against his own country, on every possible occasion, confident in her protection, and in that of the King of Prussia, brother to his Princess. The States General, indignant at this patricidal conduct, applied to France for aid, according to the stipulations of the treaty concluded with her in '85. It was assured to them readily, and in cordial terms, in a letter from the Count de Vergennes, to the Marquis de Verac, Ambassador of France at the Hague, of which the following is an extract:

Extract from the despatch of the Count de Vergennes, to the Marquis de Verac, Ambassador from France, at the Hague, dated March 1, 1786:

"The King will give his aid, as far as may be in his power, towards the success of the affair, and will, on his part, invite the Patriots to communicate to him their views, their plans, and their discontents. You may assure them that the King takes a real interest in themselves as well as their cause, and that they may rely upon his protection. On this they may place the greater dependence, as we do not conceal, that if the Stadtholder resumes his former influence, the English System will soon prevail, and our alliance become a mere affair of the imagination. The Patriots will readily feel, that this position would be incompatible both with the dignity and consideration of his Majesty. But in case the Chief of the Patriots should have to fear a division, they would have time sufficient to reclaim those whom the Anglomaniacs had misled, and to prepare matters in such a manner, that the question when again agitated, might be decided according to their wishes. In such a hypothetical case, the King authorizes you to act in concert with them, to pursue the direction which they may think proper to give you, and to employ every means to augment the number of the partisans of the good cause. It remains for me to speak of the personal security of the Patriots. You may assure them, that under every circumstance, the King will take them under his immediate protection, and you will make known wherever you may judge necessary, that his Majesty will regard as a personal offence every undertaking against their liberty. It is to be presumed that this language, energetically maintained, may have some effect on the audacity of the Anglomaniacs, and that the

Prince de Nassau will feel that he runs some risk in provoking the resentment of his Majesty."[1]

This letter was communicated by the Patriots to me, when at Amsterdam, in 1788, and a copy sent by me to Mr. Jay, in my letter to him of March 16, 1788.

The object of the Patriots was, to establish a representative and republican government. The majority of the States General were with them, but the majority of the populace of the towns was with the Prince of Orange; and that populace was played off with great effect, by the triumvirate of . . . Harris, the English Ambassador, afterwards Lord Malmesbury, the Prince of Orange, a stupid man, and the Princess as much a man as either of her colleagues, in audaciousness, in enterprise, and in the thirst of domination. By these, the mobs of the Hague were excited against the members of the States General; their persons were insulted and endangered in the streets; the sanctuary of their houses was violated; and the Prince, whose function and duty it was to repress and punish these violations of order, took no steps for that purpose. The States General, for their own protection, were therefore obliged to place their militia under the command of a Committee. The Prince filled the courts of London and Berlin with complaints at this usurpation of his prerogatives, and, forgetting that he was but the first servant of a Republic, marched his regular troops against the city of Utrecht, where the States were in session. They were repulsed by the militia. His interests now became marshalled with those of the public enemy, and against his own country. The States, therefore, exercising their rights of sovereignty, deprived him of all his powers. The great Frederic had died in August, '86. He had never intended to break with France in support of the Prince of Orange. During the illness of which he died, he had, through the Duke of Brunswick, declared to the Marquis de La Fayette, who was then at Berlin, that he meant not to support the English interest in Holland: that he might assure the government of France, his only wish was, that some honorable place in the Constitution should be reserved for the Stadtholder and his children, and that he would take no part in the quarrel, unless an entire abolition of the

[1]Translation supplied by editors of Memorial Edition, in Jefferson's text this appears in French.

Stadtholderate should be attempted. But his place was now occupied by Frederic William, his great nephew, a man of little understanding, much caprice, and very inconsiderate; and the Princess, his sister, although her husband was in arms against the legitimate authorities of the country, attempting to go to Amsterdam, for the purpose of exciting the mobs of that place, and being refused permission to pass a military post on the way, he put the Duke of Brunswick at the head of twenty thousand men, and made demonstrations of marching on Holland. The King of France hereupon declared, by his Chargé des Affaires in Holland, that if the Prussian troops continued to menace Holland with an invasion, his Majesty, in quality of Ally, was determined to succor that province. In answer to this, Eden gave official information to Count Montmorin, that England must consider as at an end its convention with France relative to giving notice of its naval armaments, and that she was arming generally. War being now imminent, Eden, since Lord Aukland, questioned me on the effect of our treaty with France, in the case of a war, and what might be our dispositions. I told him frankly, and without hesitation, that our dispositions would be neutral, and that I thought it would be the interest of both these powers that we should be so; because, it would relieve both from all anxiety as to feeding their West India islands; that England, too, by suffering us to remain so, would avoid a heavy land war on our Continent, which might very much cripple her proceedings elsewhere; that our treaty, indeed, obliged us to receive into our ports the armed vessels of France, with their prizes, and to refuse admission to the prizes made on her by her enemies: that there was clause, also, by which we guaranteed to France her American possessions, which might perhaps force us into the war, if these were attacked. "Then it will be war," said he, "for they will assuredly be attacked." Liston, at Madrid, about the same time, made the same inquiries of Carmichael. The Government of France then declared a determination to form a camp of observation at Givet, commenced arming her marine, and named the Bailli de Suffrein their Generalissimo on the Ocean. She secretly engaged, also, in negotiations with Russia, Austria, and Spain, to form a quadruple alliance. The Duke of Brunswick having advanced to the confines of Holland, sent some of his officers to Givet, to reconnoitre the state of things there, and report them to him. He said afterwards, that "if there had been only a few tents at that place, he should not have advanced further, for that the King would not, merely for the interest of his sister, engage in a war with France." But, finding that there was not a single company there, he boldly entered the country, took their towns as fast as he presented himself before them, and advanced on Utrecht. The States had appointed the Rhingrave of Salm their Commander-in-Chief; a Prince without talents, without courage, and without principle. He might have held out in Utrecht for a considerable time, but he surrendered the place without firing a gun, literally ran away and hid himself, so that for months it was not known what had become of him. Amsterdam was then attacked, and capitulated. In the meantime, the negotiations for the quadruple alliance were proceeding favorably; but the secrecy with which they were attempted to be conducted, was penetrated by Fraser, Chargé d'Affaires of England at St. Petersburg, who instantly notified his court and gave the alarm to Prussia. The King saw at once what would be his situation, between the jaws of France, Austria, and Russia. In great dismay, he besought the court of London not to abandon him, sent Alvensleben to Paris to explain and soothe; and England, through the Duke of Dorset and Eden, renewed her conferences for accommodation. The Archbishop, who shuddered at the idea of war, and preferred a peaceful surrender of right to an armed vindication of it, received them with open arms, entered into cordial conferences, and a declaration, and counter-declaration, were cooked up at Versailles, and sent to London for approbation. They were approved there, reached Paris at one o'clock of the 27th, and were signed that night at Versailles. It was said and believed at Paris, that M. de Montmorin, literally "pleuroit comme un enfant," when obliged to sign this counter-declaration; so distressed was he by the dishonor of sacrificing the Patriots, after assurances so solemn of protection, and absolute encouragement to proceed. The Prince of Orange was reinstated in all his powers, now become regal. A great emigration of the Patriots took place; all were deprived of office, many exiled, and their property confiscated. They were received in France, and subsisted, for some time, on her bounty. Thus fell Holland, by the treachery of her Chief, from her honorable independence, to become a province of England; and so, also, her Stadtholder, from the high station of the first citizen of a free Republic, to be the servile Viceroy of a foreign Sovereign. And this was effected by a mere scene of bullying and demonstration; not one of the parties, France, England, or Prussia, having ever really meant to encounter actual war for the interest of the Prince of Orange. But it had all the effect of a real and decisive war.

Our first essay, in America, to establish a federative government had fallen, on trial, very short of its object. During the war of Independence, while the pressure of an external enemy hooped us together, and their enterprises kept us necessarily on the alert, the spirit of the people, excited by danger, was a supplement to the Confederation, and urged them to zealous exertions, whether claimed by that instrument or not; but, when peace and safety were restored, and every man became engaged in useful and profitable occupation, less attention was paid to the calls of Congress. The fundamental defect of the Confederation was, that Congress was not authorized to act immediately on the people, and by its own officers. Their power was only requisitory, and these requisitions were addressed to the several Legislatures, to be by them carried into execution, without other coercion than the moral principle of duty. This allowed, in fact, a negative to every Legislature, on every measure proposed by Congress; a negative so frequently exercised in practice, as to benumb the action of the Federal government, and to render it inefficient in its general objects, and more especially in pecuniary and foreign concerns. The want, too, of a separation of the Legislative, Executive, and Judiciary functions, worked disadvantageously in practice. Yet this state of things afforded a happy augury of the future march of our Confederacy, when it was seen that the good sense and good dispositions of the people, as soon as they perceived the incompetence of their first compact, instead of leaving its correction to insurrection and civil war, agreed, with one voice, to elect deputies to a general Convention, who should peaceably met and agree on such a Constitution as "would ensure peace, justice, liberty, the common defence and general welfare."

This Convention met at Philadelphia on the 25th of May, '87. It sat with closed doors, and kept all its proceedings secret, until its dissolution on the 17th of September, when the results of its labors were published all together. I received a copy, early in November, and read and contemplated its provisions with great satisfaction. As not a member of the Convention, however, nor probably a single citizen of the Union, had approved it in all its parts, so I, too, found articles which I thought objectionable. The absence of express declarations ensuring freedom of religion, freedom of the press, freedom of the person under the uninterrupted protection of the Habeas corpus, and trial by jury in Civil as well as in Criminal cases, excited my jealousy; and the re-eligibility of the President for life, I quite disapproved. I expressed freely, in letters to my friends, and most particularly to Mr. Madison and General Washington, my approbations and objections. How the good should be secured and the ill brought to rights was the difficulty. To refer it back to a new Convention might endanger the loss of the whole. My first idea was, that the nine States first acting, should accept it unconditionally, and thus secure what in it was good, and that the four last should accept on the previous condition, that certain amendments should be agreed to; but a better course was devised, of accepting the whole, and trusting that the good sense and honest intentions of our citizens, would make the alterations which should be deemed necessary. Accordingly, all accepted, six without objection, and seven with recommendations of specified amendments. Those respecting the press, religion, and juries, with several others, of great value, were accordingly made; but the Habeas corpus was left to the discretion of Congress, and the amendment against the re-eligibility of the President was not proposed. My fears of that feature were founded on the importance of the office, on the fierce contentions it might excite among ourselves, if continuable for life, and the dangers of interference, either with money or arms, by foreign nations, to whom the choice of an American President might become interesting. Examples of this abounded in history; in the case of the Roman Emperors, for instance; of the Popes, while of any significance; of the German Emperors; the Kings of Poland, and the Deys of Barbary. I had observed, too, in the feudal history, and in the recent instance, particularly, of the Stadtholder of Holland, how easily offices, or tenures for life, slide into inheritances. My wish, therefore, was, that the President should be elected for seven years, and be ineligible afterwards. This term I thought sufficient to enable him, with the concurrence of the Legislature, to carry through and establish any system of improvement he should propose for the general good. But the practice adopted, I think, is better, allowing his continuance for eight years, with a liability to be dropped at half way of the term, making that a period of probation. That his continuance should be restrained seven years was the opinion of the Convention at an earlier stage of its session, when it voted that term, by a majority of eight against two, and by a simple majority that he should be ineligible a second time. This opinion was confirmed by the House so late as July 26, referred to the Committee of detail, reported favorably by them, and changed to the present form by final vote, on the last day but one only of their session. Of this change, three States expressed their disapprobation; New York, by recommending an amendment, that the President should not be eligible a third time, and Virginia and North Carolina that he should not be capable of serving more than eight, in any term of sixteen years; and though this amendment has not been made in form, yet practice seems to have established it. The example of four Presidents voluntarily retiring at the end of their eighth year, and the progress of public opinion, that the principle is salutary, have given it in practice the force of precedent and usage; insomuch, that, should a President consent to be a candidate for a third election, I trust he would be rejected, on this demonstration of ambitious views.

But there was another amendment, of which none of us thought at the time, and in the omission of which, lurks the germ that is to destroy this happy combination of National powers in the General government, for matters of National concern, and independent powers in the States, for what concerns the States severally. In England, it was a great point gained at the Revolution, that the commissions of the Judges, which had hitherto been during pleasure, should thenceforth be made during good behavior. A Judiciary, dependent on the will of the King, had proved itself the most oppressive of all tools, in the hands of that Magistrate. Nothing, then, could be more salutary, than a change there, to the tenure of good behavior; and the question of good behavior, left to the vote of a simple majority in the two Houses of Parliament. Before the Revolution, we were all good English Whigs, cordial in their free principles, and in their jealousies of their Executive Magistrate. These jealousies are very apparent in all our state Constitutions; and, in the General government in this instance, we have gone even beyond the English caution, by requiring a vote of two-thirds, in one of the Houses, for removing a Judge; a vote so impossible, where[1] any defence is made, before men of ordinary prejudices and passions, that our Judges are effectually independent of the nation. But this ought not to be. I would not, indeed, make them dependent on the Executive authority, as they formerly were in England; but I deem it indispensable to the continuance of this government, that they should be submitted to some practical and impartial control; and that this, to be imparted, must be compounded of a mixture of State and Federal authorities. It is not enough that honest men are appointed Judges. All know the influence of interest on the mind of man, and how unconsciously his judgment is warped by that influence. To this bias add that of the *esprit de corps*, of their peculiar maxim and creed, that "it is the office of a good Judge to enlarge his jurisdiction," and the absence of responsibility; and how can we expect impartial decision between the General government, of which they are themselves so eminent a part, and an individual State, from which they have nothing to hope or fear? We have seen, too, that contrary to all correct example, they are in the habit of going out of the question before them, to throw an anchor ahead, and grapple further hold for future advances of power. They are then, in fact, the corps of sappers and miners, steadily working to undermine the independent rights of the States, and to consolidate all power in the hands of that government in which they have so important a freehold estate. But it is not by the consolidation, or concentration of powers, but by their distribution, that good government is effected. Were not this great country already divided into States, that division must be made, that each might do for itself what concerns itself directly, and what it can so much better do than a distant authority. Every State again is divided into counties, each to take care of what lies within its local bounds; each county again into townships or wards, to manage minuter details; and every ward into farms, to be governed each by its individual proprietor. Were we directed from Washington when to sow, and when to reap, we should soon want bread. It is by this partition of cares, descending in gradation

---

[1]In the impeachment of Judge Pickering, of New Hampshire, a habitual and maniac drunkard, no defence was made. Had there been, the party vote of more than one-third of the Senate would have acquitted him. [Jefferson's footnote.]

from general to particular, that the mass of human affairs may be best managed, for the good and prosperity of all. I repeat, that I do not charge the Judges with wilful and ill-intentioned error; but honest error must be arrested, where its toleration leads to public ruin. As, for the safety of society, we commit honest maniacs to Bedlam, so judges should be withdrawn from their bench, whose erroneous biases are leading us to dissolution. It may, indeed, injure them in fame or in fortune; but it saves the Republic, which is the first and supreme law.

Among the debilities of the government of the Confederation, no one was more distinguished or more distressing, than the utter impossibility of obtaining, from the States, the moneys necessary for the payment of debts, or even for the ordinary expenses of the government. Some contributed a little, some less, and some nothing; and the last furnished at length an excuse for the first to do nothing also. Mr. Adams, while residing at the Hague, had a general authority to borrow what sums might be requisite, for ordinary and necessary expenses. Interest on the public debt, and the maintenance of the diplomatic establishment in Europe, had been habitually provided in this way. He was now elected Vice-President of the United States, was soon to return to America, and had referred our bankers to me for future counsel, on our affairs in their hands. But I had no powers, no instructions, no means, and no familiarity with the subject. It had always been exclusively under his management, except as to occasional and partial deposits in the hands of Mr. Grand, banker in Paris, for special and local purposes. These last had been exhausted for some time, and I had fervently pressed the Treasury board to replenish this particular deposit, as Mr. Grand now refused to make further advances. They answered candidly, that no funds could be obtained until the new government should get into action, and have time to make its arrangements. Mr. Adams had received his appointment to the court of London, while engaged at Paris, with Dr. Franklin and myself, in the negotiations under our joint commissions. He had repaired thence to London, without returning to the Hague, to take leave of that government. He thought it necessary, however, to do so now, before he should leave Europe, and accordingly went there. I learned his departure from London, by a letter from Mrs. Adams, received on the very day on which he would arrive at the Hague. A consultation with him, and some provision for the future, was indispensable, while we could yet avail ourselves of his powers; for when they would be gone, we should be without resource. I was daily dunned by a Company who had formerly made a small loan to the United States, the principal of which was now become due; and our bankers in Amsterdam, had notified me that the interest on our general debt would be expected in June; that if we failed to pay it, it would be deemed an act of bankruptcy, and would effectually destroy the credit of the United States, and all future prospect of obtaining money there; that the loan they had been authorized to open, of which a third only was filled, had now ceased to get forward, and rendered desperate that hope of resource. I saw that there was not a moment to lose, and set out for the Hague on the second morning after receiving the information of Mr. Adams's journey. I went the direct road by Louvres, Senlis, Roye, Pont St. Maxence, Bois le duc, Gournay, Peronne, Cambray, Bouchain, Valenciennes, Mons, Bruxelles, Malines, Antwerp, Mordick, and Rotterdam, to the Hague, where I happily found Mr. Adams. He concurred with me at once in opinion, that something must be done, and that we ought to risk ourselves on doing it without instructions, to save the credit of the United States. We foresaw, that before the new government could be adopted, assembled, establish its financial system, get the money into the Treasury, and place it in Europe, considerable time would elapse; that, therefore, we had better provide at once, for the years '88, '89, and '90, in order to place our government at its ease, and our credit in security, during that trying interval. We set out, therefore, by the way of Leyden, for Amsterdam, where we arrived on the 10th. I had prepared an estimate, showing that

		Florins.
There would be necessary for the year '88		531,937–10
'89		538,540
'90		473,540
Total.		1,544,017–10

		Florins.
To meet this, the bankers had in hand . . .	79,268–2–8	
and the unsold bonds would yield	542,800	
		622,068–2–8
Leaving a deficit of		921,949–7–4
We proposed then to borrow a million, yielding		920,000
Which would leave a small deficiency of		1,949–7–4

Mr. Adams accordingly executed 1000 bonds, for 1000 florins each, and deposited them in the hands of our bankers, with instructions, however, not to issue them until Congress should ratify the measure. This done, he returned to London, and I set out for Paris; and, as nothing urgent forbade it, I determined to return along the banks of the Rhine, to Strasburg, and thence strike off to Paris. I accordingly left Amsterdam on the 30th of March, and proceeded by Utrecht, Nimeguen, Cleves, Duysberg, Dusseldorf, Cologne, Bonne, Coblentz, Nassau, Hocheim, Frankfort, and made an excursion to Hanau, thence to Mayence, and another excursion to Rudesheim, and Johansberg; then by Oppenheim, Worms, and Manheim, making an excursion to Heidelberg, then by Spire, Carlsruh, Rastadt and Kelh, to Strasburg, where I arrived April the 16th, and proceeded again on the 18th, by Phalsbourg, Fenestrange, Dieuze, Moyenvie, Nancy, Toul, Ligny, Bar-le-duc, St. Diziers, Vitry, Chalons sur Marne, Epernay, Chateau Thierri, Meaux, to Paris, where I arrived on the 23d of April; and I had the satisfaction to reflect, that by this journey our credit was secured, the new government was placed at ease for two years to come, and that, as well as myself, relieved from the torment of incessant duns, whose just complaints could not be silenced by any means within our power.

A Consular Convention had been agreed on in '84, between Dr. Franklin and the French government, containing several articles, so entirely inconsistent with the laws of the several States, and the general spirit of our citizens, that Congress withheld their ratification, and sent it back to me, with instructions to get those articles expunged, or modified so as to render them compatible with our laws. The Minister unwillingly released us from these concessions, which, indeed, authorized the exercise of powers very offensive in a free State. After much discussion, the Convention was reformed in a considerable degree, and was signed by the Count Montmorin and myself, on the 14th of November, '88; not, indeed, such as I would have wished, but such as could be obtained with good humor and friendship.

On my return from Holland, I found Paris as I had left it, still in high fermentation. Had the Archbishop, on the close of the Assembly of Notables, immediately carried into operation the measures contemplated, it was believed they would all have been registered by the Parliament; but he was slow, presented his edicts, one after another, and at considerable intervals, which gave time for the feelings excited by the proceedings of the Notables to cool off, new claims to be advanced, and a pressure to arise for a fixed constitution, not subject to changes at the will of the King. Nor should we wonder at this pressure, when we consider the monstrous abuses of power under which this people were ground to powder; when we pass in review the weight of their taxes, and the inequality of their distribution; the oppressions of the tithes, the tailles, the corvees, the gabelles, the farms and the barriers; the shackles on commerce by monopolies; on industry by guilds and corporations; on the freedom of conscience, of thought, and of speech; on the freedom of the press by the Censure; and of the person by Lettres de Cachet; the cruelty of the Criminal code generally; the atrocities of the Rack; the venality of the Judges, and their partialities to the rich; the monopoly of Military honors by the Noblesse; the enormous expenses of the Queen, the Princes and the Court; the prodigalities of pensions; and the riches, luxury, indolence and immorality of the Clergy. Surely under such a mass of misrule and oppression, a people might justly press for a thorough reformation, and might even dismount their rough-shod riders, and leave them to walk on their own legs. The edicts, relative to the corvees and free circulation of grain, were first presented to the Parliament and registered; but those for the impôt territorial, and stamp tax, offered some time after, were refused by the Parliament, which proposed a call of the States General, as alone competent to their authorization. Their refusal produced a Bed of justice, and their exile to Troyes. The Advocates, however, refusing to attend them, a suspension in the administration of justice took place. The Parliament held out for awhile, but the ennui of their exile and absence from Paris, began at length to be felt, and some dispositions for compromise to appear. On their consent, therefore, to prolong some of the former taxes, they were recalled from exile, the King met them in session November 19, '87, promised to call the States General in the year '92, and a majority expressed their assent to register an edict for successive and annual loans from 1788 to '92; but a protest being entered by the Duke of Orleans, and this encouraging others in a disposition to retract, the King ordered peremptorily the registry of the edict, and left the Assembly abruptly. The Parliament immediately protested, that the votes for the enregistry had not been legally taken, and that they gave no sanction to the loans proposed. This was enough to discredit and defeat them. Hereupon issued another edict, for the establishment of a cour plenière, and the suspension of all the Parliaments in the kingdom. This being opposed, as might be expected, by reclamations from all the Parliaments and Provinces, the King gave way, and by an edict of July 5th, '88, renounced his cour plenière, and promised the States General for the 1st of May, of the ensuing year; and the Archbishop, finding the times beyond his faculties, accepted the promise of a Cardinal's hat, was removed [September '88] from the Ministry, and M. Necker was called to the department of finance. The innocent rejoicings of the people of Paris on this change provoked the interference of an officer of the city guards, whose order for their dispersion not being obeyed, he charged them with fixed bayonets, killed two or three, and wounded many. This dispersed them for the moment, but they collected the next day in great numbers, burnt ten or twelve guard-houses, killed two or three of the guards, and lost six or eight more of their own number. The city was hereupon put under Martial law, and after awhile the tumult subsided. The effect of this change of ministers, and the promise of the States General at an early day, tranquillized the nation. But two great questions now occurred. 1st. What proportion shall the number of deputies of the Tiers État bear to those of the Nobles and Clergy? And 2d, shall they sit in the same or in distinct apartments? M. Necker, desirous of avoiding himself these knotty questions, proposed a second call of the same Notables, and that their advice should be asked on the subject. They met, November 9, '88; and, by five bureaux against one, they recommended the forms of the States General of 1614; wherein the Houses were separate, and voted by orders, not by persons. But the whole nation declaring at once against this, and that the Tiers État should be, in numbers, equal to both the other orders, and the Parliament deciding for the same proportion, it was determined so to be, by a declaration of December 27th, '88. A Report of M. Necker, to the King, of about the same date, contained other very important concessions. 1. That the King could neither lay a new tax, nor prolong an old one. 2. It expressed a readiness to agree on the periodical meeting of the States. 3. To consult on the necessary restriction on

Lettres de Cachet; and 4. How far the press might be made free. 5. It admits that the States are to appropriate the public money; and 6. That Ministers shall be responsible for public expenditures. And these concessions came from the very heart of the King. He had not a wish but for the good of the nation; and for that object, no personal sacrifice would ever have cost him a moment's regret; but his mind was weakness itself, his constitution timid, his judgment null, and without sufficient firmness even to stand by the faith of his word. His Queen, too, haughty and bearing no contradiction, had an absolute ascendency over him; and around her were rallied the King's brother d'Artois, the court generally, and the aristocratic part of his Ministers, particularly Breteuil, Broglio, Vauguyon, Foulon, Luzerne, men whose principles of government were those of the age of Louis XIV. Against this host, the good counsels of Necker, Montmorin, St. Priest, although in unison with the wishes of the King himself, were of little avail. The resolutions of the morning, formed under their advice, would be reversed in the evening, by the influence of the Queen and court. But the hand of heaven weighed heavily indeed on the machinations of this junto; producing collateral incidents, not arising out of the case, yet powerfully co-exciting the nation to force a regeneration of its government, and overwhelming with accumulated difficulties, this liberticide resistance. For, while laboring under the want of money for even ordinary purposes, in a government which required a million of livres a day, and driven to the last ditch by the universal call for liberty, there came on a winter of such severe cold, as was without example in the memory of man, or in the written records of history. The Mercury was at times 50° below the freezing point of Fahrenheit, and 22° below that of Reaumur. All out-door labor was suspended, and the poor, without the wages of labor were, of course, without either bread or fuel. The government found its necessities aggravated by that of procuring immense quantities of firewood, and of keeping great fires at all the cross streets, around which the people gathered in crowds, to avoid perishing with cold. Bread, too, was to be bought, and distributed daily, gratis, until a relaxation of the season should enable the people to work; and the slender stock of bread stuff had for some time threatened famine, and had raised that article to an enormous price. So great, indeed, was the scarcity of bread, that, from the highest to the lowest citizen, the bakers were permitted to deal but a scanty allowance per head, even to those who paid for it; and, in cards of invitation to dine in the richest houses, the guest was notified to bring his own bread. To eke out the existence of the people, every person who had the means, was called on for a weekly subscription, which the Curés collected, and employed in providing messes for the nourishment of the poor, and vied with each other in devising such economical compositions of food, as would subsist the greatest number with the smallest means. This want of bread had been foreseen for some time past, and M. de Montmorin had desired me to notify it in America, and that, in addition to the market price, a premium should be given on what should be brought from the United States. Notice was accordingly given, and produced considerable supplies. Subsequent information made the importations from America, during the months of March, April, and May, into the Atlantic ports of France, amount to about twenty-one-thousand barrels of flour, besides what went to other ports, and in other months; while our supplies to their West Indian islands relieved them also from that drain. This distress for bread continued till July.

Hitherto no acts of popular violence had been produced by the struggle for political reformation. Little riots, on ordinary incidents, had taken place as at other times, in different parts of the kingdom, in which some lives, perhaps a dozen or twenty, had been lost; but in the month of April, a more serious one occurred in Paris, unconnected, indeed, with the Revolutionary principle, but making part of the history of the day. The Fauxbourg St. Antoine is a quarter of the city inhabited entirely by the class of day laborers and journeymen in every line. A rumor was spread among them, that a great paper manufacturer, of the name of Reveillon, had proposed, on some occasion, that their wages should be lowered to fifteen sous a day. Inflamed at once into rage, and without inquiring into its truth, they flew to his house in vast numbers, destroyed everything in it, and in his magazines and work-shops, without secreting, however, a pin's worth to themselves, and were continuing this work of devastation, when the regular troops were called in. Admonitions being disregarded, they were of necessity fired on, and a regular action ensued, in which about one hundred of them were killed, before the rest would disperse There had rarely passed a year without such a riot, in some part or other of the Kingdom; and this is distinguished only as contemporary with the Revolution, although not produced by it.

The States General were opened on the 5th of May, '89, by speeches from the King, the Garde des Sceaux, Lamoignon, and M. Necker. The last was thought to trip too lightly over the constitutional reformations which were expected. His notices of them in this speech, were not as full as in his previous 'Rapport au Roi.' This was observed, to his disadvantage; but much allowance should have been made for the situation in which he was placed, between his own counsels, and those of the ministers and party of the court. Overruled in his own opinions, compelled to deliver, and to gloss over those of his opponents, and even to keep their secrets, he could not come forward in his own attitude.

The composition of the Assembly, although equivalent, on the whole, to what had been expected, was something different in its elements. It had been supposed, that a superior education would carry into the scale of the Commons a respectable portion of the Noblesse. It did so as to those of Paris, of its vicinity, and of the other considerable cities, whose greater intercourse with enlightened society had liberalized their minds, and prepared them to advance up to the measure of the times. But the Noblesse of the country, which constituted two-thirds of that body, were far in their rear. Residing constantly on their patrimonial feuds, and familiarized, by daily habit, with Seigneurial powers and practices, they had not yet learned to suspect their inconsistence with reason and right. They were willing to submit to equality of taxation, but not to descend from their rank and prerogatives to be incorporated in session with the Tiers État. Among the Clergy, on the other hand, it had been apprehended that the higher orders of the Hierarchy, by their wealth and connections, would have carried the elections generally; but it turned out, that in most cases, the lower clergy had obtained the popular majorities. These consisted of the Curés, sons of the peasantry, who had been employed to do all the drudgery of parochial services for ten, twenty, or thirty Louis ayear; while their superiors were consuming their princely revenues in palaces of luxury and indolence.

The objects for which this body was convened, being of the first order of importance, I felt it very interesting to understand the views of the parties of which it was composed, and especially the ideas prevalent as to the organization contemplated for their government. I went, therefore, daily from Paris to Versailles, and attended their debates, generally till the hour of adjournment. Those of the Noblesse were impassioned and tempestuous. They had some able men on both sides, actuated by equal zeal. The debates of the Commons were temperate, rational, and inflexibly firm. As preliminary to all other business, the awful questions came on, shall the States sit in one, or in distinct apartments? And shall they vote by heads or houses? The opposition was soon found to consist of the Episcopal order among the clergy, and two-thirds of the Noblesse; while the Tiers État were, to a man, united and determined. After various propositions of compromise had failed, the Commons undertook to cut the Gordian knot. The Abbe Sieyes, the most logical head of the nation, (author of the pamphlet "Qu'est ce que le Tiers État?" which had electrified that country, as Paine's Common Sense did us,) after an impressive speech on the 10th of June, moved that a last invitation should be sent to the Noblesse and Clergy, to attend in the hall of the States, collectively or individually, for the verification of powers, to which the Commons would proceed immediately, either in their presence or absence. This verification being finished, a motion was made, on the 15th, that they should constitute themselves a National Assembly; which was decided on the 17th, by a majority of four-fifths. During the debates on this question, about twenty of the Curés had joined them, and a proposition was made, in the chamber of the Clergy, that their whole body should join. This was rejected, at first, by a small majority only; but, being afterwards somewhat modified, it was decided affirmatively, by a majority of eleven. While this was under debate, and unknown to the court, to wit, on the 19th, a council was held in the afternoon, at Marly, wherein it was proposed that the King should interpose, by a declaration of his sentiments, in a *séance royale*. A form of declaration was proposed by Necker, which, while it censured, in general, the proceedings, both of the Nobles and Commons, announced the King's views, such as substantially to coincide with the Commons. It was agreed to in Council, the *séance* was fixed for the 22d, the meetings of the States were till then to be suspended, and everything, in the meantime, kept secret. The members, the next morning (the 20th) repairing to their house, as usual, found the doors shut and guarded, a proclamation posted up for a *séance royale* on the 22d, and a suspension of their meetings in the meantime. Concluding that their dissolution was now to take place, they repaired to a building called the "Jeu de paume" (or Tennis court) and there bound themselves by oath to each other, never to separate, of their own accord, till they had settled a constitution for the nation, on a solid basis, and, if separated by force, that they would reassemble in some other place. The next day they met in the church of St. Louis, and were joined by a majority of the clergy. The heads of the Aristocracy saw that all was lost without some bold exertion. The King was still at Marly. Nobody was permitted to approach him but their friends. He was assailed by falsehoods in all shapes. He was made to believe that the Commons were about to absolve the army from their oath of fidelity to him, and to raise their pay. The court party were now all rage and desperation. They procured a committee to be held, consisting of the King and his Ministers, to which Monsieur and the Count d'Artois should be admitted. At this committee, the latter attacked M. Necker personally, arraigned his declaration, and proposed one which some of his prompters had put into his hands. M. Necker was brow-beaten and intimidated, and the King shaken. He determined that the two plans should be deliberated on the next day, and the *séance royale* put off a day longer. This encouraged a fiercer attack on M. Necker the next day. His draught of a declaration was entirely broken up, and that of the Count d'Artois inserted into it. Himself and Montmorin offered their resignation, which was refused; the Count d'Artois saying to M. Necker, "No, sir, you must be kept as the hostage; we hold you responsible for all the ill which shall happen." This change of plan was immediately whispered without doors. The Noblesse were in triumph; the people in consternation. I was quite alarmed at this state of things. The soldiery had not yet indicated which side they should take, and that which they should support would be sure to prevail. I considered a successful reformation of government in France, as insuring a general reformation through Europe, and the resurrection, to a new life, of their people, now ground to dust by the abuses of the governing powers. I was much acquainted with the leading patriots of the Assembly. Being from a country which had successfully passed through a similar reformation, they were disposed to my acquaintance, and had some confidence in me. I urged, most stren-uously, an immediate compromise; to secure what the government was now ready to yield, and trust to future occasions for what might still be wanting. It was well understood that the King would grant, at this time, 1. Freedom of the person by Habeas corpus: 2. Freedom of con-science: 3. Freedom of the press: 4. Trial by jury: 5. A representative Legislature: 6. Annual meetings: 7. The origination of laws: 8. The exclusive right of taxation and appropriation: and 9. The responsibility of Ministers; and with the exercise of these powers they could obtain, in future, whatever might be further necessary to improve and preserve their constitution. They thought otherwise, however, and events have proved their lamentable error. For, after thirty years of war, foreign and domestic, the loss of millions of lives, the prostration of private happiness, and the foreign subjugation of their own country for a time, they have obtained no more, nor even that securely. They were uncon-scious of (for who could foresee?) the melancholy sequel of their well-meant perseverance; that their physical force would be usurped by a first tyrant to trample on the independence, and even the existence, of other nations: that this would afford a fatal example for the atrocious conspiracy of Kings against their people; would generate their unholy and homicide alliance to make common cause among themselves, and to crush, by the power of the whole, the efforts of any part to moder-ate their abuses and oppressions.

When the King passed, the next day, through the lane formed from the Chateau to the "Hotel des États," there was a dead silence. He was about an hour in the House, delivering his speech and declara-tion. On his coming out, a feeble cry of "vive le Roi" was raised by some children, but the people remained silent and sullen. In the close of his speech, he had ordered that the members should follow him, and resume their deliberations the next day. The Noblesse followed him, and so did the Clergy, except about thirty, who, with the Tiers, remained in the room, and entered into deliberation. They protested against what the King had done, adhered to all their former proceed-ings, and resolved the inviolability of their own persons. An officer came, to order them out of the room in the King's name. "Tell those who sent you," said Mirabeau, "that we shall not move hence but at our own will, or the point of the bayonet." In the afternoon, the people, uneasy, began to assemble in great numbers in the courts, and vicinities of the palace. This produced alarm. The Queen sent for M. Necker. He was conducted, amidst the shouts and acclamations of the multitude, who filled all the apartments of the palace. He was a few minutes only with the Queen, and what passed between them did not transpire. The King went out to ride. He passed through the crowd to his carriage, and into it, without being in the least noticed. As M. Necker followed him, universal acclamations were raised of "vive Monsieur Necker, vive le sauveur de la France opprimée." He was conducted back to his house with the same demonstrations of affection and anxiety. About two hundred deputies of the Tiers, catching the enthusiasm of the moment, went to his house, and extorted from him a promise that he would not resign. On the 25th, forty-eight of the Nobles joined the Tiers, and among them the Duke of Orleans. There were then with them one hundred and sixty-four members of the Clergy, although the minority of that body still sat apart, and called themselves the Chamber of the Clergy. On the 26th, the Archbishop of Paris joined the Tiers, as did some others of the Clergy and of the Noblesse.

These proceedings had thrown the people into violent ferment. It gained the soldiery, first of the French guards, extended to those of every other denomination, except the Swiss, and even to the body guards of the King. They began to quit their barracks, to assemble in squads, to declare they would defend the life of the King, but would not be the murderers of their fellow-citizens. They called themselves the soldiers *of the nation*, and left now no doubt on which side they would be, in case of rupture. Similar accounts came in from the troops in other parts of the kingdom, giving good reason to believe they would side with their fathers and brothers, rather than with their officers. The operation of this medicine at Versailles was as sudden as it was powerful. The alarm there was so complete, that in the afternoon of the 27th, the King wrote, with his own hand, letters to the Presidents of the Clergy and Nobles, engaging them immediately to join the Tiers. These two bodies were debating, and hesitating, when notes from the Count d'Artois decided their compliance. They went in a body, and took their seats with the Tiers, and thus rendered the union of the orders in one chamber complete.

The Assembly now entered on the business of their mission, and first proceeded to arrange the order in which they would take up the heads of their constitution, as follows:

First, and as Preliminary to the whole, a general Declaration of the Rights of Man. Then, specifically, the Principles of the Monarchy; Rights of the Nation; Rights of the King; Rights of the Citizens; Organization and Rights of the National Assembly; Forms necessary for the enactment of Laws; Organization and Functions of the Provincial and Municipal Assemblies; Duties and Limits of the Judiciary power; Functions and Duties of the Military power.

A Declaration of the Rights of Man, as the preliminary of their work, was accordingly prepared and proposed by the Marquis de La Fayette.

But the quiet of their march was soon disturbed by information that troops, and particularly the foreign troops, were advancing on Paris from various quarters. The King had probably been advised to this, on the pretext of preserving peace in Paris. But his advisers were believed to have other things in contemplation. The Marshal de Broglio was appointed to their command, a high-flying aristocrat, cool and capable of everything. Some of the French guards were soon arrested, under other pretexts, but really, on account of their dispositions in favor of the National cause. The people of Paris forced their prison, liberated them, and sent a deputation to the Assembly to solicit a pardon. The Assembly recommended peace and order to the people of Paris, the prisoners to the King, and asked from him the removal of the troops. His answer was negative and dry, saying they might remove themselves, if they pleased, to Noyons or Soissons. In the meantime, these troops, to the number of twenty or thirty thousand, had arrived, and were posted in, and between Paris and Versailles. The bridges and passes were guarded. At three o'clock in the afternoon of the 11th of July, the Count de La Luzerne was sent to notify M. Necker of his dismission, and to enjoin him to retire instantly, without saying a word of it to anybody. He went home, dined, and proposed to his wife a visit to a friend, but went in fact to his country house at St. Ouen, and at midnight set out for Brussels. This was not known till the next day (the 12th,) when the whole Ministry was changed, except Villedeuil, of the domestic department, and Barenton Garde des Sceaux. The changes were as follows:

The Baron de Breteuil, President of the Council of Finance; de la Galaisiere, Comptroller General, in the room of M. Necker; the Marshal de Broglio, Minister of War, and Foulon under him, in the room of Puy-Segur; the Duke de la Vauguyon, Minister of Foreign Affairs, instead of the Count de Montmorin; de La Porte, Minister of Marine, in place of the Count de La Luzerne; St. Priest was also removed from the Council. Luzerne and Puy-Segur had been strongly of the Aristocratic party in the Council, but they were not considered equal to the work now to be done. The King was now completely in the hands of men, the principal among whom had been noted, through their lives, for the Turkish despotism of their characters, and who were associated around the King, as proper instruments for what was to be executed. The news of this change began to be known at Paris, about one or two o'clock. In the afternoon, a body of about one hundred German cavalry were advanced, and drawn up in the Place Louis XV., and about two hundred Swiss posted at a little distance in their rear. This drew people to the spot, who thus accidentally found themselves in front of the troops, merely at first as spectators; but, as their numbers increased, their indignation rose. They retired a few steps, and posted themselves on and behind large piles of stones, large and small, collected in that place for a bridge, which was to be built adjacent to it. In this position, happening to be in my carriage on a visit, I passed through the lane they had formed, without interruption. But the moment after I had passed, the people attacked the cavalry with stones. They charged, but the advantageous position of the people, and the showers of stones, obliged the horse to retire, and quit the field altogether, leaving one of their number on the ground and the Swiss in the rear not moving to their aid. This was the signal for universal insurrection, and this body of cavalry, to avoid being massacred, retired towards Versailles. The people now armed themselves with such weapons as they could find in armorer's shops, and private houses, and with bludgeons; and were roaming all night, through all parts of the city, without any decided object. The next day (the 13th,) the Assembly pressed on the King to send away the troops, to permit the Bourgeoisie of Paris to arm for the preservation of order in the city, and offered to send a deputation from their body to tranquillize them; but their propositions were refused. A committee of magistrates and electors of the city were appointed by those bodies, to take upon them its government. The people, now openly joined by the French guards, forced the prison of St. Lazare, released all the prisoners, and took a great store of corn, which they carried to the corn-market. Here they got some arms, and the French guards began to form and train them. The city-committee determined to raise forty-eight thousand Bourgeoise, or rather to restrain their numbers to forty-eight thousand. On the 14th, they sent one of their members (Monsieur de Corny) to the Hotel des Invalides, to ask arms for their Garde Bourgeoise. He was followed by, and he found there, a great collection of people. The Governor of the Invalids came out, and represented the impossibility of his delivering arms, without the orders of those from whom he received them. De Corny advised the people then to retire, and retired himself; but the people took possession of the arms. It was remarkable, that not only the Invalids themselves made no opposition, but that a body of five thousand foreign troops, within four hundred yards, never stirred. M. de Corny, and five others, were then sent to ask arms of M. de Launay, Governor of the Bastile. They found a great collection of people already before the place, and they immediately planted a flag of truce, which was answered by a like flag hoisted on the parapet. The deputation prevailed on the people to fall back a little, advanced themselves to make their demand of the Governor, and in that instant, a discharge from the Bastile killed four persons of those nearest to the deputies. The deputies retired. I happened to be at the house of M. de Corny, when he returned to it, and received from him a narrative of these transactions. On the retirement of the deputies, the people rushed forward, and almost in an instant, were in possession of a fortification of infinite strength, defended by one hundred men, which in other times had stood several regular sieges, and had never been taken. How they forced their entrance has never been explained. They took all the arms, discharged the prisoners, and such of the garrison as were not killed in the first moment of fury; carried the Governor and Lieutenant Governor, to the Place de Grève, (the place of public execution,) cut off their heads, and sent them through the city, in triumph, to the Palais royal. About the same instant, a treacherous correspondence having been discovered in M. de Flesselles, Prevôt des Marchands, they seized him in the Hotel de Ville, where he was in the execution of his office, and cut off his head. These events, carried imperfectly to Versailles, were the subject of two successive deputations from the Assembly to the King, to both of which he gave dry and hard answers; for nobody had as yet been permitted to inform him, truly and fully, of what had passed at Paris. But at night, the Duke de Liancourt forced his way into the King's bed chamber, and obliged him to hear a full and animated detail of the disasters of the day in Paris. He went to bed fearfully impressed. The decapitation of de Launay worked powerfully through the night on the whole Aristocratic party; insomuch, that in the morning, those of the greatest influence on the Count d'Artois, represented to him the absolute necessity that the King should give up everything to the Assembly. This according with the dispositions of the King, he went about eleven o'clock, accompanied only by his brothers, to the Assembly, and there read to them a speech in which he asked their interposition to re-establish order. Although couched in terms of some caution, yet the manner in which it was delivered, made it evident that it was meant as a surrender at discretion. He returned to the Chateau on foot, accompanied by the Assembly. They sent off a deputation to quiet Paris, at the head of which was the Marquis de La Fayette, who had, the same morning, been named Commandant en chef of the Milice Bourgeoise; and Monsieur Bailly, former President of the States General, was called for as Prevôt des Marchands. The demolition of the Bastile was now ordered and begun. A body of the Swiss guards, of the regiment of Ventimille, and the city horse guards joined the people. The alarm at Versailles increased. The foreign troops were ordered off instantly. Every Minister resigned. The King confirmed Bailly as Prevôt des Marchands, wrote to M. Necker, to recall him, sent his letter open to the Assembly, to be forwarded by them, and invited them to go with him to Paris the next day, to satisfy the city of his dispositions; and that night, and the next morning, the Count d'Artois, and M. de Montesson, a deputy connected with him, Madame de Polignac, Madame de Guiche, and the Count de Vaudreuil, favorites of the Queen, the Abbé de Vermont her confessor, the Prince of Condé, and Duke of Bourbon fled. The King came to Paris, leaving the Queen in consternation for his return. Omitting the less important figures of the procession, the King's carriage was in the centre; on each side of it, the Assembly, in two ranks a foot; at their head the Marquis de La Fayette, as Commander-in-chief, on horseback, and Bourgeois guards before and behind. About sixty thousand citizens, of all forms and conditions, armed with the conquest of the Bastile and Invalids, as far as they would go, the rest with pistols, swords, pikes, pruning-hooks, scythes, &c., lined all the streets through which the procession passed, and with the crowds of people in the streets, doors, and windows, saluted them everywhere with the cries of "vive la nation," but not a single "vive le Roi" was heard. The King stopped at the Hotel de Ville. There M. Bailly presented, and put into his hat, the popular cockade, and addressed him. The King being unprepared, and unable to answer, Bailly went to him, gathered from him some scraps of sentences, and made out an answer, which he delivered to the audience, as from the King. On their return, the popular cries were "vive le Roi et la nation." He was conducted by a garde Bourgeoise to his palace at Versailles, and thus concluded an "amende honorable," as no sovereign ever made, and no people ever received.

And here, again, was lost another precious occasion of sparing to France the crimes and cruelties through which she has since passed, and to Europe, and finally America, the evils which flowed on them also from this mortal source. The King was now become a passive machine in the hands of the National Assembly, and had he been left to himself, he would have willingly acquiesced in whatever they should devise as best for the nation. A wise constitution would have been formed, hereditary in his line, himself placed at its head; with powers so large as to enable him to do all the good of his station, and so limited, as to restrain him from its abuse. This he would have faithfully administered, and more than this, I do not believe, he ever wished. But he had a Queen of absolute sway over his weak mind and timid virtue, and of a character the reverse of his in all points. This angel, as gaudily painted in the rhapsodies of Burke, with some smartness of fancy, but no sound sense, was proud, disdainful of restraint, indignant at all obstacles to her will, eager in the pursuit of pleasure, and firm enough to hold to her desires, or perish in their wreck. Her inordinate gambling and dissipations, with those of the Count d'Artois, and others of her *clique*, had been a sensible item in the exhaustion of the treasury, which called into action the reforming hand of the nation; and her opposition to it, her inflexible perverseness, and dauntless spirit, led herself to the Guillotine, drew the King on with her, and plunged the world into crimes and calamities which will forever stain the pages of modern history. I have ever believed, that had there been no Queen, there would have been no revolution. No force would have been provoked, nor exercised. The King would have gone hand in hand with the wisdom of his sounder counsellors. who, guided by the increased lights of the age, wished only, with the same pace, to advance the principles of their social constitution. The deed which closed the mortal course of these sovereigns, I shall neither approve nor condemn. I am not prepared to say, that the first magistrate of a nation cannot commit treason against his country, or is unamenable to its punishment; nor yet, that where there is no written law, no regulated tribunal, there is not a law in our hearts, and a power in our hands, given for righteous employment in maintaining right, and redressing wrong. Of those who judged the King, many thought him wilfully criminal; many, that his existence would keep the nation in perpetual conflict with the horde of Kings who would war against a generation which might come home to themselves, and that it were better that one should die than all. I should not have voted with this portion of the legislature. I should have shut up the Queen in a convent, putting harm out of her power and placed the King in his station, investing him with limited powers, which, I verily believe, he would have honestly exercised, according to the measure of his understanding. In this way, no void would have been created, courting the usurpation of a military adventurer, nor occasion given for those enormities which demoralized the nations of the world, and destroyed, and is yet to destroy, millions and millions of its inhabitants. There are three epochs in history, signalized by the total extinction of national morality. The first was of the successors of Alexander, not omitting himself: The next, the successors of the first Caesar: The third, our own age. This was begun by the partition of Poland, followed by that of the treaty of Pilnitz; next the conflagration of Copenhagen; then the enormities of Bonaparte, partitioning the earth at his will, and devastating it with fire and sword; now the conspiracy of Kings, the successors of Bonaparte, blasphemously calling themselves the Holy Alliance, and treading in the footsteps of their incarcerated leader; not yet, indeed, usurping the government of other nations, avowedly and in detail, but controlling by their armies the forms in which they will permit them to be governed; and reserving, *in petto,* the order and extent of the usurpations further meditated. But I will return from a digression, anticipated, too, in time, into which I have been led by reflection on the criminal passions which refused to the world a favorable occasion of saving it from the afflictions it has since suffered.

M. Necker had reached Basle before he was overtaken by the letter of the King, inviting him back to resume the office he had recently left. He returned immediately, and all the other Ministers having resigned, a new administration was named, to wit: St. Priest and Montmorin were restored; the Archbishop of Bordeaux was appointed Garde des Sceaux, La Tour du Pin, Minister of War; La Luzerne, Minister of Marine. This last was believed to have been effected by the friendship of Montmorin; for although differing in politics, they continued firm in friendship, and Luzerne, although not an able man, was thought an honest one. And the Prince of Bauvau was taken into the Council.

Seven Princes of the blood Royal, six ex-Ministers, and many of the high Noblesse, having fled, and the present Ministers, except Luzerne, being all of the popular party, all the functionaries of government moved, for the present, in perfect harmony.

In the evening of August the 4th, and on the motion of the Viscount de Noailles, brother in law of La Fayette, the Assembly abolished all titles of rank, all the abusive privileges of feudalism, the tithes and casuals of the Clergy, all Provincial privileges, and, in fine, the Feudal regimen generally. To the suppression of tithes, the Abbé Sieyes was vehemently opposed; but his learned and logical arguments were unheeded, and his estimation lessened by a contrast of his egoism (for he was beneficed on them), with the generous abandonment of rights by the other members of the Assembly. Many days were employed in putting into the form of laws, the numerous demolitions of ancient abuses; which done, they proceeded to the preliminary work of a Declaration of Rights. There being much concord of sentiment on the elements of this instrument it was liberally framed, and passed with a very general approbation. They then appointed a Committee for the "reduction of a projet" of a constitution, at the head of which was the Archbishop of Bordeaux. I received from him, as chairman of the Committee, a letter of July 20th, requesting me to attend and assist at their deliberations; but I excused myself, on the obvious considerations, that my mission was to the King as Chief Magistrate of the nation, that my duties were limited to the concerns of my own country, and forbade me to intermeddle with the internal transactions of that, in which I had been received under a specific character only. Their plan of a constitution was discussed in sections, and so reported from time to time, as agreed to by the Committee. The first respected the general frame of the government; and that this should be formed into three departments, Executive, Legislative and Judiciary, was generally agreed. But when they proceeded to subordinate developments, many and various shades of opinion came into conflict, and schism, strongly marked, broke the Patriots into fragments of very discordant principles. The first question, Whether there should be a King? met with no open opposition; and it was readily agreed, that the government of France should be monarchical and hereditary. Shall the King have a negative on the laws? shall that negative be absolute, or suspensive only? Shall there be two Chambers of Legislation, or one only? If two, shall one of them be hereditary? or for life? or for a fixed term? and named by the King? or elected by the people? These questions found strong differences of opinion, and produced repulsive combinations among the Patriots. The Aristocracy was cemented by a common principle, of preserving the ancient regime, or whatever should be nearest to it. Making this their polar star, they moved in phalanx, gave preponderance on every question to the minorities of the Patriots, and always to those who advocated the least change. The features of the new constitution were thus assuming a fearful aspect, and great alarm was produced among the honest Patriots by these dissensions in their ranks. In this uneasy state of things, I received one day a note from the Marquis de La Fayette, informing me that he should bring a party of six or eight friends to ask a dinner of me the next day. I assured him of their welcome. When they arrived, they were La Fayette himself, Duport, Barnave, Alexander la Meth, Blacon, Mounier, Maubourg, and Dagout. These were leading Patriots, of honest but differing opinions, sensible of the necessity of effecting a coalition by mutual sacrifices, knowing each other, and not afraid, therefore, to unbosom themselves mutually. This last was a material principle in the selection. With this view, the Marquis had invited the conference, and had fixed the time and place inadvertently, as to the embarrassment under which it might place me. The cloth being removed, and wine set on the table, after the American manner, the Marquis introduced the objects of the conference, by summarily reminding them of the state of things in the Assembly, the course which the principles of the Constitution were taking, and the inevitable result, unless checked by more concord among the Patriots themselves. He observed, that although he also had his opinion, he was ready to sacrifice it to that of his brethren of the same cause; but that a common opinion must now be formed, or the Aristocracy would carry everything, and that, whatever they should now agree on, he, at the head of the National force, would maintain. The discussions began at the hour of four, and were continued till ten o'clock in the evening; during which time, I was a silent witness to a coolness and candor of argument, unusual in the conflicts of political opinion; to a logical reasoning, and chaste eloquence, disfigured by no gaudy tinsel of rhetoric or declamation, and truly worthy of being placed in parallel with the finest dialogues of antiquity, as handed to us by Xenophon, by Plato and Cicero. The result was, that the King should have a suspensive veto on the laws, that the legislature should be composed of a single body only, and that to be chosen by the people. This Concordate decided the fate of the constitution. The Patriots all rallied to the principles thus settled, carried every question agreeably to them, and reduced the Aristocracy to insignificance and impotence. But duties of exculpation were now incumbent on me. I waited on Count Montmorin the next morning, and explained to him, with truth and candor, how it had happened that my house had been made the scene of conferences of such a character. He told me, he already knew everything which had passed, that so far from taking umbrage at the use made of my house on that occasion, he earnestly wished I would habitually assist at such conferences, being sure I should be useful in moderating the warmer spirits, and promoting a wholesome and practicable reformation only. I told him, I knew too well the duties I owed to the King, to the nation, and to my own country, to take any part in councils concerning their internal government, and that I should persevere, with care, in the character of a neutral and passive spectator, with wishes only, and very sincere ones, that those measures might prevail which would be for the greatest good of the nation. I have no doubts, indeed, that this conference was previously known and approved by this honest Minister, who was in confidence and communication with the Patriots, and wished for a reasonable reform of the Constitution.

Here I discontinue my relation of the French Revolution. The minuteness with which I have so far given its details, is disproportioned to the general scale of my narrative. But I have thought it justified by the interest which the whole world must take in this Revolution. As yet, we are but in the first chapter of its history. The appeal to the rights of man, which had been made in the United States, was taken up by France, first of the European nations. From her, the spirit has spread over those of the South. The tyrants of the North have allied indeed against it; but it is irresistible. Their opposition will only multiply its millions of human victims, their own satellites will catch it, and the condition of man through the civilized world, will be finally and greatly ameliorated. This is a wonderful instance of great events from small causes. So inscrutable is the arrangement of causes and consequences in this world, that a two-penny duty on tea, unjustly imposed in a sequestered part of it, changes the condition of all its inhabitants. I have been more minute in relating the early transactions of this regeneration, because I was in circumstances peculiarly favorable for a knowledge of the truth. Possessing the confidence and intimacy of the leading Patriots, and more than all, of the Marquis Fayette, their head and Atlas, who had no secrets from me, I learned with correctness the views and proceedings of that party; while my intercourse with the diplomatic missionaries of Europe at Paris, all of them with the court, and eager in prying into its councils and proceedings, gave me a knowledge of these also. My information was always, and immediately committed to writing, in letters to Mr. Jay, and often to my friends, and a recurrence to these letters now insures me against errors of memory.

These opportunities of information ceased at this period, with my retirement from this interesting scene of action. I had been more than a year soliciting leave to go home, with a view to place my daughters in the society and care of their friends, and to return for a short time to my station at Paris. But the metamorphosis through which our government was then passing from its Chrysalid to its Organic form suspended its action in a great degree; and it was not till the last of August, that I received the permission I had asked. And here, I cannot leave this great and good country, without expressing my sense of its pre-eminence of character among the nations of the earth. A more benevolent people I have never known, nor greater warmth and devotedness in their select friendships. Their kindness and accommodation to strangers is unparalleled, and the hospitality of Paris is beyond anything I had conceived to be practicable in a large city. Their eminence, too, in science, the communicative dispositions of their scientific men, the politeness of the general manners, the ease and vivacity of their conversation, give a charm to their society, to be found nowhere else. In a comparison of this, with other countries, we have the proof of primacy, which was given to Themistocles, after the battle of Salamis. Every general voted to himself the first reward of valor, and the second to Themistocles. So, ask the travelled inhabitant of any nation, in what country on earth would you rather live?—Certainly, in my own, where are all my friends, my relations, and the earliest and sweetest affections and recollections of my life. Which would be your second choice? France.

On the 26th of September I left Paris for Havre, where I was detained by contrary winds until the 8th of October. On that day, and the 9th, I crossed over to Cowes, where I had engaged the Clermont, Capt. Colley, to touch for me. She did so; but here again we were detained by contrary winds, until the 22d, when we embarked, and landed at Norfolk on the 23d of November. On my way home, I passed some days at Eppington, in Chesterfield, the residence of my friend and connection, Mr. Eppes; and, while there, I received a letter from the President, General Washington, by express, covering an appointment to be Secretary of State. I received it with real regret. My wish had been to return to Paris, where I had left my household establishment, as if there myself, and to see the end of the Revolution, which I then thought would be certainly and happily closed in less than a year. I then meant to return home, to withdraw from political life, into which I had been impressed by the circumstances of the times, to sink into the bosom of my family and friends, and devote myself to studies more congenial to my mind. In my answer of December 15th, I expressed these dispositions candidly to the President, and my preference of a return to Paris; but assured him, that if it was believed I could be more useful in the administration of the government, I would sacrifice my own inclinations without hesitation, and repair to that destination; this I left to his decision. I arrived at Monticello on the 23d of December, where I received a second letter from the President, expressing his continued wish that I should take my station there, but leaving me still at liberty to continue in my former office, if I could not reconcile myself to that now proposed. This silenced my reluctance, and I accepted the new appointment.

In the interval of my stay at home, my eldest daughter had been happily married to the eldest son of the Tuckahoe branch of Randolphs, a young gentleman of genius, science, and honorable mind, who afterwards filled a dignified station in the General Government, and the most dignified in his own State. I left Monticello on the first of March, 1790, for New York. At Philadelphia I called on the venerable and beloved Franklin. He was then on the bed of sickness from which he never rose. My recent return from a country in which he had left so many friends, and the perilous convulsions to which they had been exposed, revived all his anxieties to know what part they had taken, what had been their course, and what their fate. He went over all in succession, with a rapidity and animation almost too much for his strength. When all his inquiries were satisfied, and a pause took place, I told him I had learned with much pleasure that, since his return to America, he had been occupied in preparing for the world the history of his own life. I cannot say much of that, said he; but I will give you a sample of what I shall leave; and he directed his little grandson (William Bache) who was standing by the bedside, to hand him a paper from the table, to which he pointed. He did so; and the Doctor putting it into my hands, desired me to take it and read it at my leisure. It was about a quire of folio paper, written in a large and running hand, very like his own. I looked into it slightly, then shut it, and said I would accept his permission to read it, and would carefully return it. He said "no, keep it." Not certain of his meaning, I again looked into it, folded it for my pocket, and said again, I would certainly return it. "No," said he, "keep it." I put it into my pocket and shortly after took leave of him. He died on the 17th of the ensuing month of April; and as I understood that he had bequeathed all his papers to his grandson, William Temple Franklin, I immediately wrote to Mr. Franklin, to inform him I possessed this paper, which I should consider as his property, and would deliver to his order. He came on immediately to New York, called on me for it, and I delivered it to him. As he put it into his pocket, he said carelessly, he had either the original, or another copy of it, I do not recollect which. This last expression struck my attention forcibly, and for the first time suggested to me the thought that Dr. Franklin had meant it as a confidential deposit in my hands, and that I had done wrong in parting from it. I have not yet seen the collection he published of Dr. Franklin's works, and, therefore, know not if this is among them. I have been told it is not. It contained a narrative of the negotiations between Dr. Franklin and the British Ministry, when he was endeavoring to prevent the contest of arms which followed. The negotiation was brought about by the intervention of Lord Howe and his sister, who, I believe, was called Lady Howe, but I may misremember her title. Lord Howe seems to have been friendly to America, and exceedingly anxious to prevent a rupture. His intimacy with Dr. Franklin, and his position with the Ministry, induced him to undertake a mediation between them; in which his sister seemed to have been associated. They carried from one to the other, backwards and forwards, the several propositions and answers which passed, and seconded with their own intercessions, the importance of mutual sacrifices, to preserve the peace and connection of the two countries. I remember that Lord North's answers were dry, unyielding, in the spirit of unconditional submission, and betrayed an absolute indifference to the occurrence of a rupture; and he said to the mediators distinctly, at last, that "a rebellion was not to be deprecated on the part of Great Britain; that the confiscations it would produce would provide for many of their friends." This expression was reported by the mediators to Dr. Franklin, and indicated so cool and calculated a purpose in the Ministry, as to render compromise hopeless, and the negotiation was discontinued. If this is not among the papers published, we ask, what has become of it? I delivered it with my own hands, into those of Temple Franklin. It certainly established views so atrocious in the British government, that its suppression would, to them, be worth a great price. But could the grandson of Dr. Franklin be, in such degree, an accomplice in the parricide of the memory of his immortal grandfather? The suspension for more than twenty years of the general publication, bequeathed and confided to him, produced, for awhile, hard suspicions against him; and if, at last, all are not published, a part of these suspicions may remain with some.

I arrived at New York on the 21st of March, where Congress was in session.

The Anas

Introduction

Jefferson's *Anas,* or Notes, amounts virtually to a continuation of the
Autobiography from his second year as Secretary of State until his last
year as President, 1791–1809. During these stormy years, which saw the
growth and eventual decline of the Federalist Party, Jefferson was in the
habit of making frequent memoranda concerning the struggles and
intrigues between the Federalists and the Republicans. These notes,
written during the peak of the "passions of the times," were several
years later revised by Jefferson, with the purpose of removing any data
which might have been "incorrect, or doubtful, or merely personal or
private." The following selections from the *Anas* consist of Jefferson's
long explanatory note, dated Feb. 4, 1818, and three or four isolated
anecdotes which are characteristic of the tone and temper of the whole.

The Anas

In these three volumes will be found copies of the official opinions given in writing by me to General Washington, while I was Secretary of State, with sometimes the documents belonging to the case. Some of these are the rough draughts, some press copies, some fair ones. In the earlier part of my acting in that office, I took no other note of the passing transactions; but after awhile, I saw the importance of doing it in aid of my memory. Very often, therefore, I made memorandums on loose scraps of paper, taken out of my pocket in the moment, and laid by to be copied fair at leisure, which, however, they hardly ever were. These scraps, therefore, ragged, rubbed, and scribbled as they were, I had bound with the others by a binder who came into my cabinet, did it under my own eye, and without the opportunity of reading a single paper. At this day, after the lapse of twenty-five years, or more, from their dates, I have given to the whole a calm revisal, when the passions of the time are passed away, and the reasons of the transactions act alone on the judgment. Some of the informations I had recorded, are now cut out from the rest, because I have seen that they were incorrect, or doubtful, or merely personal or private, with which we have nothing to do. I should perhaps have thought the rest not worth preserving, but for their testimony against the only history of that period, which pretends to have been compiled from authentic and unpublished documents.

But a short review of facts . . . will show, that the contests of that day were contests of principle, between the advocates of republican, and those of kingly government, and that had not the former made the efforts they did, our government would have been, even at this early day, a very different thing from what the successful issue of those efforts have made it.

The alliance between the States under the old Articles of Confederation, for the purpose of joint defence against the aggression of Great Britain, was found insufficient, as treaties of alliance generally are, to enforce compliance with their mutual stipulations; and these, once fulfilled, that bond was to expire of itself, and each State to become sovereign and independent in all things. Yet it could not but occur to every one, that these separate independencies, like the petty States of Greece, would be eternally at war with each other, and would become at length the mere partisans and satellites of the leading powers of Europe. All then must have looked forward to some further bond of union, which would insure eternal peace, and a political system of our own, independent of that of Europe. Whether all should be consolidated into a single government, or each remain independent as to internal matters, and the whole form a single nation as to what was foreign only, and whether that national government should be a monarchy or republic, would of course divide opinions, according to the constitutions, the habits, and the circumstances of each individual. Some officers of the army, as it has always been said and believed (and Steuben and Knox have ever been named as the leading agents), trained to monarchy by military habits, are understood to have proposed to General Washington to decide this great question by the army before its disbandment, and to assume himself the crown on the assurance of their support. The indignation with which he is said to have scouted this parricide proposition was equally worthy of his virtue and wisdom.

The next effort was (on suggestion of the same individuals, in the moment of their separation), the establishment of an hereditary order under the name of the Cincinnati, ready prepared by that distinction to be ingrafted into the future frame of government, and placing General Washington still at their head. The General wrote to me on this subject, while I was in Congress at Annapolis, and an extract from my letter is inserted in 5th Marshall's history, page 28. He afterwards called on me at that place on his way to a meeting of the society, and after a whole evening of consultation, he left that place fully determined to use all his endeavors for its total suppression. But he found it so firmly riveted in the affections of the members, that, strengthened as they happened to be by an adventitious occurrence of the moment, he could effect no more than the abolition of its hereditary principle. He called again on his return, and explained to me fully the opposition which had been made, the effect of the occurrence from France, and the difficulty with which its duration had been limited to the lives of the present members. Further details will be found among my papers, in his and my letters, and some in the *Encyclopédie Méthodique et Dictionnaire d'Economie Politique,* communicated by myself to M. Meusnier, its author, who had made the establishment of this society the ground, in that work, of a libel on our country.

The want of some authority which should procure justice to the public creditors, and an observance of treaties with foreign nations, produced, some time after, the call of a convention of the States at Annapolis. Although, at this meeting, a difference of opinion was evident on the question of a republican or kingly government, yet, so general through the States was the sentiment in favor of the former, that the friends of the latter confined themselves to a course of obstruction only, and delay, to everything proposed; they hoped, that nothing being done, and all things going from bad to worse, a kingly government might be usurped, and submitted to by the people, as better than anarchy and wars internal and external, the certain consequences of the present want of a general government. The effect of their manoeuvres, with the defective attendance of Deputies from the States, resulted in the measure of calling a more general convention, to be held at Philadelphia. At this, the same party exhibited the same practices, and with the same views of preventing a government of concord, which they foresaw would be republican, and of forcing through anarchy their way to monarchy. But the mass of that convention was too honest, too wise, and too steady, to be baffled and misled by their manoeuvres.

One of these was a form of government proposed by Colonel Hamilton, which would have been in fact a compromise between the two parties of royalism and republicanism. According to this, the executive and one branch of the legislature were to be during good behavior, i.e. for life, and the governors of the States were to be named by these two permanent organs. This, however, was rejected; on which Hamilton left the convention, as desperate, and never returned again until near its final conclusion. These opinions and efforts, secret or avowed, of the advocates for monarchy, had begotten great jealousy through the States generally; and this jealousy it was which excited the strong opposition to the conventional constitution; a jealousy which yielded at last only to a general determination to establish certain amendments as barriers against a government either monarchical or consolidated. In what passed through the whole period of these conventions, I have gone on the information of those who were members of them, being absent myself on my mission to France.

I returned from that mission in the first year of the new government, having landed in Virginia in December, 1789, and proceeded to New York in March, 1790, to enter on the office of Secretary of State. Here, certainly, I found a state of things which, of all I had ever contemplated, I the least expected. I had left France in the first year of her revolution, in the fervor of natural rights, and zeal for reformation. My conscientious devotion to these rights could not be heightened, but it had been aroused and excited by daily exercise. The President received me cordially, and my colleages and the circle of principal citizens apparently with welcome. The courtesies of dinner parties given me, as a stranger newly arrived among them, placed me at once in their familiar society. But I cannot describe the wonder and mortification with which the table conversations filled me. Politics were the chief topic, and a preference of kingly over republican government was evidently the favorite sentiment. An apostate I could not be, nor yet a hypocrite; and I found myself, for the most part, the only advocate on the republican side of the question, unless among the guests there chanced to be some member of that party from the legislative Houses. Hamilton's financial system had then passed. It had two objects; 1st, as a puzzle, to exclude popular understanding and inquiry; 2d, as a machine for the corruption of the legislature; for he avowed the opinion, that man could be governed by one of two motives only, force or interest; force, he observed, in this country was out of the question, and the interests, therefore, of the members must be laid hold of, to keep the legislative in unison with the executive. And with grief and shame it must be acknowledged that his machine was not without effect; that even in this, the birth of our government, some members were found sordid enough to bend their duty to their interests, and to look after personal rather than public good.

It is well known that during the war the greatest difficulty we encountered was the want of money or means to pay our soldiers who fought, or our farmers, manufacturers and merchants, who furnished the necessary supplies of food and clothing for them. After the expedient of paper money had exhausted itself, certificates of debt were given to the individual creditors, with assurance of payment so soon as the United States should be able. But the distresses of these people often obliged them to part with these for the half, the fifth, and even a tenth of their value; and speculators had made a trade of cozening them from the holders by the most fraudulent practices, and persuasions that they would never be paid. In the bill for funding and paying these, Hamilton made no difference between the original holders and the fraudulent purchasers of this paper. Great and just repugnance arose at putting these two classes of creditors on the same footing, and great exertions were used to pay the former the full value, and to the latter, the price only which they had paid, with interest. But this would have prevented the game which was to be played, and for which the minds of greedy members were already tutored and prepared. When the trial of strength on these several efforts had indicated the form in which the bill would finally pass, this being known within doors sooner than without, and especially, than to those who were in distant parts of the Union, the base scramble began. Couriers and relay horses by land, and swift sailing pilot boats by sea, were flying in all directions. Active partners and agents were associated and employed in every State, town, and country neighborhood, and this paper was bought up at five shillings, and even as low as two shillings in the pound, before the holder knew that Congress had already provided for its redemption at par. Immense sums were thus filched from the poor and ignorant, and fortunes accumulated by those who had themselves been poor enough before. Men thus enriched by the dexterity of a leader, would follow of course the chief who was leading them to fortune, and become the zealous instruments of all his enterprises.

This game was over, and another was on the carpet at the moment of my arrival; and to this I was most ignorantly and innocently made to hold the candle. This fiscal manoeuvre is well known by the name of the Assumption. Independently of the debts of Congress, the States had during the war contracted separate and heavy debts; and Massachusetts particularly, in an absurd attempt, absurdly conducted, on the British post of Penobscot: and the more debt Hamilton could rake up, the more plunder for his mercenaries. This money, whether wisely or foolishly spent, was pretended to have been spent for general purposes, and ought, therefore, to be paid from the general purse. But it was objected, that nobody knew what these debts were, what their amount, or what their proofs. No matter; we will guess them to be twenty millions. But of these twenty millions, we do not know how much should be reimbursed to one State, or how much to another. No matter; we will guess. And so another scramble was set on foot among the several States, and some got much, some little, some nothing. But the main object was obtained, the phalanx of the Treasury was reinforced by additional recruits. This measure produced the most bitter and angry contest ever known in Congress, before or since the Union of the States. I arrived in the midst of it. But a stranger to the ground, a stranger to the actors on it, so long absent as to have lost all familiarity with the subject, and as yet unaware of its object, I took no concern in it.

The great and trying question, however, was lost in the House of Representatives. So high were the feuds excited by this subject, that on its rejection business was suspended. Congress met and adjourned from day to day without doing anything, the parties being too much out of temper to do business together. The eastern members particularly, who, with Smith from South Carolina, were the principal gamblers in these scenes, threatened a secession and dissolution. Hamilton was in despair. As I was going to the President's one day, I met him in the street. He walked me backwards and forwards before the President's door for half an hour. He painted pathetically the temper into which the legislature had been wrought; the disgust of those who were called the creditor States; the danger of the *secession* of their members, and the separation of the States. He observed that the members of the administration ought to act in concert; that though this question was not of my department, yet a common duty should make it a common concern; that the President was the centre on which all administrative questions ultimately rested, and that all of us should rally around him, and support, with joint efforts, measures approved by him; and that the question having been lost by a small majority only, it was probable that an appeal from me to the judgment and discretion of some of my friends, might effect a change in the vote, and the machine of government, now suspended, might be again set into motion. I told him that I was really a stranger to the whole subject; that not having yet informed myself of the system of finances adopted, I knew not how far this was a necessary sequence; that undoubtedly, if its rejection endangered a dissolution of our Union at this incipient stage, I should deem that the most unfortunate of all consequences, to avert which all partial and temporary evils should be yielded. I proposed to him, however, to dine with me the next day, and I would invite another friend or two, bring them into conference together, and I thought it impossible that reasonable men, consulting together coolly, could fail, by some mutual sacrifices of opinion, to form a compromise which was to save the Union.

The discussion took place. I could take no part in it but an exhortatory one, because I was a stranger to the circumstances which should govern it. But it was finally agreed, that whatever importance had been attached to the rejection of this proposition, the preservation of the Union and of concord among the States was more important, and that therefore it would be better that the vote of rejection should be rescinded, to effect which, some members should change their votes. But it was observed that this pill would be peculiarly bitter to the southern States, and that some concomitant measure should be adopted, to sweeten it a little to them. There had before been propositions to fix the seat of government either at Philadelphia, or at Georgetown on the Potomac; and it was thought that by giving it to Philadelphia for ten years, and to Georgetown permanently afterwards, this might, as an anodyne, calm in some degree the ferment which might be excited by the other measure alone. So two of the Potomac members (White and Lee, but White with a revulsion of stomach almost convulsive) agreed to change their votes, and Hamilton undertook to carry the other point. In doing this, the influence he had established over the eastern members, with the agency of Robert Morris with those of the middle States, effected his side of the engagement; and so the Assumption was passed, and twenty millions of stock divided among favored States, and thrown in as a pabulum to the stock-jobbing herd. This added to the number of votaries to the Treasury, and made its chief the master of every vote in the legislature, which might give to the government the direction suited to his political views.

I know well, and so must be understood, that nothing like a majority in Congress had yielded to this corruption. Far from it. But a division, not very unequal, had already taken place in the honest part of that body, between the parties styled republican and federal. The latter being monarchists in principle, adhered to Hamilton of course, as their leader in that principle, and this mercenary phalanx added to them, insured him always a majority in both Houses; so that the whole action of legislature was now under the direction of the Treasury. Still the machine was not complete. The effect of the funding system, and of the Assumption, would be temporary; it would be lost with the loss of the individual members whom it has enriched, and some engine of influence more permanent must be contrived, while these myrmidons were yet in place to carry it through all opposition. This engine was the Bank of the United States. All that history is known, so I shall say nothing about it. While the government remained at Philadelphia, a selection of members of both Houses were constantly kept as directors who, on every question interesting to that institution, or to the views of the federal head, voted at the will of that head; and, together with the stock-holding members, could always make the federal vote that of the majority. By this combination, legislative expositions were given to the constitution, and all the administrative laws were shaped on the model of England, and so passed. And from this influence we were not relieved, until the removal from the precincts of the bank, to Washington.

Here then was the real ground of the opposition which was made to the course of administration. Its object was to preserve the legislature pure and independent of the executive, to restrain the administration to republican forms and principles, and not permit the constitution to be construed into a monarchy, and to be warped, in practice, into all the principles and pollutions of their favorite English model. Nor was this an opposition to General Washington. He was true to the republican charge confided to him; and has solemnly and repeatedly protested to me, in our conversations, that he would lose the last drop of his blood in support of it; and he did this the oftener and with the more earnestness, because he knew my suspicions of Hamilton's designs against it, and wished to quiet them. For he was not aware of the drift, or of the effect of Hamilton's schemes. Unversed in financial projects and calculations and budgets, his approbation of them was bottomed on his confidence in the man.

But Hamilton was not only a monarchist, but for a monarchy bottomed on corruption. In proof of this, I will relate an anecdote, for the truth of which I attest the God who made me. Before the President set out on his southern tour in April, 1791, he addressed a letter of the fourth of that month, from Mount Vernon, to the Secretaries of State, Treasury and War, desiring that if any serious and important cases should arise during his absence, they would consult and act on them. And he requested that the Vice President should also be consulted. This was the only occasion on which that officer was ever requested to take part in a cabinet question. Some occasion for consultation arising, I invited those gentlemen (and the Attorney General, as well as I remember) to dine with me, in order to confer on the subject. After the cloth was removed, and our question agreed and dismissed, conversation began on other matters, and by some circumstance, was led to the British constitution, on which Mr. Adams observed, "purge that constitution of its corruption, and give to its popular branch equality of representation, and it would be the most perfect constitution ever devised by the wit of man." Hamilton paused and said, "purge it of its corruption, and give to its popular branch equality of representation, and it would become an *impracticable* government: as it stands at present, with all its supposed defects, it is the most perfect government which ever existed." And this was assuredly the exact line which separated the political creeds of these two gentlemen. The one was for two hereditary branches and an honest elective one; the other, for an hereditary King, with a House of Lords and Commons corrupted to his will, and standing between him and the people.

Hamilton was, indeed, a singular character. Of acute understanding, disinterested, honest, and honorable in all private transactions, amiable in society, and duly valuing virtue in private life, yet so bewitched and perverted by the British example, as to be under thorough conviction that corruption was essential to the government of a nation. Mr. Adams had originally been a republican. The glare of royalty and nobility, during his mission to England, had made him believe their fascination a necessary ingredient in government; and Shay's [sic] rebellion, not sufficiently understood where he then was, seemed to prove that the absence of want and oppression, was not a sufficient guarantee of order. His book on the American constitutions having made known his political bias, he was taken up by the monarchical federalists in his absence, and on his return to the United States, he was by them made to believe that the general disposition of our citizens was favorable to monarchy. He here wrote his "Davila," as a supplement to a former work, and his election to the Presidency confirmed him in his errors. Innumerable addresses too, artfully and industriously poured in upon him, deceived him into a confidence that he was on the pinnacle of popularity, when the gulf was yawning at his feet, which was to swallow up him and his deceivers. For when General Washington was withdrawn, these *energumeni* of royalism, kept in check hitherto by the dread of his honesty, his firmness, his patriotism, and the authority of his name, now mounted on the car of State and free from control, like Phaeton on that of the sun, drove headlong and wild, looking neither to right nor left, nor regarding anything but the objects they were driving at; until, displaying these fully, the eyes of the nation were opened, and a general disbandment of them from the public councils took place.

Mr. Adams, I am sure, has been long since convinced of the treacheries with which he was surrounded during his administration. He has since thoroughly seen, that his constituents were devoted to republican government, and whether his judgment is re-settled on its ancient basis, or not, he is conformed as a good citizen to the will of the majority, and would now, I am persuaded, maintain its republican structure with the zeal and fidelity belonging to his character. For even an enemy has said, "he is always an honest man, and often a great one." But in the fervor of the fury and follies of those who made him their stalking horse, no man who did not witness it can form an idea of their unbridled madness, and the terrorism with which they surrounded themselves. The horrors of the French revolution, then raging, aided them mainly, and using that as a raw head and bloody bones, they were enabled by their stratagems of X. Y. Z. in which this historian[1] was a

---

[1] I.e., Jefferson. Deleted from Memorial Edition.

leading mountebank, their tales of tub-plots, ocean massacres, bloody buoys, and pulpit lyings and slanderings, and maniacal ravings of their Gardeners, their Osgoods and parishes, to spread alarm into all but the firmest breasts. Their Attorney General had the impudence to say to a republican member, that deportation must be resorted to, of which, said he, "you republicans have set the example"; thus daring to identify us with the murderous Jacobins of France.

These transactions, now recollected but as dreams of the night, were then sad realities; and nothing rescued us from their liberticide effect, but the unyielding opposition of those firm spirits who sternly maintained their post in defiance of terror, until their fellow citizens could be aroused to their own danger, and rally and rescue the standard of the constitution. This has been happily done. Federalism and monarchism have languished from that moment, until their treasonable combinations with the enemies of their country during the late war, their plots of dismembering the Union, and their Hartford convention, have consigned them to the tomb of the dead; and I fondly hope, "we may now truly say, we are all republicans, all federalists," and that the motto of the standard to which our country will forever rally, will be, "federal union, and republican government"; and sure I am we may say, that we are indebted for the preservation of this point of ralliance, to that opposition of which so injurious an idea is so artfully insinuated and excited in this history.

Much of this relation is notorious to the world; and many intimate proofs of it will be found in these notes. From the moment where they end, of my retiring from the administration, the federalists got unchecked hold of General Washington. His memory was already sensibly impaired by age, the firm tone of mind for which he had been remarkable, was beginning to relax, its energy was abated, a listlessness of labor, a desire for tranquility had crept on him, and a willingness to let others act, and even think for him. Like the rest of mankind, he was disgusted with atrocities of the French revolution, and was not sufficiently aware of the difference between the rabble who were used as instruments of their perpetration, and the steady and rational character of the American people, in which he had not sufficient confidence. The opposition too of the republicans to the British treaty, and the zealous support of the federalists in that unpopular but favorite measure of theirs, had made him all their own. Understanding, moreover, that I disapproved of that treaty, and copiously nourished with falsehoods by a malignant neighbor of mine, who ambitioned to be his correspondent, he had become alienated from myself personally, as from the republican body generally of his fellow-citizens; and he wrote the letters to Mr. Adams and Mr. Carroll, over which, in devotion to his imperishable fame, we must forever weep as monuments of mortal decay.

February 4th, 1818.

Conversation with President Washington

February the 7th, 1793

. . . . as to a coalition with Mr. Hamilton, if by that was meant that either was to sacrifice his general system to the other, it was impossible. We had both, no doubt, formed our conclusions after the most mature consideration; and principles conscientiously adopted, could not be given up on either side. My wish was, to see both Houses of Congress cleansed of all persons interested in the bank or public stocks; and that a pure legislature being given us, I should always be ready to acquiesce under their determinations, even if contrary to my own opinions; for that I subscribe to the principle, that the will of the majority, honestly expressed, should give law. . . .

February the 16th, 1793

E. Randolph tells J. Madison and myself, a curious fact which he had from Lear. When the President went to New York, he resisted for three weeks the efforts to introduce levees. At length he yielded, and left it to Humphreys and some others to settle the forms. Accordingly, an ante-chamber and presence room were provided, and when those who were to pay their court were assembled, the President set out, preceded by Humphreys. After passing through the ante-chamber, the door of the inner room was thrown open, and Humphreys entered first, calling out with a loud voice, "the President of the United States." The President was so much disconcerted with it, that he did not recover from it the whole time of the levee, and when the company was gone, he said to Humphreys, "Well, you have taken me in once, but by God you shall never take me in a second time."

May the 23d, [1793]

. . . . He [President Washington] adverted to a piece in Freneau's paper[1] of yesterday; he said he despised all their attacks on him personally, but that there never had been an act of the Government, not meaning in the executive line only, but in any line, which that paper had not abused. He had also marked the word republic thus, where it was applied to the French republic. . . . He was evidently sore and warm, and I took his intention to be, that I should interpose in some way with Freneau, perhaps withdraw his appointment of translating clerk to my office. But I will not do it. His paper has saved our Constitution, which was galloping fast into monarchy, and has been checked by no one means so powerfully as by that paper. It is well and universally known, that it has been that paper which has checked the career of the monocrats; and the President, not sensible of the designs of the party, has not with his usual good sense and *sang froid*, looked on the efforts and effects of this free press, and seen that, though some bad things have passed through it to the public, yet the good have preponderated immensely.

January the 24th, [1800]

Mr. Smith, a merchant of Hamburg, gives me the following information: The St. Andrew's Club of New York (all of Scotch tories) gave a public dinner lately. Among other guests, Alexander Hamilton was one. After dinner, the first toast was, "The President of the United States." It was drunk without any particular approbation. The next was, "George the Third." Hamilton started up on his feet, and insisted on a bumper and three cheers. The whole company accordingly rose and gave the cheers. . . .

[1]Philip Freneau's anti-federalist paper, *The National Gazette.*

Travel Journals

Introduction

During his five-year residence in Paris as Minister to the Court of Louis XVI, Jefferson made only occasional trips from the capital: one to England in March and April of 1786, during which he was presented to the King, made a perfunctory visit to Shakespeare's grave, and had his portrait painted by Mather Brown; one to Southern France and Northern Italy in March, April, May, and June of the following year; and a third to Amsterdam and Strasburg in February, March, and April of 1788. A man with a keen eye for detail, and an infinite capacity for taking pains, Jefferson was in the habit of making daily entries in a journal concerning the sights he had seen, the places he had visited, the people he had talked with, and the useful products and inventions he might borrow for America. Selections from the journal of his second trip, that to France and Italy, together with an interesting "traveler's guide" compiled for two fellow Americans, appear on the following pages.

Travel Journals

✍

Memoranda taken on a Journey from Paris into the Southern Parts of France, and Northern of Italy, in the year 1787.

CHAMPAGNE. March 3. *Sens to Vermanton.* The face of the country is in large hills, not too steep for the plough, somewhat resembling the Elk hill, and Beaver-dam hills of Virginia. The soil is generally a rich mulatto loam, with a mixture of coarse sand and some loose stone. The plains of the Yonne are of the same color. The plains are in corn, the hills in vineyard, but the wine not good. There are a few apple trees, but none of any other kind, and no inclosures. No cattle, sheep, or swine; fine mules.

Few châteaux; no farm-houses, all the people being gathered in villages. Are they thus collected by that dogma of their religion, which makes them believe, that to keep the Creator in good humor with His own works, they must mumble a mass every day? Certain it is, that they are less happy and less virtuous in villages, than they would be insulated with their families on the grounds they cultivate. The people are illy clothed. Perhaps they have put on their worst clothes at this moment, as it is raining. But I observe women and children carrying heavy burdens, and laboring with the hoe. This is an unequivocal indication of extreme poverty. Men, in a civilized country, never expose their wives and children to labor above their force and sex, as long as their own labor can protect them from it. I see few beggars. Probably this is the effect of a police.

BURGUNDY. March 4. *Lucy le bois. Cussy les forges. Rouvray. Maison-neuve. Vitteaux. La Chaleure. Pont de Panis. Dijon.* The hills are higher and more abrupt. The soil, a good red loam and sand, mixed with more or less grit, small stone, and sometimes rock. All in corn.

127

Some forest wood here and there, broom, whins and holly, and a few inclosures of quick hedge. Now and then a flock of sheep.

The people are well clothed, but it is Sunday. They have the appearance of being well fed. The Château de Sevigny, near Cussy les forges, is a charming situation. Between Maison-neuve and Vitteaux the road leads through an avenue of trees, eight American miles long, in a right line. It is impossible to paint the ennui of this avenue. . . .

March 7 and 8. From *la Baraque* to *Chagny*

. . . . The corn lands here rent for about fifteen livres the arpent. They are now planting, pruning, and sticking their vines. When a new vineyard is made, they plant the vines in gutters about four feet apart. As the vines advance, they lay them down. They put out new shoots, and fill all the intermediate space, till all trace of order is lost. They have ultimately about one foot square to each vine. They begin to yield good profit at five or six years old, and last one hundred, or one hundred and fifty years. A vigneron at Voulenay carried me into his vineyard, which was of about ten arpents. He told me that some years it produced him sixty pieces of wine, and some, not more than three pieces. The latter is the most advantageous produce, because the wine is better in quality, and higher in price in proportion as less is made, and the expenses at the same time diminish in the same proportion. Whereas, when much is made, the expenses are increased, while the price and quality become less. In very plentiful years, they often give one half the wine for casks to contain the other half. The cask for two hundred and fifty bottles, costs six livres in scarce years, and ten in plentiful. The Feuillette is of one hundred and twenty-five bottles, the Piece of two hundred and fifty, and the Queue or Botte, of five hundred. An arpent rents at from twenty to sixty livres. A farmer of ten arpents has about three laborers engaged by the year. He pays four louis to a man, and half as much to a woman, and feeds them. He kills one hog, and salts it, which is all the meat used in the family during the year. Their ordinary food is bread and vegetables At Pommard and Voulenay, I observed them eating good wheat bread; at Meursault, rye. I asked the reason of this difference. They told me that the white wines fail in quality much oftener than the red, and remain on hand. The farmer, therefore, cannot afford to feed his laborers so well. At Meursault, only white wines are made, because there is too much stone for the red. On such slight circumstances depends the condition of man! The wines which have given such celebrity to Burgundy, grow only on the Cote, an extent of about five leagues long, and half a league wide. They begin at Chambertin, and go through Vougeau, Romanie, Veaune, Nuys, Beaune, Pommard, Voulenay, Meursault, and end at Monrachet. Those of the two last are white, the others red. Chambertin, Vougeau and Veaune are strongest, and will bear transportation and keeping. They sell, therefore, on the spot for twelve hundred livres the queue, which is forty-eight sous the bottle. Voulenay is the best of the other reds, equal in flavor to Chambertin, etc., but being lighter, will not keep, and therefore sells for not more than three hundred livres the queue, which is twelve sous the bottle. It ripens sooner than they do, and consequently is better for those who wish to broach at a year old. In like manner of the white wines, and for the same reason, Monrachet sells for twelve hundred livres the queue (forty-eight sous the bottle), and Meursault of the best quality, viz., the Goutte d'or, at only one hundred and fifty livres (six sous the bottle). It is remarkable, that the best of each kind, that is, of the red and white, is made at the extremities of the line, to wit, at Chambertin and Monrachet. It is pretended that the adjoining vineyards produce the same qualities, but that belonging to obscure individuals, they have not obtained a name, and therefore sell as other wines. The aspect of the Cote is a little south of east. The western side is also covered with vines, and is apparently of the same soil, yet the wines are of the coarsest kinds. Such, too, are those which are produced in the plains; but there the soil is richer and less strong. Vougeau is the property of the monks of Citeaux, and produces about two hundred pieces. Monrachet contains about fifty arpents, and produces, one year with another, about one hundred and twenty pieces. It belongs to two proprietors only, Monsieur de Clarmont, who leases to some wine merchants, and the Marquis de Sarsnet, of Dijon, whose part is farmed to a Monsieur de la Tour, whose family for many generations have had the farm. The best wines are carried to Paris by land. The transportation costs thirty-six livres the piece. The more indifferent go by water. Bottles cost four and a half sous each. . . .

BEAUJOLOIS. *Maison blanche. St. George. Château de Laye-Epinaye.*
. . . . The wages of a laboring man here, are five louis; of a woman,

one half. The women do not work with the hoe; they only weed the vines, the corn, etc., and spin. They speak a patois very difficult to understand. I passed some time at the Château de Laye-Epinaye. Monsieur de Laye has a seignory of about fifteen thousand arpents, in pasture, corn, vines, and wood. He has over this, as is usual, a certain jurisdiction, both criminal and civil. But this extends only to the first crude examination, which is before his judges. The subject is referred for final examination and decision, to the regular judicatures of the country. The Seigneur is keeper of the peace on his domains. He is therefore subject to the expenses of maintaining it. A criminal prosecuted to sentence and execution, costs M. de Laye about five thousand livres. This is so burdensome to the Seigneurs, that they are slack in criminal prosecutions. A good effect from a bad cause. Through all Champagne, Burgundy, and the Beaujolois, the husbandry seems good, except that they manure too little. This proceeds from the shortness of their leases. The people of Burgundy and Beaujolois are well clothed, and have the appearance of being well fed. But they experience all the oppressions which result from the nature of the general government, and from that of their particular tenures, and of the seignorial government to which they are subject. What a cruel reflection, that a rich country cannot long be a free one. M. de Laye has a Diana and Endymion, a very superior morsel of sculpture by Michael Angelo Slodtz, done in 1740. The wild gooseberry is in leaf; the wild pear and sweet briar in bud.

Lyons. There are some feeble remains here, of an amphitheatre of two hundred feet diameter, and of an aqueduct in brick. The Pont d'Ainay has nine arches of forty feet from centre to centre. The piers are of six feet. The almond is in bloom.

. . . . *Nice.* The pine bur is used here for kindling fires. The people are in separate establishments. With respect to the orange, there seems to be no climate on this side of the Alps, sufficiently mild in itself to preserve it without shelter. At Olioules, they are between two high mountains; at Hieres, covered on the north by a very high mountain; at Antibes and Nice, covered by mountains, and also within small high enclosures. Quere. To trace the true line from east to west, which forms the northern and natural limit of that fruit? Saw an elder tree (sambucus) near Nice, fifteen inches in diameter, and eight feet stem.

The wine made in this neighborhood is good, though not of the first quality. There are one thousand mules, loaded with merchandise, which pass every week between Nice and Turin, counting those coming as well as going.

. . . . April 14th. *Ciandola. Tende.*

. . . . Tende is a very inconsiderable village, in which they have not yet the luxury of glass windows; nor in any of the villages on this passage, have they yet the fashion of powdering the hair. Common stone and limestone are so abundant, that the apartments of every story are vaulted with stone, to save wood.

April 15th. *Limone. Coni.*

. . . . A great deal of golden willow all along the rivers, on the whole of this passage through the Alps. The southern parts of France, but still more the passage through the Alps, enable one to form a scale of the tenderer plants, arranging them according to their several powers of resisting cold. Ascending three different mountains, Braus, Brois, and Tende, they disappear one after another; and descending on the other side, they show themselves again one after another. This is their order, from the tenderest to the hardiest. Caper, orange, palm, aloe, olive, pomegranate, walnut, fig, almond. But this must be understood of the plant; for as to the fruit, the order is somewhat different. The caper, for example, is the tenderest plant, yet being so easily protected, it is the most certain in its fruit. The almond, the hardiest plant, loses its fruit the oftenest, on account of its forwardness. The palm hardier than the caper and the orange, never produces perfect fruit in these parts. Coni is a considerable town, and pretty well built. It is walled.

. . . . April 19th. *Settimo. Chivasco. Ciliano. S. Germano. Vercelli.* The country continues plain and rich, the soil black. The culture, corn, pasture, maize, vines, mulberries, walnuts, some willow and poplar. The maize bears a very small proportion to the small grain. The earth is formed into ridges from three to four feet wide, and the maize sowed in the broadcast on the higher parts of the ridge, so as to cover a third or half of the whole surface. It is sowed late in May. This country is plentifully and beautifully watered at present. Much of it is by torrents which are dry in summer. These torrents make a great deal of waste ground, covering it with sand and stones. These wastes are sometimes planted in trees, sometimes quite unemployed. They make hedges of willows, by setting the plants from one to three feet apart. When they are grown to the height of eight or ten feet, they bend them down, and interlace them one with another. I do not see any of these, however, which are become old. Probably, therefore, they soon die. The women here smite on the anvil, and work with the maul and spade. The people of this country are ill dressed in comparison with those of France, and there are more spots of uncultivated ground. The plough here is made with a single handle, which is a beam twelve feet long, six inches in diameter below, and tapered to about two inches at the upper end. They use goads for the oxen, not whips. The first swallows I have seen, are to-day. . . .

April 21st, 22d. *Milan.* Figs and pomegranates grow here unsheltered, as I am told. I saw none, and therefore suppose them rare. They had formerly olives; but a great cold in 1709 killed them, and they have not been replanted. Among a great many houses painted *al fresco*, the Casa Roma and Casa Candiani, by Appiani, and Casa Belgioiosa, by Martin, are superior. In the second is a small cabinet, the ceiling of which is in small hexagons, within which are cameos and heads painted alternately, no two the same. The salon of the Casa Belgioiosa is superior to anything I have ever seen. The mixture called Scaiola, of which they make their walls and floors, is so like the finest marble as to be scarcely distinguishable from it. The nights of the 20th and 21st instant the rice ponds froze half an inch thick. Drouths of two or three months are not uncommon here in summer. About five years ago, there was such a hail as to kill cats. The Count del Verme tells me of a pendulum odometer for the wheel of a carriage. Leases here are mostly for nine years. Wheat costs a louis d'or the one hundred and forty pounds. A laboring man receives sixty livres, and is fed and lodged. The trade of this country is principally rice, raw silk, and cheese.

April 23d. *Casino,* five miles from Milan. I examined another rice-beater of six pestles. They are eight feet nine inches long. Their ends, instead of being a truncated cone, have nine teeth of iron, bound closely together. Each tooth is a double pyramid, joined at the base. When put together, they stand with the upper ends placed in contact, so as to form them into one great cone, and the lower ends diverging. The upper are socketed into the end of the pestle, and the lower, when a little blunted by use, are not unlike the jaw teeth of the mammoth, with their studs. They say here, that pestles armed with these teeth, clean the rice faster, and break it less.

. . . . *Rozzano*. Parmesan cheese. It is supposed this was formerly made at Parma, and took its name thence, but none is made there now. It is made through all the country extending from Milan for one hundred and fifty miles. . . .

The milk, . . . receives its due quantity of rennet, and is gently warmed, if the season requires it. In about four hours it becomes a slip. Then the whey begins to separate. A little of it is taken out. The curd is then thoroughly broken by a machine like a chocolate mill. A quarter of an ounce of saffron is put to seven brenta of milk, to give color to the cheese. The kettle is then moved over the hearth, and heated by a quick fire till the curd is hard enough, being broken into small lumps by continued stirring. It is moved off the fire, most of the whey taken out, the curd compressed into a globe by the hand, a linen cloth slipped under it, and it is drawn out in that. A loose hoop is then laid on a bench, and the curd, as wrapped in the linen, is put into the hoop; it is a little pressed by the hand, the hoop drawn tight and made fast. A board two inches thick is laid on it, and a stone on that of about twenty pounds weight. In an hour, the whey is run off, and the cheese finished. They sprinkle a little salt on it every other day in summer, and every day in winter, for six weeks. Seven brentas of milk make a cheese of fifty pounds, which requires six months to ripen, and is then dried to forty-five pounds. It sells on the spot for eighty-eight livres the one hundred pounds. There are now one hundred and fifty cheeses in this dairy. They are nineteen inches diameter, and six inches thick. They make a cheese a day in summer, and two in three days, or one in two days, in winter.

. . . . April 26th. *Genoa*. Strawberries at Genoa. Scaffold poles for the upper parts of a wall, as for the third story, rest on the window sills of the story below. Slate is used here for paving, for steps, for stairs, (the rise as well as tread) and for fixed Venetian blinds. At the Palazzo Marcello Durazzo, benches with straight legs, and bottoms of cane. At the Palazzo del prencipe Lomellino, at Sestri, a phaeton with a canopy. At the former, tables folding into one plane. At Nervi they have peas, strawberries, etc., all the year round. The gardens of the

Count Durazzo at Nervi exhibit as rich a mixture of the *utile dulci*, as I ever saw. All the environs in Genoa, are in olives figs, oranges, mulberries, corn, and garden stuff. Aloes in many places, but they never flower.

April 28th. *Noli*. The Apennine and Alps appear to me, to be one and the same continued ridge of mountains, separating everywhere the waters of the Adriatic Gulf from those of the Mediterranean. Where it forms an elbow, touching the Mediterranean, as a smaller circle touches a larger. within which it is inscribed, in the manner of a tangent, the name changes from Alps to Apennine. It is the beginning of the Apennine which constitutes the State of Genoa, the mountains there generally falling down in barren naked precipices into the sea. . . . Noli, into which I was obliged to put, by a change of wind, is forty miles from Genoa. There are twelve hundred inhabitants in the village, and many separate houses round about. One of the precipices hanging over the sea is covered with aloes. But neither here, nor anywhere else I have been, could I procure satisfactory information that they ever flower. The current of testimony is to the contrary. Noli furnishes many fishermen. Paths penetrate up into the mountains in several directions, about three-fourths of a mile; but these are practicable only for asses and mules. I saw no cattle nor sheep in the settlement. The wine they make, is white and indifferent. A curious cruet for oil and vinegar in one piece, I saw here. A bishop resides here, whose revenue is two thousand livres, equal to sixty-six guineas. I heard a nightingale here.

April 29th. *Albenga*. In walking along the shore from Louano to this place, I saw no appearance of shells. The tops of the mountains are covered with snow, while there are olive trees, etc., on the lower parts. I do not remember to have seen assigned anywhere, the cause of the apparent color of the sea. Its water is generally clear and colorless, if taken up and viewed in a glass. That of the Mediterranean is remarkably so. Yet in the mass, it assumes, *by reflection*, the color of the sky or atmosphere, black, green, blue, according to the state of the weather. If any person wished to retire from his acquaintance, to live absolutely unknown, and yet in the midst of physical enjoyments, it should be in some of the little villages of this coast, where air, water and earth concur to offer what each has most precious. Here are nightingales, beccaficas, ortolans, pheasants, partridges, quails, a superb climate, and the power of changing it from summer to winter at any moment, by ascending the mountains. The earth furnishes wine, oil, figs, oranges, and every production of the garden, in every season. The sea yields lobsters, crabs, oysters, thunny, sardines, anchovies, etc.

May 15. *Bezieres. Argilies. Le Saumal.*

. . . . The canal of Languedoc, along which I now travel, is six toises wide at bottom, and ten toises at the surface of the water, which is one toise deep. The barks which navigate it are seventy and eighty feet long, and seventeen or eighteen feet wide. They are drawn by one horse, and worked by two hands, one of which is generally a woman. The locks are mostly kept by women, but the necessary operations are much too laborious for them. The encroachments by the men, on the offices proper for the women, is a great derangement in the order of things. Men are shoemakers, tailors, upholsterers, stay-makers, man-tua-makers, cooks, housekeepers, house-cleaners, bed-makers; they *coiffe* the ladies, and bring them to bed: the women, therefore, to live, are obliged to undertake the offices which they abandon. They become porters, carters, reapers, sailors, lock-keepers, smiters on the anvil, cultivators of the earth, etc. Can we wonder, if such of them as have a little beauty, prefer easier courses to get their livelihood, as long as that beauty lasts? Ladies who employ men in the offices which should be reserved for their sex, are they not bawds in effect? For every man whom they thus employ, some girl, whose place he has thus taken, is driven to whoredom.

. . . . June 6th, 7th, 8th. *Nantes. Ancenis, Angers. Tours,*

. . . . Tours is at the one hundred and nineteenth milestone. Being desirous of inquiring here into a fact stated by Voltaire, in his Questions Encyclopédiques, article Coquilles, relative to the growth of shells unconnected with animal bodies, at the Chateau of Monsieur de la Sauvagiere, near Tours, I called on Monsieur Gentil, premier secretaire de l'Intendance, to whom the Intendant had written on my behalf, at the request of the Marquis de Chastellux. I stated to him the fact as advanced by Voltaire, and found he was, of all men, the best to whom I could have addressed myself. He told me he had been in correspondence with Voltaire on that very subject, and was perfectly acquainted with Monsieur de la Sauvagiere, and the Faluniere where the fact is said to have taken place. It is at the Chateau de Grillemont, six leagues from Tours, on the road to Bordeaux, belong now to Monsieur d'Orcai. He says, that de la Sauvagiere was a man of truth, and might be relied on for whatever facts he stated as of his own observations; but that he was overcharged with imagination, which, in matters of opinion and theory, often led him beyond his facts; that this feature in his character had appeared principally in what he wrote on the antiquities of Touraine; but that, as to the fact in question, he believed him. That he himself, indeed, had not watched the same identical shells, as Sauvagiere had done, growing from small to great; but that he had often seen such masses of those shells of all sizes, from a point to a full size, as to carry conviction to his mind that they were in the act of growing; that he had once made a collection of shells for the Emperor's cabinet, reserving duplicates of them for himself; and that these afforded proofs of the same fact; that he afterwards gave those duplicates to a Monsieur du Verget, a physician of Tours, of great science and candor, who was collecting on a larger scale, and who was perfectly in sentiment with Monsieur de la Sauvagiere, that not only the Faluniere, but many other places about Tours, would convince any unbiased observer, that shells are a fruit of the earth, spontaneously produced; and he gave me a copy of de la Sauvagiere's Recueil de Dissertations, presented by the author, wherein is one Sur la vegetation spontanée des coquilles du Chateau des Places. So far, I repeat from him. What are we to conclude? That we have not materials enough yet, to form any conclusion. The fact stated by Sauvagiere is not against any law of nature, and is therefore possible; but it is so little analogous to her habitual processes, that, if true, it would be extraordinary; that to command our belief, therefore, there should be such a suite of observations, as that their untruth would be more extraordinary than the existence of the fact they affirm. The bark of trees, the skin of fruits and animals, the feathers of birds, receive their growth and nutriment from the internal circulation of a juice through the vessels of the individual they cover. We conclude from analogy, then, that the shells of the testaceous tribe, receive also their growth from a like internal circulation. If it be urged, that this does not exclude the possibility of a like shell being produced by the passage of a fluid through the pores of the circumjacent body, whether of earth, stone, or water; I answer, that it is not within the usual economy of nature, to use two processes for one species of production. While I withhold my assent, however, from this hypothesis, I must deny it to every other I have ever seen, by which their authors pretend to account for the origin of shells in high places. Some of these are against the laws of nature, and therefore impossible; and others are built on positions more difficult to assent to, than that of de la Sauvagiere. They all suppose the shells to have covered submarine animals, and have then to answer the question, How came they fifteen thousand feet above the level of the sea? And they answer it, by demanding what cannot be conceded. One, therefore, who had rather have no opinion than a false one, will suppose this question one of those beyond the investigation of human sagacity; or wait till further and fuller observations enable him to decide it.

Chanteloup. I heard a nightingale to-day at Chanteloup. The gardener says, it is the male who alone sings, while the female sits; and that when the young are hatched, he also ceases. In the border at Chanteloup, is an ingenious contrivance to hide the projecting steps of a stair-case. Three steps were of necessity to project into the boudoir: they are therefore made triangular steps; and instead of being rested on the floor, as usual, they are made fast at their broad end to the stair door, swinging out and in, with that. When it shuts, it runs them under the other steps; when open, it brings them out to their proper place.

TRAVELLING NOTES FOR MR. RUTLEDGE AND MR. SHIPPEN, JUNE 3, 1788

General Observations.—On arriving at a town, the first thing is to buy the plan of the town, and the book noting its curiosities. Walk round the ramparts when there are any, go to the top of a steeple to have a view of the town and its environs.

When you are doubting whether a thing is worth the trouble of going to see, recollect that you will never again be so near it, that you may repent the not having seen it, but can never repent having seen it. But there is an opposite extreme too, that is, the seeing too much. A judicious selection is to be aimed at, taking care that the indolence of the moment have no influence in the decision. Take care particularly not to let the porters of churches, cabinets, etc., lead you through all the little details of their profession, which will load the memory with trifles, fatigue the attention, and waste that and your time. It is difficult to confine these people to the few objects worth seeing and remembering. They wish for your money, and suppose you give it the more willingly the more they detail to you.

When one calls in the taverns for the *vin du pays,* they give what is natural and unadulterated and cheap: when *vin etrangere* is called for, it only gives a pretext for charging an extravagant price for an unwholesome stuff, very often of their own brewery. The people you will naturally see the most of will be tavern keepers, *valets de place,* and postilions. These are the hackneyed rascals of every country. Of course they must never be considered when we calculate the national character.

Objects of attention for an American.—1. Agriculture. Everything belonging to this art, and whatever has a near relation to it. Useful or agreeable animals which might be transported to America. Species of plants for the farmer's garden, according to the climate of the different States.

2. Mechanical arts, so far as they respect things necessary in America, and inconvenient to be transported thither ready-made, such as forges, stone quarries, boats, bridges, (very especially,) etc., etc.

3. Lighter mechanical arts, and manufactures. Some of these will be worth a superficial view; but circumstances rendering it impossible that America should become a manufacturing country during the time of any man now living, it would be a waste of attention to examine these minutely.

4. Gardens peculiarly worth the attention of an American, because it is the country of all others where the noblest gardens may be made without expense. We have only to cut out the superabundant plants.

5. Architecture worth great attention. As we double our numbers every twenty years, we must double our houses. Besides, we build of such perishable materials, that one half of our houses must be rebuilt in every space of twenty years, so that in that time, houses are to be built for three-fourths of our inhabitants. It is, then, among the most important arts; and it is desirable to introduce taste into an art which shows so much.

6. Painting. Statuary. Too expensive for the state of wealth among us. It would be useless, therefore, and preposterous, for us to make

ourselves connoisseurs in those arts. They are worth seeing, but not studying.

7. Politics of each country, well worth studying so far as respects internal affairs. Examine their influence on the happiness of the people. Take every possible occasion for entering into the houses of the laborers, and especially at the moments of their repast; see what they eat, how they are clothed, whether they are obliged to work too hard; whether the government or their landlord takes from them an unjust proportion of their labor; on what footing stands the property they call their own, their personal liberty, etc., etc.

8. Courts. To be seen as you would see the tower of London or menagerie of Versailles with their lions, tigers, hyenas, and other beasts of prey, standing in the same relation to their fellows. A slight acquaintance with them will suffice to show you that, under the most imposing exterior, they are the weakest and worst part of mankind. Their manners, could you ape them, would not make you beloved in your own country, nor would they improve it could you introduce them there to the exclusion of that honest simplicity now prevailing in America, and worthy of being cherished.

Essay on Anglo-Saxon

Introduction

In his interest in the Anglo-Saxon language Thomas Jefferson was a pioneer and trail blazer. In an age in which Anglo-Saxon was generally neglected, he advocated its study in American colleges and universities, made provisions for teaching it in his own University of Virginia, and wrote a book on the subject. Portions from this book, the *Essay on Anglo-Saxon*, appear on the following pages. Jefferson first became interested in Anglo-Saxon while he was reading law in Williamsburg, Virginia, at which time he "devoted some time to its study," attempting to simplify the grammar, modernize the spelling, and the like. Later, in 1798, he sent the results of his labors to the English philologist, Herbert Crofts. This section was revised and rewritten, in 1818, for the proposed University of Virginia. Still later, less than a year before his death, Jefferson added a prolonged P. S., making use of recent British research in the field of Anglo-Saxon. These two sections comprise Jefferson's *Essay on Anglo-Saxon* in its final form, and were first printed twenty-five years after his death, in 1851.

To Herbert Croft, Esq., LL.B., London
Monticello, October 30th, 1798

Sir,—The copy of your printed letter on the English and German languages, which you have been so kind as to send me, has come to hand; and I pray you to accept my thanks for this mark of your attention. I have perused it with singular pleasure, and, having long been sensible of the importance of a knowledge of the Northern languages to the understanding of English, I see it, in this letter, proved and specifically exemplified by your collations of the English and German. I shall look with impatience for the publication of your "English and German Dictionary." Johnson, besides the want of precision in his definitions, and of accurate distinction in passing from one shade of meaning to another of the same word, is most objectionable in his derivations. From a want probably of intimacy with our own language while in the Anglo-Saxon form and type, and of its kindred languages of the North, he has a constant leaning towards Greek and Latin for English etymon. Even Skinner has a little of this, who, when he has given the true Northern parentage of a word, often tells you from what Greek and Latin source it might be derived by those who have that kind of partiality. He is, however, on the whole, our best etymologist, unless we ascend a step higher to the Anglo-Saxon vocabulary; and he has set the good example of collating the English word with its kindred word in the several Northern dialects, which often assist in ascertaining its true meaning.

Your idea is an excellent one, in producing authorities for the meaning of words, "to select the prominent passages in our best writers, to make your dictionary a general index to English literature, and thus intersperse with verdure and flowers the barren deserts of Philology." And I believe with you that "wisdom, morality, religion, thus thrown down, as if without intention, before the reader, in quotations, may

often produce more effect than the very passages in the books themselves."—"that the cowardly suicide, in search of a strong word for
his dying letter, might light on a passage which would excite him to
blush at his want of fortitude, and to forego his purpose;"—"and that
a dictionary with examples at the words may, in regard to every branch
of knowledge, produce more real effect than the whole collection of
books which it quotes." I have sometimes myself used Johnson as a
Repertory, to find favorite passages which I wished to recollect, but too
rarely with success.

I was led to set a due value on the study of the Northern languages,
and especially of our Anglo-Saxon, while I was a student of the law,
by being obliged to recur to that source for explanation of a multitude
of law-terms. A preface to Fortescue on Monarchies, written by Fortescue Aland, and afterwards premised to his volume of Reports, devel-
ops the advantages to be derived to the English student generally, and
particularly the student of law, from an acquaintance with the Anglo-
Saxon; and mentions the books to which the learner may have recourse
for acquiring the language. I accordingly devoted some time to its
study, but my busy life has not permitted me to indulge in a pursuit
to which I felt great attraction. While engaged in it, however, some
ideas occurred for facilitating the study by simplifying its grammar, by
reducing the infinite diversities of its unfixed orthography to single and
settled forms, indicating at the same time the pronunciation of the word
by its correspondence with the characters and powers of the English
alphabet. Some of these ideas I noted at the time on the blank leaves
of my Elstob's Anglo-Saxon Grammar: but there I have left them, and
must leave them, unpursued, although I still think them sound and useful. Among the works which I proposed for the Anglo-Saxon student,
you will find such literal and verbal translations of the Anglo-Saxon
writers recommended, as you have given us of the German in your
printed letter. Thinking that I cannot submit those ideas to a better
judge than yourself, and that if you find them of any value you may put
them to some use, either as hints in your dictionary, or in some other
way, I will copy them as a sequel to this letter, and commit them without reserve to your better knowledge of the subject. Adding my sincere wishes for the speedy publication of your valuable dictionary, I
tender you the assurance of my high respect and consideration.

An Essay on the Anglo-Saxon Language

The importance of the Anglo-Saxon dialect toward a perfect under-standing of the English language seems not to have been duly esti-mated by those charged with the education of youth; and yet it is unquestionably the basis of our present tongue. It was a full-formed language; its frame and construction, its declension of nouns and verbs, and its syntax were peculiar to the Northern languages, and funda-mentally different from those of the South. It was the language of all England, properly so called, from the Saxon possession of that coun-try in the sixth century to the time of Henry III in the thirteenth, and was spoken pure and unmixed with any other. Although the Romans had been in possession of that country for nearly five centuries from the time of Julius Caesar, yet it was a military possession chiefly, by their soldiery alone, and with dispositions intermutually jealous and unamicable. They seemed to have aimed at no lasting settlements there, and to have had little familiar mixture with the native Britons. In this state of connection there would probably be little incorpora-tion of the Roman into the native language, and on their subsequent evacuation of the island its traces would soon be lost altogether. And had it been otherwise, these innovations would have been carried with the natives themselves when driven into Wales by the invasion and entire occupation of the rest of the Southern portion of the island by the Anglo-Saxons.

The language of these last became that of the country from that time forth, for nearly seven centuries; and so little attention was paid among them to the Latin, that it was known to a few individuals only as a matter of science, and without any chance of transfusion into the vulgar language. We may safely repeat the affirmation, therefore, that the pure Anglo-Saxon constitutes at this day the basis of our language.

That it was sufficiently copious for the purposes of society in the existing condition of arts and manners, reason alone would satisfy us from
the necessity of the case. Its copiousness, too, was much favored by the
latitude it allowed of combining primitive words so as to produce any
modification of idea desired. In this characteristic it was equal to the
Greek, but it is more especially proved by the actual fact of the books
they have left us in the various branches of history, geography, religion, law, and poetry. And although since the Norman conquest it has
received vast additions and embellishments from the Latin, Greek,
French, and Italian languages, yet these are but engraftments on its
idiomatic stem; its original structure and syntax remain the same, and
can be but imperfectly understood by the mere Latin scholar. Hence
the necessity of making the Anglo-Saxon a regular branch of acade-
mic education. In the sixteenth and seventeenth centuries it was assiduously cultivated by a host of learned men. The names of Lambard,
Parker, Spelman, Wheeloc, Wilkins, Gibson, Hickes, Thwaites, Som-
ner, Benson, Mareschal, Elstob, deserve to be ever remembered with
gratitude for the Anglo-Saxon works which they have given us through
the press, the only certain means of preserving and promulgating them.
For a century past this study has been too much neglected. The reason of this neglect, and its remedy, shall be the subject of some
explanatory observations. These will respect—I. The Alphabet. II.
Orthography. III. Pronunciation. IV. Grammar.

I. THE ALPHABET

The Anglo-Saxon alphabet, as known to us in its printed forms, consists of twenty-six characters, about the half of which are Roman, the
others of forms peculiarly Saxon. These, mixed with the others, give an
aspect to the whole rugged, uncouth, and appalling to an eye accustomed to the roundness and symmetry of the Roman character. This is
a first discouragement to the English student. Next, the task of learning new alphabet, and the time and application necessary to render it
easy and familiar to the reader, often decides the doubting learner
against an enterprise so apparently irksome.

The earliest remains extant of Saxon writing are said to be of the
seventh century; and the latest of the thirteenth. The black letter seems

to have been introduced by William the Conqueror, whose laws are written in Norman French, and in that letter. The full alphabet of Roman characters was first used about the beginning of the sixteenth century. But the expression of the same sounds, by a different character did not change these sounds, nor the language which they constituted; did not make the language of Alfred a different one from that of Piers Ploughman, of Chaucer, Douglas, Spenser, and Shakespeare, any more than the second revolution, which substituted the Roman for the English black letter, made theirs a different language from that of Pope and Bolingbroke; or the writings of Shakespeare, printed in black letter, different from the same as now done in Roman type. The life of Alfred, written in Latin and in Roman character by Asser, was reprinted by Archbishop Parker in Anglo-Saxon letters. But it is Latin still, although the words are represented by characters different from those of Asser's original. And the extracts given us by Dr. Hickes from the Greek Septuagint, in Anglo-Saxon characters, are Greek still, although the Greek sounds are represented by other types. Here then I ask, why should not this Roman character, with which we are all familiar, be substituted now for the Anglo-Saxon, by printing in the former the works already edited in the latter type? and also the manuscripts still inedited? This may be done letter for letter, and would remove entirely the first discouraging obstacle to the general study of the Anglo-Saxon.

II. ORTHOGRAPHY

In the period during which the Anglo-Saxon alphabet was in use, reading and writing were rare arts. The highest dignitaries of the church subscribed their marks, not knowing how to write their names. Alfred himself was taught to read in his thirty-sixth year only, or, as some editions of Asser say, in his thirty-ninth. Speaking of learning in his Preface to the Pastoral of Gregory, Alfred says, "Swa clean hi was othfallen on Angelkin that swithe few were on behinan Humber the hior thenung cuthon understandan on Englisc, oth furthon an errand y-write of Latin on Englisc areckon. And I ween that not many beyondan Humber nay aren; swa few hior weron that I furthon ane on lepne nay may y-thinkan be-Suthan Thames tha tha I to ric fang." Or, as literally translated into later English by Archbishop Parker, "So clean was it fallen amongst the English nation, that very few were on this side Humber which their service could understand in English, or else furthermore an epistle from Latin into English to declare. And I ween that not many beyond Humber were not. So few of them were that I also one only may not remember by South Tamise when as I to reign undertook." In this benighted state, so profoundly illiterate, few read at all, and fewer wrote: and the writer having no examples of orthography to recur to, thinking them indeed not important, had for his guide his own ideas only of the power of the letters, unpractised and indistinct as they might be. He brought together, therefore, those letters which he supposed must enter into the composition of the sound he meant to express, and was not even particular in arranging them in the order in which the sounds composing the word followed each other. Thus, *birds* was spelt brides; *grass*, gaers; *run*, yrnan, *cart*, craett; *fresh*, fersh. They seemed to suppose, too, that a final vowel was necessary to give sound to the consonant preceding it, and they used for that purpose any vowel indifferently. A *son* was suna, sune, sunu; *maera*, maere, maero, maeru; *fines*, limites; ge, ye, y, i, are various spellings of the same prefix. The final *e* mute in English is a remain of this, as in *give*, *love*, *curse*.

The vowels were used indiscriminately also for every vowel sound. Thus,

The comparative ended in *ar*, *er*, *ir*, *or*, *ur*, *yr*.
The superlative ended in *ast*, *est*, *ist*, *ost*, *ust*, *yst*.
The participle present ended in *and*, *end*, *ind*, *ond*, *und*, *ynd*.
The participle past ended in *ad*, *ed*, *id*, *od*, *ud*, *yd*.
Other examples are, betweox, betwix, betwox, betwux, betwyx, for
    betwixt; egland, igland, ygland, for *island*.

Of this promiscuous use of the vowels we have also abundant remains still in English. For according to the powers given to our letters we often use them indifferently for the same sound, as in *bulwark*, *assert*, *stir*, *work*, *lurk*, *myrtle*. The single word *many*, in Anglo-Saxon, was spelt, as Dr. Hickes has observed, in twenty different ways; to wit, maenigeo, maenio, maeniu, menio, meniu, maenigo, maenego, manige, menigo, manegeo, maenegeo, menegeo, maenygeo, menigeo, manegu, maenigu, menegu, menego, menigu manigo. To prove, indeed, that every one spelt according to his own notions, without regard to any standard, we have only to compare different editions of the same composition. . . .[1]

This unsettled orthography renders it necessary to swell the volume of the dictionaries, by giving to each word as many places in order of the alphabet as there are different modes of spelling it; and in proportion as this is omitted, the difficulty of finding the words increases on the student.

Since, then, it is apparent that the Anglo-Saxon writers had established no particular standard of orthography, but each followed arbitrarily his own mode of combining the letters, we are surely at liberty equally to adopt any mode which, establishing uniformity, may be more consonant with the power of the letters, and with the orthography of the present dialect, as established by usage. The latter attention has the advantage of exhibiting more evidently the legitimate parentage of the two dialects.

III. PRONUNCIATION

To determine what that was among the Anglo-Saxons, our means are as defective as to determine the long-agitated question what was the original pronunciation of the Greek and Latin languages. The presumption is certainly strong that in Greece and Italy, the countries occupied by those languages, their pronunciation has been handed down, by tradition, more nearly than it can be known to other countries: and the rather, as there has been no particular point of time at which those ancient languages were changed into the modern ones occupying the same grounds. They have been gradually worn down to their present forms by time, and changes of modes and circumstances. In like manner there has been no particular point of time at which the Anglo-Saxon has been changed into its present English form. The languages of Europe have generally, in like manner, under-

[1]Here Jefferson cites various printed versions of Alfred's Preface to Pope Gregory's Pastoral Care.

gone a gradual metamorphosis, some of them in name as well as in form. We should presume, therefore, that in those countries of Great Britain which were occupied earliest, longest, and latest by the Saxon immigrants, the pronunciation of their language has been handed down more nearly than elsewhere; and should be searched for in the provincial dialects of those countries. But the fact is, that these countries have divaricated in their dialects, so that it would be difficult to decide among them which is the most genuine. Under these doubts, therefore, we may as well take the pronunciation now in general use as the legitimate standard, and that form which it is most promotive of our object to infer the Anglo-Saxon pronunciation. It is, indeed, the forlorn hope of all aim at their probably pronunciation; for were we to regard the powers of the letters only, no human organ could articulate their uncouth jumble. We will suppose, therefore, the power of the letters to have been generally the same in Anglo-Saxon as now in English; and to produce the same sounds we will combine them, as nearly as may be, conformably with the present English orthography. This is, indeed, a most irregular and equivocal standard; but a conformity with it will bring the two dialects nearer together in sound and semblance, and facilitate the transition from the one to the other more auspiciously than a rigorous adherence to any uniform system of orthography which speculation might suggest.

IV. GRAMMAR

Some observations on Anglo-Saxon grammar may show how much easier that also may be rendered to the English student. Dr. Hickes may certainly be considered as the father of this branch of modern learning. He has been the great restorer of the Anglo-Saxon dialect from the oblivion into which it was fast falling. His labors in it were great, and his learning not less than his labors. His grammar may be said to be the only one we yet possess: for that edited at Oxford in 1711 is but an extract from Hickes, and the principal merit of Mrs. Elstob's is, that it is written in English, without anything original in it. Some others have been written, taken also, and almost entirely from Hickes. In his time there was too exclusive a prejudice in favor of the Greek and Latin languages. They were considered as the standards of perfection, and the endeavor generally was to force other languages to a conformity with these models. But nothing can be more radically unlike than the frames of the ancient languages, Southern and Northern, of the Greek and Latin languages, from those of the Gothic family. Of this last are the Anglo-Saxon and English; and had Dr. Hickes, instead of keeping his eye fixed on the Greek and Latin languages, as his standard, viewed the Anglo-Saxon in its conformity with the English only, he would greatly have enlarged the advantages for which we are already so much indebted to him. His labors, however, have advanced us so far on the right road, and a correct pursuit of it will be a just homage to him.

A noun is to be considered under its accidents of genders, cases, and numbers. The word gender is, in nature, synonymous with sex. To all the subjects of the animal kingdom nature has given sex, and that is twofold only, male or female, masculine or feminine. Vegetable and mineral subjects have no distinction of sex, consequently are of no gender. Words, like other inanimate things, have no sex, are of no gender. Yet in the construction of the Greek and Latin languages, and of the modern ones of the same family, their adjectives being varied in termination, and made distinctive of animal sex, in conformity with the nouns or names of animal subject, the two real genders, which nature has established, are distinguished in these languages. But, not stopping here, they have by usage, thrown a number of unsexual subjects into the sexual classes, leaving the residuary mass to a third class, which grammarians call neutral—that is to say, of no gender or sex: and some Latin grammarians have so far lost sight of the real and natural genders as to ascribe to that language seven genders, the masculine, feminine, neuter, gender common to two, common to three, the doubtful, and the epicene; than which nothing can be more arbitrary, and nothing more useless. But the language of the Anglo-Saxons and English is based on principles totally different from those of the Greek and Latin, and is constructed on laws peculiar and idiomatic to itself. Its adjectives have no changes of termination on account of gender, number or case. Each has a single one applicable to every noun, whether it be the name of a thing having sex, or not. To ascribe gender to nouns in such a case would be to embarrass the learner with unmeaning and useless distinctions.

It will be said, e.g., that a priest is of one gender, and a priestess of another; a poet of one, a poetess of another, etc.; and that therefore the words designating them must be of different genders. I say, not at all; because although the thing designated may have sex, the word designating it, like other inanimate things, has no sex, no gender. In Latin, we well know that the thing may be of one gender and the word designating it of another. See Martial vii., Epig. 17. The ascription of gender to it is artificial and arbitrary, and, in English and Anglo-Saxon, absolutely useless. Lowthe, therefore, among the most correct of our English grammarians, has justly said that in the nouns of the English language there is no other distinction of gender but that of nature, its adjectives admitting no change but of the degrees of comparison. We must guard against the conclusion of Dr. Hickes that the change of termination in the Anglo-Saxon adjectives, as god, gode, for example, is an indication of gender; this, like others of his examples of inflection, is only an instance of unsettled orthography. In the languages acknowledged to ascribe genders to their words, as Greek, Latin, Italian, Spanish, French, their dictionaries indicate the gender of every noun; but the Anglo-Saxon and English dictionaries give no such indication; a proof of the general sense that gender makes no part of the character of the noun. We may safely therefore dismiss the learning of genders from our language, whether in its ancient or modern form.

2. Our law of Cases is different. They exist in nature, according to the difference of accident they announce. No language can be without them, and it is an error to say that the Greek is without an ablative. Its ablative indeed is always like its dative; but were that sufficient to deny its existence, we might equally say that the Latins had no ablative plural, because in all nouns of every declension, their ablative plural is the same with the dative. It would be to say that to go *to* a place, or *from* a place, means the same thing. The grammarians of Port-Royal, therefore, have justly restored the ablative to Greek nouns. Our cases are generally distinguished by the aid of the prepositions *of, to, by, from,* or *with,* but sometimes also by change of termination. But these changes are not so general or difficult as to require, or to be capable of a distribution into declensions. Yet Dr. Hickes, having in view the Saxon declensions of the Latin, and ten of the Greek lan-

guage, has given six, and Thwaytes seven to the Anglo-Saxon. The whole of them, however, are comprehended under the three simple canons following:

(1.) The datives and ablatives plural of all nouns end in *um*.

(2.) Of the other cases, some nouns inflect their genitive singular only, and some their nominative, accusative and vocative plural also in *s*, as in English.

(3.) Others, preserving the primitive form in their nominative and vocative singular, inflect all the other cases and numbers in *en*.

3. Numbers. Every language, as I presume, has so formed its nouns and verbs as to distinguish a single and a plurality of subjects, and all, as far as I know, have been contented with the simple distinction of singular and plural, except the Greeks, who have interposed between them a dual number, so distinctly formed by actual changes of termination and inflection, as to leave no doubt of its real distinction from the other numbers. But they do not uniformly use their dual for its appropriate purpose. The number two is often expressed plurally, and sometimes by a dual noun and plural verb. Dr. Hickes supposes the Anglo-Saxon to have a dual number also, not going through the whole vocabulary of nouns and verbs, as in Greek, but confined to two particular pronouns, *i.e., wit* and *yit,* which he translates we two, and ye two. But Benson renders *wit* by *nos,* and does not give *yit* at all. And is it worth while to embarrass grammar with an extra distinction for two or three, or half a dozen words? And why may not *wit,* we two, and *yit,* ye two, be considered plural, as well as we three, or we four? as duo, ambo, with the Latins? We may surely say then that neither the Anglo-Saxon nor English have a dual number.

4. Verbs, moods. To the verbs in Anglo-Saxon Dr. Hickes gives six moods. The Greeks, besides the four general moods, Indicative, Subjunctive, Imperative, and Infinitive, have really an Optative mood, distinguished from the others by actual differences of termination. And some Latin grammarians, besides the Optative, have added, in that language, a Potential mood; neither of them distinguished by differences of termination or inflection. They have therefore been disallowed by later and sounder grammarians; and we may, in like manner, disembarrass our Anglo-Saxon and English from the Optatives and Potentials of Dr. Hickes.

Supines and Gerunds

He thinks, too, that the Anglo-Saxon has supines and gerunds among its variations; accidents certainly peculiar to Latin verbs only. He considers *lufian,* to love, as the infinitive, and *to lufian,* a supine. The exclusion, therefore, of the preposition *to,* makes with him the infinitive, while we have ever considered it as the essential sign of that mood. And what all grammarians have hitherto called the infinitive, he considers as a supine or gerund. . . .

From these aberrations, into which our great Anglo-Saxon leader, Dr. Hickes, has been seduced by too much regard to the structure of the Greek and Latin languages and too little to their radical difference from that of the Gothic family, we have to recall our footsteps into the right way, and we shall find our path rendered smoother, plainer, and more direct to the object of profiting of the light which each dialect throws on the other. . . .

As we are possessed in America of the printed editions of the Anglo-Saxon writings, they furnish a fit occasion for this country to make some return to the older nations for the science for which we are indebted to them; and in this task I hope an honorable part will in time be borne by our University for which, at an hour of life too late for anything elaborate, I hazard these imperfect hints, for consideration chiefly on a subject on which I pretend not to be profound. The publication of the inedited manuscripts which exist in the libraries of Great Britain only, must depend on the learned of that nation. Their means of science are great. They have done much, and much is yet expected from them. Nor will they disappoint us. Our means are as yet small; but the widow's mite was piously given and kindly accepted. How much would contribute to the happiness of these two nations a brotherly emulation in doing good to each other, rather than the mutual vituperations so unwisely and unjustifiably sometimes indulged in by both. And this too by men on both sides of the water, who think themselves of a superior order of understanding, and some of whom are truly of an elevation far above the ordinary stature of the human mind. No two people on earth can so much help or hurt each other. Let us then yoke ourselves jointly to the same car of mutual happiness, and vie in common efforts to do each other all the good we can—to reflect on each other the lights of mutual science particularly, and the kind affections of kindred blood. Be it our task, in the case under consideration, to reform and republish, in forms more advantageous, what we already possess, and theirs to add to the common stock the inedited treasures which have been too long buried in their depositories.

P. S. January, 1825. In the year 1818, by authority of the legislature of Virginia, a plan for the establishment of an University was prepared and proposed by them. In that plan the Anglo-Saxon language was comprehended as a part of the circle of instruction to be given to the students; and the preceding pages were then committed to writing for the use of the University. I pretend not to be an Anglo-Saxon scholar. From an early period of my studies, indeed, I have been sensible of the importance of making it a part of the regular education of our youth; and at different times, as leisure permitted, I applied myself to the study of it, with some degree of attention. But my life has been too busy in pursuits of another character to have made much proficiency in this. The leading idea which very soon impressed itself on my mind, and which has continued to prevail through the whole of my observations on the language, was, that it was nothing more than the Old English of a period of some ages earlier than that of Piers Ploughman; and under this view my cultivation of it has been continued. It was apparent to me that the labors of Dr. Hickes, and other very learned men, have been employed in a very unfortunate direction, in endeavors to give it the complicated structure of the Greek and Latin languages. I have just now received a copy of a new work, by Mr. Bosworth, on the elements of Anglo-Saxon grammar, and it quotes two other works, by Turner and Jamieson, both of great erudition, but not yet known here.

Mr. Bosworth's is, indeed, a treasure of that venerable learning. It proved the assiduity with which he has cultivated it, the profound knowledge in it which he has attained, and that he has advanced far beyond all former grammarians in the science of its structure. Yet, I own, I was disappointed on finding that in proportion as he has advanced on and beyond the footsteps of his predecessors, he has the more embarrassed the language with rules and distinctions, in imitation of the grammars of Greek and Latin; has led it still further from its genuine type of old English, and increased its difficulties by the multitude and variety of new and minute rules with which he has charged

it. . . . And this leads to such an infinitude of minute rules and obser-
vances, as are beyond the power of any human memory to retain. If,
indeed, this be the true genius of the Anglo-Saxon language, then its
difficulties go beyond its worth, and render a knowledge of it no longer
a compensation for the time and labor its acquisition will require; and,
in that case, I would recommend its abandonment in our University, as
an unattainable and unprofitable pursuit.

But if, as I believe, we may consider it as merely an antiquated form
of our present language, if we may throw aside the learned difficulties
which mask its real character, liberate it from these foreign shackles,
and proceed to apply ourselves to it with little more preparation than
to Piers Ploughman, Douglas, or Chaucer, then I am persuaded its
acquisition will require little time or labor, and will richly repay us by
the intimate insight it will give us into the genuine structure, powers,
and meanings of the language we now read and speak. We shall then
read Shakespeare and Milton with a superior degree of intelligence and
delight, heightened by the new and delicate shades of meaning developed to us by a knowledge of the original sense of the same words.

This rejection of the learned labors of our Anglo-Saxon doctors,
may be considered, perhaps, as a rebellion against science. My hope,
however, is, that it may prove a revolution. Two great works, indeed,
will be wanting to effect all its advantages. 1. A grammar on the simple principles of the English grammar, analogizing the idiom, the rules
and principles of the one and the other, eliciting their common origin,
the identity of their structure, laws, and composition, and their total
unlikeness to the genius of the Greek and Latin. 2. A dictionary, on
the plan of Stephens or Scapula, in which the Anglo-Saxon roots
should be arranged alphabetically, and the derivatives from each root,
Saxon and English, entered under it in their proper order and connection. Such works as these, with new editions of the Saxon writings, on
the plan I venture to propose, would show that the Anglo-Saxon is
really old English, little more difficult to understand than works we
possess, and read, and still call English. They would recruit and reno-
vate the vigor of the English language, too much impaired by the
neglect of its ancient constitution and dialects, and would remove, for
the student, the principal difficulties of ascending to the source of the
English language, the main object of what has been here proposed.

Biographical Sketches

Introduction

As one of the founding fathers of the Republic and as a man who knew intimately most of the outstanding men connected with the early history of the United States, Thomas Jefferson, in his later years particularly, was frequently asked to furnish material to historians and biographers. The following biographical sketches were all written in compliance with such requests and are reprinted in their entirety.

Biographical Sketches

—

The Character of George Washington[1]

. . . . I think I knew General Washington intimately and thoroughly; and were I called on to delineate his character, it should be in terms like these.

His mind was great and powerful, without being of the very first order; his penetration strong, though not so acute as that of a Newton, Bacon, or Locke; and as far as he saw, no judgment was ever sounder. It was slow in operation, being little aided by invention or imagination, but sure in conclusion. Hence the common remark of his officers, of the advantage he derived from councils of war, where hearing all suggestions, he selected whatever was best; and certainly no general ever planned his battles more judiciously. But if deranged during the course of the action, if any member of his plan was dislocated by sudden circumstances, he was slow in re-adjustment. The consequence was, that he often failed in the field, and rarely against an enemy in station, as at Boston and York He was incapable of fear, meeting personal dangers with the calmest unconcern. Perhaps the strongest feature in his character was prudence, never acting until every circumstance, every consideration, was maturely weighed; refraining if he saw a doubt, but, when once decided, going through with his purpose, whatever obstacles opposed. His integrity was most pure, his justice the most inflexible I have ever known, no motives of interest or consanguinity, of friendship or hatred, being able to bias his decision.

[1]From Jefferson's letter to Dr. Walter Jones, January 2, 1814. Dr. Jones had written Jefferson saying he was having trouble, with a historical work under preparation, in depicting Washington's role during the Federalist-Republican struggle.

He was, indeed, in every sense of the words, a wise, a good, and a great man. His temper was naturally irritable and high toned; but reflection and resolution had obtained a firm and habitual ascendency over it. If ever, however, it broke its bonds, he was most tremendous in his wrath. In his expenses he was honorable, but exact; liberal in contributions to whatever promised utility; but frowning and unyielding on all visionary projects, and all unworthy calls on his charity. His heart was not warm in its affections; but he exactly calculated every man's value, and gave him a solid esteem proportioned to it. His person, you know, was fine, his stature exactly what one would wish, his deportment easy, erect and noble; the best horseman of his age, and the most graceful figure that could be seen on horseback. Although in the circle of his friends, where he might be unreserved with safety, he took a free share in conversation, his colloquial talents were not above mediocrity, possessing neither copiousness of ideas, nor fluency of words. In public, when called on for a sudden opinion, he was unready, short and embarrassed. Yet he wrote readily, rather diffusely, in an easy and correct style. This he had acquired by conversation with the world, for his education was merely reading, writing and common arithmetic, to which he added surveying at a later day. His time was employed in action chiefly, reading little, and that only in agriculture and English history. His correspondence became necessarily extensive, and, with journalizing his agricultural proceedings, occupied most of his leisure hours within doors. On the whole, his character was, in its mass, perfect, in nothing bad, in few points indifferent; and it may truly be said, that never did nature and fortune combine more perfectly to make a man great, and to place him in the same constellation with whatever worthies have merited from man an everlasting remembrance. For his was the singular destiny and merit, of leading the armies of his country successfully through an arduous war, for the establishment of its independence; of conducting its councils through the birth of a government, new in its forms and principles, until it had settled down into a quiet and orderly train; and of scrupulously obeying the laws through the whole of his career, civil and military, of which the history of the world furnishes no other example.

. . . . I am satisfied the great body of republicans think of him as I do. We were, indeed, dissatisfied with him on his ratification of the

British treaty. But this was short lived. We knew his honesty, the wiles with which he was encompassed, and that age had already begun to relax the firmness of his purposes; and I am convinced he is more deeply seated in the love and gratitude of the republicans, than in the Pharisaical homage of the federal monarchists. For he was no monarchist from preference of his judgment. The soundness of that gave him correct views of the rights of man, and his severe justice devoted him to them. He has often declared to me that he considered our new Constitution as an experiment on the practicability of republican government, and with what dose of liberty man could be trusted for his own good; that he was determined the experiment should have a fair trial, and would lose the last drop of his blood in support of it. And these declarations he repeated to me the oftener and more pointedly, because he knew my suspicions of Colonel Hamilton's views, and probably had heard from him the same declarations which I had, to wit, "that the British constitution, with its unequal representation, corruption and other existing abuses, was the most perfect government which had ever been established on earth, and that a reformation of those abuses would make it an impracticable government." I do believe that General Washington had not a firm confidence in the durability of our government. He was naturally distrustful of men, and inclined to gloomy apprehensions; and I was ever persuaded that a belief that we must at length end in something like a British constitution, had some weight in his adoption of the ceremonies of levees, birthdays, pompous meetings with Congress, and other forms of the same character, calculated to prepare us gradually for a change which he believed possible, and to let it come on with as little shock as might be to the public mind.

These are my opinions of General Washington, which I would vouch at the judgment seat of God, having been formed on an acquaintance of thirty years. I served with him in the Virginia legislature from 1769 to the Revolutionary war, and again, a short time in Congress, until he left us to take command of the army. During the war and after it we corresponded occasionally, and in the four years of my continuance in the office of Secretary of State, our intercourse was daily, confidential and cordial. After I retired from that office, great and malignant pains were taken by our federal monarchists, and not entirely without effect, to make him view me as a theorist, holding French principles of government, which would lead infallibly to licentiousness and anarchy. And to this he listened the more easily, from my known dis-approbation of the British treaty. I never saw him afterwards, or these malignant insinuations should have been dissipated before his just judgment, as mists before the sun. I felt on his death, with my countrymen, that "verily a great man hath fallen this day in Israel."

Anecdotes of Benjamin Franklin[1]

Our revolutionary process, as is well known, commenced by petitions, memorials, remonstrances, etc., from the old Congress. These were followed by a non-importation agreement, as a pacific instrument of coercion. While that was before us, and sundry exceptions, as of arms, ammunition, etc., were moved from different quarters of the house, I was sitting by Dr. Franklin and observed to him that I thought we should except books; that we ought not to exclude science, even coming from an enemy. He thought so too, and I proposed the exception, which was agreed to. Soon after it occurred that medicine should be excepted, and I suggested that also to the Doctor. "As to that," said he, "I will tell you a story. When I was in London, in such a year, there was a weekly club of physicians, of which Sir John Pringle was president, and I was invited by my friend Dr. Fothergill to attend when convenient. Their rule was to propose a thesis one week and discuss it the next. I happened there when the question to be considered was whether physicians had, on the whole, done most good or harm? The young members, particularly, having discussed it very learnedly and eloquently till the subject was exhausted, one of them observed to Sir John Pringle, that although it was not usual for the President to take part in a debate, yet they were desirous to know his opinion on the question. He said they must first tell him whether, under the appellation of physicians, they meant to include *old women*, if they did he thought they had done more good than harm, otherwise more harm than good."

The confederation of the States, while on the carpet before the old Congress, was strenuously opposed by the smaller States, under appre-

[1]These anecdotes were written by Jefferson at the request of Robert Walsh, journalist and publisher, and were inclosed to him with a letter of December 4, 1818.

hensions that they would be swallowed up by the larger ones. We were long engaged in the discussion; it produced great heats, much ill humor, and intemperate declarations from some members. Dr. Franklin at length brought the debate to a close with one of his little apologues. He observed that "at the time of the union of England and Scotland, the Duke of Argyle was most violently opposed to that measure, and among other things predicted that, as the whale had swallowed Jonah, so Scotland would be swallowed by England. However," said the Doctor, "when Lord Bute came into the government, he soon brought into its administration so many of his countrymen, that it was found in event that Jonah swallowed the whale." This little story produced a *general* laugh, and restored good humor, and the article of difficulty was passed.

When Dr. Franklin went to France, on his revolutionary mission, his eminence as a philosopher, his venerable appearance, and the cause on which he was sent, rendered him extremely popular. For all ranks and conditions of men there, entered warmly into the American interest. He was, therefore, feasted and invited into all the court parties. At these he sometimes met the old Duchess of Bourbon, who, being a chess player of about his force, they very generally played together. Happening once to put her king into prize, the Doctor took it. "Ah," said she, "we do not take kings so." "We do in America," said the Doctor.

At one of these parties the Emperor Joseph III, then at Paris, incog., under the title of Count Falkenstein, was overlooking the game in silence, while the company was engaged in animated conversations on the American question. "How happens it M. le Comte," said the Duchess, "that while we all feel so much interest in the cause of the Americans, you say nothing for them?" "I am a king by trade," said he.

When the Declaration of Independence was under the consideration of Congress, there were two or three unlucky expressions in it which gave offence to some members. The words "Scotch and other foreign auxiliaries" excited the ire of a gentleman or two of that country. Severe strictures on the conduct of the British king, in negotiating our repeated repeals of the law which permitted the importation of slaves, were disapproved by some Southern gentlemen, whose reflections were not yet matured to the full abhorrence of that traffic. Although the offensive expressions were immediately yielded these gentlemen continued their depredations on other parts of the instrument. I was sitting by Dr. Franklin, who perceived that I was not insensible to these mutilations. "I have made it a rule," said he, "whenever in my power, to avoid becoming the draughtsmen of papers to be reviewed by a public body. I took my lesson from an incident which I will relate to you. When I was a journeyman printer, one of my companions, an apprentice hatter, having served out his time, was about to open shop for himself. His first concern was to have a handsome signboard, with a proper inscription. He composed it in these words, 'John Thompson, *Hatter, makes* and *sells hats* for ready money,' with a figure of a hat subjoined; but he thought he would submit it to his friends for their amendments. The first he showed it to thought the word '*Hatter*' tautologous, because followed by the words 'makes hats,' which show he was a hatter. It was struck out. The next observed that the word '*makes*' might as well be omitted, because his customers would not care who made the hats. If good and to their mind, they would buy, by whomsoever made. He struck it out. A third said he thought the words '*for ready money*' were useless, as it was not the custom of the place to sell on credit. Every one who purchased expected to pay. They were parted with, and the inscription now stood, 'John Thompson sells hats.' '*Sells hats!*' says his next friend. Why nobody will expect you to give them away, what then is the use of that word? It was stricken out, and '*hats*' followed it, the rather as there was one painted on the board. So the inscription was reduced ultimately to 'John Thompson' with the figure of a hat subjoined."

The Doctor told me at Paris the two following anecdotes of the Abbé Raynal. He had a party to dine with him one day at Passy, of whom one half were Americans, the other half French, and among the last was the Abbé. During the dinner he got on his favorite theory of the degeneracy of animals, and even of man, in America, and urged it with his usual eloquence The Doctor at length noticing the accidental stature and position of his guests, at table, "Come," says he, "M. l'Abbé, let us try this question by the fact before us. We are here one half Americans, and one half French, and it happens that the Americans have placed themselves on one side of the table, and our French friends are on the other. Let both parties rise, and we will see on which side nature has degenerated." It happened that his American guests were Carmichael, Harmer, Humphreys, and others of the finest stature and form; while those of the other side were remarkably diminutive, and the Abbé himself particularly, was a mere shrimp. He parried the appeal, however, by a complimentary admission of exceptions among which the Doctor himself was a conspicuous one.

The Doctor and Silas Deane were in conversation one day at Passy, on the numerous errors in the Abbé's *Histoire des deux Indes,* when he happened to step in. After the usual salutations, Silas Deane said to him, "The Doctor and myself, Abbé, were just speaking of the errors of fact into which you have been led in your history." "Oh, no Sir," said the Abbé, "that is impossible. I took the greatest care not to insert a single fact, for which I had not the most unquestionable authority." "Why," says Deane, "there is the story of Polly Baker, and the eloquent apology you have put into her mouth, when brought before a court of Massachusetts to suffer punishment under a law which you cite, for having had a bastard. I know there never was such a law in Massachusetts." "Be assured," said the Abbé, "you are mistaken, and that that is a true story. I do not immediately recollect indeed the particular information on which I quote it; but I am certain that I had for it unquestionable authority." Doctor Franklin, who had been for some time shaking with unrestrained laughter at the Abbé's confidence in his authority for that tale, said, "I will tell you, Abbé, the origin of that story. When I was a printer and editor of a newspaper, we were sometimes slack of news, and to amuse our customers, I used to fill up our vacant columns with anecdotes and fables, and fancies of my own, and this of Polly Baker is a story of my making, on one of these occasions. The Abbé, without the least disconcert, exclaimed with a laugh, "Oh, very well, Doctor, I had rather relate your stories than other men's truths."

Notes for the Biography of George Wythe[1]

George Wythe was born about the year 1727, or 1728, of a respectable family in the County of Elizabeth City, on the shores of

[1]This biographical sketch was furnished to John Saunderson, who had written Jefferson concerning a proposed biography of Wythe. It was sent him with a letter of August 31, 1820.

the Chesapeake. He inherited, from his father, a fortune sufficient for independence and ease. He had not the benefit of a regular education in the schools, but acquired a good one of himself, and without assistance; insomuch, as to become the best Latin and Greek scholar in the State. It is said, that while reading the Greek Testament, his mother held an English one, to aid him in rendering the Greek text conformably with that. He also acquired, by his own reading, a good knowledge of Mathematics, and of Natural and Moral Philosophy. He engaged in the study of the law under the direction of a Mr. Lewis, of that profession, and went early to the bar of the General Court, then occupied by men of great ability, learning and dignity in their profession. He soon became eminent among them, and, in process of time, the first at the bar, taking into consideration his superior learning, correct elocution, and logical style of reasoning; for in pleading he never indulged himself with an useless or declamatory thought or word; and became as distinguished by correctness and purity of conduct in his profession, as he was by his industry and fidelity to those who employed him. He was early elected to the House of Representatives, then called the House of Burgesses, and continued in it until the Revolution. On the first dawn of that, instead of higgling on half-way principles, as others did who feared to follow their reason, he took his stand on the solid ground that the only link of political union between us and Great Britain, was the identity of our Executive; that that nation and its Parliament had no more authority over us, than we had over them, and that we were co-ordinate nations with Great Britain and Hanover.

In 1774, he was a member of a Committee of the House of Burgesses, appointed to prepare a Petition to the King, a Memorial to the House of Lords, and a Remonstrance to the House of Commons, on the subject of the proposed Stamp Act. He was made draughtsman of the last, and, following his own principles, he so far overwent the timid hesitations of his colleagues, that his draught was subjected by them to material modifications; and, when the famous Resolutions of Mr. Henry, in 1775, were proposed, it was not on any difference of principle that they were opposed by Wythe, Randolph, Pendleton, Nicholas, Bland, and other worthies, who had long been the habitual leaders of the House; but because those papers of the preceding session had already expressed the same sentiments and assertions of right, and that an answer to them was yet to be expected.

In August, 1775, he was appointed a member of Congress, and in 1776, signed the Declaration of Independence, of which he had, in debate, been an eminent supporter. And subsequently, in the same year, he was appointed, by the Legislature of Virginia, one of a Committee to revise the laws of the State, as well of British as of Colonial enactment, and to prepare bills for re-enacting them, with such alterations as the change in the form and principles of the government, and other circumstances, required; and of this work, he executed the period commencing with the revolution in England, and ending with the establishment of the new government here; excepting the Acts for regulating descents, for religious freedom, and for proportioning crimes and punishments. In 1777, he was chosen Speaker of the House of Delegates, being of distinguished learning in Parliamentary law and proceedings; and towards the end of the same year, he was appointed one of the three Chancellors, to whom that department of the Judiciary was confided, on the first organization of the new government. On a subsequent change of the form of that court, he was appointed sole Chancellor, in which office he continued to act until his death, which happened in June, 1806, about the seventy-eighth or seventy-ninth year of his age.

Mr. Wythe had been twice married: first, I believe, to a daughter of Mr. Lewis, with whom he had studied law, and afterwards to a Miss Taliaferro, of a wealthy and respectable family in the neighborhood of Williamsburg; by neither of whom did he leave issue.

No man ever left behind him a character more venerated than George Wythe. His virtue was of the purest tint; his integrity inflexible, and his justice exact; of warm patriotism, and, devoted as he was to liberty, and the natural and equal rights of man, he might truly be called the Cato of his country, without the avarice of the Roman; for a more disinterested person never lived. Temperance and regularity in all his habits, gave him general good health, and his unaffected modesty and suavity of manners endeared him to every one. He was of easy elocution, his language chaste, methodical in the arrangement of his matter, learned and logical in the use of it, and of great urbanity in debate; not quick of apprehension, but, with a little time, profound in penetration, and sound in conclusion. In his philosophy he was firm, and neither troubling, nor perhaps trusting, any one with his religious creed, he left the world to the conclusion, that that religion must be good which could produce a life of such exemplary virtue.

His stature was of the middle size, well formed and proportioned, and the features of his face were manly, comely, and engaging. Such was George Wythe, the honor of his own, and the model of future times.

Notes on Virginia[1]

~~~~~~~~~~~~~~~~~~~~~~~~~~~~~~~~~~~~ ✍ ~~~~~~~~~~~~~~~~~~~~~~~~~~~~~~~~~~~~

[1]The full title is: *Notes on the State of Virginia*; written in the year 1781, somewhat corrected and enlarged in the winter of 1782, for the use of a Foreigner of distinction, in answer to certain queries proposed by him respecting its boundaries; rivers; sea ports; mountains; cascades and caverns; productions mineral, vegetable and animal; climate; population; military force; marine force; aborigines; counties and towns; constitution; laws; colleges, buildings, and roads; proceedings as to tories; religion; manners; manufactures; subjects of commerce; Weights, Measures, and Money; public revenue and expenses; histories, memorials and state papers.

Introduction

Jefferson's *Notes on Virginia*, his only original full-length book, was written, for the most part, in answer to inquiries made to him by the Marquis de Barbé-Marbois, then Secretary of the French Legation in Philadelphia. Following his resignation as Governor of Virginia, during a rare period of leisure while recuperating from the effects of being thrown from a horse, Jefferson had occasion to work over the material concerning Virginia he had assiduously collected over a period of many years. These notes were revised and enlarged during the winter of 1782–83, but were not immediately published in this country, largely for financial reasons. The *Notes on Virginia* were first anonymously published at Jefferson's expense in an edition of 200 copies, Paris, 1784 (dated 1782), shortly after Jefferson's arrival in that capital. This very limited edition was followed, within the next five years, by popular French, English, German, and American printings, authorized and unauthorized. The *Notes* made a great impression on the French political world, where French liberals paid particular attention to the sections on the free institutions of republican government.

Important not only as a notable contribution to American scientific writing (formulating principles of scientific geography later developed by von Humboldt), it has been praised by reputable twentieth-century historians of science as the most influential scientific book written by an American. The *Notes* continue to be of interest for the clarity, vigor, and occasional beauty of Jefferson's prose.

With the exception of statistical tables, insignificant on repetitive detail, and technical footnotes, the *Notes on Virginia* is printed complete.

Notes on Virginia

✍

QUERY I

*An exact description of the limits and boundaries of
the State of Virginia?*

Virginia is bounded on the east by the Atlantic; on the north by a line
of latitude crossing the eastern shore through Watkin's Point, being
about 37° 57' north latitude; from thence by a straight line to Cinquac,
near the mouth of the Potomac; thence by the Potomac, which is common to Virginia and Maryland, to the first fountain of its northern
branch; thence by a meridian line, passing through that fountain till it
intersects a line running east and west, in latitude 39° 43' 42.4" which
divides Maryland from Pennsylvania, and which was marked by
Messrs. Mason and Dixon; thence by that line, and a continuation of
it westwardly to the completion of five degrees of longitude from the
eastern boundary of Pennsylvania, in the same latitude, and thence by
a meridian line to the Ohio; on the west by the Ohio and Mississippi,
to latitude 36° 3o' north, and on the south by the line of latitude last
mentioned. . . . These boundaries include an area somewhat triangular of one hundred and twenty-one thousand five hundred and twenty-
five square miles, whereof seventy-nine thousand six hundred and fifty
lie westward of the Alleghany mountains, and fifty-seven thousand and
thirty-four westward of the meridian of the mouth of the Great Kanhaway. This State is therefore one-third larger than the islands of Great
Britain and Ireland, which are reckoned at eighty-eight thousand three
hundred and fifty-seven square miles.

These limits result from, 1. The ancient charters from the crown
of England. 2. The grant of Maryland to the Lord Baltimore, and the
subsequent determinations of the British court as to the extent of that

grant. 3. The grant of Pennsylvania to William Penn, and a compact between the general assemblies of the commonwealths of Virginia and Pennsylvania as to the extent of that grant. 4. The grant of Carolina, and actual location of its northern boundary, by consent of both parties. 5. The treaty of Paris of 1763. 6. The confirmation of the charters of the neighboring States by the convention of *Virginia* at the time of constituting their commonwealth. 7. The cession made by *Virginia* to Congress of all the lands to which they had title on the north side of the Ohio.

QUERY II

A notice of its rivers, rivulets, and how far they are navigable?

An inspection of a map of *Virginia*, will give a better idea of the geography of its rivers, than any description in writing. Their navigation may be imperfectly noted.

Roanoke, so far as it lies within the State, is nowhere navigable but for canoes, or light batteaux; and even for these in such detached parcels as to have prevented the inhabitants from availing themselves of it at all.

James River, and its waters, afford navigation as follows:

The whole of *Elizabeth River*, the lowest of those which run into James River, is a harbor, and would contain upwards of three hundred ships. The channel is from one hundred and fifty to two hundred fathoms wide and at common flood tide affords eighteen feet water to Norfolk. The Stafford, a sixty gun ship, went there, lightening herself to cross the bar at Sowel's Point. The Fier Rodrigue, pierced for sixty-four guns, and carrying fifty, went there without lightening. Craney Island, at the mouth of this river, commands its channel tolerably well.

Nansemond River is navigable to Sleepy Hole for vessels of two hundred and fifty tons; to Suffolk for those of one hundred tons; and to Milner's for those of twenty-five.

Pagan Creek affords eight or ten feet water to Smithfield, which admits vessels of twenty tons.

Chickahominy has at its mouth a bar, on which is only twelve feet water at common flood tide. Vessels passing that, may go eight miles up the river; those of ten feet draught may go four miles further, and those of six tons burden twenty miles further.

Appomattox may be navigated as far as Broadways, by any vessel which has crossed Harrison's bar in James River; it keeps eight or ten feet water a mile or two higher up to Fisher's bar, and four feet on that and upwards to Petersburg, where all navigation ceases.

James River itself affords a harbor for vessels of any size in Hampton Road, but not in safety through the whole winter; and there is navigable water for them as far as Mulberry Island. A forty gun ship goes to Jamestown, and lightening herself, may pass Harrison's bar; on which there is only fifteen feet water. Vessels of two hundred and fifty tons may go to Warwick; those of one hundred and twenty-five go to Rocket's, a mile below Richmond; from thence is about seven feet water to Richmond; and about the centre of the town, four feet and a half, where the navigation is interrupted by falls, which in a course of six miles, descend about eighty-eight feet perpendicular; above these it is resumed in canoes and batteaux, and is prosecuted safely and advantageously to within ten miles of the Blue Ridge; and even through the Blue Ridge a ton weight has been brought; and the expense would not be great, when compared with its object, to open a tolerable navigation up Jackson's river and Carpenter's creek, to within twenty-five miles of Howard's creek of Green Briar, both of which have then water enough to float vessels into the Great Kanhaway. In some future state of population I think it possible that its navigation may also be made to interlock with that of the Potomac, and through that to communicate by a short portage with the Ohio. It is to be noted that this river is called in the maps *James River*, only to its confluence with the Rivanna; thence to the Blue Ridge it is called the Fluvanna; and thence to its source Jackson's river. But in common speech, it is called James River to its source.

The *Rivanna*, a branch of James River, is navigable for canoes and batteaux to its intersection with the South-West mountains, which is about twenty-two miles; and may easily be opened to navigation through these mountains to its fork above Charlottesville. . . .

The *Mississippi* will be one of the principal channels of future commerce for the country westward of the Alleghany. From the mouth of this river to where it receives the Ohio, is one thousand miles by water, but only five hundred by land, passing through the Chickasaw country. From the mouth of the Ohio to that of the Missouri, is two hundred and thirty miles by water, and one hundred and forty by land, from thence to the mouth of the Illinois river, is about twenty-five miles. The Mississippi, below the mouth of the Missouri, is always muddy, and abounding with sand bars, which frequently change their places. However, it carries fifteen feet water to the mouth of the Ohio, to which place it is from one and a half to two miles wide, and thence to Kaskaskia from one mile to a mile and a quarter wide. Its current is so rapid, that it never can be stemmed by the force of the wind alone, acting on sails. Any vessel, however, navigated with oars, may come up at any time, and receive much aid from the wind. A batteau passes from the mouth of Ohio to the mouth of Mississippi in three weeks, and is from two to three months getting up again. During its floods, which are periodical as those of the Nile, the largest vessels may pass down it, if their steerage can be insured. These floods begin in April, and the river returns into its banks early in August. The inundation extends further on the western than eastern side, covering the lands in some places for fifty miles from its banks. Above the mouth of the Missouri it becomes much such a river as the Ohio, like it clear and gentle in its current, not quite so wide, the period of its floods nearly the same, but not rising to so great a height. The streets of the village at Cohoes are not more than ten feet above the ordinary level of the water, and yet were never overflowed. Its bed deepens every year. Cohoes, in the memory of many people now living, was insulated by every flood of the river. What was the eastern channel has now become a lake, nine miles in length and one in width, into which the river at this day never flows. This river yields turtle of a peculiar kind, perch, trout, gar, pike, mullets, herrings, carp, spatula-fish of fifty pounds weight, cat-fish of one hundred pounds weight, buffalo fish, and sturgeon. Alligators or crocodiles have been seen as high up as the Acansas. It also abounds in herons, cranes, ducks, brant, geese, and swans. Its passage is commanded by a fort established by this State, five miles below the mouth of the Ohio, and ten miles above the Carolina boundary.

The Missouri, since the treaty of Paris, the Illinois and northern branches of the Ohio, since the cession to Congress, are no longer within our limits. Yet having been so heretofore, and still opening to us channels of extensive communication with the western and north-western country, they shall be noted in their order.[1]

QUERY III

A notice of the best Seaports of the State and how big are the vessels they can receive?

Having no ports but our rivers and creeks, this *Query* has been answered under the preceding one.

QUERY IV

A notice of its Mountains?

For the particular geography of our mountains I must refer to Fry and Jefferson's map of Virginia; and to Evans' analysis of this map of America, for a more philosophical view of them than is to be found in any other work. It is worthy of notice, that our mountains are not solitary and scattered confusedly over the face of the country; but that they commence at about one hundred and fifty miles from the sea-coast, are disposed in ridges, one behind another, running nearly parallel with the sea-coast, though rather approaching it as they advance north-eastwardly. To the south-west, as the tract of country between the sea-coast and the Mississippi becomes narrower, the mountains converge into a single ridge, which, as it approaches the Gulf of Mexico, subsides into plain country, and gives rise to some of the waters of that gulf, and particularly to a river called the Apalachiocola, probably from the Apalachies, an Indian nation formerly residing on it. Hence, the mountains giving rise to that river, and seen from its various parts, were called the Apalachian mountains, being in fact the end or termination only of the great ridges passing through the continent. European geographers, however, extended the name northwardly as far as the mountains extended; some giving it, after their separation into different

---

[1]The remainder of this Query enumerates and describes the following rivers: Missouri, Illinois, Kaskaskia, Ohio, Tennessee, Cumberland, Wabash, Green, Kentucky, Great Miami, Salt River, Little Miami, Sioto, Great Sandy, Guiandot, Great Kanhaway, Hockhocking, Little Kanhaway, Muskingum, Monongahela, and Alleghany.

ridges, to the Blue Ridge, others to the North Mountain, others to the Alleghany, others to the Laurel Ridge, as may be seen by their different maps. But the fact I believe is, that none of these ridges were ever known by that name to the inhabitants, either native or emigrant, but as they saw them so called in European maps. In the same direction, generally, are the veins of limestone, coal, and other minerals hitherto discovered; and so range the falls of our great rivers. But the courses of the great rivers are at right angles with these. James and Potomac penetrate through all the ridges of mountains eastward of the Alleghany; that is, broken by no water course. It is in fact the spine of the country between the Atlantic on one side, and the Mississippi and St. Lawrence on the other. The passage of the Potomac through the Blue Ridge is, perhaps, one of the most stupendous scenes in nature. You stand on a very high point of land. On your right comes up the Shenandoah, having ranged along the foot of the mountain an hundred miles to seek a vent. On your left approaches the Potomac, in quest of a passage also. In the moment of their junction, they rush together against the mountain, rend it asunder, and pass off to the sea. The first glance of this scene hurries our senses into the opinion, that this earth has been created in time, that the mountains were formed first, that the rivers began to flow afterwards, that in this place, particularly, they have been dammed up by the Blue Ridge of mountains, and have formed an ocean which filled the whole valley; that continuing to rise they have at length broken over at this spot, and have torn the mountain down from its summit to its base. The piles of rock on each hand, but particularly on the Shenandoah, the evident marks of their disrupture and avulsion from their beds by the most powerful agents of nature, corroborate the impression. But the distant finishing which nature has given to the picture, is of a very different character. It is a true contrast to the foreground. It is as placid and delightful as that is wild and tremendous. For the mountain being cloven asunder, she presents to your eye, through the cleft, a small catch of smooth blue horizon, at an infinite distance in the plain country, inviting you, as it were, from the riot and tumult roaring around, to pass through the breach and participate of the calm below. Here the eye ultimately composes itself; and that way, too, the road happens actually to lead. You cross the Potomac above the junction, pass along its side through the base of the mountain for three miles, its terrible precipices hanging in fragments over you, and within about twenty miles reach Fredericktown, and the fine country round that. This scene is worth a voyage across the Atlantic. Yet here, as in the neighborhood of the Natural Bridge, are people who have passed their lives within half a dozen miles, and have never been to survey these monuments of a war between rivers and mountains, which must have shaken the earth itself to its centre. . . .

The height of our mountains has not yet been estimated with any degree of exactness. The Alleghany being the great ridge which divides the waters of the Atlantic from those of the Mississippi, its summit is doubtless more elevated above the ocean than that of any other mountain. But its relative height, compared with the base on which it stands, is not so great as that of some others, the country rising behind the successive ridges like the steps of stairs. The mountains of the Blue Ridge, and of these the Peaks of Otter, are thought to be of a greater height, measured from their base, than any others in our country, and perhaps in North America. From data, which may found a tolerable conjecture, we suppose the highest peak to be about four thousand feet perpendicular, which is not a fifth part of the height of the mountains of South America, nor one-third of the height which would be necessary in our latitude to preserve ice in the open air unmelted through the year. The ridge of mountains next beyond the Blue Ridge, called by us the North mountain, is of the greatest extent; for which reason they were named by the Indians the endless mountains.

A substance supposed to be Pumice, found floating on the Mississippi, has induced a conjecture that there is a volcano on some of its waters; and as these are mostly known to their sources, except the Missouri, our expectations of verifying the conjecture would of course be led to the mountains which divide the waters of the Mexican Gulf from those of the South Sea; but no volcano having ever yet been known at such a distance from the sea, we must rather suppose that this floating substance has been erroneously deemed Pumice.

QUERY V
Its Cascades and Caverns?

The only remarkable cascade in this country is that of the Falling Spring in Augusta. It is a water of James' river where it is called Jackson's river, rising in the warm spring mountains, about twenty miles southwest of the warm spring, and flowing into that valley. About three-quarters of a mile from its source it falls over a rock two hundred feet into the valley below. The sheet of water is broken in its breadth by the rock, in two or three places, but not at all in its height. Between the sheet and the rock, at the bottom, you may walk across dry. This cataract will bear no comparison with that of Niagara as to the quantity of water composing it; the sheet being only twelve or fifteen feet wide above and somewhat more spread below; but it is half as high again, the latter being only one hundred and fifty-six feet, according to the mensuration made by order of M. Vaudreuil, Governor of Canada, and one hundred and thirty according to a more recent account.

In the lime-stone country there are many caverns of very considerable extent. The most noted is called Madison's Cave,[1] and is on the north side of the Blue Ridge, near the intersection of the Rockingham and Augusta line with the south fork of the southern river of Shenandoah. It is in a hill of about two hundred feet perpendicular height, the ascent of which, on one side, is so steep that you may pitch a biscuit from its summit into the river which washes its base. The entrance of the cave is, in this side, about two-thirds of the way up. It extends into the earth about three hundred feet, branching into subordinate caverns, sometimes ascending a little, but more generally descending, and at length terminates, in two different places, at basins of water of unknown extent, and which I should judge to be nearly on a level with the water of the river; however, I do not think they are formed by refluent water from that, because they are never turbid; because they do not rise and fall in correspondence with that in times of flood or of drought; and because the water is always cool. It is probably one of the

---

[1]Jefferson includes a diagram of Madison's Cave which is omitted in the present edition.

many reservoirs with which the interior parts of the earth are supposed to abound, and yield supplies to the fountains of water, distinguished from others only by being accessible. The vault of this cave is of solid lime-stone, from twenty to forty or fifty feet high; through which water is continually percolating. This, trickling down the sides of the cave, has incrusted them over in the form of elegant drapery; and dripping from the top of the vault generates on that and on the base below, stalactites of a conical form, some of which have met and formed massive columns.

Another of these caves is near the North Mountain, in the county of Frederic, on the lands of Mr. Zane. The entrance into this is on the top of an extensive ridge. You descend thirty or forty feet, as into a well, from whence the cave extends, nearly horizontally, four hundred feet into the earth, preserving a breadth of from twenty to fifty feet, and a height of from five to twelve feet. After entering this cave a few feet, the mercury, which in the open air was 50°, rose to 57° of Fahrenheit's thermometer, answering to 11° of Reaumur's, and it continued at that to the remotest parts of the cave. The uniform temperature of the cellars of the observatory of Paris, which are ninety feet deep, and of all subterraneous cavities of any depth, where no chemical agencies may be supposed to produce a factitious heat, has been found to be 10° of Reaumur, equal to 54½° of Fahrenheit. The temperature of the cave above mentioned so nearly corresponds with this, that the difference may be ascribed to a difference of instruments.

At the Panther gap, in the ridge which divides the waters of the Cow and the Calf pasture, is what is called the *Blowing Cave*. It is in the side of a hill, is of about one hundred feet diameter, and emits constantly a current of air of such force as to keep the weeds prostrate to the distance of twenty yards before it. This current is strongest in dry, frosty weather, and in long spells of rain weakest. Regular inspirations and expirations of air, by caverns and fissures, have been probably enough accounted for by supposing them combined with intermitting fountains; as they must of course inhale air while their reservoirs are emptying themselves, and again emit it while they are filling. But a constant issue of air, only varying in its force as the weather is drier or damper, will require a new hypothesis There is another blowing cave in the Cumberland mountain, about a mile from where it crosses the

Carolina line. All we know of this is, that it is not constant, and that a fountain of water issues from it.

The *Natural Bridge*, the most sublime of nature's works, though not comprehended under the present head, must not be pretermitted. It is on the ascent of a hill, which seems to have been cloven through its length by some great convulsion. The fissure, just at the bridge, is, by some admeasurements, two hundred and seventy feet deep, by others only two hundred and five. It is about forty-five feet wide at the bottom and ninety feet at the top; this of course determines the length of the bridge, and its height from the water. Its breadth in the middle is about sixty feet, but more at the ends, and the thickness of the mass, at the summit of the arch, about forty feet. A part of this thickness is constituted by a coat of earth, which gives growth to many large trees. The residue, with the hill on both sides, is one solid rock of lime-stone. The arch approaches the semi-elliptical form; but the larger axis of the ellipsis, which would be the cord of the arch, is many times longer than the transverse. Though the sides of this bridge are provided in some parts with a parapet of fixed rocks, yet few men have resolution to walk to them, and look over into the abyss. You involuntarily fall on your hands and feet, creep to the parapet, and peep over it. Looking down from this height about a minute, gave me a violent headache. If the view from the top be painful and intolerable, that from below is delightful in an equal extreme. It is impossible for the emotions arising from the sublime to be felt beyond what they are here; so beautiful an arch, so elevated, so light, and springing as it were up to heaven! The rapture of the spectator is really indescribable! The fissure continuing narrow, deep, and straight, for a considerable distance above and below the bridge, opens a short but very pleasing view of the North mountain on one side and the Blue Ridge on the other, at the distance each of them of about five miles. This bridge is in the county of Rockbridge, to which it has given name, and affords a public and commodious passage over a valley which cannot be crossed elsewhere for a considerable distance. The stream passing under it is called Cedar creek. It is a water of James' river, and sufficient in the driest seasons to turn a grist-mill, though its fountain is not more than two miles above.[1]

---

[1]A long footnote supplied by Jefferson is omitted here.

QUERY VI

*A notice of the mines and other subterraneous riches;
its trees, plants, fruits, etc.*

I knew a single instance of gold found in this State. It was interspersed in small specks through a lump of ore of about four pounds weight, which yielded seventeen pennyweights of gold, of extraordinary ductility. This ore was found on the north side of Rappahanoc, about four miles below the falls. I never heard of any other indication of gold in its neighborhood. . . .

Near the eastern foot of the North mountain are immense bodies of *Schist*, containing impressions of shells in a variety of forms. I have received petrified shells of very different kinds from the first sources of Kentucky, which bear no resemblance to any I have ever seen on the tide-waters. It is said that shells are found in the Andes, in South America, fifteen thousand feet above the level of the ocean. This is considered by many, both of the learned and unlearned, as a proof of an universal deluge. To the many considerations opposing this opinion, the following may be added: The atmosphere, and all its contents, whether of water, air, or other matter, gravitate to the earth; that is to say, they have weight. Experience tells us, that the weight of all these together never exceeds that of a column of mercury of thirty-one inches height, which is equal to one of rain water of thirty-five feet high. If the whole contents of the atmosphere, then, were water, instead of what they are, it would cover the globe but thirty-five feet deep; but as these waters, as they fell, would run into the seas, the superficial measure of which is to that of the dry parts of the globe, as two to one, the seas would be raised only fifty-two and a half feet above their present level, and of course would overflow the lands to that height only. In Virginia this would be a very small proportion even of the champaign country, the banks of our tide waters being frequently, if not generally, of a greater height. Deluges beyond this extent, then, as for instance, to the North mountain or to Kentucky, seem out of the laws of nature. But within it they may have taken place to a greater or less degree, in proportion to the combination of natural causes which may be supposed to have produced them. History renders probably some instances of a partial deluge in the country lying round the Mediterranean sea. It has been often[1] supposed, and it is not unlikely, that that sea was once a lake. While such, let us admit an extraordinary collection of the waters of the atmosphere from the other parts of the globe to have been discharged over that and the countries whose waters run into it. Or without supposing it a lake, admit such an extraordinary collection of the waters of the atmosphere, and an influx from the Atlantic ocean, forced by long-continued western winds. The lake, or that sea, may thus have been so raised as to overflow the low lands adjacent to it, as those of Egypt and Armenia, which, according to a tradition of the Egyptians and Hebrews, were overflowed about two thousand three hundred years before the Christian era; those of Attica, said to have been overflowed in the time of Ogyges, about five hundred years later; and those of Thessaly, in the time of Deucalion, still three hundred years posterior. But such deluges as these will not account for the shells found in the higher lands. A second opinion has been entertained, which is, that in times anterior to the records either of history or tradition, the bed of the ocean, the principal residence of the shelled tribe, has, by some great convulsion of nature, been heaved to the heights at which we now find shells and other marine animals. The favorers of this opinion do well to suppose the great events on which it rests to have taken place beyond all the eras of history; for within these, certainly, none such are to be found; and we may venture to say farther, that no fact has taken place, either in our own days, or in the thousands of years recorded in history, which proves the existence of any natural agents, within or without the bowels of the earth, of forces sufficient to heave, to the height of fifteen thousand feet, such masses as the Andes. The difference between the power necessary to produce such an effect, and that which shuffled together the different parts of Calabria in our days, is so immense, that from the existence of the latter, we are not authorized to infer that of the former.

M. de Voltaire has suggested a third solution of this difficulty. (Quest. Encycl. Coquilles.) He cites an instance in Touraine, where, in the space of eighty years, a particular spot of earth had been twice metamorphosed into soft stone, which had become hard when

---

[1]Buffon Epoques, 96. [Jefferson's footnote.] Jefferson evidently means Vol. II of Buffon's Epoques.—Eds.

employed in building. In this stone shells of various kinds were produced, discoverable at first only with a microscope, but afterwards
growing with the stone. From this fact, I suppose, he would have us
infer, that, besides the usual process for generating shells by the elaboration of earth and water in animal vessels, nature may have provided
an equivalent operation, by passing the same materials through the
pores of calcareous earths and stones; as we see calcareous drop-stones
generating every day, by the percolation of water through lime-stone,
and new marble forming in the quarries from which the old has been
taken out. And it might be asked, whether is it more difficult for
nature to shoot the calcareous juice into the form of a shell, than other
juices into the forms of crystals, plants, animals, according to the construction of the vessels through which they pass? There is a wonder
somewhere. Is it greatest on this branch of the dilemma; on that which
supposes the existence of a power, of which we have no evidence in any
other case; or on the first, which requires us to believe the creation of
a body of water and its subsequent annihilation? The establishment
of the instance, cited by M. de Voltaire, of the growth, of shells unat-
tached to animal bodies, would have been that of his theory. But he has
not established it. He has not even left it on ground so respectable as
to have rendered it an object of inquiry to the *literati* of his own country. Abandoning this fact, therefore, the three hypotheses are equally
unsatisfactory; and we must be contented to acknowledge, that this
great phenomenon is as yet unsolved. Ignorance is preferable to error;
and he is less remote from the truth who believes nothing, than he who
believes what is wrong.

. . . . Our *farms* produce wheat, rye, barley, oats, buck-wheat,
broom corn, and Indian corn. The climate suits rice well enough,
wherever the lands do. Tobacco, hemp, flax, and cotton, are staple
commodities. Indigo yields two cuttings. The silk-worm is a native,
and the mulberry, proper for its food, grows kindly.

We cultivate, also, potatoes, both the long and the round, turnips,
carrots, parsnips, pumpkins, and ground nuts (Arachis). Our grasses
are lucerne, st. foin, burnet, timothy, ray, and orchard grass; red,
white, and yellow clover; greensward, blue grass, and crab grass.

The *gardens* yield musk-melons, water-melons, tomatoes, okra,
pomegranates, figs, and the esculent plants of Europe.

The *orchards* produce apples, pears, cherries, quinces, peaches, nectarines, apricots, almonds, and plums.

Our quadrupeds have been mostly described by Linnæus and Mons. de Buffon. Of these the mammoth, or big buffalo, as called by the Indians, must certainly have been the largest. Their tradition is, that he was carnivorous, and still exists in the northern parts of America. A delegation of warriors from the Delaware tribe having visited the Governor of Virginia, during the revolution, on matters of business, after these had been discussed and settled in council, the Governor asked them some questions relative to their country, and among others, what they knew or had heard of the animal whose bones were found at the Saltlicks on the Ohio. Their chief speaker immediately put himself into an attitude of oratory, and with a pomp suited to what he conceived the elevation of his subject, informed him that it was a tradition handed down from their fathers, "That in ancient times a herd of these tremendous animals came to the Big-bone licks, and began an universal destruction of the bear, deer, elks, buffaloes, and other animals which had been created for the use of the Indians; that the Great Man above, looking down and seeing this, was so enraged that he seized his lightning, descended on the earth, seated himself on a neighboring mountain, on a rock of which his seat and the print of his feet are still to be seen, and hurled his bolts among them till the whole were slaughtered, except the big bull, who presenting his forehead to the shafts, shook them off as they fell; but missing one at length, it wounded him in the side; whereon, springing round, he bounded over the Ohio, over the Wabash, the Illinois, and finally over the great lakes, where he is living at this day." It is well known, that on the Ohio, and in many parts of America further north, tusks, grinders, and skeletons of unparalleled magnitude, are found in great numbers, some lying on the surface of the earth, and some a little below it. A Mr. Stanley, taken prisoner near the mouth of the Tennessee, relates, that after being transferred through several tribes, from one to another, he was at length carried over the mountains west of the Missouri to a river which runs westwardly; that these bones abounded there, and that the natives described to him the animal to which they belonged as still existing in the northern parts of their country; from which description he judged it to be an elephant. Bones of the same kind have been lately found, some feet below the surface of the earth, in salines opened on the North Holston, a branch of the Tennessee, about the latitude of 36½° north. From the accounts published in Europe, I suppose it to be decided that these are of the same kind with those found in Siberia. Instances are mentioned of like animal remains found in the more southern climates of both hemispheres; but they are either so loosely mentioned as to leave a doubt of the fact, so inaccurately described as not to authorize the classing them with the great northern bones, or so rare as to found a suspicion that they have been carried thither as curiosities from the northern regions. So that, on the whole, there seem to be no certain vestiges of the existence of this animal farther south than the salines just mentioned. It is remarkable that the tusks and skeletons have been ascribed by the naturalists of Europe to the elephant, while the grinders have been given to the hippopotamus, or river horse. Yet it is acknowledged, that the tusks and skeletons are much larger than those of the elephant, and the grinders many times greater than those of the hippopotamus, and essentially different in form. Wherever these grinders are found, there also we find the tusks and skeleton; but no skeleton of the hippopotamus nor grinders of the elephant. It will not be said that the hippopotamus and elephant came always to the same spot, the former to deposit his grinders, and the latter his tusks and skeleton. For what became of the parts not deposited there? We must agree then, that these remains belong to each other, that they are of one and the same animal, that this was not a hippopotamus, because the hippopotamus had no tusks, nor such a frame, and because the grinders differ in their size as well as in the number and form of their points. That this was not an elephant, I think ascertained by proofs equally decisive. I will not avail myself of the authority of the celebrated[1] anatomist, who, from an examination of the form and structure of the tusks, has declared they were essentially different from those of the elephant; be cause another[2] anatomist, equally celebrated, has declared, on a like examination, that they are precisely the same. Between two such authorities I will suppose this circumstance equivocal. But, 1. The skeleton of the mammoth (for so the incognitum

[1]Hunter. [Jefferson's footnote.]

[2]D'Aubenton. [Jefferson's footnote.]

has been called) bespeaks an animal of five or six times the cubic volume of the elephant, as Mons. de Buffon has admitted. 2. The grinders are five times as large, are square, and the grinding surface studded with four or five rows of blunt points; whereas those of the elephant are broad and thin, and their grinding surface flat. 3. I have never heard an instance, and suppose there has been none, of the grinder of an elephant being found in America. 4. From the known temperature and constitution of the elephant, he could never have existed in those regions where the remains of the mammoth have been found. The elephant is a native only of the torrid zone and its vicinities; if, with the assistance of warm apartments and warm clothing, he has been preserved in the temperate climates of Europe, it has only been for a small portion of what would have been his natural period, and no instance of his multiplication in them has ever been known. But no bones of the mammoth, as I have before observed, have been ever found further south than the salines of Holston, and they have been found as far north as the Arctic circle. Those, therefore, who are of opinion that the elephant and mammoth are the same, must believe, 1. That the elephant known to us can exist and multiply in the frozen zone; or, 2. That an eternal fire may once have warmed those regions, and since abandoned them, of which, however, the globe exhibits no unequivocal indications; or, 3. That the obliquity of the ecliptic, when these elephants lived, was so great as to include within the tropics all those regions in which the bones are found; the tropics being, as is before observed, the natural limits of habitation for the elephant. But if it be admitted that this obliquity has really decreased, and we adopt the highest rate of decrease yet pretended, that is, of one minute in a century, to transfer the northern tropic to the Arctic circle, would carry the existence of these supposed elephants two hundred and fifty thousand years back; a period far beyond our conception of the duration of animal bones less exposed to the open air than these are in many instances. Besides, though these regions would then be supposed within the tropics, yet their winters would have been too severe for the sensibility of the elephant. They would have had, too, but one day and one night in the year, a circumstance to which we have no reason to suppose the nature of the elephant fitted. However, it has been demonstrated, that, if a variation of obliquity in the ecliptic takes place at all, it is vibratory, and never exceeds the limits of nine degrees, which is not sufficient to bring these bones within the tropics. One of these hypotheses, or some other equally voluntary and inadmissible to cautious philosophy, must be adopted to support the opinion that these are the bones of the elephant. For my own part, I find it easier to believe that an animal may have existed, resembling the elephant in his tusks, and general anatomy, while his nature was in other respects extremely different. From the 30th degree of south latitude to the 30th degree of north, are nearly the limits which nature has fixed for the existence and multiplication of the elephant known to us. Proceeding thence northwardly to 36½ degrees, we enter those assigned to the mammoth. The farther we advance north, the more their vestiges multiply as far as the earth has been explored in that direction; and it is as probable as otherwise, that this progression continues to the pole itself, if land extends so far. The centre of the frozen zone, then, may be the acmé of their vigor, as that of the torrid is of the elephant. Thus nature seems to have drawn a belt of separation between these two tremendous animals, whose breadth, indeed, is not precisely known, though at present we may suppose it about 6½ degrees of latitude; to have assigned to the elephant the region south of these confines, and those north to the mammoth, founding the constitution of the one in her extreme of heat, and that of the other in the extreme of cold. When the Creator has therefore separated their nature as far as the extent of the scale of animal life allowed to this planet would permit, it seems perverse to declare it the same, from a partial resemblance of their tusks and bones. But to whatever animal we ascribe these remains, it is certain such a one has existed in America, and that it has been the largest of all terrestrial beings. It should have sufficed to have rescued the earth it inhabited, and the atmosphere it breathed, from the imputation of impotence in the conception and nourishment of animal life on a large scale; to have stifled, in its birth, the opinion of a writer, the most learned, too, of all others in the science of animal history, that in the new world, "La nature vivante est beaucoup moins agissante, beaucoup moins forte:"[1] that nature is less active, less energetic on one side of the globe than she is on the other. As if both sides were not warmed by the

[1]Buffon, xviii. 112 edit. Paris, 1764. [Jefferson's footnote]

same genial sun; as if a soil of the same chemical composition was less capable of elaboration into animal nutriment; as if the fruits and grains from that soil and sun yielded a less rich chyle, gave less extension to the solids and fluids of the body, or produced sooner in the cartilages, membranes, and fibres, that rigidity which restrains all further extension, and terminates animal growth. The truth is, that a pigmy and a Patagonian, a mouse and a mammoth, derive their dimensions from the same nutritive juices. The difference of increment depends on circumstances unsearchable to beings with our capacities. Every race of animals seems to have received from their Maker certain laws of extension at the time of their formation. Their elaborate organs were formed to produce this, while proper obstacles were opposed to its further progress. Below these limits they cannot fall, nor rise above them. What intermediate station they shall take may depend on soil, on climate, on food, on a careful choice of breeders. But all the manna of heaven would never raise the mouse to the bulk of the mammoth.

The opinion advanced by the Count de Buffon,[1] is 1. That the animals common both to the old and new world are smaller in the latter. 2. That those peculiar to the new are on a smaller scale. 3. That those which have been domesticated in both have degenerated in America; and 4. That on the whole it exhibits fewer species. And the reason he thinks is, that the heats of America are less; that more waters are spread over its surface by nature, and fewer of these drained off by the hand of man. In other words, that *heat is* friendly, and *moisture* adverse to the production and development of large quadrupeds. I will not meet this hypothesis on its first doubtful ground, whether the climate of America be comparatively more humid? Because we are not furnished with observations sufficient to decide this question. And though, till it be decided, we are as free to deny as others are to affirm the fact, yet for a moment let it be supposed. The hypothesis, after this supposition, proceeds to another; that *moisture* is unfriendly to animal growth. The truth of this is inscrutable to us by reasonings *a priori*. Nature has hidden from us her *modus agendi*. Our only appeal on such questions is to experience; and I think that experience is against the supposition. It is by the assistance of *heat* and *moisture* that vegetables are elaborated

[1]Buffon, xviii. 100, 156. [Jefferson's footnote.]

from the elements of earth, air, water, and fire. We accordingly see the more humid climates produce the greater quantity of vegetables. Vegetables are mediately or immediately the food of every animal; and in proportion to the quantity of food, we see animals not only multiplied in their numbers, but improved in their bulk, as far as the laws of their nature will admit. Of this opinion is the Count de Buffon himself in another part of his work;[1] "in general, it appears that rather cold countries are more suitable to our oxen than rather warm countries, and that they (the oxen) are all the larger and greater in proportion as the climate is damper and more abounding in pasturage . . . "[2] Here then a race of animals, and one of the largest too, has been increased in its dimensions by *cold* and *moisture,* in direct opposition to the hypothesis, which supposes that these two circumstances diminish animal bulk, and that it is their contraries *heat* and *dryness* which enlarge it. But when we appeal to experience we are not to rest satisfied with a single fact. Let us, therefore, try our question on more general ground. Let us take two portions of the earth, Europe and America for instance, sufficiently extensive to give operation to general causes; let us consider the circumstances peculiar to each, and observe their effect on animal nature. America, running through the torrid as well as temperate zone, has more *heat* collectively taken, than Europe. But Europe, according to our hypothesis, is the *dryest.* They are equally adapted then to animal productions; each being endowed with one of those causes which befriends animal growth, and with one which opposes it. If it be thought unequal to compare Europe with America, which is so much larger, I answer, not more so than to compare America with the whole world. Besides, the purpose of the comparison is to try an hypothesis, which makes the size of animals depend on the *heat* and *moisture* of climate. If, therefore, we take a region so extensive as to comprehend a sensible distinction of climate, and so extensive, too, as that local accidents, or the intercourse of animals on its borders, may not materially affect the size of those in its interior parts, we shall comply with those conditions which the hypothesis may reasonably demand. The objection would be the weaker in the present case, because any intercourse of animals which

[1]viii, 134. [Jefferson's note.]

[2]In Jefferson's text, this is given in French.

may take place on the confines of Europe and Asia, is to the advantage of the former, Asia producing certainly larger animals than Europe. Let us then take a comparative view of the quadrupeds of Europe and America, presenting them to the eye in three different tables, in one of which shall be enumerated those found in both countries; in a second, those found in one only; in a third, those which have been domesticated in both.[1] To facilitate the comparison, let those of each table be arranged in gradation according to their sizes, from the greatest to the smallest, so far as their sizes can be conjectured. The weights of the large animals shall be expressed in the English avoirdupois and its decimals; those of the smaller, in the same ounce and its decimals. . . . The white bear of America is as large as that of Europe. The bones of the mammoth which has been found in America, are as large as those found in the old world. It may be asked, why I insert the mammoth, as if it still existed? I ask in return, why I should omit it, as if it did not exist? Such is the economy of nature, that no instance can be produced, of her having permitted any one race of her animals to become extinct; of her having formed any link in her great work so weak as to be broken. To add to this, the traditionary testimony of the Indians, that this animal still exists in the northern and western parts of America, would be adding the light of a taper to that of the meridian sun. Those parts still remain in their aboriginal state, unexplored and undisturbed by us, or by others for us. He may as well exist there now, as he did formerly where we find his bones. If he be a carnivorous animal, as some anatomists have conjectured, and the Indians affirm, his early retirement may be accounted for from the general destruction of the wild game by the Indians, which commences in the first instant of their connection with us, for the purpose of purchasing match-coats, hatchets, and fire-locks, with their skins. There remain then the buffalo, red deer, fallow deer, wolf, roe, glutton, wild cat, monax, bison, hedgehog, marten, and water-rat, of the comparative sizes of which we have not sufficient testimony. It does not appear that Messieurs de Buffon and D'Aubenton have measured, weighed, or seen those of America. It is said of some of them, by some travellers, that they are smaller than the European. But who were these travellers? Have they not been men

---

[1]These tables have been omitted in the present edition.

of a very different description from those who have laid open to us the other three quarters of the world? Was natural history the object of their travels? Did they measure or weigh the animals they speak of? or did they not judge of them by sight, or perhaps even from report only? Were they acquainted with the animals of their own country, with which they undertake to compare them? Have they not been so ignorant as often to mistake the species? A true answer to these questions would probably lighten their authority, so as to render it insufficient for the foundation of an hypothesis. How unripe we yet are, for an accurate comparison of the animals of the two countries, will appear from the work of Monsieur de Buffon. The ideas we should have formed of the sizes of some animals, from the formation he had received at his first publications concerning them, are very different from what his subsequent communications give us. And indeed his candor in this can never be too much praised. One sentence of his book must do him immortal honor. "I like a person who points out a mistake just as much as one who teaches me a truth, because, in effect, a corrected mistake is a truth."[1] . . .

Hitherto I have considered this hypothesis as applied to brute animals only, and not in its extension to the man of America, whether aboriginal or transplanted. It is the opinion of Mons. de Buffon that the former furnishes no exception to it . . .[2]

An afflicting picture, indeed, which for the honor of human nature, I am glad to believe has no original. Of the Indian of South America I know nothing; for I would not honor with the appellation of knowledge, what I derive from the fables published of them. These I believe to be just as true as the fables of Æsop. This belief is founded on what I have seen of man, white, red, and black, and what has been written of him by authors, enlightened themselves, and writing among an enlightened people. The Indian of North America being more within our reach, I can speak of him somewhat from my own knowledge, but more from the information of others better acquainted with him, and on whose truth and judgment I can rely. From these sources I am able to say, in contradiction to this representation, that he is neither more defective

[1]In Jefferson's text, this is given in French.

[2]Jefferson cites Buffon's thesis at this point.

in ardor, nor more impotent with his female, than the white reduced to the same diet and exercise; that he is brave, when an enterprise depends on bravery; education with him making the point of honor consist in the destruction of an enemy by stratagem, and in the preservation of his own person free from injury; or, perhaps, this is nature, while it is education which teaches us to[1] honor force more than finesse; that he will defend himself against a host of enemies, always choosing to be killed, rather than to surrender,[2] though it be to the whites, who he knows will treat him well; that in other situations, also, he meets death with more deliberation, and endures tortures with a firmness unknown almost to religious enthusiasm with us; that he is affectionate to his children, careful of them, and indulgent in the extreme; that his affections comprehend his other connections, weakening, as with us, from circle to circle, as they recede from the centre; that his friendships are strong and faithful to the uttermost[3] extremity; that his sensibility is keen, even the warriors weeping most bitterly on the loss of their children, though in general they endeavor to appear superior to human events; that his vivacity and activity of mind is equal to ours in the same situation; hence his eagerness for hunting, and for games of chance. The women are submitted to unjust drudgery. This I believe is the case with every barbarous people. With such, force is law. The stronger sex imposes on the weaker. It is civilization alone which replaces women in the enjoyment of their natural equality. That first teaches us to subdue the selfish passions, and to respect those rights in others which we value in ourselves. Were we in equal barbarism, our females would be equal drudges. The man with them is less strong than with us, but their women stronger than ours; and both for the same obvious reason; because our man and their woman is habituated to labor, and formed by it. With both races the sex which is indulged with ease is the least athletic. An Indian man is small in the hand and wrist, for the same reason for which a sailor is large and strong in the arms and shoulders, and a porter in the legs and thighs. They raise fewer

[1]Jefferson's footnote omitted.

[2]Jefferson's footnote omitted.

[3]Jeffersons footnote omitted.

children than we do. The causes of this are to be found, not in a difference of nature, but of circumstance. The women very frequently attending the men in their parties of war and of hunting, child-bearing becomes extremely inconvenient to them. It is said, therefore, that they have learned the practice of procuring abortion by the use of some vegetable; and that it even extends to prevent conception for a considerable time after. During these parties they are exposed to numerous hazards, to excessive exertions, to the greatest extremities of hunger. Even at their homes the nation depends for food, through a certain part of every year, on the gleanings of the forest; that is, they experience a famine once in every year. With all animals, if the female be badly fed, or not fed at all, her young perish; and if both male and female be reduced to like want, generation becomes less active, less productive. To the obstacles, then, of want and hazard, which nature has opposed to the multiplication of wild animals, for the purpose of restraining their numbers within certain bounds, those of labor and of voluntary abortion are added with the Indian. No wonder, then, if they multiply less than we do. Where food is regularly supplied, a single farm will show more of cattle, than a whole country of forests can of buffaloes. The same Indian women, when married to white traders, who feed them and their children plentifully and regularly, who exempt them from excessive drudgery, who keep them stationary and unexposed to accident, produce and raise as many children as the white women. Instances are known, under these circumstances, of their rearing a dozen children. An inhuman practice once prevailed in this country, of making slaves of the Indians. It is a fact well known with us, that the Indian women so enslaved produced and raised as numerous families as either the whites or blacks among whom they lived. It has been said that Indians have less hair than the whites, except on the head. But this is a fact of which fair proof can scarcely be had. With them it is disgraceful to be hairy on the body. They say it likens them to hogs. They therefore pluck the hair as fast as it appears. But the traders who marry their women, and prevail on them to discontinue this practice, say, that nature is the same with them as with the whites. Nor, if the fact be true, is the consequence necessary which has been drawn from it. . . .

Before we condemn the Indians of this continent as wanting genius, we must consider that letters have not yet been introduced among them. Were we to compare them in their present state with the Europeans, north of the Alps, when the Roman arms and arts first crossed those mountains, the comparison would be unequal, because, at that time, those parts of Europe were swarming with numbers; because numbers produce emulation, and multiply the chances of improvement, and one improvement begets another. Yet I may safely ask, how many good poets, how many able mathematicians, how many great inventors in arts or sciences, had Europe, north of the Alps, then produced? And it was sixteen centuries after this before a Newton could be formed. I do not mean to deny that there are varieties in the race of man, distinguished by their powers both of body and mind. I believe there are, as I see to be the case in the races of other animals. I only mean to suggest a doubt, whether the bulk and faculties of animals depend on the side of the Atlantic on which their food happens to grow, or which furnishes the elements of which they are compounded? Whether nature has enlisted herself as a Cis or Trans-Atlantic partisan? I am induced to suspect there has been more eloquence than sound reasoning displayed in support of this theory; that it is one of those cases where the judgment has been seduced by a glowing pen; and whilst I render every tribute of honor and esteem to the celebrated zoologist, who has added, and is still adding, so many precious things to the treasures of science, I must doubt whether in this instance he has not cherished error also, by lending her for a moment his vivid imagination and bewitching language. . . .

So far the Count de Buffon has carried this new theory of the tendency of nature to belittle her productions on this side the Atlantic. Its application to the race of whites transplanted from Europe, remained for the Abbé Raynal. "One must be astonished (he says) that America has not yet produced a good poet, an able mathematician, a man of genius in a single art or single science."[1] When we shall have existed as a people as long as the Greeks did before they produced a Homer, the Romans a Virgil, the French a Racine and Voltaire, the English a Shakespeare and Milton, should this reproach be still true, we will inquire from what unfriendly causes it has proceeded, that the other countries of Europe and quarters of the earth shall not have inscribed

[1]In Jefferson's text, this is given in French.

any name in the roll of poets.[1] But neither has America produced "one able mathematician, one man of genius in a single art or a single science." In war we have produced a Washington, whose memory will be adored while liberty shall have votaries, whose name shall triumph over time, and will in future ages assume its just station among the most celebrated worthies of the world, when that wretched philosophy shall be forgotten which would have arranged him among the degeneracies of nature. In physics we have produced a Franklin, than whom no one of the present age has made more important discoveries, nor has enriched philosophy with more, or more ingenious solutions of the phenomena of nature. We have supposed Mr. Rittenhouse second to no astronomer living; that in genius he must be the first, because he is self taught. As an artist he has exhibited as great a proof of mechanical genius as the world has ever produced. He has not indeed made a world; but he has by imitation approached nearer its Maker than any man who has lived from the creation to this day.[2] As in philosophy and war, so in government, in oratory, in painting, in the plastic art, we might show that America, though but a child of yesterday, has already given hopeful proofs of genius, as well as of the nobler kinds, which arouse the best feelings of man, which call him into action, which substantiate his freedom, and conduct him to happiness, as of the subordinate, which serve to amuse him only. We therefore suppose, that this reproach is as unjust as it is unkind: and that, of the geniuses which adorn the present age, America contributes its full share For comparing it with those countries where genius is most cultivated, where are the most excellent models for art, and scaffoldings for the attainment of science, as France and England for instance, we calculate thus: The United States contains

[1]Has the world as yet produced more than two poets, acknowledged to be such by all nations? An Englishman only reads Milton with delight, an Italian, Tasso, a Frenchman the Henriade; a Portuguese, Camoens; but Homer and Virgil have been the rapture of every age and nation; they are read with enthusiasm in their originals by those who can read the originals, and in translations by those who cannot. [Jefferson's footnote.]

[2]There are various ways of keeping truth out of sight. Mr. Rittenhouse's model of the planetary system has the plagiary application of an Orrery; and the quadrant invented by Godfrey, an American also, and with the aid of which the European nations traverse the globe, is called Hadley's quadrant. [Jefferson's footnote.]

three millions of inhabitants; France twenty millions; and the British islands ten. We produce a Washington, a Franklin, a Rittenhouse. France then should have half a dozen in each of these lines, and Great Britain half that number, equally eminent. It may be true that France has; we are but just becoming acquainted with her, and our acquaintance so far gives us high ideas of the genius of her inhabitants. It would be injuring too many of them to name particularly a Voltaire, a Buffon, the constellation of Encyclopedists, the Abbé Raynal himself, etc., etc. We, therefore, have reason to believe she can produce her full quota of genius. The present war having so long cut off all communication with Great Britain, we are not able to make a fair estimate of the state of science in that country. The spirit in which she wages war, is the only sample before our eyes, and that does not seem the legitimate offspring either of science or of civilization. The sun of her glory is fast descending to the horizon. Her philosophy has crossed the channel, her freedom the Atlantic, and herself seems passing to that awful dissolution whose issue is not given human foresight to scan.[1]

QUERY VII

A notice of all that can increase the progress of Human Knowledge?

[This section, which is concerned with an analysis of local climatic conditions, is omitted in the present.]

QUERY VIII

The number of its inhabitants?

. . . . During the infancy of the colony, while numbers were small, wars, importations, and other accidental circumstances render the progression fluctuating and irregular. By the year 1654, however, it becomes tolerably uniform, importations having in a great measure ceased from the dissolution of the company, and the inhabitants become too numerous to be sensibly affected by Indian wars. Beginning at that period, therefore, we find that from thence to the year 1772, our tythes had increased from 7,209 to 153,000. The whole term

[1]Jefferson's footnote omitted.

being of one hundred and eighteen years, yields a duplication once in every twenty-seven and a quarter years. The intermediate enumerations taken in 1700, 1748, and 1759, furnish proofs of the uniformity of this progression. Should this rate of increase continue, we shall have between six and seven millions of inhabitants within ninety-five years. If we suppose our country to be bounded, at some future day, by the meridian of the mouth of the Great Kanhaway, (within which it has been before conjectured, are 64,461 square miles) there will then be one hundred inhabitants for every square mile, which is nearly the state of population in the British Islands.

Here I will beg leave to propose a doubt. The present desire of America is to produce rapid population by as great importations of foreigners as possible. But is this founded in good policy? The advantage proposed is the multiplication of numbers. Now let us suppose (for example only) that, in this state, we could double our numbers in one year by the importation of foreigners; and this is a greater accession than the most sanguine advocate for emigration has a right to expect. Then I say, beginning with a double stock, we shall attain any given degree of population only twenty-seven years, and three months sooner than if we proceed on our single stock. If we propose four millions and a half as a competent population for this State, we should be fifty-four and a half years attaining it, could we at once double our numbers; and eighty-one and three quarter years, if we rely on natural propagation, as may be seen by the following tablet:

	Proceeding on our present stock.	Proceeding on a double stock.
1781	567,614	1,135,228
1808¼	1,135,228	2,270,456
1835½	2,270,456	4,540,912
1862¾	4,540,912	

In the first column are stated periods of twenty-seven and a quarter years; in the second are our numbers at each period, as they will be if we proceed on our actual stock; and in the third are what they would be, at the same periods, were we to set out from the double of our present stock. I have taken the term of four million and a half of inhabitants for example's sake only. Yet I am persuaded it is a greater number than the country spoken of, considering how much inarable land it contains, can clothe and feed without a material change in the quality of their diet. But are there no inconveniences to be thrown into the scale against the advantage expected from a multiplication of numbers by the importation of foreigners? It is for the happiness of those united in society to harmonize as much as possible in matters which they must of necessity transact together. Civil government being the sole object of forming societies, its administration must be conducted by common consent. Every species of government has its specific principles. Ours perhaps are more peculiar than those of any other in the universe. It is a composition of the freest principles of the English constitution, with others derived from natural right and natural reason. To these nothing can be more opposed than the maxims of absolute monarchies. Yet from such we are to expect the greatest number of emigrants. They will bring with them the principles of the governments they leave, imbibed in their early youth; or, if able to throw them off, it will be in exchange for an unbounded licentiousness, passing, as is usual, from one extreme to another. It would be a miracle were they to stop precisely at the point of temperate liberty. These principles, with their language, they will transmit to their children. In proportion to their numbers, they will share with us the legislation. They will infuse into it their spirit, warp and bias its directions, and render it a heterogeneous, incoherent, distracted mass. I may appeal to experience, during the present contest, for a verification of these conjectures. But, if they be not certain in event, are they not possible, are they not probable? Is it not safer to wait with patience twenty-seven years and three months longer, for the attainment of any degree of population desired or expected? May not our government be more homogeneous, more peaceable, more durable? Suppose twenty millions of republican Americans thrown all of a sudden into France, what would be the condition of that kingdom? If it would be more turbulent, less happy, less strong, we may believe that the addition of half a million of foreigners to our present numbers would produce a similar effect here. If they come of themselves they are entitled to all the rights of citizenship; but I doubt the expediency of inviting them by extraordinary encouragements. I mean not that these doubts should be extended to the importation of useful artificers. The policy of that measure depends on very different considerations. Spare no expense in obtaining them. They will after a while go to the plough and the hoe; but, in the mean time, they will teach us something we do not know. It is not so in agriculture. The indifferent state of that among us does not proceed from a want of knowledge merely; it is from our having such quantities of land to waste as we please. In Europe the object is to make the most of their land, labor being abundant; here it is to make the most of our labor, land being abundant. . . .

During the regal government we had at one time obtained a law which imposed such a duty on the importation of slaves as amounted nearly to a prohibition, when one inconsiderate assembly, placed under a peculiarity of circumstance, repealed the law. This repeal met a joyful sanction from the then reigning sovereign, and no devices, no expedients, which could ever be attempted by subsequent assemblies, and they seldom met without attempting them, could succeed in getting the royal assent to a renewal of the duty. In the very first session held under the republican government, the assembly passed a law for the perpetual prohibtion of the importation of slaves. This will in some measure stop the increase of this great political and moral evil, while the minds of our citizens may be ripening for a complete emancipation of human nature.

QUERY IX
The number and condition of the Militia and Regular Troops, and their Pay?

. . . .

Every able-bodied freeman, between the ages of sixteen and fifty, is enrolled in the militia. Those of every county are formed into companies, and these again into one or more battalions, according to the numbers in the county. They are commanded by colonels, and other subordinate officers, as in the regular service. In every county is a county-lieutenant, who commands the whole militia of his county, but ranks only as a colonel in the field. We have no general officers always existing. These are appointed occasionally, when an invasion or insurrection happens, and their commission determines with the occasion. The Governor is head of the military, as well as civil power. The law requires every militia-man to provide himself with the arms usual in the regular service. But this injunction was always indifferently complied with, and the arms they had, have been so frequently called for to arm the regulars, that in the lower parts of the country they are entirely disarmed. In the middle country a fourth or fifth part of them may have such firelocks as they had provided to destroy the noxious animals which infest their farms; and on the western side of the Blue Ridge they are generally armed with rifles. The pay of our militia, as well as of our regulars, is that of the continental regulars. The condition of our regulars, of whom we have none but continentals, and part of a battalion of state troops, is so constantly on the change, that a state of it at this day would not be its state a month hence. It is much the same with the condition of the other continental troops, which is well enough known.

QUERY X
The Marine?

Before the present invasion of this State by the British, under the command of General Phillips, we had three vessels of sixteen guns, one of fourteen, five small gallies, and two or three armed boats. They were generally so badly manned as seldom to be in a condition for service. Since the perfect possession of our rivers assumed by the enemy, I believe we are left with a single armed boat only.

QUERY XI
A description of the Indians established in that State?

When the first effectual settlement of our colony was made, which was in 1607, the country from the seacoast to the mountains, and from the Potomac to the most southern waters of James' river, was occupied by upwards of forty different tribes of Indians. Of these the *Powhatans*, the *Mannahoacs*, and *Monacans*, were the most powerful. Those between the sea-coast and falls of the rivers, were in amity with one another, and attached to the Powhatans as their link of union. Those between the falls of the rivers and the mountains, were divided into two confederacies; the tribes inhabiting the head waters of Potomac and

Rappahannock, being attached to the *Mannahoacs;* and those on the upper parts of James' river to the *Monacans.* But the *Monacans* and their friends were in amity with the *Mannahoacs* and their friends, and waged joint and perpetual war against the *Powhatans.* We are told that the *Powhatans, Mannahoacs,* and *Monacans,* spoke languages so radically different, that interpreters were necessary when they transacted business. Hence we may conjecture, that this was not the case between all the tribes, and, probably, that each spoke the language of the nation to which it was attached; which we know to have been the case in many particular instances. Very possibly there may have been anciently three different stocks, each of which, multiplying in a long course of time, had separated into so many little societies. This practice results from the circumstance of their having never submitted themselves to any laws, any coercive power, any shadow of government. Their only controls are their manners, and that moral sense of right and wrong, which, like the sense of tasting and feeling in every man, makes a part of his nature. An offence against these is punished by contempt, by exclusion from society, or, where the case is serious, as that of murder, by the individuals whom it concerns. Imperfect as this species of coercion may seem, crimes are very rare among them; insomuch that were it made a question, whether no law, as among the savage Americans, or too much law, as among the civilized Europeans, submits man to the greatest evil, one who has seen both conditions of existence would pronounce it to be the last; and that the sheep are happier of themselves, than under care of the wolves. It will be said, the great societies cannot exist without government. The savages, therefore, break them into small ones.

The territories of the *Powhatan* confederacy, south of the Potomac, comprehended about eight thousand square miles, thirty tribes, and two thousand four hundred warriors. Captain Smith tells us, that within sixty miles of Jamestown were five thousand people, of whom one thousand five hundred were warriors. From this we find the proportion of their warriors to their whole inhabitants, was as three to ten. The *Powhatan* confederacy, then, would consist of about eight thousand inhabitants, which was one for every square mile; being about the twentieth part of our present population in the same territory, and the hundredth of that of the British islands.

Besides these were the *Nottoways,* living on Nottoway river, the

Meherrins and *Tuteloes* on Meherrin river, who were connected with the Indians of Carolina, probably with the *Chowanocs*. . . .

I know of no such thing existing as an Indian monument; for I would not honor with that name arrow points, stone hatchets, stone pipes, and half shapen images. Of labor on the large scale, I think there is no remain as respectable as would be a common ditch for the draining of lands; unless indeed it would be the barrows, of which many are to be found all over this country. These are of different sizes, some of them constructed of earth, and some of loose stones. That they were repositories of the dead, has been obvious to all; but on what particular occasion constructed, was a matter of doubt. Some have thought they covered the bones of those who have fallen in battles fought on the spot of interment. Some ascribed them to the custom, said to prevail among the Indians, of collecting, at certain periods, the bones of all their dead, wheresoever deposited at the time of death. Others again supposed them the general sepulchres for towns, conjectured to have been on or near these grounds; and this opinion was supported by the quality of the lands in which they are found (those constructed of earth being generally in the softest and most fertile meadow-grounds on river sides), and by a tradition, said to be handed from the aboriginal Indians, that when they settled in a town, the first person who died was placed erect, and earth put about him, so as to cover and support him; that when another died, a narrow passage was dug to the first, the second reclined against him, and the cover of earth replaced, and so on. There being one of these in my neighborhood, I wished to satisfy myself whether any, and which of these opinions were just. For this purpose I determined to open and examine it thoroughly. It was situated on the low grounds of the Rivanna, about two miles above its principal fork, and opposite to some hills, on which had been an Indian town. It was of a spheroidical form, of about forty feet diameter at the base, and had been of about twelve feet altitude, though now reduced by the plough to seven and a half, having been under cultivation about a dozen years. Before this it was covered with trees of twelve inches diameter, and round the base was an excavation of five feet depth and width, from whence the earth had been taken of which the hillock was formed. I first dug superficially in several parts of it, and came to collections of human bones, at different depth, from six inches to three feet below the surface. These were lying in the utmost confusion, some vertical, some oblique, some horizontal, and directed to every point of the compass, entangled and held together in clusters by the earth. Bones of the most distant parts were found together, as, for instance, the small bones of the foot in the hollow of a scull; many sculls would sometimes be in contact, lying on the face, on the side, on the back, top or bottom, so as, on the whole, to give the idea of bones emptied promiscuously from a bag or a basket, and covered over with earth, without any attention to their order. The bones of which the greatest numbers remained, were sculls, jaw-bones, teeth, the bones of the arms, thighs, legs, feet and hands. A few ribs remained, some vertebrae of the neck and spine, without their processes, and one instance only of the bone[1] which serves as a base to the vertebral column. The sculls were so tender, that they generally fell to pieces on being touched. The other bones were stronger. There were some teeth which were judged to be smaller than those of an adult; a scull, which on a slight view, appeared to be that of an infant, but it fell to pieces on being taken out, so as to prevent satisfactory examination; a rib, and a fragment of the under-jaw of a person about half grown; another rib of an infant; and a part of the jaw of a child, which had not cut its teeth. This last furnishing the most decisive proof of the burial of children here, I was particular in my attention to it. It was part of the right half of the under-jaw. The processes, by which it was attenuated to the temporal bones, were entire, and the bone itself firm to where it had been broken off, which, as nearly as I could judge, was about the place of the eye-tooth. Its upper edge, wherein would have been the sockets of the teeth, was perfectly smooth. Measuring it with that of an adult, by placing their hinder processes together, its broken end extended to the penultimate grinder of the adult. This bone was white, all the others of a sand color. The bones of infants being soft, they probably decay sooner, which might be the cause so few were found here. I proceeded then to make a perpendicular cut through the body of the barrow, that I might examine its internal structure. This passed about three feet from its centre, was opened to the former surface of the earth, and was wide enough for a man to walk through and examine its sides. At the bottom, that is,

---

[1]The os sacrum. [Jefferson's note.]

on the level of the circumjacent plain, I found bones; above these a few stones, brought from a cliff a quarter of a mile off; then a large interval of earth, then a stratum of bones, and so on. At one end of the section were four strata of bones plainly distinguishable; at the other, three; the strata in one part not ranging with those in another. The bones nearest the surface were least decayed. No holes were discovered in any of them, as if made with bullets, arrows, or other weapons. I conjectured that in this barrow might have been a thousand skeletons. Every one will readily seize the circumstances above related, which militate against the opinion, that it covered the bones only of persons fallen in battle; and against the tradition also, which would make it the common sepulchre of a town, in which the bodies were placed upright, and touching each other. Appearances certainly indicate that it has derived both origin and growth from the accustomary collection of bones, and deposition of them together; that the first collection had been deposited on the common surface of the earth, a few stones put over it, and then a covering of earth, that the second had been laid on this, had covered more or less of it in proportion to the number of bones, and was then also covered with earth; and so on. The following are the particular circumstances which give it this aspect. 1. The number of bones. 2. Their confused position. 3. Their being in different strata. 4. The strata in one part having no correspondence with those in another. 5. The different states of decay in these strata which seem to indicate a difference in the time of inhumation. The existence of infant bones among them.

But on whatever occasion they may have been made, they are of considerable notoriety among the Indians; for a party passing, about thirty years ago, through the part of the country where this barrow is, went through the woods directly to it, without any instructions or inquiry, and having staid about it for some time, with expressions which were construed to be those of sorrow, they returned to the high road, which they had left about half a dozen miles to pay this visit, and pursued their journey. There is another barrow much resembling this, in the low grounds of the south branch of Shenandoah, where it is crossed by the road leading from the Rockfish gap to Staunton. Both of these have, within these dozen years, been cleared of their trees and put under cultivation, are much reduced in their height, and spread in width, by the plough, and will probably disappear in time. There is another on a hill in the Blue Ridge of mountains, a few miles north of Wood's gap, which is made up of small stones thrown together. This has been opened and found to contain human bones, as the others do. There are also many others in other parts of the country.

Great question has arisen from whence came those aboriginals of America? Discoveries, long ago made, were sufficient to show that the passage from Europe to America was always practicable, even to the imperfect navigation of ancient times. In going from Norway to Iceland, from Iceland to Greenland, from Greenland to Labrador, the first traject is the widest; and this having been practised from the earliest times of which we have any account of that part of the earth, it is not difficult to suppose that the subsequent trajects may have been sometimes passed. Again, the late discoveries of Captain Cook, coasting from Kamschatka to California, have proved that if the two continents of Asia and America be separated at all, it is only by a narrow strait. So that from this side also, inhabitants may have passed into America; and the resemblance between the Indians of America and the eastern inhabitants of Asia, would induce us to conjecture, that the former are the descendants of the latter, or the latter of the former; excepting indeed the Esquimaux, who, from the same circumstance of resemblance, and from identity of language, must be derived from the Greenlanders, and these probably from some of the northern parts of the old continent. A knowledge of their several languages would be the most certain evidence of their derivation which could be produced. In fact, it is the best proof of the affinity of nations which ever can be referred to. How many ages have elapsed since the English, the Dutch, the Germans, the Swiss, the Norwegians, Danes and Swedes have separated from their common stock? Yet how many more must elapse before the proofs of their common origin, which exist in their several languages, will disappear? It is to be lamented then, very much to be lamented, that we have suffered so many of the Indian tribes already to extinguish, without our having previously collected and deposited in the records of literature, the general rudiments at least of the languages they spoke. Were vocabularies formed of all the languages spoken in North and South America, preserving their appellations of the most common objects in nature, of those which must be present to every nation barbarous or civilized, with the inflections of their nouns and verbs, their principles of regimen and concord, and these deposited in all the public libraries, it would furnish opportunities to those skilled in the languages of the old world to compare them with these, now, or at any future time, and hence to construct the best evidence of the derivation of this part of the human race.

But imperfect as is our knowledge of the tongues spoken in America, it suffices to discover the following remarkable fact: Arranging them under the radical ones to which they may be palpably traced, and doing the same by those of the red men of Asia, there will be found probably twenty in America, for one in Asia, of those radical languages, so called because if they were ever the same they have lost all resemblance to one another. A separation into dialects may be the work of a few ages only, but for two dialects to recede from one another till they have lost all vestiges of their common origin, must require an immense course of time; perhaps not less than many people give to the age of the earth. A greater number of those radical changes of language having taken place among the red men of America, proves them of greater antiquity than those of Asia.

. . . .

QUERY XII
A notice of the counties, cities, townships, and villages?

The counties have been enumerated under Query IX. They are seventy-four in number, of very unequal size and population. Of these thirty-five are on the tide waters, or in that parallel; twenty-three are in the midlands, between the tide waters and Blue Ridge of mountains; eight between the Blue Ridge and Alleghany; and eight westward of the Alleghany.

The State, by another division, is formed into parishes, many of which are commensurate with the counties; but sometimes a county comprehends more than one parish, and sometimes a parish more than one county. This division had relation to the religion of the State, a portion of the Anglican church, with a fixed salary, having been heretofore established in each parish. The care of the poor was another object of the parochial division.

We have no townships. Our country being much intersected with navigable waters, and trade brought generally to our doors, instead of our being obliged to go in quest of it, has probably been one of the causes why we have no towns of any consequence. Williamsburg, which, till the year 1780, was the seat of our government, never contained above 1,800 inhabitants; and Norfolk, the most populous town we ever had, contained but 6,000. . . .

There are other places at which, like some of the foregoing, the *laws* have said there shall be towns; but *nature* has said there shall not, and they remain unworthy of enumeration. *Norfolk* will probably be the emporium for all the trade of the Chesapeake bay and its waters; and a canal of eight or ten miles will bring to it all that of Albemarle sound and its waters. Secondary to this place, are the towns at the head of the tide waters, to wit, Petersburg on Appomattox; Richmond on James' river; Newcastle on York river; Alexandria on Potomac, and Baltimore on Patapsco. From these the distribution will be to subordinate situations in the country. Accidental circumstances, however, may control the indications of nature, and in no instance do they do it more frequently than in the rise and fall of towns.

QUERY XIII
The constitution of the State and its several charters?

Queen Elizabeth by her letters patent, bearing date March 25, 1584, licensed Sir Walter Raleigh to search for remote heathen lands, not inhabited by Christian people, and granted to him in fee simple, all the soil within two hundred leagues of the places where his people should, within six years, make their dwellings or abidings; reserving only to herself and her successors, their allegiance and one-fifth part of all the gold and silver ore they should obtain. Sir Walter immediately sent out two ships, which visited Wococon island in North Carolina, and the next year despatched seven with one hundred and seven men, who settled in Roanoke island, about latitude 35 ° 50'. Here Okisko, king of the Weopomeiocs, in a full council of his people is said to have acknowledged himself the homager of the Queen of England, and, after her, of Sir Walter Raleigh. A supply of fifty men were sent in 1586, and one hundred and fifty in 1587. With these last Sir Walter sent a governor, appointed him twelve assistants, gave them a charter of incorporation, and instructed them to settle on Chesapeake bay. They landed, however, at Hatorask. In 1588, when a fleet was ready to sail with a new supply of colonists and necessaries, they were detained by the Queen to assist against the Spanish armada. Sir Walter having now expended £40,000 in these enterprises, obstructed occasionally by the crown without a shilling of aid from it, was under a necessity of engaging others to adventure their money. He, therefore, by deed bearing date the 7th of March, 1589, by the name of Sir Walter Raleigh, Chief Governor of Assamàcòmoc, (probably Acomàc,) alias Wingadacoia, alias Virginia, granted to Thomas Smith and others, in consideration of their adventuring certain sums of money, liberty to trade to this new country free from all customs and taxes for seven years, excepting the fifth part of the gold and silver ore to be obtained; and stipulated with them and the other assistants, then in Virginia, that he would confirm the deed of incorporation which he had given in 1587, with all the prerogatives, jurisdictions, royalties and privileges granted to him by the Queen. Sir Walter, at different times, sent five other adventurers hither, the last of which was in 1602; for in 1603 he was attainted and put into close imprisonment, which put an end to his cares over his infant colony. What was the particular fate of the colonists he had before sent and seated, has never been known; whether they were murdered, or incorporated with the savages.

Some gentlemen and merchants, supposing that by the attainder of Sir Walter Raleigh the grant to him was forfeited, not inquiring over carefully whether the sentence of an English court could affect lands not within the jurisdiction of that court, petitioned king James for a new grant of Virginia to them. He accordingly executed a grant to Sir Thomas Gates and others, bearing date the 9th of March, 1607, under which, in the same year, a settlement was effected at Jamestown, and ever after maintained. Of this grant, however, no particular notice need be taken, as it was superseded by letters patent of the same king, of May 23, 1609, to the Earl of Salisbury and others, incorporating them by the name of "The Treasurer and company of Adventurers and Planters of the City of London for the first colony in Virginia," granting to them and their successors all the lands in Virginia from Point Comfort along the sea-coast, to the northward two hundred miles, and from the same point along the sea-coast to the southward two hundred miles, and all the space from this precinct on the sea-coast up into the land, west and north-west, from sea to sea, and the islands within one hundred miles of it, with all the communities, jurisdictions, royalties, privileges, franchises, and pre-eminencies, within the same, and thereto and thereabouts, by sea and land, appertaining in as ample manner as had before been granted to any adventurer; to be held of the king and his successors, in common soccage, yielding one-fifth part of the gold and silver ore to be therein found, for all manner of services; establishing a counsel in England for the direction of the enterprise, the members of which were to be chosen and displaced by the voice of the majority of the company and adventurers, and were to have the nomination and revocation of governors, officers, and ministers, which by them should be thought needful for the colony, the power of establishing laws and forms of government and magistracy, obligatory not only within the colony, but also on the seas in going and coming to and from it; authorizing them to carry thither any persons who should consent to go, freeing them forever from all taxes and impositions on any goods or merchandise on importations into the colony, or exportation out of it, except the five per cent. due for custom on all goods imported into the British dominions, according to the ancient trade of merchants; which five per cent. only being paid they might, within thirteen months, re-export the same goods into foreign parts, without any custom, tax, or other duty, to the king or any of his officers, or deputies; with powers of waging war against those who should annoy them; giving to the inhabitants of the colony all the rights of natural subjects, as if born and abiding in England; and declaring that these letters should be construed, in all doubtful parts, in such manner as should be most for the benefit of the grantees.

Afterwards on the 12th of March, 1612, by other letters patent, the king added to his former grants, all islands in any part of the ocean between the 30th and 41st degrees of latitude, and within three hundred leagues of any of the parts before granted to the treasurer and company, not being possessed or inhabited by any other Christian prince or state, nor within the limits of the northern colony.

In pursuance of the authorities given to the company by these charters, and more especially of that part in the charter of 1609, which authorized them to establish a form of government, they on the 24th of July, 1621, by charter under their common seal, declared that from thenceforward there should be two supreme councils in Virginia, the one to be called the council of state, to be placed and displaced by the treasurer, council in England, and company from time to time, whose office was to be that of assisting and advising the governor; the other to be called the general assembly, to be convened by the governor once yearly or oftener, which was to consist of the council of state, and two burgesses out of every town, hundred, or plantation, to be respectively chosen by the inhabitants. In this all matters were to be decided by the greater part of the votes present; reserving to the governor a negative voice; and they were to have power to treat, consult, and conclude all emergent occasions concerning the public weal, and to make laws for the behoof and government of the colony, imitating and following the laws and policy of England as nearly as might be; providing that these laws should have no force till ratified in a general court of the company in England, and returned under their common seal; and declaring that, after the government of the colony should be well framed and settled, no orders of the council in England should bind the colony unless ratified in the said general assembly. The king and company quarrelled, and by a mixture of law and force, the latter were ousted of all their rights without retribution, after having expended one hundred thousand pounds in establishing the colony, without the smallest aid from government. King James suspended their powers by proclamation of July 15, 1624, and Charles I. took the government into his own hands. Both sides had their partisans in the colony, but, in truth, the people of the colony in general thought themselves little concerned in the dispute. There being three parties interested in these several charters, what passed between the first and second, it was thought could not affect the third. If the king seized on the powers of the company, they only passed into other hands, without increase or diminution, while the rights of the people remained as they were. But they did not remain so long. The northern parts of their country were granted away to the lords Baltimore and Fairfax; the first of these obtaining also the rights of separate jurisdiction and government. And in 1650 the parliament, considering itself as standing in the place of their deposed king, and as having succeeded to all his powers, without as well as within the realm, began to assume a right over the colonies, passing an act for inhibiting their trade with foreign nations. This succession to the exercise of kingly authority gave the first color for parliamentary interference with the colonies, and produced that fatal precedent which they continued to follow, after they had retired, in other respects, within their proper functions. When this colony, therefore, which still maintained its opposition to Cromwell and the parliament, was induced in 1651 to lay down their arms, they previously secured their most essential rights by a solemn convention, which, having never seen in print, I will here insert literally from the records.

"ARTICLES *agreed on and concluded at James Cittie in Virginia for the surrendering and settling of that plantation under the obedience and government of the commonwealth of England by the commissioners of the Councill of State by authoritie of the parliamt of England, and by the Grand assembly of the Governour, Councill, and Burgesses of that countrey.*

"First it is agreed and consted that the plantation of Virginia, and all the inhabitants thereof, shall be and remain in due obedience and Subjection to the Commonwealth of England, according to the laws there established, and that this submission and subscription bee acknowledged a voluntary act not forced nor constrained by a conquest upon the countrey, and that they shall have and enjoy such freedoms and priviledges as belong to the free borne people of England, and that the former government by the Commissions and Instructions be void and null.

"2ly. That the Grand assembly as formerly shall convene and transact the affairs of Virginia, wherein nothing is to be acted or done contrairie to the government of the Commonwealth of England and the lawes there established.

"3ly. That there shall be a full and totall remission and indempnitie of all acts, words, or writeings done or spoken against the parliament of England in relation to the same.

"4ly. That Virginia shall have and enjoy the antient bounds and lymitts granted by the charters of the former kings, and that we shall seek a new charter from the parliament to that purpose against any that have intrencht upon the rights thereof.

"5ly. That all the pattents of land granted under the colony seal by any of the precedent governours shall be and remaine in their full force and strength.

"6ly. That the priviledge of haveing ffiftie acres of land for every person transported in that collonie shall continue as formerly granted.

"7ly. That the people of Virginia have free trade as the people of England do enjoy to all places and with all nations according to the lawes of that commonwealth, and that Virginia shall enjoy all priviledges equall with any English plantations in America.

"8ly. That Virginia shall be free from all taxes, customs and impositions whatsoever, and none to be imposed on them without consent of the Grand assembly; and soe that neither fforts nor castle bee erected or garrisons maintained without their consent.

"9ly. That noe charge shall be required from this country in respect of this present ffleet.

"10ly. That for the future settlement of the countrey in their due obedience, the engagement shall be tendred to all the inhabitants according to act of parliament made to that purpose, that all persons who shall refuse to subscribe the said engagement, shall have a yeare's time if they please to remove themselves and their estates out of Virginia, and in the meantime during the said yeare to have equall justice as formerly.

"11ly. That the use of the booke of common prayer shall be permitted for one yeare ensueinge with referrence to the consent of the major part of the parishes, provided that those which relate to kingshipp or that government be not used publiquely, and the continuance of ministers in their places, they not misdemeaning themselves, and the payment of their accustomed dues and agreements made with them respectively shall be left as they now stand dureing this ensueing yeare.

"12ly. That no man's cattell shall be questioned as the companies unless such as have been entrusted with them or have disposed of them without order.

"13ly. That all ammunition, powder and armes, other than for private use, shall be delivered up, securitie being given to make satisfaction for it.

"14ly. That all goods allreadie brought hither by the Dutch or others which are now on shoar shall be free from surprizall.

"15ly. That the quittrents granted unto us by the late kinge for seaven yeares bee confirmed.

"16ly. That the commissioners for the parliament subscribeing these articles engage themselves and the honour of parliament for the full performance thereof; and that the present governour, and the councill, and the burgesses do likewise subscribe and engage the whole collony on their parts.

RICHARD BENNETT.—Seale.
WILLIAM CLAIBORNE.—Seale.
EDMOND CURTIS.—Seale.

"Theise articles were signed and sealed by the Commissioners of the Councill of state for the Commonwealth of England the twelveth day of March 1651."

The colony supposed, that, by this solemn convention, entered into with arms in their hands, they had secured the ancient limits of their country, its free trade, its exemption from taxation but by their own assembly, and exclusion of military force from among them. Yet in every of these points was this convention violated by subsequent kings and parliaments, and other infractions of their constitution, equally dangerous committed. Their general assembly, which was composed of the council of state and burgesses, sitting together and deciding by plurality of voices, was split into two houses, by which the council obtained a separate negative on their laws. Appeals from their supreme court, which had been fixed by law in their general assembly, were arbitrarily revoked to England, to be there heard before the king and council. Instead of four hundred miles on the seacoast, they were reduced, in the space of thirty years, to about one hundred miles. Their trade with foreigners was totally suppressed, and when carried to Great Britain, was there loaded with imposts. It is unnecessary, however, to glean up the several instances of injury, as scattered through American and British history, and the more especially as, by passing on to the accession of the present king, we shall find specimens of them all, aggravated, multiplied and crowded within a small compass of time, so as to evince a fixed design of considering our rights natural, conventional and chartered as mere nullities. The following is an epitome of the first sixteen years of his reign: The colonies were taxed internally and externally; their essential interests sacrificed to individuals in Great Britain; their legislatures suspended; charters annulled; trials by juries taken away; their persons subjected to transportation across the Atlantic, and to trial before foreign judicatories; their supplications for redress thought beneath answer; themselves published as cowards in the councils of their mother country and courts of Europe; armed troops sent among them to enforce submission to these violences; and actual hostilities commenced against them. No alternative was presented but resistance, or unconditional submission. Between these could be no hesitation. They closed in the appeal to arms. They declared themselves independent states. They confederated together into one great republic; thus securing to every State the benefit of an union of their whole force. In each State separately a new form of government was established. Of ours particularly the following are the outlines: The executive powers are lodged in the hands of a governor, chosen annually, and incapable of acting more than three years in seven. He is assisted by a council of eight members. The judiciary powers are divided among several courts, as will be hereafter explained. Legislation is exercised by two houses of assembly, the one called the house of Delegates, composed of two members from each county, chosen annually by the citizens, possessing an estate for life in one hundred acres of uninhabited land, or twenty-five acres with a house on it, or in a house or lot in some town: the other called the Senate, consisting of twenty-four members, chosen quadrenially by the same electors, who for this purpose are distributed into twenty-four districts. The concurrence of both houses is necessary to the passage of a law. They have the appointment of the governor and council, the judges of the superior courts, auditors, attorney-general, treasurer, register of the land office, and delegates to Congress. As the dismemberment of the State had never had its confirmation, but, on the contrary, had always been the subject of protestation and complaint, that it might never be in our own power to raise scruples on that subject, or to disturb the harmony of our new confederacy, the grants to Maryland, Pennsylvania, and the two Carolinas, were ratified.

This constitution was formed when we were new and unexperienced in the science of government. It was the first, too, which was formed in the whole United States. No wonder then that time and trial have discovered very capital defects in it.

1. The majority of the men in the State, who pay and fight for its support, are unrepresented in the legislature, the roll of freeholders entitled to vote not including generally the half of those on the roll of the militia, or of the tax-gatherers.

2. Among those who share the representation, the shares are very unequal. Thus the county of Warwick, with only one hundred fighting men, has an equal representation with the county of Loudon, which has one thousand seven hundred and forty-six. So that every man in Warwick has as much influence in the government as seventeen men in Loudon. But lest it should be thought that an equal interspersion of small among large counties, through the whole State, may prevent any danger of injury to particular parts of it, we will divide it into districts, and show the proportions of land, of fighting men, and of representation in each. . . .[1]

3. The senate is, by its constitution, too homogeneous with the house of delegates. Being chosen by the same electors, at the same time, and out of the same subjects, the choice falls of course on men of the same description. The purpose of establishing different houses of legislation is to introduce the influence of different interests or different principles. Thus in Great Britain it is said their constitution relies on the house of commons for honesty, and the lords for wisdom; which would be a rational reliance, if honesty were to be bought with money, and if wisdom were hereditary. In some of the American States, the delegates and senators are so chosen, as that the first represent the persons, and the second the property of the State. But with us, wealth and wisdom have equal chance for admission into both houses. We do not, therefore, derive from the separation of our legislature into two houses, those benefits which a proper complication of principles are capable of producing, and those which alone can compensate the evils which may be produced by their dissensions

4. All the powers of government, legislative, executive, and judiciary, result to the legislative body. The concentrating these in the same hands is precisely the definition of despotic government. It will be no allevia-

[1]A table, compiled by Jefferson, is omitted here.

tion that these powers will be exercised by a plurality of hands, and not by a single one. One hundred and seventy-three despots would surely be as oppressive as one. Let those who doubt it turn their eyes on the republic of Venice. As little will it avail us that they are chosen by ourselves. An *elective despotism* was not the government we fought for, but one which should not only be founded on free principles, but in which the powers of government should be so divided and balanced among several bodies of magistracy, as that no one could transcend their legal limits, without being effectually checked and restrained by the others. For this reason that convention which passed the ordinance of government, laid its foundation on this basis, that the legislative, executive, and judiciary departments should be separate and distinct, so that no person should exercise the powers of more than one of them at the same time. But no barrier was provided between these several powers. The judiciary and executive members were left dependent on the legislative, for their subsistence in office, and some of them for their continuance in it. If, therefore, the legislature assumes executive and judiciary powers, no opposition is likely to be made; nor, if made, can it be effectual; because in that case they may put their proceedings into the form of an act of assembly, which will render them obligatory on the other branches. They have, accordingly, in many instances, decided rights which should have been left to judiciary controversy; and the direction of the executive, during the whole time of their session, is becoming habitual and familiar. And this is done with no ill intention. The views of the present members are perfectly upright. When they are led out of their regular province, it is by art in others, and inadvertance in themselves. And this will probably be the case for some time to come. But it will not be a very long time. Mankind soon learn to make interested uses of every right and power which they possess, or may assume. The public money and public liberty, intended to have been deposited with three branches of magistracy, but found inadvertently to be in the hands of one only, will soon be discovered to be sources of wealth and dominion to those who hold them; distinguished, too, by this tempting circumstance, that they are the instrument, as well as the object of acquisition. With money we will get men, said Cæsar, and with men we will get money. Nor should our assembly be deluded by the integrity of their own purposes, and conclude that these unlimited powers will never be abused, because themselves are not disposed to abuse them. They should look forward to a time, and that not a distant one, when a corruption in this, as in the country from which we derive our origin, will have seized the heads of government, and be spread by them through the body of the people; when they will purchase the voices of the people, and make them pay the price. Human nature is the same on every side of the Atlantic, and will be alike influenced by the same causes. The time to guard against corruption and tyranny, is before they shall have gotten hold of us. It is better to keep the wolf out of the fold, than to trust to drawing his teeth and claws after he shall have entered. To render these considerations the more cogent, we must observe in addition:

5. That the ordinary legislature may alter the constitution itself. On the discontinuance of assemblies, it became necessary to substitute in their place some other body, competent to the ordinary business of government, and to the calling forth the powers of the State for the maintenance of our opposition to Great Britain. Conventions were therefore introduced, consisting of two delegates from each county, meeting together and forming one house, on the plan of the former house of burgesses, to whose places they succeeded. These were at first chosen anew for every particular session. But in March 1775, they recommended to the people to choose a convention, which should continue in office a year. This was done, accordingly, in April 1775, and in the July following that convention passed an ordinance for the election of delegates in the month of April annually. It is well known, that in July 1775, a separation from Great Britain and establishment of republican government, had never yet entered into any person's mind. A convention, therefore, chosen under that ordinance, cannot be said to have been chosen for the purposes which certainly did not exist in the minds of those who passed it. Under this ordinance, at the annual election in April 1776, a convention for the year was chosen. Independence, and the establishment of a new form of government, were not even yet the objects of the people at large. One extract from the pamphlet called Common Sense had appeared in the Virginia papers in February, and copies of the pamphlet itself had got in a few hands. But the idea had not been opened to the mass of the people in April, much less can it be said that they had made up their minds in its favor.

So that the electors of April 1776, no more than the legislators of July 1775, not thinking of independence and a permanent republic, could not mean to vest in these delegates powers of establishing them, or any authorities other than those of the ordinary legislature. So far as a temporary organization of government was necessary to render our opposition energetic, so far their organization was valid. But they received in their creation no powers but what were given to every legislature before and since. They could not, therefore, pass an act transcendent to the powers of other legislatures. If the present assembly pass an act, and declare it shall be irrevocable by subsequent assemblies, the declaration is merely void, and the act repealable, as other acts are. So far, and no farther authorized, they organized the government by the ordinance entitled a constitution or form of government. It pretends to no higher authority than the other ordinances of the same session; it does not say that it shall be perpetual; that it shall be unalterable by other legislatures; that it shall be transcendent above the powers of those who they knew would have equal power with themselves. Not only the silence of the instrument is a proof they thought it would be alterable, but their own practice also; for this very convention, meeting as a house of delegates in general assembly with the Senate in the autumn of that year, passed acts of assembly in contradiction to their ordinance of government; and every assembly from that time to this has done the same. I am safe, therefore, in the position that the constitution itself is alterable by the ordinary legislature. Though this opinion seems founded on the first elements of common sense, yet is the contrary maintained by some persons. 1. Because, say they, the conventions were vested with every power necessary to make effectual opposition to Great Britain. But to complete this argument, they must go on, and say further, that effectual opposition could not be made to Great Britain without establishing a form of government perpetual and unalterable by the legislature; which is not true. An opposition which at some time or other was to come to an end, could not need a perpetual institution to carry it on; and a government amendable as its defects should be discovered, was as likely to make effectual resistance, as one that should be unalterably wrong. Besides, the assemblies were as much vested with all powers requisite for resistance as the conventions were. If, therefore, these powers included that of

modelling the form of government in the one case, they did so in the
other. The assemblies then as well as the conventions may model the
government; that is, they may alter the ordinance of government. 2.
They urge, that if the convention had meant that this instrument
should be alterable, as their other ordinances were, they would have
called it an ordinance; but they have called it a *constitution*, which, *ex
vi termini*, means "an act above the power of the ordinary legislature."
I answer that *constitutio, constitutium, statutum, lex,* are convertible
terms. . . . Thus in the statute 25 Hen. VIII. c. 19, § 1, *"Constitutions
and ordinances"* are used as synonymous. The term *constitution* has
many other significations in physics and politics; but in jurisprudence,
whenever it is applied to any act of the legislature, it invariably means
a statute, law, or ordinance which is the present case. No inference
then of a different meaning can be drawn from the adoption of this
title; on the contrary, we might conclude that, by their affixing to it a
term synonymous with ordinance, or statute, they meant it to be an
ordinance, or statute. But of what consequence is their meaning, where
their power is denied? If they meant to do more than they had power
to do, did this give them power? It is not the name, but the authority
that renders an act obligatory. . . . To get rid of the magic supposed
to be in the word *constitution,* let us translate it into its definition as
given by those who think it above the power of the law; and let us suppose the convention, instead of saying, "We the ordinary legislature,
establish a *constitution,"* had said, "We the ordinary legislature, establish an act *above the power of the ordinary legislature."* Does not this
expose the absurdity of the attempt? 3. But, say they, the people have
acquiesced, and this has given it an authority superior to the laws. It
is true that the people did not rebel against it; and was that a time for
the people to rise in rebellion? Should a prudent acquiescence, at a critical time, be construed into a confirmation of every illegal thing done
during that period? Besides, why should they rebel? At an annual election they had chosen delegates for the year, to exercise the ordinary
powers of legislation, and to manage the great contest in which they
were engaged. These delegates thought the contest would be best managed by an organized government. They therefore, among others,
passed an ordinance of government. They did not presume to call it
perpetual and unalterable. They well knew they had no power to make

it so; that our choice of them had been for no such purpose, and at a time when we could have no such purpose in contemplation. Had an unalterable form of government been meditated, perhaps we should have chosen a different set of people. There was no cause then for the people to rise in rebellion. But to what dangerous lengths will this argument lead? Did the acquiescence of the colonies under the various acts of power exercised by Great Britain in our infant State, confirm these acts, and so far invest them with the authority of the people as to render them unalterable, and our present resistance wrong? On every unauthoritative exercise of power by the legislature must the people rise in rebellion, or their silence be construed into a surrender of that power to them? If so, how many rebellions should we have had already? One certainly for every session of assembly. The other States in the union have been of opinion that to render a form of government unalterable by ordinary acts of assembly, the people must delegate persons with special powers. They have accordingly chosen special conventions to form and fix their governments. The individuals then who maintain the contrary opinion in this country, should have the modesty to suppose it possible that they may be wrong, and the rest of America right. But if there be only a possibility of their being wrong, if only a plausible doubt remains of the validity of the ordinance of government, is it not better to remove that doubt by placing it on a bottom which none will dispute? If they be right we shall only have the unnecessary trouble of meeting once in convention. If they be wrong, they expose us to the hazard of having no fundamental rights at all. True it is, this is no time for deliberating on forms of government. While an enemy is within our bowels, the first object is to expel him. But when this shall be done, when peace shall be established, and leisure given us for intrenching within good forms, the rights for which we have bled, let no man be found indolent enough to decline a little more trouble for placing them beyond the reach of question. If anything more be requisite to produce a conviction of the expediency of calling a convention at a proper season to fix our form of government, let it be the reflection:

6. That the assembly exercises a power of determining the quorum of their own body which may legislate for us. After the establishment of the new form they adhered to the *Lex majoris partis*, founded in

common law as well as common right. It is the natural law of every assembly of men, whose numbers are not fixed by any other law. They continued for some time to require the presence of a majority of their whole number, to pass an act. But the British parliament fixes its own quorum; our former assemblies fixed their own quorum; and one precedent in favor of power is stronger than an hundred against it. The house of delegates, therefore, have lately voted that, during the present dangerous invasion, forty members shall be a house to proceed to business. They have been moved to this by the fear of not being able to collect a house. But this danger could not authorize them to call that a house which was none; and if they may fix it at one number, they may at another, till it loses its fundamental character of being a representative body. As this vote expires with the present invasion, it is probable the former rule will be permitted to revive; because at present no ill is meant. The power, however, of fixing their own quorum has been avowed, and a precedent set. From forty it may be reduced to four, and from four to one; from a house to a committee, from a committee to a chairman or speaker, and thus an oligarchy or monarchy be substituted under forms supposed to be regular. "All bad precedents arise out of good; but where power comes into the hands of the ignorant or the indifferent, that new precedent proceeds from the worthy and the fit to the unworthy and the unfit."[1]

When, therefore, it is considered, that there is no legal obstacle to the assumption by the assembly of all the powers legislative, executive, and judiciary, and that these may come to the hands of the smallest rag of delegation, surely the people will say, and their representatives, while yet they have honest representatives, will advise them to say, that they will not acknowledge as laws any acts not considered and assented to by the major part of their delegates.

In enumerating the defects of the Constitution, it would be wrong to count among them what is only the error of particular persons. In December 1776, our circumstances being much distressed, it was proposed in the house of delegates to create a *dictator*, invested with every power legislative, executive, and judiciary, civil and military, of life and

---

[1] In Jefferson's text this is given in Latin.

of death, over our persons and over our properties; and in June 1781, again under calamity, the same proposition was repeated, and wanted a few votes only of being passed. One who entered into this contest from a pure love of liberty, and a sense of injured rights, who determined to make every sacrifice, and to meet every danger, for the re-establishment of those rights on a firm basis, who did not mean to expend his blood and substance for the wretched purpose of changing this matter for that, but to place the powers of governing him in a plurality of hands of his own choice, so that the corrupt will of no one man might in future oppress him, must stand confounded and dismayed when he is told, that a considerable portion of that plurality had mediated the surrender of them into a single hand, and, in lieu of a limited monarchy, to deliver him over to a despotic one! How must we find his efforts and sacrifices abused and baffled, if he may still, by a single vote, be laid prostrate at the feet of one man! In God's name, from whence have they derived this power? Is it from our ancient laws? None such can be produced. Is it from any principle in our new Constitution expressed or implied? Every lineament expressed or implied, is in full opposition to it. Its fundamental principle is, that the State shall be governed as a commonwealth. It provides a republican organization, proscribes under the name of *prerogative* the exercise of all powers undefined by the laws; places on this basis the whole system of our laws; and by consolidating them together, chooses that they should be left to stand or fall together, never providing for any circumstances, nor admitting that such could arise, wherein either should be suspended; no, not for a moment. Our ancient laws expressly declare, that those who are but delegates themselves shall not delegate to others powers which require judgment and integrity in their exercise. Or was this proposition moved on a supposed right in the movers, of abandoning their posts in a moment of distress? The same laws forbid the abandonment of that post, even on ordinary occasions; and much more a transfer of their powers into other hands and other forms, without consulting the people. They never admit the idea that these, like sheep or cattle, may be given from hand to hand without an appeal to their own will. Was it from the necessity of the case? Necessities which dissolve a government, do not convey its authority to an oligarchy or a monarchy. They throw back, into the hands of the people, the powers they had delegated, and leave them as individuals to shift for themselves. A leader may offer, but not impose himself, nor be imposed on them. Much less can their necks be submitted to his sword, their breath to be held at his will or caprice. The necessity which should operate these tremendous effects should at least be palpable and irresistible. Yet in both instances, where it was feared, or pretended with us, it was belied by the event. It was belied, too, by the preceding experience of our sister States, several of whom had grappled through greater difficulties without abandoning their forms of government. When the proposition was first made, Massachusetts had found even the government of committees sufficient to carry them through an invasion. But we at the time of that proposition, were under no invasion. When the second was made, there had been added to this example those of Rhode Island, New York, New Jersey, and Pennsylvania, in all of which the republican form had been found equal to the task of carrying them through the severest trials. In this State alone did there exist so little virtue, that fear was to be fixed in the hearts of the people, and to become the motive of their exertions, and principle of their government? The very thought alone was treason against the people; was treason against mankind in general; as riveting forever the chains which bow down their necks, by giving to their oppressors a proof, which they would have trumpeted through the universe, of the imbecility of republican government, in times of pressing danger, to shield them from harm. Those who assume the right of giving away the reins of government in any case, must be sure that the herd, whom they hand on to the rods and hatchet of the dictator, will lay their necks on the block when they shall nod to them. But if our assemblies supposed such a recognition in the people, I hope they mistook their character. I am of opinion, that the government, instead of being braced and invigorated for greater exertions under their difficulties, would have been thrown back upon the bungling machinery of county committees for administration, till a convention could have been called, and its wheels again set into regular motion. What a cruel moment was this for creating such an embarrassment, for putting to the proof the attachment of our countrymen to republican government! Those who meant well, of the advocates of this measure, (and most of them meant well, for I know them personally, had been their fellow-laborer in the common cause, and had often proved the purity of their principles,) had been seduced in their judgment by the example of an ancient republic, whose constitution and circumstances were fundamentally different. They had sought this precedent in the history of Rome, where alone it was to be found, and where at length, too, it had proved fatal. They had taken it from a republic rent by the most bitter factions and tumults, where the government was of a heavy-handed unfeeling aristocracy, over a people ferocious, and rendered desperate by poverty and wretchedness; tumults which could not be allayed under the most trying circumstances, but by the omnipotent hand of a single despot. Their constitution, therefore, allowed a temporary tyrant to be erected, under the name of a dictator; and that temporary tyrant, after a few examples, became perpetual. They misapplied this precedent to a people mild in their dispositions, patient under their trial, united for the public liberty, and affectionate to their leaders. But if from the constitution of the Roman government there resulted to their senate a power of submitting all their rights to the will of one man, does it follow that the assembly of Virginia have the same authority? What clause in our constitution has substituted that of Rome, by way of residuary provision, for all cases not otherwise provided for? Or if they may step *ad libitum* into any other form of government for precedents to rule us by, for what oppression may not a precedent be found in this world of the *ballum omnium in omnia?* Searching for the foundations of this proposition, I can find none which may pretend a color of right or reason but the defect before developed, that there being no barrier between the lgislative, executive, and judiciary departments, the legislature may seize the whole; that having seized it, and possessing a right to fix their own quorum, they may reduce that quorum to one, whom they may call a chairman, speaker, dictator, or by any other name they please. Our situation is indeed perilous, and I hope my countrymen will be sensible of it, and will apply, at a proper season, the proper remedy; which is a convention to fix the constitution, to amend its defects, to bind up the several branches of government by certain laws, which, when they transgress, their acts shall become nullities; to render unnecessary an appeal to the people, or in other words a rebellion, on every infraction of their rights, on the peril that their acquiescence shall be construed into an intention to surrender those rights.

QUERY XIV

The administration of justice and the description of the laws?

The State is divided into counties. In every county are appointed magistrates, called justices of the peace, usually from eight to thirty or forty in number, in proportion to the size of the county, of the most discreet and honest inhabitants. They are nominated by their fellows, but commissioned by the governor, and act without reward. These magistrates have jurisdiction both criminal and civil. If the question before them be a question of law only, they decide on it themselves; but if it be of fact, or of fact and law combined, it must be referred to a jury. In the latter case, of a combination of law and fact, it is usual for the jurors to decide the fact, and to refer the law arising on it to the decision of the judges. But this division of the subject lies with their discretion only. And if the question relate to any point of public liberty, or if it be one of those in which the judges may be suspected of bias, the jury undertake to decide both law and fact. If they be mistaken, a decision against right, which is casual only, is less dangerous to the State, and less afflicting to the loser, than one which makes part of a regular and uniform system. In truth, it is better to toss up cross and pile in a cause, than to refer it to a judge whose mind is warped by any motive whatever, in that particular case. But the common sense of twelve honest men gives still a better chance of just decision, than the hazard of cross and pile. These judges execute their process by the sheriff or coroner of the county, or by constables of their own appointment. If any free person commit an offense against the commonwealth, if it be below the degree of felony, he is bound by a justice to appear before their court, to answer it on an indictment or information. If it amount to felony, he is committed to jail; a court of these justices is called; if they on examination think him guilty, they send him to the jail of the general court, before which court he is to be tried first by a grand jury of twenty-four, of whom thirteen must concur in opinion; if they find him guilty, he is then tried by a jury of twelve men of the county where the offence was committed, and by their verdict, which must be unanimous, he is acquitted or condemned without appeal. If the criminal be a slave, the trial by the county court is final. In every case, however, except that of high treason, there resides in the governor a power of pardon. In high treason the pardon can only flow from the general assembly. In civil matters these justices have jurisdiction in all cases of whatever value, not appertaining to the department of the admiralty. This jurisdiction is twofold. If the matter in dispute be of less value than four dollars and one-sixth, a single member may try it at any time and place within his county, and may award execution on the goods of the party cast. If it be of that or greater value, it is determinable before the county court, which consists of four at the least of those justices and assembles at the courthouse of the county on a certain day in every month. From their determination, if the matter be of the value of ten pounds sterling, or concern the title or bounds of land, an appeal lies to one of the superior courts.

. . . .

The laws of England seem to have been adopted by consent of the settlers, which might easily enough be done whilst they were few and living all together. Of such adoption, however, we have no other proof than their practice till the year 1661, when they were expressly adopted by an act of the assembly, except so far as "a difference of condition" rendered them inapplicable. Under this adoption, the rule, in our courts of judicature was, that the common law of England, and the general statutes previous to the fourth of James, were in force here; but that no subsequent statutes were, *unless we were named in them*, said the judges and other partisans of the crown, but *named or not named*, said those who reflected freely. It will be unnecessary to attempt a description of the laws of England, as that may be found in English publications. To those which were established here, by the adoption of the legislature, have been since added a number of acts of assembly passed during the monarchy, and ordinances of convention and acts of assembly enacted since the establishment of the republic. The following variations from the British model are perhaps worthy of being specified:

Debtors unable to pay their debts, and making faithful delivery of their whole effects, are released from confinement, and their persons forever discharged from restraint for such previous debts; but any property they may afterwards acquire will be subject to their creditors.

The poor unable to support themselves, are maintained by an assessment on the tytheable persons in their parish. This assessment is levied and administered by twelve persons in each parish, called vestrymen, originally chosen by the housekeepers of the parish, but afterwards filling vacancies in their own body by their own choice. These are usually the most discreet farmers, so distributed through their parish, that every part of it may be under the immediate eye of some one of them. They are well acquainted with the details and economy of private life, and they find sufficient inducements to execute their charge well, in their philanthropy, in the approbation of their neighbors, and the distinction which that gives them. The poor who have neither property, friends, nor strength to labor, are boarded in the houses of good farmers, to whom a stipulated sum is annually paid. To those who are able to help themselves a little, or have friends from whom they derive some succors, inadequate however to their full maintenance, supplementary aids are given which enable them to live comfortably in their own houses, or in the houses of their friends. Vagabonds without visible property or vocation, are placed in work houses, where they are well clothed, fed, lodged and made to labor. Nearly the same method of providing for the poor prevails through all our States; and from Savannah to Portsmouth you will seldom meet a beggar. In the large towns, indeed, they sometimes present themselves. These are usually foreigners, who have never obtained a settlement in any parish. I never yet saw a native American begging in the streets or highways. A subsistence is easily gained here; and if, by misfortunes, they are thrown on the charities of the world, those provided by their own country are so comfortable and so certain, that they never think of relinquishing them to become strolling beggars. Their situation too, when sick, in the family of a good farmer, where every member is emulous to do them kind offices, where they are visited by all the neighbors, who bring them the little rarities which their sickly appetites may crave, and who take by rotation the nightly watch over them, when their condition requires it, is without comparison better than in a general hospital, where the sick, the dying and the dead are crammed together in the same rooms, and often in the same beds. The disadvantages, inseparable from general hospitals, are such as can never be counterpoised by all the regularities of medicine and regimen. Nature and kind nursing save a much greater proportion in our plain way, at a smaller expense, and with less abuse. One branch only of hospital institutions is wanting with us; that is, a general establishment for those laboring under difficult cases of chirurgery. The aids of this art are not equivocal. But an able chirurgeon cannot be had in every parish. Such a receptacle should therefore be provided for those patients; but no others should be admitted.

Marriages must be solemnized either on special license, granted by the first magistrate of the county, on proof of the consent of the parent or guardian of either party under age, or after solemn publication, on three several Sundays, at some place of religious worship, in the parishes where the parties reside. The act of solemnization may be by the minister of any society of Christians, who shall have been previously licensed for this purpose by the court of the county. Quakers and Menonists, however, are exempted from all these conditions, and marriage among them is to be solemnized by the society itself.

A foreigner of any nation, not in open war with us, becomes naturalized by removing to the State to reside, and taking an oath of fidelity; and thereupon acquires every right of a native citizen; and citizens may divest themselves of that character, by declaring, by solemn deed, or in open court, that they mean to expatriate themselves, and no longer to be citizens of this State.

Conveyances of land must be registered in the court of the county wherein they lie, or in the general court, or they are void, as to creditors, and subsequent purchasers.

Slaves pass by descent and dower as lands do. Where the descent is from a parent, the heir is bound to pay an equal share of their value in money to each of their brothers and sisters.

Slaves, as well as lands, were entailable during the monarchy; but by an act of the first republican assembly, all donees in tail, present and future, were vested with the absolute dominion of the entailed subject.

Bills of exchange, being protested, carry ten per cent interest from their date.

No person is allowed, in any other case, to take more than five per cent per annum simple interest for the loan of moneys.

Gaming debts are made void, and moneys actually paid to discharge such debts (if they exceed forty shillings) may be recovered by the payer within three months, or by any other person afterwards.

Tobacco, flour, beef, pork, tar, pitch, and turpentine must be inspected by persons publicly appointed, before they can be exported.

The erecting iron-works and mills is encouraged by many privileges; with necessary cautions however to prevent their dams from obstructing the navigation of the water-courses. The general assembly have on several occasions shown a great desire to encourage the opening the great falls of James and Potomac rivers. As yet, however, neither of these have been effected.

The laws have also descended to the preservation and improvement of the races of useful animals, such as horses, cattle, deer; to the extirpation of those which are noxious, as wolves, squirrels, crows, blackbirds; and to the guarding our citizens against infectious disorders, by obliging suspected vessels coming into the State, to perform quarantine, and by regulating the conduct of persons having such disorders within the State.

The mode of acquiring lands, in the earliest times of our settlement, was by petition to the general assembly. If the lands prayed for were already cleared of the Indian title, and the assembly thought the prayer reasonable, they passed the property by their vote to the petitioner. But if they had not yet been ceded by the Indians, it was necessary that the petitioner should previously purchase their right. This purchase the assembly verified, by inquiries of the Indian proprietors; and being satisfied of its reality and fairness, proceeded further to examine the reasonableness of the petition, and its consistence with policy; and according to the result, either granted or rejected the petition. The company also sometimes, though very rarely, granted lands, independently of the general assembly. As the colony increased, and individual applications for land multiplied, it was found to give too much occupation to the general assembly to inquire into and execute the grant in every special case. They therefore thought it better to establish general rules, according to which all grants should be made, and to leave to the governor the execution of them, under these rules. This they did by what have been usually called the land laws, amending them from time to time, as their defects were developed. According to these laws, when an individual wished a portion of unappropriated land, he was to locate and survey it by a public officer, appointed for that purpose, its breadth was to bear a certain proportion to its length: the grant was to be executed by the governor; and the lands were to be improved in a certain manner, within a given time. From these regulations there resulted to the State a sole and exclusive power of taking conveyances of the Indian right of soil; since, according to them, an Indian conveyance alone could give no right to an individual, which the laws would acknowledge. The State, or the crown, thereafter, made general purchases of the Indians from time to time, and the governor parcelled them out by special grants, conformable to the rules before described, which it was not in his power, or in that of the crown, to dispense with. Grants, unaccompanied by their proper legal circumstances, were set aside regularly by *fieri facies*, or by bill in chancery. Since the establishment of our new Government, this order of things is but little changed. An individual, wishing to appropriate to himself lands still unappropriated by any other, pays to the public treasurer a sum of money proportioned to the quantity he wants. He carries the treasurer's receipt to the auditors of public accounts, who thereupon debit the treasurer with the sum, and order the register of the land-office to give the party a warrant for his land. With this warrant from the register, he goes to the surveyor of the county where the land lies on which he has cast his eye. The surveyor lays it off for him, gives him its exact description, in the form of a certificate, which certificate he returns to the land-office, where a grant is made out, and is signed by the governor. This vests in him a perfect dominion in his lands, transmissible to whom he pleases by deed or will, or by descent to his heirs, if he die intestate.

Many of the laws which were in force during the monarchy being relative merely to that form of government, or inculcating principles inconsistent with republicanism, the first assembly which met after the establishment of the commonwealth appointed a committee to revise the whole code, to reduce it into proper form and volume, and report it to the assembly. This work has been executed by three gentlemen, and reported;[1] but probably will not be taken up till a restoration of peace shall leave to the legislature leisure to go through such a work.

The plan of the revisal was this. The common law of England, by which is meant, that part of the English law which was anterior to the

---

[1] This revisal was performed by Jefferson, Wythe, and Pendleton.

date of the oldest statutes extant, is made the basis of the work. It was thought dangerous to attempt to reduce it to a text; it was therefore left to be collected from the usual monuments of it. Necessary alterations in that, and so much of the whole body of the British statutes, and of acts of assembly, as were thought proper to be retained, were digested into one hundred and twenty-six new acts, in which simplicity of style was aimed at, as far as was safe. The following are the most remarkable alterations proposed:

To change the rules of descent, so as that the lands of any person dying intestate shall be divisible equally among all his children, or other representatives, in equal degree.

To make slaves distributable among the next of kin, as other movables.

To have all public expenses, whether of the general treasury, or of a parish or county, (as for the maintenance of the poor, building bridges, courthouses, &c.,) supplied by assessment on the citizens, in proportion to their property.

To hire undertakers for keeping the public roads in repair and indemnify individuals through whose lands new roads shall be opened.

To define with precision the rules whereby aliens should become citizens, and citizens make themselves aliens.

To establish religious freedom on the broadest bottom.

To emancipate all slaves born after the passing the act. The bill reported by the revisers does not itself contain this proposition; but an amendment containing it was prepared, to be offered to the legislature whenever the bill should be taken up, and farther directing, that they should continue with their parents to a certain age, then to be brought up, at the public expense, to tillage, arts, or sciences, according to their geniuses, till the females should be eighteen, and the males twenty-one years of age, when they should be colonized to such place as the circumstances of the time should render most proper, sending them out with arms, implements of household and of the handicraft arts, seeds, pairs of the useful domestic animals, &c., to declare them a free and independent people, and extend to them our alliance and protection, till they have acquired strength; and to send vessels at the same time to other parts of the world for an equal number of white inhabitants; to induce them to migrate hither proper encouragements were to be proposed. It will probably be asked, Why not retain and incorporate the blacks into the State, and thus save the expense of supplying by importation of white settlers, the vacancies they will leave? Deep-rooted prejudices entertained by the whites; ten thousand recollections, by the blacks, of the injuries they have sustained; new provocations; the real distinctions which nature has made; and many other circumstances, will divide us into parties, and produce convulsions, which will probably never end but in the extermination of the one or the other race. To these objections, which are political, may be added others, which are physical and moral. The first difference which strikes us is that of color. Whether the black of the negro resides in the reticular membrane between the skin and scarf-skin, or in the scarf-skin itself; whether it proceeds from the color of the blood, the color of the bile, or from that of some other secretion, the difference is fixed in nature, and is as real as if its seat and cause were better known to us. And is this difference of no importance? Is it not the foundation of a greater or less share of beauty in the two races? Are not the fine mixtures of red and white, the expressions of every passion by greater or less suffusions of color in the one, preferable to that eternal monotony, which reigns in the countenances, that immovable veil of black which covers the emotions of the other race? Add to these, flowing hair, a more elegant symmetry of form, their own judgment in favor of the whites, declared by their preference of them, as uniformly as is the preference of the Oran-utan for the black woman over those of his own species. The circumstance of superior beauty, is thought worthy attention in the propagation of our horses, dogs, and other domestic animals; why not in that of man? Besides those of color, figure, and hair, there are other physical distinctions proving a difference of race. They have less hair on the face and body. They secrete less by the kidneys, and more by the glands of the skin, which gives them a very strong and disagreeable odor. This greater degree of transpiration, renders them more tolerant of heat, and less so of cold than the whites. Perhaps, too, a difference of structure in the pulmonary apparatus, which a late ingenious experimentalist has discovered to be the principal regulator of animal heat, may have disabled them from extricating, in the act of inspiration, so much of that fluid from the outer air, or obliged them in expiration, to part with more of it. They seem to require less sleep. A black after hard labor through the day, will be induced by the slightest amusements to sit up till midnight, or later, though knowing he must be out with first dawn of the morning. They are at least as brave, and more adventuresome. But this may perhaps proceed from a want of forethought, which prevents their seeing a danger till it be present. When present, they do not go through it with more coolness or steadiness than the whites. They are more ardent after their female; but love seems with them to be more an eager desire, than a tender delicate mixture of sentiment and sensation. Their griefs are transient. Those numberless afflictions, which render it doubtful whether heaven has given life to us in mercy or in wrath, are less felt, and sooner forgotten with them. In general, their existence appears to participate more of sensation than reflection. To this must be ascribed their disposition to sleep when abstracted from their diversions, and unemployed in labor. An animal whose body is at rest, and who does not reflect must be disposed to sleep of course. Comparing them by their faculties of memory, reason, and imagination, it appears to me that in memory they are equal to the whites; in reason much inferior, as I think one could scarcely be found capable of tracing and comprehending the investigations of Euclid; and that in imagination they are dull, tasteless, and anomalous. It would be unfair to follow them to Africa for this investigation. We will consider them here, on the same stage with the whites, and where the facts are not apocryphal on which a judgment is to be formed. It will be right to make great allowances for the difference of condition, of education, of conversation, of the sphere in which they move. Many millions of them have been brought to, and born in America. Most of them, indeed, have been confined to tillage, to their own homes, and their own society; yet many have been so situated, that they might have availed themselves of the conversation of their masters; many have been brought up to the handicraft arts, and from that circumstance have always been associated with the whites. Some have been liberally educated, and all have lived in countries where the arts and sciences are cultivated to a considerable degree, and all have had before their eyes samples of the best works from abroad. The Indians, with no advantages of this kind, will often carve figures on their pages not destitute of design and merit. They will crayon out an animal, a plant, or a country, so as to prove the existence of a germ in their minds which only wants cultivation. They astonish you with strokes of the most sublime oratory; such as prove their reason and sentiment strong, their imagination glowing and elevated. But never yet could I find that a black had uttered a thought above the level of plain narration; never saw even an elementary trait of painting or sculpture. In music they are more generally gifted than the whites with accurate ears for tune and time, and they have been found capable of imagining a small catch.[1] Whether they will be equal to the composition of a more extensive run of melody, or of complicated harmony, is yet to be proved. Misery is often the parent of the most affecting touches in poetry. Among the blacks is misery enough, God knows, but no poetry. Love is the peculiar oestrum of the poet. Their love is ardent, but it kindles the senses only, not the imagination. Religion, indeed, has produced a Phyllis Whately;[2] but it could not produce a poet. The compositions published under her name are below the dignity of criticism The heroes of the Dunciad are to her, as Hercules to the author of that poem. Ignatius Sancho[3] has approached nearer to merit in composition; yet his letters do more honor to the heart than the head. They breathe the purest effusions of friendship and general philanthropy, and show how great a degree of the latter may be compounded with strong religious zeal. He is often happy in the turn of his compliments, and his style is easy and familiar, except when he affects a Shandean fabrication of words. But his imagination is wild and extravagant, and escapes incessantly from every restraint of reason and taste, and, in the course of its vagaries, leaves a tract of thought as incoherent and eccentric, as is the course of a meteor through the sky. His subjects should often have led him to a process of sober reasoning; yet we find him always substituting sentiment for demonstration. Upon the whole, though we admit him to the first place among those of his own color who have presented themselves to the public judgment, yet when we compare him with the writers of the race among whom he lived and

[1]The instrument proper to them is the Banjar, which they brought hither from Africa, and which is the original of the guitar, its chords being precisely the four lower chords of the guitar. [Jefferson's note.]

[2]Phyllis Wheatley, (correct spelling) whose collected poems were published in London in 1773.

[3]Sancho, born in 1729 on a slaveship, was a longtime resident of England; his *Letters, with Memoirs of his Life* appeared in 1782.

particularly with the epistolary class in which he has taken his own stand, we are compelled to enrol him at the bottom of the column. This criticism supposes the letters published under his name to be genuine, and to have received amendment from no other hand; points which would not be of easy investigation. The improvement of the blacks in body and mind, in the first instance of their mixture with the whites, has been observed by every one, and proves that their inferiority is not the effect merely of their condition of life. We know that among the Romans, about the Augustan age especially, the condition of their slaves was much more deplorable than that of the blacks on the continent of America. The two sexes were confined in separate apartments, because to raise a child cost the master more than to buy one. Cato, for a very restricted indulgence to his slaves in this particular,[1] took from them a certain price. But in this country the slaves multiply as fast as the free inhabitants. Their situation and manners place the commerce between the two sexes almost without restraint. The same Cato, on a principle of economy, always sold his sick and superannuated slaves. He gives it as a standing precept to a master visiting his farm, to sell his old oxen, old wagons, old tools, old and diseased servants, and everything else become useless . . . The American slaves cannot enumerate this among the injuries and insults they receive. It was the common practice to expose in the island Aesculapius, in the Tyber, diseased slaves whose cure was like to become tedious. The emperor Claudius by an edict, gave freedom to such of them as should recover, and first declared that if any person chose to kill rather than to expose them, it should not be deemed homicide. The exposing them is a crime of which no instance has existed with us; and were it to be followed by death, it would be punished capitally. We are told of a certain Vedius Pollio, who, in the presence of Augustus, would have given a slave as food to his fish, for having broken a glass. With the Roman, the regular method of taking the evidence of their slaves was under torture. Here it has been thought better never to resort to their evidence. When a master was murdered, all his slaves, in the same house, or within hearing, were condemned to death. Here punishment falls on the guilty only, and as precise proof is required against him as against a freeman.

[1]Jefferson's footnote omitted.

Yet notwithstanding these and other discouraging circumstances among the Romans, their slaves were often their rarest artists. They excelled too in science, insomuch as to be usually employed as tutors to their master's children. Epictetus, Terence, and Phaedrus, were slaves. But they were of the race of whites. It is not their condition then, but nature, which has produced the distinction. Whether further observation will or will not verify the conjecture, that nature has been less bountiful to them in the endowments of the head, I believe that in those of the heart she will be found to have done them justice. That disposition to theft with which they have been branded, must be ascribed to their situation, and not to any depravity of the moral sense. The man in whose favor no laws of property exist, probably feels himself less bound to respect those made in favor of others. When arguing for ourselves, we lay it down as a fundamental, that laws, to be just, must give a reciprocation of right; that, without this, they are mere arbitrary rules of conduct, founded in force, and not in conscience; and it is a problem which I give to the master to solve, whether the religious precepts against the violation of property were not framed for him as well as his slave? And whether the slave may not as justifiably take a little from one who has taken all from him, as he may slay one who would slay him? That a change in the relations in which a man is placed should change his ideas of moral right or wrong, is neither new, nor peculiar to the color of the blacks. Homer tells us it was so two thousand six hundred years ago.

> Jove fix'd it certain, take whatever day
> Makes man a slave, takes half his worth away.

But the slaves of which Homer speaks were whites. Notwithstanding these considerations which must weaken their respect for the laws of property, we find among them numerous instances of the most rigid integrity, and as many as among their better instructed masters, of benevolence, gratitude and unshaken fidelity. The opinion that they are inferior in the faculties of reason and imagination, must be hazarded with great diffidence. To justify a general conclusion, requires many observations, even where the subject may be submitted to the anatomical knife, to optical glasses, to analysis by fire or by solvents.

How much more then where it is a faculty, not a substance, we are examining; where it eludes the research of all the senses; where the conditions of its existence are various and variously combined; where the effects of those which are present or absent bid defiance to calculation; let me add too, as a circumstance of great tenderness, where our conclusion would degrade a whole race of men from the rank in the scale of beings which their Creator may perhaps have given them. To our reproach it must be said, that though for a century and a half we have had under our eyes the races of black and of red men, they have never yet been viewed by us as subjects of natural history. I advance it, therefore, as a suspicion only, that the blacks, whether originally a distinct race, or made distinct by time and circumstances, are inferior to the whites in the endowments both of body and mind. It is not against experience to suppose that different species of the same genus, or varieties of the same species, may possess different qualifications. Will not a lover of natural history then, one who views the gradations in all the races of animals with the eye of philosophy, excuse an effort to keep those in the department of man as distinct as nature has formed them? This unfortunate difference of color, and perhaps of faculty, is a powerful obstacle to the emancipation of these people. Many of their advocates, while they wish to vindicate the liberty of human nature, are anxious also to preserve its dignity and beauty. Some of these, embarrassed by the question, "What further is to be done with them?" join themselves in opposition with those who are actuated by sordid avarice only. Among the Romans emancipation required but one effort. The slave, when made free, might mix with, without staining the blood of his master. But with us a second is necessary, unknown to history. When freed, he is to be removed beyond the reach of mixture. . . .

Another object of the revisal is to diffuse knowledge more generally through the mass of the people. This bill proposes to lay off every county into small districts of five or six miles square, called hundreds, and in each of them to establish a school for teaching, reading, writing, and arithmetic. The tutor to be supported by the hundred, and every person in it entitled to send their children three years gratis, and as much longer as they please, paying for it. These schools to be under a visitor who is annually to choose the boy of best genius in the school, of those whose parents are too poor to give them further education, and to send him forward to one of the grammar schools, of which twenty are proposed to be erected in different parts of the country, for teaching Greek, Latin, Geography, and the higher branches of numerical arithmetic. Of the boys thus sent in one year, trial is to be made at the grammar schools one or two years, and the best genius of the whole selected, and continued six years, and the residue dismissed. By this means twenty of the best geniuses will be raked from the rubbish annually, and be instructed, at the public expense, so far as the grammar schools go. At the end of six years' instruction, one half are to be discontinued (from among whom the grammar schools will probably be supplied with future masters); and the other half, who are to be chosen for the superiority of their parts and disposition, are to be sent and continued three years in the study of such sciences as they shall choose, at William and Mary College, the plan of which is proposed to be enlarged, as will be hereafter explained, and extended to all the useful sciences. The ultimate result of the whole scheme of education would be the teaching all the children of the State reading, writing, and common arithmetic; turning out ten annually, of superior genius, well taught in Greek, Latin, Geography, and the higher branches of arithmetic; turning out ten others annually, of still superior parts, who, to those branches of learning, shall have added such of the sciences as their genius shall have led them to; the furnishing to the wealthier part of the people convenient schools at which their children may be educated at their own expense. The general objects of this law are to provide an education adapted to the years, to the capacity, and the condition of every one, and directed to their freedom and happiness. Specific details were not proper for the law. These must be the business of the visitors entrusted with its execution. The first stage of this education being the schools of the hundreds, wherein the great mass of the people will receive their instruction, the principal foundations of future order will be laid here. Instead, therefore, of putting the Bible and Testament into the hands of the children at an age when their judgments are not sufficiently matured for religious inquiries, their memories may here be stored with the most useful facts from Grecian, Roman, European and American history. The first elements of morality too may be instilled into their minds; such as, when further devel-

oped as their judgments advance in strength, may teach them how to
work out their own greatest happiness, by showing them that it does
not depend on the condition of life in which chance has placed them,
but is always the result of a good conscience, good health, occupation,
and freedom in all just pursuits. Those whom either the wealth of their
parents or the adoption of the State shall destine to higher degrees of
learning, will go on to the grammar schools, which constitute the next
stage, there to be instructed in the languages. The learning Greek and
Latin, I am told, is going into disuse in Europe. I know not what their
manners and occupations may call for; but it would be very ill-judged
in us to follow their example in this instance. There is a certain period
of life, say from eight to fifteen or sixteen years of age, when the mind
like the body is not yet firm enough for laborious and close operations.
If applied to such, it falls an early victim to premature exertion;
exhibiting, indeed, at first, in these young and tender subjects, the flattering appearance of their being men while they are yet children, but
ending in reducing them to be children when they should be men. The
memory is then most susceptible and tenacious of impressions; and the
learning of languages being chiefly a work of memory, it seems precisely fitted to the powers of this period, which is long enough, too, for
acquiring the most useful languages, ancient and modern. I do not pretend that language is science. It is only an instrument for the attainment of science. But that time is not lost which is employed in
providing tools for future operation; more especially as in this case the
books put into the hands of the youth for this purpose may be such
as will at the same time impress their minds with useful facts and good
principles. If this period be suffered to pass in idleness, the mind
becomes lethargic and impotent, as would the body it inhabits if unexercised during the same time. The sympathy between body and mind
during their rise, progress and decline, is too strict and obvious to
endanger our being missed while we reason from the one to the other.
As soon as they are of sufficient age, it is supposed they will be sent on
from the grammar schools to the university, which constitutes our
third and last stage, there to study those sciences which may be
adapted to their views. By that part of our plan which prescribes the
selection of the youths of genius from among the classes of the poor,
we hope to avail the State of those talents which nature has sown as

liberally among the poor as the rich, but which perish without use, if not sought for and cultivated. But of the views of this law none is more important, none more legitimate, than that of rendering the people the safe, as they are the ultimate, guardians of their own liberty. For this purpose the reading in the first stage, where *they* will receive their whole education, is proposed, as has been said, to be chiefly historical. History, by apprizing them of the past, will enable them to judge of the future; it will avail them of the experience of other times and other nations; it will qualify them as judges of the actions and designs of men; it will enable them to know ambition under every disguise it may assume; and knowing it, to defeat its views. In every government on earth is some trace of human weakness, some germ of corruption and degeneracy, which cunning will discover, and wickedness insensibly open, cultivate and improve. Every government degenerates when trusted to the rulers of the people alone. The people themselves therefore are its only safe depositories. And to render even them safe, their minds must be improved to a certain degree. This indeed is not all that is necessary, though it be essentially necessary. An amendment of our constitution must here come in aid of the public education. The influence over government must be shared among all the people. If every individual which composes their mass participates of the ultimate authority, the government will be safe; because the corrupting the whole mass will exceed any private resources of wealth; and public ones cannot be provided but by levies on the people. In this case every man would have to pay his own price. The government of Great Britain has been corrupted, because but one man in ten has a right to vote for members of parliament. The sellers of the government, therefore, get nine-tenths of their price clear. It has been thought that corruption is restrained by confining the right of suffrage to a few of the wealthier of the people; but it would be more effectually restrained by an extension of that right to such members as would bid defiance to the means of corruption.

Lastly, it is proposed, by a bill in this revisal, to begin a public library and gallery, by laying out a certain sum annually in books, paintings, and statues.

QUERY XV

The Colleges and Public Establishments, the Roads, Buildings, &c.

The college of William and Mary is the only public seminary of learning in this State. It was founded in the time of king William and queen Mary, who granted to it twenty thousand acres of land, and a penny a pound duty on certain tobaccoes exported from Virginia and Maryland, which had been levied by the statute of 25 Car. II. The assembly also gave it, by temporary laws, a duty on liquors imported, and skins and furs exported. From these resources it received upwards of three thousand pounds *communibus annis*. The buildings are of brick, sufficient for an indifferent accommodation of perhaps an hundred students. By its charter it was to be under the government of twenty visitors, who were to be its legislators, and to have a president and six professors, who were incorporated. It was allowed a representative in the general assembly. Under this charter, a professorship of the Greek and Latin languages, a professorship of mathematics, one of moral philosophy, and two of divinity, were established. To these were annexed, for a sixth professorship, a considerable donation by Mr. Boyle, of England, for the instruction of the Indians, and their conversion to Christianity. This was called the professorship of Brafferton, from an estate of that name in England, purchased with the monies given. The admission of the learners of Latin and Greek filled the college with children. This rendering it disagreeable and degrading to young gentlemen already prepared for entering on the sciences, they were discouraged from resorting to it, and thus the schools for mathematics and moral philosophy, which might have been of some service, became of very little. The revenues, too, were exhausted in accommodating those who came only to acquire the rudiments of science. After the present revolution, the visitors, having no power to change those circumstances in the constitution of the college which were fixed by the charter, and being therefore confined in the number of the professorships, undertook to change the objects of the professorships. They excluded the two schools for divinity, and that for the Greek and Latin languages, and substituted others; so that at present they stand thus:

A Professorship for Law and Police;

    Anatomy and Medicine;

A Natural Philosophy and Mathematics;
   Moral Philosophy, the Law of Nature and Nations, the Fine
      Arts;
   Modern Languages;
   For the Brafferton.

And it is proposed, so soon as the legislature shall have leisure to take up this subject, to desire authority from them to increase the number of professorships, as well for the purpose of subdividing those already instituted, as of adding others for other branches of science. To the professorships usually established in the universities of Europe, it would seem proper to add one for the ancient languages and literature of the north, on account of their connection with our own language, laws, customs, and history. The purposes of the Brafferton institution would be better answered by maintaining a perpetual mission among the Indian tribes, the object of which, besides instructing them in the principles of Christianity, as the founder requires, should be to collect their traditions, laws, customs, languages, and other circumstances which might lead to a discovery of their relation with one another, or descent from other nations. When these objects are accomplished with one tribe, the missionary might pass on to another.

The roads are under the government of the county courts, subject to be controlled by the general court. They order new roads to be opened wherever they think them necessary. The inhabitants of the county are by them laid off into precincts, to each of which they allot a convenient portion of the public roads to be kept in repair. Such bridges as may be built without the assistance of artificers, they are to build. If the stream be such as to require a bridge of regular workmanship, the court employs workmen to build it, at the expense of the whole county. If it be too great for the county, application is made to the general assembly, who authorize individuals to build it, and to take a fixed toll from all passengers, or give sanction to such other proposition as to them appears reasonable.

Ferries are admitted only at such places as are particularly pointed out by law, and the rates of ferriage are fixed.

Taverns are licensed by the courts, who fix their rates from time to time.

The private buildings are very rarely constructed of stone or brick, much the greatest portion being of scantling and boards, plastered with lime. It is impossible to devise things more ugly, uncomfortable, and happily more perishable. There are two or three plans, on one of which, according to its size, most of the houses in the State are built. The poorest people build huts of logs, laid horizontally in pens, stopping the interstices with mud. These are warmer in winter, and cooler in summer, than the more expensive construction of scantling and plank. The wealthy are attentive to the raising of vegetables, but very little so to fruits. The poorer people attend to neither, living principally on milk and animal diet. This is the more inexcusable, as the climate requires indispensably a free use of vegetable food, for health as well as comfort, and is very friendly to the raising of fruits. The only public buildings worthy of mention are the capitol, the palace, the college, and the hospital for lunatics, all of them in Williamsburg, heretofore the seat of our government. The capitol is a light and airy structure, with a portico in front of two orders, the lower of which, being Doric, is tolerably just in its proportions and ornaments, save only that the intercolonations are too large. The upper is Ionic, much too small for that on which it is mounted, its ornaments not proper to the order, nor proportioned within themselves. It is crowned with a pediment, which is too high for its span. Yet, on the whole, it is the most pleasing piece of architecture we have. The palace is not handsome without, but it is spacious and commodious within, is prettily situated, and with the grounds annexed to it, is capable of being made an elegant seat. The college and hospital are rude, misshapen piles, which, but that they have roofs, would be taken for brick-kilns. There are no other public buildings but churches and courthouses, in which no attempts are made at elegance. Indeed, it would not be easy to execute such an attempt, as a workman could scarcely be found capable of drawing an order. The genius of architecture seems to have shed its maledictions over this land. Buildings are often erected, by individuals, of considerable expense. To give these symmetry and taste, would not increase their cost. It would only change the arrangement of the materials, the form and combination of the members. This would often cost less than the burthen of barbarous ornaments with which these buildings are sometimes charged. But the first principles of the art are unknown, and there exists scarcely a model among us sufficiently chaste to give an idea of them.

Architecture being one of the fine arts, and as such within the department of a professor of the college, according to the new arrangement, perhaps a spark may fall on some young subjects of natural taste, kindle up their genius, and produce a reformation in this elegant and useful art. But all we shall do in this way will produce no permanent improvement to our country, while the unhappy prejudice prevails that houses of brick or stone are less wholesome than those of wood. A dew is often observed on the walls of the former in rainy weather, and the most obvious solution is, that the rain has penetrated through these walls. The following facts, however, are sufficient to prove the error of this solution: 1. This dew upon the walls appears when there is no rain, if the state of the atmosphere be moist. 2. It appears upon the partition as well as the exterior walls. 3. So, also, on pavements of brick or stone. 4. It is more copious in proportion as the walls are thicker; the reverse of which ought to be the case, if this hypothesis were just. If cold water be poured into a vessel of stone, or glass, a dew forms instantly on the outside; but if it be poured into a vessel of wood, there is no such appearance. It is not supposed, in the first case, that the water has exuded through the glass, but that it is precipitated from the circumambient air; as the humid particles of vapor, passing from the boiler of an alembic through its refrigerant, are precipitated from the air, in which they are suspended, on the internal surface of the refrigerant. Walls of brick and stone act as the refrigerant in this instance. They are sufficiently cold to condense and precipitate the moisture suspended in the air of the room, when it is heavily charged therewith. But walls of wood are not so. The question then is, whether the air in which this moisture is left floating, or that which is deprived of it, be most wholesome? In both cases the remedy is easy. A little fire kindled in the room, whenever the air is damp, prevents the precipitation on the walls; and this practice, found healthy in the warmest as well as coldest seasons, is as necessary in a wooden as in a stone or brick house. I do not mean to say that the rain never penetrates through walls of brick. On the contrary, I have seen instances of it. But with us it is only through the northern and eastern walls of the house, after a northeasterly storm, this being the only one which continues long enough to force through the walls. This, however, happens too rarely to give a just character of unwholesomeness to such houses. In a house, the walls of which are of well-burnt brick and good mortar, I have seen the rain penetrate through but twice in a dozen or fifteen years. The inhabitants of Europe, who dwell chiefly in houses of stone or brick, are surely as healthy as those of Virginia. These houses have the advantage, too, of being warmer in winter and cooler in summer than those of wood; of being cheaper in their first construction, where lime is convenient, and infinitely more durable. The latter consideration renders it of great importance to eradicate this prejudice from the minds of our countrymen A country whose buildings are of wood, can never increase in its improvements to any considerable degree. Their duration is highly estimated at fifty years. Every half century then our country becomes a *tabula rasa,* whereon we have to set out anew, as in the first moment of seating it. Whereas when buildings are of durable materials, every new edifice is an actual and permanent acquisition to the State, adding to its value as well as to its ornament.

QUERY XVI

The measures taken with regard to the estates and possessions of the Rebels, commonly called Tories?

A tory has been properly defined to be a traitor in thought but not in deed. The only description, by which the laws have endeavored to come at them, was that of non-jurors, or persons refusing to take the oath of fidelity to the State. Persons of this description were at one time subjected to double taxation, at another to treble, and lastly were allowed retribution, and placed on a level with good citizens. It may be mentioned as a proof, both of the lenity of our government, and unanimity of its inhabitants, that though this war has now raged near seven years, not a single execution for treason has taken place.

Under this query I will state the measures which have been adopted as to British property, the owners of which stand on a much fairer footing than the tories. By our laws, the same as the English as in this respect, no alien can hold lands, nor alien enemy maintain an action for money, or other movable thing. Lands acquired or held by aliens become forfeited to the State; and, on an action by an alien enemy to recover money, or other movable property, the defendant may plead that he is an alien enemy. This extinguishes his right in the hands of the debtor or holder of his movable property. By our separation from Great Britain, British subjects became aliens, and being at war, they were alien enemies. Their lands were of course forfeited, and their debts irrecoverable. The assembly, however, passed laws at various times, for saving their property. They first sequestered their lands, slaves, and other property on their farms in the hands of commissioners, who were mostly the confidential friends or agents of the owners, and directed their clear profits to be paid into the treasury; and they gave leave to all persons owing debts to British subjects to pay them also into the treasury. The monies so to be brought in were declared to remain the property of the British subject, and if used by the State, were to be repaid, unless an improper conduct in Great Britain should render a detention of it reasonable. Depreciation had at that time, though unacknowledged and unperceived by the whigs, begun in some small degree. Great sums of money were paid in by debtors. At a later period, the assembly, adhering to the political principles which forbid an alien to hold lands in the State, ordered all British property to be sold; and, become sensible of the real progress of depreciation, and of the losses which would thence occur, if not guarded against, they ordered that the proceeds of the sales should be converted into their then worth in tobacco, subject to the future direction of the legislature. This act has left the question of retribution more problematical. In May, 1780, another act took away the permission to pay into the public treasury debts due to British subjects.

QUERY XVII

The different religions received into that State?

The first settlers in this country were emigrants from England, of the English Church, just at a point of time when it was flushed with complete victory over the religious of all other persuasions. Possessed, as they became, of the powers of making, administering, and executing the laws, they showed equal intolerance in this country with their Presbyterian brethren, who had emigrated to the northern government. The poor Quakers were flying from persecution in England. They cast their eyes on these new countries as asylums of civil and religious freedom; but they found them free only for the reigning sect. Several acts of the

Virginia assembly of 1659, 1662, and 1693, had made it penal in parents to refuse to have their children baptized; had prohibited the unlawful assembling of Quakers; had made it penal for any master of a vessel to bring a Quaker into the State; had ordered those already here, and such as should come thereafter, to be imprisoned till they should abjure the country; provided a milder punishment for their first and second return, but death for their third; had inhibited all persons from suffering their meetings in or near their houses, entertaining them individually, or disposing of books which supported their tenets. If no execution took place here, as did in New England, it was not owing to the moderation of the church, or spirit of the legislature, as may be inferred from the law itself; but to historical circumstances which have not been handed down to us. The Anglicans retained full possession of the country about a century. Other opinions began then to creep in, and the great care of the government to support their own church, having begotten an equal degree of indolence in its clergy, two-thirds of the people had become dissenters at the commencement of the present revolution. The laws, indeed, were still oppressive on them, but the spirit of the one party had subsided into moderation, and of the other had risen to a degree of determination which commanded respect.

The present state of our laws on the subject of religion is this. The convention of May, 1776, in their declaration of rights, declared it to be a truth, and a natural right, that the exercise of religion should be free; but when they proceeded to form on that declaration the ordinance of government, instead of taking up every principle declared in the bill of rights, and guarding it by legislative sanction, they passed over that which asserted our religious rights, leaving them as they found them. The same convention, however, when they met as a member of the general assembly in October, 1776, repealed all *acts of Parliament* which had rendered criminal the maintaining any opinions in matters of religion, the forbearing to repair to church, and the exercising any mode of worship; and suspended the laws giving salaries to the clergy, which suspension was made perpetual in October, 1779. Statutory oppressions in religion being thus wiped away, we remain at present under those only imposed by the common law, or by our own acts of assembly. At the common law, *heresy* was a capital offence, punishable by burning. Its definition was left to the ecclesiastical judges, before whom the conviction was, till the statute of the I El. c. I circumscribed it, by declaring, that nothing should be deemed heresy, but what had been so determined by authority of the canonical scriptures, or by one of the four first general councils, or by other council, having for the grounds of their declaration the express and plain words of the scriptures. Heresy, thus circumscribed, being an offence against the common law, our act of assembly of October 1777, c. 17, gives cognizance of it to the general court, by declaring that the jurisdiction of that court shall be general in all matters at the common law. The execution is by the writ *De haeretico comburendo*. By our own act of assembly of 1705, c. 30, if a person brought up in the Christian religion denies the being of a God, or the Trinity, or asserts there are more gods than one, or denies the Christian religion to be true, or the scriptures to be of divine authority, he is punishable on the first offence by incapacity to hold any office or employment ecclesiastical, civil, or military; on the second by disability to sue, to take any gift or legacy, to be guardian, executor, or administrator, and by three years' imprisonment without bail. A father's right to the custody of his own children being founded in law on his right of guardianship, this being taken away, they may of course be severed from him, and put by the authority of a court into more orthodox hands. This is a summary view of that religious slavery under which a people have been willing to remain, who have lavished their lives and fortunes for the establishment of their civil freedom. The error[1] seems not sufficiently eradicated, that the operations of the mind, as well as the acts of the body, are subject to the coercion of the laws. But our rulers can have no authority over such natural rights, only as we have submitted to them. The rights of conscience we never submitted, we could not submit. We are answerable for them to our God. The legitimate powers of government extend to such acts only as are injurious to others. But it does me no injury for my neighbor to say there are twenty gods, or no God. It neither picks my pocket nor breaks my leg. If it be said, his testimony in a court of justice cannot be relied on, reject it then, and be the stigma on him. Constraint may make him worse by making him a hypocrite, but it will never make him a truer man. It may fix him obstinately in his errors, but will not cure them.

---

[1]Jefferson's footnote omitted.

Reason and free inquiry are the only effectual agents against error. Give a loose to them, they will support the true religion by bringing every false one to their tribunal, to the test of their investigation. They are the natural enemies of error, and of error only. Had not the Roman government permitted free inquiry, Christianity could never have been introduced. Had not free inquiry been indulged at the era of the Reformation, the corruptions of Christianity could not have been purged away. If it be restrained now, the present corruptions will be protected, and new ones encouraged. Was the government to prescribe to us our medicine and diet, our bodies would be in such keeping as our souls are now. Thus in France the emetic was once forbidden as a medicine, the potato as an article of food. Government is just as infallible, too, when it fixes systems in physics. Galileo was sent to the Inquisition for affirming that the earth was a sphere; the government had declared it to be as flat as a trencher, and Galileo was obliged to abjure his error. This error, however, at length prevailed, the earth became a globe, and Descartes declared it was whirled round its axis by a vortex. The government in which he lived was wise enough to see that this was no question of civil jurisdiction, or we should all have been involved by authority in vortices. In fact, the vortices have been exploded, and the Newtonian principle of gravitation is now more firmly established, on the basis of reason, than it would be were the government to step in, and to make it an article of necessary faith. Reason and experiment have been indulged, and error has fled before them. It is error alone which needs the support of government. Truth can stand by itself. Subject opinion to coercion: whom will you make your inquisitors? Fallible men; men governed by bad passions, by private as well as public reasons. And why subject it to coercion? To produce uniformity. But is uniformity of opinion desirable? No more than of face and stature. Introduce the bed of Procrustes then, and as there is danger that the large men may beat the small, make us all of a size, by lopping the former and stretching the latter. Difference of opinion is advantageous in religion. The several sects perform the office of a *censor morum* over such other. Is uniformity attainable? Millions of innocent men, women, and children, since the introduction of Christianity, have been burnt, tortured, fined, imprisoned; yet we have not advanced one inch towards uniformity. What has been the effect of coercion? To make one half the world fools, and the other half hypocrites. To support roguery and error all over the earth. Let us reflect that it is inhabited by a thousand millions of people. That these profess probably a thousand different systems of religion. That ours is but one of that thousand. That if there be but one right, and ours that one, we should wish to see the nine hundred and ninety-nine wandering sects gathered into the fold of truth. But against such a majority we cannot effect this by force. Reason and persuasion are the only practicable instruments. To make way for these, free inquiry must be indulged; and how can we wish others to indulge it while we refuse it ourselves. But every State, says an inquisitor, has established some religion. No two, say I, have established the same. Is this a proof of the infallibility of establishments? Our sister States of Pennsylvania and New York, however, have long subsisted without any establishment at all. The experiment was new and doubtful when they made it. It has answered beyond conception. They flourish infinitely. Religion is well supported; of various kinds, indeed, but all good enough; all sufficient to preserve peace and order; or if a sect arises, whose tenets would subvert morals, good sense has fair play, and reasons and laughs it out of doors, without suffering the State to be troubled with it. They do not hang more malefactors than we do. They are not more disturbed with religious dissensions. On the contrary, their harmony is unparalleled, and can be ascribed to nothing but their unbounded tolerance, because there is no other circumstance in which they differ from every nation on earth. They have made the happy discovery, that the way to silence religious disputes, is to take no notice of them. Let us too give this experiment fair play, and get rid, while we may, of those tyrannical laws. It is true, we are as yet secured against them by the spirit of the times. I doubt whether the people of this country would suffer an execution for heresy, or a three years' imprisonment for not comprehending the mysteries of the Trinity. But is the spirit of the people an infallible, a permanent reliance? Is it government? Is this the kind of protection we receive in return for the rights we give up? Besides, the spirit of the times may alter, will alter. Our rulers will become corrupt, our people careless. A single zealot may commence persecutor, and better men be his victims. It can never be too often repeated, that the time for fixing every essential right on a legal basis is while our rulers are honest, and ourselves united. From the conclusion of this war we shall be going down hill. It will not then be necessary to resort every moment to the people for support. They will be forgotten, therefore, and their rights disregarded. They will forget themselves, but in the sole faculty of making money, and will never think of uniting to effect a due respect for their rights. The shackles, therefore, which shall not be knocked off at the conclusion of this war, will remain on us long, will be made heavier and heavier, till our rights shall revive or expire in a convulsion.

QUERY XVIII

The particular customs and manners that may happen to be received in that State?

It is difficult to determine on the standard by which the manners of a nation may be tried, whether *catholic* or *particular*. It is more difficult for a native to bring to that standard the manners of his own nation, familiarized to him by habit. There must doubtless be an unhappy influence on the manners of our people produced by the existence of slavery among us. The whole commerce between master and slave is a perpetual exercise of the most boisterous passions, the most unremitting despotism on the one part, and degrading submissions on the other. Our children see this, and learn to imitate it; for man is an imitative animal. This quality is the germ of all education in him. From his cradle to his grave he is learning to do what he sees others do. If a parent could find no motive either in his philanthropy or his self-love, for restraining the intemperance of passion towards his slave, it should always be a sufficient one that his child is present. But generally it is not sufficient. The parent storms, the child looks on, catches the lineaments of wrath, puts on the same airs in the circle of smaller slaves, gives a loose to the worst of passions, and thus nursed, educated, and daily exercised in tyranny, cannot but be stamped by it with odious peculiarities. The man must be a prodigy who can retain his manners and morals undepraved by such circumstances. And with what execration should the statesman be loaded, who, permitting one half the citizens thus to trample on the rights of the other, transforms those into despots, and these into enemies, destroys the morals of the one part, and the *amor patriae* of the other. For if a slave can have a country in this world, it must be any other in preference to that in which he is born to live and labor for another; in which he must lock up the faculties of his nature, contribute as far as depends on his individual endeavors to the evanishment of the human race, or entail his own miserable condition on the endless generations proceeding from him. With the morals of the people, their industry also is destroyed. For in a warm climate, no man will labor for himself who can make another labor for him. This is so true, that of the proprietors of slaves a very small proportion indeed are ever seen to labor. And can the liberties of a nation be thought secure when we have removed their only firm basis, a conviction in the minds of the people that these liberties are of the gift of God? That they are not to be violated but with His wrath? Indeed I tremble for my country when I reflect that God is just; that his justice cannot sleep forever; that considering numbers, nature and natural means only, a revolution of the wheel of fortune, an exchange of situation is among possible events; that it may become probably by supernatural interference! The Almighty has no attribute which can take side with us in such a contest But it is impossible to be temperate and to pursue this subject through the various considerations of policy, of morals, of history natural and civil. We must be contented to hope they will force their way into every one's mind. I think a change already perceptible, since the origin of the present revolution. The spirit of the master is abating, that of the slave rising from the dust, his condition mollifying, the way I hope preparing, under the auspices of heaven, for a total emancipation, and that this is disposed, in the order of events, to be with the consent of the masters, rather than by their extirpation.

QUERY XIX

The present state of manufactures, commerce, interior and exterior trade?

We never had an interior trade of any importance. Our exterior commerce has suffered very much from the beginning of the present contest. During this time we have manufactured within our families the most necessary articles of clothing. Those of cotton will bear some comparison with the same kinds of manufacture in Europe; but those of wool, flax and hemp are very coarse, unsightly, and unpleasant; and such is our attachment to agriculture, and such our preference for foreign manufactures, that be it wise or unwise, our people will certainly return as soon as they can, to the raising raw materials, and exchanging them for finer manufactures than they are able to execute themselves.

The political economists of Europe have established it as a principle, that every State should endeavor to manufacture for itself; and this principle, like many others, we transfer to America, without calculating the difference of circumstance which should often produce a difference of result. In Europe the lands are either cultivated, or locked up against the cultivator. Manufacture must therefore be resorted to of necessity not of choice, to support the surplus of their people. But we have an immensity of land courting the industry of the husbandman. Is it best then that all our citizens should be employed in its improvement, or that one half should be called off from that to exercise manufactures and handicraft arts for the other? Those who labor in the earth are the chosen people of God, if ever He had a chosen people, whose breasts He has made His peculiar deposit for substantial and genuine virtue. It is the focus in which he keeps alive that sacred fire, which otherwise might escape from the face of the earth. Corruption of morals in the mass of cultivators is a phenomenon of which no age nor nation has furnished an example. It is the mark set on those, who, not looking up to heaven, to their own soil and industry, as does the husbandman, for their subsistence, depend for it on casualties and caprice of customers. Dependence begets subservience and venality, suffocates the germ of virtue, and prepares fit tools for the designs of ambition. This, the natural progress and consequence of the arts, has sometimes perhaps been retarded by accidental circumstances; but, generally speaking, the proportion which the aggregate of the other classes of citizens bears in any State to that of its husbandmen, is the proportion of its unsound to its healthy parts, and is a good enough barometer whereby to measure its degree of corruption. While we have land to labor then, let us never wish to see our citizens occupied at a workbench, or twirling a distaff. Carpenters, masons, smiths, are wanting in husbandry; but, for the general operations of manufacture, let our workshops remain in Europe. It is better to carry provisions and materials to workmen there, than bring them to the provisions and materials, and with them their manners and principles. The loss by the transportation of commodities across the Atlantic will be made up in happiness and permanence of government. The mobs of great cities add just so much to the support of pure government, as sores do to the strength of the human body. It is the manners and spirit of a people which preserve a republic in vigor. A degeneracy in these is a canker which soon eats to the heart of its laws and constitution.

QUERY XX

A notice of the commercial productions particular to the State, and of those objects which the inhabitants are obliged to get from Europe and from other parts of the world?

. . . .

In the year 1758 we exported seventy thousand hogsheads of tobacco, which was the greatest quantity ever produced in this country in one year. But its culture was fast declining at the commencement of this war and that of wheat taken its place; and it must continue to decline on the return of peace. I suspect that the change in the temperature of our climate has become sensible to that plant, which to be good, requires an extraordinary degree of heat. But it requires still more indispensably an uncommon fertility of soil; and the price which it commands at market will not enable the planter to produce this by manure. Was the supply still to depend on Virginia and Maryland alone as its culture becomes more difficult, the price would rise so as to enable the planter to surmount those difficulties and to live. But the western country on the Mississippi and the midlands of Georgia, having fresh and fertile lands in abundance, and a hotter sun, will be able to undersell these two States, and will oblige them to abandon the raising of tobacco altogether. And a happy obligation for them it will be. It is a culture productive of infinite wretchedness. Those employed in it are in a continual state of exertion beyond the power of nature to support. Little food of any kind is raised by them; so that the men and animals on these farms are badly fed, and the earth is rapidly impoverished. The cultivation of wheat is the reverse in every circumstance. Besides clothing the earth with herbage, and preserving its fertility, it feeds the laborers plentifully, requires from them only a moderate toil, except in the season of harvest, raises great numbers of animals for food and service, and diffuses plenty and happiness among the whole. We find it easier to make an hundred bushels of wheat than a thousand weight of tobacco, and they are worth more when made. The weavil indeed is a formidable obstacle to the cultivation of this grain with us. But principles are already known which must lead to a remedy. Thus a certain degree of heat, to wit, that of the common air in summer, is necessary to hatch the eggs. If subterranean granaries, or others, therefore, can be contrived below that temperature, the evil will be cured by cold. A degree of heat beyond that which hatches the egg we know will kill it. But in aiming at this we easily run into that which produces putrefaction. To produce putrefaction, however, three agents are requisite, heat, moisture, and the external air. If the absence of any one of these be secured, the other two may safely be admitted. Heat is the one we want. Moisture then, or external air, must be excluded. The former has been done by exposing the grain in kilns to the action of fire, which produces heat, and extracts moisture at the same time; the latter, by putting the grain into hogsheads, covering it with a coating of lime, and heading it up. In this situation its bulk produced a heat sufficient to kill the eggs; the moisture is suffered to remain indeed, but the external air is excluded. A nicer operation yet has been attempted; that is, to produce an intermediate temperature of heat between that which kills the egg, and that which produces putrefaction. The threshing the grain as soon as it is cut, and laying it in its chaff in large heaps, has been found very nearly to hit this temperature, though not perfectly, nor always. The heap generates heat sufficient to kill most of the eggs, whilst the chaff commonly restrains it from rising into putrefaction. But all these methods abridge too much the quantity which the farmer can manage, and enable other countries to undersell him, which are not infested with this insect. There is still a desideratum then to give with us decisive triumph to this branch of agriculture over that of tobacco. The culture of wheat by enlarging our pasture, will render the Arabian horse an article of very considerable profit. Experience has shown that ours is the particular climate of America where he may be raised without degeneracy. Southwardly the heat of the sun occasions a deficiency of pasture, and northwardly the winters are too cold for the short and fine hair, the particular sensibility and constitution of that race. Animals transplanted into unfriendly climates, either change their nature and acquire new senses against the new difficulties in which they are placed, or they multiply poorly and become extinct. A good foundation is laid for their propagation here by our possessing already great numbers of horses of that blood, and by a decided taste and preference for them established among the people. Their patience of heat without injury, their superior wind, fit them better in this and the more southern climates even for the drudgeries of the plough and wagon. Northwardly they will become an object only to persons of taste and fortune, for the saddle and light carriages. To those, and for these uses, their fleetness and beauty will recommend them. Besides these there will be other valuable substitutes when the cultivation of tobacco shall be discontinued such as cotton in the eastern parts of the State, and hemp and flax in the western.

It is not easy to say what are the articles either of necessity, comfort, or luxury, which we cannot raise, and which we therefore shall be under a necessity of importing from abroad, as everything hardier than the olive, and as hardy as the fig, may be raised here in the open air. Sugar, coffee and tea, indeed, are not between these limits; and habit having placed them among the necessaries of life with the wealthy part of our citizens, as long as these habits remain we must go for them to those countries which are able to furnish them.

QUERY XXI

The weights, measures and the currency of the hard money?
Some details relating to exchange with Europe?

Our weights and measures are the same which are fixed by acts of parliament in England. Now it has happened that in this as well as the other American States the nominal value of coin was made to differ from what it was in the country we had left, and to differ among ourselves too, I am not able to say with certainty. . . .

The first symptom of the depreciation of our present paper money, was that of silver dollars selling at six shillings, which had before been worth but five shillings and ninepence. The assembly thereupon raised them by law to six shillings. As the dollar is now likely to become the money-unit of America, as it passes at this rate in some of our sister States, and as it facilitates their computation in pounds and shillings, &c., converso, this seems to be more convenient than its former denomination. But as this particular coin now stands higher than any other in the proportion of one hundred and thirty-three and a half to one hundred and twenty-five, or sixteen to fifteen, it will be necessary to raise the others in proportion.

QUERY XXII
The public Income and Expenses?

. . . .

To this estimate of our [financial] abilities, let me add a word as to the application of them. If, when cleared of the present contest, and of the debts with which that will charge us, we come to measure force hereafter with any European power, such events are devoutly to be deprecated. Young as we are, and with such a country before us to fill with people and with happiness, we should point in that direction the whole generative force of nature, wasting none of it in efforts of mutual destruction. It should be our endeavor to cultivate the peace and friendship of every nation, even of that which has injured us most, when we shall have carried our point against her. Our interest will be to throw open the doors of commerce, and to knock off all its shackles, giving perfect freedom to all persons for the vent of whatever they may choose to bring into our ports, and asking the same in theirs. Never was so much false arithmetic employed on any subject, as that which has been employed to persuade nations that it is their interest to go to war. Were the money which it has cost to gain, at the close of a long war, a little town, or a little territory, the right to cut wood here, or to catch fish there, expended in improving what they already possess, in making roads, opening rivers, building ports, improving the arts, and finding employment for their idle poor, it would render them much stronger, much wealthier and happier. This I hope will be our wisdom. And, perhaps, to remove as much as possible the occasions of making war, it might be better for us to abandon the

ocean altogether, that being the element whereon we shall be principally exposed to jostle with other nations; to leave to others to bring
what we shall want, and to carry what we can spare. This would make
us invulnerable to Europe, by offering none of our property to their
prize, and would turn all our citizens to the cultivation of the earth;
and, I repeat it again, cultivators of the earth are the most virtuous
and independent citizens. It might be time enough to seek employment for them at sea, when the land no longer offers it. But the actual
habits of our countrymen attach them to commerce. They will exercise it for themselves. Wars then must sometimes be our lot; and all
the wise can do, will be to avoid that half of them which would be
produced by our own follies and our own acts of injustice; and to
make for the other half the best preparations we can. Of what nature
should these be? A land army would be useless for offence, and not
the best nor safest instrument of defence. For either of these purposes,
the sea is the field on which we should meet an European enemy. On
that element it is necessary we should possess some power. To aim
at such a navy as the greater nations of Europe possess, would be a
foolish and wicked waste of the energies of our countrymen. It would
be to pull on our own heads that load of military expense which makes
the European laborer go supperless to bed, and moistens his bread
with the sweat of his brows. It will be enough if we enable ourselves
to prevent insults from those nations of Europe which are weak on the
sea, because circumstances exist, which render even the stronger ones
weak as to us. Providence has placed their richest and most defence-
less possessions at our door; has obliged their most precious commerce
to pass, as it were, in review before us. To protect this, or to assail, a
small part only of their naval force will ever be risked across the
Atlantic. The dangers to which the elements expose them here are
too well known, and the greater dangers to which they would be
exposed at home were any general calamity to involve their whole
fleet. They can attack us by detachment only; and it will suffice to
make ourselves equal to what they may detach. Even a smaller force
than they may detach will be rendered equal or superior by the quick-
ness with which any check may be repaired with us, while losses with
them will be irreparable till too late. A small naval force then is suf-

ficient for us, and a small one is necessary. What this should be, I will not undertake to say. I will only say, it should by no means be so great as we are able to make it. Suppose the million of dollars, or three hundred thousand pounds, which Virginia could annually spare without distress, to be applied to the creating a navy. A single year's contribution would build, equip, man, and send to sea a force which should carry three hundred guns. The rest of the confederacy, exerting themselves in the same proportion, would equip in the same time fifteen hundred guns more. So that one year's contributions would set up a navy of eighteen hundred guns. The British ships of the line average seventy-six guns; their frigates thirty-eight. Eighteen hundred guns then would form a fleet of thirty ships, eighteen of which might be of the line, and twelve frigates. Allowing eight men, the British average, for every gun, their annual expense, including subsistence, clothing, pay, and ordinary repairs, would be about $1,280 for every gun, or $2,304,000 for the whole. I state this only as one year's possible exertion, without deciding whether more or less than a year's exertion should be thus applied.

QUERY XXIII

The histories of the State, the memorials published in its name in the time of its being a colony, and the pamphlets relating to its interior or exterior affairs present or ancient?

Captain Smith, who next to Sir Walter Raleigh may be considered as the founder of our colony, has written its history from the first adventures to it, till the year 1624. He was a member of the council, and afterwards president of the colony; and to his efforts principally may be ascribed its support against the opposition of the natives. He was honest, sensible, and well informed; but his style is barbarous and uncouth. His history, however, is almost the only source from which we derive any knowledge of the infancy of our State.

The reverend William Stith, a native of Virginia, and president of its college, has also written the history of the same period, in a large octavo volume of small print. He was a man of classical learning, and very exact, but of no taste in style. He is inelegant, therefore, and his details often too minute to be tolerable, even to a native of the country, whose history he writes.

Beverley, a native also, has run into the other extreme; he has comprised our history from the first propositions of Sir Walter Raleigh to the year 1700, in the hundredth part of the space which Stith employs for the fourth part of the period.

Sir Walter Keith has taken it up at its earliest period, and continued it to the year 1725. He is agreeable enough in style, and passes over events of little importance. Of course he is short and would be preferred by a foreigner.

During the regal government, some contest arose on the exaction of an illegal fee by Governor Dinwiddie, and doubtless there were others on other occasions not at present recollected. It is supposed that these are not sufficiently interesting to a foreigner to merit a detail.

The petition of the council and burgesses of Virginia to the king, their memorials to the lords, and remonstrance to the commons in the year 1764, began the present contest; and these having proved ineffectual to prevent the passage of the stamp-act, the resolutions of the house of burgesses of 1765 were passed declaring the independence of the people of Virginia of the parliament of Great Britain, in matters of taxation. From that time till the Declaration of Independence by Congress in 1776, their journals are filled with assertions of the public rights. The pamphlets published in this State on the controverted question, were:

1766, An Inquiry into the rights of the British Colonies, by Richard Bland.

1769, The Monitor's Letters, by Dr. Arthur Lee.

1774, A summary View of the rights of British America.[1]

1774, Considerations, &c., by Robert Carter Nicholas.

Since the Declaration of Independence this State has had no controversy with any other, except with that of Pennsylvania, on their common boundary. Some papers on this subject passed between the executive and legislative bodies of the two States, the result of which was a happy accommodation of their rights.

To this account of our historians, memorials, and pamphlets, it may

---

[1]By the author of these "Notes." [Jefferson's note.]

not be unuseful to add a chronological catalogue of American state-papers, as far as I have been able to collect their titles.[1] It is far from being either complete or correct. Where the title alone, and not the paper itself, has come under my observation, I cannot answer for the exactness of the date. Sometimes I have not been able to find any date at all, and sometimes have not been satisfied that such a paper exists. An extensive collection of papers of this description has been for some time in a course of preparation by a gentleman[2] fully equal to the task, and from whom, therefore, we may hope ere long to receive it. In the meantime accept this as the result of my labors, and as closing the tedious detail which you have so undesignedly drawn upon yourself.

[1]Jefferson was a pioneer in collecting and preserving early American manuscripts and printed laws. The exhaustive bibliography he includes at this point is omitted from the present edition.

[2]Ebenezer Hazard. [Jefferson's note.]

Public Papers

Introduction

When Jefferson came to Congress in the notable year 1775, John Adams remarked he "brought with him a reputation for literature, science and a happy talent of composition." Jefferson's happy talent of composition seems to have won him the role of writing more bills, reports and official documents than any of his contemporaries. It is generally conceded that his talent as an organizer and writer of public papers was one of the solid pillars of his statesmanship. Jefferson's official papers range from those written as a member of the Virginia Assembly, the Virginia Convention, and the Continental Congress, to those prepared as Governor of Virginia, Minister to France, Secretary of State, Vice-President, and, finally, President. However, when an enterprising publisher wanted to publish every last one of these papers, Jefferson declined, saying many of them "would be like old newspapers, materials for future historians, but no longer interesting to the readers of the day."

Guided by Jefferson's criterion, the editors have selected papers the extraordinary importance or interest of which is not obscured by technical exposition. Jefferson's stylistic triumph, *The Declaration of Independence,* is not included in this section since it appears in his *Autobiography.* Another work, far less known but almost as great a literary contribution to the American Revolution, is here printed in full. This, A *Summary View of the Rights of British America,* was prepared as Jefferson's instructions for the delegates from Virginia to the proposed first Congress of the Colonies. It is an uncompromising argument that the natural right of emigration and conquest made the American colonies free of British Parliamentary jurisdiction, and that their only tie was that of voluntary submission to the "same common Sovereign," the Briting King. These resolutions were not adopted. "Tamer sentiments were preferred," Jefferson observed many years later. However, admirers of the vibrant manifesto subscribed a sum for its publication, gave it its present title, and published the work (Williamsburg, 1774) as that of "a native of Virginia."

The Bill for Establishing Religious Freedom, introduced into the Virginia Assembly June 13, 1779, by John Harvie, was briskly attacked by the opposition. Jefferson regarded this bill as one of his most genuine contributions to humanity. It proclaimed the religious independence of the individual, and formulated Jefferson's belief in freedom of thought. When word came to Jefferson in Paris in 1786 that the Assembly had finally passed this bill, he hastened to order an edition printed there. It was subsequently reprinted in America.

The First Inaugural Address, typically Jeffersonian in political sentiment, is a lasting definition of democratic principles. The Second Inaugural Address is the *performance,* as Jefferson said, of which the First is the *promise.* The famous passage on the Indians was included for its own sake, but also for the more urgent purpose of combatting "the hue and cry raised against philosophy and the rights of man." Jefferson was aiming at the "anti-social doctrines" of the aroused Federalist opposition.

Additional papers, and excerpts from papers, are included.

Public Papers

—— ✍ ——

A Summary View of the Rights of British America, 1774

Resolved, That it be an instruction to the said deputies, when assembled in General Congress, with the deputies from the other states of British America, to propose to the said Congress, that an humble and dutiful address be presented to his Majesty, begging leave to lay before him, as Chief Magistrate of the British empire, the united complaints of his Majesty's subjects in America; complaints which are excited by many unwarrantable encroachments and usurpations, attempted to be made by the legislature of one part of the empire, upon the rights which God, and the laws, have given equally and independently to all. To represent to his Majesty that these, his States, have often individually made humble application to his imperial Throne, to obtain, through its intervention, some redress of their injured rights; to none of which, was ever even an answer condescended. Humbly to hope that this, their joint address, penned in the language of truth, and divested of those expressions of servility, which would persuade his Majesty that we are asking favors, and not rights, shall obtain from his Majesty a more respectful acceptance; and this his Majesty will think we have reason to expect, when he reflects that he is no more than the chief officer of the people, appointed by the laws, and circumscribed with definite powers, to assist in working the great machine of government, erected for their use, and, consequently, subject to their superintendence; and, in order that these, our rights, as well as the invasions of them, may be laid more fully before his Majesty, to take a view of them, from the origin and first settlement of these countries.

To remind him that our ancestors, before their emigration to America, were the free inhabitants of the British dominions in Europe, and

possessed a right, which nature has given to all men, of departing from
the country in which chance, not choice, has placed them, of going in
quest of new habitations, and of there establishing new societies, under
such laws and regulations as, to them, shall seem most likely to promote public happiness. That their Saxon ancestors had, under this universal law, in like manner, left their native wilds and woods in the
North of Europe, had possessed themselves of the Island of Britain,
then less charged with inhabitants, and had established there that system of laws which has so long been the glory and protection of that
country. Nor was ever any claim of superiority or dependence asserted
over them, by that mother country from which they had migrated: and
were such a claim made, it is believed his Majesty's subjects in Great
Britain have too firm a feeling of the rights derived to them from their
ancestors, to bow down the sovereignty of their state before such
visionary pretensions. And it is thought that no circumstance has
occurred to distinguish, materially, the British from the Saxon emigration. America was conquered, and her settlements made and firmly
established, at the expense of individuals, and not of the British public. Their own blood was spilt in acquiring lands for their settlement,
their own fortunes expended in making that settlement effectual. For
themselves they fought, for themselves they conquered, and for themselves alone they have right to hold. No shilling was ever issued from
the public treasures of his Majesty, or his ancestors, for their assistance, till of very late times, after the colonies had become established
on a firm and permanent footing. That then, indeed, having become
valuable to Great Britain for her commercial purposes, his Parliament
was pleased to lend them assistance against an enemy who would fain
have drawn to herself the benefits of their commerce, to the great
aggrandisement of herself, and danger of Great Britain. Such assistance, and in such circumstances, they had often before given to Portugal and other allied states, with whom they carry on a commercial
intercourse. Yet these states never supposed that by calling in her aid,
they thereby submitted themselves to her sovereignty. Had such terms
been proposed, they would have rejected them with disdain, and
trusted for better, to the moderation of their enemies, or to a vigorous
exertion of their own force. We do not, however, mean to underrate
those aids, which, to us, were doubtless valuable, on whatever princi-

ples granted: but we would shew that they cannot give a title to that authority which the British Parliament would arrogate over us; and that may amply be repaid by our giving to the inhabitants of Great Britain such exclusive privileges in trade as may be advantageous to them, and, at the same time, not too restrictive to ourselves. That settlement having been thus effected in the wilds of America, the emigrants thought proper to adopt that system of laws, under which they had hitherto lived in the mother country, and to continue their union with her, by submitting themselves to the same common sovereign, who was thereby made the central link, connecting the several parts of the empire thus newly multiplied.

But that not long were they permitted, however far they thought themselves removed from the hand of oppression, to hold undisturbed the rights thus acquired at the hazard of their lives and loss of their fortunes. A family of Princes was then on the British throne, whose treasonable crimes against their people, brought on them, afterwards, the exertion of those sacred and sovereign rights of punishment, reserved in the hands of the people for cases of extreme necessity, and judged by the constitution unsafe to be delegated to any other judicature. While every day brought forth some new and unjustifiable exertion of power over their subjects on that side of the water, it was not to be expected that those here, much less able at that time to oppose the designs of despotism, should be exempted from injury. Accordingly, this country which had been acquired by the lives, the labors, and fortunes of individual adventurers, was by these Princes, several times, parted out and distributed among the favorites and followers of their fortunes; and, by an assumed right of the Crown alone, were erected into distinct and independent governments; a measure, which it is believed, his Majesty's prudence and understanding would prevent him from imitating at this day; as no exercise of such power, of dividing and dismembering a country, has ever occurred in his Majesty's realm of England, though now of very ancient standing; nor could it be justified or acquiesced under there, or in any part of his Majesty's empire.

That the exercise of a free trade with all parts of the world, possessed by the American colonists, as of natural right, and which no law of their own had taken away or abridged, was next the object of unjust encroachment. Some of the colonies having thought proper to continue the administration of their government in the name and under the authority of his Majesty, King Charles the first, whom, notwithstanding his late deposition by the Commonwealth of England, they continued in the sovereignty of their State, the Parliament, for the Commonwealth, took the same in high offence, and assumed upon themselves the power of prohibiting their trade with all other parts of the world, except the Island of Great Britain. This arbitrary act, however, they soon recalled, and by solemn treaty entered into on the 12th day of March, 1651, between the said Commonwealth, by their Commissioners, and the colony of Virginia by their House of Burgesses, it was expressly stipulated by the eighth article of the said treaty, that they should have 'free trade as the people of England do enjoy to all places and with all nations, according to the laws of that Commonwealth.' But that, upon the restoration of his Majesty, King Charles the second, their rights of free commerce fell once more a victim to arbitrary power; and by several acts of his reign, as well as of some of his successors, the trade of the colonies was laid under such restrictions, as show what hopes they might form from the justice of a British Parliament, were its uncontrolled power admitted over these States. History has informed us, that bodies of men as well as of individuals, are susceptible of the spirit of tyranny. A view of these acts of Parliament for regulation, as it has been affectedly called, of the American trade, if all other evidences were removed out of the case, would undeniably evince the truth of this observation. Besides the duties they impose on our articles of export and import, they prohibit our going to any markets Northward of Cape Finisterra, in the kingdom of Spain, for the sale of commodities which Great Britain will not take from us, and for the purchase of others, with which she cannot supply us; and that, for no other than the arbitrary purpose of purchasing for themselves, by a sacrifice of our rights and interests, certain privileges in their commerce with an allied state, who, in confidence, that their exclusive trade with America will be continued, while the principles and power of the British Parliament be the same, have indulged themselves in every exorbitance which their avarice could dictate or our necessity extort: have raised their commodities called for in America, to the double and treble of what they sold for, before such exclusive privileges were given them, and of what better commodities of the same kind would cost us elsewhere; and, at the same time, give us much less for what we carry thither, than might be had at more convenient ports. That these acts prohibit us from carrying, in quest of other purchasers, the surplus of our tobaccos, remaining after the consumption of Great Britain is supplied: so that we must leave them with the British merchant, for whatever he will please to allow us, to be by him re-shipped to foreign markets, where he will reap the benefits of making sale of them for full value. That, to heighten still the idea of Parliamentary justice, and to show with what moderation they are like to exercise power, where themselves are to feel no part of its weight, we take leave to mention to his Majesty, certain other acts of the British Parliament, by which they would prohibit us from manufacturing, for our own use, the articles we raise on our own lands, with our own labor. By an act passed in the fifth year of the reign of his late Majesty, King George the second, an American subject is forbidden to make a hat for himself, of the fur which he has taken, perhaps, on his own soil; an instance of despotism, to which no parallel can be produced in the most arbitrary ages of British history. By one other act, passed in the twenty-third year of the same reign, the iron which we make, we are forbidden to manufacture; and, heavy as that article is, and necessary in every branch of husbandry, besides commission and insurance, we are to pay freight for it to Great Britain, and freight for it back again, for the purpose of supporting, not men, but machines, in the island of Great Britain. In the same spirit of equal and impartial legislation, is to be viewed the act of Parliament, passed in the fifth year of the same reign, by which American lands are made subject to the demands of British creditors, while their own lands were still continued unanswerable for their debts; from which, one of these conclusions must necessarily follow, either that justice is not the same thing in America as in Britain, or else, that the British Parliament pay less regard to it here than there. But, that we do not point out to his Majesty the injustice of these acts, with intent to rest on that principle the cause of their nullity; but to show that experience confirms the propriety of those political principles, which exempt us from the jurisdiction of the British Parliament. The true ground on which we declare these acts void, is, that the British Parliament has no right to exercise authority over us.

That these exercises of usurped power have not been confined to instances alone, in which themselves were interested; but they have also intermeddled with the regulation of the internal affairs of the colonies. The act of the 9th of Anne for establishing a post office in America, seems to have had little connection with British convenience, except that of accommodating his Majesty's ministers and favorites with the sale of a lucrative and easy office.

That thus have we hastened through the reigns which preceded his Majesty's, during which the violation of our rights were less alarming, because repeated at more distant intervals, than that rapid and bold succession of injuries, which is likely to distinguish the present from all other periods of American story. Scarcely have our minds been able to emerge from the astonishment into which one stroke of Parliamentary thunder has involved us, before another more heavy and more alarming is fallen on us. Single acts of tyranny may be ascribed to the accidental opinion of a day; but a series of oppressions, begun at a distinguished period, and pursued unalterably through every change of ministers, too plainly prove a deliberate, systematical plan of reducing us to slavery.[1]

That the act, passed in the 4th year of his majesty's reign, entitled "An act for granting certain duties in the British colonies and plantations in America, &c."

One other act, passed in the 5th year of his reign, entitled "An act for granting and applying certain stamp duties and other duties in the British colonies and plantations in America, &c."

One other act, passed in the 6th year of his reign, entitled "An act for the better securing the dependency of his majesty's dominions in America upon the crown and parliament of Great Britain;" and one other act, passed in the 7th year of his reign entitled "An act for granting duties on paper, tea, &c." form that connected chain of parliamentary usurpation, which has already been the subject of frequent applications to his majesty, and the houses of lords and commons of Great Britain; and no answers having yet been condescended to any

[1]The following passage, naming the acts of tyranny, is taken from Ford. [Paul Leicester Ford, ed., *The Works of Thomas Jefferson*, Federal Edition, 12 vols., G. P. Putnam's Sons: New York and London, 1904–05.] The version given in the Memorial Edition is not intelligible.

of these, we shall not trouble his majesty with a repetition of the matters they contained.

But that one other act, passed in the same 7th year of the reign, having been a peculiar attempt, must ever require peculiar mention; it is entitled "An act for suspending the legislature of New York."[1]

One free and independent legislature, hereby takes upon itself to suspend the powers of another, free and independent as itself. Thus exhibiting a phenomenon unknown in nature, the creator, and creature of its own power. Not only the principles of common sense, but the common feelings of human nature must be surrendered up, before his Majesty's subjects here, can be persuaded to believe, that they hold their political existence at the will of a British Parliament. Shall these governments be dissolved, their property annihilated, and their people reduced to a state of nature, at the imperious breath of a body of men whom they never saw, in whom they never confided, and over whom they have no powers of punishment or removal, let their crimes against the American public be ever so great? Can any one reason be assigned, why one hundred and sixty thousand electors in the island of Great Britain, should give law to four millions in the States of America, every individual of whom is equal to every individual of them in virtue, in understanding, and in bodily strength? Were this to be admitted, instead of being a free people, as we have hitherto supposed, and mean to continue ourselves, we should suddenly be found the slaves, not of one, but of one hundred and sixty thousand tyrants; distinguished, too, from all others, by this singular circumstance, that they are removed from the reach of fear, the only restraining motive which may hold the hand of a tyrant.

That, by 'an act to discontinue in such manner, and for such time as are therein mentioned, the landing and discharging, lading or shipping of goods, wares and merchandize, at the town and within the harbor of Boston, in the province of Massachusetts bay, in North America,' which was passed at the last session of the British Parliament, a large and populous town, whose trade was their sole subsistence, was deprived of that trade, and involved in utter ruin. Let us for a while, suppose the question of right suspended, in order to examine

---

[1]This ends the inserted material from Ford.

this act on principles of justice. An act of Parliament had been passed, imposing duties on teas, to be paid in America, against which act the Americans had protested, as inauthoritative. The East India Company, who till that time, had never sent a pound of tea to America on their own account, step forth on that occasion, the asserters of Parliamentary right, and send hither many ship loads of that obnoxious commodity. The masters of their several vessels, however, on their arrival in America, wisely attended to admonition, and returned with their cargoes. In the province of New-England alone, the remonstrances of the people were disregarded, and a compliance, after being many days waited for, was flatly refused. Whether in this, the master of the vessel was governed by his obstinacy, or his instructions, let those who know, say. There are extraordinary situations which require extraordinary interposition. An exasperated people, who feel that they possess power, are not easily restrained within limits strictly regular. A number of them assembled in the town of Boston, threw the tea into the ocean, and dispersed without doing any other act of violence. If in this they did wrong, they were known, and were amenable to the laws of the land; against which, it could not be objected, that they had ever, in any instance, been obstructed or diverted from the regular course, in favor of popular offenders. They should, therefore, not have been distrusted on this occasion. But that ill-fated colony had formerly been bold in their enmities against the House of Stuart, and were now devoted to ruin, by that unseen hand which governs the momentous affairs of this great empire. On the partial representations of a few worthless ministerial dependants, whose constant office it has been to keep that government embroiled, and who, by their treacheries, hope to obtain the dignity of British knighthood, without calling for a party accused, without asking a proof, without attempting a distinction between the guilty and the innocent, the whole of that ancient and wealthy town, is in a moment reduced from opulence to beggary. Men who had spent their lives in extending the British commerce, who had invested, in that place, the wealth their honest endeavors had merited, found themselves and their families, thrown at once on the world, for subsistence by its charities. Not the hundredth part of the inhabitants of that town, had been concerned in the act complained of; many of them were in Great Britain, and in other parts beyond the sea; yet all were involved in one indiscriminate ruin, by a new executive power, unheard of till then, that of a British Parliament. A property of the value of many millions of money, was sacrificed to revenge, not repay, the loss of a few thousands. This is administering justice with a heavy hand indeed! And when is this tempest to be arrested in its course? Two wharves are to be opened again when his Majesty shall think proper: the residue, which lined the extensive shores of the bay of Boston, are forever interdicted the exercise of commerce. This little exception seems to have been thrown in for no other purpose, than that of setting a precedent for investing his Majesty with legislative powers. If the pulse of his people shall beat calmly under this experiment, another and another will be tried, till the measure of despotism be filled up. It would be an insult on common sense, to pretend that this exception was made, in order to restore its commerce to that great town. The trade, which cannot be received at two wharves alone, must of necessity be transferred to some other place; to which it will soon be followed by that of the two wharves. Considered in this light, it would be an insolent and cruel mockery at the annihilation of the town of Boston. By the act for the suppression of riots and tumults in the town of Boston, passed also in the last session of Parliament, a murder committed there, is, if the Governor pleases, to be tried in the court of King's bench, in the island of Great Britain, by a jury of Middlesex. The witnesses, too, on receipt of such a sum as the Governor shall think it reasonable for them to expend, are to enter into recognizance to appear at the trial. This is, in other words, taxing them to the amount of their recognizance; and that amount may be whatever a Governor pleases. For who does his Majesty think can be prevailed on to cross the Atlantic for the sole purpose of bearing evidence to a fact? His expenses are to be borne, indeed, as they shall be estimated by a Governor; but who are to feed the wife and children whom he leaves behind, and who have had no other subsistence but his daily labor? Those epidemical disorders, too, so terrible in a foreign climate, is the cure of them to be estimated among the articles of expense, and their danger to be warded off by the Almighty power of a Parliament? And the wretched criminal, if he happen to have offended on the American side, stripped of his privilege of trial by peers of his vicinage, removed from the place where alone full evidence could be obtained, without money, without counsel, without friends, without exculpatory proof, is tried before Judges predetermined to condemn. The cowards who would suffer a countryman to be torn from the bowels of their society, in order to be thus offered a sacrifice to Parliamentary tyranny, would merit that everlasting infamy now fixed on the authors of the act! A clause, for a similar purpose, had been introduced into an act passed in the twelfth year of his Majesty's reign, entitled, 'an act for the better securing and preserving his Majesty's Dock-yards, Magazines, Ships, Ammunition and Stores;' against which, as meriting the same censures, the several colonies have already protested.

That these are the acts of power, assumed by a body of men foreign to our constitutions, and unacknowledged by our laws; against which we do, on behalf of the inhabitants of British America, enter this, our solemn and determined protest. And we do earnestly intreat his Majesty, as yet the only mediatory power between the several States of the British empire, to recommend to his Parliament of Great Britain, the total revocation of these acts, which, however nugatory they may be, may yet prove the cause of further discontents and jealousies among us.

That we next proceed to consider the conduct of his Majesty, as holding the Executive powers of the laws of these States, and mark out his deviations from the line of duty. By the Constitution of Great Britain, as well as of the several American States, his Majesty possesses the power of refusing to pass into a law, any bill which has already passed the other two branches of the legislature. His Majesty, however, and his ancestors, conscious of the impropriety of opposing their single opinion to the united wisdom of two Houses of Parliament, while their proceedings were unbiassed by interested principles, for several ages past, have modestly declined the exercise of this power, in that part of his empire called Great Britain. But, by change of circumstances, other principles than those of justice simply, have obtained an influence on their determinations. The addition of new States to the British empire has produced an addition of new, and, sometimes, opposite interests. It is now, therefore, the great office of his Majesty to resume the exercise of his negative power, and to prevent the passage of laws by any one legislature of the empire, which might bear injuriously on the rights and interests of another. Yet this will not excuse the wanton exercise of this power, which we have seen his Majesty practice on the laws of the American legislature. For the most trifling reasons, and, sometimes for no conceivable reason at all, his Majesty has rejected laws of the most salutary tendency. The abolition of domestic slavery is the great object of desire in those colonies, where it was, unhappily, introduced in their infant state. But previous to the enfranchisement of the slaves we have, it is necessary to exclude all further importations from Africa. Yet our repeated attempts to effect this, by prohibitions, and by imposing duties which might amount to a prohibition, having been hitherto defeated by his Majesty's negative: thus preferring the immediate advantages of a few British corsairs, to the lasting interests of the American States, and to the rights of human nature, deeply wounded by this infamous practice. Nay, the single interposition of an interested individual against a law was scarcely ever known to fail of success, though, in the opposite scale, were placed the interests of a whole country. That this is so shameful an abuse of a power, trusted with his Majesty for other purposes, as if, not reformed, would call for some legal restrictions.

With equal inattention to the necessities of his people here, has his Majesty permitted our laws to lie neglected, in England, for years, neither confirming them by his assent, nor annulling them by his negative: so, that such of them as have no suspending clause, we hold on the most precarious of all tenures, his Majesty's will; and such of them as suspend themselves till his Majesty's assent be obtained, we have feared might be called into existence at some future and distant period, when time and change of circumstances shall have rendered them destructive to his people here. And, to render this grievance still more oppressive, his Majesty, by his instructions, has laid his Governors under such restrictions, that they can pass no law, of any moment, unless it have such suspending clause: so that, however immediate may be the call for legislative interposition, the law cannot be executed, till it has twice crossed the Atlantic, by which time the evil may have spent its whole force.

But in what terms reconcilable to Majesty, and at the same time to truth, shall we speak of a late instruction to his Majesty's Governor of the colony of Virginia, by which he is forbidden to assent to any law for the division of a county, unless the new county will consent to have no representative in Assembly? That colony has as yet affixed no boundary to the Westward. Their Western counties, therefore, are of an indefinite extent. Some of them are actually seated many hundred miles from their Eastern limits. Is it possible, then, that his Majesty can have bestowed a single thought on the situation of those people, who, in order to obtain justice for injuries, however great or small, must, by the laws of that colony, attend their county court at such a distance, with all their witnesses, monthly, till their litigation be determined? Or does his Majesty seriously wish, and publish it to the world, that his subjects should give up the glorious right of representation, with all the benefits derived from that, and submit themselves the absolute slaves of his sovereign will? Or is it rather meant to confine the legislative body to the present numbers, that they may be the cheaper bargain, whenever they shall become worth the purchase?

One of the articles of impeachment against Tresilian, and the other Judges of Westminster Hall, in the reign of Richard the Second, for which they suffered death, as traitors to their country, was, that they had advised the King, that he might dissolve his Parliament at any time; and succeeding kings have adopted the opinion of these unjust Judges. Since the establishment, however, of the British constitution, at the glorious Revolution, on its free and ancient principles, neither his Majesty, nor his ancestors, have exercised such a power of dissolution in the island of Great Britain;[1] and when his Majesty was petitioned, by the united voice of his people there, to dissolve the present Parliament, who had become obnoxious to them, his Ministers were heard to declare, in open Parliament, that his Majesty possessed no such power by the constitution. But how different their language, and his practice, here! To declare, as their duty required, the known rights of their country, to oppose the usurpation of every foreign judicature, to disregard the imperious mandates of a Minister or Governor, have been the avowed causes of dissolving Houses of Representatives in America. But if such powers be really vested in his Majesty, can he suppose they

[1]On further inquiry, I find two instances of dissolutions before the Parliament would, of itself, have been at an end: viz., the Parliament called to meet August 24, 1698, was dissolved by King William, December 19 1700, and a new one called, to meet February 6, 1701, which was also dissolved, November 11, 1701, and a new one met December 30, 1701. [Jefferson's note.]

are there placed to awe the members from such purposes as these? When the representative body have lost the confidence of their constituents, when they have notoriously made sale of their most valuable rights, when they have assumed to themselves powers which the people never put into their hands, then, indeed, their continuing in office becomes dangerous to the State, and calls for an exercise of the power of dissolution. Such being the cause for which the representative body should, and should not, be dissolved, will it not appear strange, to an unbiassed observer, that that of Great Britain was not dissolved, while those of the colonies have repeatedly incurred that sentence?

But your Majesty, or your Governors, have carried this power beyond every limit known or provided for by the laws. After dissolving one House of Representatives, they have refused to call another, so that, for a great length of time, the legislature provided by the laws, has been out of existence. From the nature of things, every society must, at all times, possess within itself the sovereign powers of legislation. The feelings of human nature revolt against the supposition of a State so situated, as that it may not, in any emergency, provide against dangers which, perhaps, threaten immediate ruin. While those bodies are in existence to whom the people have delegated the powers of legislation, they alone possess, and may exercise, those powers. But when they are dissolved, by the lopping off one or more of their branches, the power reverts to the people, who may use it to unlimited extent, either assembling together in person, sending deputies, or in any other way they may think proper. We forbear to trace consequences further; the dangers are conspicuous with which this practice is replete.

That we shall, at this time also, take notice of an error in the nature of our land holdings, which crept in at a very early period of our settlement. The introduction of the Feudal tenures into the kingdom of England, though ancient, is well enough understood to set this matter in a proper light. In the earlier ages of the Saxon settlement, feudal holdings were certainly altogether unknown, and very few, if any, had been introduced at the time of the Norman conquest. Our Saxon ancestors held their lands, as they did their personal property in absolute dominion, disincumbered with any superior, answering nearly to the nature of those possessions which the Feudalist term Allodial.

William the Norman, first introduced that system generally. The lands which had belonged to those who fell in the battle of Hastings, and in the subsequent insurrections of his reign, formed a considerable proportion of the lands of the whole kingdom. These he granted out, subject to feudal duties, as did he also those of a great number of his new subjects, who, by persuasions or threats, were induced to surrender them for that purpose. But still, much was left in the hands of his Saxon subjects, held of no superior, and not subject to feudal conditions. These, therefore, by express laws, enacted to render uniform the system of military defence, were made liable to the same military duties as if they had been feuds; and the Norman lawyers soon found means to saddle them, also, with the other feudal burthens. But still they had not been surrendered to the King, they were not derived from his grant, and therefore they were not holden of him. A general principle was introduced, that "all lands in England were held either mediately or immediately of the Crown;" but this was borrowed from those holdings which were truly feudal, and only applied to others for the purposes of illustration. Feudal holdings were, therefore, but exceptions out of the Saxon laws of possession, under which all lands were held in absolute right. These, therefore, still form the basis or groundwork of the Common law, to prevail wheresoever the exceptions have not taken place. America was not conquered by William the Norman, nor its lands surrendered to him or any of his successors. Possessions there are, undoubtedly, of the Allodial nature. Our ancestors, however, who migrated hither, were laborers, not lawyers. The fictitious principle, that all lands belong originally to the King, they were early persuaded to believe real, and accordingly took grants of their own lands from the Crown. And while the Crown continued to grant for small sums and on reasonable rents, there was no inducement to arrest the error, and lay it open to public view. But his majesty has lately taken on him to advance the terms of purchase and holding, to the double of what they were; by which means, the acquisition of lands being rendered difficult, the population of our country is likely to be checked. It is time, therefore, for us to lay this matter before his Majesty, and to declare, that he has no right to grant lands of himself. From the nature and purpose of civil institutions, all the lands within the limits, which any particular party has circumscribed around itself, are assumed by that society, and subject to their allotment; this may be done by themselves assembled collectively, or by their legislature, to whom they may have delegated sovereign authority; and, if they are allotted in neither of these ways, each individual of the society, may appropriate to himself such lands as he finds vacant, and occupancy will give him title.

That, in order to enforce the arbitrary measures before complained of, his Majesty has, from time to time, sent among us large bodies of armed forces, not made up of the people here, nor raised by the authority of our laws. Did his Majesty possess such a right as this, it might swallow up all our other rights, whenever he should think proper. But his Majesty has no right to land a single armed man on our shores; and those whom he sends here are liable to our laws, for the suppression and punishment of riots, routs, and unlawful assemblies, or are hostile bodies invading us in defiance of law. When, in the course of the late war, it became expedient that a body of Hanoverian troops should be brought over for the defence of Great Britain, his Majesty's grandfather, our late sovereign, did not pretend to introduce them under any authority he possessed. Such a measure would have given just alarm to his subjects of Great Britain, whose liberties would not be safe if armed men of another country, and of another spirit, might be brought into the realm at any time, without the consent of their legislature. He, therefore, applied to Parliament, who passed an act for that purpose, limiting the number to be brought in, and the time they were to continue. In like manner is his Majesty restrained in every part of the empire. He possesses indeed the executive power of the laws in every State; but they are the laws of the particular State, which he is to administer within that State, and not those of any one within the limits of another. Every State must judge for itself, the number of armed men which they may safely trust among them, of whom they are to consist, and under what restrictions they are to be laid. To render these proceedings still more criminal against our laws, instead of subjecting the military to the civil power, his majesty has expressly made the civil subordinate to the military. But can his Majesty thus put down all law under his feet? Can he erect a power superior to that which erected himself? He has done it indeed by force; but let him remember that force cannot give right.

That these are our grievances, which we have thus laid before his

Majesty, with that freedom of language and sentiment which becomes
a free people claiming their rights as derived from the laws of nature,
and not as the gift of their Chief Magistrate. Let those flatter, who
fear: it is not an American art. To give praise where it is not due might
be well from the venal, but would ill beseem those who are asserting
the rights of human nature. They know, and will, therefore, say, that
Kings are the servants, not the proprietors of the people. Open your
breast, Sire, to liberal and expanded thought. Let not the name of
George the Third, be a blot on the page of history. You are surrounded
by British counsellors, but remember that they are parties. You have
no ministers for American affairs, because you have none taken from
among us, nor amenable to the laws on which they are to give you
advice. It behooves you, therefore, to think and to act for yourself and
your people. The great principles of right and wrong are legible to
every reader; to pursue them, requires not the aid of many counsellors. The whole art of government consists in the art of being honest.
Only aim to do your duty, and mankind will give you credit where you
fail. No longer persevere in sacrificing the rights of one part of the
empire to the inordinate desires of another; but deal out to all, equal
and impartial right. Let no act be passed by any one legislature, which
may infringe on the rights and liberties of another. This is the important post in which fortune has placed you, holding the balance of a
great, if a well-poised empire. This, Sire, is the advice of your great
American council, on the observance of which may perhaps depend
your felicity and future fame, and the preservation of that harmony
which alone can continue, both to Great Britain and America,
the reciprocal advantages of their connection. It is neither our
wish nor our interest to separate from her. We are willing, on our
part, to sacrifice everything which reason can ask, to the restoration
of that tranquillity for which all must wish. On their part, let them
be ready to establish union on a generous plan. Let them name their
terms, but let them be just. Accept of every commercial preference it is
in our power to give, for such things as we can raise for their use, or
they make for ours. But let them not think to exclude us from going
to other markets to dispose of those commodities which they cannot
use, nor to supply those wants which they cannot supply. Still less, let
it be proposed, that our properties, within our own territories, shall

be taxed or regulated by any power on earth, but our own. The God who gave us life, gave us liberty at the same time: the hand of force may destroy, but cannot disjoin them. This, Sire, is our last, our determined resolution. And that you will be pleased to interpose, with that efficacy which your earnest endeavors may insure, to procure redress of these our great grievances, to quiet the minds of your subjects in British America against any apprehensions of future encroachment, to establish fraternal love and harmony through the whole empire, and that that may continue to the latest ages of time, is the fervent prayer of all British America.

An Act for establishing Religious Freedom [1779], passed in the Assembly of Virginia in the beginning of the year 1786

Well aware that Almighty God hath created the mind free; that all attempts to influence it by temporal punishments or burdens, or by civil incapacitations, tend only to beget habits of hypocrisy and meanness, and are a departure from the plan of the Holy Author of our religion, who being Lord both of body and mind, yet chose not to propagate it by coercions on either, as was in his Almighty power to do; that the impious presumption of legislators and rulers, civil as well as ecclesiastical, who, being themselves but fallible and uninspired men have assumed dominion over the faith of others, setting up their own opinions and modes of thinking as the only true and infallible, and as such endeavoring to impose them on others, hath established and maintained false religions over the greatest part of the world, and through all time; that to compel a man to furnish contributions of money for the propagation of opinions which he disbelieves, is sinful and tyrannical; that even the forcing him to support this or that teacher of his own religious persuasion, is depriving him of the comfortable liberty of giving his contributions to the particular pastor whose morals he would make his pattern, and whose powers he feels most persuasive to righteousness, and is withdrawing from the ministry those temporal rewards, which proceeding from an approbation of their personal conduct, are an additional incitement to earnest and unremitting labors for the instruction of mankind; that our civil rights have no dependence on our religious opinions, more than our opinions in physics or geometry; that, therefore, the proscribing any citizen as unworthy the public confidence by laying upon him an incapacity of being called to the offices of trust and emolument, unless he profess or renounce this or that religious opinion, is depriving him injuriously of those privileges and advantages to which in common with his fellow citizens he has a natural right; that it tends also to corrupt the principles of that very religion it is meant to encourage, by bribing, with a monopoly of worldly honors and emoluments, those who will externally profess and conform to it; that though indeed these are criminal who do not withstand such temptation, yet neither are those innocent who lay the bait in their way; that to suffer the civil magistrate to intrude his powers into the field of opinion and to restrain the profession or propagation of principles, on the supposition of their ill tendency, is a dangerous fallacy, which at once destroys all religious liberty, because he being of course judge of that tendency, will make his opinions the rule of judgment, and approve or condemn the sentiments of others only as they shall square with or differ from his own; that it is time enough for the rightful purposes of civil government, for its offices to interfere when principles break out into overt acts against peace and good order; and finally, that truth is great and will prevail if left to herself, that she is the proper and sufficient antagonist to error, and has nothing to fear from the conflict, unless by human interposition disarmed of her natural weapons, free argument and debate, errors ceasing to be dangerous when it is permitted freely to contradict them.

Be it therefore enacted by the General Assembly, That no man shall be compelled to frequent or support any religious worship, place or ministry whatsoever, nor shall be enforced, restrained, molested, or burthened in his body or goods, nor shall otherwise suffer on account of his religious opinions or belief; but that all men shall be free to profess, and by argument to maintain, their opinions in matters of religion, and that the same shall in nowise diminish, enlarge, or affect their civil capacities.

And though we well know this Assembly, elected by the people for the ordinary purposes of legislation only, have no power to restrain the acts of succeeding assemblies, constituted with the powers equal to our own, and that therefore to declare this act irrevocable, would be of no effect in law, yet we are free to declare, and do declare, that the rights hereby asserted are of the natural rights of mankind, and that if any act shall be hereafter passed to repeal the present or to narrow its operation, such act will be an infringement of natural right.

Report of Government for the Western Territory.[1] March 22, 1784

The Committee to whom was re-committed the report of a plan for a temporary government of the Western territory have agreed to the following resolutions.

Resolved, that so much of the territory ceded or to be ceded by individual states to the United States as is already purchased or shall be purchased of the Indian inhabitants & offered for sale by Congress, shall be divided into distinct states, ...

That the settlers on any territory so purchased & offered for sale shall, either on their own petition, or on the order of Congress, receive authority from them with appointments of time & place for their free males of full age, within the limits of their state to meet together for the purpose of establishing a temporary government, to adopt the constitution and laws of any one of the original states, so that such laws nevertheless shall be subject to alteration by their ordinary legislature; & to erect, subject to a like alteration, counties or townships for the election of members for their legislature.

That such temporary government shall only continue in force in any state until it shall have acquired 20,000 free inhabitants, when giving due proof thereof to Congress, they shall receive from them authority with appointment of time & place to call a convention of representatives to establish a permanent Constitution & Government for themselves. Provided that both the temporary and permanent governments be established on these principles as their basis. 1. That they shall forever remain a part of this confederacy of the United States of America. 2. That in their persons, property and territory they shall be subject to the Government of the United States in Congress assembled, & to the articles of Confederation in all those cases in which the orig-

[1]This document has been included because of its important proposal to limit the spread of slavery in the entire western territory of the United States. [The text is taken from Ford.]

inal states shall be so subject. 3. That they shall be subject to pay a part of the federal debts contracted or to be contracted, to be apportioned on them by Congress, according to the same common rule & measure, by which apportionments thereof shall be made on the other states. 4. That their respective Governments shall be in republican forms and shall admit no person to be a citizen who holds any hereditary title. 5. That after the year 1800 of the Christian era, there shall be neither slavery nor involuntary servitude in any of the sd states, otherwise than in punishment of crimes whereof the party shall have been convicted to have been personally guilty.

That whensoever any of ths sd states shall have, of free inhabitants, as many as shall then be in any one the least numerous, of the thirteen original states, such state shall be admitted by it's delegates into the Congress of the United States on an equal footing with the said original states: provided nine States agree to such admission according to the reservation of the 11th of the articles of Confederation, and in order to adopt the sd articles of Confederation, to the state of Congress when it's numbers shall be thus increased, it shall be proposed to the legislatures of states originally parties thereto, to require the assent of two thirds of the United States in Congress assembled in all those cases wherein by the said articles the assent of nine states is now required; which being agreed to by them shall be binding on the new states. Until such admission by their delegates into Congress, any of the said states after the establishment of their temporary government shall have authority to keep a sitting member in Congress, with a right of debating, but not of voting.

That the preceding articles shall be formed into a charter of compact, shall be duly executed by the president of the United States in Congress assembled, under his hand & the seal of the United States, shall be promulgated & shall stand as fundamental constitutions between the thirteen original states and each of the several states now newly described, unalterable but by the joint consent of the United States in Congress assembled, & of the particular state within which such alteration is proposed to be made.

That measures not inconsistent with the principles of the Confedn. & necessary for the preservation of peace & good order among the settlers in any of the said new states until they shall assume a temporary

Government as aforesaid, may from time to time be taken by the U S in C. assembled.

> *Opinion upon the question whether the President should veto the Bill, declaring that the seat of government shall be transferred to the Potomac, in the year 1790. July 15, 1790*

. . . .

Every man, and every body of men on earth, posseses the right of self-government. They receive it with their being from the hand of nature. Individuals exercise it by their single will; collections of men by that of their majority; for the law of the majority is the natural law of every society of men. When a certain description of men are to transact together a particular business, the times and places of their meeting and separating, depend on their own will; they make a part of the natural right of self-government. This, like all other natural rights, may be abridged or modified in its exercise by their own consent, or by the law of those who depute them, if they meet in the right of others; but as far as it is not abridged or modified, they retain it as a natural right and may exercise them in what form they please, either exclusively by themselves, or in association with others, or by others altogether, as they shall agree.

> *March 18, 1792. Paper on the rights to navigate the Mississippi*

. . . .

But our right is built on ground still broader and more unquestionable, to wit:

On the law of nature and nations.

If we appeal to this, as we feel it written on the heart of man, what sentiment is written in deeper characters than that the ocean is free to all men, and their rivers to all their inhabitants? Is there a man, savage or civilized, unbiased by habit, who does not feel and attest this truth? Accordingly, in all tracts of country united under the same political society, we find this natural right universally acknowledged and protected by laying the navigable rivers open to all their inhabitants. When their rivers enter the limits of another society, if the right of the upper inhabitants to descend the stream is in any case obstructed, it is an act of force by a stronger society against a weaker, condemned by the judgment of mankind. The late case of Antwerp and the Scheldt was a striking proof of a general union of sentiment on this point; as it is believed that Amsterdam had scarcely an advocate out of Holland, and even there its pretensions were advocated on the ground of treaties, and not of natural right. . . . The United States hold 600,000 square miles of habitable territory on the Mississippi and its branches, and this river and its branches afford many thousands of miles of navigable waters penetrating this territory in all its parts. The inhabitable grounds of Spain below our boundary and bordering on the river, which alone can pretend any fear of being incommoded by our use of the river, are not the thousandth part of that extent. This vast portion of the territory of the United States has no other outlet for its productions, and these productions are of the bulkiest kind. And in truth, their passage down the river may not only be innocent as to the Spanish subjects on the river, but cannot fail to enrich them far beyond their present condition. The real interest then of all the inhabitants, upper and lower, concur in fact with their rights.

. . . .

Opinion on the question whether the United States have a right to renounce their treaties with France, or to hold them suspended till the government of that country shall be established. April 28, 1793

. . . .

I consider the people who constitute a society or nation as the source of all authority in that nation; as free to transact their common concerns by any agents they think proper; to change these agents individually, or the organization of them in form or function whenever they please; that all the acts done by these agents under the authority of the nation, are the acts of the nation, are obligatory to them and enure to their use, and can in no wise be annulled or affected by any change in the form of the government, or of the persons administering it, consequently the treaties between the United States and France, were not treaties between the United States and Louis Capet, but between the two nations of

America and France; and the nations remaining in existence, though both of them have since changed their forms of government, the treaties are not annulled by these changes. The law of nations, by which this question is to be determined, is composed of three branches. 1. The moral law of our nature. 2. The usages of nations. 3. Their special conventions. The first of these only concerns this question, that is to say the moral law to which man has been subjected by his creator, and of which his feelings or conscience, as it is sometimes called, are the evidence with which his creator has furnished him. The moral duties which exist between individual and individual in a state of nature, accompany them into a state of society, and the aggregate of the duties of all the individuals composing the society constitutes the duties of that society towards any other; so that between society and society the same moral duties exist as did between the individuals composing them, while in an unassociated state, and their maker not having released them from those duties on their forming themselves into a nation. Compacts then, between nation and nation, are obligatory on them by the same moral law which obliges individuals to observe their compacts. There are circumstances, however, which sometimes excuse the non-performance of contracts between man and man; so are there also between nation and nation. When performance, for instance, becomes impossible, non-performance is not immoral; so if performance becomes self-destructive to the party, the law of self-preservation overrules the laws of obligation in others. For the reality of these principles I appeal to the true fountains of evidence, the head and heart of every rational and honest man. It is there nature has written her moral laws, and where every man may read them for himself. He will never read there the permission to annul his obligations for a time, or forever, whenever they become dangerous useless, or disagreeable; certainly not when merely useless or disagreeable. . . . and though he may, under certain degrees of danger, yet the danger must be imminent, and the degree great. Of these, it is true, that nations are to be judges for themselves; since no one nation has a right to sit in judgment over another, but the tribunal of our conscience remains, and that also of the opinion of the world. These will revise the sentence we pass in our own case, and as we respect these, we must see that in judging ourselves we have honestly done the part of impartial and rigorous judges.

. . . . Questions of natural right are triable by their conformity with the moral sense and reason of man. Those who write treatises of natural law, can only declare what their own moral sense and reason dictate in the several cases they state. Such of them as happen to have feelings and a reason coincident with those of the wise and honest part of mankind, are respected and quoted as witnesses of what is morally right or wrong in particular cases. Grotius, Puffendorf, Wolf, and Vattel are of this number. Where they agree their authority is strong; but where they differ (and they often differ), we must appeal to our own feelings and reason to decide between them. . . .

Report on the privileges end restrictions on the commerce of the United States in foreign countries. December 16, 1793

. . . . As to commerce, two methods occur. 1. By friendly arrangements with the several nations with whom these restrictions exist: Or, 2. By the separate act of our own legislatures for countervailing their effects.

There can be no doubt but that of these two, friendly arrangement is the most eligible. Instead of embarrassing commerce under piles of regulating laws, duties and prohibitions, could it be relieved from all its shackles in all parts of the world, could every country be employed in producing that which nature has best fitted it to produce, and each be free to exchange with others mutual surplusses for mutual wants, the greatest mass possible would then be produced of those things which contribute to human life and human happiness; the numbers of mankind would be increased, and their condition bettered. . . .

But should any nation, contrary to our wishes, suppose it may better find its advantage by continuing its system of prohibitions, duties and regulations, it behooves us to protect our citizens, their commerce and navigation, by counter prohibitions, duties and regulations, also. Free commerce and navigation are not to be given in exchange for restrictions and vexations; nor are they likely to produce a relaxation of them. . . .

Where a nation imposes high duties on our productions, or prohibits them altogether, it may be proper for us to do the same by theirs; first burdening or excluding those productions which they bring here, in competition with our own of the same kind; selecting next, such manufactures as we take from them in greatest quantity, and which, at the same time, we could the soonest furnish to ourselves, or obtain from other countries; imposing on them duties lighter at first, but heavier and heavier afterwards as other channels of supply open. Such duties having the effect of indirect encouragement to domestic manufactures of the same kind, may induce the manufacturer to come himself into these States, where cheaper subsistence, equal laws, and a vent of his wares, free of duty, may ensure him the highest profits from his skill and industry. And here, it would be in the power of the State governments to co-operate essentially, by opening the resources of encouragement which are under their control, extending them liberally to artists in those particular branches of manufacture for which their soil, climate, population and other circumstances have matured them, and fostering the precious efforts and progress of household manufacture, by some patronage suited to the nature of its objects, guided by the local informations they possess, and guarded against abuse by their presence and attentions. The oppressions on our agriculture, in foreign ports, would thus be made the occasion of relieving it from a dependence on the councils and conduct of others, and of promoting arts, manufactures and population at home. . . .

Inauguration Address.—March 4, 1801

Friends and Fellow Citizens:—

Called upon to undertake the duties of the first executive office of our country, I avail myself of the presence of that portion of my fellow citizens which is here assembled, to express my grateful thanks for the favor with which they have been pleased to look toward me, to declare a sincere consciousness that the task is above my talents, and that I approach it with those anxious and awful presentiments which the greatness of the charge and the weakness of my powers so justly inspire. A rising nation, spread over a wise and fruitful land, traversing all the seas with the rich productions of their industry, engaged in commerce with nations who feel power and forget right, advancing rapidly to destinies beyond the reach of mortal eye—when I contemplate these transcendent objects, and see the honor, the happiness, and the hopes of this beloved country committed to the issue and the auspices of this day, I shrink from the contemplation, and humble myself before the magnitude of the undertaking. Utterly indeed, should I despair, did not the presence of many whom I here see remind me, that in the other high authorities provided by our constitution, I shall find resources of wisdom, of virtue, and of zeal, on which to rely under all difficulties. To you, then, gentlemen, who are charged with the sovereign functions of legislation, and to those associated with you, I look with encouragement for that guidance and support which may enable us to steer with safety the vessel in which we are all embarked amid the conflicting elements of a troubled world.

During the contest of opinion through which we have passed, the animation of discussion and of exertions has sometimes worn an aspect which might impose on strangers unused to think freely and to speak and to write what they think; but this being now decided by the voice of the nation, announced according to the rules of the constitution, all will, of course, arrange themselves under the will of the law, and unite in common efforts for the common good. All, too, will bear in mind this sacred principle, that though the will of the majority is in all cases to prevail, that will, to be rightful, must be reasonable; that the minority possess their equal rights, which equal laws must protect, and to violate which would be oppression. Let us, then, fellow citizens, unite with one heart and one mind. Let us restore to social intercourse that harmony and affection without which liberty and even life itself are but dreary things. And let us reflect that having banished from our land that religious intolerance under which mankind so long bled and suffered, we have yet gained little if we countenance a political intolerance as despotic, as wicked, and capable of as bitter and bloody persecutions. During the throes and convulsions of the ancient world, during the agonizing spasms of infuriated man, seeking through blood and slaughter his long-lost liberty, it was not wonderful that the agitations of the billows should reach even this distant and peaceful shore; that this should be more felt and feared by some and less by others; that this should divide opinions as to measures of safety. But every difference of opinion is not a difference of principle. We have called by different names brethren of the same principle. We are all republicans—we are federalists. If there be any among us who would wish to dissolve this Union or to change its republican form, let them stand undisturbed as monuments of the safety with which error of opinion may be tolerated where reason is left free to combat it. I know, indeed, that some honest men fear that a republican government cannot be strong; that this government is not strong enough. But would the honest patriot, in the full tide of successful experiment, abandon a government which has so far kept us free and firm, on the theoretic and visionary fear that this government, the world's best hope, may by possibility want energy to preserve itself? I trust not. I believe this, on the contrary, the strongest government on earth. I believe it is the only one where every man, at the call of the laws, would fly to the standard of the law, and would meet invasions of the public order as his own personal concern. Sometimes it is said that man cannot be trusted with the government of himself. Can he, then, be trusted with the government of others? Or have we found angels in the forms of kings to govern him? Let history answer this question.

Let us, then, with courage and confidence pursue our own federal and republican principles, our attachment to our union and representative government. Kindly separated by nature and a wide ocean from the exterminating havoc of one quarter of the globe; too high-minded to endure the degradations of the others; possessing a chosen country, with room enough for our descendants to the hundredth and thousandth generation; entertaining a due sense of our equal right to the use of our own faculties, to the acquisitions of our industry, to honor and confidence from our fellow citizens, resulting not from birth but from our actions and their sense of them; enlightened by a benign religion, professed, indeed, and practiced in various forms, yet all of them including honesty, truth, temperance, gratitude, and the love of man; acknowledging and adoring an overruling Providence, which by all its dispensations proves that it delights in the happiness of man here and his greater happiness hereafter; with all these blessings, what more is necessary to make us a happy and prosperous people? Still one thing more, fellow citizens—a wise and frugal government, which shall restrain men from injuring one another, which shall leave them otherwise free to regulate their own pursuits of industry and improvement, and shall not take from the mouth of labor the bread it has earned. This is the sum of good government, and this is necessary to close the circle of our felicities.

About to enter, fellow citizens, on the exercise of duties which comprehend everything dear and valuable to you, it is proper that you should understand what I deem the essential principles of our government, and consequently those which ought to shape its administration. I will compress them within the narrowest compass they will bear, stating the general principle, but not all its limitations. Equal and exact justice to all men, of whatever state or persuasion, religious or political; peace, commerce, and honest friendship, with all nations—entangling alliances with none; the support of the state governments in all their rights, as the most competent administrations for our domestic concerns and the surest bulwarks against anti-republican tendencies; the preservation of the general government in its whole constitutional vigor, as the sheet anchor of our peace at home and safety abroad; a jealous care of the right of election by the people—a mild and safe corrective of abuses which are lopped by the sword of the revolution where peaceable remedies are unprovided; absolute acquiescence in the decisions of the majority—the vital principle of republics, from which there is no appeal but to force, the vital principle and immediate parent of despotism; a well-disciplined militia—our best reliance in peace and for the first moments of war, till regulars may relieve them; the supremacy of the civil over the military authority; economy in the public expense, that labor may be lightly burdened; the honest payment of our debts and sacred preservation of the public faith; encouragement of agriculture, and of commerce as its handmaid; the diffusion of information and the arraignment of all abuses at the bar of public reason; freedom of religion; freedom of the press; freedom of person under the protection of the habeas corpus; and trial by juries impartially selected—these principles form the bright constellation which has gone before us, and guided our steps through an age of revolution and reformation. The wisdom of our sages and the blood of our heroes have been devoted to their attainment. They should be the creed of our political faith—the text of civil instruction—the touchstone by which to try the services of those we trust; and should we wander from them in moments of error or alarm, let us hasten to retrace our steps and to regain the road which alone leads to peace, liberty, and safety.

I repair, then, fellow citizens, to the post you have assigned me. With experience enough in subordinate offices to have seen the difficulties of this, the greatest of all, I have learned to expect that it will rarely fall to the lot of imperfect man to retire from this station with the reputation and the favor which bring him into it. Without pretensions to that high confidence reposed in our first and great revolutionary character, whose preeminent services had entitled him to the first place in his country's love, and destined for him the fairest page in the volume of faithful history, I ask so much confidence only as may give firmness and effect to the legal administration of your affairs. I shall often go wrong through defect of judgment When right, I shall often be thought wrong by those whose positions will not command a view of the whole ground. I ask your indulgence for my own errors, which will never be intentional; and your support against the errors of others, who may condemn what they would not if seen in all its parts. The approbation implied by your suffrage is a consolation to me for the past; and my future solicitude will be to retain the good opinion of those who have bestowed it in advance, to conciliate that of others by doing them all the good in my power, and to be instrumental to the happiness and freedom of all.

Relying, then, on the patronage of your good will, I advance with obedience to the work, ready to retire from it whenever you become sensible how much better choice it is in your power to make. And may that Infinite Power which rules the destinies of the universe, lead our councils to what is best, and give them a favorable issue for your peace and prosperity.

First Annual Message.—December 8, 1801

Fellow citizens of the Senate and House of Representatives:

It is a circumstance of sincere gratification to me that on meeting the great council of our nation, I am able to announce to them, on the grounds of reasonable certainty, that the wars and troubles which have for so many years afflicted our sister nations have at length come to an end, and that the communications of peace and commerce are once more opening among them. While we devoutly return thanks to the beneficent Being who has been pleased to breathe into them the spirit of conciliation and forgiveness, we are bound with peculiar gratitude to be thankful to him that our own peace has been preserved through so perilous a season, and ourselves permitted quietly to cultivate the earth and to practice and improve those arts which tend to increase our comforts. The assurances, indeed, of friendly disposition, received from all the powers with whom we have principal relations, had inspired a confidence that our peace with them would not have been disturbed. But a cessation of the irregularities which had affected the commerce of neutral nations, and of the irritations and injuries produced by them, cannot but add to this confidence; and strengthens, at the same time, the hope, that wrongs committed on unoffending friends, under a pressure of circumstances, will now be reviewed with candor, and will be considered as founding just claims of retribution for the past and new assurance for the future.

Among our Indian neighbors, also, a spirit of peace and friendship generally prevails; and I am happy to inform you that the continued efforts to introduce among them the implements and the practice of husbandry, and of the household arts, have not been without success; that they are becoming more and more sensible of the superiority of this dependence for clothing and subsistence over the precarious resources of hunting and fishing; and already we are able to announce, that instead of that constant diminution of their numbers, produced by their wars and their wants, some of them begin to experience an increase of population.

To this state of general peace with which we have been blessed, one only exception exists. Tripoli, the least considerable of the Barbary States, had come forward with demands unfounded either in right or in compact, and had permitted itself to denounce war, on our failure to comply before a given day. The style of the demand admitted but one answer. I sent a small squadron of frigates into the Mediterranean, with assurances to that power of our sincere desire to remain in peace, but with orders to protect our commerce against the threatened attack. The measure was seasonable and salutary. The bey had already declared war in form. His cruisers were out. Two had arrived at Gibraltar. Our commerce in the Mediterranean was blockaded, and that of the Atlantic in peril. The arrival of our squadron dispelled the danger. One of the Tripolitan cruisers having fallen in with, and engaged the small schooner Enterprise, commanded by Lieutenant Sterret, which had gone as a tender to our larger vessels, was captured, after a heavy slaughter of her men, without the loss of a single one on our part. The bravery exhibited by our citizens on that element will, I trust, be a testimony to the world that it is not the want of that virtue which makes us seek their peace, but a conscientious desire to direct the energies of our nation to the multiplication of the human race, and not to its destruction. Unauthorized by the constitution, without the sanction of Congress, to go beyond the line of defence, the vessel being disabled from committing further hostilities, was liberated with its crew. The legislature will doubtless consider whether, by authorizing measures of offence, also, they will place our force on an equal footing with that of its adversaries. I communicate all material information on this subject, that in the exercise of the important function confided by the constitution to the legislature exclusively, their judgment may form itself on a knowledge and consideration of every circumstance of weight. . . .

I lay before you the result of the census lately taken of our inhabitants, to a conformity with which we are to reduce the ensuing rates of representation and taxation. You will perceive that the increase of numbers during the last ten years, proceeding in geometrical ratio, promises a duplication in little more than twenty-two years. We contemplate this rapid growth, and the prospect it holds up to us, not with a view to the injuries it may enable us to do to others in some future day, but to the settlement of the extensive country still remaining vacant within our limits, to the multiplications of men susceptible of happiness, educated in the love of order, habituated to self-government, and valuing its blessings above all price.

Other circumstances, combined with the increase of numbers, have produced an augmentation of revenue arising from consumption, in a ratio far beyond that of population alone, and though the changes of foreign relations now taking place so desirably for the world, may for a season affect this branch of revenue, yet, weighing all probabilities of expense, as well as of income, there is reasonable ground of confidence that we may now safely dispense with all the internal taxes, comprehending excises, stamps, auctions, licenses, carriages, and refined sugars, to which the postage on newspapers may be added, to facilitate the progress of information, and that the remaining sources of revenue will be sufficient to provide for the support of government, to pay the interest on the public debts, and to discharge the principals in shorter periods than the laws or the general expectations had contemplated. War, indeed, and untoward events, may change this prospect of things, and call for expenses which the imposts could not meet; but sound principles will not justify our taxing the industry of our fellow citizens to accumulate treasure for wars to happen we know not when, and which might not perhaps happen but from the temptations offered by that treasure.

These views, however, of reducing our burdens, are formed on the expectation that a sensible, and at the same time a salutary reduction, may take place in our habitual expenditures. For this purpose those of the civil government, the army, and navy, will need revisal.

When we consider that this government is charged with the external and mutual relations only of these states; that the states themselves have principal care of our persons, our property, and our reputation, constituting the great field of human concerns, we may well doubt whether our organization is not too complicated, too expensive; whether offices and officers have not been multiplied unnecessarily, and sometimes injuriously to the service they were meant to promote. . . .

A statement has been formed by the secretary of war, on mature consideration, of all the posts and stations where garrisons will be expedient, and of the number of men requisite for each garrison. The whole amount is considerably short of the present military establishment. For the surplus no particular use can be pointed out. For defence against invasion, their number is as nothing; nor is it conceived needful or safe that a standing army should be kept up in time of peace for that purpose. Uncertain as we must ever be of the particular point in our circumference where an enemy may choose to invade us, the only force which can be ready at every point and competent to oppose them, is the body of neighboring citizens as formed into a militia. On these, collected from the parts most convenient, in numbers proportioned to the invading foe, it is best to rely, not only to meet the first attack, but if it threatens to be permanent, to maintain the defence until regulars may be engaged to relieve them. These considerations render it important that we should at every session continue to amend the defects which from time to time show themselves in the laws for regulating the militia, until they are sufficiently perfect. Nor should we now or at any time separate, until we can say we have done everything for the militia which we could do were an enemy at our door.

The provisions of military stores on hands will be laid before you, that you may judge of the additions still requisite.

With respect to the extent to which our naval preparations should be carried, some difference of opinion may be expected to appear; but just attention to the circumstances of every part of the Union will doubtless reconcile all. A small force will probably continue to be wanted for actual service in the Mediterranean. Whatever annual sum beyond that you may think proper to appropriate to naval preparations, would perhaps be better employed in providing those articles which may be kept without waste or consumption, and be in readiness when any exigence calls them into use. Progress has been made, as will appear by papers now communicated, in providing materials for seventy-four gun ships as directed by law. . . .

Agriculture, manufacture, commerce, and navigation, the four pillars of our prosperity, are the most thriving when left most free to individual enterprise. Protection from casual embarrassments, however, may sometimes be seasonably interposed. If in the course of your observations or inquiries they should appear to need any aid within the limits of our constitutional powers, your sense of their importance is a sufficient assurance they will occupy your attention. We cannot, indeed, but all feel an anxious solicitude for the difficulties under which our carrying trade will soon be placed. How far it can be relieved, otherwise than by time, is a subject of important consideration.

The judiciary system of the United States, and especially that portion of it recently erected, will of course present itself to the contemplation of Congress; and that they may be able to judge of the proportion which the institution bears to the business it has to perform, I have caused to be procured from the several States, and now lay before Congress, an exact statement of all the causes decided since the first establishment of the courts, and of those which were depending when additional courts and judges were brought into their aid.

And while on the judiciary organization, it will be worthy your consideration, whether the protection of the inestimable institution of juries has been extended to all the cases involving the security of our persons and property. Their impartial selection also being essential to their value, we ought further to consider whether that is sufficiently secured in those States where they are named by a marshal depending on executive will, or designated by the court or by officers dependent on them.

I cannot omit recommending a revisal of the laws on the subject of naturalization. Considering the ordinary chances of human life, a denial of citizenship under a residence of fourteen years is a denial to a great proportion of those who ask it, and controls a policy pursued from their first settlement by many of these States, and still believed of consequence to their prosperity. And shall we refuse the unhappy fugitives from distress that hospitality which the savages of the wilderness extended to our fathers arriving in this land? Shall oppressed humanity find no asylum on this globe? The constitution, indeed, has wisely provided that, for admission to certain offices of important trust, a residence shall be required sufficient to develop character and design. But might not the general character and capabilities of a citizen be safely communicated to every one manifesting a bona fide purpose of embarking his life and fortunes permanently with us? with restrictions, perhaps, to guard against the fraudulent usurpation of our flag; an abuse which brings so much embarrassment and loss on the genuine citizen, and so much danger to the nation of being involved in war, that no endeavor should be spared to detect and suppress it.

These, fellow citizens, are the matters respecting the state of the nation, which I have thought of importance to be submitted to your consideration at this time. Some others of less moment, or not yet ready for communication, will be the subject of separate messages. I am happy in this opportunity of committing the arduous affairs of our government to the collected wisdom of the Union. Nothing shall be wanting on my part to inform, as far as in my power, the legislative judgement, nor to carry that judgment into faithful execution. The prudence and temperance of your discussions will promote, within your own walls, that conciliation which so much befriends rational conclusion; and by its example will encourage among our constituents that progress of opinion which is tending to unite them in object and in will. That all should be satisfied with any one order of things is not to be expected, but I indulge the pleasing persuasion that the great body of our citizens will cordially concur in honest and disinterested efforts, which have for their object to preserve the general and State governments in their constitutional form and equilibrium; to maintain peace abroad, and order and obedience to the laws at home; to establish principles and practices of administration favorable to the security of liberty and property, and to reduce expenses to what is necessary for the useful purposes of government.

Messrs. Nehemiah Dodge, Ephraim Robbins, and Stephen S. Nelson, A Committee of the Danbury Baptist Association, in the State of Connecticut. Washington, January 1, 1802

Gentlemen:—The affectionate sentiments of esteem and approbation which you are so good as to express towards me, on behalf of the Danbury Baptist Association, give me the highest satisfaction. My duties dictate a faithful and zealous pursuit of the interests of my constituents, and in proportion as they are persuaded of my fidelity to those duties, the discharge of them becomes more and more pleasing.

Believing with you that religion is a matter which lies solely between man and his God, that he owes account to none other for his faith or his worship, that the legislative powers of government reach actions only, and not opinions, I contemplate with sovereign reverence that act of the whole American people which declared that their legislature should "make no law respecting an establishment of religion, or prohibiting the free exercise thereof," thus building a wall of separation between Church and State. Adhering to this expression of the supreme will of the nation in behalf of the rights of conscience, I shall see with sincere satisfaction the progress of those sentiments which tend to restore to man all his natural rights, convinced he has no natural right in opposition to his social duties.

I reciprocate your kind prayers for the protection and blessing of the common Father and Creator of man, and tender you for yourselves and your religious association, assurances of my high respect and esteem.

Washington, January 7, 1802

Brothers and friends of the Miamis, Powtewatamies, and Weeauks:—

I receive with great satisfaction the visit you have been so kind as to make us at this place, and I thank the Great Spirit who has conducted you to us in health and safety. It is well that friends should sometimes meet, open their minds mutually, and renew the chain of affection. Made by the same Great Spirit, and living in the same land with our brothers, the red men, we consider ourselves as of the same family; we wish to live with them as one people, and to cherish their interests as our own. The evils which of necessity encompass the life of man are sufficiently numerous. Why should we add to them by voluntarily distressing and destroying one another? Peace, brothers, is better than war. In a long and bloody war, we lose many friends, and gain nothing. Let us then live in peace and friendship together, doing to each other all the good we can. The wise and good on both sides desire this, and we must take care that the foolish and wicked among us shall not prevent it. On our part, we shall endeavor in all things to be just and generous towards you, and to aid you in meeting those difficulties which a change of circumstances is bringing on. We shall, with great pleasure, see your people become disposed to cultivate the earth, to raise herds of the useful animals, and to spin and weave, for their food and clothing. These resources are certain; they will never disappoint you: while those of hunting may fail, and expose your women and children to the miseries of hunger and cold. We will with pleasure furnish you with implements for the most necessary arts, and with persons who may instruct you how to make and use them.

Second Annual Message.—December 15, 1802

. . . .

To cultivate peace and maintain commerce and navigation in all their lawful enterprises; to foster our fisheries and nurseries of navigation and for the nurture of man, and protect the manufactures adapted to our circumstances; to preserve the faith of the nation by an exact discharge of its debts and contracts, expend the public money with the same care and economy we would practise with our own, and impose on our citizens no unnecessary burden; to keep in all things within the pale of our constitutional powers, and cherish the federal union as the only rock of safety—these, fellow citizens, are the landmarks by which we are to guide ourselves in all our proceedings. By continuing to make these our rule of action, we shall endear to our countrymen the true principles of their constitution, and promote a union of sentiment and of action equally auspicious to their happiness and safety. On my part, you may count on a cordial concurrence in every measure for the public good, and on all the information I possess which may enable you to discharge to advantage the high functions with which you are invested by your country.

Third Annual Message.—October 17, 1803

To the Senate and House of Representatives of the United States:—

In calling you together, fellow citizens, at an earlier day than was contemplated by the act of the last session of Congress, I have not been insensible to the personal inconveniences necessarily resulting from an unexpected change in your arrangements. But matters of great public concernment have rendered this call necessary, and the interest you feel in these will supersede in your minds all private considerations.

Congress witnessed, at their last session, the extraordinary agitation produced in the public mind by the suspension of our right of deposit at the port of New Orleans, no assignment of another place having been made according to treaty. They were sensible that the continuance of that privation would be more injurious to our nation than any consequences which could flow from any mode of redress, but reposing just confidence in the good faith of the government whose officer had committed the wrong, friendly and reasonable representations were resorted to, and the right of deposit was restored.

Previous, however, to this period, we had not been unaware of the danger to which our peace would be perpetually exposed while so important a key to the commerce of the western country remained under foreign power. Difficulties, too, were presenting themselves as to the navigation of other streams, which, arising within our territories, pass through those adjacent. Propositions had, therefore, been authorized for obtaining, on fair conditions, the sovereignty of New Orleans, and of other possessions in that quarter interesting to our quiet, to such extent as was deemed practicable; and the provisional appropriation of two millions of dollars, to be applied and accounted for by the president of the United States, intended as part of the price, was considered as conveying the sanction of Congress to the acquisition proposed. The enlightened Government of France saw, with just discernment, the importance to both nations of such liberal arrangements as might best and permanently promote the peace, friendship, and interests of both; and the property and sovereignty of all Louisiana, which had been restored to them, have on certain conditions been transferred to the United States by instruments bearing date the 30th of April last. When these shall have received the constitutional sanction of the senate, they will without delay be communicated to the representatives also, for the exercise of their functions, as to those conditions which are within the powers vested by the constitution in Congress. While the property and sovereignty of the Mississippi and its waters secure an independent outlet for the produce of the western States, and an uncontrolled navigation through their whole course, free from collision with other powers and the dangers to our peace from that source, the fertility of the country, its climate and extent, promise in due season important aids to our treasury, an ample provision for our posterity, and a widespread field for the blessings of freedom and equal laws.

With the wisdom of Congress it will rest to take those ulterior measures which may be necessary for the immediate occupation and temporary government of the country; for its incorporation into our Union; for rendering the change of government a blessing to our newly-adopted brethren; for securing to them the rights of conscience and of property; for confirming to the Indian inhabitants their occupancy and self-government, establishing friendly and commercial relations with them, and for ascertaining the geography of the country acquired. Such materials for your information, relative to its affairs in general, as the short space of time has permitted me to collect, will be laid before you when the subject shall be in a state for your consideration.

Another important acquisition of territory has also been made since the last session of Congress. The friendly tribe of Kaskaskia Indians with which we have never had a difference, reduced by the wars and wants of savage life to a few individuals unable to defend themselves against the neighboring tribes, has transferred its country to the United States, reserving only for its members what is sufficient to maintain them in an agricultural way. The considerations stipulated are, that we shall extend to them our patronage and protection, and give them certain annual aids in money, in implements of agriculture, and other articles of their choice. This country, among the most fertile within our limits, extending along the Mississippi from the mouth of the Illinois to and up the Ohio, though not so necessary as a barrier since the acquisition of the other bank, may yet be well worthy of being laid open to immediate settlement, as its inhabitants may descend with rapidity in support of the lower country should future circumstances expose that to foreign enterprize. As the stipulations in this treaty also involve matters within the competence of both houses only, it will be laid before Congress as soon as the senate shall have advised its ratification.

With many other Indian tribes, improvements in agriculture and household manufacture are advancing, and with all our peace and friendship are established on grounds much firmer than heretofore. The measure adopted of establishing trading houses among them, and of furnishing them necessaries in exchange for their commodities, at such moderated prices as leave no gain, but cover us from loss, has the most conciliatory and useful effect upon them, and is that which will best secure their peace and good will. . . .

Should the acquisition of Louisiana be constitutionally confirmed and carried into effect, a sum of nearly thirteen millions of dollars will then be added to our public debt, most of which is payable after fifteen years; before which term the present existing debts will all be discharged by the established operation of the sinking fund. When we contemplate the ordinary annual augmentation of imposts from increasing population and wealth, the augmentation of the same revenue by its extension to the new acquisition, and the economies which may still be introduced into our public expenditures, I cannot but hope that Congress in reviewing their resources will find means to meet the intermediate interests of this additional debt without recurring to new taxes, and applying to this object only the ordinary progression of our revenue. Its extraordinary increase in times of foreign war will be the proper and sufficient fund for any measures of safety or precaution which that state of things may render necessary in our neutral position. . . .

We have seen with sincere concern the flames of war lighted up again in Europe, and nations with which we have the most friendly and useful relations engaged in mutual destruction. While we regret the miseries in which we see others involved, let us bow with gratitude to that kind Providence which, inspiring with wisdom and moderation our late legislative councils while placed under the urgency of the greatest wrongs, guarded us from hastily entering into the sanguinary contest, and left us only to look on and to pity its ravages. These will be heaviest on those immediately engaged. Yet the nations pursuing peace will not be exempt from all evil. In the course of this conflict, let it be our endeavor, as it is our interest and desire, to cultivate the friendship of the belligerent nations by every act of justice and of incessant kindness; to receive their armed vessels with hospitality from the distresses of the sea, but to administer the means of annoyance to none; to establish in our harbors such a police as may maintain law and order; to restrain our citizens from embarking individually in a war in which their country takes no part; to punish severely those persons, citizen or alien, who shall usurp the cover of our flag for vessels not entitled to it, infecting thereby with suspicion those of real Americans, and committing us into controversies for the redress of wrongs not our own; to exact from every nation the observance, toward our vessels and citizens, of those principles and practices which all civilized people acknowledge; to merit the character of a just nation, and maintain that of an independent one, preferring every consequence to insult and habitual wrong . . . . Separated by a wide ocean from the nations of Europe, and from the political interests which entangle them together, with productions and wants which render our commerce and friendship useful to them and theirs to us, it cannot be the interest of any to assail us, nor ours to disturb them. We should be most unwise, indeed, were we to cast away the singular blessings of the position in which nature has placed us, the opportunity she has endowed us with of pursuing, at a distance from foreign contentions, the paths of industry, peace, and happiness; of cultivating general friendship, and of bringing collisions of interest to the umpirage of reason rather than of force. . . .

Fourth Annual Message.—*November 8, 1804*

. . . .

While noticing the irregularities committed on the ocean by others, those on our own part should not be omitted nor left unprovided for. Complaints have been received that persons residing within the United States have taken on themselves to arm merchant vessels, and to force a commerce into certain ports and countries in defiance of the laws of those countries That individuals should undertake to wage private war, independently of the authority of their country, cannot be permitted in a well-ordered society. Its tendency to produce aggression on the laws and rights of other nations, and to endanger the peace of our own is so obvious, that I doubt not you will adopt measures for restraining it effectually in future. . . .

Second Inaugural Address.—*March 4, 1805*

Proceeding, fellow citizens, to that qualification which the constitution requires, before my entrance on the charge again conferred upon me, it is my duty to express the deep sense I entertain of this new proof of confidence from my fellow citizens at large, and the zeal with which it inspires me, so to conduct myself as may best satisfy their just expectations.

On taking this station on a former occasion, I declared the principles on which I believed it my duty to administer the affairs of our commonwealth. My conscience tells me that I have, on every occasion, acted up to that declaration, according to its obvious import, and to the understanding of every candid mind.

In the transaction of your foreign affairs, we have endeavored to cultivate the friendship of all nations, and especially of those with which we have the most important relations. We have done them justice on all occasions, favored where favor was lawful and cherished mutual interests and intercourse on fair and equal terms. We are firmly convinced, and we act on that conviction, that with nations as with individuals, our interests soundly calculated, will ever be found inseparable from our moral duties; and history bears witness to the fact, that a just nation is taken on its word, when recourse is had to armaments and wars to bridle others.

At home, fellow citizens, you best know whether we have done well or ill. The suppression of unnecessary offices, of useless establishments and expenses, enabled us to discontinue our internal taxes. These covering our land with officers, and opening our doors to their intrusions, had already begun that process of domiciliary vexation which, once entered, is scarcely to be restrained from reaching successively every article of produce and property. If among these taxes some minor ones fell which had not been inconvenient, it was because their amount would not have paid the officers who collected them, and because, if they had any merit, the state authorities might adopt them, instead of others less approved.

The remaining revenue on the consumption of foreign articles, is paid cheerfully by those who can afford to add foreign luxuries to domestic comforts, being collected on our seaboards and frontiers only, and incorporated with the transactions of our mercantile citizens, it may be the pleasure and pride of an American to ask, what farmer, what mechanic, what laborer, ever sees a taxgatherer of the United States? These contributions enable us to support the current expenses of the government, to fulfill contracts with foreign nations, to extinguish the native right of soil within our limits, to extend those limits, and to apply such a surplus to our public debts, as places at a short day their final redemption, and that redemption once effected, the revenue thereby liberated may, by a just repartition among the states, and a corresponding amendment of the constitution, be applied, *in time of peace*, to rivers, canals, roads, arts, manufactures, education, and other great objects within each state. *In time of war*, if injustice, by ourselves or others, must sometimes produce war, increased as the same revenue will be increased by population and consumption, and aided by other resources reserved for that crisis, it may meet within the year all the expenses of the year, without encroaching on the rights of future generations, by burdening them with the debts of the past. War will then be but a suspension of useful works, and a return to a state of peace, a return to the progress of improvement.

I have said, fellow citizens, that the income reserved had enabled us to extend our limits; but that extension may possibly pay for itself before we are called on, and in the meantime, may keep down the accruing interest; in all events, it will repay the advances we have made. I know that the acquisition of Louisiana has been disapproved by some, from a candid apprehension that the enlargement of our territory would endanger its union. But who can limit the extent to which the federative principle may operate effectively? The larger our association, the less will it be shaken by local passions; and in any view, is it not better that the opposite bank of the Mississippi should be settled by our own brethren and children, than by strangers of another family? With which shall we be most likely to live in harmony and friendly intercourse?

In matters of religion, I have considered that its free exercise is placed by the constitution independent of the powers of the general government. I have therefore undertaken, on no occasion, to prescribe the religious exercises suited to it; but have left them, as the constitution found them, under the direction and discipline of State or Church authorities acknowledged by the several religious societies.

The aboriginal inhabitants of these countries I have regarded with the commiseration their history inspires. Endowed with the faculties and the rights of men, breathing an ardent love of liberty and independence, and occupying a country which left them no desire but to be undisturbed, the stream of overflowing population from other regions directed itself on these shores; without power to divert, or habits to contend against, they have been overwhelmed by the current, or driven before it; now reduced within limits too narrow for the hunter's state, humanity enjoins us to teach them agriculture and the domestic arts; to encourage them to that industry which alone can enable them to maintain their place in existence, and to prepare them in time for that state of society, which to bodily comforts adds the improvement of the mind and morals. We have therefore liberally furnished them with the implements of husbandry and household use; we have placed among them instructors in the arts of first necessity; and they are covered with the aegis of the law against aggressors from among ourselves.

But the endeavors to enlighten them on the fate which awaits their present course of life, to induce them to exercise their reason, follow its dictates, and change their pursuits with the change of circumstances, have powerful obstacles to encounter; they are combated by the habits of their bodies, prejudice of their minds, ignorance, pride, and the influence of interested and crafty individuals among them, who feel themselves something in the present order of things, and fear to become nothing in any other. These persons inculcate a sanctimonious reverence for the customs of their ancestors; that whatsoever they did, must be done through all time; that reason is a false guide, and to advance under its counsel, in their physical, moral or political condition, is perilous innovation; that their duty is to remain as their Creator made them, ignorance being safety, and knowledge full of danger; in short, my friends, among them is seen the action and counteraction of good sense and bigotry; they, too, have their anti-philosophers, who find an interest in keeping things in their present state, who dread reformation, and exert all their faculties to maintain the ascendency of habit over the duty of improving our reason, and obeying its mandates.

In giving these outlines, I do not mean, fellow citizens, to arrogate to myself the merit of the measures; that is due, in the first place, to the reflecting character of our citizens at large, who, by the weight of public opinion, influence and strengthen the public measures; it is due to the sound discretion with which they select from among themselves those to whom they confide the legislative duties; it is due to the zeal and wisdom of the characters thus selected, who lay the foundations of public happiness in wholesome laws, the execution of which alone remains for others; and it is due to the able and faithful auxiliaries, whose patriotism has associated with me in the executive functions.

During this course of administration, and in order to disturb it, the artillery of the press has been levelled against us, charged with whatsoever its licentiousness could devise or dare These abuses of an institution so important to freedom and science, are deeply to be regretted, inasmuch as they tend to lessen its usefulness, and to sap its safety; they might, indeed, have been corrected by the wholesome punishments reserved and provided by the laws of the several States against falsehood and defamation; but public duties more urgent press on the time of public servants, and the offenders have therefore been left to find their punishment in the public indignation.

Nor was it uninteresting to the world, that an experiment should be fairly and fully made, whether freedom of discussion unaided by power, is not sufficient for the propagation and protection of truth— whether a government, conducting itself in the true spirit of its constitution, with zeal and purity, and doing no act which it would be unwilling the whole world should witness, can be written down by falsehood and defamation. The experiment has been tried; you have witnessed the scene, our fellow citizens have looked on, cool and collected; they saw the latent source from which these outrages proceeded; they gathered around their public functionaries, and when the constitution called them to the decision by suffrage, they pronounced their verdict, honorable to those who had served them, and consolatory to the friend of man, who believes he may be intrusted with his own affairs.

No inference is here intended, that the laws, provided by the State against false and defamatory publications, should not be enforced; he who has time, renders a service to public morals and public tranquillity, in reforming these abuses by the salutary coercions of the law; but the experiment is noted, to prove that, since truth and reason have maintained their ground against false opinions in league with false facts, the press, confined to truth, needs no other legal restraint; the public judgment will correct false reasonings and opinions, on a full hearing of all parties; and no other definite line can be drawn between the inestimable liberty of the press and its demoralizing licentiousness. If there be still improprieties which this rule would not restrain, its supplement must be sought in the censorship of public opinion.

Contemplating the union of sentiment now manifested so generally, as auguring harmony and happiness to our future course, I offer to our country sincere congratulations. With those, too, not yet rallied to the same point, the disposition to do so is gaining strength; facts are piercing through the veil drawn over them; and our doubting brethren will at length see, that the mass of their fellow citizens, with whom they cannot yet resolve to act, as to principles and measures, think as they think, and desire what they desire; that our wish, as well as theirs, is, that the public efforts may be directed honestly to the public good, that peace be cultivated, civil and religious liberty unassailed, law and order preserved, equality of rights maintained, and that state of property, equal or unequal, which results to every man from his own industry, or that of his fathers. When satisfied of these views, it is not in human nature that they should not approve and support them; in the meantime, let us cherish them with patient affection; let us do them justice, and more than justice, in all competitions of interest; and we need not doubt that truth, reason, and their own interests, will at length prevail, will gather them into the fold of their country, and will complete their entire union of opinion, which gives to a nation the blessing of harmony, and the benefit of all its strength.

I shall now enter on the duties to which my fellow citizens have again called me, and shall proceed in the spirit of those principles which they have approved. I fear not that any motives of interest may lead me astray; I am sensible of no passion which could seduce me knowingly from the path of justice; but the weakness of human nature, and the limits of my own understanding, will produce errors of judgment sometimes injurious to your interests. I shall need, therefore, all the indulgence I have heretofore experienced—the want of it will certainly not lessen with increasing years. I shall need, too, the favor of that Being in whose hands we are, who led our forefathers, as Israel of old, from their native land, and planted them in a country flowing with all the necessaries and comforts of life; who has covered our infancy with his providence, and our riper years with his wisdom and power; and to whose goodness I ask you to join with me in supplications, that he will so enlighten the minds of your servants, guide their councils, and prosper their measures, that whatsoever they do, shall result in your good, and shall secure to you the peace, friendship, and approbation of all nations.

To the General Assembly of North Carolina. Washington, January 10, 1808

The wrongs our country has suffered, fellow citizens, by violations of those moral rules which the Author of our nature has implanted in man as the law of his nature, to govern him in his associated, as well as individual character, have been such as justly to excite the sensibilities you express, and a deep abhorrence at indications threatening a substitution of power for right in the intercourse between nations. Not less worthy of your indignation have been the machinations of parricides who have endeavored to bring into danger the union of these States, and to subvert, for the purposes of inordinate ambition, a government founded in the will of its citizens, and directed to no object but their happiness.

I learn, with the liveliest sentiments of gratitude and respect, your approbation of my conduct, in the various charges which my country has been pleased to confide to me at different times; and especially that the administration of our public affairs, since my accession to the chief magistracy, has been so far satisfactory, that my continuance in that office after its present term, would be acceptable to you. But, that I should lay down my charge at a proper period, is as much a duty as to have borne it faithfully. If some termination to the services of the chief magistrate be not fixed by the Constitution, or supplied by practice, his office, nominally for years, will in fact become for life; and history shows how easily that degenerates into an inheritance. Believing that a representative government, responsible at short periods of election, is that which produces the greatest sum of happiness to mankind, I feel it a duty to do no act which shall essentially impair that principle; and I should unwillingly be the person who, disregarding the sound precedent set by an illustrious predecessor, should furnish the first example of prolongation beyond the second term of office.

Truth also obliges me to add, that I am sensible of that decline which advancing years bring on; and feeling their physical, I ought not to doubt their mental effect. Happy if I am the first to perceive and obey this admonition of nature, and to solicit a retreat from cares too great for the wearied faculties of age.

Declining a re-election on grounds which cannot but be approved, it will be the great comfort of my future days, and the satisfactory reward of a service of forty years, to carry into retirement such testimonies as you have been pleased to give, of the approbation and good will of my fellow citizens generally. And I supplicate the Being in whose hands we all are, to preserve our county in freedom and independence, and to bestow on yourselves the blessings of His favor.

To the Society of Tammany, or Columbian Order, No. 1, of the City of New York. Washington, February 29, 1808

I have received your address, fellow citizens, and, thankful for the expressions so personally gratifying to myself, I contemplate with high satisfaction the ardent spirit it breathes of love to our country, and of devotion to its liberty and independence. The crisis in which it is placed, cannot but be unwelcome to those who love peace, yet spurn at a tame submission to wrong. So fortunately remote from the theatre of European contests, and carefully avoiding to implicate ourselves in them, we had a right to hope for an exemption from the calamities which have afflicted the contending nations, and to be permitted unoffendingly to pursue paths of industry and peace.

But the ocean, which, like the air, is the common birthright of mankind, is arbitrarily wrested from us, and maxims consecrated by time, by usage, and by an universal sense of right, are trampled on by superior force. To give time for this demoralizing tempest to pass over, one measure only remained which might cover our beloved country from its overwhelming fury: an appeal to the deliberate understanding of our fellow citizens in a cessation of all intercourse with the belligerent nations, until it can be resumed under the protection of a returning sense of the moral obligations which constitute a law for nations as well as individuals. There can be no question, in a mind truly American, whether it is best to send our citizens and property into certain captivity, and then wage war for their recovery, or to keep them at home, and to turn seriously to that policy which plants the manufacturer and the husbandman side by side, and establishes at the door of every one that exchange of mutual labors and comforts, which we have hitherto sought in distant regions, and under perpetual risks of broils with them.

Eighth Annual Message.—November 8, 1808

. . . .

Considering the extraordinary character of the times in which we live, our attention should unremittingly be fixed on the safety of our country. For a people who are free, and who mean to remain so, a well-organized and armed militia is their best security. It is, therefore, incumbent on us, at every meeting, to revise the condition of the militia, and to ask ourselves if it is prepared to repel a powerful enemy at every point of our territories exposed to invasion. Some of the States have paid a laudable attention to this object; but every degree of neglect is to be found among others. Congress alone have power to produce a uniform state of preparation in this great organ of defence; the interests which they so deeply feel in their own and their country's security will present this as among the most important objects of their deliberation. . . .

The suspension of our foreign commerce, produced by the injustice of the belligerent powers, and the consequent losses and sacrifices of our citizens, are subjects of just concern. The situation into which we have thus been forced, has impelled us to apply a portion of our industry and capital to internal manufactures and improvements. The extent of this conversion is daily increasing, and little doubt remains that the establishments formed and forming will—under the auspices of cheaper materials and subsistence, the freedom of labor from taxation with us, and of protecting duties and prohibitions—become permanent. . . .

Availing myself of this the last occasion which will occur of addressing the two houses of the legislature at their meeting, I cannot omit the expression of my sincere gratitude for the repeated proofs of confidence manifested to me by themselves and their predecessors since my call to the administration, and the many indulgences experienced at their hands. The same grateful acknowledgments are due to my fellow citizens generally, whose support has been my great encouragement under all embarrassments. In the transaction of their business I cannot have escaped error. It is incident to our imperfect nature. But I may say with truth, my errors have been of the understanding, not of intention; and that the advancement of their rights and interests has been the constant motive for every measure. On these considerations I solicit their indulgence. Looking forward with anxiety to their future destinies, I trust that, in their steady character unshaken by difficulties, in their love of liberty, obedience to law, and support of the public authorities, I see a sure guaranty of the permanence of our republic; and retiring from the charge of their affairs, I carry with me the consolation of a firm persuasion that Heaven has in store for our beloved country long ages to come of prosperity and happiness.

Letters

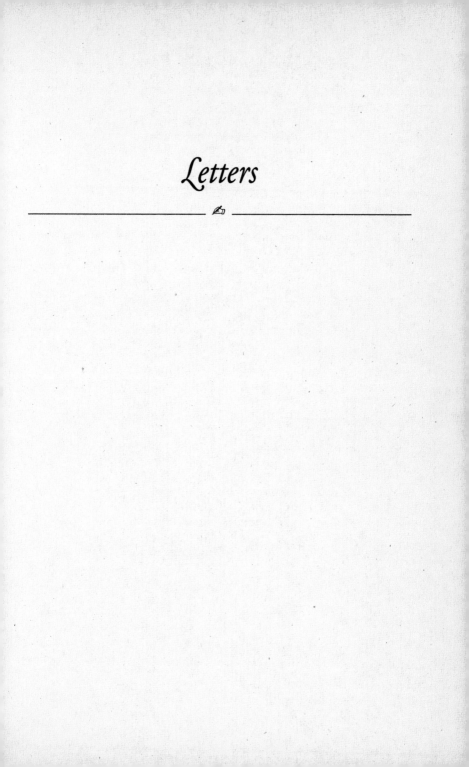

Introduction

Reflecting upon his long and active life, Jefferson observed "the letters of a person . . . . form the only full and genuine journal of his life." This statement is particularly true of Jefferson himself, who wrote a staggering number of letters, probably between fifty and seventy-five thousand. Although many of these have been published, many unpublished ones are in public or private collections. These letters, with their phenomenal range of interest, not only re-create the most versatile American of his time, but the age in which he lived.

The majority of these letters are taken from the twenty-volume Memorial Edition, which modernizes spelling and punctuation. Letters from manuscript collections, published here for the first time, or from other printed sources, retain, in most cases, Jefferson's spelling and punctuation. The Memorial Edition contains frequent textual inaccuracies. Only such inaccuracies as impede the reader's understanding have been cited and corrected in the following selections.

Letters

---------------------------------- 🖎 ----------------------------------

TO JOHN HARVIE[1]

Shadwell, Jan. 14, 1760

SIR,—I was at Colo. Peter Randolph's about a Fortnight ago, & my Schooling falling into Discourse, he said he thought it would be to my Advantage to go to the College,[2] & was desirous I should go, as indeed I am myself for several Reasons. In the first place as long as I stay at the Mountains the loss of one fourth of my Time is inevitable, by Company's coming here & detaining me from School. And likewise my Absence will in a great measure put a Stop to so much Company, & by that Means lessen the Expences of the Estate in House-Keeping. And on the other Hand by going to the College I shall get a more universal Acquaintance, which may hereafter be serviceable to me; & I suppose I can pursue my studies in the Greek & Latin as well there as here, & likewise learn something of the Mathematics. I shall be glad of your opinion.

TO JOHN PAGE[3]

Fairfield, December 25, 1762

DEAR PAGE,—This very day, to others the day of greatest mirth and jollity, sees me overwhelmed with more and greater misfortunes

[1]John Harvie, after Peter Jefferson's death, was one of Thomas Jefferson's guardians.

[2]William and Mary, Williamsburg, Virginia.

[3]John Page, later to become governor of Virginia, was Jefferson's closest friend at William and Mary.

than have befallen a descendant of Adam for these thousand years past, I am sure; and perhaps, after excepting Job, since the creation of the world. I think his misfortunes were somewhat greater than mine; for, although we may be pretty nearly on a level in other respects, yet, I thank my God, I have the advantage of brother Job in this, that Satan has not as yet put forth his hand to load me with bodily afflictions. You must know, dear Page, that I am now in a house surrounded with enemies, who take counsel together against my soul; and when I lay me down to rest, they say among themselves, come let us destroy him. I am sure if there is such a thing as a Devil in this world, he must have been here last night, and have had some hand in contriving what happened to me. Do you think the cursed rats (at his instigation, I suppose) did not eat up my pocket-book, which was in my pocket, within a foot of my head? And not contented with plenty for the present, they carried away my jemmy-worked silk garters, and half a dozen new minuets I had just got, to serve, I suppose, as provision for the winter. But of this I should not have accused the Devil (because, you know rats will be rats, and hunger, without the addition of his instigations, might have urged them to do this), if something worse, and from a different quarter, had not happened. You know it rained last night, or if you do not know it, I am sure I do. When I Went to bed, I laid my watch in the usual place, and going to take her up after I arose this morning, I found her in the same place, it's true, but *Quantum mutatus ab illo!*[1] all afloat in water, let in at a leak in the roof of the house, and as silent and still as the rats that had eaten my pocket-book. Now, you know, if chance had had anything to do in this matter, there were a thousand other spots where it might have chanced to leak as well as at this one, which was perpendicularly over my watch. But I'll tell you, it's my opinion that the Devil came and bored the hole over it on purpose. Well, as I was saying, my poor watch had lost her speech. I should not have cared much for this, but something worse attended it; the subtle particles of the water with which the case was filled, had, by their penetration, so overcome the cohesion of the particles of the paper, of which my

---

[1]"How changed from what it was!"

dear picture and watch-paper were composed,[1] that, in attempting to take them out to dry them, good God! *Mens horret referre!*[2] My cursed fingers gave them such a rent, as I fear I never shall get over. This, cried I, was the last stroke Satan had in reserve for me; he knew I cared not for anything else he could do to me, and was determined to try his last most fatal expedient. *"Multis fortunæ vulneribus percussus, huic uni me imperem sensi, et penitus succubui!"*[3] I would have cried bitterly, but I thought it beneath the dignity of a man, . . . However, whatever misfortunes may attend the picture or lover, my hearty prayers shall be, that all the health and happiness which Heaven can send may be the portion of the original, and that so much goodness may ever meet with what may be most agreeable in this world, as I am sure it must be in the next. And now, although the picture be defaced, there is so lively an image of her imprinted in my mind, that I shall think of her too often, I fear, for my peace of mind; and too often, I am sure, to get through old Coke this winter; for God knows I have not seen him since I packed him up in my trunk in Williamsburg. Well, Page, I do wish the Devil had old Coke, for I am sure I never was so tired of an old dull scoundrel in my life. What! are there so few inquietudes tacked to this momentary life of ours, that we must need be loading ourselves with a thousand more? Or, as brother Job says (who, by-the-bye, I think began to whine a little under his afflictions), "Are not my days few? Cease then, that I may take comfort a little before I go whence I shall not return, even to the land of darkness, and the shadow of death." But the old fellows say we must read to gain knowledge, and gain knowledge to make us happy and admired. *Mere jargon!* Is there any such thing as happiness in this world? No. And as for admiration, I am sure the man who pow- ders most, perfumes most, embroiders most, and talks most nonsense, is most admired. Though to be candid, there are some who have too much good sense to esteem such monkey-like animals as these, in

[1]This refers to a portrait of Rebecca Burwell whose brother was a classmate of Jefferson at William and Mary.

[2]"The mind shudders to recall it."

[3]"Pierced through by the many wounds of fate, I felt myself unequal to this one and succumbed utterly!"

whose formation, as the saying is, the tailors and barbers go halves with God Almighty; and since these are the only persons whose esteem is worth a wish, I do not know but that, upon the whole, the advice of these old fellows may be worth following.

You cannot conceive the satisfaction it would give me to have a letter from you. Write me very circumstantially everything which happened at the wedding. Was she there? because, if she was, I ought to have been at the Devil for not being there too. If there is any news stirring in town or country, such as deaths, courtships, or marriages, in the circle of my acquaintance, let me know it. Remember me affectionately to all the young ladies of my acquaintance, particularly the Miss Burwells, and Miss Potters, and tell them that though that heavy earthly part of me, my body, be absent, the better half of me, my soul, is ever with them, and that my best wishes shall ever attend them. Tell Miss Alice Corbin that I verily believe the rats knew I was to win a pair of garters from her, or they never would have been so cruel as to carry mine away. This very consideration makes me so sure of the bet, that I shall ask everybody I see from that part of the world what pretty gentleman is making his addresses to her. I would fain ask the favor of Miss Becca Burwell to give me another watch-paper of her own cutting, which I should esteem much more, though it were a plain round one, than the nicest in the world cut by other hands; however, I am afraid she would think this presumption, after my suffering the other to get spoiled. If you think you can excuse me to her for this, I should be glad if you would ask her. Tell Miss Sukey Potter that I heard, just before I came out of town, that she was offended with me about something, what it is I do not know; but this I know, that I never was guilty of the least disrespect to her in my life, either in word or deed; as far from it as it has been possible for one to be. I suppose when we meet next, she will be *endeavoring* to repay an imaginary affront with a real one; but she may save herself the trouble, for nothing that she can say or do to me shall ever lessen her in my esteem, and I am determined always to look upon her as the same honest-hearted, good-humored, agreeable lady I ever did. Tell—tell—in short, tell them all ten thousand things more than either you or I can now or ever shall think of as long as we live.

My mind has been so taken up with thinking of my acquaintances, that, till this moment, I almost imagined myself in Williamsburg, talking to you in our old unreserved way; and never observed, till I turned over the leaf, to what an immoderate size I had swelled my letter; however, that I may not tire your patience by further additions, I will make but this one more, that I am sincerely and affectionately,

Dear Page, your friend and servant.

P. S. I am now within an easy day's ride of Shadwell, whither I shall proceed in two or three days.

TO JOHN PAGE

Shadwell, July 15th, 1763

. . . . The most fortunate of us, in our journey through life, frequently meet with calamities and misfortunes which may greatly afflict us; and, to fortify our minds against the attacks of these calamities and misfortunes, should be one of the principal studies and endeavors of our lives. The only method of doing this is to assume a perfect resignation to the Divine will, to consider that whatever does happen, must happen; and that, by our uneasiness, we cannot prevent the blow before it does fall, but we may add to its force after it has fallen. These considerations, and others such as these, may enable us in some measure to surmount the difficulties thrown in our way; to bear up with a tolerable degree of patience under this burthen of life; and to proceed with a pious and unshaken resignation, till we arrive at our journey's end, when we may deliver up our trust into the hands of him who gave it, and receive such reward as to him shall seem proportioned to our merit. Such, dear Page, will be the language of the man who considers his situation in this life, and such should be the language of every man who would wish to render that situation as easy as the nature of it will admit. Few things will disturb him at all: nothing will disturb him much. . . .

TO JOHN PAGE

Williamsburg, October 7, 1763

DEAR PAGE,—In the most melancholy fit that ever any poor soul was, I sit down to write to you. Last night, as merry as agreeable company and dancing with Belinda in the Apollo could make me, I never could have thought the succeeding sun would have seen me so wretched as I now am! I was prepared to say a great deal: I had dressed up, in my own mind, such thoughts as occurred to me, in as moving a language as I knew how, and expected to have performed in a tolerably creditable manner. But, good God! When I had an opportunity of venting them, a few broken sentences, uttered in great disorder, and interrupted with pauses of uncommon length, were the too visible marks of my strange confusion! The whole confab I will tell you, word for word, if I can, when I see you, which God send may be soon. Affairs at W. and M. are in the greatest confusion. Walker, M'Clurg and Wat Jones are expelled *pro tempore*, or, as Horrox softens it, rusticated for a month. Lewis Burwell, Warner Lewis, and one Thompson, have fled to escape flagellation. I should have excepted Warner Lewis, who came off of his own accord. Jack Walker leaves town on Monday. The court is now at hand, which I must attend constantly, so that unless you come to town, there is little probability of my meeting with you anywhere else. For God sake come. I am, dear Page, your sincere friend.

TO ROBERT SKIPWITH[1]

Monticello, Aug. 3, 1771

. . . . A little attention however to the nature of the human mind evinces that the entertainments of fiction are useful as well as pleasant. That they are pleasant when well written every person feels who reads. But wherein is its utility asks the reverend sage, big with the notion that nothing can be useful but the learned lumber of Greek and Roman reading with which his head is stored?

I answer, everything is useful which contributes to fix in the principles and practices of virtue. When any original act of charity or of gratitude, for instance, is presented either to our sight or imagination, we are deeply impressed with its beauty and feel a strong desire in our-

[1]Robert Skipwith was a member of a well-to-do Virginia family and an in-law of Jefferson.

selves of doing charitable and grateful acts also. On the contrary when
we see or read of any atrocious deed, we are disgusted with its defor-
mity, and conceive an abhorrence of vice. Now every emotion of this
kind is an exercise of our virtuous dispositions, and dispositions of the
mind, like limbs of the body acquire strength by exercise. But exercise
produces habit, and in the instance of which we speak the exercise being
of the moral feelings produces a habit of thinking and acting virtuously.
We never reflect whether the story we read be truth or fiction. If the
painting be lively, and a tolerable picture of nature, we are thrown into
a reverie, from which if we awaken it is the fault of the writer. I appeal
to every reader of feeling and sentiment whether the fictitious murder
of Duncan by Macbeth in Shakespeare does not excite in him as great
a horror of villainy, as the real one of Henry IV by Ravaillac as related
by Davila? And whether the fidelity of Nelson and generosity of
Blandford in Marmontel do not dilate his breast and elevate his sentiments as much as any similar incident which real history can furnish?
Does he not in fact feel himself a better man while reading them, and
privately covenant to copy the fair example? We neither know nor care
whether Lawrence Sterne really went to France, whether he was there
accosted by the Franciscan, at first rebuked him unkindly, and then
gave him a peace offering: or whether the whole be not fiction. In
either case we equally are sorrowful at the rebuke, and secretly resolve
we will never do so: we are pleased with the subsequent atonement,
and view with emulation a soul candidly acknowledging its fault and
making a just reparation. Considering history as a moral exercise, her
lessons would be too infrequent if confined to real life. Of those
recorded by historians few incidents have been attended with such circumstances as to excite in any high degree this sympathetic emotion
of virtue. We are, therefore, wisely framed to be as warmly interested
for a fictitious as for a real personage. The field of imagination is thus
laid open to our use and lessons may be formed to illustrate and carry
home to the heart every moral rule of life. Thus a lively and lasting
sense of filial duty is more effectually impressed on the mind of a son
or daughter by reading King Lear, than by all the dry volumes of
ethics, and divinity that ever were written. This is my idea of well-writ-
ten Romance, of Tragedy, Comedy and Epic poetry. . . .

TO DR. WILLIAM SMALL[1]

May 7, 1775

DEAR SIR,—Within this week we have received the unhappy news of an action of considerable magnitude, between the King's troops and our brethren of Boston, in which it is said five hundred of the former, with the Earl of Percy, are slain. That such an action has occurred, is undoubted, though perhaps the circumstances may not have reached us with truth. This accident has cut off our last hope of reconciliation, and a phrensy of revenge seems to have seized all ranks of people. It is a lamentable circumstance, that the only mediatory power acknowledged by both parties, instead of leading to a reconciliation his divided people, should pursue the incendiary purpose of still blowing up the flames, as we find him constantly doing, in every speech and public declaration. This may, perhaps, be intended to intimidate into acquiescence, but the effect has been most unfortunately otherwise. A little knowledge of human nature, and attention to its ordinary workings, might have foreseen that the spirits of the people here were in a state, in which they were more likely to be provoked, than frightened, by haughty deportment. And to fill up the measure of irritation, a proscription of individuals has been substituted in the room of just trial. Can it be believed, that a grateful people will suffer those to be consigned to execution, whose sole crime has been the developing and asserting their rights? Had the Parliament possessed the power of reflection, they would have avoided a measure as impotent, as it was inflammatory. When I saw Lord Chatham's bill, I entertained high hope that a reconciliation could have been brought about. The difference between his terms, and those offered by our Congress, might have been accommodated, if entered on, by both parties, with a disposition to accommodate. But the dignity of Parliament, it seems, can brook no opposition to its power. Strange, that a set of men, who have made sale of their virtue to the Minister, should yet talk of retaining dignity! But I am getting into politics, though I

[1]Dr. William Small, Scottish professor at William and Mary, was the greatest intellectual influence on Jefferson during his college days.

sat down only to ask your acceptance of the wine, and express my constant wishes for your happiness.

TO JOHN RANDOLPH, ESQ.[1]

Philadelphia, November 29, 1775

.... This day, certain intelligence has reached us, that our General, Montgomery, is received into Montreal; and we expect, every hour, to be informed that Quebec has opened its arms to Colonel Arnold, who, with eleven hundred men, was sent from Boston up the Kennebec, and down the Chaudière river to that place. He expected to be there early this month. Montreal acceded to us on the 13th, and Carleton set out, with the shattered remains of his little army, for Quebec, where we hope he will be taken up by Arnold. In a short time, we have reason to hope, the delegates of Canada will join us in Congress, and complete the American union, as far as we wish to have it completed. We hear that one of the British transports has arrived at Boston; the rest are beating off the coast, in very bad weather. You will have heard, before this reaches you, that Lord Dunmore has commenced hostilities in Virginia. That people bore with everything, till he attempted to burn the town of Hampton. They opposed and repelled him, with considerable loss on his side, and none on ours. It has raised our countrymen into a perfect phrensy. It is an immense misfortune, to the whole empire, to have a King of such a disposition at such a time. We are told, and everything proves it true, that he is the bitterest enemy we have. His Minister is able, and that satisfies me that ignorance or wickedness, somewhere, controls him. In an earlier part of this contest, our petitions told him, that from our King there was but one appeal. The admonition was despised, and that appeal forced on us. To undo his empire, he has but one truth more to learn; that, after colonies have drawn the sword, there is but one step more they can take. That step is now pressed upon us, by the measures adopted, as

[1]At the beginning of hostilities between the Colonies and England, this friend and kinsman of Thomas Jefferson sided with the Crown and forsook Virginia to live in England. (Not to be confused with John Randolph of Roanoke.)

if they were afraid we would not take it. Believe me, dear Sir, there is not in the British empire a man who more cordially loves a union with Great Britain than I do. But by the God that made me, I will cease to exist before I yield to a connection on such terms as the British Parliament propose; and in this, I think I speak the sentiments of America. We want neither inducement nor power, to declare and assert a separation. It is will, alone, which is wanting, and that is growing apace under the fostering hand of our King. One bloody campaign will probably decide, everlastingly, our future course, and I am sorry to find a bloody campaign is decided on. If our winds and waters should not combine to rescue their shores from slavery, and General Howe's reinforcements should arrive in safety, we have hopes he will be inspirited to come out of Boston and take another drubbing; and we must drub him soundly, before the sceptred tyrant will know we are not mere brutes, to crouch under his hand, and kiss the rod with which he designs to scourge us.

TO FRANCIS EPPES[1]

Philadelphia, July 15th, 1776

. . . . Admiral Howe is himself arrived at New York, and two or three vessels, supposed to be of his fleet, were coming in. The whole is expected daily.

Washington's numbers are greatly increased, but we do not know them exactly. I imagine he must have from 30 to 35,000 by this time. The enemy the other day ordered two of their men-of-war to hoist anchor and push by our batteries up the Hudson River. Both wind and tide were very fair. They passed all the batteries with ease, and, as far as is known, without receiving material damage; though there was an incessant fire kept up on them. This experiment of theirs, I suppose, is a prelude to the passage of their whole fleet, and seems to indicate an intention of landing above New York. I imagine General Washing-

---

[1]Francis Eppes, member of a distinguished Virginia family, had married one of the sisters of Jefferson's wife, Martha [Wayles] Skelton.

ton, finding he cannot prevent their going up the river, will prepare to amuse them wherever they shall go. Our army from Canada is now at Crown Point, but still one half down with the small pox. You ask about Arnold's behavior at the Cedars. It was this. The scoundrel, Major Butterfield, having surrendered three hundred and ninety men, in a fort with twenty or thirty days' provision, and ammunition enough, to about forty regulars, one hundred Canadians, and five hundred Indians, before he had lost a single man—and Major Sherburne, who was coming to the relief of the fort with one hundred men, having, after bravely engaging the enemy an hour and forty minutes, killing twenty of them and losing twelve of his own, been surrounded by them, and taken prisoners also—General Arnold appeared on the opposite side of the river and prepared to attack them. His numbers I know not, but believe they were about equal to the enemy. Captain Foster, commander of the king's troops, sent over a flag to him, proposing an exchange of prisoners for as many of the king's in our possession, and, moreover, informed Arnold that if he should attack, the Indians would put every man of the prisoners to death. Arnold refused, called a council of war, and, it being now in the night, it was determined to attack next morning. A second flag came over; he again refused, though in an excruciating situation, as he saw the enemy were in earnest about killing the prisoners. His men, too, began to be importunate for the recovery of their fellow-soldiers. A third flag came, the men grew more clamorous and Arnold, now almost raving with rage and compassion, was obliged to consent to the exchange and six days suspension of hostilities, Foster declaring he had not boats to deliver them in less time. However, he did deliver them so much sooner as that before the six days were expired, himself and party had fled out of all reach. Arnold then retired to Montreal. You have long before this heard of General Thompson's defeat. The truth of that matter has never appeared till lately. You will see it in the public papers. No men on earth ever behaved better than ours did. The enemy behaved dastardly. Colonel Allen (who was in the engagement) assured me this day, that such was the situation of our men, half way up to the thighs in mud for several hours, that five hundred men of spirit must have taken the whole; yet the enemy were repulsed several times, and our people had time to extricate themselves and come off. It is believed the enemy suffered considerably. The above account of Arnold's affair you may rely on, as I was one of a committee appointed to inquire into the whole of that matter, and have it from those who were in the whole transaction, and were taken prisoners.

My sincere affections to Mrs. Eppes, and adieu.

TO [JOHN FABRONI][1]

Williamsburg, Virginia, June 8th, 1778

. . . . If there is a gratification, which I envy any people in this world, it is to your country its music. This is the favorite passion of my soul, and fortune has cast my lot in a country where it is in a state of deplorable barbarism. From the line of life in which we conjecture you to be, I have for some time lost the hope of seeing you here. Should the event prove so, I shall ask your assistance in procuring a substitute, who may be a proficient in singing, &, on the Harpsichord. I should be contented to receive such an one two or three years hence; when it is hoped he may come more safely and find here a greater plenty of those useful things which commerce alone can furnish.

The bounds of an American fortune will not admit the indulgence of a domestic band of musicians, yet I have thought that a passion for music might be reconciled with that economy which we are obliged to observe. I retain among my domestic servants a gardener, a weaver, a cabinet-maker, and a stone-cutter, to which I would add a *vigneron*.[2] In a country where, like yours, music is cultivated and practiced by every class of men, I suppose there might be found persons of these trades who could perform on the French horn, clarinet, or hautboy and bas-

[1]John Fabroni, an Italian musician, had instructed both Jefferson and Mrs. Jefferson in music.

[2]The complete text, as it appears in Ford, is: "I retain for instance among my domestic servants a gardener (Ortolans), a weaver (Tessitore di lino e lin), a cabinet-maker (Stipeltaro) and a stone-cutter (Scalpellino laborante in piano) to which I would add a vigneron.

soon, so that one might have a band of two French horns, two clarinets, two hautboys, and a bassoon, without enlarging their domestic
expenses. A certainty of employment for a half dozen years, and at the
end of that time, to find them, if they chose, a conveyance to their own
country, might induce them to come here on reasonable wages. Without meaning to give you trouble, perhaps it might be practicable for
you, in your ordinary intercourse with your people, to find out such
men disposed to come to America. Sobriety and good nature would
be desirable parts of their characters. If you think such a plan practicable, and will be so kind as to inform me what will be necessary to
be done on my part, I will take care that it shall be done. The necessary expenses, when informed of them, I can remit before they are
wanting, to any port in France, with which country alone we have safe
correspondence. I am, Sir, with much esteem, your humble servant.

TO COLONEL JAMES MONROE[1]

Monticello, May 20th, 1782

. . . . If we are made in some degree for others, yet, in a greater, are
we made for ourselves. It were contrary to feeling, and indeed ridiculous to suppose that a man had less rights in himself than one of his
neighbors, or indeed all of them put together. This would be slavery,
and not that liberty which the bill of rights has made inviolable, and
for the preservation of which our government has been charged.
Nothing could so completely divest us of that liberty as the establishment of the opinion, that the State has a perpetual right to the services
of all its members. This, to men of certain ways of thinking, would
be to annihilate the blessings of existence, and to contradict the Giver
of life, who gave it for happiness and not for wretchedness. And certainly, to such it were better that they had never been born. However, with these, I may think public service and private misery
inseparably linked together. I have not the vanity to count myself

---

[1]James Monroe, later fifth President of the United States, was a close friend and fol-
lower of Jefferson until the latter's death.

among those whom the State would think worth oppressing with perpetual service. I have received a sufficient memento to the contrary. I am persuaded that, having hitherto dedicated to them the whole of the active and useful part of my life, I shall be permitted to pass the rest in mental quiet. I hope, too, that I did not mistake modes any more than the matter of right when I preferred a simple act of renunciation, to the taking sanctuary under those disqualifications (provided by the law for other purposes indeed but) after affording asylum also for rest to the wearied. I dare say you did not expect by the few words you dropped on the right of renunciation to expose yourself to the fatigue of so long a letter, but I wished you to see that, if I had done wrong, I had been betrayed by a semblance of right at least. . . .

TO FRANÇOIS JEAN, CHEVALIER DE CHASTELLUX[1]

Ampthill Nov. 26, 1782

. . . . It [your letter] found me a little emerging from the stupor of mind which had rendered me as dead to the world as she whose loss occasioned it.[2] Your letter recalled to my memory that there were persons still living of much value to me. If you should have thought me remiss in not testifying to you sooner how deeply I had been impressed with your worth in the little time I had the happiness of being with you, you will I am sure ascribe it to it's true cause, the state of the dreadful suspense in which I had been kept all the summer & the catastrophe which closed it. Before that event my scheme of life had been determined. I had folded myself in the arms of retirement, and rested all prospects of future happiness on domestic & literary objects. A single event wiped away all my plans and left me a blank which I had not the spirits to fill up. In this state of mind an appointment from Congress found me, requiring me to cross the Atlantic. . . .

---

[1]The Marquis de Chastellux, celebrated French soldier and writer, had visited Jefferson at Monticello in the spring of 1782. His impressions are recorded in his book, *Travels in North America*. [Ford.]

[2]Jefferson refers to the death of his wife. After this event, Jefferson virtually ceased writing letters for almost a year.

TO MARTHA JEFFERSON[1]

Annapolis, Dec. 22, 1783

. . . . I omitted . . . to advise you on the subject of dress, which I know you are a little apt to neglect. I do not wish you to be gaily clothed at this time of life, but what you wear should be fine of its kind. But above all things and at all times let your clothes be clean, whole, and properly put on. Do not fancy you must wear them till the dirt is visible to the eye. You will be the last who is sensible of this. Some ladies think they may, under the privileges of the *dishabillé*, be loose and negligent of their dress in the morning. But be you, from the moment you rise till you go to bed, as cleanly and properly dressed as at the hours of dinner or tea. A lady who has been seen as a sloven or a slut in the morning, will never efface the impression she has made, with all the dress and pageantry she can afterwards involve herself in. Nothing is so disgusting to our sex as a want of cleanliness and delicacy in yours. I hope, therefore, the moment you rise from bed, your first work will be to dress yourself in such style, as that you may be seen by any gentleman without his being able to discover a pin amiss, or any other circumstance of neatness wanting. . . .

TO COLONEL MONROE

Paris, June 17, 1785

. . . . I sincerely wish you may find it convenient to come here; the pleasure of the trip will be less than you expect, but the utility greater. It will make you adore your own country, its soil, its climate, its equality, liberty, laws, people, and manners. My God! how little do my countrymen know what precious blessings they are in possession of, and which no other people on earth enjoy. I confess I had no idea of it myself. While we shall see multiplied instances of Europeans going to live in America, I will venture to say, no man now living will ever

[1]Martha Jefferson was Jefferson's oldest daughter. [Henry S. Randall, *The Life of Thomas Jefferson*, 3 vols., Derby and Jackson: New York, 1858. Hereafter referred to as Randall.]

see an instance of an American removing to settle in Europe, and continuing there. Come, then, and see the proofs of this, and on your return add your testimony to that of every thinking American, in order to satisfy our countrymen how much it is their interest to preserve, uninfected by contagion, those peculiarities in their governments and manners, to which they are indebted for those blessings. . . .

TO DR. PRICE[1]

Paris, August 7, 1785

SIR,—Your favor of July the 2d came duly to hand. The concern you therein express as to the effect of your pamphlet in America, induces me to trouble you with some observations on that subject.

From my acquaintance with that country, I think I am able to judge, with some degree of certainty, of the manner in which it will have been received. Southward of the Chesapeake, it will find but few readers concurring with it in sentiment, on the subject of slavery. From the mouth to the head of the Chesapeake, the bulk of the people will approve it in theory, and it will find a respectable minority ready to adopt it in practice; a minority, which for weight and worth of character, preponderates against the greater number, who have not the courage to divest their families of a property, which, however, keeps their conscience unquiet. Northward of the Chesapeake, you may find, here and there, an opponent to your doctrine, as you may find, here and there, a robber and murderer; but in no greater number. In that part of America, there being but few slaves, they can easily disencumber themselves of them; and emancipation is put into such a train, that in a few years there will be no slaves northward of Maryland. In Maryland, I do not find such a disposition to begin the redress of this enormity, as in Virginia. This is the next State to which we may turn our eyes for the interesting spectacle of justice, in conflict with avarice and oppression; a conflict wherein the sacred side is gaining daily recruits, from the influx into office of young men grown, and growing up.

[1]Richard Price, the English moral and political philosopher, defended the cause of American independence in Great Britain.

These have sucked in the principles of liberty, as it were, with their mother's milk; and it is to them I look with anxiety to turn the fate of this question. Be not therefore discouraged. What you have written will do a great deal of good; and could you still trouble yourself with our welfare, no man is more able to give aid to the laboring side. The College of William and Mary, in Williamsburg, since the remodeling of its plan, is the place where are collected together all the young men of Virginia, under preparation for public life. They are there under the direction (most of them) of a Mr. Wythe, one of the most virtuous of characters, and whose sentiments on the subject of slavery are unequivocal. I am satisfied, if you could resolve to address an exhortation to those young men, with all that eloquence of which you are master, that its influence on the future decision of this important question would be great, perhaps decisive. Thus you see, that, so far from thinking you have cause to repent of what you have done, I wish you to do more, and wish it, on an assurance of its effect. The information I have received from America, of the reception of your pamphlet in the different States, agrees with the expectations I had formed.

Our country is getting into a ferment against yours, or rather has caught it from yours. God knows how this will end; but assuredly in one extreme or the other. There can be no medium between those who have loved so much. I think the decision is in your power as yet, but will not be so long.

I pray you to be assured of the sincerity of the esteem and respect with which I have the honor to be, Sir, your most obedient humble servant.

TO THE COUNT DE VERGENNES[1]

Paris, August 15, 1785

. . . . The monopoly of the purchase of tobacco in France discourages both the French and American merchant from bringing it here, and from taking in exchange the manufactures and productions of

---

[1]The Count de Vergennes was Secretary of Foreign Affairs under Louis XVI, and chief of the royal council of finances.

France. It is contrary to the spirit of trade, and to the dispositions of merchants, to carry a commodity to any market where but one person is allowed to buy it, and where, of course, that person fixes its price, which the seller must receive, or re-export his commodity, at the loss of his voyage thither. Experience accordingly shows, that they carry it to other markets, and that they take in exchange the merchandise of the place where they deliver it. I am misinformed if France has not been furnished from a neighboring nation with considerable quantities of tobacco since the peace, and been obliged to pay there in coin, what might have been paid here in manufactures, had the French and American merchants brought the tobacco originally here. I suppose, too, that the purchases made by the Farmers General, in America, are paid for chiefly in coin, which coin is also remitted directly hence to England, and makes an important part of the balance supposed to be in favor of that nation against this. Should the Farmers General, by themselves, or by the company to whom they may commit the procuring these tobaccos from America, require, for the satisfaction of government on this head, the exportation of a proportion of merchandise in exchange for them, it would be an unpromising expedient. It would only commit the exports, as well as imports, between France and America, to a monopoly, which, being secure against rivals in the sale of the merchandise of France, would not be likely to sell at such moderate prices as might encourage its consumption there, and enable it to bear a competition with similar articles from other countries. I am persuaded this exportation of coin may be prevented, and that of commodities effected, by leaving both operations to the French and American merchants, instead of the Farmers General. They will import a sufficient quantity of tobacco, if they are allowed a perfect freedom in the sale; and they will receive in payment, wines, oils, brandies, and manufactures, instead of coin; forcing each other, by their competition, to bring tobaccos of the best quality; to give to the French manufacturer the full worth of his merchandise, and to sell to the American consumer at the lowest price they can afford; thus encouraging him to use, in preference, the merchandise of this country. . . .

While the advantages of an increase of revenue to the crown, a diminution of impost on the people, and a payment in merchandise, instead of money, are conjectured as likely to result to France from a suppression of the monopoly on tobacco, we have also reason to hope some advantages on our part; and this hope alone could justify my entering into the present details. I do not expect this advantage will be by any augmentation of price. The other markets of Europe have too much influence on this article to admit any sensible augmentation of price to take place. But the advantage I principally expect is an increase of consumption. This will give us a vent for so much more, and, of consequence, find employment for so many more cultivators of the earth; and in whatever proportion it increases this production for us, in the same proportion will it procure additional vent for the merchandise of France, and employment for the hands which produce it. I expect, too, that by bringing our merchants here, they would procure a number of commodities in exchange, better in kind, and cheaper in price. It is with sincerity I add, that warm feelings are indulged in my breast by the further hope, that it would bind the two nations still closer in friendship, by binding them in interest. In truth, no two countries are better calculated for the exchanges of commerce. France wants rice, tobacco, potash, furs, and ship-timber. We want wines, brandies, oils, and manufactures. There is an affection, too, between the two people, which disposes them to favor one another. If they do not come together, then, to make the exchanges in their own ports, it shows there is some substantial obstructions in the way. We have had the benefit of too many proofs of his Majesty's friendly disposition towards the United States, and know too well his affectionate care of his own subjects, to doubt his willingness to remove these obstructions, if they can be unequivocally pointed out. It is for his wisdom to decide, whether the monopoly, which is the subject of this letter, be deservedly classed with the principal of these. It is a great comfort to me, too, that, in presenting this to the mind of his Majesty, your Excellency will correct my ideas where an insufficient knowledge of facts may have led me into error; and that, while the interests of the King and of his people are the first objects of your attention, an additional one will be presented by those dispositions toward us, which have heretofore so often befriended our nation.

I avail myself of this occasion to repeat the assurance of that high respect and esteem, with which I have the honor to be your Excellency's most obedient, and most humble servant.

TO MRS. TRIST[1]

Paris, August 18, 1785

DEAR MADAM,—

I am much pleased with the people of this country. The roughness of the human mind is so thoroughly rubbed off with them, that it seems as if one might glide through a whole life among them without a jostle. Perhaps, too, their manners may be the best calculated for happiness to a people in their situation, but I am convinced they fall far short of effecting a happiness so temperate, so uniform, and so lasting as is generally enjoyed with us. The domestic bonds here are absolutely done away, and where can their compensation be found? Perhaps they may catch some moments of transport above the level of the ordinary tranquil joy we experience, but they are separated by long intervals, during which all the passions are at sea without rudder or compass. Yet, fallacious as the pursuits of happiness are, they seem on the whole to furnish the most effectual abstraction from a contemplation of the hardness of their government. Indeed, it is difficult to conceive how so good a people, with so good a King, so well-disposed rulers in general, so genial a climate, so fertile a soil, should be rendered so ineffectual for producing human happiness by one single curse—that of a bad form of government. But it is a fact, in spite of the mildness of their governors, the people are ground to powder by the vices of the form of government. Of twenty millions of people supposed to be in France, I am of opinion there are nineteen millions more wretched, more accursed in every circumstance of human existence than the most conspicuously wretched individual of the whole United States. I beg your pardon for

---

[1]Mrs. Trist had taken care of Jefferson's oldest daughter Martha during her stay in Philadelphia. Her grandson Nicholas P. Trist married one of Jefferson's granddaughters, Virginia Jefferson Randolph.

getting into politics. I will add only one sentiment more of that character, that is, nourish peace with their persons, but war against their manners. Every step we take towards the adoption of their manners is a step to perfect misery. I pray you to write to me often. Do not you turn politician too; but write me all the small news—the news about persons and about states; tell me who dies, that I may meet these disagreeable events in detail, and not all at once when I return; who marry, who hang themselves because they cannot marry, &c. . . .

TO PETER CARR[1]

Paris, August 19, 1785

DEAR PETER,—I received, by Mr. Mazzei, your letter of April the 20th. I am much mortified to hear that you have lost so much time; and that, when you arrived in Williamsburg, you were not at all advanced from what you were when you left Monticello. Time now begins to be precious to you. Every day you lose will retard a day your entrance on that public stage whereon you may begin to be useful to yourself. However, the way to repair the loss is to improve the future time. I trust, that with your dispositions, even the acquisition of science is a pleasing employment. I can assure you, that the possession of it is, what (next to an honest heart) will above all things render you dear to your friends, and give you fame and promotion in your own country. When your mind shall be well improved with science, nothing will be necessary to place you in the highest points of view, but to pursue the interests of your country, the interests of your friends, and your own interests also, with the purest integrity, the most chaste honor. The defect of these virtues can never be made up by all the other acquirements of body and mind. Make these, then, your first object. Give up money, give up fame, give up science, give up the earth itself and all it contains, rather than do an immoral act. And never suppose, that in any possible situation, or under any circumstances, it is best for you to do

[1]Peter Carr was one of Jefferson's favorite nephews, the son of Jefferson's school-boy friend Dabney Carr and Martha Jefferson, his fourth sister.

a dishonorable thing, however slightly so it may appear to you. Whenever you are to do a thing, though it can never be known but to yourself, ask yourself how you would act were all the world looking at you, and act accordingly. Encourage all your virtuous dispositions, and exercise them whenever an opportunity arises; being assured that they will gain strength by exercise, as a limb of the body does, and that exercise will make them habitual. From the practice of the purest virtue, you may be assured you will derive the most sublime comforts in every moment of life, and in the moment of death. If ever you find yourself environed with difficulties and perplexing circumstances, out of which you are at a loss how to extricate yourself, do what is right, and be assured that that will extricate you the best out of the worst situations. Though you cannot see, when you take one step, what will be the next, yet follow truth, justice, and plain dealing, and never fear their leading you out of the labyrinth, in the easiest manner possible. The knot which you thought a Gordian one, will untie itself before you. Nothing is so mistaken as the supposition, that a person is to extricate himself from a difficulty, by intrigue, by chicanery, by dissimulation, by trimming, by an untruth, by an injustice. This increases the difficulties tenfold; and those, who pursue these methods, get themselves so involved at length, that they can turn no way but their infamy becomes more exposed. It is of great importance to set a resolution, not to be shaken, never to tell an untruth. There is no vice so mean, so pitiful, so contemptible; and he who permits himself to tell a lie once, finds it much easier to do it a second and third time, till at length it becomes habitual; he tells lies without attending to it, and truths without the world's believing him. This falsehood of the tongue leads to that of the heart, and in time depraves all its good dispositions.

An honest heart being the first blessing, a knowing head is the second. It is time for you now to begin to be choice in your reading; to begin to pursue a regular course in it; and not to suffer yourself to be turned to the right or left by reading anything out of that course. I have long ago digested a plan for you, suited to the circumstances in which you will be placed. This I will detail to you, from time to time, as you advance. For the present, I advise you to begin a course of ancient history, reading everything in the original and not in translations. First read Goldsmith's history of Greece. This will give you a digested view of that field. Then take up ancient history in the detail, reading the following books, in the following order: Herodotus, Thucydides, Xenophontis Anabasis, Arrian, Quintus Curtius, Diodorus Siculus, Justin. This shall form the first stage of your historical reading, and is all I need mention to you now. The next will be of Roman history.[1] From that, we will come down to modern history. In Greek and Latin poetry, you have read or will read at school, Virgil, Terence, Horace, Anacreon, Theocritus, Homer, Euripides, Sophocles. Read also Milton's "Paradise Lost," Shakespeare, Ossian, Pope's and Swift's works, in order to form your style in your own language. In morality, read Epictetus, Xenophontis Memorabilia, Plato's Socratic dialogues, Cicero's philosophies, Antoninus, and Seneca. In order to assure a certain progress in this reading, consider what hours you have free from the school and the exercises of the school. Give about two of them, every day, to exercise; for health must not be sacrificed to learning. A strong body makes the mind strong. As to the species of exercise, I advise the gun. While this gives a moderate exercise to the body, it gives boldness, enterprise, and independence to the mind. Games played with the ball, and others of that nature, are too violent for the body, and stamp no character on the mind. Let your gun, therefore, be the constant companion of your walks. Never think of taking a book with you. The object of walking is to relax the mind. You should therefore not permit yourself even to think while you walk; but divert yourself by the objects surrounding you. Walking is the best possible exercise. Habituate yourself to walk very far. The Europeans value themselves on having subdued the horse to the uses of man; but I doubt whether we have not lost more than we have gained, by the use of this animal. No one has occasioned so much the degeneracy of the human body. An Indian goes on foot nearly as far in a day, for a long journey, as an enfeebled white does on his horse; and he will tire the best horses. There is no habit you will value so much as that of walking far without fatigue. I would advise you to take your exercise in the after-

[1]Livy, Sallust, Caesar, Cicero's epistles, Suetonius, Tacitus, Gibbon. [Jefferson's footnote.]

noon: not because it is the best time for exercise, for certainly it is not; but because it is the best time to spare from your studies; and habit will soon reconcile it to health, and render it nearly as useful as if you gave to that the more precious hours of the day. A little walk of half an hour, in the morning, when you first rise, is advisable also. It shakes off sleep, and produces other good effects in the animal economy. Rise at a fixed and an early hour, and go to bed at a fixed and early hour also. Sitting up late at night is injurious to the health, and not useful to the mind. Having ascribed proper hours to exercise, divide what remain (I mean of your vacant hours) into three portions. Give the principal to History, the other two, which should be shorter, to Philosophy and Poetry. Write to me once every month or two, and let me know the progress you make. Tell me in what manner you employ every hour in the day. The plan I have proposed for you is adapted to your present situation only. When that is changed, I shall propose a corresponding change of plan. I have ordered the following books to be sent to you from London, to the care of Mr. Madison: Herodotus, Thucydides, Xenophon's Hellenics, Anabasis and Memorabilia, Cicero's works, Baretti's Spanish and English Dictionary, Martin's Philosophical Grammar, and Martin's Philosophia Britannica. I will send you the following from hence: Bezout's Mathematics, De la Lande's Astronomy, Muschenbrock's Physics, Quintus Curtius, Justin, Spanish Grammar, and some Spanish books. You will observe that Martin, Bezout, De la Lande, and Muschenbrock, are not in the preceding plan. They are not to be opened till you go to the University. You are now, I expect, learning French. You must push this; because the books which will be put into your hands when you advance into Mathematics, Natural philosophy, Natural history, &c., will be mostly French, these sciences being better treated by the French than the English writers. Our future connection with Spain renders that the most necessary of the modern languages, after the French. When you become a public man, you may have occasion for it, and the circumstance of your possessing that language, may give you a preference over other candidates. I have nothing further to add for the present, but husband well your time, cherish your instructors, strive to make everybody your friend; and be assured that nothing will be so pleasing as your success to, Dear Peter,

Yours affectionately.

TO JOHN JAY[1]
(*Private*)

Paris, August 23, 1785

. . . . We have now lands enough to employ an infinite number of people in their cultivation. Cultivators of the earth are the most valuable citizens. They are the most vigorous, the most independent, the most virtuous, and they are tied to their country, and wedded to its liberty and interests, by the most lasting bonds. As long, therefore, as they can find employment in this line, I would not convert them into mariners, artisans, or anything else. But our citizens will find employment in this line, till their numbers, and of course their productions, become too great for the demand, both internal and foreign. This is not the case as yet, and probably will not be for a considerable time. As soon as it is, the surplus of hands must be turned to something else. I should then, perhaps, wish to turn them to the sea in preference to manufactures; because, comparing the characters of the two classes, I find the former the most valuable citizens. I consider the class of artificers as the panders of vice, and the instruments by which the liberties of a country are generally overturned. However, we are not free to decide this question on principles of theory only. Our people are decided in the opinion, that it is necessary for us to take a share in the occupation of the ocean, and their established habits induce them to require that the sea be kept open to them, and that that line of policy be pursued, which will render the use of that element to them as great as possible. I think it a duty in those entrusted with the administration of their affairs, to conform themselves to the decided choice of their constituents; and that therefore, we should, in every instance, preserve an equality of right to them in the transportation of commodities, in the right of fishing, and in the other uses of the sea.

But what will be the consequence? Frequent wars without a doubt. Their property will be violated on the sea, and in foreign ports, their persons will be insulted, imprisoned, &c., for pretended debts, con-

[1]John Jay, American statesman and diplomat, was later Chief Justice of the Supreme Court.

tracts, crimes, contraband, &c., &c. These insults must be resented, even if we had no feelings, yet to prevent their eternal repetition; or, in other words, our commerce on the ocean and in other countries, must be paid for by frequent war. The justest dispositions possible in ourselves, will not secure us against it. It would be necessary that all other nations were just also. Justice indeed, on our part, will save us from those wars which would have been produced by a contrary disposition. But how can we prevent those produced by the wrongs of other nations? By putting ourselves in a condition to punish them. Weakness provokes insult and injury, while a condition to punish, often prevents them. This reasoning leads to the necessity of some naval force; that being the only weapon by which we can reach an enemy. I think it to our interest to punish the first insult; because an insult unpunished is the parent of many others. We are not, at this moment, in a condition to do it, but we should put ourselves into it, as soon as possible. . . .

TO BARON GEISMER[1]

Paris, September 6, 1785

DEAR SIR,—Your letter of March the 28th, which I received about a month after its date, gave me a very real pleasure, as it assured me of an existence which I valued, and of which I had been led to doubt. You are now too distant from America, to be much interested in what passes there. From the London gazettes, and the papers copying them, you are led to suppose that all there is anarchy, discontent and civil war. Nothing, however, is less true. There are not, on the face of the earth, more tranquil governments than ours, nor a happier and more contented people. Their commerce has not as yet found the channels, which their new relations with the world will offer to best advantage, and the old ones remain as yet unopened by new conventions. This occasions a stagnation in the sale of their produce, the only truth among all the circumstances published about them. Their hatred against Great Britain, having lately received from that nation new

[1]German brigade major in the American Revolutionary war, Baron Geismer was made prisoner in Virginia.

cause and new aliment, has taken a new spring. . . . The character in which I am here at present, confines me to this place, and will confine me as long as I continue in Europe. How long this will be, I cannot tell. I am now of an age which does not easily accommodate itself to new manners and new modes of living; and I am savage enough to prefer the woods, the wilds, and the independence of Monticello, to all the brilliant pleasures of this gay Capital. I shall, therefore, rejoin myself to my native country, with new attachments, and with exaggerated esteem for its advantages; for though there is less wealth there, there is more freedom, more ease, and less misery. I should like it better, however, if it could tempt you once more to visit it; but that is not to be expected. Be this as it may, and whether fortune means to allow or deny me the pleasure of ever seeing you again, be assured that the worth which gave birth to my attachment, and which still animates it, will continue to keep it up while we both live, and that it is with sincerity I subscribe myself, dear Sir, your friend and servant.

TO JAMES MADISON[1]

Paris, September 20, 1785

. . . . I received this summer a letter from Messrs. Buchanan and Hay, as Directors of the public buildings, desiring I would have drawn for them, plans of sundry buildings, and, in the first place, of a capitol.[2] They fixed, for their receiving this plan, a day which was within about six weeks of that on which their letter came to my hand. I engaged an architect of capital abilities in this business. Much time was requisite, after the external form was agreed on, to make the internal distribution convenient for the three branches of government. This time was much lengthened by my avocations to other objects, which I had no right to neglect. The plan, however, was settled. The gentlemen had sent me one which they had thought of. The one agreed on here, is more convenient, more beautiful, gives more room, and will not cost

[1]James Madison, fourth President of the United States, was, until Jefferson's death, one of his closest friends and staunchest followers.

[2]For Richmond, Virginia.

more than two-thirds of what that would. We took for our model what is called the *Maison Quarrée* of Nismes, one of the most beautiful, if not the most beautiful and precious morsel of architecture left us by antiquity. It was built by Caius and Lucius Cæsar, and repaired by Louis XIV., and has the suffrage of all the judges of architecture who have seen it, as yielding to no one of the beautiful monuments of Greece, Rome, Palmyra, and Balbec, which late travellers have communicated to us. It is very simple, but it is noble beyond expression, and would have done honor to our country, as presenting to travellers a specimen of taste in our infancy, promising much for our maturer age. I have been much mortified with information, which I received two days ago from Virginia, that the first brick of the capitol would be laid within a few days. But surely, the delay of this piece of a summer would have been repaired by the savings in the plan preparing here, were we to value its other superiorities as nothing. But how is a taste in this beautiful art to be formed in our countrymen unless we avail ourselves of every occasion when public buildings are to be erected, of presenting to them models for their study and imitation? Pray try if you can effect the stopping of this work. . . .

The loss will be only of the laying the bricks already laid or a part of them. The bricks themselves will do again for the interior walls, and one side wall and one end wall may remain, as they will answer equally well for our plan. This loss is not to be weighed against the saving of money which will arise, against the comfort of laying out the public money for something honorable, the satisfaction of seeing an object and proof of national good taste, and the regret and mortification of erecting a monument of our barbarism, which will be loaded with execrations as long as it shall endure. The plans are in good forwardness, and I hope will be ready within three or four weeks. They could not be stopped now, but on paying their whole price, which will be considerable. If the undertakers are afraid to undo what they have done, encourage them to it by a recommendation from the Assembly. You see I am an enthusiast on the subject of the arts. But it is an enthusiasm of which I am not ashamed, as its object is to improve the taste of my countrymen, to increase their reputation, to reconcile to them the respect of the world, and procure them its praise. . . .

TO MR. BELLINI[1]

Paris, September 30, 1785

. . . . Behold me at length on the vaunted scene of Europe! It is not necessary for your information, that I should enter into details concerning it. But you are, perhaps, curious to know how this new scene has struck a savage of the mountains of America. Not advantageously, I assure you. I find the general fate of humanity here most deplorable. The truth of Voltaire's observation, offers itself perpetually, that every man here must be either the hammer or the anvil. It is a true picture of that country to which they say we shall pass hereafter, and where we are to see God and his angels in splendor, and crowds of the damned trampled under their feet. While the great mass of the people are thus suffering under physical and moral oppression, I have endeavored to examine more nearly the condition of the great, to appreciate the true value of the circumstances in their situation, which dazzle the bulk of spectators, and, especially, to compare it with that degree of happiness which is enjoyed in America, by every class of people. Intrigues of love occupy the younger, and those of ambition, the elder part of the great. Conjugal love having no existence among them, domestic happiness, of which that is the basis, is utterly unknown. In lieu of this, are substituted pursuits which nourish and invigorate all our bad passions, and which offer only moments of ecstasy, amidst days and months of restlessness and torment. Much, very much inferior, this, to the tranquil, permanent felicity with which domestic society in America blesses most of its inhabitants; leaving them to follow steadily those pursuits which health and reason approve, and rendering truly delicious the intervals of those pursuits.

In science, the mass of the people are two centuries behind ours; their literati, half a dozen years before us. Books, really good, acquire just reputation in that time, and so become known to us, and communicate to us all their advances in knowledge. Is not this delay compensated,

[1]Charles Bellini, an *émigré* resident of Virginia, became the first professor of modern languages at William and Mary.

by our being placed out of the reach of that swarm of nonsensical publications which issues daily from a thousand presses, and perishes almost in issuing? With respect to what are termed polite manners, without sacrificing too much the sincerity of language, I would wish my countrymen to adopt just so much of European politeness, as to be ready to make all those little sacrifices of self, which really render European manners amiable, and relieve society from the disagreeable scenes to which rudeness often subjects it. Here, it seems that a man might pass a life without encountering a single rudeness. In the pleasures of the table, they are far before us, because, with good taste they unite temperance. They do not terminate the most sociable meals by transforming themselves into brutes. I have never yet seen a man drunk in France, even among the lowest of the people. Were I to proceed to tell you how much I enjoy their architecture, sculpture, painting, music, I should want words. It is in these arts they shine. The last of them, particularly, is an enjoyment, the deprivation of which with us, cannot be calculated. I am almost ready to say, it is the only thing which from my heart I envy them, and which, in spite of all the authority of the Decalogue, I do covet. But I am running on in an estimate of things infinitely better known to you than to me, and which will only serve to convince you, that I have brought with me all the prejudices of country, habit, and age. But whatever I may allow to be charged to me as prejudice, in every other instance, I have one sentiment at least, founded on reality: it is that of the perfect esteem which your merit and that of Mrs. Bellini have produced, and which will forever enable me to assure you of the sincere regard with which I am, dear Sir, your friend and servant.

TO HOGENDORP[1]

Paris, October 13, 1785

. . . . You ask what I think on the expediency of encouraging our States to be commercial? Were I to indulge my own theory, I should wish them to practise neither commerce nor navigation, but to stand,

[1]Charles Van Hogendorp was a Dutch business man.

with respect to Europe, precisely on the footing of China. We should thus avoid wars, and all our citizens would be husbandmen. Whenever, indeed, our numbers should so increase as that our produce would overstock the markets of those nations who should come to seek it, the farmers must either employ the surplus of their time in manufactures, or the surplus of our hands must be employed in manufactures or in navigation. But that day would, I think, be distant, and we should long keep our workmen in Europe, while Europe should be drawing rough materials, and even subsistence from America. But this is theory only, and a theory which the servants of America are not at liberty to follow. Our people have a decided taste for navigation and commerce. They take this from their mother country; and their servants are in duty bound to calculate all their measures on this datum: we wish to do it by throwing open all the doors of commerce, and knocking off its shackles. But as this cannot be done for others, unless they will do it for us, and there is no great probability that Europe will do this, I suppose we shall be obliged to adopt a system which may shackle them in our ports, as they do us in theirs.

With respect to the sale of our lands, that cannot begin till a considerable portion shall have been surveyed. They cannot begin to survey till the fall of the leaf of this year, nor to sell probably till the ensuing spring. So that it will be yet a twelvemonth before we shall be able to judge of the efficacy of our land office to sink our national debt. It is made a fundamental, that the proceeds shall be solely and sacredly applied as a sinking fund to discharge the capital only of the debt.

It is true that the tobaccos of Virginia go almost entirely to England. The reason is, the people of that State owe a great debt there, which they are paying as fast as they can. I think I have now answered your several queries, and shall be happy to receive your reflections on the same subjects, and at all times to hear of your welfare, and to give you assurances of the esteem, with which I have the honor to be, dear Sir, your most obedient, and most humble servant.

TO J. BANISTER, JUNIOR[1]

Paris, October 15, 1785

DEAR SIR,—I should sooner have answered the paragraph in your letter, of September the 19th, respecting the best seminary for the education of youth in Europe, but that it was necessary for me to make inquiries on the subject. The result of these has been, to consider the competition as resting between Geneva and Rome. They are equally cheap, and probably are equal in the course of education pursued. The advantage of Geneva is, that students acquire there the habit of speaking French. The advantages of Rome are, the acquiring a local knowledge of a spot so classical and so celebrated; the acquiring the true pronunciation of the Latin language; a just taste in the fine arts, more particularly those of painting, sculpture, architecture, and music; a familiarity with those objects and processes of agriculture which experience has shown best adapted to a climate like ours; and lastly, the advantage of a fine climate for health. It is probable, too, that by being boarded in a French family, the habit of speaking that language may be obtained. I do not count on any advantage to be derived, in Geneva, from a familiar acquaintance with the principles of that government. The late revolution has rendered it a tyrannical aristocracy, more likely to give ill than good ideas to an American. I think the balance in favor of Rome. Pisa is sometimes spoken of as a place of education. But it does not offer the first and third of the advantages of Rome. But why send an American youth to Europe for education? What are the objects of an useful American education? Classical knowledge, modern languages, chiefly French, Spanish, and Italian; Mathematics, Natural philosophy, Natural history, Civil history, and Ethics. In Natural philosophy, I mean to include Chemistry and Agriculture, and in Natural history, to include Botany, as well as the other branches of those departments. It is true that the habit of speaking the modern languages cannot be so well acquired in America; but every other article can be as well acquired at William and Mary college, as at any place in

---

[1] This young man, sent abroad because of ill health, was being educated in France, where he was recommended to Jefferson's care.

Europe. When college education is done with, and a young man is to prepare himself for public life, he must cast his eyes (for America) either on Law or Physics. For the former, where can he apply so advantageously as to Mr. Wythe? For the latter, he must come to Europe: the medical class of students, therefore, is the only one which need come to Europe. Let us view the disadvantages of sending a youth to Europe. To enumerate them all, would require a volume. I will select a few. If he goes to England, he learns drinking, horse racing, and boxing. These are the peculiarities of English education. The following circumstances are common to education in that, and the other countries of Europe. He acquires a fondness for European luxury and dissipation, and a contempt for the simplicity of his own country; he is fascinated with the privileges of the European aristocrats, and sees, with abhorrence, the lovely equality which the poor enjoy with the rich, in his own country; he contracts a partiality for aristocracy or monarchy; he forms foreign friendships which will never be useful to him, and loses the seasons of life for forming, in his own country, those friendships which, of all others, are the most faithful and permanent; he is led, by the strongest of all the human passions, into a spirit for female intrigue, destructive of his own and others' happiness, or a passion for whores, destructive of his health, and, in both cases, learns to consider fidelity to the marriage bed as an ungentlemanly practice, and inconsistent with happiness; he recollects the voluptuary dress and arts of the European women, and pities and despises the chaste affections and simplicity of those of his own country; he retains, through life, a fond recollection, and a hankering after those places, which were the scenes of his first pleasures and of his first connections; he returns to his own country, a foreigner, unacquainted with the practices of domestic economy necessary to preserve him from ruin, speaking and writing his native tongue as a foreigner, and therefore unqualified to obtain those distinctions, which eloquence of the pen and tongue ensures in a free country; for I would observe to you, that what is called style in writing or speaking is formed very early in life, while the imagination is warm, and impressions are permanent. I am of opinion, that there never was an instance of a man's writing or speaking his native tongue with elegance, who passed from fifteen to twenty years of age out of the country where it was spoken. Thus, no instance exists of a person's writing two languages perfectly. That will always appear to be his native language, which was most familiar to him in his youth. It appears to me, then, that an American, coming to Europe for education, loses in his knowledge, in his morals, in his health, in his habits, and in his happiness. I had entertained only doubts on this head before I came to Europe: what I see and hear, since I came here, proves more than I had even suspected. Cast your eye over America: who are the men of most learning, of most eloquence, most beloved by their countrymen and most trusted and promoted by them? They are those who have been educated among them, and whose manners morals, and habits, are perfectly homogeneous with those of the country.

Did you expect by so short a question, to draw such a sermon on yourself? I dare say you did not. But the consequences of foreign education are alarming to me, as an American. I sin, therefore, through zeal, whenever I enter on the subject. You are sufficiently American to pardon me for it. Let me hear of your health, and be assured of the esteem with which I am, dear Sir, your friend and servant.

REVEREND JAMES MADISON[1]

Fontainebleau, Oct. 28, 1785

DEAR SIR,—Seven o'clock, and retired to my fireside, I have determined to enter into conversation with you. This is a village of about 15,000 inhabitants when the court is not here, and 20,000 when they are, occupying a valley through which runs a brook and on each side of it a ridge of small mountains, most of which are naked rock. The King comes here, in the fall always, to hunt. His court attends him, as do also the foreign diplomatic corps; but as this is not indispensably required and my finances do not admit the expense of a continued residence here, I propose to come occasionally to attend the King's levees, returning again to Paris, distant forty miles. This being the first trip,

---

[1]Bishop Madison, not to be confused with his statesman cousin of the same name, was the President of William and Mary, and first Bishop of the Protestant-Episcopal Church in Virginia.

I set out yesterday morning to take a view of the place. For this purpose I shaped my course towards the highest of the mountains in sight, to the top of which was about a league.

As soon as I had got clear of the town I fell in with a poor woman walking at the same rate with myself and going the same course. Wishing to know the condition of the laboring poor I entered into conversation with her, which I began by enquiries for the path which would lead me to the mountain: and thence proceeded to enquiries into her vocation, condition and circumstances. She told me she was a day laborer at 8 sous or 4d. sterling the day: that she had two children to maintain, and to pay a rent of 30 livres for her house (which would consume the hire of 75 days), that often she could get no employment and of course was without bread. As we had walked together near a mile and she had so far served me as a guide, I gave her, on parting, 24 sous. She burst into tears of a gratitude which I could perceive was unfeigned because she was unable to utter a word. She had probably never before received so great an aid. This little *attendrissement*, with the solitude of my walk, led me into a train of reflections on that unequal division of property which occasions the numberless instances of wretchedness which I had observed in this country and is to be observed all over Europe.

The property of this country is absolutely concentrated in a very few hands, having revenues of from half a million of guineas a year downwards. These employ the flower of the country as servants, some of them having as many as 200 domestics, not laboring. They employ also a great number of manufacturers and tradesmen, and lastly the class of laboring husbandmen. But after all these comes the most numerous of all classes, that is, the poor who cannot find work. I asked myself what could be the reason so many should be permitted to beg who are willing to work, in a country where there is a very considerable proportion of uncultivated lands? These lands are undisturbed only for the sake of game. It should seem then that it must be because of the enormous wealth of the proprietors which places them above attention to the increase of their revenues by permitting these lands to be labored. I am conscious that an equal division of property is impracticable, but the consequences of this enormous inequality producing so much misery to the bulk of mankind, legislators cannot invent too many devices for subdividing property, only taking care to let their subdivisions go hand in hand with the natural affections of the human mind. The descent of property of every kind therefore to all the children, or to all the brothers and sisters, or other relations in equal degree, is a politic measure and a practicable one. Another means of silently lessening the inequality of property is to exempt all from taxation below a certain point, and to tax the higher portions or property in geometrical progression as they rise. Whenever there are in any country uncultivated lands and unemployed poor, it is clear that the laws of property have been so far extended as to violate natural right. The earth is given as a common stock for man to labor and live on. If for the encouragement of industry we allow it to be appropriated, we must take care that other employment be provided to those excluded from the appropriation. If we do not, the fundamental right to labor the earth returns to the unemployed. It is too soon yet in our country to say that every man who cannot find employment, but who can find uncultivated land, shall be at liberty to cultivate it, paying a moderate rent. But it is not too soon to provide by every possible means that as few as possible shall be without a little portion of land. The small landholders are the most precious part of a state. . . .

TO A. STUART, ESQ.[1]

Paris, January 25, 1786

. . . . The quiet of Europe, at this moment, furnishes little which can attract your notice. Nor will that quiet be soon disturbed, at least for the current year. Perhaps it hangs on the life of the King of Prussia, and that hangs by a very slender thread. American reputation in Europe is not such as to be flattering to its citizens. Two circumstances are particularly objected to us: the non-payment of our debts, and the want of energy in our government. These discourage a connection with us. I own it to be my opinion, that good will arise from

[1] After a distinguished career as a soldier during the Revolution, Stuart became a legislator and jurist, for years leading the conservative wing of Jeffersonian democrats in Virginia.

the destruction of our credit. I see nothing else which can restrain our disposition to luxury, and to the change of those manners which alone can preserve republican government. As it is impossible to prevent credit, the best way would be to cure its ill effects, by giving an instantaneous recovery to the creditor. This would be reducing purchases on credit to purchases for ready money. A man would then see a prison painted on everything he wished, but had not ready money to pay for.

I fear from an expression in your letter, that the people of Kentucky think of separating, not only from Virginia (in which they are right), but also from the confederacy. I own, I should think this a most calamitous event, and such a one as every good citizen should set himself against. Our present federal limits are not too large for good government, nor will the increase of votes in Congress produce any ill effect. On the contrary, it will drown the little divisions at present existing there. Our confederacy must be viewed as the nest, from which all America, North and South, is to be peopled. We should take care, too, not to think it for the interest of that great Continent to press too soon on the Spaniards. Those countries cannot be in better hands. My fear is, that they are too feeble to hold them till our population can be sufficiently advanced to gain it from them, piece by piece. The navigation of the Mississippi we must have. This is all we are, as yet, ready to receive. I have made acquaintance with a very sensible, candid gentleman here, who was in South America during the revolt which took place there, while our Revolution was going on. He says, that those disturbances (of which we scarcely heard anything) cost, on both sides, an hundred thousand lives.

I have made a particular acquaintance here, with Monsieur de Buffon, and have a great desire to give him the best idea I can of our elk. Perhaps your situation may enable you to aid me in this. You could not oblige me more than by sending me the horns, skeleton, and skin of an elk, were it possible to procure them. The most desirable form of receiving them would be, to have the skin slit from the under jaw along the belly to the tail, and down the thighs to the knee, to take the animal out, leaving the legs and hoofs, the bones of the head, and the horns attached to the skin. By sewing up the belly, &c., and stuffing the skin, it would present the form of the animal. However, as an opportunity of doing this is scarcely to be expected, I shall be glad to receive them detached, packed in a box, and sent to Richmond, to the care of Dr. Currie. Everything of this kind is precious here. . . .

TO JAMES MADISON

Paris, February 8, 1786

. . . . I am persuaded, that a gift of lands by the State of Virginia to the Marquis de La Fayette would give a good opinion here of our character, and would reflect honor on the Marquis. Nor, am I sure that the day will not come when it might be an useful asylum to him. The time of life at which he visited America was too well adapted to receive good and lasting impressions to permit him ever to accommodate himself to the principles of monarchical government; and it will need all his own prudence, and that of his friends, to make this country a safe residence for him. How glorious, how comfortable in reflection, will it be, to have prepared a refuge for him in case of a reverse. In the meantime, he could settle it with tenants from the freest part of this country, Bretaigne. I have never suggested the smallest idea of this kind to him; because the execution of it should convey the first notice. If the State has not a right to give him lands with their own officers, they could buy up, at cheap prices, the shares of others. . . .

TO JOHN PAGE

Paris, May 4, 1786

. . . . I returned but three or four days ago from a two months' trip to England. I traversed that country much, and own both town and country fell short of my expectations. Comparing it with this, I found a much greater proportion of barrens, a soil, in other parts, not naturally so good as this, not better cultivated, but better manured, and, therefore, more productive. This proceeds from the practice of long leases there, and short ones here. The laboring people here are poorer than in England. They pay about one half their produce in rent; the English, in general, about a third. The gardening, in that country, is the article in which it surpasses all the earth. I mean their pleasure gardening. This, indeed, went far beyond my ideas. The city of London, though handsomer than Paris, is not so handsome as Philadelphia. Their architecture is in the most wretched style I ever saw, not meaning to except America, where it is bad, nor even Virginia, where it is worse than in any other part of America which I have seen. The mechanical arts in London are carried to a wonderful perfection. But of these I need not speak, because of them my countrymen have unfortunately too many samples before their eyes. I consider the extravagance, which has seized them, as a more baneful evil than toryism was during the war. It is the more so, as the example is set by the best and most amiable characters among us. Would a missionary appear, who would make frugality the basis of his religious system, and go through the land, preaching it up as the only road to salvation, I would join his school, though not generally disposed to seek my religion out of the dictates of my own reason, and feelings of my own heart. These things have been more deeply impressed on my mind, by what I have heard and seen in England. That nation hate us, their ministers hate us, and their King, more than all other men. They have the impudence to avow this, though they acknowledge our trade important to them. But they think, we cannot prevent our countrymen from bringing that into their laps. A conviction of this determines them to make no terms of commerce with us. They say, they will pocket our carrying trade as well as their own. Our overtures of commercial arrangements have been treated with a derision, which shows their firm persuasion, that we shall never unite to suppress their commerce, or even to impede it. I think their hostility towards us is much more deeply rooted at present, than during the war. In the arts, the most striking thing I saw there, new, was the application of the principle of the steam-engine to grist mills. I saw eight pair of stones which are worked by steam, and there are to be set up thirty pair in the same house. An hundred bushels of coal a day, are consumed at present. I do not know in what proportion the consumption will be increased by the additional geer. . . .

TO MR. WYTHE[1]

Paris, August 13, 1786

. . . . If all the sovereigns of Europe were to set themselves to work, to emancipate the minds of their subjects from their present ignorance and prejudices, and that, as zealously as they now endeavor the contrary, a thousand years would not place them on that high ground, on which our common people are now setting out. Ours could not have been so fairly placed under the control of the common sense of the people, had they not been separated from their parent stock, and kept from contamination, either from them, or the other people of the old world, by the intervention of so wide an ocean. To know the worth of this, one must see the want of it here. I think by far the most important bill in our whole code, is that for the diffusion of knowledge among the people. No other sure foundation can be devised, for the preservation of freedom and happiness. If anybody thinks that kings, nobles, or priests are good conservators of the public happiness, send him here. It is the best school in the universe to cure him of that folly. He will see here, with his own eyes, that these descriptions of men are an abandoned confederacy against the happiness of the mass of the people. The omnipotence of their effect cannot be better proved, than in this country particularly, where, notwithstanding the finest soil upon earth, the finest climate under heaven, and a people of the most benevolent, the most gay and amiable character of which the human form is susceptible; where such a people, I say, surrounded by so many blessings from nature, are loaded with misery, by kings, nobles, and priests, and by them alone. Preach, my dear Sir, a crusade against ignorance; establish and improve the law for educating the common people. Let our countrymen know, that the people alone can protect us against these evils, and that the tax which will be paid for this purpose, is not more than the thousandth part of what will be paid to kings, priests and

[1]After graduating from William and Mary, Jefferson studied law under George Wythe, one of the most celebrated jurists of his day, who later became Jefferson's warm friend.

nobles, who will rise up among us if we leave the people in ignorance. The people of England, I think, are less oppressed than here. But it needs but half an eye to see, when among them, that the foundation is laid in their dispositions for the establishment of a despotism. Nobility, wealth, and pomp are the objects of their admiration. They are by no means the free-minded people we suppose them in America. Their learned men, too, are few in number, and are less learned, and infinitely less emancipated from prejudice, than those of this country. . . .

TO MRS. COSWAY[1]

Paris, October 12, 1786

MY DEAR MADAM,—Having performed the last sad office of handing you into your carriage, at the pavillon de St. Denis, and seen the wheels get actually into motion, I turned on my heel and walked, more dead than alive, to the opposite door, where my own was awaiting me. Mr. Danquerville was missing. He was sought for, found, and dragged down stairs. We were crammed into the carriage, like recruits for the Bastille, and not having soul enough to give orders to the coachman, he presumed Paris our destination, and drove off. After a considerable interval, silence was broke, with a *"Je suis vraiment affligé du départ de ces bons gens."* This was a signal for a mutual confession of distress. We began immediately to talk of Mr. and Mrs. Cosway, of their goodness, their talents, their amiability; and, though we spoke of nothing else, we seemed hardly to have entered into the matter, when the coachman announced the rue St. Denis, and that we were opposite Mr. Danquerville's. He insisted on descending there, and traversing a short passage to his lodgings. I was carried home. Seated by my fireside, solitary and sad, the following dialogue took place between my Head and my Heart.

Head. Well, friend, you seem to be in a pretty trim.

Heart. I am indeed the most wretched of all earthly beings. Over-

[1]Maria Cosway, a famous Italian-English beauty and accomplished painter, captivated Jefferson during his stay in Paris.

whelmed with grief, every fibre of my frame distended beyond its natural powers to bear, I would willingly meet whatever catastrophe
should leave me no more to feel, or to fear.

Head. These are the eternal consequences of your warmth and precipitation. This is one of the scrapes into which you are ever leading
us. You confess your follies, indeed; but still you hug and cherish
them; and no reformation can be hoped where there is no repentance.

Heart. Oh, my friend! this is no moment to upbraid my foibles. I
am rent into fragments by the force of my grief! If you have any balm,
pour it into my wounds; if none, do not harrow them by new torments.
Spare me in this awful moment! At any other, I will attend with
patience to your admonitions.

Head. On the contrary, I never found that the moment of triumph,
with you, was the moment of attention to my admonitions. While suffering under your follies, you may perhaps be made sensible of them,
but the paroxysm over, you fancy it can never return. Harsh, therefore,
as the medicine may be, it is my office to administer it. You will be
pleased to remember, that when our friend Trumbull used to be telling
us of the merits and talents of these good people, I never ceased whis-
pering to you that we had no occasion for new acquaintances; that the
greater their merits and talents, the more dangerous their friendship
to our tranquillity, because the regret at parting would be greater.

Heart. Accordingly, Sir, this acquaintance was not the consequence
of my doings. It was one of your projects, which threw us in the way
of it. It was you, remember, and not I, who desired the meeting at
Legrand and Molinos. I never trouble myself with domes nor arches.
The Halle aux Bleds might have rotted down, before I should have
gone to see it. But you, forsooth, who are eternally getting us to sleep
with your diagrams and crotchets, must go and examine this wonderful piece of architecture; and when you had seen it, oh! it was the most
superb thing on earth! What you had seen there was worth all you
had yet seen in Paris! I thought so, too. But I meant it of the lady and
gentleman to whom we had been presented; and not of a parcel of
sticks and chips put together in pens. You, then, Sir, and not I, have
been the cause of the present distress.

Head. It would have been happy for you if my diagrams and crotchets had gotten you to sleep on that day, as you are pleased to say they

eternally do. My visit to Legrand and Molinos had public utility for its object. A market is to be built in Richmond. What a commodious plan is that of Legrand and Molinos; especially, if we put on it the noble dome of the Halle aux Bleds. If such a bridge as they showed us can be thrown across the Schuylkill, at Philadelphia, the floating bridges taken up, and the navigation of that river opened, what a copious resource will be added, of wood and provisions, to warm and feed the poor of that city? While I was occupied with these objects, you were dilating with your new acquaintances, and contriving how to prevent a separation from them. Every soul of you had an engagement for the day. Yet all these were to be sacrificed, that you might dine together. Lying messengers were to be despatched into every quarter of the city, with apologies for your breach of engagement. You, particularly, had the effrontery to send word to the Duchess Danville, that on the moment we were setting out to dine with her, despatches came to hand, which required immediate attention. You wanted me to invent a more ingenious excuse; but I knew you were getting into a scrape, and I would have nothing to do with it. Well; after dinner to St. Cloud, from St. Cloud to Ruggieri's, from Ruggieri's to Krumfoltz; and if the day had been as long as a Lapland summer day, you would still have contrived means among you to have filled it.

Heart. Oh! my dear friend, how you have revived me by recalling to my mind the transactions of that day! How well I remember them all, and that, when I came home at night, and looked back to the morning, it seemed to have been a month agone. Go on, then, like a kind comforter, and paint to me the day we went to St. Germains. How beautiful was every object! the Port de Neuilly, the hills along the Seine, the rainbows of the machine of Marly, the terrace of St. Germains, the chateaux, the gardens, the statues of Marly, the pavillon of Lucienne. Recollect, too, Madrid, Bagatelle, the King's garden, the Dessert. How grand the idea excited by the remains of such a column. The spiral staircase, too, was beautiful. Every moment was filled with something agreeable. The wheels of time moved on with a rapidity, of which those of our carriage gave but a faint idea. And yet, in the evening, when one took a retrospect of the day, what a mass of happiness had we travelled over! Retrace all those scenes to me, my good companion, and I will forgive the unkindness with which you were chiding me. The day we went to St. Germains was a little too warm, I think; was it not?

Head. Thou art the most incorrigible of all the beings that ever sinned! I reminded you of the follies of the first day, intending to deduce from thence some useful lessons for you; but instead of listening to them, you kindle at the recollection, you retrace the whole series with a fondness, which shows you want nothing, but the opportunity, to act it over again. I often told you, during its course, that you were imprudently engaging your affections, under circumstances that must have cost you a great deal of pain; that the persons, indeed, were of the greatest merit, possessing good sense, good humor, honest hearts, honest manners, and eminence in a lovely art, that the lady had, moreover, qualities and accomplishments belonging to her sex, which might form a chapter apart for her; such as music, modesty, beauty, and that softness of disposition, which is the ornament of her sex and charm of ours; but that all those considerations would increase the pang of separation; that their stay here was to be snort; that you rack our whole system when you are parted from those you love, complaining that such a separation is worse than death, inasmuch as this ends our sufferings, whereas that only begins them; and that the separation would, in this instance, be the more severe, as you would probably never see them again.

Heart. But they told me they would come back again, the next year.

Head. But, in the meantime, see what you suffer; and their return, too, depends on so many circumstances, that if you had a grain of prudence, you would not count upon it. Upon the whole, it is improbable, and therefore you should abandon the idea of ever seeing them again.

Heart. May heaven abandon me if I do!

Head. Very well. Suppose, then, they come back. They are to stay two months, and, when these are expired, what is to follow? Perhaps you flatter yourself they may come to America?

Heart. God only knows what is to happen. I see nothing impossible in that supposition; and I see things wonderfully contrived sometimes, to make us happy. Where could they find such objects as in America, for the exercise of their enchanting art? especially the lady, who paints landscapes so inimitably. She wants only subjects worthy of immortality, to render her pencil immortal. The Falling Spring, the Cascade of Niagara, the passage of the Potomac through the Blue Mountains, the Natural Bridge; it is worth a voyage across the Atlantic to see these objects; much more to paint, and make them, and thereby ourselves, known to all ages. And our own dear Monticello; where has nature spread so rich a mantle under the eye? mountains, forest, rocks, rivers. With what majesty do we there ride above the storms! How sublime to look down into the workhouse of nature, to see her clouds, hail, snow, rain, thunder, all fabricated at our feet! and the glorious sun, when rising as if out of a distant water, just gilding the tops of the mountains, and giving life to all nature! I hope in God, no circumstance may ever make either seek an asylum from grief! With what sincere sympathy I would open every cell of my composition, to receive the effusion of their woes! I would pour my tears into their wounds; and if a drop of balm could be found on the top of the Cordilleras, or at the remotest sources of the Missouri, I would go thither myself to seek and to bring it. Deeply practised in the school of affliction, the human heart knows no joy which I have not lost, no sorrow of which I have not drunk! Fortune can present no grief of unknown form to me! Who, then, can so softly bind up the wound of another, as he who has felt the same wound himself? But heaven forbid they should ever know a sorrow! Let us turn over another leaf, for this has distracted me.

Head. Well. Let us put this possibility to trial then, on another point. When you consider the character which is given of our country, by the lying newspapers of London, and their credulous copiers in other countries; when you reflect that all Europe is made to believe we are a lawless banditti, in a state of absolute anarchy, cutting one another's throats, and plundering without distinction, how could you expect that any reasonable creature would venture among us?

Heart. But you and I know that all this is false: that there is not a country on earth, where there is greater tranquillity; where the laws are milder, or better obeyed; where every one is more attentive to his own business, or meddles less with that of others; where strangers are better received, more hospitably treated, and with a more sacred respect.

Head. True, you and I know this, but your friends do not know it.

Heart. But they are sensible people, who think for themselves. They will ask of impartial foreigners, who have been among us, whether they saw or heard on the spot, any instance of anarchy. They will judge, too, that a people, occupied as we are, in opening rivers, digging navigable canals, making roads, building public schools, establishing academies, erecting busts and statues to our great men, protecting religious freedom, abolishing sanguinary punishments, reforming and improving our laws in general; they will judge, I say, for themselves, whether these are not the occupations of a people at their ease; whether this is not better evidence of our true state, than a London newspaper, hired to lie, and from which no truth can ever be extracted but by reversing everything it says.

Head. I did not begin this lecture, my friend, with a view to learn from you what America is doing. Let us return, then, to our point. I wish to make you sensible how imprudent it is to place your affections, without reserve, on objects you must so soon lose, and whose loss, when it comes, must cost you such severe pangs. Remember the last night. You knew your friends were to leave Paris to-day. This was enough to throw you into agonies. All night you tossed us from one side of the bed to the other; no sleep, no rest. The poor crippled wrist, too, never left one moment in the same position; now up, now down, now here, now there; was it to be wondered at, if its pains returned? The surgeon then was to be called, and to be rated as an ignoramus, because he could not divine the cause of this extraordinary change. In fine, my friend, you must mend your manners. This is not a world to live at random in, as you do. To avoid those eternal distresses, to which you are forever exposing us, you must learn to look forward, before you take a step which may interest our peace. Everything in this world is a matter of calculation. Advance then with caution, the balance in your hand. Put into one scale the pleasures which any object may offer; but put fairly into the other, the pains which are to follow, and see which preponderates. The making an acquaintance, is not a matter of indifference. When a new one is proposed to you, view it all round. Consider what advantages it presents, and to what inconveniences it may expose you. Do not bite at the bait of pleasure, till you know there is no hook beneath it. The art of life is the art of avoiding pain; and he is the best pilot, who steers clearest of the rocks and shoals with which it is beset. Pleasure is always before us; but misfortune is at our side: while running after that, this arrests us. The most effectual means of being secure against pain, is to retire within ourselves, and to suffice for our own happiness. Those which depend on ourselves, are the only pleasures a wise man will count on: for nothing is ours, which another may deprive us of. Hence the inestimable value of intellectual pleasures. Ever in our power, always leading us to something new, never cloying, we ride serene and sublime above the concerns of this mortal world, contemplating truth and nature, matter and motion, the laws which bind up their existence, and that Eternal Being who made and bound them up by those laws. Let this be our employ. Leave the bustle and tumult of society to those who have not talents to occupy themselves without them. Friendship is but another name for an alliance with the follies and the misfortunes of others. Our own share of miseries is sufficient: why enter then as volunteers into those of an other? Is there so little gall poured into our cup, that we must need help to drink that of our neighbor? A friend dies, or leaves us: we feel as if a limb were cut off. He is sick: we must watch over him, and participate of his pains. His fortune is shipwrecked: ours must be laid under contribution. He loses a child, a parent, or a partner: we must mourn the loss as if it were our own.

Heart. And what more sublime delight than to mingle tears with one whom the hand of heaven hath smitten! to watch over the bed of sickness, and to beguile its tedious and its painful moments! to share our bread with one to whom misfortune has left none. This world abounds indeed with misery; to lighten its burthen, we must divide it with one another. But let us now try the virtue of your mathematical balance, and as you have put into one scale the burthens of friendship, let me put its comforts into the other. When languishing then under disease, how grateful is the solace of our friends! how are we penetrated with their assiduities and attentions! how much are we supported by their encouragements and kind offices! When heaven has taken from us some object of our love, how sweet is it to have a bosom whereon to recline our heads, and into which we may pour the torrent of our tears! Grief, with such a comfort, is almost a luxury! In a life, where we are perpetually exposed to want and accident, yours is a wonderful proposition, to insulate ourselves, to retire from all aid, and to wrap ourselves in the mantle of self-sufficiency! For, assuredly, nobody will care for him who cares for nobody. But friendship is precious, not only in the shade, but in the sunshine of life; and thanks to a benevolent arrangement of things, the greater part of life is sunshine. I will recur for proof to the days we have lately passed. On these, indeed, the sun shone brightly. How gay did the face of nature appear! Hills, valleys, chateaux, gardens, rivers, every object wore its liveliest hue! Whence did they borrow it? From the presence of our charming companion. They were pleasing, because she seemed pleased. Alone, the scene would have been dull and insipid: the participation of it with her gave it relish. Let the gloomy monk, sequestered from the world, seek unsocial pleasures in the bottom of his cell! Let the sublimated philosopher grasp visionary happiness, while pursuing phantoms dressed in the garb of truth! Their supreme wisdom is supreme folly; and they mistake for happiness the mere absence of pain. Had they ever felt the solid pleasure of one generous spasm of the heart, they would exchange for it all the frigid speculations of their lives, which you have been vaunting in such elevated terms. Believe me, then, my friend, that that is a miserable arithmetic which could estimate friendship at nothing, or at less than nothing. Respect for you has induced me to enter into this discussion, and to hear principles uttered which I detest and abjure. Respect for myself now obliges me to recall you into the proper limits of your office. When nature assigned us the same habitation, she gave us over it a divided empire. To you, she allotted the field of science; to me, that of morals. When the circle is to be squared, or the orbit of a comet to be traced; when the arch of greatest strength, or the solid of least resistance, is to be investigated, take up the problem; it is yours; nature has given me no cognizance of it. In like manner, in denying to you the feelings of sympathy, of benevolence, of gratitude, of justice, of love, of friendship, she has excluded you from their control. To these, she has adapted the mechanism of the heart. Morals were too essential to the happiness of man, to be risked on the uncertain combinations of the head. She laid their foundation, therefore, in sentiment, not in science. That she gave to all, as necessary to all; this to a few only, as sufficing with a few. I know, indeed, that you pretend authority to the sovereign control of our conduct, in all its parts; and a respect for your grave saws and maxims, a desire to do what is right, has sometimes induced me to conform to your counsels. A few facts, however, which I can readily recall to your memory, will suffice to prove to you, that nature has not organized you for our moral direction. When the poor, wearied soldier whom we overtook at Chickahominy, with his pack on his back, begged us to let him get up behind our chariot, you began to calculate that the road was full of soldiers, and that if all should be taken up, our horses would fail in their journey. We drove on therefore. But, soon becoming sensible you had made me do wrong, that, though we cannot relieve all the distressed, we should relieve as many as we can, I turned about to take up the soldier; but he had entered a bye-path, and was no more to be found; and from that moment to this, I could never find him out, to ask his forgiveness. Again, when the poor woman came to ask a charity in Philadelphia, you whispered that she looked like a drunkard, and that half a dollar was enough to give her for the ale-house. Those who want the dispositions to give, easily find reasons why they ought not to give. When I sought her out afterwards, and did what I should have done at first, you know that she employed the money immediately towards placing her child at school. If our country, when pressed with wrongs at the point of the bayonet, had been governed by its heads instead of its hearts, where should we have been now? Hanging on a gallows as high as Haman's. You began to calculate, and to compare wealth and numbers: we threw up a few pulsations of our blood; we supplied enthusiasm against wealth and numbers; we put our existence to the hazard, when the hazard seemed against us, and we saved our country: justifying, at the same time, the ways of Providence, whose precept is, to do always what is right, and leave the issue to Him. In short, my friend, as far as my rec-ollection serves me, I do not know that I ever did a good thing on your suggestion, or a dirty one without it. I do forever, then, disclaim your interference in my province. Fill paper as you please with triangles and squares: try how many ways you can hang and combine them together. I shall never envy nor control your sublime delights. But leave me to decide, when and where friendships are to be contracted. You say, I contract them at random. So you said the woman at Philadelphia was a drunkard. I receive none into my esteem, till I know they are worthy of it. Wealth, title, office, are no recommendations to my friendship. On the contrary, great good qualities are requisite to make amends for their having wealth, title, and office. You confess, that, in the present case, I could not have made a worthier choice. You only object, that I was so soon to lose them. We are not immortal ourselves, my friend; how can we expect our enjoyments to be so? We have no rose without its thorn; no pleasure without alloy. It is the law of our existence, and we must acquiesce. It is the condition annexed to all our pleasures, not by us who receive, but by him who gives them. True, this condition is pressing cruelly on me at this moment. I feel more fit for death than life. But, when I look back on the pleasures of which it is the consequence, I am conscious they were worth the price I am paying. Notwithstanding your endeavors, too, to damp my hopes, I comfort myself with expectations of their promised return. Hope is sweeter than despair; and they were too good to mean to deceive me. "In the summer," said the gentleman; but "in the spring," said the lady; and I should love her forever, were it only for that! Know, then, my friend, that I have taken these good people into my bosom; that I have lodged them in the warmest cell I could find; that I love them, and will continue to love them through life; that if fortune should dispose them on one side the globe, and me on the other, my affections shall pervade its whole mass to reach them. Knowing then my determination, attempt not to disturb it. If you can, at any time, furnish matter for their amusement, it will be the office of a good neighbor to do it. I will, in like manner, seize any occasion which may offer, to do the like good turn for you with Condorcet, Rittenhouse, Madison, La Cretelle, or any other of those worthy sons of science, whom you so justly prize.

I thought this a favorable proposition whereon to rest the issue of the dialogue. So I put an end to it by calling for my nightcap. Methinks, I hear you wish to heaven I had called a little sooner, and so spared you the ennui of such a sermon. I did not interrupt them sooner, because I was in a mood for hearing sermons. You too were the subject; and on such thesis, I never think the theme long; not even if I am to write it, and that slowly and awkwardly, as now, with the left hand. But, that you may not be discouraged from a correspondence which begins so formidably, I will promise you, on my honor, that my future letters shall be of a reasonable length. I will even agree to express but half my esteem for you, for fear of cloying you with too full a dose. But, on your part, no curtailing. If your letters are as long as the Bible, they will appear short to me. Only let them be brimful of affection. I shall read them with the dispositions with which Arlequin, in *Les deux billets*, spelt the words *"je t'aime,"* and wished that the whole alphabet had entered into their composition.

We have had incessant rains since your departure. These make me fear for your health, as well as that you had an uncomfortable journey. The same cause has prevented me from being able to give you any account of your friends here. This voyage to Fontainebleau will probably send the Count de Moustier and the Marquise de Brehan, to America. Danquerville promised to visit me, but has not done it as yet. De la Tude comes sometimes to take family soup with me, and entertains me with anecdotes of his five and thirty years' imprisonment. How fertile is the mind of man, which can make the Bastile and dungeon of Vincennes yield interesting anecdotes! You know this was for making four verses on Madame de Pompadour. But I think you told me you did not know the verses. They were these: *"Sans esprit, sans sentiments, Sans etre belle, ni neuve, En France on peut avoir le premier ament; Pompadour en est l'épreuve."*[1] I have read the memoir of his three escapes. As to myself, my health is good, except my wrist which mends slowly, and my mind which mends not at all, but broods constantly over your departure. The lateness of the season obliges me to decline my journey into the south of France. Present me in the most friendly terms to Mr. Cosway, and receive me into your own recollection with a partiality and warmth, proportioned not to my own poor merit, but to the sentiments of sincere affection and esteem, with which I have the honor to be, my dear Madam, your most obedient humble servant.

TO JAMES MADISON

Paris, December 16, 1786

. . . . To make us one nation as to foreign concerns, and keep us distinct in domestic ones, gives the outline of the proper division of powers between the general and particular governments. But, to enable the federal head to exercise the powers given it to best advantage, it should be organized as the particular ones are, into legisla-

---

[1] "Without brains or feeling, /Without beauty or youth, / In France one may have the first of lovers: / There's Pompadour for proof."

tive, executive, and judiciary. The first and last are already separated. The second should be. When last with Congress, I often proposed to members to do this, by making of the committee of the States, an executive committee during the recess of Congress, and, during its sessions, to appoint a committee to receive and despatch all executive business, so that Congress itself should meddle only with what should be legislative. But I question if any Congress (much less all successively) can have self-denial enough to go through with this distribution. The distribution, then, should be imposed on them. I find Congress have reversed their division of the western States, and proposed to make them fewer and larger. This is reversing the natural order of things. A tractable people may be governed in large bodies; but, in proportion as they depart from this character, the extent of their government must be less. We see into what small divisions the Indians are obliged to reduce their societies. This measure, with the disposition to shut up the Mississippi, gives me serious apprehensions of the severance of the eastern and western parts of our confederacy. It might have been made the interest of the western States to remain united with us, by managing their interests honestly, and for their own good. But, the moment we sacrifice their interest to our own, they will see it better to govern themselves. The moment they resolve to do this, the point is settled. A forced connection is neither our interest, nor within our power.

The Virginia act for religious freedom has been received with infinite approbation in Europe, and propagated with enthusiasm. I do not mean by the governments, but by the individuals who compose them. It has been translated into French and Italian, has been sent to most of the courts of Europe, and has been the best evidence of the falsehood of those reports which stated us to be in anarchy. It is inserted in the new "Encyclopédie," and is appearing in most of the publications respecting America. In fact, it is comfortable to see the standard of reason at length erected, after so many ages, during which the human mind has been held in vassalage by kings, priests, and nobles; and it is honorable for us, to have produced the first legislature who had the courage to declare, that the reason of man may be trusted with the formation of his own opinions. . . .

TO JOHN JAY

Paris, January 9, 1787

. . . . You will have seen in the public papers, that the King has called an assembly of the Notables of this country. This has not been done for one hundred and sixty years past. Of course, it calls up all the attention of the people. The objects of this assembly are not named: several are conjectured. The tolerating the Protestant religion; removing all the internal Custom houses to the frontier; equalizing the gabelles on salt through the kingdom; the sale of the King's domains, to raise money; or, finally, the effecting this necessary end by some other means, are talked of. But in truth, nothing is known about it. This government practises secrecy so systematically, that it never publishes its purposes or its proceedings, sooner or more extensively than necessary. I send you a pamphlet, which, giving an account of the last Assemblée des Notables, may give an idea of what the present will be. . . .

TO MONSIEUR DE CREVE-COEUR[1]

Paris, January 15, 1787

DEAR SIR,—I see by the Journal of this morning, that they are robbing us of another of our inventions to give it to the English. The writer, indeed, only admits them to have revived what he thinks was known to the Greeks, that is, the making the circumference of a wheel of one single piece. The farmers in New Jersey were the first who practised it, and they practised it commonly. Dr. Franklin, in one of his trips to London, mentioned this practice to the man now in London, who has the patent for making those wheels. The idea struck him. The Doctor promised to go to his shop, and assist him in trying to make the wheel of one piece. The Jersey farmers do it by cutting a young

---

[1]This distinguished French *émigré* and acquaintance of Jefferson was the author of *Letters of an American Farmer*.

sapling, and bending it, while green and juicy, into a circle; and leaving it so until it becomes perfectly seasoned. But in London there are no saplings. The difficulty was, then, to give to old wood the pliancy of young. The Doctor and the workman labored together some weeks, and succeeded; and the man obtained a patent for it, which has made his fortune. I was in his shop in London, he told me the whole story himself, and acknowledged, not only the origin of the idea, but how much the assistance of Dr. Franklin had contributed to perform the operation on dry wood. He spoke of him with love and gratitude. I think I have had a similar account from Dr. Franklin, but cannot be quite certain. I know, that being in Philadelphia when the first set of patent wheels arrived from London, and were spoken of by the gentleman (an Englishman) who brought them, as a wonderful discovery, the idea of its being a new discovery was laughed at by the Philadelphians, who, in their Sunday parties across the Delaware, had seen every farmer's cart mounted on such wheels. The writer in the paper, supposes the English workman got his idea from Homer. But it is more likely the Jersey farmer got his idea from thence, because ours are the only farmers who can read Homer; because, too, the Jersey practice is precisely that stated by Homer: the English practice very different. Homer's words are (comparing a young hero killed by Ajax to a poplar felled by a workman) literally thus: "He fell on the ground, like a poplar, which has grown smooth, in the west part of a great meadow; with its branches shooting from its summit. But the chariot maker, with the sharp axe, has felled it, that he may bend a wheel for a beautiful chariot. It lies drying on the banks of the river." Observe the circumstances which coincide with the Jersey practice. 1. It is a tree growing in a moist place, full of juices and easily bent. 2. It is cut while green. 3. It is bent into the circumference of a wheel. 4. It is left to dry in that form. You, who write French well and readily, should write a line for the Journal, to reclaim the honor of our farmers. Adieu. Yours affectionately.

TO COLONEL EDWARD CARRINGTON[1]

Paris, January 16, 1787

. . . . The tumults in America I expected would have produced in Europe an unfavorable opinion of our political state. But it has not. On the contrary, the small effect of these tumults seems to have given more confidence in the firmness of our governments. The interposition of the people themselves on the side of government has had a great effect on the opinion here. I am persuaded myself that the good sense of the people will always be found to be the best army. They may be led astray for a moment, but will soon correct themselves. The people are the only censors of their governors; and even their errors will tend to keep these to the true principles of their institution. To punish these errors too severely would be to suppress the only safeguard of the public liberty. The way to prevent these irregular interpositions of the people, is to give them full information of their affairs through the channel of the public papers, and to contrive that those papers should penetrate the whole mass of the people. The basis of our governments being the opinion of the people, the very first object should be to keep that right; and were it left to me to decide whether we should have a government without newspapers, or newspapers without a government, I should not hesitate a moment to prefer the latter. But I should mean that every man should receive those papers, and be capable of reading them. I am convinced that those societies (as the Indians) which live without government, enjoy in their general mass an infinitely greater degree of happiness than those who live under the European governments. Among the former, public opinion is in the place of law, and restrains morals as powerfully as laws ever did anywhere. Among the latter, under pretence of governing, they have divided their nations into two classes, wolves and sheep. I do not exaggerate. This is a true picture of Europe. Cherish, therefore, the spirit of our people, and keep alive their attention. Do not be too severe upon their errors, but reclaim them by enlightening them. If once they become inattentive

---

[1]Carrington was a member of a prominent Virginia family who served in the Revolution and was a member of the Continental Congress.

to the public affairs, you and I, and Congress and Assemblies, Judges and Governors, shall all become wolves. It seems to be the law of our general nature, in spite of individual exceptions; and experience declares that man is the only animal which devours his own kind; for I can apply no milder term to the governments of Europe, and to the general prey of the rich on the poor. . . .

TO JAMES MADISON

Paris, January 30, 1787

. . . . I am impatient to learn your sentiments on the late troubles in the Eastern States. So far as I have yet seen, they do not appear to threaten serious consequences. Those States have suffered by the stoppage of the channels of their commerce, which have not yet found other issues. This must render money scarce, and make the people uneasy. This uneasiness has produced acts absolutely unjustifiable; but I hope they will provoke no severities from their governments. A consciousness of those in power that their administration of the public affairs has been honest, may, perhaps, produce too great a degree of indignation; and those characters, wherein fear predominates over hope, may apprehend too much from these instances of irregularity. They may conclude too hastily, that nature has formed man insusceptible of any other government than that of force, a conclusion not founded in truth nor experience. Societies exist under three forms, sufficiently distinguishable. 1. Without government, as among our Indians. 2. Under governments, wherein the will of every one has a just influence; as is the case in England, in a slight degree, and in our States, in a great one. 3. Under governments of force; as is the case in all other monarchies, and in most of the other republics. To have an idea of the curse of existence under these last, they must be seen. It is a government of wolves over sheep. It is a problem, not clear in my mind, that the first condition is not the best. But I believe it to be inconsistent with any great degree of population. The second state has a great deal of good in it. The mass of mankind under that, enjoys a precious degree of liberty and happiness. It has its evils, too; the principal of which is the turbulence to which it is subject. But weigh this against the oppressions of monarchy, and it becomes nothing. *Malo periculosem libertatem quam quietam servitutem.*[1] Even this evil is productive of good. It prevents the degeneracy of government, and nourishes a general attention to the public affairs. I hold it, that a little rebellion, now and then, is a good thing, and as necessary in the political world as storms in the physical. Unsuccessful rebellions, indeed, generally establish the encroachments on the rights of the people, which have produced them. An observation of this truth should render honest republican governors so mild in their punishment of rebellions, as not to discourage them too much. It is a medicine necessary for the sound health of government.

. . . . The Marquis de La Fayette is a most valuable auxiliary to me. His zeal is unbounded, and his weight with those in power, great. His education having been merely military, commerce was an unknown field to him. But his good sense enabling him to comprehend perfectly whatever is explained to him, his agency has been very efficacious. He has a great deal of sound genius, is well remarked by the King, and rising in popularity. He has nothing against him, but the suspicion of republican principles. I think he will one day be of the ministry. His foible is, a canine appetite for popularity and fame; but he will get above this. *The Count de Vergennes is ill.* The possibility of his *recovery,* renders it dangerous for us to express a doubt of it; but he is in danger. He is a great minister in European affairs, but has very imperfect ideas of our *institutions,* and no confidence in them. His devotion to the principles of pure despotism, renders him unaffectionate to our governments. But his fear of England makes him value us as a make weight. He is cool, reserved in political conversations, but free and familiar on other subjects, and a very attentive, agreeable person to do business with. It is impossible to have a clearer, better organized head; but age has chilled his heart. . . . .

[1] I prefer freedom with danger to slavery with ease.

TO MADAME LA COMTESSE DE TESSÉ[1]

Nismes, March 20, 1787

Here I am, Madam, gazing whole hours at the Maison Quarrée, like a lover at his mistress. The stocking weavers and silk spinners around it consider me a hypochondriac Englishman, about to write with a pistol the last chapter of his history. This is the second time I have been in love since I left Paris. The first was with a Diana at the Chateau de Laye-Epinaye in Beaujolois, a delicious morsel of sculpture, by M. A. Slodtz. This, you will say, was in rule, to fall in love with a female beauty; but with a house! it is out of all precedent. No, Madam, it is not without a precedent in my own history. While in Paris, I was violently smitten with the Hotel de Salm, and used to go to the Tuileries almost daily, to look at it. . . .

From Lyons to Nismes I have been nourished with the remains of Roman grandeur. They have always brought you to my mind, because I know your affection for whatever is Roman and noble. At Vienna I thought of you. But I am glad you were not there; for you would have seen me more angry than, I hope, you will ever see me. The Prætorian Palace as it is called, comparable, for its fine proportions, to the Maison Quarrée, defaced by the barbarians who have converted it to its present purpose, its beautiful fluted Corinthian columns cut out, in part, to make space for Gothic windows, and hewed down, in the residue, to the plane of the building, was enough, you must admit, to disturb my composure. At Orange, too, I thought of you. I was sure you had seen with pleasure the sublime triumphal arch of Marius at the entrance of the city. I went then to the Arenæ. Would you believe, Madam, that in this eighteenth century, in France, under the reign of Louis XVI., they are at this moment pulling down the circular wall of this superb remain, to pave a road? . . .

A propos of Paris. I have now been three weeks from there, without knowing anything of what has passed. I suppose I shall meet it all at Aix, where I have directed my letters to be lodged, *poste restante*. My

---

[1]Madame de Tessé was Lafayette's older cousin whom Jefferson greatly admired and frequently visited while he was in Paris.

journey has given me leisure to reflect on this Assemblée des Notables. Under a good and a young King, as the present, I think good may be made of it. I would have the deputies then, by all means, so conduct themselves as to encourage him to repeat the calls of this Assembly. Their first steps should be, to get themselves divided into two chambers instead of seven; the Noblesse and the Commons separately. The second, to persuade the King, instead of choosing the deputies of the Commons himself, to summon those chosen by the people for the Provincial administrations. The third, as the Noblesse is too numerous to be all of the Assemblée, to obtain permission for that body to choose its own deputies. Two Houses, so elected, would contain a mass of wisdom which would make the people happy, and the King great; would place him in history where no other act can possibly place him. They would thus put themselves in the track of the best guide they can follow; they would soon overtake it, become its guide in turn, and lead to the wholesome modifications wanting in that model, and necessary to constitute a rational government. Should they attempt more than the established habits of the people are ripe for, they may lose all, and retard indefinitely the ultimate object of their aim. These, Madam, are my opinions; but I wish to know yours, which, I am sure, will be better.

From a correspondent at Nismes, you will not expect news. Were I to attempt to give you news, I should tell you stories one thousand years old. I should detail to you the intrigues of the courts of the Cæsars, how they affect us here, the oppressions of their prætors, prefects, &c. I am immersed in antiquities from morning to night. For me, the city of Rome is actually existing in all the splendor of its empire. I am filled with alarms for the event of the irruptions daily making on us, by the Goths, the Visigoths, Ostrogoths, and Vandals, lest they should re-conquer us to our original barbarism. If I am sometimes induced to look forward to the eighteenth century, it is only when recalled to it by the recollection of your goodness and friendship, and by those sentiments of sincere esteem and respect with which I have the honor to be Madam, your most obedient, and most humble servant.

TO MARTHA JEFFERSON[1]

Aix-en Provence, March 28, 1787

I was happy, my dear Patsy, to receive, on my arrival here, your letter, informing me of your good health and occupations. I have not written you sooner because I have been almost constantly on the road. My journey hitherto has been a very pleasing one. It was undertaken with the hope that the mineral waters of this place might restore strength to my wrist. Other considerations also concurred, instruction, amusement, and abstraction from business, of which I had too much at Paris. I am glad to learn that you are employed in things new and good, in your music and drawing. You know what have been my fears for some time past—that you do not employ yourself so closely as I could wish. You have promised me a more assiduous attention, and I have great confidence in what you promise. It is your future happiness which interests me, and nothing can contribute more to it (moral rectitude always excepted) than the contracting a habit of industry and activity. Of all the cankers of human happiness none corrodes with so silent, yet so baneful a tooth, as indolence. Body and mind both unemployed, our being becomes a burthen, and every object about us loathsome, even the dearest. Idleness begets ennui, ennui the hypochondria, and that a diseased body. No laborious person was ever yet hysterical. Exercise and application produce order in our affairs, health of body, cheerfulness of mind, and these make us precious to our friends. It is while we are young that the habit of industry is formed. If not then, it never is afterwards. The fortune of our lives, therefore, depends on employing well the short period of youth. If at any moment, my dear, you catch yourself in idleness, start from it as you would from the precipice of a gulf. You are not, however, to consider yourself as unemployed while taking exercise. That is necessary for your health, and health is the first of all objects. For this reason, if you leave your dancing-master for the summer, you must increase your other exercise.

I do not like your saying that you are unable to read the ancient

[1]Martha, Jefferson's oldest daughter, had accompanied her father on his mission to France. She was fifteen years old when this letter was written. [Randall.]

print of your Livy, but with the aid of your master. We are always equal to what we undertake with resolution. A little degree of this will enable you to decipher your Livy. If you always lean on your master, you will never be able to proceed without him. It is a part of the American character to consider nothing as desperate—to surmount every difficulty by resolution and contrivance. In Europe there are shops for every want: its inhabitants therefore have no idea that their wants can be furnished otherwise. Remote from all other aid, we are obliged to invent and to execute; to find means within ourselves, and not to lean on others. Consider, therefore, the conquering your Livy as an exercise in the habit of surmounting difficulties; a habit which will be necessary to you in the country where you are to live, and without which you will be thought a very helpless animal, and less esteemed. Music, drawing, books, invention, and exercise, will be so many resources to you against ennui. But there are others which, to this object, add that of utility. These are the needle and domestic economy. The latter you cannot learn here, but the former you may. In the country life of America there are many moments when a woman can have recourse to nothing but her needle for employment. In a dull company and in dull weather, for instance, it is ill manners to read; it is ill manners to leave them; no card-playing there among genteel people—that is abandoned to blackguards. The needle is then a valuable resource. Besides, without knowing how to use it herself, how can the mistress of a family direct the works of her servants?

You ask me to write you long letters. I will do it, my dear, on condition you will read them from time to time, and practice what they will inculcate. Their precepts will be dictated by experience, by a perfect knowledge of the situation in which you will be placed, and by the fondest love for you. This it is which makes me wish to see you more qualified than common. My expectations from you are high—yet not higher than you may attain. Industry and resolution are all that are wanting. Nobody in this world can make me so happy, or so miserable, as you. Retirement from public life will ere long become necessary for me. To your sister and yourself I look to render the evening of my life serene and contented. Its morning has been clouded by loss after loss, till I have nothing left but you. I do not doubt either your affection or dispositions. But great exertions are necessary, and you have little time left to make them. Be industrious, then, my dear child. Think nothing unsurmountable by resolution and application and you will be all that I wish you to be.

. . . . Continue to love me with all the warmth with which you are beloved. . . . . my dear Patsy. . . .

TO MARTHA JEFFERSON

Toulon, April 7, 1787[1]

MY DEAR PATSY:

I received yesterday at Marseilles your letter of March 25th; and I received it with pleasure, because it announced to me that you were well. Experience learns us to be always anxious about the health of those whom we love. I have not been able to write to you as often as I expected, because I am generally on the road; and when I stop anywhere, I am occupied in seeing what is to be seen. It will be some time now, perhaps three weeks, before I shall be able to write you again. But this need not slacken your writing to me, because you have leisure, and your letters come regularly to me. I have received letters which inform me that our dear Polly[2] will certainly come to us this summer. By the time I return, it will be time to expect her. When she arrives, she will become a precious charge on your hands. The difference of your age and your common loss of a mother, will put that office on you. Teach her to be always true; no vice is so mean as the want of truth, and at the same time so useless. Teach her never to be angry: anger only serves to torment ourselves, to divert others, and alienate their esteem. And teach her industry and application to useful pursuits. I will venture to assure you, that if you inculcate this in her mind, you will make her a happy being herself, a most inestimable friend to you, and precious to all the world. In teaching her these dispositions of mind, you will be more fixed in them yourself, and render yourself dear to all your acquaintances. Practice them, then, my dear, without ceasing. If ever you find yourself in difficulty, and doubt how to extricate your-

---

[1][Ford.]

[2]Maria Jefferson, Martha's younger sister.

self, do what is right, and you will find it the easiest way of getting out of the difficulty. Do it for the additional incitement of increasing the happiness of him who loves you infinitely, ...

TO THE MARQUIS DE LAFAYETTE[1]

Nice, April 11, 1787

Your head, my dear friend, is full of notable things; and being better employed, therefore, I do not expect letters from you. I am constantly roving about, to see what I have never seen before, and shall never see again. In the great cities, I go to see what travellers think alone worthy of being seen; but I make a job of it, and generally gulp it all down in a day. On the other hand, I am never satiated with rambling through the fields and farms, examining the culture and cultivators, with a degree of curiosity which makes some take me to be a fool, and others to be much wiser than I am. I have been pleased to find among the people a less degree of physical misery than I had expected. They are generally well clothed, and have a plenty of food, not animal indeed, but vegetable, which is as wholesome. Perhaps they are overworked, the excess of the rent required by the landlord obliging them to too many hours of labor in order to produce that, and wherewith to feed and clothe themselves. The soil of Champagne and Burgundy I have found more universally good than I had expected, and as I could not help making a comparison with England, I found that comparison more unfavorable to the latter than is generally admitted. The soil, the climate, and the productions are superior to those of England, and the husbandry as good, except in one point; that of manure. In England, long leases for twenty-one years, or three lives, to wit, that of the farmer, his wife, and son, renewed by the son as soon as he comes to the possession, for his own life, his wife's and eldest child's, and so on, render the farms there almost hereditary, make it worth the farmer's while to manure the lands highly, and give

---

[1]Lafayette, brilliant volunteer fighter for American freedom and one of Jefferson's dearest friends for half a century, was political contact man for him while he was Minister to France.

the landlord an opportunity of occasionally making his rent keep pace with the improved state of the lands. Here the leases are either during pleasure, or for three, six, or nine years, which does not give the farmer time to repay himself for the expensive operation of well manuring, and, therefore, he manures ill, or not at all. I suppose, that could the practice of leasing for three lives be introduced in the whole kingdom, it would, within the term of your life, increase agricultural productions fifty per cent.; or were any one proprietor to do it with his own lands, it would increase his rents fifty per cent.; in the course of twenty-five years. But I am told the laws do not permit it. The laws then, in this particular, are unwise and unjust, and ought to give that permission. In the southern provinces, where the soil is poor, the climate hot and dry, and there are few animals, they would learn the art, found so precious in England, of making vegetable manure, and thus improving these provinces in the article in which nature has been least kind to them. Indeed, these provinces afford a singular spectacle. Calculating on the poverty of their soil, and their climate by its latitude only, they should have been the poorest in France. On the contrary, they are the richest, from one fortuitous circumstance. Spurs or ramifications of high mountains, making down from the Alps, and, as it were, reticulating these provinces, give to the valleys the protection of a particular inclosure to each, and the benefit of a general stagnation of the northern winds produced by the whole of them, and thus countervail the advantage of several degrees of latitude. From the first olive fields of Pierrelatte, to the orangeries of Hieres, has been continued rapture to me. I have often wished for you. I think you have not made this journey. It is a pleasure you have to come, and an improvement to be added to the many you have already made. It will be a great comfort to you, to know, from your own inspection, the condition of all the provinces of your own country, and it will be interesting to them at some future day, to be known to you. This is, perhaps, the only moment of your life in which you can acquire that knowledge. And to do it most effectually, you must be absolutely incognito, you must ferret the people out of their hovels as I have done, look into their kettles, eat their bread, loll on their beds under pretence of resting yourself, but in fact, to find if they are soft. You will feel á sublime pleasure in the course of this investigation, and a sublimer one hereafter, when you shall be able to apply your knowledge to the softening of their beds, or the throwing a morsel of meat into their kettle of vegetables.

You will not wonder at the subjects of my letters; they are the only ones which have been presented to my mind for some time past; and the waters must always be what are the fountains from which they flow. According to this, indeed, I should have intermixed, from beginning to end, warm expressions of friendship to you. But according to the ideas of our country, we do not permit ourselves to speak even truths, when they may have the air of flattery. I content myself, therefore, with saying once for all, that I love you, your wife and children. Tell them so, and adieu. Yours affectionately.

TO JAMES MADISON

Paris, June 20, 1787

. . . . The idea of separating the executive business of the confederacy from Congress, as the judiciary is already, in some degree, is just and necessary. I had frequently pressed on the members individually, while in Congress, the doing this by a resolution of Congress for appointing an executive committee, to act during the sessions of Congress, as the committee of the States was to act during their vacations. But the referring to this committee all executive business, as it should present itself, would require a more persevering self-denial than I suppose Congress to possess. It will be much better to make that separation by a federal act. The negative, proposed to be given them on all the acts of the several legislatures, is now, for the first time, suggested to my mind. *Prima facie*, I do not like it. It fails in an essential character; that the hole and the patch should be commensurate. But this proposes to mend a small hole by covering the whole garment. Not more than one out of one hundred State acts concern the confederacy. This proposition, then, in order to give them one degree of power, which they ought to have, gives them ninety-nine more, which they ought not to have, upon a presumption that they will not exercise the ninety-nine. But upon every act, there will be a preliminary question, Does this act concern the confederacy? And was there ever a proposition so plain, as to pass Congress without a debate? Their decisions are almost always wise; they are like pure metal. But you know of how much dross this is the result. Would not an appeal from the State judicature to a federal court, in all cases where the act of Confederation controlled the question, be as effectual a remedy, and exactly commensurate to the defect? A British creditor, for example, sues for his debt in Virginia; the defendant pleads an act of the State, excluding him from their courts; the plaintiff urges the Confederation, and the treaty made under that, as controlling the State law; the judges are weak enough to decide according to the views of their legislature. An appeal to a federal court sets all to rights. It will be said, that this court may encroach on the jurisdiction of the State courts. It may. But there will be a power, to wit, Congress, to watch and restrain them. But place the same authority in Congress itself, and there will be no power above them, to perform the same office. They will restrain within due bounds, a jurisdiction exercised by others, much more rigorously than if exercised by themselves. . . .

The late changes in the ministry here excite considerable hopes. I think we gain in them all. I am particularly happy at the re-entry of Malesherbes into the Council. His knowledge and integrity render his value inappreciable, and the greater to me, because, while he had no views of office, we had established together the most unreserved intimacy. So far, too, I am pleased with Montmorin. His honesty proceeds from the heart as well as the head, and therefore may be more surely counted on. The King loves business, economy, order, and justice, and wishes sincerely the good of his people; but he is irascible, rude, very limited in his understanding, and religious, bordering on bigotry. He has no mistress, loves his queen, and is too much governed by her. She is capricious like her brother, and governed by him; devoted to pleasure and expense; and not remarkable for any other vices or virtues. Unhappily the King shows a propensity for the pleasures of the table. That for drink has increased lately, or, at least, it has become more known. . . .

To T. M. Randolph, Junior[1]

Paris, July 6, 1787

. . . . I am glad to find, that among the various branches of science presenting themselves to your mind, you have fixed on that of politics as your principal pursuit. Your country will derive from this a more immediate and sensible benefit. She has much for you to do. For, though we may say with confidence, that the worst of the American constitutions is better than the best which ever existed before, in any other country, and that they are wonderfully perfect for a first essay, yet every human essay must have defects. It will remain, therefore, to those now coming on the stage of public affairs, to perfect what has been so well begun by those going off it. Mathematics, Natural Philosophy, Natural History, Anatomy, Chemistry, Botany, will become amusements for your hours of relaxation, and auxiliaries to your principal studies. Precious and delightful ones they will be. As soon as such a foundation is laid in them, as you may build on as you please, hereafter, I suppose you will proceed to your main objects, Politics, Law, Rhetoric, and History. As to these, the place where you study them is absolutely indifferent. I should except Rhetoric, a very essential member of them, and which I suppose must be taught to advantage where you are. You would do well, therefore, to attend the public exercises in this branch also, and to do it with very particular diligence. This being done, the question arises, where you shall fix yourself for studying Politics, Law, and History? I should not hesitate to decide in favor of France, because you will, at the same time, be learning to speak the language of that country, become absolutely essential under our present circumstances. The best method of doing this, would be to fix yourself in some family where there are women and children, in Passy, Auteuil, or some other of the little towns in reach of Paris. The principal hours of the day, you will attend to your studies, and in those of relaxation, associate with the family. You will learn to speak better from women and children in three months, than from men in a year.

[1]Randolph was Jefferson's nephew who later married Martha Jefferson, his second cousin and Thomas Jefferson's older daughter.

Such a situation, too will render more easy a due attention to economy of time and money. Having pursued your main studies here,
about two years, and acquired a facility in speaking French, take a tour
of four or five months through this country and Italy, return then to
Virginia, and pass a year in Williamsburg, under the care of Mr.
Wythe; and you will be ready to enter on the public stage, with superior advantages. I have proposed to you, to carry on the study of the
law with that of politics and history. Every political measure will, forever, have an intimate connection with the laws of the land; and he,
who knows nothing of these, will always be perplexed, and often foiled
by adversaries having the advantage of that knowledge over him.
Besides, it is a source of infinite comfort to reflect, that under every
chance of fortune, we have a resource in ourselves from which we may
be able to derive an honorable subsistence. I would, therefore, propose not only the study, but the practice of the law for some time, to
possess yourself of the habit of public speaking. With respect to modern languages, French, as I have before observed, is indispensable.
Next to this, the Spanish is most important to an American. Our connection with Spain is already important, and will become daily more
so. Besides this, the ancient part of American history is written chiefly
in Spanish. To a person who would make a point of reading and speaking French and Spanish, I should doubt the utility of learning Italian.
These three languages, being all degeneracies from the Latin, resem-
ble one another so much, that I doubt the probability of keeping in
the head a distinct knowledge of them all. I suppose that he who learns
them all, will speak a compound of the three, and neither perfectly.
The journey which I propose to you need not be expensive, and would
be very useful. With your talents and industry, with science, and that
steadfast honesty which eternally pursues right, regardless of consequences, you may promise yourself everything—but health, without
which there is no happiness. An attention to health, then, should take
place of every other object. The time necessary to secure this by active
exercises, should be devoted to it, in preference to every other pursuit.
I know the difficulty with which a studious man tears himself from his
studies, at any given moment of the day. But his happiness, and that
of his family, depend on it. The most uninformed mind, with a healthy
body, is happier than the wisest valetudinarian. I need not tell you, that

if I can be useful to you in any part of this, or any other plan you shall adopt, you will make me happy by commanding my services. . . .

TO EDWARD CARRINGTON

Paris, August 4, 1787

DEAR SIR,—Since mine of the 16th of January, I have been honored by your favors of April the 24th and June the 9th. I am happy to find that the States have come so generally into the schemes of the federal convention, from which, I am sure, we shall see wise propositions. I confess, I do not go as far in the reforms thought necessary, as some of my correspondents in America, but if the convention should adopt such propositions, I shall suppose them necessary. My general plan would be, to make the States one as to everything connected with foreign nations, and several as to everything purely domestic. But with all the imperfections of our present government, it is without comparison the best existing, or that ever did exist. Its greatest defect is the imperfect manner in which matters of commerce have been provided for. It has been so often said, as to be generally believed, that Congress have no power by the Confederation to enforce anything; for example, contributions of money. It was not necessary to give them that power expressly; they have it by the law of nature. When two parties make a compact, there results to each a power of compelling the other to execute it. Compulsion was never so easy as in our case, where a single frigate would soon levy on the commerce of any State the deficiency of its contributions; nor more safe than in the hands of Congress, which has always shown that it would wait, as it ought to do, to the last extremities, before it would execute any of its powers which are disagreeable. I think it very material, to separate, in the hands of Congress, the executive and legislative powers, as the judiciary already are, in some degree. This, I hope, will be done. The want of it has been the source of more evil than we have experienced from any other cause. Nothing is so embarrassing nor so mischievous, in a great assembly, as the details of execution. The smallest trifle of that kind occupies as long as the most important act of legislation, and takes place of everything else. Let any man recollect, or look over, the files of Congress; he will observe the most important propositions hanging over, from week to week, and month to month, till the occasions have passed them, and the things never done. I have ever viewed the executive details as the greatest cause of evil to us, because they in fact place us as if we had no federal head, by diverting the attention of that head from great to small subjects; and should this division of power not be recommended by the convention, it is my opinion Congress should make it itself, by establishing an executive committee. . . .

TO COLONEL MONROE

Paris, August 5, 1787

DEAR SIR,—A journey of between three and four months, into the southern parts of France and northern of Italy, has prevented my writing to you. In the meantime, you have changed your ground, and engaged in different occupations, so that I know not whether the news of this side the water will even amuse you. However, it is all I have for you. The storm which seemed to be raised suddenly in Brabant, will probably blow over. The Emperor, on his return to Vienna, pretended to revoke all the concessions which had been made by his Governors General, to his Brabantine subjects; but he, at the same time, called for deputies from among them to consult with. He will use their agency to draw himself out of the scrape, and all there, I think, will be quieted. Hostilities go on occasionally in Holland. France espouses the cause of the Patriots, as you know, and England and Prussia that of the Stadtholder. France and England are both unwilling to bring on war, but a hasty move of the King of Prussia will perplex them. He has thought the stopping his sister sufficient cause for sacrificing a hundred or two thousand of his subjects, and as many Hollanders and French. He has therefore ordered twenty thousand men to march, without consulting England, or even his own ministers. He may thus drag England into a war, and of course this country, against their will. But it is certain they will do everything they can to prevent it; and that in this at least they agree. Though such a war might be gainful to us, yet it is much to be deprecated by us at this time. In all probability, France would be unequal to such a war by sea and by land, and it is not our interest, or even safe for us, that she should be weakened. The great improvements in their constitution, effected by the Assemblée des Notables, you are apprized of. That of partitioning the country into a number of subordinate governments, under the administration of Provincial Assemblies, chosen by the people, is a capital one. But to the delirium of joy which these improvements gave the nation, a strange reverse of temper has suddenly succeeded. The deficiencies of their revenue were exposed, and they were frightful. Yet there was an appearance of intention to economise, and reduce the expenses of government. But expenses are still very inconsiderately incurred, and all reformation in that point despaired of. The public credit is affected; and such a spirit of discontent has arisen, as has never been seen. The parliament refused to register the edict for a stamp tax, or any other tax, and call for the States General, who alone, they say, can impose a new tax. They speak with a boldness unexampled. The King has called them to Versailles tomorrow, where he will hold a *lit de justice*, and compel them to register the tax. How the chapter will finish, we must wait to see . . .

TO PETER CARR

Paris, August 10, 1787

DEAR PETER,—I have received your two letters of December the 30th and April the 18th, and am very happy to find by them, as well as by letters from Mr. Wythe, that you have been so fortunate as to attract his notice and good will; I am sure you will find this to have been one of the most fortunate events of your life, as I have ever been sensible it was of mine. I enclose you a sketch of the sciences to which I would wish you to apply, in such order as Mr. Wythe shall advise; I mention, also, the books in them worth your reading, which submit to his correction. Many of these are among your father's books, which you should have brought to you. As I do not recollect those of them not in his library, you must write to me for them, making out a catalogue of such as you think you shall have occasion for, in eighteen months from the date of your letter, and consulting Mr. Wythe on the subject. To this sketch, I will add a few particular observations:

1. Italian. I fear the learning this language will confound your French and Spanish. Being all of them degenerated dialects of the Latin, they are apt to mix in conversation. I have never seen a person speaking the three languages, who did not mix them. It is a delightful language, but late events having rendered the Spanish more useful, lay it aside to prosecute that.

2. Spanish. Bestow great attention on this, and endeavor to acquire an accurate knowledge of it. Our future connections with Spain and Spanish America, will render that language a valuable acquisition. The ancient history of that part of America, too, is written in that language. I send you a dictionary.

3. Moral Philosophy. I think it lost time to attend lectures on this branch. He who made us would have been a pitiful bungler, if he had made the rules of our moral conduct a matter of science. For one man of science, there are thousands who are not. What would have become of them? Man was destined for society. His morality, therefore, was to be formed to this object. He was endowed with a sense of right and wrong, merely relative to this. This sense is as much a part of his nature, as the sense of hearing, seeing, feeling; it is the true foundation of morality, and not the το καλου,[1] truth, &c., as fanciful writers have imagined. The moral sense, or conscience, is as much a part of man as his leg or arm. It is given to all human beings in a stronger or weaker degree, as force of members is given them in a greater or less degree. It may be strengthened by exercise, as may any particular limb of the body. This sense is submitted, indeed, in some degree, to the guidance of reason; but it is a small stock which is required for this: even a less one than what we call common sense. State a moral case to a ploughman and a professor. The former will decide it as well, and often better than the latter, because he has not been led astray by artificial rules. In this branch, therefore, read good books, because they will encourage, as well as direct your feelings. The writings of Sterne, particularly, form the best course of morality that ever was written. Besides these, read the books mentioned in the enclosed paper; and, above all things, lose no occasion of exercising your dispositions to be grateful, to be generous, to be charitable, to be humane, to be true,

[1]The beautiful.

just, firm, orderly, courageous, &c. Consider every act of this kind will strengthen your moral faculties and increase your worth.

4. Religion. Your reason is now mature enough to examine this object. In the first place, divest yourself of all bias in favor of novelty and singularity of opinion. Indulge them in any other subject rather than that of religion. It is too important, and the consequences of error may be too serious. On the other hand, shake off all the fears and servile prejudices, under which weak minds are servilely crouched. Fix reason firmly in her seat, and call to her tribunal every fact, every opinion. Question with boldness even the existence of a God; because, if there be one, he must more approve of the homage of reason, than that of blind-folded fear. You will naturally examine first, the religion of your own country. Read the Bible, then, as you would read Livy or Tacitus. The facts which are within the ordinary course of nature, you will believe on the authority of the writer, as you do those of the same kind in Livy and Tacitus. The testimony of the writer weighs in their favor, in one scale, and their not being against the laws of nature, does not weigh against them. But those facts in the Bible which contradict the laws of nature, must be examined with more care, and under a variety of faces. Here you must recur to the pretensions of the writer to inspiration from God. Examine upon what evidence his pretensions are founded, and whether that evidence is so strong, as that its falsehood would be more improbable than a change in the laws of nature, in the case he relates. For example, in the book of Joshua, we are told, the sun stood still several hours. Were we to read that fact in Livy or Tacitus, we should class it with their showers of blood, speaking of statues, beasts, etc. But it is said, that the writer of that book was inspired. Examine, therefore, candidly, what evidence there is of his having been inspired. The pre-tension is entitled to your inquiry, because millions believe it. On the other hand, you are astronomer enough to know how contrary it is to the law of nature that a body revolving on its axis, as the earth does, should have stopped, should not, by that sudden stoppage, have pros-trated animals, trees, buildings, and should after a certain time have resumed its revolution, and that without a second general prostration. Is this arrest of the earth's motion, or the evidence which affirms it, most within the law of probabilities? You will next read the New Tes-tament. It is the history of a personage called Jesus. Keep in your eye

the opposite pretensions: 1, of those who say he was begotten by God, born of a virgin, suspended and reversed the laws of nature at will, and ascended bodily into heaven; and 2, of those who say he was a man of illegitimate birth, of a benevolent heart, enthusiastic mind, who set out without pretensions to divinity, ended in believing them, and was punished capitally for sedition, by being gibbeted, according to the Roman law, which punished the first commission of that offence by whipping, and the second by exile, or death *in furea*. . . . .

Do not be frightened from this inquiry by any fear of its consequences. If it ends in a belief that there is no God, you will find incitements to virtue in the comfort and pleasantness you feel in its exercise, and the love of others which it will procure you. If you find reason to believe there is a God, a consciousness that you are acting under his eye, and that he approves you, will be a vast additional incitement; if that there be a future state, the hope of a happy existence in that increases the appetite to deserve it; if that Jesus was also a God, you will be comforted by a belief of his aid and love. In fine, I repeat, you must lay aside all prejudice on both sides, and neither believe nor reject anything, because any other persons, or description of persons, have rejected or believed it. Your own reason is the only oracle given you by heaven, and you are answerable, not for the rightness, but uprightness of the decision. I forgot to observe, when speaking of the New Testament, that you should read all the histories of Christ, as well of those whom a council of ecclesiastics have decided for us, to be Pseudo-evangelists, as those they named Evangelists. Because these Pseudo-evangelists pretended to inspiration, as much as the others, and you are to judge their pretensions by your own reason, and not by the reason of those ecclesiastics. Most of these are lost. There are some, however, still extant, collected by Fabricius, which I will endeavor to get and send you.

5. Travelling. This makes men wiser, but less happy. When men of sober age travel, they gather knowledge, which they may apply usefully for their country; but they are subject ever after to recollections mixed with regret; their affections are weakened by being extended over more objects; and they learn new habits which cannot be gratified when they return home. Young men, who travel, are exposed to all these inconveniences in a higher degree, to others still more serious,

and do not acquire that wisdom for which a previous foundation is requisite, by repeated and just observations at home. The glare of pomp and pleasure is analogous to the motion of the blood; it absorbs all their affection and attention, they are torn from it as from the only good in this world, and return to their home as to a place of exile and condemnation. Their eyes are forever turned back to the object they have lost, and its recollection poisons the residue of their lives. Their first and most delicate passions are hackneyed on unworthy objects here, and they carry home the dregs, insufficient to make themselves or anybody else happy. Add to this, that a habit of idleness, an inability to apply themselves to business is acquired, and renders them useless to themselves and their country. These observations are founded in experience. There is no place where your pursuit of knowledge will be so little obstructed by foreign objects, as in your own country, nor any, wherein the virtues of the heart will be less exposed to be weakened. Be good, be learned, and be industrious, and you will not want the aid of travelling, to render you precious to your country, dear to your friends, happy within yourself. I repeat my advice, to take a great deal of exercise, and on foot. Health is the first requisite after morality. Write to me often, and be assured of the interest I take in your success, as well as the warmth of those sentiments of attachment with which I am, dear Peter, your affectionate friend.

TO JOHN ADAMS[1]

Paris, August 30, 1787

. . . , all tongues in Paris (and in France as it is said) have been let loose, and never was a license of speaking against the government exercised in London more freely or more universally. Caricatures, placards, bons mots, have been indulged in by all ranks of people, and I know of no well-attested instance of a single punishment. For some time mobs of ten, twenty and thirty thousand people collected daily,

[1]Jefferson and Adam's mutual friendship and respect, interrupted for some years because of political differences and personal misunderstandings, was particularly strong in the later years of their lives. Their correspondence is notable for its philosophic and spirited character.

surrounded the parliament house, huzzaed the members, even entered the doors and examined into their conduct, took the horses out of the carriages of those who did well, and drew them home. The government thought it prudent to prevent these, drew some regiments into the neighborhood, multiplied the guards, had the streets constantly patrolled by strong parties, suspended privileged places, forbade all clubs, etc. The mobs have ceased; perhaps this may be partly owing to the absence of parliament. The Count d'Artois, sent to hold a bed of justice in the Cour des Aides, was hissed and hooted without reserve, by the populace; the carriage of Madame de (I forget the name) in the Queen's livery was stopped by the populace, under a belief that it was Madame de Polignac, whom they would have insulted; the Queen, going to the theatre at Versailles with Madame de Polignac, was received with a general hiss. The King, long in the habit of drowning his cares in wine, plunges deeper and deeper. The Queen cries, but sins on. The Count d'Artois is detested, and Monsieur, the general favorite.. . .

TO JOHN ADAMS

Paris, November 13, 1787

. . . . How do you like our new constitution? I confess there are things in it which stagger all my disposition to subscribe to what such an Assembly has proposed. The house of federal representatives will not be adequate to the management of affairs, either foreign or federal. Their President seems a bad edition of a Polish King. He may be elected from four years to four years, for life. Reason and experience prove to us, that a chief magistrate, so continuable, is an office for life When one or two generations shall have proved that this is an office for life, it becomes, on every occasion, worthy of intrigue, of bribery, of force, and even of foreign interference. It will be of great consequence to France and England, to have America governed by a Galloman or Angloman. Once in office, and possessing the military force of the Union, without the aid or check of a council, he would not be easily dethroned, even if the people could be induced to withdraw their votes from him. I wish that at the end of the four years, they had made him forever ineligible a second time. Indeed, I think all the good of this new constitution might have been couched in three or four new articles, to be added to the good, old and venerable fabric, which should have been preserved even as a religious relique. . . .

TO COLONEL SMITH[1]

Paris, November 13, 1787

. . . . can history produce an instance of rebellion[2] so honorably conducted? I say nothing of its motives. They were founded in ignorance, not wickedness. God forbid we should ever be twenty years without such a rebellion. The people cannot be all, and always, well informed. The part which is wrong will be discontented, in proportion to the importance of the facts they misconceive. If they remain quiet under such misconceptions, it is a lethargy, the forerunner of death to the public liberty. We have had thirteen States independent for eleven years. There has been one rebellion. That comes to one rebellion in a century and a half, for each State. What country before, ever existed a century and a half without a rebellion? And what country can preserve its liberties, if its rulers are not warned from time to time, that this people preserve the spirit of resistance? Let them take arms. The remedy is to set them right as to facts, pardon and pacify them. What signify a few lives lost in a century or two? The tree of liberty must be refreshed from time to time, with the blood of patriots and tyrants. It is its natural manure. . . .

TO JAMES MADISON

Paris, December 20, 1787

. . . . I like much the general idea of framing a government, which should go on of itself, peaceably, without needing continual recurrence

[1]Colonel William Stephens Smith was an American diplomat and son-in-law of John Adams.

[2]Jefferson has been discussing Shays's insurrection in Massachusetts.

to the State legislatures. I like the organization of the government into legislative, judiciary and executive. I like the power given the legislature to levy taxes, and for that reason solely, I approve of the greater House being chosen by the people directly. For though I think a House so chosen, will be very far inferior to the present Congress, will be very illy qualified to legislate for the Union, for foreign nations, etc., yet this evil does not weigh against the good, of preserving inviolate the fundamental principle, that the people are not to be taxed but by representatives chosen immediately by themselves. I am captivated by the compromise of the opposite claims of the great and little States, of the latter to equal, and the former to proportional influence. I am much pleased, too, with the substitution of the method of voting by person, instead of that of voting by States; and I like the negative given to the Executive, conjointly with a third of either House; though I should have liked it better, had the judiciary been associated for that purpose, or invested separately with a similar power. There are other good things of less moment. I will now tell you what I do not like. First, the omission of a bill of rights, providing clearly, and without the aid of sophism, for freedom of religion, freedom of the press, protection against standing armies, restriction of monopolies, the eternal and unremitting force of the habeas corpus laws, and trials by jury in all matters of fact triable by the laws of the land, and not by the laws of nations. To say, as Mr. Wilson does, that a bill of rights was not necessary, because all is reserved in the case of the general government which is not given, while in the particular ones, all is given which is not reserved, might do for the audience to which it was addressed; but it is surely a *gratis dictum,* the reverse of which might just as well be said; and it is opposed by strong inferences from the body of the instrument, as well as from the omission of the cause of our present Confederation, which had made the reservation in express terms. It was hard to conclude, because there has been a want of uniformity among the States as to the cases triable by jury, because some have been so incautious as to dispense with this mode of trial in certain cases, therefore, the more prudent States shall be reduced to the same level of calamity. It would have been much more just and wise to have concluded the other way, that as most of the States had preserved with jealousy this sacred palladium of liberty, those who had wandered, should be brought back to it; and to have established general right rather than general wrong. For I consider all the ill as established, which may be established. I have a right to nothing, which another has a right to take away; and Congress will have a right to take away trials by jury in all civil cases. Let me add, that a bill of rights is what the people are entitled to against every government on earth, general or particular; and what no just government should refuse, or rest on inference.

The second feature I dislike, and strongly dislike, is the abandonment, in every instance, of the principle of rotation in office, and most particularly in the case of the President. Reason and experience tell us, that the first magistrate will always be re-elected if he may be re-elected. He is then an officer for life. This once observed, it becomes of so much consequence to certain nations to have a friend or a foe at the head of our affairs, that they will interfere with money and with arms. A Galloman, or an Angloman, will be supported by the nation he befriends. If once elected, and at a second or third election out-voted by one or two votes, he will pretend false votes, foul play, hold possession of the reins of government, be supported by the States voting for him, especially if they be the central ones, lying in a compact body themselves, and separating their opponents; and they will be aided by one nation in Europe, while the majority are aided by another. The election of a President of America, some years hence, will be much more interesting to certain nations of Europe, than ever the election of a King of Poland was. Reflect on all the instances in history, ancient and modern, of elective monarchies, and say if they do not give foundation for my fears; the Roman Emperors, the Popes while they were of any importance, the German Emperors till they became hereditary in practice, the Kings of Poland, the Deys of the Ottoman dependencies. It may be said, that if elections are to be attended with these disorders, the less frequently they are repeated the better. But experience says, that to free them from disorder, they must be rendered less interesting by a necessity of change. No foreign power, nor domestic party, will waste their blood and money to elect a person, who must go out at the end of a short period. The power of removing every fourth year by the vote of the people, is a power which they will not exercise, and if they were disposed to exercise it, they would not be permitted. The King of Poland is removable every day by the diet. But they never remove him. Nor would Russia, the Emperor, etc., permit them to do it. Smaller objections are, the appeals on matters of fact as well as laws; and the binding all persons, legislative, executive, and judiciary by oath, to maintain that constitution. I do not pretend to decide, what would be the best method of procuring the establishment of the manifold good things in this constitution, and of getting rid of the bad. Whether by adopting it, in hopes of future amendment; or after it shall have been duly weighed and canvassed by the people, after seeing the parts they generally dislike, and those they generally approve, to say to them, "We see now what you wish. You are willing to give to your federal government such and such powers; but you wish, at the same time, to have such and such fundamental rights secured to you, and certain sources of convulsion taken away. Be it so. Send together deputies again. Let them establish your fundamental rights by a sacrosanct declaration, and let them pass the parts of the Constitution you have approved. These will give powers to your federal government sufficient for your happiness."

This is what might be said, and would probably produce a speedy, more perfect and more permanent form of government. At all events, I hope you will not be discouraged from making other trials, if the present one should fail. We are never permitted to despair of the commonwealth. I have thus told you freely what I like, and what I dislike, merely as a matter of curiosity; for I know it is not in my power to offer matter of information to your judgment, which has been formed after hearing and weighing everything which the wisdom of man could offer on these subjects. I own, I am not a friend to a very energetic government. It is always oppressive. It places the governors indeed more at their ease, at the expense of the people. The late rebellion in Massachusetts has given more alarm, than I think it should have done. Calculate that one rebellion in thirteen States in the course of eleven years, is but one for each State in a century and a half. No country should be so long without one. Nor will any degree of power in the hands of government, prevent insurrections. In England, where the hand of power is heavier than with us, there are seldom half a dozen years without an insurrection. In France, where it is still heavier, but less despotic, as Montesquieu supposes, than in some other countries, and where there are always two or three hundred thousand men ready to crush insurrections, there have been three in the course of the three years I have been here, in every one of which greater numbers were engaged than in Massachusetts, and a great deal more blood was spilt. In Turkey, where the sole nod of the despot is death, insurrections are the events of every day. Compare again the ferocious depredations of their insurgents, with the order, the moderation and the almost self-extinguishment of ours. And say, finally, whether peace is best preserved by giving energy to the government, or information to the people. This last is the most certain, and the most legitimate engine of government. Educate and inform the whole mass of the people. Enable them to see that it is their interest to preserve peace and order, and they will preserve them. And it requires no very high degree of education to convince them of this. They are the only sure reliance for the preservation of our liberty. After all, it is my principle that the will of the majority should prevail. If they approve the proposed constitution in all its parts, I shall concur in it cheerfully, in hopes they will amend it, whenever they shall find it works wrong. This reliance cannot deceive us, as long as we remain virtuous; and I think we shall be so, as long as agriculture is our principal object, which will be the case, while there remains vacant lands in any part of America. When we get piled upon one another in large cities, as in Europe, we shall become corrupt as in Europe, and go to eating one another as they do there. I have tired you by this time with disquisitions which you have already heard repeated by others a thousand and a thousand times; and therefore, shall only add assurances of the esteem and attachment with which I have the honor to be, dear Sir, your affectionate friend and servant.

P S. The instability of our laws is really an immense evil. I think it would be well to provide in our constitutions, that there shall always be a twelvemonth between the engrossing a bill and passing it; that it should then be offered to its passage without changing a word; and that if circumstances should be thought to require a speedier passage, it should take two-thirds of both Houses, instead of a bare majority.

TO E. CARRINGTON

Paris, Dec. 21, 1787

. . . . I often doubt whether I should trouble Congress or my friends with . . . details of European politics. I know they do not excite that interest in America, of which it is impossible for one to divest himself here. I know, too, that it is a maxim with us, and I think it a wise one, not to entangle ourselves with the affairs of Europe. Still, I think, we should know them. The Turks have practiced the same maxim of not meddling in the complicated wrangles of this continent. But they have unwisely chosen to be ignorant of them also, and it is this total ignorance of Europe, its combinations and its movements, which exposes them to that annihilation possibly about taking place. While there are powers in Europe which fear our views, or have views on us, we should keep an eye on them, their connections and oppositions, that in a moment of need, we may avail ourselves of their weakness with respect to others as well as ourselves, and calculate their designs and movements, on all the circumstances under which they exist. Though I am persuaded, therefore, that these details are read by many with great indifference, yet I think it my duty to enter into them, and to run the risk of giving too much, rather than too little information. . . .

TO MR. A. DONALD[1]

Paris, February 7, 1788

. . . . I wish with all my soul, that the nine first conventions may accept the new constitution, because this will secure to us the good it contains, which I think great and important. But I equally wish, that the four latest conventions, whichever they be, may refuse to accede to it, till a declaration of rights be annexed. This would probably command the offer of such a declaration, and thus give to the whole fab-

[1]Alexander Donald, a friend of Jefferson, was engaged in the tobacco trade in Richmond, Virginia.

ric, perhaps, as much perfection as any one of that kind ever had. By a declaration of rights, I mean one which shall stipulate freedom of religion, freedom of the press, freedom of commerce against monopolies, trial by juries in all cases, no suspensions of the habeas corpus, no standing armies. These are fetters against doing evil, which no honest government should decline. There is another strong feature in the new Constitution, which I as strongly dislike. That is, the perpetual re-eligibility of the President. Of this I expect no amendment at present, because I do not see that anybody has objected to it on your side the water. But it will be productive of cruel distress to our country, even in your day and mine. The importance to France and England, to have our government in the hands of a friend or a foe, will occasion their interference by money, and even by arms. Our President will be of much more consequence to them than a King of Poland. We must take care, however, that neither this, nor any other objection to the new form, produces a schism in our Union. That would be an incurable evil, because near friends falling out, never re-unite cordially; whereas, all of us going together, we shall be sure to cure the evils of our new Constitution, before they do great harm. . . . I do not see, at present, any symptoms strongly indicating war. It is true, that the distrust existing between the two courts of Versailles and London, is so great, that they can scarcely do business together. However, the difficulty and doubt of obtaining money make both afraid to enter into war. The little preparations for war, which we see, are the effect of distrust, rather than of a design to commence hostilities. And in such a state of mind, you know, small things may produce a rupture; so that though peace is rather probable, war is very possible.

Your letter has kindled all the fond recollections of ancient times; recollections much dearer to me than anything I have known since. There are minds which can be pleased by honors and preferments; but I see nothing in them but envy and enmity. It is only necessary to possess them, to know how little they contribute to happiness, or rather how hostile they are to it. No attachments soothe the mind so much as those contracted in early life; nor do I recollect any societies which have given me more pleasure, than those of which you have partaken with me. I had rather be shut up in a very modest cottage, with my books, my family and a few old friends, dining on simple bacon, and letting the world roll on as it liked, than to occupy the most splendid post, which any human power can give. . . .

TO THE COUNT DE MOUSTIER[1]

Paris, May 17, 1788

DEAR SIR,—I have at length an opportunity of acknowledging the receipt of your favors of February, and March the 14th, and congratulating you on your resurrection from the dead, among whom you had been confidently entombed by the newsdealers of Paris. I am sorry that your first impressions have been disturbed by matters of etiquette, where surely they should least have been expected to occur. These disputes are the most insusceptible of determination, because they have no foundation in reason. Arbitrary and senseless in their nature, they are arbitrarily decided by every nation for itself. These decisions are meant to prevent disputes, but they produce ten where they prevent one. It would have been better, therefore, in a new country, to have excluded etiquette altogether; or if it must be admitted in some form or other, to have made it depend on some circumstance founded in nature, such as the age or station of the parties. However, you have got over all this, and, I am in hopes, have been able to make up a society suited to your own dispositions. Your situation will doubtless be improved by the adoption of the new constitution, which I hope will have taken place before you receive this. I see in this instrument, a great deal of good. The consolidation of our government, a just representation, an administration of some permanence, and other features of great value, will be gained by it. There are, indeed, some faults, which revolted me a good deal in the first moment; but we must be contented to travel on towards perfection, step by step. We must be contented with the ground which this constitution will gain for us, and hope that a favorable moment will come for correcting what is amiss in it. I view in the same light, the innovations making here. The new organization of the judiciary department is undoubtedly for the better. The reformation

[1]General and diplomat, Moustier was French Minister to the United States in 1787.

of the criminal code, is an immense step taken towards good. The composition of the Plenary court is, indeed, vicious in the extreme; but the basis of that court may be retained, and its composition changed. Make of it a representative of the people, by composing it of members sent from the Provincial Assemblies, and it becomes a valuable member of the constitution. But it is said, the court will not consent to do this; the court, however, has consented to call the States General, who will consider the Plenary court but as a canvas for them to work on. The public mind is manifestly advancing on the abusive prerogatives of their governors, and bearing them down. No force in the government can withstand this, in the long run. Courtiers had rather give up power than pleasures; they will barter, therefore, the usurped prerogatives of the King, for the money of the people. This is the agent by which modern nations will recover their rights. I sincerely wish that in this country, they may be contented with a peaceable and passive opposition. At this moment, we are not sure of this, though as yet it is difficult to say what form the opposition will take. It is a comfortable circumstance, that their neighboring enemy is under the administration of a minister disposed to keep the peace. Engage in war who will, may my country long continue your peaceful residence, and merit your good offices with that nation, whose affections it is their duty and interest to cultivate.

TO WILLIAM CARMICHAEL[1]

Paris, May 27, 1788

. . . . A riot has taken place in New York, which I will state to you from an eye witness. It has long been a practice with the surgeons of that city, to steal from the grave bodies recently buried. A citizen had lost his wife: he went the first or second evening after her burial, to pay a visit to her grave. He found that it had been disturbed, and suspected from what quarter. He found means to be admitted to the anatomical lecture of that day, and on his entering the room, saw the body of his wife, naked and under dissection. He raised the people immediately.

---

[1]Carmichael was an American diplomat, at this time chargé d'affaires at the Court of Spain.

The body, in the meantime, was secreted. They entered into, and searched the houses of the physicians whom they most suspected, but found nothing. One of them, however, more guilty or more timid than the rest, took asylum in the prison. The mob considered this an acknowledgment of guilt. They attacked the prison. The Governor ordered militia to protect the culprit, and suppress the mob. The militia, thinking the mob had just provocation, refused to turn out. Hereupon the people of more reflection, thinking it more dangerous that even a guilty person should be punished without the forms of law, than that he should escape, armed themselves, and went to protect the physician. They were received by the mob with a volley of stones, which wounded several of them. They hereupon fired on the mob, and killed four. By this time, they received a reinforcement of other citizens of the militia horse, the appearance of which, in the critical moment, dispersed the mob. So ended this chapter of history, which I have detailed to you, because it may be represented as a political riot, when politics had nothing to do with it. Mr. Jay and Baron Steuben were both grievously wounded in the head by stones. The former still kept his bed, and the latter his room, when the packet sailed, which was the 24th of April. . . .

TO COLONEL CARRINGTON

Paris, May 27, 1788

I learn with great pleasure the progress of the new Constitution. Indeed I have presumed it would gain on the public mind, as I confess it has on my own. At first, though I saw that the great mass and groundwork was good, I disliked many appendages. Reflection and discussion have cleared off most of these. You have satisfied me as to the query I had put to you about the right of direct taxation. My first wish was that nine States would adopt it in order to ensure what was good in it, and that the others might, by holding off, produce the necessary amendments. But the plan of Massachusetts is far preferable, and will, I hope, be followed by those who are yet to decide. There are two amendments only which I am anxious for: 1. A bill of rights, which it is so much the interest of all to have, that I conceive it must be yielded.

The 1st amendment proposed by Massachusetts will in some degree answer this end, but not so well. It will do too much in some instances, and too little in others. It will cripple the Federal Government in some cases where it ought to be free, and not restrain in some others where restraint would be right. The 2d amendment which appears to me essential is the restoring the principle of necessary rotation, particularly to the Senate and Presidency: but most of all to the last. Re-eligibility makes him an officer for life, and the disasters inseparable from an elective monarchy, render it preferable if we cannot tread back that step, that we should go forward and take refuge in an hereditary one. Of the correction of this article, however, I entertain no present hope, because I find it has scarcely excited an objection in America. And if it does not take place erelong, it assuredly never will The natural progress of things is for liberty to yield and government to gain ground. As yet our spirits are free. Our jealousy is only put to sleep by the unlimited confidence we all repose in the person to whom we all look as our president. After him inferior characters may perhaps succeed, and awaken us to the danger which his merit has led us into. For the present, however, the general adoption is to be prayed for, and I wait with great anxiety for the news from Maryland and South Carolina, which have decided before this, and with that Virginia, now in session, may give the ninth vote of approbation There could then be no doubt of North Carolina, New York, and New Hampshire. But what do you propose to do with Rhode Island? As long as there is hope we should give her time. I cannot conceive but that she will come to rights in the long run. Force, in whatever form, would be a dangerous precedent. . . .

TO MR. IZARD[1]

Paris, July 17, 1788

. . . . The war in Europe threatens to spread. Sweden, we suppose, has commenced hostilities against Russia, though we do not yet certainly know it. I have hoped this country would settle her internal disputes advantageously and without bloodshed. As yet none has been

[1]Ralph Izard was a South Carolinian, patriot, and diplomat.

spilt, though the British newspapers give the idea of a general civil war. Hitherto, I had supposed both the King and parliament would lose authority, and the nation gain it, through the medium of its States General and provincial Assemblies, but the arrest of the deputies of Bretagne two days ago, may kindle a civil war. Its issue will depend on two questions. 1. Will other provinces rise? 2. How will the army conduct itself? A stranger cannot predetermine these questions. Happy for us that abuses have not yet become patrimonies, and that every description of interest is in favor of national and moderate government. That we are yet able to send our wise and good men together to talk over our form of government, discuss its weaknesses and establish its remedies with the same *sang-froid* as they would a subject of agriculture. The example we have given to the world is single, that of changing our form of government under the authority of reason only, without bloodshed. . . .

TO E. RUTLEDGE[1]

Paris, July 18, 1788

. . . . We can surely boast of having set the world a beautiful example of a government reformed by reason alone, without bloodshed. But the world is too far oppressed, to profit by the example. On this side of the Atlantic, the blood of the people is become an inheritance, and those who fatten on it will not relinquish it easily. The struggle in this country is, as yet, of doubtful issue. It is, in fact, between the monarchy and the parliaments. The nation is no otherwise concerned, but as both parties may be induced to let go some of its abuses, to court the public favor. The danger, is that the people, deceived by a false cry of liberty, may be led to take side with one party, and thus give the other a pretext for crushing them still more. If they can avoid the appeal to arms, the nation will be sure to gain much by this controversy. But if that appeal is made, it will depend entirely on the disposition of the army, whether it issue in liberty or despotism. Those

---

[1]Edward Rutledge, South Carolina lawyer and statesman, had been, with Jefferson, one of the signers of the Declaration of Independence.

dispositions are not as yet known. In the meantime, there is great probability that the war kindled in the east, will spread from nation to nation and in the long run, become general. . . .

TO MR. CUTTING[1]

Paris, July 24, 1788

. . . . The internal affairs here do not yet clear up. Most of the late innovations have been much for the better. Two only must be fundamentally condemned; the abolishing, in so great a degree, of the parliaments, and the substitution of so ill-composed a body as the *cour plenière*. If the King has power to do this, the government of this country is a pure despotism. I think it a pure despotism in theory, but moderated in practice by the respect which the public opinion commands. But the nation repeats, after Montesquieu, that the different bodies of magistracy, of priests and nobles, are barriers between the King and the people. It would be easy to prove that these barriers can only appeal to public opinion, and that neither these bodies, nor the people, can oppose any legal check to the will of the monarch. But they are manifestly advancing fast to a constitution. Great progress is already made. The provincial assemblies, which will be a very perfect representative of the people, will secure them a great deal against the power of the crown. The confession lately made by the government, that it cannot impose a new tax, is a great thing: the convocation of the States General, which cannot be avoided, will produce a national assembly, meeting at certain epochs, possessing at first probably only a negative on the laws, but which will grow into the right of original legislation, and prescribing limits to the expenses of the King. These are improvements which will assuredly take place, and which will give an energy to this country they have never yet had. Much may be hoped from the States General, because the King's dispositions are solidly good; he is capable of great sacrifices; all he wants to induce him to do a thing, is to be assured it will be for the good of the nation. He will probably

---

[1]Mr. John B. Cutting later earned Jefferson's appreciation for his efforts in liberating American seamen who had been impressed in British ports.

believe what the States General shall tell him, and will do it. It is supposed they will reduce the parliament to a mere judiciary. I am in hopes all this will be effected without convulsions. . . .

TO JAMES MADISON

Paris, July 31, 1788

I sincerely rejoice at the acceptance of our new constitution by nine States. It is a good canvas, on which some strokes only want retouching. What these are, I think are sufficiently manifested by the general voice from north to south, which calls for a bill of rights. It seems pretty generally understood, that this should go to juries, habeas corpus, standing armies, printing, religion and monopolies. I conceive there may be difficulty in finding general modifications of these, suited to the habits of all the States. But if such cannot be found, then it is better to establish trials by jury, the right of habeas corpus, freedom of the press and freedom of religion, in all cases, and to abolish standing armies in time of peace, and monopolies in all cases, than not to do it in any. The few cases wherein these things may do evil, cannot be weighed against the multitude wherein the want of them will do evil. In disputes between a foreigner and a native, a trial by jury may be improper. But if this exception cannot be agreed to, the remedy will be to model the jury, by giving the *mediatas linguæ*, in civil as well as criminal cases. Why suspend the habeas corpus in insurrections and rebellions? The parties who may be arrested, may be charged instantly with a well-defined crime; of course, the judge will remand them. If the public safety requires that the government should have a man imprisoned on less probable testimony, in those than in other emergencies, let him be taken and tried, retaken and retried, while the necessity continues, only giving him redress against the government, for damages. Examine the history of England. See how few of the cases of the suspension of the habeas corpus law, have been worthy of that suspension. They have been either real treason, wherein the parties might as well have been charged at once, or sham plots, where it was shameful they should ever have been suspected. Yet for the few cases wherein the suspension of the habeas corpus has done real good, that operation is now become habitual, and the minds of the nation almost prepared to live under its constant suspension. A declaration, that the federal government will never restrain the presses from printing anything they please, will not take away the liability of the printers for false facts printed. The declaration, that religious faith shall be unpunished, does not give impunity to criminal acts, dictated by religious error. The saying there shall be no monopolies, lessens the incitements to ingenuity, which is spurred on by the hope of a monopoly for a limited time, as of fourteen years; but the benefit of even limited monopolies is too doubtful, to be opposed to that of their general suppression. If no check can be found to keep the number of standing troops within safe bounds, while they are tolerated as far as necessary, abandon them altogether, discipline well the militia, and guard the magazines with them. More than magazine guards will be useless, if few, and dangerous, if many. No European nation can ever send against us such a regular army as we need fear, and it is hard, if our militia are not equal to those of Canada or Florida. My idea then, is, that though proper exceptions to these general rules are desirable, and probably practicable, yet if the exceptions cannot be agreed on, the establishment of the rules, in all cases, will do ill in very few. I hope, therefore, a bill of rights will be formed, to guard the people against the federal government, as they are already guarded against their State governments, in most instances. The abandoning the principle of necessary rotation in the Senate, has, I see, been disapproved by many; in the case of the President, by none. I readily, therefore, suppose my opinion wrong, when opposed by the majority, as in the former instance, and the totality, as in the latter. In this, however, I should have done it with more complete satisfaction, had we all judged from the same position. . . .

TO JAMES MADISON

Paris, November 18, 1788

. . . . With respect to the Federalist, the three authors had been named to me. I read it with care, pleasure and improvement, and was satisfied there was nothing in it by one of those hands, and not a great deal by a second. It does the highest honor to the third, as being, in my opinion, the best commentary on the principles of government, which ever was written. In some parts, it is discoverable that the author means only to say what may be best said in defence of opinions, in which he did not concur. But in general, it establishes firmly the plan of government. I confess, it has rectified me on several points. As to the bill of rights, however, I still think it should be added; and I am glad to see, that three States have at length considered the perpetual re-eligibility of the President, as an article which should be amended. . . .

TO DR. PRICE

Paris, January 8, 1789

DEAR SIR,—I was favored with your letter of October 26th, and far from finding any of its subjects uninteresting as you apprehend, they were to me, as everything which comes from you, pleasing and instructive. I concur with you strictly in your opinion of the comparative merits of atheism and demonism, and really see nothing but the latter in the Being worshipped by many who think themselves Christians. Your opinions and writings will have effect in bringing others to reason on this subject. Our new Constitution, of which you speak also, has succeeded beyond what I apprehended it would have done. I did not at first believe that eleven States out of thirteen would have consented to a plan consolidating them as much into one. A change in their dispositions, which had taken place since I left them, had rendered this consolidation necessary, that is to say, had called for a federal government which could walk upon its own legs, without leaning for support on the State legislatures. A sense of necessity, and a submission to it, is to me a new and consolatory proof that, whenever the people are well-informed, they can be trusted with their own government; that, whenever things get so far wrong as to attract their notice, they may be relied on to set them to rights. You say you are not sufficiently informed about the nature and circumstances of the present struggle here. Having been on the spot from its first origin, and watched its movements as an uninterested spectator, with no other bias than a love of mankind, I will give you my ideas of it. Though celebrated writers of this and other countries had already sketched good principles on the subject of government, yet the American war seems first to have awakened the thinking part of this nation in general from the sleep of despotism in which they were sunk. The officers too who had been to America, were mostly young men, less shackled by habit and prejudice, and more ready to assent to the dictates of common sense and common right. They came back impressed with these. The press, notwithstanding its shackles, began to disseminate them; conversation, too, assumed new freedom; politics became the theme of all societies, male and female, and a very extensive and zealous party was formed, which may be called the Patriotic party, who, sensible of the abusive government under which they lived, longed for occasions of reforming it. This party comprehended all the honesty of the kingdom, sufficiently at its leisure to think; the men of letters, the easy bourgeois, the young nobility, partly from reflection, partly from mode; for those sentiments became a matter of mode, and as such united most of the young women to the party. Happily for the nation, it happened that, at the same moment, the dissipations of the court had exhausted the money and credit of the State, and M. de Calonnes found himself obliged to appeal to the nation, and to develop to it the ruin of their finances. He had no idea of supplying the deficit by economies, he saw no means but new taxes. To tempt the nation to consent to these some douceurs were necessary. The Notables were called in 1787. The leading vices of the constitution and administration were ably sketched out, good remedies proposed, and under the splendor of the proposition, a demand for more money was couched. The Notables concurred with the minister in the necessity of reformation, adroitly avoided the demand of money, got him displaced, and one of their leading men placed in his room. The archbishop of Thoulouse, by the aid of the hopes formed of him, was able to borrow some money, and he reformed considerably the expenses of the court. Notwithstanding the prejudices since formed against him, he appeared to me to pursue the reformation of the laws and constitution as steadily as a man could do who had to drag the court after him, and even to conceal from them the consequences of the measures he was leading them into. In his time the criminal laws were reformed, provincial assemblies and States established in most of the provinces, the States General promised, and a solemn acknowledgment made by the King that he could not impose

a new tax without the consent of the nation. It is true he was continually goaded forward by the public clamors, excited by the writings
and workings of the Patriots, who were able to keep up the public fermentation at the exact point which borders on resistance, without
entering on it. They had taken into their alliance the Parliaments also,
who were led, by very singular circumstances, to espouse, for the first
time, the rights of the nation. They had from old causes had personal
hostility against M. de Calonnes. They refused to register his laws or
his taxes, and went so far as to acknowledge they had no power to do
it. They persisted in this with his successor, who therefore exiled them.
Seeing that the nation did not interest themselves much for their recall,
they began to fear that the new judicatures proposed in their place
would be established and that their own suppression would be perpetual. In short, they found their own strength insufficient to oppose that
of the King. They, therefore, insisted that the States General should be
called. Here they became united with and supported by the Patriots,
and their joint influence was sufficient to produce the promise of that
assembly. I always suspected that the archbishops had no objections
to this force under which they laid him. But the Patriots and Parliament insisted it was their efforts which extorted the promise against his
will. The re-establishment of the Parliament was the effect of the same
coalition between the Patriots and Parliament; but, once re-established,
the latter began to see danger in that very power, the States General,
which they had called for in a moment of despair, but which they now
foresaw might very possibly abridge their powers. They began to prepare grounds for questioning their legality, as a rod over the head of
the States, and as a refuge if they should really extend their reformations to them. Mr. Neckar came in at this period and very dexterously
disembarrassed the administration of these disputes by calling the
Notables to advise the form of calling and constituting the States. The
court was well disposed towards the people, not from principles of justice or love to them; but they want money. No more can be had from
the people. They are squeezed to the last drop. The clergy and nobles,
by their privileges and influence, have kept their property in a great
measure untaxed hitherto. They then remain to be squeezed, and no
agent is powerful enough for this but the people. The court therefore
must ally itself with the people. But the Notables, consisting mostly

of privileged characters, had proposed a method of composing the States, which would have rendered the voice of the people, or Tiers États, in the States General, inefficient for the purpose of the court. It concurred then with the Patriots in intriguing with the Parliament to get them to pass a vote in favor of the rights of the people. This vote, balancing that of the Notables, has placed the court at liberty to follow its own views, and they have determined that the Tiers État shall have in the States General as many votes as the clergy and nobles put together. Still a great question remains to be decided, that is, shall the States General vote by orders, or by persons? precedents are both ways. The clergy will move heaven and earth to obtain the suffrage by orders, because that parries the effect of all hitherto done for the people. The people will probably send their deputies expressly instructed to consent to no tax, to no adoption of the public debts, unless the unprivileged part of the nation has a voice equal to that of the privileged; that is to say, unless the voice of the Tiers État be equalled to that of the clergy and nobles. They will have the young noblesse in general on their side, and the King and court. Against them will be the ancient nobles and the clergy. So that I hope, upon the whole, that by the time they meet, there will be a majority of the nobles themselves in favor of the Tiers État. So far history. We are now to come to prophecy; for you will ask, to what will all this lead? I answer, if the States General do not stumble at the threshold on the question before stated, and which must be decided before they can proceed to business, then they will in their first session easily obtain, 1. Their future periodical convocation of the States. 2. Their exclusive right to raise and appropriate money which includes that of establishing a civil list. 3. A participation in legislation; probably at first, it will only be a transfer to them of the portion of it now exercised by parliament, that is to say, a right to propose amendments and a negative. But it must infallibly end in a right of origination. 4. Perhaps they may make a declaration of rights. It will be attempted at least. Two other objects will be attempted, viz., a habeas corpus law and a free press. But probably they may not obtain these in the first session, or with modifications only, and the nation must be left to ripen itself more for their unlimited adoption. Upon the whole, it has appeared to me that the basis of the present struggle is an illumination of the public mind as to the rights of the nation, aided by fortunate incidents; that they can never retrograde, but from the natural progress of things, must press forward to the establishment of a constitution which shall assure to them a good degree of liberty. They flatter themselves they shall form a better constitution than the English. I think it will be better in some points— worse in others. It will be better in the article of representation, which will be more equal. It will be worse, as their situation obliges them to keep up the dangerous machine of a standing army. I doubt, too, whether they will obtain the trial by jury, because they are not sensible of its value.

I am sure I have by this time heartily tired you with this long epistle, and that you will be glad to see it brought to an end, with assurances of the sentiments of esteem and respect with which I have the honor to be, dear Sir, your most obedient, and most humble servant.

TO JOHN JAY

Paris, January 11, 1789

. . . . As the character of the Prince of Wales is becoming interesting, I have endeavored to learn what it truly is. This is less difficult in his case, than in that of other persons of his rank, because he has taken no pains to hide himself from the world. The information I most rely on, is from a person here with whom I am intimate, who divides his time between Paris and London, an Englishman by birth, of truth, sagacity and science. He is of a circle, when in London, which has had good opportunities of knowing the Prince; but he has also, himself, had special occasions of verifying their information, by his own personal observation. He happened, when last in London, to be invited to a dinner of three persons. The Prince came by chance, and made the fourth. He ate half a leg of mutton; did not taste of small dishes, because small; drank Champagne and Burgundy, as small beer during dinner, and Bordeaux after dinner, as the rest of the company. Upon the whole, he ate as much as the other three, and drank about two bottles of wine without seeming to feel it. My informant sat next him, and being till then unknown to the Prince, personally (though not by character), and lately from France, the Prince confined his conversation almost entirely to him. Observing to the Prince that he spoke French without the least foreign accent, the Prince told him, that when very young, his father had put only French servants about him, and that it was to that circumstance he owed his pronunciation. He led him from this to give an account of his education, the total of which was the learning a little Latin. He has not a single element of Mathematics, of Natural or Moral Philosophy, or of any other science on earth, nor has the society he has kept been such as to supply the void of education. It has been that of the lowest, the most illiterate and profligate persons of the kingdom, without choice of rank or mind, and with whom the subjects of conversation are only horses, drinking-matches, bawdy houses, and in terms the most vulgar. The young nobility, who begin by associating with him, soon leave him, disgusted with the insupportable profligacy of his society; and Mr. Fox, who has been supposed his favorite, and not over-nice in the choice of company, would never keep his company habitually. In fact, he never associated with a man of sense. He has not a single idea of justice, morality, religion, or of the rights of men, or any anxiety for the opinion of the world. He carries that indifference for fame so far, that he would probably not be hurt were he to lose his throne, provided he could be assured of having always meat, drink, horses, and women. In the article of women, nevertheless, he is become more correct, since his connection with Mrs. Fitzherbert, who is an honest and worthy woman: he is even less crapulous than he was. He had a fine person, but it is becoming coarse. He possesses good native common sense; is affable, polite, and very good humored. Saying to my informant, on another occasion, "your friend, such a one, dined with me yesterday, and I made him damned drunk;" he replied, "I am sorry for it; I had heard that your royal highness had left off drinking:" the Prince laughed, tapped him on the shoulder very good naturedly, without saying a word, or ever after showing any displeasure. . . .

TO FRANCIS HOPKINSON[1]

Paris, March 13, 1789

DEAR SIR,—Since my last, which was of December the 21st, yours of December the 9th and 21st are received. Accept my thanks for the papers and pamphlets which accompanied them, and mine and my daughter's, for the book of songs. I will not tell you how much they have pleased us, nor how well the last of them merits praise for its pathos, but relate a fact only, which is, that while my elder daughter was playing it on the harpsichord, I happened to look towards the fire, and saw the younger one all in tears. I asked her if she was sick? She said "no; but the tune was so mournful."

The Editor of the Encyclopédie has published something as to an advanced price on his future volumes, which, I understand, alarms the subscribers. It was in a paper which I do not take, and therefore I have not yet seen it, nor can I say what it is. I hope that by this time you have ceased to make wry faces about your vinegar, and that you have received it safe and good. You say that I have been dished up to you as an anti-federalist, and ask me if it be just. My opinion was never worthy enough of notice to merit citing; but since you ask it, I will tell you. I am not a federalist, because I never submitted the whole system of my opinions to the creed of any party of men whatever, in religion, in philosophy, in politics or in anything else, where I was capable of thinking for myself. Such an addiction, is the last degradation of a free and moral agent. If I could not go to heaven but with a party, I would not go there at all. Therefore, I am not of the party of federalists. But I am much farther from that of the anti-federalists. I approved, from the first moment, of the great mass of what is in the new Constitution; the consolidation of the government; the organization into executive, legislative, and judiciary; the subdivision of the legislative; the happy compromise of interests between the great and little States, by the different manner of voting in the different Houses; the voting by persons instead of States; the qualified negative on laws given to the executive, which,

---

[1]Francis Hopkinson, accomplished statesman, musician, and author, frequently corresponded with Jefferson.

however, I should have liked better if associated with the judiciary also, as in New York; and the power of taxation. I thought at first that the latter might have been limited. A little reflection soon convinced me it ought not to be. What I disapproved from the first moment also, was the want of a bill of rights, to guard liberty against the legislative as well as the executive branches of the government; that is to say, to secure freedom in religion, freedom of the press, freedom from monopolies, freedom from unlawful imprisonment, freedom from a permanent military, and a trial by jury, in all cases determinable by the laws of the land. I disapproved, also, the perpetual re-eligibility of the President. To these points of disapprobation I adhere. My first wish was, that the nine first conventions might accept the constitution, as the means of securing to us the great mass of good it contained, and that the four last might reject it, as the means of obtaining amendments. But I was corrected in this wish, the moment I saw the much better plan of Massachusetts, and which had never occurred to me. With respect to the declaration of rights, I suppose the majority of the United States are of my opinion; for I apprehend, all the anti-federalists and a very respectable proportion of the federalists, think that such a declaration should be now annexed. The enlightened part of Europe have given us the greatest credit for inventing the instrument of security for the rights of the people, and have been not a little surprised to see us so soon give it up. With respect to the re-eligibility of the President, I find myself differing from the majority of my countrymen; for I think there are but three States out of the eleven which have desired an alteration of this. And indeed, since the thing is established, I would wish it not to be altered during the life of our great leader, whose executive talents are superior to those, I believe, of any man in the world, and who, alone, by the authority of his name and the confidence reposed in his perfect integrity, is fully qualified to put the new government so under way, as to secure it against the efforts of opposition. But, having derived from our error all the good there was in it, I hope we shall correct it, the moment we can no longer have the same name at the helm.

These, my dear friend, are my sentiments, by which you will see I was right in saying I am neither federalist nor anti-federalist; that I am of neither party, nor yet a trimmer between parties. These, my opinions, I wrote within a few hours after I had read the Constitution, to one or two friends in America. I had not then read one single word printed on the subject. I never had an opinion in politics or religion, which I was afraid to own. A costive reserve on these subjects might have procured me more esteem from some people, but less from myself. My great with is, to go on in a strict but silent performance of my duty; to avoid attracting notice, and to keep my name out of newspapers, because I find the pain of a little censure, even when it is unfounded, is more acute than the pleasure of much praise. The attaching circumstance of my present office, is, that I can do its duties unseen by those for whom they are done. You did not think, by so short a phrase in your letter, to have drawn on yourself such an egotistical dissertation. I beg your pardon for it, and will endeavor to merit that pardon by the constant sentiments of esteem and attachment with which I am, dear Sir, your sincere friend and servant.

TO JAMES MADISON

Paris, March 15, 1789

. . . . Your thoughts on the subject of the declaration of rights, in the letter of October the 17th, I have weighed with great satisfaction. Some of them had not occurred to me before, but were acknowledged just in the moment they were presented to my mind. In the arguments in favor of a declaration of rights, you omit one which has great weight with me; the legal check which it puts into the hands of the judiciary. This is a body, which, if rendered independent and kept strictly to their own department, merits great confidence for their learning and integrity. In fact, what degree of confidence would be too much, for a body composed of such men as Wythe, Blair and Pendleton? On characters like these, the *"civium ardor prava jubentium"*[1] would make no impression. I am happy to find that, on the whole, you are a friend to this amendment. The declaration of rights is, like all other human blessings, alloyed with some inconveniences, and not accomplishing fully its object. But the good in this instance, vastly overweighs the evil. I cannot refrain from making short answers to the objections which your

---

[1]"The wayward zeal of the ruling citizens."

letter states to have been raised. 1. That the rights in question are reserved, by the manner in which the federal powers are granted. Answer. A constitutive act may, certainly, be so formed, as to need no declaration of rights. The act itself has the force of a declaration, as far as it goes, and if it goes to all material points, nothing more is wanting. In the draught of a constitution which I had once a thought of proposing in Virginia, and printed afterwards, I endeavored to reach all the great objects of public liberty, and did not mean to add a declaration of rights. Probably the object was imperfectly executed; but the deficiencies would have been supplied by others, in the course of discussion. But in a constitutive act which leaves some precious articles unnoticed, and raises implications against others, a declaration of rights becomes necessary, by way of supplement. This is the case of our new federal Constitution. This instrument forms us into one State, as to certain objects, and gives us a legislative and executive body for these objects. It should, therefore, guard us against their abuses of power, within the field submitted to them. 2. A positive declaration of some essential rights could not be obtained in the requisite latitude. Answer. Half a loaf is better than no bread. If we cannot secure all our rights, let us secure what we can. 3. The limited powers of the federal government, and jealousy of the subordinate governments, afford a security which exists in no other instance. Answer. The first member of this seems resolvable into the first objection before stated. The jealousy of the subordinate governments is a precious reliance. But observe that those governments are only agents. They must have principles furnished them, whereon to found their opposition. The declaration of rights will be the text, whereby they will try all the acts of the federal government. In this view, it is necessary to the federal government also; as by the same text, they may try the opposition of the subordinate governments. 4. Experience proves the inefficacy of a bill of rights. True. But though it is not absolutely efficacious under all circumstances, it is of great potency always, and rarely inefficacious. A brace the more will often keep up the building which would have fallen, with that brace the less. There is a remarkable difference between the characters of the inconveniences which attend a declaration of rights, and those which attend the want of it. The inconveniences of the declaration are, that it may cramp government in its useful exertions. But the evil of this is short-lived, moderate and reparable. The inconveniences of the want of a declaration are permanent, afflicting and irreparable. They are in constant progression from bad to worse. The executive, in our governments, is not the sole, it is scarcely the principal object of my jealousy. The tyranny of the legislatures is the most formidable dread at present, and will be for many years. That of the executive will come in its turn; but it will be at a remote period. I know there are some among us, who would now establish a monarchy. But they are inconsiderable in number and weight of character. The rising race are all republicans. We were educated in royalism; no wonder, if some of us retain that idolatry still. Our young people are educated in republicanism; an apostasy from that to royalism, is unprecedented and impossible. I am much pleased with the prospect that a declaration of rights will be added; and I hope it will be done in that way, which will not endanger the whole frame of government, or any essential part of it. . . .

TO COLONEL HUMPHREYS[1]

Paris, March 18, 1789

The change in this country since you left it, is such as you can form no idea of. The frivolities of conversation have given way entirely to politics. Men, women and children talk nothing else; and all, you know, talk a great deal. The press groans with daily productions, which, in point of boldness, makes an Englishman stare, who hitherto has thought himself the boldest of men. A complete revolution in this government has, within the space of two years (for it began with the Notables of 1787), been effected merely by the force of public opinion, aided, indeed, by the want of money, which the dissipations of the court had brought on. And this revolution has not cost a single life, unless we charge to it a little riot lately in Bretagne, which began about the price of bread, became afterwards political, and ended in the loss of four or five lives. The assembly of the States General begins the 27th of April.

[1]David Humphreys, distinguished Revolutionary soldier, statesman, and verse writer, had served as an American diplomat in Paris during Jefferson's first years in that capital.

The representation of the people will be perfect. But they will be alloyed by an equal number of nobility and clergy. The first great question they will have to decide will be, whether they shall vote by orders or persons. And I have hopes that the majority of the Nobles are already disposed to join the Tiers État, in deciding that the vote shall be by persons. This is the opinion à *la mode* at present, and mode has acted a wonderful part in the present instance. All the handsome young women, for example, are for the Tiers État, and this is an army more powerful in France, than the two hundred thousand men of the King. Add to this, that the court itself is for the Tiers État, as the only agent which can relieve their wants; not by giving money themselves (they are squeezed to the last drop), but by pressing it from the non-contributing orders. The King stands engaged to pretend no more to the power of laying, continuing or appropriating taxes; to call the States General periodically; to submit *lettres de cachet* to legal restrictions; to consent to freedom of the press; and that all this shall be fixed by a fundamental constitution, which shall bind his successors. He has not offered a participation in the legislature, but it will surely be insisted on. The public mind is so ripened on all these subjects, that there seems to be now but one opinion. The clergy, indeed, think separately, and the old men among the Nobles; but their voice is suppressed by the general one of the nation. The writings published on this occasion are, some of them, very valuable; because, unfettered by the prejudices under which the English labor, they give a full scope to reason, and strike out truths, as yet unperceived and unacknowledged on the other side the channel. An Englishman, dosing under a kind of half reformation, is not excited to think by such gross absurdities as stare a Frenchman in the face, wherever he looks, whether it be towards the throne or the altar. In fine, I believe this nation will, in the course of the present year, have as full a portion of liberty dealt out to them, as the nation can bear at present, considering how uninformed the mass of their people is. . . .

There are rights which it is useless to surrender to the government, and which governments have yet always been found to invade. These are the rights of thinking, and publishing our thoughts by speaking or writing; the right of free commerce; the right of personal freedom. There are instruments for administering the government, so peculiarly trust-worthy, that we should never leave the legislature at liberty to change them. The new Constitution has secured these in the executive and legislative department; but not in the judiciary. It should have established trials by the people themselves, that is to say, by jury. There are instruments so dangerous to the rights of the nation, and which place them so totally at the mercy of their governors, that those governors, whether legislative or executive, should be restrained from keeping such instruments on foot, but in well-defined cases. Such an instrument is a standing army. We are now allowed to say, such a declaration of rights, as a supplement to the Constitution where that is silent, is wanting, to secure us in these points. The general voice has legitimated this objection. It has not, however, authorized me to consider as a real defect, what I thought and still think one, the perpetual re-eligibility of the President. But three States out of eleven, having declared against this, we must suppose we are wrong, according to the fundamental law of every society, the *lex majoris partis*, to which we are bound to submit. And should the majority change their opinion, and become sensible that this trait in their Constitution is wrong, I would wish it to remain uncorrected, as long as we can avail ourselves of the services of our great leader, whose talents and whose weight of character, I consider as peculiarly necessary to get the government so under way, as that it may afterwards be carried on by subordinate characters. . . .

TO DOCTOR WILLARD[1]

Paris, March 24, 1789

. . . In the arts, I think two of our countrymen have presented the most important inventions. Mr. Paine, the author of "Common Sense," has invented an iron bridge, which promises to be cheaper by a great deal than stone, and to admit of a much greater arch. He supposes it may be ventured for an arch of five hundred feet. He has obtained a patent for it in England, and is now executing the first experiment with an arch of between ninety and one hundred feet. Mr. Rumsey has also obtained a patent for his navigation by the force of steam, in England,

[1]Dr. Joseph Willard at this time was President of Harvard University.

and is soliciting a similar one here. His principal merit is in the improvement of the boiler, and, instead of the complicated machinery of oars and paddles, proposed by others, the substitution of so simple a thing as the reaction of a stream of water on his vessel. He is building a sea vessel at this time in England, and she will be ready for an experiment in May. He has suggested a great number of mechanical improvements in a variety of branches; and upon the whole, is the most original and the greatest mechanical genius I have ever seen. The return of La Peyrouse (whenever that shall happen) will probably add to our knowledge in Geography, Botany and Natural History. What a field have we at our doors to signalize ourselves in! The Botany of America is far from being exhausted, its Mineralogy is untouched, and its Natural History or Zoology, totally mistaken and misrepresented. As far as I have seen, there is not one single species of terrestrial birds common to Europe and America, and I question if there be a single species of quadrupeds. (Domestic animals are to be excepted.) It is for such institutions as that over which you preside so worthily, Sir, to do justice to our country, its productions and its genius. It is the work to which the young men, whom you are forming, should lay their hands. We have spent the prime of our lives in procuring them the precious blessing of liberty. Let them spend theirs in showing that it is the great parent of *science* and of virtue; and that a nation will be great in both, always in proportion as it is free. Nobody wishes more warmly for the success of your good exhortations on this subject, than he who has the honor to be, with sentiments of great esteem and respect, Sir, your most obedient humble servant.

TO GENERAL WASHINGTON[1]

Paris, May 10, 1789

. . . I am in great pain for the Marquis de La Fayette. His principles, you know, are clearly with the people; but having been elected for

[1]Jefferson abandoned his career as Minister to Paris to accept, at Washington's personal request, the office of first Secretary of State. Despite occasional political differences arising from the Federalist-Republican struggle, Washington and Jefferson maintained cordial and sympathetic relations until Washington's death.

the Noblesse of Auvergne, they have laid him under express instructions, to vote for the decision by orders and not persons. This would ruin him with the Tiers État, and it is not possible he could continue long to give satisfaction to the Noblesse. I have not hesitated to press on him to burn his instructions, and follow his conscience as the only sure clue, which will eternally guide a man clear of all doubts and inconsistencies. If he cannot effect a conciliatory plan, he will surely take his stand manfully at once, with the Tiers État. He will in that case be what he pleases with them, and I am in hopes that base is now too solid to render it dangerous to be mounted on it. . . .

TO MONSIEUR DE ST. ETIENNE[1]

Paris, June 3, 1789

SIR,—After you quitted us yesterday evening, we continued our conversation (Monsieur de La Fayette, Mr. Short and myself) on the subject of the difficulties which environ you. The desirable object being, to secure the good which the King has offered, and to avoid the ill which seems to threaten, an idea was suggested, which appearing to make an impression on Monsieur de La Fayette, I was encouraged to pursue it on my return to Paris, to put it into form, and now to send it to you and him. It is this; that the King, in a *séance royale* should come forward with a Charter of Rights in his hand, to be signed by himself and by every member of the three orders. This charter to contain the five great points which the Resultat of December offered, on the part of the King, the abolition of pecuniary privileges offered by the privileged orders, and the adoption of the national debt, and a grant of the sum of money asked from the nation. This last will be a cheap price for the preceding articles; and let the same act declare your immediate separation till the next anniversary meeting. You will carry back to your constituents more good than ever was effected before without violence, and you will stop exactly at the point where violence would otherwise begin. Time will be gained, the public mind will continue to ripen and to be informed, a basis of support may be prepared with the

[1]Rabaud de Saint Etienne was a well-known advocate of the Protestant cause.

people themselves, and expedients occur for gaining still something further at your next meeting, and for stopping again at the point of force. I have ventured to send to yourself and Monsieur de La Fayette a sketch of my ideas of what this act might contain, without endangering any dispute. But it is offered merely as a canvas for you to work on, if it be fit to work on at all. I know too little of the subject, and you know too much of it, to justify me in offering anything but a hint. I have done it, too, in a hurry; insomuch, that since committing it to writing, it occurs to me that the fifth article may give alarm; that it is in a good degree included in the fourth, and is, therefore, useless. But after all, what excuse can I make, Sir, for this presumption. I have none but an unmeasurable love for your nation, and a painful anxiety lest despotism, after an unaccepted offer to bind its own hands, should seize you again with tenfold fury. Permit me to add to these, very sincere assurances of the sentiments of esteem and respect, with which I have the honor to be, Sir, your most obedient, and most humble servant.

[The annexed is the Charter accompanying the two preceding letters.]

A Charter of Rights, solemnly established by the King and Nation

1. The States General shall assemble, uncalled, on the first day of November, annually, and shall remain together so long as they shall see cause. They shall regulate their own elections and proceedings, and until they shall ordain otherwise, their elections shall be in the forms observed in the present year, and shall be triennial.

2. The States General alone shall levy money on the nation, and shall appropriate it.

3. Laws shall be made by the States General only, with the consent of the King.

4. No person shall be restrained of his liberty, but by regular process from a court of justice, authorized by a general law. (Except that a Noble may be imprisoned by order of a court of justice, on the prayer of twelve of his nearest relations.) On complaint of an unlawful imprisonment, to any judge whatever, he shall have the prisoner immediately brought before him, and shall discharge him, if his imprisonment be unlawful. The officer in whose custody the prisoner is, shall obey the

orders of the judge; and both judge and officer shall be responsible, civilly and criminally, for a failure of duty herein.

5. The military shall be subordinate to the civil authority.

6. Printers shall be liable to legal prosecution for printing and publishing false facts, injurious to the party prosecuting; but they shall be under no other restraint.

7. All pecuniary privileges and exemptions, enjoyed by any description of persons, are abolished.

8. All debts already contracted by the King, are hereby made the debts of the nation; and the faith thereof is pledged for their payment in due time.

9. Eighty millions of livres are now granted to the King, to be raised by loan, and reimbursed by the nation; and the taxes heretofore paid, shall continue to be paid to the end of the present year, and no longer.

10. The States General shall now separate, and meet again on the 1st day of November next.

Done, on behalf of the whole nation, by the King and their representatives in the States General, at Versailles, this —— day of June, 1789.

Signed by the King, and by every member individually, And in his presence.

TO JOHN JAY

Paris, June 24, 1789

SIR,—My letter of the 17th and 18th instant, gave you the progress of the States General to the 17th, when the Tiers had declared the illegality of all the existing taxes, and their discontinuance from the end of their present session. The next day being a *jour de fête*, could furnish no indication of the impression that vote was likely to make on the government. On the 19th, a Council was held at Marly, in the afternoon. It was there proposed, that the King should interpose by a declaration of his sentiments in a *séance royale*. The declaration prepared by Mr. Neckar, while it censured in general the proceedings both of the Nobles and Commons, announced the King's views, such as substantially to coincide with the Commons. It was agreed to in Council, as also that the *séance royale* should be held on the 22d, and the meetings till then be suspended. While the Council was engaged in this deliberation at Marly, the Chamber of the Clergy was in debate, whether they should accept the invitation of the Tiers to unite with them in the common chamber. On the first question, to unite simply and unconditionally, it was decided in the negative by a very small majority. As it was known, however, that some members who had voted in the negative, would be for the affirmative with some modifications, the question was put with these modifications, and it was determined by a majority of eleven members, that their body should join the Tiers. These proceedings of the Clergy were unknown to the Council at Marly, and those of the Council were kept secret from everybody. The next morning (the 20th), the members repaired to the House as usual, found the doors shut and guarded, and a proclamation posted up for holding a *séance royale* on the 22d, and a suspension of their meetings till then. They presumed, in the first moment, that their dissolution was decided, and repaired to another place, where they proceeded to business. They there bound themselves to each other by an oath, never to separate of their own accord, till they had settled a constitution for the ration on a solid basis, and if separated by force, that they would reassemble in some other place. It was intimated to them, however, that day, privately, that the proceedings of the *séance royale* would be favorable to them. The next day they met in a church, and were joined by a majority of the Clergy. The heads of the aristocracy saw that all was lost without some violent exertion. The King was still at Marly. Nobody was permitted to approach him but their friends. He was assailed by lies in all shapes. He was made to believe that the Commons were going to absolve the army from their oath of fidelity to him, and to raise their pay. . . . They procured a committee to be held, consisting of the King and his ministers, to which Monsieur and the Count d'Artois should be admitted. At this committee, the latter attacked Mr. Neckar personally, arraigned his plans, and proposed one which some of his engines had put into his hands. Mr. Neckar, whose characteristic is the want of firmness, was browbeaten and intimidated, and the King shaken. He determined that the two plans should be deliberated on the next day, and the *séance royale* put off a day longer. This encouraged a fiercer attack on Mr. Neckar the next day; his plan was totally dislocated, and that of the Count d'Artois inserted into it. Himself and Monsieur de Montmorin offered their resignation, which was refused; the Count d'Artois saying to Mr. Neckar, "No, Sir, you must be kept as the hostage; we hold you responsible for all the ill which shall happen." This change of plan was immediately whispered without doors. The nobility were in triumph, the people in consternation. When the King passed the next day through the lane they formed from the Chateau to the Hotel des États (about half a mile), there was a dead silence. He was about an hour in the House, delivering his speech and declaration, copies of which I enclose you. On his coming out, a feeble cry of *"vive le roy"* was raised by some children, but the people remained silent and sullen. When the Duke d'Orleans followed, however, their applauses were excessive. This must have been sensible to the King. He had ordered, in the close of his speech, that the members should follow him, and resume their deliberations the next day. The Noblesse followed him, and so did the Clergy, except about thirty, who, with the Tiers, remained in the room, and entered into deliberation. They protested against what the King had done, adhered to all their former proceedings, and resolved the inviolability of their own persons. An officer came twice to order them out of the room, in the King's name, but they refused to obey. In the afternoon, the people, uneasy, began to assemble in great numbers in the courts and vicinities of the palace. The Queen was alarmed, and sent for Mr. Neckar. He was conducted amidst the shouts and acclamations of the multitude, who filled all the apartments of the palace. He was a few minutes only with the Queen, and about three-quarters of an hour with the King. Not a word has transpired of what passed at these interviews. The King was just going to ride out. He passed through the crowd to his carriage, and into it, without being in the least noticed. As Mr. Neckar followed him, universal acclamations were raised of "Vive Monsieur Neckar, vive le sauveur de la France opprimée." He was conducted back to his house with the same demonstration of affection and anxiety. About two hundred deputies of the Tiers, catching the enthusiasm of the moment, went to his house, and extorted from him a promise that he would not resign. These circumstances must wound the heart of the King, desirous as he is, to possess the affections of his subjects. As soon as the proceedings at Versailles were known at Paris, a run began on the *caisse d'escompte,* which is the first symptom always of the public diffidence and alarm. It is the less in condition to meet the run, as Mr. Neckar has been forced to make free with its funds, for the daily support of the government. This is the state of things, as late as I am able to give them with certainty, at this moment. My letter not being to go off till to-morrow evening, I shall go to Versailles to-morrow, and be able to add the transactions of this day and to-morrow.

June 25. Just returned from Versailles, I am enabled to continue my narration. On the 24th, nothing remarkable passed, except an attack by the mob of Versailles on the Archbishop of Paris, who had been one of the instigators of the court, to the proceedings of the *séance royale.* They threw mud and stones at his carriage, broke the windows of it, and he in a fright promised to join the Tiers.

This day (the 25th) forty-eight of the Nobles have joined the Tiers. Among these, is the Duke d'Orleans. The Marquis de La Fayette could not be of the number, being restrained by his instructions. He is writing to his constituents, to change his instructions or to accept his resignation. There are with the Tiers now, one hundred and sixty-four members of the Clergy, so that the common chamber consists of upwards of eight hundred members. The minority of the Clergy, however, call themselves the chamber of the Clergy, and pretend to go on with business. I found the streets of Versailles much embarassed with soldiers. There was a body of about one hundred horse drawn up in front of the Hotel of the States, and all the avenues and doors guarded by soldiers. Nobody was permitted to enter but the members, and this was by order of the King; for till now, the doors of the common room have been open, and at least two thousand spectators attending their debates constantly. They have named a deputation to wait on the King, and desire a removal of the soldiery from their doors, and seem determined, if this is not complied with, to remove themselves elsewhere.

Instead of being dismayed with what has passed, they seem to rise in their demands, and some of them to consider the erasing every vestige of a difference of order as indispensable to the establishment and preservation of a good constitution. I apprehend there is more courage than calculation in this project. I did imagine, that seeing that Mr. Neckar and themselves were involved as common enemies in the hatred of the aristocrats, they would have been willing to make common cause with him, and to wish his continuance in office; and that Mr. Neckar, seeing that all the trimmings he has used towards the court and Nobles, has availed him nothing, would engage himself heartily and solely on the popular side, and view his own salvation in that alone. The confidence which the people place in him, seems to merit some attention. However, the mass of the common chamber are absolutely indifferent to his remaining in office. They consider his head as unequal to the planning a good constitution, and his fortitude to a co-operation in the effecting it. His dismission is more credited to-day than it was yesterday. If it takes place, he will retain his popularity with the nation, as the members of the States will not think it important to set themselves against it, but on the contrary, will be willing that he should continue on their side, on his retirement. The run on the *casse d'escompte* continues. The members of the States admit, that Mr. Neckar's departure out of office will occasion a stoppage of public payments. But they expect to prevent any very ill effect, by assuring the public against any loss, and by taking immediate measures for continuing payment. They may, perhaps, connect these measures with their own existence, so as to interest the public in whatever catastrophe may be aimed at them. The gazettes of France and Leyden accompany this. During the continuance of this crisis and my own stay, I shall avail myself of every private conveyance to keep you informed of what passes. I have the honor to be, with the most perfect esteem and respect, Sir, your most obedient, and most humble servant.

TO JOHN JAY

Paris, June 29, 1789

SIR—My letter of the 25th gave you the transactions of the States General to the afternoon of that day. On the next, the Archbishop of Paris joined the Tiers, as did some others of the Clergy and Noblesse. On the 27th, the question of the St. Domingo deputation came on, and it was decided that it should be received. I have before mentioned to you the ferment into which the proceedings at the *séance royale* of the 23d, had thrown the people. The soldiery also were affected by it. It began in the French guards, extended to those of every other denomination, (except the Swiss) and even to the bodyguards of the King. They began to quit their barracks, to assemble in squads, to declare they would defend the life of the King, but would not cut the throats of their fellow-citizens. They were treated and caressed by the people, carried in triumph through the streets, called themselves the soldiers of the nation, and left no doubt on which side they would be, in case of a rupture. Similar accounts came in from the troops in other parts of the kingdom, as well those which had not heard of the *séance royale*, as those which had, and gave good reason to apprehend that the soldiery, in general, would side with their fathers and brothers, rather than with their officers. The operation of this medicine, at Versailles, was as sudden as it was powerful. The alarm there was so complete, that in the afternoon of the 27th, the King wrote a letter to the President of the Clergy, the Cardinal de La Rochefoucault, in these words:[1]

"MY COUSIN,—*Wholly engaged in promoting the general good of my kingdom, and desirous, above all things, that the Assembly of the States General should apply themselves to objects of general interest, after the voluntary acceptance by your order of my declaration of the 23d of the present month; I pass my word that my faithful Clergy will, without delay, unite themselves with the other two orders, to hasten the accomplishment of my paternal views. Those, whose powers are too limited, may decline voting until new powers are procured. This will be a new mark of attachment which my Clergy will give me. I pray God, my Cousin, to have you in his holy keeping. Louis.*"

A like letter was written to the Duke de Luxemburgh, President of the Noblesse. The two chambers entered into debate on the question, whether they should obey the letter of the King. There was a considerable opposition; when notes written by the Count d'Artois to sundry members, and handed about among the rest, decided the matter, and they went in a body and took their seats with the Tiers, and thus rendered the union of the orders in one chamber complete. As soon as this was known to the people of Versailles, they assembled about the palace, demanded the King and Queen, who came and showed them-

---

[1]The following is a literal translation of the King's letter. [Editors' footnote, Memorial Edition.]

selves in a balcony. They rent the skies with cries of *"vive le roy,"* *"vive le reine."* They called for the Dauphin, who was also produced, and was the subject of new acclamations. After feasting themselves and the royal family with this tumultuary reconciliation, they went to the house of Mr. Neckar and M. de Montmorin, with shouts of thankfulness and affection. Similar emotions of joy took place in Paris, and at this moment, the triumph of the Tiers is considered as complete. To-morrow they will recommence business, voting by persons on all questions; and whatever difficulties may be opposed in debate by the malcontents of the Clergy and Nobility, everything must be finally settled at the will of the Tiers. It remains to see whether they will leave to the Nobility anything but their titulary appellations. I suppose they will not. Mr. Neckar will probably remain in office. It would seem natural that he should endeavor to have the hostile part of the Council removed, but I question if he finds himself firm enough for that. A perfect co-operation with the Tiers will be his wisest game. This great crisis being now over, I shall not have matter interesting enough to trouble you with, as often as I have done lately. There has nothing remarkable taken place in any other part of Europe. I have the honor to be, with the most perfect esteem and respect, Sir, your most obedient, and most humble servant.

TO THOMAS PAINE[1]

Paris, July 11, 1789

. . . . The *National Assembly* then (for this is the name they take), having shown through every stage of these transactions a coolness, wisdom, and resolution to set fire to the four corners of the kingdom and to perish with it themselves, rather than to relinquish an iota from their plan of a total change of government, are now in complete and undisputed possession of the sovereignty. The executive and aristocracy are at their feet; the mass of the nation, the mass of the clergy, and the army are with them; they have prostrated the old government, and are

[1]Jefferson's admiration for Paine's revolutionary political writings, as well as for his inventive genius, led him to sponsor Paine in the trying years after Paine's expulsion from England.

now beginning to build one from the foundation. A committee, charged with the arrangement of their business, gave in, two days ago, the following order of proceedings.

"1. Every government should have for its only end, the preservation of the rights of man; whence it follows, that to recall constantly the government to the end proposed, the constitution should begin by a declaration of the natural and imprescriptable rights of man.

"2. Monarchical government being proper to maintain those rights, it has been chosen by the French nation. It suits especially a great society; it is necessary for the happiness of France. The declaration of the principles of this government, then, should follow immediately the declaration of the rights of man.

"3. It results from the principles of monarchy, that the nation, to assure its own rights, has yielded particular rights to the monarch; the constitution, then, should declare, in a precise manner, the rights of both. It should begin by declaring the rights of the French nation, and then it should declare the rights of the King.

"4. The rights of the King and nation not existing but for the happiness of the individuals who compose it, they lead to an examination of the rights of citizens.

"5. The French nation not being capable of assembling individually, to exercise all its rights, it ought to be represented. It is necessary, then, to declare the form of its representation and the rights of its representatives.

"6. From the union of the powers of the nation and King, should result the enacting and execution of the laws; thus then, it should first be determined how the laws shall be established, afterwards should be considered, how they shall be executed.

"7. Laws have for their object the general administration of the kingdom, the property and the actions of the citizens. The execution of the laws which concern the general administration, requires Provincial and Municipal Assemblies. It is necessary to examine, therefore, what should be the organization of the Provincial Assemblies, and what of the Municipal.

"8. The execution of the laws which concern the property and actions of the citizens, call for the judiciary power. It should be determined how that should be confided, and then its duties and limits.

"9. For the execution of the laws and the defence of the kingdom, there exists a public force. It is necessary, then, to determine the principles which should direct it, and how it should be employed.

"Recapitulation

"Declaration of the rights of man. Principles of the monarchy. Rights of the nation. Rights of the King. Rights of the citizens.

"Organization and rights of the National Assembly. Forms necessary for the enaction of laws. Organization and functions of the Provincial and Municipal Assemblies. Duties and limits of the judiciary power. Functions and duties of the military power."

You see that these are the materials of a superb edifice, and the hands which have prepared them, are perfectly capable of putting them together, and of filling up the work of which these are only the outlines. While there are some men among them of very superior abilities, the mass possess such a degree of good sense, as enables them to decide well. I have always been afraid their numbers might lead to confusion. Twelve hundred men in one room are too many. I have still that fear. Another apprehension is, that a majority cannot be induced to adopt the trial by jury; and I consider that as the only anchor ever yet imagined by man, by which a government can be held to the principles of its constitution. . . .

TO JOHN JAY

Paris, July 19, 1789

. . . . My letter of the 29th of June, brought down the proceedings of the States and government to the re-union of the orders, which took place on the 27th. Within the Assembly, matters went on well. But it was soon observed, that troops, and particularly the foreign troops, were on their march towards Paris from various quarters, and that this was against the opinion of Mr. Neckar. The King was probably advised to this, under pretext of preserving peace in Paris and Versailles, and saw nothing else in the measure. That his advisers are supposed to have had in view, when he should be secured and inspirited by the presence of the troops, to take advantage of some favorable moment, and surprise him into an act of authority for establishing the declaration of the 23d of June, and perhaps dispersing the States General, is probable. The Marshal de Broglio was appointed to command all the troops within the isle of France, a high flying aristocrat, cool and capable of everything. Some of the French guards were soon arrested under other pretexts, but in reality, on account of their dispositions in favor of the national cause. The people of Paris forced the prison, released them, and sent a deputation to the States General, to solicit a pardon. The States, by a most moderate and prudent Arreté, recommended these prisoners to the King, and peace to the people of Paris. Addresses came in to them from several of the great cities, expressing sincere allegiance to the King, but a determined resolution to support the States General. On the 8th of July, they voted an address to the King to remove the troops. This piece of masculine eloquence, written by Monsieur de Mirabeau, is worth attention on account of the bold matter it expresses and discovers through the whole. The King refused to remove the troops, and said they might remove themselves, if they pleased, to Noyons or Soissons. They proceeded to fix the order in which they will take up the several branches of their future constitution, from which it appears, they mean to build it from the bottom, confining themselves to nothing in their ancient form, but a King. A declaration of rights, which forms the first chapter of their work, was then proposed by the Marquis de La Fayette. This was on the 11th. In the meantime, troops, to the number of about twenty-five or thirty thousand, had arrived, and were posted in and between Paris and Versailles. The bridges and passes were guarded. At three o'clock in the afternoon, the Count de La Luzerne was sent to notify Mr. Neckar of his dismission, and to enjoin him to retire instantly, without saying a word of it to anybody. He went home, dined, proposed to his wife a visit to a friend, but went in fact to his country-house at St. Ouen, and at midnight, set out from thence, as is supposed, for Brussels. This was not known till the next day, when the whole ministry was changed, except Villedeuil, of the domestic department, and Barentin, Garde des Sceaux. These changes were as follows: the Baron de Breteuil, President of the Council of Finance; and de La Galaisiere, Comptroller General in the room of Mr. Neckar; the Marshal de Broglio, minister of war, and Foulon under him, in the room of Puy-Segur; Monsieur de La Vauguyon, minister of foreign affairs, instead of Monsieur de Montmorin; de La Porte, minister of marine, in place of the Count de La Luzerne; St. Priest was also removed from the Council. It is to be observed, that Luzerne and Puy-Segur had been strongly of the aristocratical party in Council; but they were not considered as equal to bear their shares in the work now to be done. For this change, however sudden it may have been in the mind of the King, was, in that of his advisers, only one chapter of a great plan, of which the bringing together the foreign troops had been the first. He was now completely in the hands of men, the principal among whom, had been noted through their lives, for the Turkish despotism of their characters, and who were associated about the King, as proper instruments for what was to be executed. The news of this change began to be known in Paris about one or two o'clock. In the afternoon, a body of about one hundred German cavalry were advanced and drawn up in the Place Louis XV. and about two hundred Swiss posted at a little distance in their rear. This drew the people to that spot, who naturally formed themselves in front of the troops, at first merely to look at them. But as their numbers increased their indignation arose; they retired a few steps, posted themselves on and behind large piles of loose stone, collected in that place for a bridge adjacent to it, and attacked the horse with stones. The horse charged, but the advantageous position of the people, and the showers of stones, obliged them to retire, and even to quit the field altogether, leaving one of their number on the ground. The Swiss in their rear were observed never to stir. This was the signal for universal insurrection, and this body of cavalry, to avoid being massacred, retired towards Versailles. The people now armed themselves with such weapons as they could find in armorers' shops and private houses, and with bludgeons, and were roaming all night through all parts of the city, without any decided practicable object. The next day, the States pressed on the King to send away the troops, to permit the Bourgeoise of Paris to arm for the preservation of order in the city, and offered to send a deputation from their body to tranquillize them. He refused all the propositions. A committee of magistrates and electors of the city were appointed by their bodies, to take upon them its government. The mob, now openly joined by the

French guards, forced the prison of St. Lazare, released all the prisoners, and took a great store of corn, which they carried to the corn market. Here they got some arms, and the French guards began to form and train them. The committee determined to raise forty-eight thousand Bourgeoise, or rather to restrain their numbers to forty-eight thousand. On the 14th, they sent one of their members (Monsieur de Corny, whom we knew in America) to the Hotel des Invalides, to ask arms for their Garde Bourgeoise. He was followed by, or he found there, a great mob. The Governor of the Invalides came out, and represented the impossibility of his delivering arms, without the orders of those from whom he received them. De Corny advised the people then to retire, and retired himself; and the people took possession of the arms. It was remarkable, that not only the Invalides themselves made no opposition, but that a body of five thousand foreign troops, encamped within four hundred yards, never stirred. Monsieur de Corny and five others were then sent to ask arms of Monsieur de Launai, Governor of the Bastile. They found a great collection of people already before the place, and they immediately planted a flag of truce, which was answered by a like flag hoisted on the parapet. The deputation prevailed on the people to fall back a little, advanced themselves to make their demand of the Governor, and in that instant a discharge from the Bastile killed four people of those nearest to the deputies. The deputies retired; the people rushed against the place, and almost in an instant were in possession of a fortification, defended by one hundred men, of infinite strength, which in other times had stood several regular sieges, and had never been taken. How they got in, has, as yet, been impossible to discover. Those who pretend to have been of the party tell so many different stories, as to destroy the credit of them all. They took all the arms, discharged the prisoners, and such of the garrison as were not killed in the first moment of fury, carried the Governor and Lieutenant Governor to the Gréve (the place of public execution), cut off their heads, and sent them through the city in triumph to the Palais Royal. About the same instant, a treacherous correspondence having been discovered in Monsieur de Flesselles, Prevost des Marchands, they seized him in the Hotel de Ville, where he was in the exercise of his office, and cut off his head. These events, carried imperfectly to Versailles, were the subject of two successive deputations from the States to the King, to both of which he gave dry and hard answers; for it has transpired, that it had been proposed and agitated in Council, to seize on the principal members of the States General, to march the whole army down upon Paris, and to suppress its tumults by the sword. But at night, the Duke de Liancourt forced his way into the King's bed chamber, and obliged him to hear a full and animated detail of the disasters of the day in Paris. He went to bed deeply impressed. The decapitation of de Launai worked powerfully through the night on the whole aristocratical party, insomuch, that in the morning, those of the greatest influence on the Count d'Artois, represented to him the absolute necessity that the King should give up everything to the States. This according well enough with the dispositions of the King, he went about eleven o'clock, accompanied only by his brothers, to the States General, and there read to them a speech, in which he asked their interposition to re-establish order. Though this be couched in terms of some caution, yet the manner in which it was delivered, made it evident that it was meant as a surrender at discretion. He returned to the chateau a foot, accompanied by the States. They sent off a deputation, the Marquis de La Fayette at their head, to quiet Paris. He had, the same morning, been named Commandant-in-Chief of the Milice Bourgeoise, and Monsieur Bailly, former President of the States General, was called for as Prevost des Marchands. The demolition of the Bastile was now ordered, and begun. A body of the Swiss guards of the regiment of Ventimille; and the city horse guards, joined the people. The alarm at Versailles increased instead of abating. They believed that the aristocrats of Paris were under pillage and carnage, that one hundred and fifty thousand men were in arms, coming to Versailles to massacre the royal family, the court, the ministers, and all connected with them, their practices and principles. The aristocrats of the Nobles and Clergy in the States General, vied with each other in declaring how sincerely they were converted to the justice of voting by persons, and how determined to go with the nation all its lengths. The foreign troops were ordered off instantly. Every minister resigned. The King confirmed Bailly as Prevost des Marchands, wrote to Mr. Neckar to recall him, sent his letter open to the States General, to be forwarded by them, and invited them to go with him to Paris the next day, to satisfy the city of his dispositions; and that night and the next morning, the Count d'Artois and Monsieur de Montisson (a deputy connected with him), Madame de Polignac, Madame de Guiche and the Count de Vaudreuil, favorites of the Queen, the Abbé de Vermont, her confessor, the Prince of Condé and Duke de Bourbon, all fled; we know not whither. The King came to Paris, leaving the Queen in consternation for his return. Omitting the less important figures of the procession, I will only observe, that the King's carriage was in the centre, on each side of it the States General, in two ranks, a foot, and at their head the Marquis de La Fayette, as Commander-in-Chief, on horseback, and Bourgeoise guards before and behind. About sixty thousand citizens of all forms and colors, armed with the muskets of the Bastile and Invalides, as far as they would go, the rest with pistols, swords, pikes, pruning hooks, scythes, etc., lined all the streets through which the procession passed, and, with the crowds of people in the streets, doors and windows, saluted them everywhere with cries of *"vive la nation;"* but not a single *"vive le roy"* was heard. The King stopped at the Hotel de Ville. There Monsieur Bailly presented and put into his hat the popular cockade, and addressed him. The King being unprepared and unable to answer, Bailly went to him, gathered from him some scraps of sentences, and made out an answer, which he delivered to the audience as from the King. On their return, the popular cries were *"vive le roy et la nation."* He was conducted by a Garde Bourgeoise to his palace at Versailles, and thus concluded such an *amende honorable*, as no sovereign ever made, and no people ever received. Letters written with his own hand to the Marquis de La Fayette, remove the scruples of his position. Tranquillity is now restored to the capital: the shops are again opened; the people resuming their labors, and if the want of bread does not disturb our peace, we may hope continuance of it. The demolition of the Bastile is going on, and the Milice Bourgeoise organizing and training. The ancient police of the city is abolished by the authority of the people, the introduction of the King's troops will probably be proscribed, and a watch or city guards substituted, which shall depend on the city alone. But we cannot suppose this paroxysm confined to Paris alone. The whole country must pass successively through it, and happy if they get through it as soon and as well as Paris has done.

I went yesterday to Versailles, to satisfy myself what had passed there; for nothing can be believed, but what one sees, or has from an eye witness. They believe there still, that three thousand people have fallen victims to the tumults of Paris. Mr. Short and myself have been every day among them, in order to be sure what was passing. We cannot find, with certainty, that anybody has been killed but the three before mentioned, and those who fell in the assault or defence of the Bastile. How many of the garrison were killed, nobody pretends to have ever heard. Of the assailants, accounts vary from six to six hundred. The most general belief is, that there fell about thirty. There have been many reports of instantaneous executions by the mob, on such of their body as they caught in acts of theft or robbery. Some of these may perhaps be true. There was a severity of honesty observed, of which no example has been known. Bags of money offered on various occasions through fear or guilt, have been uniformly refused by the mobs. The churches are now occupied in singing *"De profundis"* and *"Requiems"* "for the repose of the souls of the brave and valiant citizens who have sealed with their blood the liberty of the nation." Monsieur de Montmorin is this day replaced in the department of foreign affairs, and Monsieur de St. Priest is named to the home department. The gazettes of France and Leyden accompany this. I send, also, a paper (called the Point du Jour), which will give you some idea of the proceedings of the National Assembly. It is but an indifferent thing; however, it is the best. . . .

TO JAMES MADISON

Paris, September 6, 1789

DEAR SIR,—I sit down to write to you without knowing by what occasion I shall send my letter. I do it, because a subject comes into my head, which I would wish to develop a little more than is practicable in the hurry of the moment of making up general despatches.

The question, whether one generation of men has a right to bind another, seems never to have been started either on this or our side of the water. Yet it is a question of such consequences as not only to merit decision, but place also among the fundamental principles of every government. The course of reflection in which we are immersed here, on the elementary principles of society, has presented this question to my mind; and that no such obligation can be transmitted, I think very capable of proof. I set out on this ground, which I suppose to be self-evident, that the *earth belongs in usufruct to the living*; that the dead have neither powers nor rights over it. The portion occupied by any individual ceases to be his when himself ceases to be, and reverts to the society. If the society has formed no rules for the appropriation of its lands in severalty, it will be taken by the first occupants, and these will generally be the wife and children of the decedent. If they have formed rules of appropriation, those rules may give it to the wife and children, or to some one of them, or to the legatee of the deceased. So they may give it to its creditor. But the child, the legatee or creditor, takes it, not by *natural right*, but by a law of the society of which he is a member, and to which he is subject. Then, no man can, by natural right, oblige the lands he occupied, or the persons who succeed him in that occupation, to the payment of debts contracted by him. For if he could, he might during his own life, eat up the usufruct of the lands for several generations to come; and then the lands would belong to the dead, and not to the living, which is the reverse of our principle.

What is true of every member of the society, individually, is true of them all collectively; since the rights of the whole can be no more than the sum of the rights of the individuals. To keep our ideas clear when applying them to a multitude, let us suppose a whole generation of men to be born on the same day, to attain mature age on the same day, and to die on the same day, leaving a succeeding generation in the moment of attaining their mature age, all together. Let the ripe age be supposed of twenty-one years, and their period of life thirty-four years more, that being the average term given by the bills of mortality to persons of twenty-one years of age. Each successive generation would, in this way, come and go off the stage at a fixed moment, as individuals do now. Then I say, the earth belongs to each of these generations during its course, fully and in its own right. The second generation receives it clear of the debts and incumbrances of the first, the third of the second, and so on. For if the first could charge it with a debt, then the earth would belong to the dead and not to the living generation. Then, no generation can contract debts greater than may be paid during the course of its own existence At twenty-one years of age, they may bind themselves and their lands for thirty-four years to come; at twenty-two, for thirty-three; at twenty-three, for thirty-two; and at fifty-four, for one year only; because these are the terms of life which remain to them at the respective epochs. But a material difference must be noted, between the succession of an individual and that of a whole generation. Individuals are parts only of a society, subject to the laws of a whole. These laws may appropriate the portion of land occupied by a decedent, to his creditor, rather than to any other, or to his child, on condition he satisfies the creditor. But when a whole generation, that is, the whole society, dies, as in the case we have supposed, and another generation or society succeeds, this forms a whole, and there is no superior who can give their territory to a third society, who may have lent money to their predecessors, beyond their faculties of paying.

What is true of generations succeeding one another at fixed epochs, as has been supposed for clearer conception, is true for those renewed daily, as in the actual course of nature. As a majority of the contracting generation will continue in being thirty-four years, and a new majority will then come into possession, the former may extend their engagement to that term, and no longer. The conclusion then, is, that neither the representatives of a nation, nor the whole nation itself assembled, can validly engage debts beyond what they may pay in their own time, that is to say, within thirty-four years of the date of the engagement.

To render this conclusion palpable, suppose that Louis the XIV. and XV. had contracted debts in the name of the French nation, to the amount of ten thousand milliards, and that the whole had been contracted in Holland. The interest of this sum would be five hundred milliards, which is the whole rent-roll or net proceeds of the territory of France. Must the present generation of men have retired from the territory in which nature produces them, and ceded it to the Dutch creditors? No; they have the same rights over the soil on which they were produced, as the preceding generations had. They derive these rights not from them, but from nature. They, then, and their soil are, by nature, clear of the debts of their predecessors. To present this in another point of view, suppose Louis XV. and his contemporary generation, had said to the money lenders of Holland, give us money, that we may eat, drink, and be merry in our day; and on condition you will

demand no interest till the end of thirty-four years, you shall then, forever after, receive an annual interest of fifteen per cent. The money is
lent on these conditions, is divided among the people, eaten, drunk,
and squandered. Would the present generation be obliged to apply the
produce of the earth and of their labor, to replace their dissipations?
Not at all.

I suppose that the received opinion, that the public debts of one
generation devolve on the next, has been suggested by our seeing,
habitually, in private life, that he who succeeds to lands is required to
pay the debts of his predecessor; without considering that this requi-
sition is municipal only, not moral, flowing from the will of the society, which has found it convenient to appropriate the lands of a
decedent on the condition of a payment of his debts; but that between
society and society, or generation and generation, there is no municipal
obligation, no umpire but the law of nature.

The interest of the national debt of France being, in fact, but a two
thousandth part of its rent-roll, the payment of it is practicable enough;
and so becomes a question merely of honor or of expediency. But with
respect to future debts, would it not be wise and just for that nation
to declare in the constitution they are forming, that neither the legislature nor the nation itself, can validly contract more debt than they
may pay within their own age, or within the term of thirty-four years?
And that all future contracts shall be deemed void, as to what shall
remain unpaid at the end of thirty-four years from their date? This
would put the lenders, and the borrowers also, on their guard. By
reducing, too, the faculty of borrowing within its natural limits, it
would bridle the spirit of war, to which too free a course has been procured by the inattention of money lenders to this law of nature, that
succeeding generations are not responsible for the preceding.

On similar ground it may be proved, that no society can make a
perpetual constitution, or even a perpetual law. The earth belongs
always to the living generation: they may manage it, then, and what
proceeds from it, as they please, during their usufruct. They are masters, too, of their own persons, and consequently may govern them as
they please. But persons and property make the sum of the objects of
government. The constitution and the laws of their predecessors are
extinguished then, in their natural course, with those whose will gave

them being. This could preserve that being, till it ceased to be itself, and no longer. Every constitution, then, and every law, naturally expires at the end of thirty-four years. If it be enforced longer, it is an act of force, and not of right. It may be said, that the succeeding generation exercising, in fact, the power of repeal, this leaves them as free as if the constitution or law had been expressly limited to thirty-four years only. In the first place, this objection admits the right, in proposing an equivalent. But the power of repeal is not an equivalent. It might be, indeed, if every form of government were so perfectly contrived, that the will of the majority could always be obtained, fairly and without impediment. But this is true of no form. The people cannot assemble themselves; their representation is unequal and vicious. Various checks are opposed to every legislative proposition. Factions get possession of the public councils, bribery corrupts them, personal interests lead them astray from the general interests of their constituents; and other impediments arise, so as to prove to every practical man, that a law of limited duration is much more manageable than one which needs a repeal.

This principle, that the earth belongs to the living and not to the dead, is of very extensive application and consequences in every country, and most especially in France. It enters into the resolution of the questions, whether the nation may change the descent of lands holden in tail; whether they may change the appropriation of lands given anciently to the church, to hospitals, colleges, orders of chivalry, and otherwise in perpetuity; whether they may abolish the charges and privileges attached on lands, including the whole catalogue, ecclesiastical and feudal; it goes to hereditary offices, authorities and jurisdictions, to hereditary orders, distinctions and appellations, to perpetual monopolies in commerce, the arts or sciences, with a long train of *et ceteras;* renders the question of reimbursement, a question of generosity and not of right. In all these cases, the legislature of the day could authorize such appropriations and establishments for their own time, but no longer; and the present holders, even where they or their ancestors have purchased, are in the case of *bona fide* purchasers of what the seller had no right to convey.

Turn this subject in your mind, my dear Sir, and particularly as to the power of contracting debts, and develop it with that cogent logic which is so peculiarly yours. Your station in the councils of our country gives you an opportunity of producing it to public consideration, of forcing it into discussion. At first blush it may be laughed at, as the dream of a theorist; but examination will prove it to be solid and salutary. It would furnish matter for a fine preamble to our first law for appropriating the public revenue; and it will exclude, at the threshold of our new government, the ruinous and contagious errors of this quarter of the globe, which have armed despots with means which nature does not sanction, for binding in chains their fellow-men. We have already given, in example, one effectual check to the dog of war, by transferring the power of declaring war from the executive to the legislative body, from those who are to spend, to those who are to pay. I should be pleased to see this second obstacle held out by us also, in the first instance. No nation can make a declaration against the validity of long-contracted debts, so disinterestedly as we, since we do not owe a shilling which will not be paid, principal and interest, by the measures you have taken, within the time of our own lives. I write you no news, because when an occasion occurs, I shall write a separate letter for that.

I am always, with great and sincere esteem, dear Sir, your affectionate friend and servant.

TO WM. HUNTER, ESQ., MAYOR OF ALEXANDRIA

Alexandria, March 11, 1790

. . . . Convinced that the republican is the only form of government which is not eternally at open or secret war with the rights of mankind, my prayers and efforts shall be cordially distributed to the support of that we have so happily established. It is indeed an animating thought, that while we are securing the rights of ourselves and our posterity, we are pointing out the way to struggling nations, who wish like us to emerge from their tyrannies also. Heaven help their struggles, and lead them, as it has done us, triumphantly through them. . . .

New York, April 2, 1790

Behold me, my dear friend, elected Secretary of State, instead of returning to the far more agreeable position which placed me in the daily participation of your friendship. I found the appointment in the newspapers the day of my arrival in Virginia. I had indeed been asked while in France, whether I would accept of any appointment at home, and I had answered that, not meaning to remain long where I was, I meant it to be the last office I should ever act in. Unfortunately this letter had not arrived at the time of arranging the new Government. I expressed freely to the President my desire to return. He left me free, but still showing his own desire. This, and the concern of others, more general than I had a right to expect, induced, after three months parleying, to sacrifice my own inclinations. I have been here, then, ten days harnessed in new gear. Wherever I am, or ever shall be, I shall be sincere in my friendship to you and to your nation. I think with others, that nations are to be governed with regard to their own interests, but I am convinced that it is their interest, in the long run, to be grateful, faithful to their engagements, even in the worst of circumstances, and honorable and generous always. If I had not known that the head of our government was in these sentiments, and that his national and private ethics were the same, I would never have been where I am. I am sorry to tell you his health is less firm than it used to be. However, there is nothing in it to give alarm. The opposition to our new Constitution has almost totally disappeared. Some few indeed had gone such lengths in their declarations of hostility, that they feel it awkward perhaps to come over; but the amendments proposed by Congress, have brought over almost all their followers. If the President can be preserved a few years till habits of authority and obedience can be established generally, we have nothing to fear. The little vautrien, Rhode Island, will come over with a little more time. Our last news from Paris is of the 8th of January. So far it seemed that your revolution had got along with a steady peace; meeting indeed occasional difficulties and dangers, but we are not to expect to be translated from despotism to liberty in a feather-bed. I have never feared for the ultimate result, though I have feared for you personally. Indeed, I hope you will never see such another 5th or 6th of October. Take care of yourself, my dear friend, for though I think your nation would in any event work out her salvation, I am persuaded, were she to lose you, it would cost her oceans of blood, and years of confusion and anarchy. Kiss and bless your dear children for me. Learn them to be as you are, a cement between our two nations. I write to Madame de LaFayette, so have only to add assurances of the respect of your affectionate friend and humble servant.

TO MARIA JEFFERSON

New York, April 11, 1790[1]

Where are you, my dear Maria? how do you do? how are you occupied? Write me a letter by the first post, and answer me all these questions. Tell me whether you see the sun rise every day? how many pages a day you read in Don Quixote? how far you are advanced in him? whether you repeat a grammar lesson every day? what else you read? how many hours a day you sew? whether you have an opportunity of continuing your music? whether you know how to make a pudding yet, to cut out a beefsteak, to sow spinach? or to set a hen? Be good, my dear, as I have always found you; never be angry with anybody, nor speak harm of them; try to let everybody's faults be forgotten, as you would wish yours to be; take more pleasure in giving what is best to another than in having it yourself, and then all the world will love you, and I more than all the world. If your sister is with you, kiss her and tell her how much I love her also, and present my affections to Mr. Randolph. Love your aunt and uncle and be dutiful and obliging to them for all their kindness to you. What would you do without them and with such a vagrant for a father? Say to both of them a thousand affectionate things for me; and adieu, my dear Maria.

TH. JEFFERSON.

[1]Randall.

TO MR. THOMAS MANN RANDOLPH

New York, May 30, 1790

. . . . Your resolution to apply to the study of the law, is wise in my opinion, and at the same time to mix with it a good degree of attention to the farm. The one will relieve the other. The study of the law is useful in a variety of points of view. It qualifies a man to be useful to himself, to his neighbors, and to the public. It is the most certain stepping-stone to preferment in the political line. In political economy, I think Smith's Wealth of Nations the best book extant; in the science of government, Montesquieu's Spirit of Laws is generally recommended. It contains, indeed, a great number of political truths; but also an equal number of heresies: so that the reader must be constantly on his guard. There has been lately published a letter of Helvetius, who was the intimate friend of Montesquieu, and whom he consulted before the publication of his book. Helvetius advised him not to publish it; and in this letter to a friend he gives us a solution for the mixture of truth and error found in this book. He says Montesquieu was a man of immense reading; that he had commonplaced all his reading, and that his object was to throw the whole contents of his commonplace book into systematical order, and to show his ingenuity by reconciling the contradictory facts it presents. Locke's little book on Government, is perfect as far as it goes. Descending from theory to practice there is no better book than the Federalist. Burgh's Political Disquisitions are good also, especially after reading De Lome. Several of Hume's Political Essays are good. There are some excellent books of theory written by Turgot and the economists of France. For parliamentary knowledge, the Lex Parliamentaria is the best book. . . .

TO JOHN GARLAND JEFFERSON[1]

New York, June 11, 1790

DEAR SIR,—Your uncle mr Garland informs me, that, your education being finished, you are desirous of obtaining some clerkship or something else under government whereby you may turn your talents to some account for yourself and he had supposed it might be in my power to provide you with some such office. His commendations of you are such as to induce me to wish sincerely to be of service to you. But there is not, and has not been, a single vacant office at my disposal. Nor would I, as your friend, ever think of putting you into the petty clerkships in the several offices, where you would have to drudge through life for a miserable pittance, without a hope of bettering your situation. But he tells me you are also disposed to the study of the law. This therefore brings it more within my power to serve you. It will be necessary for you in that case to go and live somewhere in my neighborhood in AIbemarle. The inclosed letter to Colo. Lewis near Charlottesville will show you what I have supposed could be best done for you there. It is a general practice to study the law in the office of some lawyer. This indeed gives to the student the advantage of his instruction. But I have ever seen that the services expected in return have been more than the instructions have been worth. All that is necessary for a student is access to a library, and directions in what order the books are to be read. This I will take the liberty of suggesting to you, observing previously that as other branches of science, and especially history, are necessary to form a lawyer, these must be carried on together. I will arrange the books to be read into three columns, and propose that you should read those in the first column till 12. oclock every day; those in the 2d. from 12. to 2. those in the 3d. after candlelight, leaving all the afternoon for exercise and recreation, which are as necessary as reading: I will rather say more necessary, because health is worth more than learning.

---

[1]John Garland Jefferson was the son of George Jefferson, Thomas Jefferson's cousin. [Ford].

1st.	2d.	3d.
Coke on Littleton	Dalrymple's feudal	Mallet's North antiq-
Coke's 2d. 3d & 4th.	system.	uit'.
institutes.	Hale's history of the	History of England in
Coke's reports.	Com. law.	3 vols. folio com-
Vaughan's do	Gilbert on Devises	piled by Kennet.
Salkeld's	Uses	Ludlow's memoirs
Ld. Raymond's	Tenures.	Burnet's history
Strange's	Rents	Ld. Orrery's
Burrows's	Distresses.	history.
Kaim's Principles of	Ejectments.	Burke's George III.
equity.	Executions.	Robertson's hist. of
Vernon's reports.	Evidence.	Scotl'd.
Peere Williams.	Sayer's lay of costs.	Robertson's hist. of
Precedents in	Lambard's circonan-	America.
Chancery.	tia.	Other American his-
Tracy Atheyns.	Bacon. voce Pleas &	tories.
Verey.	Pleadings	Voltaire's historical
Hawkin's Pleas of the	Cummingham's law	works.
crown.	of bills.	
Blackstone	Molley de jure mar-	
Virginia laws.	itimo.	
	Locke on govern-	
	ment.	
	Montesquieu's Spirit	
	of law.	
	Smith's wealth of	
	nations.	
	Beccaria.	
	Kaim's moral essays.	
	Vattel's law of	
	nations.	

Should there by any little intervals in the day not otherwise occupied fill them up by reading Lowthe's grammar, Blair's lectures on
rhetoric, Mason on poetic & prosaic numbers, Bolingbroke's works for

the sake of the stile, which is declamatory & elegant, the English poets for the sake of style also.

As mr Peter Carr in Goochland is engaged in a course of law reading, and has my books for that purpose, it will be necessary for you to go to mrs Carr's, and to receive such as he shall be then done with, and settle with him a plan of receiving from him regular[ly] the before mentioned books as fast as he shall get through them. The losses I have sustained by lending my books will be my apology to you for asking your particular attention to the replacing them in the presses as fast as you finish them, and not to lend them to anybody else, nor suffer anybody to have a book out of the Study under cover of your name. You will find, when you get there, that I have had reason to ask this exactness.

I would have you determine beforehand to make yourself a thorough lawyer, & not be contented with a mere smattering. It is superiority of knowledge which can alone lift you above the heads of your competitors, and ensure you success. I think therefore you must calculate on devoting between two & three years to this course of reading, before you think of commencing practice. Whenever that begins, there is an end of reading.

I shall be glad to hear from you from time to time, and shall hope to see you in the fall in Albemarle, to which place I propose a visit in that season. In the meantime wishing you all the industry of patient perseverance which this course of reading will require I am with great esteem Dear Sir Your most obedient friend & servant.

TO MARIA JEFFERSON[1]

New York, June 13th, 1790

MY DEAR MARIA:

I have received your letter of May 23d, which was in answer to mine of May 2d, but I wrote you also on the 23d of May, so that you still owe me an answer to that, which I hope is now on the road. In mat-

[1][Randall.]

ters of correspondence as well as of money, you must never be in debt. I am much pleased with the account you give me of your occupations, and the making the pudding is as good an article of them as any. When I come to Virginia I shall insist on eating a pudding of your own making, as well as on trying other specimens of your skill. You must make the most of your time while you are with so good an aunt who can learn you everything. We had not peas nor strawberries here till the 8th day of this month. On the same day I heard the first whip-poor-will whistle. Swallows and martins appeared here on the 21st of April. When did they appear with you? and when had you peas, strawberries, and whip-poor-wills in Virginia? Take notice hereafter whether the whip-poor-wills always come with the strawberries and peas. Send me a copy of the maxims I gave you, also a list of the books I promised you. I have had a long touch of my periodical headache, but a very moderate one. It has not quite left me yet. Adieu, my dear; love your uncle, aunt, and cousins, and me more than all.

TO COUNT DE MOUSTIER

Philadelphia, December 3, 1790

. . . . The powers of the government for the collection of taxes, are found to be perfect, so far as they have been tried. This has been as yet only by duties on consumption. As these fall principally on the rich, it is a general desire to make them contribute the whole money we want, if possible. And we have a hope that they will furnish enough for the expenses of government and the interest of our whole public debt foreign and domestic. If they do this for the present, their increase, from the increase of population and consumption, (which is at the rate of five per centum per annum), will sink the capital in thirteen or fourteen years, as it will operate in the way of compound interest. Independent of this prospect, which is itself a good one, we make the produce of our land office, and some other articles, a sinking fund for the principal. . . .

TO MARTHA JEFFERSON RANDOLPH

Philadelphia, Dec. 23, 1790

MY DEAR DAUGHTER:

This is a scolding letter for you all. I have not received a scrip of a pen from home since I left it. I think it so easy for you to write me one letter every week, which will be but once in the three weeks for each of you, when I write one every week, who have not one moment's repose from business, from the first to the last moment of the week.

Perhaps you think you have nothing to say to me. It is a great deal to say you are well; or that one has a cold, another a fever, etc.: besides that, there is not a sprig of grass that shoots uninteresting to me; nor anything that moves from yourself down to Bergère or Grizzle.[1] Write, then, my dear daughter, punctually on your day, and Mr. Randolph and Polly on theirs. I suspect you may have news to tell me of yourself of the most tender interest to me. Why silent then? . . . .

TO MR. HAZARD[2]

Philadelphia, February 18, 1791

SIR,—I return you the two volumes of records, with thanks for the opportunity of looking into them. They are curious monuments of the infancy of our country. I learn with great satisfaction that you are about committing to the press the valuable historical and State papers you have been so long collecting. Time and accident are committing daily havoc on the originals deposited in our public offices. The late war has done the work of centuries in this business. The last cannot be recovered, but let us save what remains; not by vaults and locks which fence them from the public eye and use in consigning them to the waste of time, but by such a multiplication of copies, as shall place them beyond the reach of accident. This being the tendency of your

[1]These were the shepherd dogs Jefferson brought with him from France.

[2]Ebenezer Hazard was engaged in collecting and preparing for publication early Virginia and America documents.

undertaking, be assured there is no one who wishes it more success than, Sir, your most obedient, and most humble servant.

TO MAJOR L'ENFANT[1]

Philadelphia, April 10, 1791

SIR,—I am favored with your letter of the 4th instant, and in compliance with your request, I have examined my papers, and found the plans of Frankfort-on-the-Mayne, Carlsruhe, Amsterdam, Strasburg, Paris, Orleans, Bordeaux, Lyons, Montpelier, Marseilles, Turin, and Milan, which I send in a roll by the post. They are on large and accurate scales, having been procured by me while in those respective cities myself. As they are connected with the notes I made in my travels, and often necessary to explain them to myself, I will beg your care of them, and to return them when no longer useful to you, leaving you absolutely free to keep them as long as useful. I am happy that the President has left the planning of the town in such good hands, and have no doubt it will be done to general satisfaction. Considering that the grounds to be reserved for the public are to be paid for by the acre, I think very liberal reservations should be made for them; and if this be about the Tyber and on the back of the town, it will be of no injury to the commerce of the place, which will undoubtedly establish itself on the deep waters towards the eastern branch and mouth of Rock Creek; the water about the mouth of the Tyber not being of any depth. Those connected with the government will prefer fixing themselves near the public grounds in the centre, which will also be convenient to be resorted to as walks from the lower and upper town. Having communicated to the President, before he went away, such general ideas on the subject of the town as occurred to me, I make no doubt that, in explaining himself to you on the subject, he has interwoven with his own ideas, such of mine as he approved. For fear of repeating therefore what he did not approve, and having more confidence in the unbiassed state of his mind, than in my own, I avoided interfer-

[1]Pierre Charles L'Enfant, Paris born soldier, artist, and engineer, was at this time planning the New Federal City which was to become Washington, D. C.

ing with what he may have expressed to you. Whenever it is proposed to prepare plans for the Capitol, I should prefer the adoption of some one of the models of antiquity, which have had the approbation of thousands of years; and for the President's house, I should prefer the celebrated fronts of modern buildings, which have already received the approbation of all good judges. Such are the Galerie du Louire, the Gardes meubles, and two fronts of the Hotel de Salm. But of this it is yet time enough to consider. In the meantime I am, with great esteem, Sir, your most obedient humble servant.

TO THOMAS MANN RANDOLPH

Bennington, in Vermont, June 5, 1791

DEAR SIR,—Mr. Madison and myself are so far on the tour we had projected. We have visited, in the course of it, the principal scenes of General Burgoyne's misfortunes, to wit, the grounds at Stillwater, where the action of that name was fought, and particularly the breastworks, which cost so much blood to both parties, the encampments at Saratoga and ground where the British piled their arms, and the field of the battle of Bennington, about nine miles from this place. We have also visited Forts William, Henry and George, Ticonderoga, Crown Point, etc., which have been scenes of blood from a very early part of our history. We were more pleased, however, with the botanical objects which continually presented themselves. Those either unknown or rare in Virginia, were the sugar maple in vast abundance. The silver fir, white pine, pitch pine, spruce pine, a shrub with decumbent stems, which they call juniper, an aralea, very different from the nudiflora, with very large clusters of flowers, more thickly set on the branches, of a deeper red, and high pink-fragrance. It is the richest shrub I have seen. The honey-suckle of the gardens growing wild on the banks of Lake George, the paper-birch, an aspen with a velvet leaf, a shrub-willow with downy catkins, a wild gooseberry, the wild cherry with single fruit (not the bunch cherry), strawberries in abundance. . . .

TO T. M. RANDOLPH

Philadelphia, July 3, 1791

You will observe by the enclosed and preceding papers that I am mentioned on the subject of Paine's pamphlet on The Rights of Man; and you will have seen a note of mine prefixed to that pamphlet whence it has been inferred that I furnished the pamphlet to the printer and procured its publication. This is not true. The fact was this: Mr. Beckley had the only copy of that pamphlet in town. He lent it to Mr. Madison, who lent it to me under the injunction to return it to Mr. Beckley within the day. Beckley came for it before I had finished reading it and desired as soon as I had done I would send it to a Mr. Jonathan B. Smith whose brother was to reprint it. Being an utter stranger to Mr. J. B. Smith I explained to him in a note that I sent the pamphlet to him by order of Mr. Beckley, and to take off somewhat of the dryness of the note I added that I was glad to find it was to be reprinted here, etc., as you have seen in the printed note. I thought so little of this note that I did not even retain a copy of it; and without the least information or suspicion that it would be published, out it comes the next week at the head of the pamphlet. I knew immediately that it would give displeasure to some gentlemen just by the chair of government who were in sentiment with Burke and as much opposed to the sentiments of Paine.

I could not disavow my note, because I had written it. I could not disavow my approbation of the pamphlet, because I was fully in sentiment with it, and it would have been trifling to have disavowed merely the publication of the note approving at the same time of the pamphlet. I determined, therefore, to be utterly silent except so far as verbal explanations could be made.

The Vice-President, who is at Boston, took up the cudgels under the name of Publicola. He is in turn assailed by a host of republican champions. I think it probable he will be aided by some of his compeers, but, more cautious than he, they will mask themselves better. For my part I am determined to let them write and wrangle as they please without intermeddling in word or deed.

I am unable as yet to fix a time for my trip to Virginia. It must depend on the movements of the President. I foresee nothing in the public affairs which threatens impediment. Present me affectionately to my daughters, and believe me to be, dear Sir, yours sincerely.

TO JOHN ADAMS

Philadelphia, July 17, 1791

DEAR SIR,—I have a dozen times taken up my pen to write to you, and as often laid it down again, suspended between opposing considerations. I determine, however, to write from a conviction that truth, between candid minds, can never do harm. The first of Paine's pamphlets on the rights of man, which came to hand here, belonged to Mr. Beckley. He lent it to Mr. Madison, who lent it to me; and while I was reading it, Mr. Beckley called on me for it, and, as I had not finished it, he desired me, as soon as I should have done so, to send it to Mr. Jonathan B. Smith, whose brother meant to reprint it. I finished reading it, and, as I had no acquaintance with Mr. Jonathan B. Smith, propriety required that I should explain to him why I, a stranger to him, sent him the pamphlet. I accordingly wrote a note of compliment, informing him that I did it at the desire of Mr. Beckley, and, to take off a little of the dryness of the note, I added that I was glad it was to be reprinted here, and that something was to be publicly said against the political heresies which had sprung up among us, etc. I thought so little of this note, that I did not even keep a copy of it; nor ever heard a tittle more of it, till, the week following, I was thunderstruck with seeing it come out at the head of the pamphlet. I hoped, however, it would not attract notice. But I found, on my return from a journey of a month, that a writer came forward, under the signature of Publicola, attacking not only the author and principles of the pamphlet, but myself as its sponsor, by name. Soon after came hosts of other writers, defending the pamphlet, and attacking you, by name, as the writer of Publicola. Thus were our names thrown on the public stage as public antagonists. That you and I differ in our ideas of the best form of government, is well known to us both; but we have differed as friends should do, respecting the purity of each other's motives, and confining our difference of opinion to private conversation. And I can declare with truth, in the presence of the Almighty, that nothing was further from my intention or expectation than to have either my own or your name brought before the public on this occasion. The friendship and confidence which has so long existed between us, required this explanation from me, and I know you too well to fear any misconstruction of the motives of it. Some people here who would wish me to be, or to be thought, guilty of improprieties, have suggested that I was Agricola, that I was Brutus, etc., etc. I never did in my life, either by myself or by any other, have a sentence of mine inserted in a newspaper without putting my name to it; and I believe I never shall.

TO WILLIAM SHORT[1]

Philadelphia, July 28, 1791

Whenever jealousies are expressed as to any supposed views of ours, on the dominion of the West Indies, you cannot go farther than the truth, in asserting we have none. If there be one principle more deeply rooted than any other in the mind of every American, it is, that we should have nothing to do with conquest. As to commerce, indeed, we have strong sensations. In casting our eyes over the earth, we see no instance of a nation forbidden, as we are, by foreign powers, to deal with neighbors, and obliged, with them, to carry into another hemisphere, the mutual supplies necessary to relieve mutual wants. This is not merely a question between the foreign power and our neighbor. We are interested in it equally with the latter, and nothing but moderation, at least with respect to us, can render us indifferent to its continuance. An exchange of surplusses and wants between neighbor nations, is both a right and a duty under the moral law, and measures against right should be mollified in their exercise, if it be wished to lengthen them to the greatest term possible. Circumstances sometimes require, that rights the most unquestionable should be advanced with delicacy. It would seem that the one now spoken of, would need only a mention, to be assented to by any unprejudiced mind: but with

[1]William Short, American diplomat, was Jefferson's protégé and intimate friend. He had served as Jefferson's private secretary in Paris, and, at the time of this letter, was American chargé d'affaires in Paris.

respect to America, Europeans in general, have been too long in the habit of confounding force with right. The Marquis de La Fayette stands in such a relation between the two countries, that I should think him perfectly capable of seeing what is just as to both. Perhaps on some occasion of free conversation, you might find an opportunity of impressing these truths on his mind, and that from him, they might be let out at a proper moment as matters meriting consideration and weight, when they shall be engaged in the work of forming a constitution for our neighbors. In policy, if not in justice, they should be disposed to avoid oppression, which, falling on us, as well as on their colonies, might tempt us to act together. . . .

TO BENJAMIN BANNEKER[1]

Philadelphia, August 30, 1791

SIR,—I thank you sincerely for your letter of the 19th instant, and for the Almanac it contained. Nobody wishes more than I do to see such proofs as you exhibit, that nature has given to our black brethren, talents equal to those of the other colors of men, and that the appearance of a want of them is owing merely to the degraded condition of their existence, both in Africa and America. I can add with truth, that nobody wishes more ardently to see a good system commenced for raising the condition both of their body and mind to what it ought to be, as fast as the imbecility of their present existence, and other circumstances which cannot be neglected, will admit. I have taken the liberty of sending your Almanac to Monsieur de Condorcet, Secretary of the Academy of Sciences at Paris, and member of the Philanthropic Society, because I considered it as a document to which your color had a right for their justification against the doubts which have been entertained of them. I am, with great esteem, Sir, your most obedient humble servant.

---

[1]Benjamin Banneker, a Negro, was born in Baltimore County, Maryland; although lacking any formal education, he invented, among other things, a clock, and published an almanac for several years.

TO MARTHA JEFFERSON RANDOLPH

Philadelphia, January 15th, 1792[1]

MY DEAR MARTHA,—Having no particular subject for a letter, I find none more soothing to my mind than to indulge itself in expressions of the love I bear you, and the delight with which I recall the various scenes through which we have passed together in our wanderings over the world. These reveries alleviate the toils and inquietudes of my present situation, and leave me always impressed with the desire of being at home once more, and of exchanging labor, envy, and malice for ease, domestic occupation, and domestic love and society; where I may once more be happy with you, with Mr. Randolph and dear little Anne, with whom even Socrates might ride on a stick without being ridiculous. Indeed it is with difficulty that my resolution will bear me through what yet lies between the present day and that which, on mature consideration of all circumstances respecting myself and others, my mind has determined to be the proper one for relinquishing my office. Though not very distant, it is not near enough for my wishes. The ardor of these, however, would be abated if I thought that, on coming home, I should be left alone. On the contrary, I hope that Mr. Randolph will find a convenience in making only leisurely preparations for a settlement, and that I shall be able to make you both happier than you have been at Monticello, and relieve you of désagréments to which I have been sensible you were exposed, without the power in myself to prevent it, but by my own presence. Remember me affectionately to Mr. Randolph, and be assured of the tender love of yours.

TO THE PRESIDENT OF THE UNITED STATES[2]

Philadelphia, May 23, 1792

DEAR SIR,—I have determined to make the subject of a letter what for some time past has been a subject of inquietude to my mind, with-

[1][Ford.]

[2]George Washington.

out having found a good occasion of disburthening itself to you in conversation, during the busy scenes which occupied you here. Perhaps, too, you may be able in your present situation, or on the road, to give it more time and reflection than you could do here at any moment.

When you first mentioned to me your purpose of retiring from the government, though I felt all the magnitude of the event, I was in a considerable degree silent. I knew that, to such a mind as yours, persuasion was idle and impertinent; that before forming your decision you had weighed all the reasons for and against the measure, had made up your mind on full view of them, and that there could be little hope of changing the result. Pursuing my reflections, too, I knew we were some day to try to walk alone, and if the essay should be made while you should be alive and looking on, we should derive confidence from that circumstance, and resource, if it failed. The public mind, too, was calm and confident, and therefore in a favorable state for making the experiment. Had no change of circumstances intervened, I should not, with any hopes of success, have now ventured to propose to you a change of purpose. But the public mind is no longer confident and serene; and that from causes in which you are no ways personally mixed. Though these causes have been hackneyed in the public papers in detail, it may not be amiss, in order to calculate the effect they are capable of producing, to take a view of them in the mass, giving to each the form, real or imaginary, under which they have been presented.

It has been urged, then, that a public debt, greater than we can possibly pay, before other causes of adding new debt to it will occur, has been artificially created by adding together the whole amount of the debtor and creditor sides of accounts, instead of only taking their balances, which could have been paid off in a short time: that this accumulation of debt has taken forever out of our power those easy sources of revenue which applied to the ordinary necessities and exigencies of government, would have answered them habitually, and covered us from habitual murmurings against taxes and tax-gatherers, reserving extraordinary calls for those extraordinary occasions which would animate the people to meet them: that though the calls for money have been no greater than we must expect generally, for the same or equivalent exigencies, yet we are already obliged to strain the impost till it produces clamor, and will produce evasion and war on our own citi-

zens to collect it, and even to resort to an *excise* law of odious character with the people, partial in its operation, unproductive unless
enforced by arbitrary and vexatious means, and committing the authority of the government in parts where resistance is most probable and
coercion least practicable. They cite propositions in Congress, and suspect other projects on foot still to increase the mass of debt. They say,
that by borrowing at two-thirds of the interest, we might have paid
off the principal in two-thirds of the time; but that from this we are
precluded by its being made irredeemable but in small portions and
long terms; that this irredeemable quality was given it for the avowed
purpose of inviting its transfer to foreign countries. They predict that
this transfer of the principal, when completed, will occasion an exportation of three millions of dollars annually for the interest, a drain of
coin, of which, as there has been no examples, no calculation can be
made of its consequences: that the banishment of our coin will be complicated by the creation of ten millions of paper money, in the form
of bank bills now issuing into circulation. They think the ten or twelve
per cent. annual profit paid to the lenders of this paper medium taken
out of the pockets of the people, who would have had without interest
the coin it is banishing: that all the capital employed in paper speculation is barren and useless, producing, like that on a gaming table,
no accession to itself, and is withdrawn from commerce and agriculture, where it would have produced addition to the common mass: that
it nourishes in our citizens habits of vice and idleness, instead of industry and morality: that it has furnished effectual means of corrupting
such a portion of the legislature as turns the balance between the honest voters, whichever way it is directed: that this corrupt squadron,
deciding the voice of the legislature, have manifested their dispositions
to get rid of the limitations imposed by the Constitution on the general
legislature, limitations, on the faith of which, the States acceded to that
instrument: that the ultimate object of all this is to prepare the way
for a change from the present republican form of government to that of
a monarchy, of which the English Constitution is to be the model: that
this was contemplated by the convention is no secret, because its partisans have made more of it. To effect it then was impracticable, but
they are still eager after their object, and are predisposing everything
for its ultimate attainment. So many of them have got into the Legis-

lature, that, aided by the corrupt squadron of paper dealers, who are at their devotion, they make a majority in both houses. The republican party, who wish to preserve the government in its present form, are fewer in number; they are fewer even when joined by the two, three, or half dozen anti-federalists, who, though they dare not avow it, are still opposed to any General Government; but being less so to a republican than a monarchical one, they naturally join those whom they think pursuing the lesser evil.

Of all the mischiefs objected to the system of measures before mentioned, none is so afflicting and fatal to every honest hope, as the corruption of the Legislature. As it was the earliest of these measures, it became the instrument for producing the risk, and will be the instrument for producing in future a king, lords and commons, or whatever else those who direct it may choose. Withdrawn such a distance from the eye of their constituents, and these so dispersed as to be inaccessible to public information, and particularly to that of the conduct of their own representatives, they will form the most corrupt government on earth, if the means of their corruption be not prevented. The only hope of safety hangs now on the numerous representation which is to come forward the ensuing year. Some of the new members will be, probably, either in principle or interest, with the present majority; but it is expected that the great mass will form an accession to the republican party. They will not be able to undo all which the two preceding Legislatures, and especially the first, have done. Public faith and right will oppose this. But some parts of the system may be rightfully reformed, a liberation from the rest unremittingly pursued as fast as right will permit, and the door shut in future against similar commitments of the nation. Should the next Legislature take this course, it will draw upon them the whole monarchical and paper interest; but the latter, I think, will not go all lengths with the former, because creditors will never, of their own accord, fly off entirely from their debtors; therefore, this is the alternative least likely to produce convulsion. But should the majority of the new members be still in the same principles with the present, and show that we have nothing to expect but a continuance of the same practices, it is not easy to conjecture what would be the result, nor what means would be resorted to for correction of the evil. True wisdom would direct that they should be temperate and peaceable; but the division of sentiment and interest happens unfortunately to be so geographical, that no mortal can say that what is most wise and temperate would prevail against what is most easy and obvious? I can scarcely contemplate a more incalculable evil than the breaking of the Union into two or more parts. Yet when we consider the mass which opposed the original coalescence; when we consider that it lay chiefly in the Southern quarter; that the Legislature have availed themselves of no occasion of allaying it, but on the contrary, whenever Northern and Southern prejudices have come into conflict, the latter have been sacrificed and the former soothed; that the owners of the debt are in the Southern, and the holders of it in the Northern division; that the anti-federal champions are now strengthened in argument by the fulfillment of their predictions; that this has been brought about by the monarchical federalists themselves, who, having been for the new government merely as a stepping stone to monarchy, have themselves adopted the very constructions of the Constitution, of which, when advocating its acceptance before the tribunal of the people, they declared it unsusceptible; that the republican federalists who espoused the same government for its intrinsic merits, are disarmed of their weapons; that which they denied as prophecy, having now become true history, who can be sure that these things may not proselyte the small number which was wanting to place the majority on the other side? And this is the event at which I tremble, and to prevent which I consider your continuing at the head of affairs as of the last importance. The confidence of the whole Union is centred in you. Your being at the helm will be more than an answer to every argument which can be used to alarm and lead the people in any quarter, into violence and secession. North and South will hang together if they have you to hang on; and if the first correction of a numerous representation should fail in its effect, your presence will give time for trying others, not inconsistent with the union and peace of the States.

I am perfectly aware of the oppression under which your present office lays your mind, and of the ardor with which you pant for domestic life. But there is sometimes an eminence of character on which society have such peculiar claims as to control the predilections of the individual for a particular walk of happiness, and restrain him to that alone arising from the present and future benedictions of mankind. This seems to be your condition, and the law imposed on you by providence in forming your character, and fashioning the events on which it was to operate; and it is to motives like these, and not to personal anxieties of mine or others who have no right to call on you for sacrifices, that I appeal, and urge a revisal of it, on the ground of change in the aspect of things. Should an honest majority result from the new and enlarged representation; should those acquiesce whose principles or interest they may control, your wishes for retirement would be gratified with less danger, as soon as that shall be manifest, without awaiting the completion of the second period of four years. One or two sessions will determine the crisis; and I cannot but hope that you can resolve to add more to the many years you have already sacrificed to the good of mankind.

The fear of suspicion that any selfish motive of continuance in office may enter into this solicitation on my part, obliges me to declare that no such motive exists. It is a thing of mere indifference to the public whether I retain or relinquish my purpose of closing my tour with the first periodical renovation of the government. I know my own measure too well to suppose that my services contribute anything to the public confidence, or the public utility. Multitudes can fill the office in which you have been pleased to place me, as much to their advantage and satisfaction. I have, therefore, no motive to consult but my own inclination, which is bent irresistibly on the tranquil enjoyment of my family, my farm and my books. I should repose among them, it is true, in far greater security, if I were to know that you remained at the watch; and I hope it will be so. To the inducements urged from a view of our domestic affairs, I will add a bare mention, of what indeed need only to be mentioned, that weighty motives for your continuance are to be found in our foreign affairs. I think it probable that both the Spanish and English negotiations, if not completed before your purpose is known, will be suspended from the moment it is known, and that the latter nation will then use double diligence in fomenting the Indian War. With my wishes for the future, I shall at the same time express my gratitude for the past, at least my portion in it; and beg permission to follow you, whether in public or private life, with those sentiments of sincere attachment and respect, with which I am unalterably, dear Sir, your affectionate friend and humble servant.

TO THOMAS PAINE

Philadelphia, June 19, 1792[1]

DEAR SIR,—I received with great pleasure the present of your pamphlets, as well as for the thing itself as that it was a testimony of your recollection. Would you believe it possible that in this country there should be high & important characters who need your lessons in republicanism, & who do not heed them? It is but too true that we have a sect preaching up pouting after an English constitution of king, lords, & commons, & whose heads are itching for crowns, coronets & mitres. But our people, my good friend, are firm and unanimous in their principles of republicanism & there is no better proof of it than that they love what you write and read it with delight. The printers season every newspaper with extracts from your last, as they did before from your first part of the *Rights of Man*. They have both served here to separate the wheat from the chaff, and to prove that tho' the latter appears on the surface, it is on the surface only. The bulk below is sound & pure. Go on then in doing with your pen what in other times was done with the sword: shew that reformation is more practicable by operating on the mind than on the body of man, and be assured that it has not a more sincere votary nor you a more ardent well-wisher than Yrs. &c.

TO THE PRESIDENT OF THE UNITED STATES

Monticello, September 9, 1792

. . . . I now take the liberty of proceeding to that part of your letter wherein you notice the internal dissensions which have taken place within our government, and their disagreeable effect on its movements. That such dissensions have taken place is certain, and even among those who are nearest to you in the administration. To no one have

[1][Ford.]

they given deeper concern than myself; to no one equal mortification at being myself a part of them. Though I take to myself no more than my share of the general observations of your letter, yet I am so desirous ever that you should know the whole truth, and believe no more than the truth, that I am glad to seize every occasion of developing to you whatever I do or think relative to the government; and shall, therefore, ask permission to be more lengthy now than the occasion particularly calls for, or could otherwise perhaps justify.

When I embarked in the government, it was with a determination to intermeddle not at all with the Legislature, and as little as possible with my co-departments. The first and only instance of variance from the former part of my resolution, I was duped into by the Secretary of the Treasury, and made a tool for forwarding his schemes, not then sufficiently understood by me; and of all the errors of my political life, this has occasioned me the deepest regret. It has ever been my purpose to explain this to you, when, from being actors on the scene, we shall have become uninterested spectators only. The second part of my resolution has been religiously observed with the War Department; and as to that of the Treasury, has never been further swerved from than by the mere enunciation of my sentiments in conversation, and chiefly among those who, expressing the same sentiments, drew mine from me. If it has been supposed that I have ever intrigued among the members of the Legislature to defeat the plans of the Secretary of the Treasury, it is contrary to all truth. As I never had the desire to influence the members, so neither had I any other means than my friendships, which I valued too highly to risk by usurpation on their freedom of judgment, and the conscientious pursuit of their own sense of duty. That I have utterly, in my private conversations, disapproved of the system of the Secretary of the Treasury, I acknowledge and avow; and this was not merely a speculative difference. His system flowed from principles adverse to liberty, and was calculated to undermine and demolish the Republic, by creating an influence of his department over the members of the Legislature. I saw this influence actually produced, and its first fruits to be the establishment of the great outlines of his project by the votes of the very persons who, having swallowed his bait, were laying themselves out to profit by his plans; and that had these persons withdrawn, as those interested in a question ever should, the vote of the disinterested majority was clearly the reverse of what they made it. These were no longer the votes then of the representatives of the people, but of deserters from the rights and interests of the people; and it was impossible to consider their decisions, which had nothing in view but to enrich themselves, as the measures of the fair majority, which ought always to be respected. If, what was actually doing, begat uneasiness in those who wished for virtuous government, what was further proposed was not less threatening to the friends of the Constitution. For, in a report on the subject of manufactures, (still to be acted on), it was expressly assumed that the General Government has a right to exercise all powers which may be for the *general welfare*, that is to say, all the legitimate powers of government; since no government has a legitimate right to do what is not for the welfare of the governed. There was, indeed, a sham limitation of the universality of this power *to cases where money is to be employed*. But about what is it that money cannot be employed? Thus the object of these plans, taken together, is to draw all the powers of government into the hands of the general Legislature, to establish means for corrupting a sufficient corps in that Legislature to divide the honest votes, and preponderate, by their own, the scale which suited, and to have the corps under the command of the Secretary of the Treasury, for the purpose of subverting, step by step, the principles of the Constitution which he has so often declared to be a thing of nothing, which must be changed. Such views might have justified something more than mere expressions of dissent, beyond which, nevertheless, I never went. Has abstinence from the department, committed to me, been equally observed by him? To say nothing of other interferences equally known, in the case of the two nations, with which we have the most intimate connections, France and England, my system was to give some satisfactory distinctions to the former, of little cost to us, in return for the solid advantages yielded us by them; and to have met the English with some restrictions which might induce them to abate their severities against our commerce. I have always supposed this coincided with your sentiments. Yet the Secretary of the Treasury, by his cabals with members of the Legislature, and by high-toned declamations on other occasions, has forced down his own system, which was exactly the reverse. He undertook, of his own authority, the conferences with the ministers of those two nations, and was, on every consultation, provided with some report of a conversation with the one or the other of them, adapted to his views. These views, thus made to prevail, their execution fell, of course, to me; and I can safely appeal to you, who have seen all my letters and proceedings, whether I have not carried them into execution as sincerely as if they had been my own, though I ever considered them as inconsistent with the honor and interest of our country. That they have been inconsistent with our interest is but too fatally proved by the stab to our navigation given by the French. So that if the question be by whose fault is it that Colonel Hamilton and myself have not drawn together? the answer will depend on that to two other questions, whose principles of administration best justify, by their purity, conscientious adherence? and which of us has, notwithstanding, stepped farthest into the control of the department of the other? . . . .

When I came into this office, it was with a resolution to retire from it as soon as I could with decency. It pretty early appeared to me that the proper moment would be the first of those epochs at which the Constitution seems to have contemplated a periodical change or renewal of the public servants. In this I was confirmed by your resolution respecting the same period; from which, however, I am happy in hoping you have departed. I look to that period with the longing of a wave-worn mariner, who has at length the land in view, and shall count the days and hours which still lie between me and it. In the meanwhile, my main object will be to wind up the business of my office, avoiding as much as possible all new enterprise. With the affairs of the Legislature, as I never did intermeddle, so I certainly shall not now begin. I am more desirous to predispose everything for the repose to which I am withdrawing, than expose it to be disturbed by newspaper contests. If these, however, cannot be avoided altogether, yet a regard for your quiet will be a sufficient motive for my deferring it till I become merely a private citizen, when the propriety or impropriety of what I may say or do, may fall on myself alone. I may then, too, avoid the charge of misapplying that time which now, belonging to those who employ me, should be wholly devoted to their service. If my own justification, or the interests of the republic shall require it, I reserve to myself the right of then appealing to my country, subscribing my name to whatever I write, and using with freedom and truth the facts and names necessary to place the cause in its just form before that tribunal. To a thorough disregard of the honors and emoluments of office, I join as great a value for the esteem of my countrymen, and conscious of having merited it by an integrity which cannot be reproached, and by an enthusiastic devotion to their rights and liberty, I will not suffer my retirement to be clouded by the slanders of a man whose history, from the moment at which history can stoop to notice him, is a tissue of machinations against the liberty of the country which has not only received and given him bread, but heaped its honors on his head. Still, however, I repeat the hope that it will not be necessary to make such an appeal. Though little known to the people of America, I believe, that as far as I am known, it is not as an enemy to the Republic, nor an intriguer against it, nor a waster of its revenue, nor prostitutor of it to the purposes of corruption, as the "American" represents me; and I confide that yourself are satisfied that as to dissensions in the newspapers, not a syllable of them has ever proceeded from me, and that no cabals or intrigues of mine have produced those in the Legislature, and I hope I may promise both to you and myself, that none will receive aliment from me during the short space I have to remain in office, which will find ample employment in closing the present business of the department.

TO WILLIAM SHORT

Philadelphia, January 3, 1793

. . . . The tone of your letters had for some time given me pain, on account of the extreme warmth with which they censured the proceedings of the Jacobins of France. I considered that sect as the same with the Republican patriots, and the Feuillants as the Monarchical patriots, well known in the early part of the Revolution, and but little distant in their views, both having in object the establishment of a free constitution, differing only on the question whether their chief Executive should be hereditary or not. The Jacobins (as since called) yielded to the Feuillants, and tried the experiment of retaining their hereditary Executive. The experiment failed completely, and would have brought on the re-establishment of despotism had it been pursued. The Jacobins knew this, and that the expunging that office was of absolute necessity. And the nation was with them in opinion, for however they might have been formerly for the constitution framed by the first assembly, they were come over from their hope in it, and were now generally Jacobins. In the struggle which was necessary, many guilty persons fell without the forms of trial, and with them some innocent. These I deplore as much as anybody, and shall deplore some of them to the day of my death. But I deplore them as I should have done had they fallen in battle. It was necessary to use the arm of the people, a machine not quite so blind as balls and bombs, but blind to a certain degree. A few of their cordial friends met at their hands the fate of enemies. But time and truth will rescue and embalm their memories, while their posterity will be enjoying that very liberty for which they would never have hesitated to offer up their lives. The liberty of the whole earth was depending on the issue of the contest, and was ever such a prize won with so little innocent blood? My own affections have been deeply wounded by some of the martyrs of this cause, but rather than it should have failed I would have seen half the earth desolated; were there but an Adam and an Eve left in every country, and left free, it would be better than as it now is. . . .

TO JAMES MADISON

Philadelphia, June 9, 1793

I have to acknowledge the receipt of your two favors of May 27th and 29th, since the date of my last which was of the 2d instant. In that of the 27th you say you must not make your final exit from public life till it will be marked with justifying circumstances which all good citizens will respect, and to which your friends can appeal. To my fellow-citizens the debt of service has been fully and faithfully paid. I acknowledge that such a debt exists, that a tour of duty, in whatever line he can be most useful to his country, is due from every individual. It is not easy perhaps to say of what length exactly this tour should be, but we may safely say of what length it should not be. Not of our whole life, for instance, for that would be to be born a slave—not even of a very large portion of it. I have now been in the public service four and twenty years; one half of which has been spent in total occupation with their affairs, and absence from my own. I have served my tour then. No positive engagement, by word or deed, binds me to their further service. No commitment of their interests in any enterprise by me requires that I should see them through it. I am pledged by no act which gives any tribunal a call upon me before I withdraw. Even my enemies do not pretend this. I stand clear then of public right on all points—my friends I have not committed. No circumstances have attended my passage from office to office, which could lead them, and others through them, into deception as to the time I might remain, and particularly they and all have known with what reluctance I engaged and have continued in the present one, and of my uniform determination to return from it at an early day. If the public then has no claim on me, and my friends nothing to justify, the decision will rest on my own feelings alone. There has been a time when these were very different from what they are now; when perhaps the esteem of the world was of higher value in my eye than everything in it. But age, experience and reflection preserving to that only its due value, have set a higher on tranquillity. The motion of my blood no longer keeps time with the tumult of the world. It leads me to seek for happiness in the lap and love of my family, in the society of my neighbors and my books, in the wholesome occupations of my farm and my affairs, in an interest or affection in every bud that opens, in every breath that blows around me, in an entire freedom of rest, of motion of thought, owing account to myself alone of my hours and actions. What must be the principle of that calculation which should balance against these the circumstances of my present existence—worn down with labors from morning to night, and day to day; knowing them as fruitless to others as they are vexatious to myself, committed singly in desperate and eternal contest against a host who are systematically undermining the public liberty and prosperity, even the rare hours of relaxation sacrificed to the society of persons in the same intentions, of whose hatred I am conscious even in those moments of conviviality when the heart wishes most to open itself to the effusions of friendship and confidence, cut off from my family and friends, my affairs abandoned to chaos and derangement, in short, giving everything I love in exchange for everything I hate, and all this without a single gratification in possession or prospect, in present enjoyment or future wish. Indeed, my dear friend, duty being out of the question, inclination cuts off all argument, and so never let there be more between you and me, on this subject.

I enclose you some papers which have passed on the subject of a new town. You will see by them that the paper Coryphæus is either undaunted or desperate. I believe that the statement enclosed has secured a decision against his proposition. I dined yesterday in a company where Morris and Bingham were, and happened to sit between them. In the course of a conversation after dinner, Morris made one of his warm declarations that after the expiration of his present senatorial term, nothing on earth should ever engage him to serve again in any public capacity. He did this with such solemnity as renders it impossible he should not be in earnest. The President is not well. Little lingering fevers have been hanging about him for a week or ten days, and affected his looks most remarkably. He is also extremely affected by the attacks made and kept up on him in the public papers. I think he feels those things more than any person I ever yet met with. I am sincerely sorry to see them. I remember an observation of yours, made when I first went to New York, that the satellites and sycophants which surrounded him had wound up the ceremonials of the government to a pitch of stateliness which nothing but his personal character could have supported, and which no character after him could ever maintain. It appears now that even his will be insufficient to justify them in the appeal of the times to common sense as the arbiter of everything. Naked he would have been sanctimoniously reverenced; but enveloped in the rags of royalty, they can hardly be torn off without laceration. It is the more unfortunate that this attack is planted on popular ground, on the love of the people to France and its cause, which is universal. Genet mentions freely enough in conversation that France does not wish to involve us in the war by our guarantee. The information from St. Domingo and Martinique is, that those two islands are disposed and able to resist any attack which Great Britain can make on them by land. A blockade would be dangerous, could it be maintained in that climate for any length of time. I delivered to Genet your letter to Roland. As the latter is out of office, he will direct it to the Minister of the Interior. I found every syllable of it strictly proper. Your ploughs shall be duly attended to. Have you ever taken notice of Tull's horse-houghing plough? I am persuaded that[1] where you wish your work to be very exact, and our great plough where a less degree will suffice, leave us nothing to wish for from other countries as to ploughs, under our circumstances. I have not yet received my threshing machine. I fear the late, long, and heavy rains must have extended to us, and affected our wheat. Adieu. Yours affectionately.

TO THE PRESIDENT OF THE UNITED STATES

Philadelphia, July 31, 1793

DEAR SIR,—When you did me the honor of appointing me to the office I now hold, I engaged in it without a view of continuing any length of time, and I pretty early concluded on the close of the first four years of our Republic as a proper period for withdrawing; which I had the honor of communicating to you. When the period, however, arrived, circumstances had arisen, which, in the opinion of some of my friends, rendered it proper to postpone my purpose for awhile. These circumstances have now ceased in such a degree as to leave me free to think again of a day on which I may withdraw without its exciting disadvantageous opinions or conjectures of any kind. The close of the present quarter seems to be a convenient period, because the quarterly accounts of the domestic department are then settled of course, and by that time, also, I may hope to receive from abroad the materials for bringing up the foreign account to the end of its third year. At the close, therefore, of the ensuing month of September, I shall beg leave to retire to scenes of greater tranquillity, from those which I am every day more and more convinced that neither my talents, tone of mind, nor time of life fit me. I have thought it my duty to mention the matter thus early, that there may be time for the arrival of a successor, from any part of the Union from which you may think proper to call one. That you may find one more able to lighten the burthen of your labors, I most sincerely wish; for no man living more sincerely wishes that your administration could be rendered as pleasant to your-

[1]Correct in Ford; unintelligible in Memorial Edition.

self, as it is useful and necessary to our country, nor feels for you a more rational or cordial attachment and respect than, dear Sir, your most obedient, and most humble servant.

TO ELI WHITNEY

Germantown, November. 16, 1793[1]

SIR,—Your favor of Oct. 15. inclosing a drawing of your cotton gin, was received on the 6th inst. The only requisite of the law now uncomplied with is the forwarding a model, which being received, your patent may be made out & delivered to your order immediately.

As the state of Virginia, of which I am, carries on household manufactures of cotton to a great extent, as I also do myself, and one of our great embarrassments is the clearing the cotton of the seed, I feel a considerable interest in the success of your invention for family use. Permit me therefore to ask information from you on these points. Has the machine been thoroughly tried in the ginning of cotton, or is it as yet but a machine of theory? What quantity of cotton has it cleaned on on average of several days, & worked by hand, & by how many hands? What will be the cost of one of them made to be worked by hand? Favorable answers to these questions would induce me to engage one of them to be forwarded to Richmond for me. . . .

TO JOHN ADAMS

Monticello, Apr. 25, 1794[2]

DEAR SIR,—I am to thank you for the book you were so good as to transmit me, as well as the letter covering it, and your felicitations on my present quiet. The difference of my present & past situation is such as to leave me nothing to regret, but that my retirement has been postponed four years too long. The principles on which I calculate the value of life, are entirely in favor of my present course. I return to farming

[1][Ford.]

[2][Ford.]

with an ardor which I scarcely knew in my youth, and which has got the better entirely of my love of study. Instead of writing 10. or 12. letters a day, which I have been in the habit of doing as a thing of course, I put off answering my letters now, farmer-like, till a rainy day, & then find it sometimes postponed by other necessary occupations. The case of the Pays de Vaud is new to me. The claims of both parties are on grounds which, I fancy, we have taught the world to set little store by. The rights of one generation will scarcely be considered hereafter as depending on the paper transactions of another. My countrymen are groaning under the insults of Gr Britain. I hope some means will turn up of reconciling our faith & honor with peace. I confess to you I have seen enough of one war never to wish to see another. With wishes of every degree of happiness to you, both public & private, and with my best respects to Mrs. Adams, I am, your affectionate & humble servant.

TO TENCH COXE[1]

Monticello, May 1, 1794

. . . . Your letters give a comfortable view of French affairs, and later events seem to confirm it. Over the foreign powers I am convinced they will triumph completely, and I cannot but hope that that triumph, and the consequent disgrace of the invading tyrants, is destined, in order of events, to kindle the wrath of the people of Europe against those who have dared to embroil them in such wickedness, and to bring at length, kings, nobles and priests to the scaffolds which they have been so long deluging with human blood. I am still warm whenever I think of these scoundrels, though I do it as seldom as I can, preferring infinitely to contemplate the tranquil growth of my lucerne and potatoes. I have so completely withdrawn myself from these spectacles of usurpation and misrule, that I do not take a single newspaper, nor read one a month; and I feel myself infinitely the happier for it.

We are alarmed here with the apprehensions of war; and sincerely anxious that it may be avoided; but not at the expense either of our

[1]Tench Coxe, American political economist and statesman, was a staunch Federalist who later deserted the Federalists and became an ardent Jeffersonian.

faith or honor. It seems much the general opinion here, the latter has been too much wounded not to require reparation, and to seek it even in war, if that be necessary. As to myself, I love peace, and I am anxious that we should give the world still another useful lesson, by showing to them other modes of punishing injuries than by war, which is as much a punishment to the punisher as to the sufferer. I love, therefore, . . . [the] proposition of cutting off all communication with the nation which has conducted itself so atrociously. This, you will say, may bring on war. If it does, we will meet it like men; but it may not bring on war, and then the experiment will have been a happy one. I believe this war would be vastly more unanimously approved than any one we ever were engaged in; because the aggressions have been so wanton and bare-faced, and so unquestionably against our desire. . . .

TO JAMES MADISON

Monticello, December 28, 1794

. . . . The denunciation[1] of the democratic societies is one of the extraordinary acts of boldness of which we have seen so many from the faction of monocrats. It is wonderful indeed, that the President should have permitted himself to be the organ of such an attack on the freedom of discussion, the freedom of writing, printing and publishing. It must be a matter of rare curiosity to get at the modifications of these rights proposed by them, and to see what line their ingenuity would draw between democratical societies, whose avowed object is the nourishment of the republican principles of our Constitution, and the society of the Cincinnati, *a self-created* one, carving out for itself hereditary distinctions, lowering over our Constitution eternally, meeting together in all parts of the Union, periodically, with closed doors, accumulating a capital in their separate treasury, corresponding secretly and regularly, and of which society the very persons denouncing the democrats are themselves the fathers, founders and high officers. Their sight must be perfectly dazzled by the glittering of crowns and coronets, not to see

[1]Washington, under Hamilton's influence, had written a strong denunciation of the Democratic societies in his yearly message to Congress.

the extravagance of the proposition to suppress the friends of general freedom, while those who wish to confine that freedom to the few, are permitted to go on in their principles and practices. I here put out of sight the persons whose misbehavior has been taken advantage of to slander the friends of popular rights; and I am happy to observe, that as far as the circle of my observation and information extends, everybody has lost sight of them, and views the abstract attempt on their natural and constitutional rights in all its nakedness. I have never heard, or heard of, a single expression or opinion which did not condemn it as an inexcusable aggression . . .

TO MONSIEUR D'IVERNOIS[1]

Monticello, February 6, 1795

DEAR SIR,—Your several favors on the affairs of Geneva found me here, in the month of December last. It is now more than a year that I have withdrawn myself from public affairs, which I never liked in my life, but was drawn into by emergencies which threatened our country with slavery, but ended in establishing it free. I have returned, with infinite appetite, to the enjoyment of my farm, my family and my books, and had determined to meddle in nothing beyond their limits. Your proposition, however, for transplanting the college of Geneva to my own county, was too analogous to all my attachments to science, and freedom, the first-born daughter of science, not to excite a lively interest in my mind, and the essays which were necessary to try its practicability. This depended altogether on the opinions and dispositions of our State legislature, which was then in session. I immediately communicated your papers to a member of the legislature, whose abilities and zeal pointed him out as proper for it, urging him to sound as many of the leading members of the legislature as he could, and if he found their opinions favorable, to bring forward the proposition; but if he should find it desperate, not to hazard it; because I thought it best not to commit the honor either of our State or of your college, by an

[1]Francois d'Ivernois, liberal Swiss economist and political historian, was a political exile from Geneva.

useless act of eclat. It was not till within these three days that I have had an interview with him, and an account of his proceedings. He communicated the papers to a great number of the members, and discussed them maturely, but privately, with them. They were generally well-disposed to the proposition, and some of them warmly; however, there was no difference of opinion in the conclusion, that it could not be effected. The reasons which they thought would with certainty prevail against it, were 1, that our youth, not familiarized but with their mother tongue, were not prepared to receive instructions in any other; 2, that the expense of the institution would excite uneasiness in their constituents, and endanger its permanence; and 3, that its extent was disproportioned to the narrow state of the population with us. Whatever might be urged on these several subjects, yet as the decision rested with others, there remained to us only to regret that circumstances were such, or were thought to be such, as to disappoint your and our wishes.

I should have seen with peculiar satisfaction the establishment of such a mass of science in my country, and should probably have been tempted to approach myself to it, by procuring a residence in its neighborhood, at those seasons of the year at least when the operations of agriculture are less active and interesting. I sincerely lament the circumstances which have suggested this emigration. I had hoped that Geneva was familiarized to such a degree of liberty, that they might without difficulty or danger fill up the measure to its *maximum;* a term, which, though in the insulated man, bounded only by his natural powers, must, in society, be so far restricted as to protect himself against the evil passions of his associates, and consequently, them against him. I suspect that the doctrine, that small States alone are fitted to be republics, will be exploded by experience, with some other brilliant fallacies accredited by Montesquieu and other political writers. Perhaps it will be found, that to obtain a just republic (and it is to secure our just rights that we resort to government at all) it must be so extensive as that local egoisms may never reach its greater part; that on every particular question, a majority may be found in its councils free from particular interests, and giving, therefore, an uniform prevalence to the principles of justice. The smaller the societies, the more violent and more convulsive their schisms. We have chanced to live in an age which will probably be distinguished in history, for its experiments in government on a larger scale than has yet taken place. But we shall not live to see the result. The grosser absurdities, such as hereditary magistracies, we shall see exploded in our day, long experience having already pronounced condemnation against them. But what is to be the substitute? This our children or grandchildren will answer. We may we satisfied with the certain knowledge that none can ever be tried, so stupid, so unrighteous, so oppressive, so destructive of every end for which honest men enter into government, as that which their forefathers had established, and their fathers alone venture to tumble headlong from the stations they have so long abused. It is unfortunate, that the efforts of mankind to recover the freedom of which they have been so long deprived, will be accompanied with violence, with errors, and even with crimes. But while we weep over the means, we must pray for the end.

But I have been insensibly led by the general complexion of the times, from the particular case of Geneva, to those to which it bears no similitude. Of that we hope good things. Its inhabitants must be too much enlightened, too well experienced in the blessings of freedom and undisturbed industry, to tolerate long a contrary state of things. I should be happy to hear that their government perfects itself, and leaves room for the honest, the industrious and wise; in which case, your own talents, and those of the persons for whom you have interested yourself, will, I am sure, find welcome and distinction. My good wishes will always attend you, as a consequence of the esteem and regard with which I am, dear Sir, your most obedient, and most humble servant.

TO M. DE MEUSNIER[1]

Monticello, Virginia, Apr. 29, 95

. . . . I think it fortunate for the United States to have become the asylum for so many virtuous patriots of different denominations: but

---

[1] M. de Meusnier was introduced to Jefferson by the Duc de la Rochefoucauld. He obtained much detailed information about the United States from Jefferson for his article in the *Encyolopédie Méthodique*. [Ford.]

their circumstances, with which you were so well acquainted before, enabled them to be but a bare asylum, & to offer nothing for them but an entire freedom to use their own means & faculties as they please. There is no such thing in this country as what would be called wealth in Europe. The richest are but a little at ease, & obliged to pay the most rigorous attention to their affairs to keep them together. I do not mean to speak here of the Beaujons of America. For we have some of these tho' happily they are but ephemeral. Our public economy also is such as to offer drudgery and subsistence only to those entrusted with its administration, a wise & necessary precaution against the degeneracy of the public servants. In our private pursuits it is a great advantage that every honest employment is deemed honorable. I am myself a nail-maker. On returning home after an absence of ten years, I found my farms so much deranged that I saw evidently they would be a burden to me instead of a support till I could regenerate them; & consequently that it was necessary for me to find some other resource in the meantime. I thought for awhile of taking up the manufacture of pot-ash, which requires but small advances of money. I concluded at length however to begin a manufacture of nails, which needs little or no capital, & I now employ a dozen little boys from 10. to 16. years of age, overlooking all the details of their business myself & drawing from it a profit which I can get along till I can put my farms into a course of yielding profit. My new trade of nail-making is to me in this country what an additional title of nobility or the ensigns of a new order are in Europe. . . .

TO MANN PAGE[1]

Monticello, August 30, 1795

. . . . I do most anxiously wish to see the highest degrees of education given to the higher degrees of genius, and to all degrees of it, so much as may enable them to read and understand what is going on in the world, and to keep their part of it going on right: for nothing can keep it right but their own vigilant and distrustful superintendence. I

[1]Son of Mann Page, the eminent Virginia planter and councilman.

do not believe with the Rochefoucaulds and Montaignes, that four-teen out of fifteen men are rogues: I believe a great abatement from that proportion may be made in favor of general honesty. But I have always found that rogues would be uppermost, and I do not know that the proportion is too strong for the higher orders, and for those who, rising above the swinish multitude, always contrive to nestle them-selves into the places of power and profit. These rogues set out with stealing the people's good opinion, and then steal from them the right of withdrawing it, by contriving laws and associations against the power of the people themselves. Our part of the country is in consid-erable fermentation, on what they suspect to be a recent roguery of this kind. They say that while all hands were below deck mending sails, splicing ropes, and every one at his own business, and the captain in his cabin attending to his log book and chart, a rogue of a pilot has run them into an enemy's port. But metaphor apart, there is much dissat-isfaction with Mr. Jay and his treaty. For my part, I consider myself now but as passenger, leaving the world and its government to those who are likely to live longer in it. That you may be among the longest of these, is my sincere prayer. . . .

TO GEORGE WYTHE

Monticello, January 16, 1796

In my letter which accompanied the box containing my collection of printed laws, I promised to send you by post a statement of the con-tents of the box. On taking up the subject I found it better to take a more general review of the whole of the laws I possessed, as well man-uscript as printed, as also of those which I do not possess, and sup-pose to be no longer extant. This general view you will have in the enclosed paper, whereof the articles stated to be printed constitute the contents of the box I sent you. Those in manuscript were not sent, because not supposed to have been within your view, and because some of them will not bear removal, being so rotten, that in turning over a leaf it sometimes falls into powder. These I preserve by wrap-ping and sewing them up in oil cloth, so that neither air nor moisture can have access to them. Very early in the course of my researches into the laws of Virginia, I observed that many of them were already lost, and many more on the point of being lost, as existing only in single copies in the hands of careful or curious individuals, on whose death they would probably be used for waste paper. I set myself therefore to work, to collect all which were then existing, in order that when the day should come in which the public should advert to the magnitude of their loss in these precious monuments of our property, and our history, a part of their regret might be spared by information that a portion had been saved from the wreck, which is worthy of their attention and preservation. In searching after these remains, I spared neither time, trouble, nor expense; and am of opinion that scarcely any law escaped me, which was in being as late as the year 1790 in the middle or southern parts of the State. In the northern parts, perhaps something might still be found. In the clerk's offices in the ancient counties, some of these manuscript copies of the laws may possibly still exist, which used to be furnished at the public expense to every county, before the use of the press was introduced; and in the same places, and in the hands of ancient magistrates or of their families, some of the fugitive sheets of the laws of separate sessions, which have been usually distributed since the practice commenced of printing them. But recurring to what we actually possess, the question is, what means will be the most effectual for preserving these remains from future loss? All the care I can take of them, will not preserve them from the worm, from the natural decay of the paper, from the accidents of fire, or those of removal when it is necessary for any public purposes, as in the case of those now sent you. Our experience has proved to us that a single copy, or a few, deposited in manuscript in the public offices, cannot be relied on for any great length of time. The ravages of fire and of ferocious enemies have had but too much part in producing the very loss we are now deploring. How many of the precious works of antiquity were lost while they were preserved only in manuscript! has there ever been one lost since the art of printing has rendered it practicable to multiply and disperse copies? This leads us then to the only means of preserving those remains of our laws now under consideration, that is, a multiplication of printed copies. I think therefore that there should be printed at public expense, an edition of all the laws ever passed by our legislatures which can now be found; that a copy should be deposited in every public library in America, in the principal public offices within the State, and some perhaps in the most distinguished public libraries of Europe, and the rest should be sold to individuals, towards reimbursing the expenses of the edition. . . .

TO PHILIP MAZZEI[1]

Monticello, April 24, 1796

. . . . The aspect of our politics has wonderfully changed since you left us. In place of that noble love of liberty and republican government which carried us triumphantly through the war, an Anglican monarchical aristocratical party has sprung up, whose avowed object is to draw over us the substance, as they have already done the forms, of the British government. The main body of our citizens, however, remain true to their republican principles; the whole landed interest is republican, and so is a great mass of talents. Against us are the Executive, the Judiciary, two out of three branches of the Legislature, all the officers of the government, all who want to be officers, all timid men who prefer the calm of despotism to the boisterous sea of liberty, British merchants and Americans trading on British capital, speculators and holders in the banks and public funds, a contrivance invented for the purposes of corruption, and for assimilating us in all things to the rotten as well as the sound parts of the British model. It would give you a fever were I to name to you the apostates who have gone over to these heresies, men who were Samsons in the field and Solomons in the council, but who have had their heads shorn by the harlot England. In short, we are likely to preserve the liberty we have obtained only by unremitting labors and perils. But we shall preserve it; and our mass

---

[1]Philip Mazzei, Italian born physician, merchant, horticulturist, and author of *Recherches Historiques et Politiques sur les États-Unis de l'Amerique Septentrionale*, had been Jefferson's friend and neighbor at Monticello, and had served as confidential agent for Virginia during the Revolution. In 1785 he left America, and spent the remainder of his life abroad.

of weight and wealth on the good side is so great, as to leave no danger that force will ever be attempted against us. We have only to awake and snap the Lilliputian cords with which they have been entangling us during the first sleep which succeeded our labors. . . .

TO JOHN ADAMS

Monticello, Dec. 28, 1796

DEAR SIR,—The public and the papers have been much occupied lately in placing us in a point of opposition to each other. I trust with confidence that less of it has been felt by ourselves personally. In the retired canton where I am, I learn little of what is passing: pamphlets I see never: papers but a few; and the fewer the happier. Our latest intelligence from Philadelphia at present is of the 16th instant, but though at that date your election to the first magistracy seems not to have been known as a fact, yet with me it has never been doubted. I knew it impossible you should lose a vote north of the Delaware, and even if that of Pennsylvania should be against you in the mass, yet that you would get enough south of that to place your succession out of danger. I have never one single moment expected a different issue; and though I know I shall not be believed, yet it is not the less true that I have never wished it. My neighbors as my compurgators could aver that fact, because they see my occupations and my attachment to them. Indeed it is possible that you may be cheated of your succession by a trick worthy the subtlety of your arch-friend of New York who has been able to make of your real friends tools to defeat their and your just wishes. Most probably he will be disappointed as to you; and my inclinations place me out of his reach. I leave to others the sublime delights of riding in the storm, better pleased with sound sleep and a warm berth below, with the society of neighbors, friends and fellow-laborers of the earth, than of spies and sycophants. No one then will congratulate you with purer disinterestedness than myself. . . .

TO JAMES MADISON

Monticello, Jan. 1, '97

Yours of Dec. 19 has come safely. The event of the election has never been a matter of doubt in my mind. I knew that the Eastern States were disciplined in the schools of their town meetings to sacrifice differences of opinion to the great object of operating in phalanx, and that the more free and moral agency practiced in the other States would always make up the supplement of their weight. Indeed the vote comes much nearer an equality than I had expected. I know the difficulty of obtaining belief to one's declarations of a disinclination to honors, and that it is greatest with those who still remain in the world. But no arguments were wanting to reconcile me to a relinquishment of the first office or acquiescence under the second. As to the first it was impossible that a more solid unwillingness settled on full calculation, could have existed in any man's mind, short of the degree of absolute refusal. The only view on which I would have gone into it for awhile was to put our vessel on her republican tack before she should be thrown too much to leeward of her true principles. As to the second, it is the only office in the world about which I am unable to decide in my own mind whether I had rather have it or not have it. Pride does not enter into the estimate; for I think with the Romans that the general of to-day should be a soldier to-morrow if necessary. I can particularly have no feelings which would revolt at a secondary position to Mr Adams. I am his junior in life, was his junior in Congress, his junior in the diplomatic line, his junior lately in the civil government. Before the receipt of your letter I had written the enclosed one to him. I had intended it some time, but had deferred it from time to time under the discouragement of a despair of making him believe I could be sincere in it. The papers by the last post not rendering it necessary to change anything in the letter I enclose it open for your perusal, not only that you may possess the actual state of dispositions between us, but that if anything should render the delivery of it ineligible in your opinion, you may return it to me. If Mr. Adams can be induced to administer the government on its true principles, and to relinquish his bias to an English constitution, it is to be considered whether it would

not be on the whole for the public good to come to a good understanding with him as to his future elections. He is perhaps the only
sure barrier against Hamilton's getting in. . . .

TO ELBRIDGE GERRY[1]

Philadelphia, May 13, 1797

. . . . I entirely commend your dispositions towards Mr. Adams;
knowing his worth as intimately and esteeming it as much as any one,
and acknowledging the preference of his claims, if any I could have
had, to the high office conferred on him. But in truth, I had neither
claims nor wishes on the subject, though I know it will be difficult to
obtain belief of this. When I retired from this place and the office of
Secretary of State, it was in the firmest contemplation of never more
returning here. There had indeed been suggestions in the public
papers, that I was looking towards a succession to the President's chair,
but feeling a consciousness of their falsehood, and observing that the
suggestions came from hostile quarters, I considered them as intended
merely to excite public odium against me. I never in my life exchanged
a word with any person on the subject, till I found my name brought
forward generally, in competition with that of Mr. Adams. Those with
whom I then communicated, could say, if it were necessary, whether
I met the call with desire, or even with a ready acquiescence, and
whether from the moment of my first acquiescence, I did not devoutly
pray that the very thing might happen which has happened. The second office of the government is honorable and easy, the first is but a
splendid misery.

You express apprehensions that stratagems will be used, to produce
a misunderstanding between the President and myself. Though not a
word having this tendency has ever been hazarded to me by any one,
yet I consider as a certainty that nothing will be left untried to alienate him from me. These machinations will proceed from the Hamiltonians by whom he is surrounded, and who are only a little less hostile

[1]Elbridge Gerry, American statesman, was soon to be appointed, by President John
Adams a member of the "X.Y.Z." Mission.

to him than to me. It cannot but damp the pleasure of cordiality, when we suspect that it is suspected. I cannot help thinking, that it is impossible for Mr. Adams to believe that the state of my mind is what it really is; that he may think I view him as an obstacle in my way. I have no supernatural power to impress truth on the mind of another, nor he any to discover that the estimate which he may form, on a just view of the human mind as generally constituted, may not be just in its application to a special constitution. This may be a source of private uneasiness to us; I honestly confess that it is so to me at this time. But neither of us is capable of letting it have effect on our public duties. Those who may endeavor to separate us, are probably excited by the fear that I might have influence on the executive councils; but when they shall know that I consider my office as constitutionally confined to legislative functions, and that I could not take any part whatever in executive consultations, even were it proposed, their fears may perhaps subside, and their object be found not worth a machination.

I do sincerely wish with you, that we could take our stand on a ground perfectly neutral and independent towards all nations. It has been my constant object through my public life; and with respect to the English and French, particularly, I have too often expressed to the former my wishes, and made to them propositions verbally and in writing, officially and privately, to official and private characters, for them to doubt of my views, if they would be content with equality. Of this they are in possession of several written and formal proofs, in my own handwriting. But they have wished a monopoly of commerce and influence with us; and they have in fact obtained it. When we take notice that theirs is the workshop to which we go for all we want; that with them centre either immediately or ultimately all the labors of our hands and lands; that to them belongs either openly or secretly the great mass of our navigation; that even the factorage of their affairs here, is kept to themselves by factitious citizenships; that these foreign and false citizens now constitute the great body of what are called our merchants, fill our sea ports, are planted in every little town and district of the interior country, sway everything in the former places by their own votes, and those of their dependants, in the latter, by their insinuations and the influence of their ledgers; that they are advancing fast to a monopoly of our banks and public funds, and thereby placing our public finances under their control; that they have in their alliance the most influential characters in and out of office; when they have shown that by all these bearings on the different branches of the government, they can force it to proceed in whatever direction they dictate, and bend the interests of this country entirely to the will of another; when all this, I say, is attended to, it is impossible for us to say we stand on independent ground, impossible for a free mind not to see and to groan under the bondage in which it is bound. If anything after this could excite surprise, it would be that they have been able so far to throw dust in the eyes of our own citizens, as to fix on those who wish merely to recover self-government the charge of subserving one foreign influence, because they resist submission to another. But they possess our printing presses, a powerful engine in their government of us. At this very moment, they would have drawn us into a war on the side of England, had it not been for the failure of her bank. Such was their open and loud cry, and that of their gazettes till this event. After plunging us in all the broils of the European nations, there would remain but one act to close our tragedy, that is, to break up our Union; and even this they have ventured seriously and solemnly to propose and maintain by arguments in a Connecticut paper. I have been happy, however, in believing, from the stifling of this effort, that that dose was found too strong, and excited as much repugnance there as it did horror in other parts of our country, and that whatever follies we may be led into as to foreign nations, we shall never give up our Union, the last anchor of our hope, and that alone which is to prevent this heavenly country from becoming an arena of gladiators. Much as I abhor war, and view it as the greatest scourge of mankind, and anxiously as I wish to keep out of the broils of Europe, I would yet go with my brethren into these, rather than separate from them. But I hope we may still keep clear of them, notwithstanding our present thraldom, and that time may be given us to reflect on the awful crisis we have passed through, and to find some means of shielding ourselves in future from foreign influence, political, commercial, or in whatever other form it may be attempted. I can scarcely withhold myself from joining in the wish of Silas Deane, that there were an ocean of fire between us and the old world.

A perfect confidence that you are as much attached to peace and union as myself, that you equally prize independence of all nations, and the blessings of self-government, has induced me freely to unbosom myself to you, and let you see the light in which I have viewed what has been passing among us from the beginning of the war. And I shall be happy, at all times, in an intercommunication of sentiments with you, believing that the dispositions of the different parts of our country have been considerably misrepresented and misunderstood in each part, as to the other, and that nothing but good can result from an exchange of information and opinions between those whose circumstances and morals admit no doubt of the integrity of their views.

I remain, with constant and sincere esteem, dear Sir, your affectionate friend and servant.

TO EDWARD RUTLEDGE

Philadelphia, June 24, 1797

. . . . We had, in 1793, the most respectable character in the universe. What the neutral nations think of us now, I know not; but we are low indeed with the belligerents. Their kicks and cuffs prove their contempt. If we weather the present storm, I hope we shall avail ourselves of the calm of peace, to place our foreign connections under a new and different arrangement. We must make the interest of every nation stand surety for their justice, and their own loss to follow injury to us, as effect follows its cause. As to everything except commerce, we ought to divorce ourselves from them all. But this system would require time, temper, wisdom, and occasional sacrifice of interest; and how far all of these will be ours, our children may see, but we shall not. The passions are too high at present, to be cooled in our day. You and I have formerly seen warm debates and high political passions. But gentlemen of different politics would then speak to each other, and separate the business of the Senate from that of society. It is not so now. Men who have been intimate all their lives, cross the streets to avoid meeting, and turn their heads another way, lest they should be obliged to touch their hats. This may do for young men with whom passion is enjoyment. But it is afflicting to peaceable minds. Tranquillity is the old man's milk. I go to enjoy it in a few days, and to exchange the roar and tumult of bulls and bears, for the prattle of my grandchildren and senile rest. . . .

TO ELBRIDGE GERRY

Philadelphia, January 26, 1799

I do then, with sincere zeal, wish an inviolable preservation of our present federal Constitution, according to the true sense in which it was adopted by the States, that in which it was advocated by its friends, and not that which its enemies apprehended, who therefore became its enemies; and I am opposed to the monarchising its features by the forms of its administration, with a view to conciliate a first transition to a President and Senate for life, and from that to an hereditary tenure of these offices, and thus to worm out the elective principle. I am for preserving to the States the powers not yielded by them to the Union, and to the legislature of the Union its constitutional share in the division of powers; and I am not for transferring all the powers of the States to the General Government, and all those of that government to the executive branch. I am for a government rigorously frugal and simple, applying all the possible savings of the public revenue to the discharge of the national debt; and not for a multiplication of officers and salaries merely to make partisans, and for increasing, by every device, the public debt, on the principle of its being a public blessing. I am for relying, for internal defence, on our militia solely, till actual invasion, and for such a naval force only as may protect our coasts and harbors from such depredations as we have experienced; and not for a standing army in time of peace, which may overawe the public sentiment; nor for a navy, which, by its own expenses and the eternal wars in which it will implicate us, will grind us with public burthens, and sink us under them. I am for free commerce with all nations; political connection with none; and little or no diplomatic establishment. And I am not for linking ourselves by new treaties with the quarrels of Europe; entering that field of slaughter to preserve their balance, or joining in the confederacy of kings to war against the principles of liberty. I am for freedom of religion, and against all manoeuvres to bring about a legal ascendancy of one sect over another: for freedom of the press, and against all violations of the Constitution to silence by force and not by reason the complaints or criticisms, just or unjust, of our citizens against the conduct of their agents. And I am for encouraging the progress of science in all its branches; and not for raising a hue and cry against the sacred name of philosophy; for awing the human mind by stories of raw-head and bloody bones to a distrust of its own vision, and to repose implicitly on that of others; to go backwards instead of forwards to look for improvement; to believe that government, religion, morality, and every other science were in the highest perfection in ages of the darkest ignorance, and that nothing can ever be devised more perfect than what was established by our forefathers. To these I will add, that I was a sincere well-wisher to the success of the French revolution, and still wish it may end in the establishment of a free and well-ordered republic; but I have not been insensible under the atrocious depredations they have committed on our commerce. The first object of my heart is my own country. In that is embarked my family, my fortune, and my own existence. I have not one farthing of interest, nor one fibre of attachment out of it, nor a single motive of preference of any one nation to another, but in proportion as they are more or less friendly to us. But though deeply feeling the injuries of France, I did not think war the surest means of redressing them. I did believe, that a mission sincerely disposed to preserve peace, would obtain for us a peaceable and honorable settlement and retribution; and I appeal to you to say, whether this might not have been obtained, if either of your colleagues had been of the same sentiment with yourself.

These, my friend, are my principles; they are unquestionably the principles of the great body of our fellow-citizens, and I know there is not one of them which is not yours also. In truth, we never differed but on one ground, the funding system; and as, from the moment of its being adopted by the constituted authorities, I became religiously principled in the sacred discharge of it to the uttermost farthing, we are united now even on that single ground of difference. . . .

TO EDMUND PENDLETON[1]

Philadelphia, January 29, 1799

DEAR SIR,—Your patriarchal address to your country is running through all the republican papers, and has a very great effect on the people. It is short, simple, and presents things in a view they readily comprehend. The character and circumstances too of the writer leave them without doubts of his motives. If, like the patriarch of old, you had but one blessing to give us, I should have wished it directed to a particular object. But I hope you have one for this also. You know what a wicked use has been made of the French negotiation; and particularly the X. Y. Z. dish cooked up by Marshall[2] where the swindlers are made to appear as the French government. Art and industry combined, have certainly wrought out of this business a wonderful effect on the people. Yet they have been astonished more than they have understood it, and now that Gerry's correspondence comes out, clearing the French government of that turpitude, and showing them "sincere in their dispositions for peace, not wishing us to break the British treaty, and willing to arrange a liberal one with us," the people will be disposed to suspect they have been duped. But these communications are too voluminous for them, and beyond their reach. A recapitulation is now wanting of the whole story, stating everything according to what we may now suppose to have been the truth, short, simple and levelled to every capacity. Nobody in America can do it so well as yourself, in the same character of the father of your country, any form you like better, and so concise as, omitting nothing material, may yet be printed in hand bills, of which we could print and disperse ten or twelve thousand copies under letter covers, through all the United States, by the members of Congress when they return home. If the understanding of the people could be rallied to the truth on this subject, by exposing the dupery practised on them, there are so many other things about to bear on them favorably for the resurrection of

[1]Edmund Pendleton, Virginia jurist and Revolutionary patriot, although a strict conservative, became in his later years a staunch defender of Jefferson's policies.

[2]Name deleted by editors of Memorial Edition.

their republican spirit, that a reduction of the administration to constitutional principles cannot fail to be the effect. These are the alien and sedition laws, the vexations of the stamp act, the disgusting particularities of the direct tax, the additional army without an enemy, and recruiting officers lounging at every court-house to decoy the laborer from his plough, a navy of fifty ships, five millions to be raised to build it, on the usurious interest of eight per cent., the perseverance in war on our part, when the French government shows such an anxious desire to keep at peace with us, taxes of ten millions now paid by four millions of people, and yet a necessity, in a year or two, of raising five millions more for annual expenses. These things will immediately be bearing on the public mind, and if it remain not still blinded by a supposed necessity, for the purposes of maintaining our independence and defending our country, they will set things to rights. . . .

TO MARIA JEFFERSON EPPES[1]

Philadelphia, Feb. 7, 1799

Your letter, my dear Maria, of January 21st, was received two days ago. It was, as Ossian says, or would say, like the bright beams of the moon on the desolate heath. Environed here in scenes of constant torment, malice and obliquy, worn down in a station where no effort to render service can avail anything, I feel not that existence is a blessing, but when something recalls my mind to my family or farm. This was the effect of your letter, and its affectionate expressions kindled up all those feelings of love for you and our dear connections which now constitute the only real happiness of my life. I am now feeding on the idea of my departure for Monticello, which is but three weeks distant. The roads will then be so dreadful that, as to visit you even by the direct route of Fredericksburg and Richmond would add 100 miles to the length of my journey, I must defer it in hope that about the last of March, or first of April, I may be able to take a trip express to see you. The roads will then be fine; perhaps your sister may join in a fly-

[1]Maria Jefferson Eppes, Jefferson's second daughter had married her half cousin, John Wayles Eppes, in 1797. [Randall.]

ing trip. . . . Continue always to love me, and be assured that there is no object on earth so dear to my heart as your health and happiness, and that my tenderest affections always hang on you. Adieu, my ever dear Maria.

TO EDMUND RANDOLPH[1]

Monticello, August 18, 1799

DEAR SIR,—I received only two days ago your favor of the 12th, and as it was on the eve of the return of our post, it was not possible to make so prompt a despatch of the answer. Of all the doctrines which have ever been broached by the federal government, the novel one, of the common law being in force and cognizable as an existing law in their courts, is to me the most formidable. All their other assumptions of ungiven powers have been in the detail. The bank law, the treaty doctrine, the sedition act, alien act, the undertaking to change the State laws of evidence in the State courts by certain parts of the stamp act, etc., etc., have been solitary, unconsequential, timid things, in comparison with the audacious, barefaced and sweeping pretension to a system of law for the United States, without the adoption of their Legislature, and so infinitively beyond their power to adopt. If this assumption be yielded to, the State courts may be shut up, as there will then be nothing to hinder citizens of the same State suing each other in the federal courts in every case, as on a bond for instance, because the common law obliges payment of it, and the common law they say is their law. I am happy you have taken up the subject; and I have carefully perused and considered the notes you enclosed, and find but a single paragraph which I do not approve. It is that wherein (page two) you say, that laws being emanations from the legislative department, and, when once enacted, continuing in force from a presumption that their will so continues, that that presumption fails and the laws of course fall, on the destruction of that legislative department. I do not think this is the true bottom on which laws and the administering them

---

[1] Edmund Randolph, Virginia statesman, was Attorney General under Washington and succeeded Jefferson as Secretary of State.

rest. The whole body of the nation is the sovereign legislative, judiciary and executive power for itself. The inconvenience of meeting to exercise these powers in person, and their inaptitude to exercise them, induce them to appoint special organs to declare their legislative will, to judge and to execute it. It is the will of the nation which makes the law obligatory; it is their will which creates or annihilates the organ which is to declare and announce it. They may do it by a single person, as an Emperor of Russia, (constituting his declarations evidence of their will), or by a few persons, as the aristocracy of Venice, or by a complication of councils, as in our former regal government, or our present republican one. The law being law because it is the will of the nation, is not changed by their changing the organ through which they choose to announce their future will; no more than the acts I have done by one attorney lose their obligation by my changing or discontinuing that attorney. This doctrine has been, in a certain degree, sanctioned by the federal executive. For it is precisely that on which the continuance of obligation from our treaty with France was established, and the doctrine was particularly developed in a letter to Gouverneur Morris, written with the approbation of President Washington and his cabinet. Mercer once prevailed on the Virginia Assembly to declare a different doctrine in some resolutions. These met universal disapprobation in this, as well as the other States, and if I mistake not, a subsequent Assembly did something to do away the authority of their former unguarded resolutions. In this case, as in all others, the true principle will be quite as effectual to establish the just deductions. Before the revolution, the nation of Virginia had, by the organs they then thought proper to constitute, established a system of laws, which they divided into three denominations of 1, common law; 2, statute law; 3, chancery: or if you please, into two only, of 1, common law; 2, chancery. When, by the Declaration of Independence, they chose to abolish their former organs of declaring their will, the acts of will already formally and constitutionally declared, remained untouched. For the nation was not dissolved, was not annihilated; its will, therefore, remained in full vigor; and on the establishing the new organs, first of a convention, and afterwards a more complicated legislature, the old acts of national will continued in force, until the nation should, by its new organs, declare its will changed. The common law, therefore, which was not in force when we landed here, nor till we had formed ourselves into a nation, and had manifested by the organs we constituted that the common law was to be our law, continued to be our law, because the nation continued in being, and because though it changed the organs for the future declarations of its will, yet it did not change its former declarations that the common law was its law. Apply these principles to the present case. Before the revolution there existed no such nation as the United States; they then first associated as a nation, but for special purposes only. They had all their laws to make, as Virginia had on her first establishment as a nation. But they did not, as Virginia had done, proceed to adopt a whole system of laws ready made to their hand. As their association as a nation was only for special purposes, to wit, for the management of their concerns with one another and with foreign nations, and the States composing the association chose to give it powers for those purposes and no others, they could not adopt any general system, because it would have embraced objects on which this association had no right to form or declare a will. It was not the organ for declaring a national will in these cases. In the cases confided to them, they were free to declare the will of the nation, the law; but till it was declared there could be no law. So that the common law did not become, *ipso facto,* law on the new association; it could only become so by a positive adoption, and so far only as they were authorized to adopt.

I think it will be of great importance, when you come to the proper part, to portray at full length the consequences of this new doctrine, that the common law is the law of the United States, and that their courts have, of course, jurisdiction co-extensive with that law, that is to say, general over all cases and persons. But, great heavens! Who could have conceived in 1789, that within ten years we should have to combat such windmills! Adieu. Yours affectionately.

TO DR. JOSEPH PRIESTLEY[1]

Philadelphia, January 18, 1800

. . . . We have . . . in Virginia a College (William and Mary) just well enough endowed to draw out the miserable existence to which a miserable constitution has doomed it. It is moreover eccentric in its position, exposed to all bilious diseases as all the lower country is, and therefore abandoned by the public care, as that part of the country itself is in a considerable degree by its inhabitants. We wish to establish in the upper country, and more centrally for the State, an University on a plan so broad and liberal and *modern,* as to be worth patronizing with the public support, and be a temptation to the youth of other States to come and drink of the cup of knowledge and fraternize with us. The first step is to obtain a good plan; that is, a judicious selection of the sciences, and a practicable grouping of some of them together, and ramifying of others, so as to adopt the professorships to our uses and our means. In an institution meant chiefly for use, some branches of science, formerly esteemed, may be now omitted; so may others now valued in Europe, but useless to us for ages to come. As an example of the former, the Oriental learning, and of the latter, almost the whole of the institution proposed to Congress by the Secretary of War's report of the 5th instant. Now there is no one to whom this subject is so familiar as yourself. There is no one in the world who, equally with yourself, unites this full possession of the subject with such a knowledge of the state of our existence, as enables you to fit the garment to him who is to *pay* for it and to *wear* it. To you therefore we address our solicitations, and to lessen to you as much as possible the ambiguities of our object, I will venture even to sketch the sciences which seem useful and practicable for us, as they occur to me while holding my pen. Botany, chemistry, zoology, anatomy, surgery, medicine, natural philosophy, agriculture, mathematics, astronomy, geography, politics, commerce, history, ethics, law, arts, fine arts. This list is imperfect

---

[1]Dr. Joseph Priestley, the celebrated English scientist, educator, and thinker, was at this time a resident of the United States. Until his death four years later, he was engaged in a stimulating and provocative correspondence with Jefferson.

because I make it hastily, and because I am unequal to the subject. It is evident that some of these articles are too much for one professor and must therefore be ramified; others may be ascribed in groups to a single professor. This is the difficult part of the work, and requires a head perfectly knowing the extent of each branch, and the limits within which it may be circumscribed, so as to bring the whole within the powers of the fewest professors possible, and consequently within the degree of expense practicable for us. We should propose that the professors follow no other calling, so that their whole time may be given to their academical functions; and we should propose to draw from Europe the first characters in science, by considerable temptations, which would not need to be repeated after the first set should have prepared fit successors and given reputation to the institution. . . .

TO DR. JOSEPH PRIESTLEY

Philadelphia, January 27, 1800

DEAR SIR,—In my last letter of the 18th, I omitted to say any thing of the languages as part of our proposed University. It was not that I think, as some do, that they are useless. I am of a very different opinion. I do not think them very essential to the obtaining eminent degrees of science; but I think them very useful towards it. I suppose there is a portion of life during which our faculties are ripe enough for this, and for nothing more useful. I think the Greeks and Romans have left us the present models which exist of fine composition, whether we examine them as works of reason, or of style and fancy; and to them we probably owe these characteristics of modern composition. I know of no composition of any other ancient people, which merits the least regard as a model for its matter or style. To all this I add, that to read the Latin and Greek authors in their original, is a sublime luxury; and I deem luxury in science to be at least as justifiable as in architecture, painting, gardening, or the other arts. I enjoy Homer in his own language infinitely beyond Pope's translation of him, and both beyond the dull narrative of the same events by Dares Phrygius; and it is an innocent enjoyment. I thank on my knees, Him who directed my early education, for having put into my possession this rich source of delight;

and I would not exchange it for anything which I could then have acquired, and have not since acquired. With this regard for those languages, you will acquit me of meaning to omit them. About twenty years ago, I drew a bill for our legislature, which proposed to lay off every county into hundreds or townships of five or six miles square, in the centre of each of them was to be a free English school; the whole State was further laid off into ten districts, in each of which was to be a college for teaching the languages, geography, surveying, and other useful things of that grade; and then a single University for the sciences. It was received with enthusiasm; but as I had proposed that William and Mary, under an improved form, should be the University, and that was at that time pretty highly Episcopal, the dissenters after awhile began to apprehend some secret design of a preference to that sect. About three years ago they enacted that part of my bill which related to English schools, except that instead of obliging, they left it optional in the court of every county to carry it into execution or not. I think it probable that part of the plan for the middle grade of education, may also be brought forward in due time. In the meanwhile, we are not without a sufficient number of good country schools, where the languages, geography, and the first elements of mathematics, are taught. Having omitted this information in my former letter, I thought it necessary now to supply it, that you might know on what base your superstructure was to be reared. I have a letter from Mr. Dupont since his arrival at New York, dated the 20th, in which he says he will be in Philadelphia within about a fortnight from that time; but only on a visit. How much would it delight me if a visit from you at the same time, were to show us two such illustrious foreigners embracing each other in my country, as the asylum for whatever is great and good. Pardon, I pray you, the temporary delirium which has been excited here, but which is fast passing away. The Gothic idea that we are to look backwards instead of forwards for the improvement of the human mind, and to recur to the annals of our ancestors for what is most perfect in government, in religion and in learning, is worthy of those bigots in religion and government, by whom it has been recommended, and whose purposes it would answer. But it is not an idea which this country will endure; and the moment of their showing it is fast ripening; and the signs of it will be their respect for you, and growing detestation of those who have dishonored our country by endeavors to disturb our tranquillity in it. No one has felt this with more sensibility than, my dear Sir, your respectful and affectionate friend and servant.

TO DR. WILLIAM BACHE[1]

Philadelphia, Feb. 2, 1800

. . . . You have seen the afflicting details from Paris. On what grounds a revolution has been made, we are not informed, & are still more at a loss to divine what will be its issue: whether we are to have over again the history of Robespierre, of Caesar, or the new phenomenon of an usurpation of the government for the purpose of making it free. Our citizens, however, should derive from this some useful lessons. They should see in it a necessity to rally firmly and in close bands round their Constitution. Never to suffer an iota of it to be infringed. *To inculcate on minorities the duty of acquiesence in the will of the majority; and on majorities a respect for the rights of the minority.* To beware of a military force, even of citizens; and to beware of too much confidence in any man. The confidence of the French people in Bonaparte has enabled him to kick down their Constitution and instead of that, to leave them dependent on his will & his life. *I have never seen so awful a moment as the present.* The prospects too, in this State, important as it is in our union, are very discouraging. . . .

TO SAMUEL ADAMS[2]

Philadelphia, February 26, 1800

. . . . A letter from you, my respectable friend, after three and twenty years of separation, has given me a pleasure I cannot express. It recalls

[1]Dr. William Bache was a neighbor of Jefferson's in Virginia. [MS. copy by Nicholas P. Trist, husband of Jefferson's grand-daughter, Virginia Randolph, University of Virginia.]

[2]This letter to Samuel Adams, one of the most important Revolutionary patriots and second cousin of President John Adams, was written three years before his death.

to my mind the anxious days we then passed in struggling for the cause of mankind. Your principles have been tested in the crucible of time, and have come out pure. You have proved that it was monarchy, and not merely British monarchy, you opposed. A government by representatives, elected by the people at *short* periods, was our object; and our maxim at that day was, "where annual election ends, tyranny begins;" nor have our departures from it been sanctioned by the happiness of their effects. A debt of an hundred millions growing by usurious interest, and an artificial paper phalanx overruling the agricultural mass of our country, with other *et ceteras*, have a portentous aspect.

I fear our friends on the other side of the water, laboring in the same cause, have yet a great deal of crime and misery to wade through. My confidence has been placed in the head, not in the heart of Bonaparte. I hoped he would calculate truly the difference between the fame of a Washington and a Cromwell. Whatever his views may be, he has at least transferred the destinies of the republic from the civil to the military arm. Some will use this as a lesson against the practicability of republican government. I read it as a lesson against the danger of standing armies.

Adieu, my ever respected and venerable friend. May that kind overruling providence which has so long spared you to our country, still foster your remaining years with whatever may make them comfortable to yourself and soothing to your friends. Accept the cordial salutations of your affectionate friend.

TO DR. BENJAMIN RUSH[1]

Monticello, September 23, 1800

. . . . I promised you a letter on Christianity, which I have not forgotten. On the contrary, it is because I have reflected on it, that I find much more time necessary for it than I can at present dispose of. I have a view of the subject which ought to displease neither the rational Christian nor Diests, and would reconcile many to a character they

[1]Dr. Benjamin Rush, distinguished American physician and humanitarian, and Jefferson, were fellow-members of the American Philosophical Society. They corresponded frequently.

have too hastily rejected. I do not know that it would reconcile the *genus irritabile vatum*[1] who are all in arms against me. Their hostility is on too interesting ground to be softened. The delusion into which the X. Y. Z. plot showed it possible to push the people; the successful experiment made under the prevalence of that delusion on the clause of the Constitution, which, while it secured the freedom of the press, covered also the freedom of religion, had given to the clergy a very favorite hope of obtaining an establishment of a particular form of Christianity through the United States; and as every sect believes its own form the true one, every one perhaps hoped for his own, but especially the Episcopalians and Congregationalists. The returning good sense of our country threatens abortion to their hopes, and they believe that any portion of power confided to me, will be exerted in opposition to their schemes. And they believe rightly: for I have sworn upon the altar of God, eternal hostility against every form of tyranny over the mind of man. But this is all they have to fear from me: and enough too in their opinion. . . .

TO MARTHA JEFFERSON RANDOLPH

Washington, January 26, 1801

MY DEAR MARTHA,—I wrote to Mr. Randolph on the 9th and 10th inst., and yesterday received his letter of the 10th. It gave me great joy to learn that Lilly had got a recruit of hands from Mr. Allen, though still I would not have that prevent the taking all from the nailery who are able to cut, as I desired in mine of the 9th, as I wish Craven's ground to be got ready for him without any delay. Mr. Randolph writes me you are about to wean Cornelia; this must be right and proper. I long to be in the midst of the children, and have more pleasure in their little follies than in the wisdom of the wise. Here, too, there is such a mixture of the bad passions of the heart, that one feels themselves in an enemy's country. It is an unpleasant circumstance, if I am destined to stay here, that the great proportion of those of the place who figure are Federalists, and most of them of the vio-

---

[1] The irritable tribe of priests.

lent kind. Some have been so personally bitter that they can never forgive me, though I do them with sincerity. Perhaps in time they will get tamed. Our prospect as to the election has been alarming; as a strong disposition exists to prevent an election, and that case not being provided for by the Constitution, a dissolution of the government seemed possible. At present there is a prospect that some, though Federalists, will prefer yielding to the wishes of the people rather than have no government. If I am fixed here, it will be but three easy days' journey from you, so that I should hope you and the family could pay an annual visit here at least; which with mine to Monticello of the spring and fall, might enable us to be together four or five months of the year. On this subject, however, we may hereafter converse, lest we should be counting chickens before they are hatched. I inclose for Anne a story, too long to be got by heart but worth reading. Kiss them all for me and keep them in mind of me. Tell Ellen I am afraid she has forgotten me. I shall probably be with you the first week in April, as I shall endeavor to be at our court for that month. Continue to love me, my dear Martha, and be assured of my unalterable and tenderest love to you. Adieu.

P. S. Hamilton is using his uttermost influence to procure my election rather than Colonel Burr's.

TO T. M. RANDOLPH

Washington, February 19, 1801

After exactly a week's balloting there at length appeared ten States for me, four for Burr, and two voted blanks. This was done without a single vote coming over. Morris of Vermont withdrew, so that Lyon's vote became that of the State. The four Maryland federalists put in blanks, so then the vote of the four republicans became that of their State. Mr. Hager of South Carolina (who had constantly voted for me) withdrew by agreement, his colleagues agreeing in that case to put in blanks. Bayard, the sole member of Delaware, voted blank. They had before deliberated whether they would come over in a body, when they saw they could not force Burr on the republicans, or keep their body entire and unbroken to act in phalanx on such ground of opposition as they shall hereafter be able to conjure up. Their vote showed what they had decided on, and is considered as a declaration of perpetual war; but their conduct has completely left them without support. Our information from all quarters is that the whole body of federalists concurred with the republicans in the last elections, and with equal anxiety. They had been made to interest themselves so warmly for the very choice, which while before the people they opposed, that when obtained it came as a thing of their own wishes, and they find themselves embodied with the republicans, and their quondam leaders separated from them, and I verily believe they will remain embodied with us, so that this conduct of the minority has done in one week what very probably could hardly have been effected by years of mild and impartial administration. . . .

TO JOHN DICKINSON[1]

Washington, March 6, 1801

DEAR SIR,—No pleasure can exceed that which I received from reading your letter of the 21st ultimo. It was like the joy we expect in the mansions of the blessed, when received with the embraces of our forefathers, we shall be welcomed with their blessing as having done our part not unworthily of them. The storm through which we have passed, has been tremendous indeed. The tough sides of our Argosy have been thoroughly tried. Her strength has stood the waves into which she was steered, with a view to sink her. We shall put her on her republican tack, and she will now show by the beauty of her motion the skill of her builders. Figure apart, our fellow-citizens have been led hoodwinked from their principles, by a most extraordinary combination of circumstances. But the band is removed, and they now see for themselves. I hope to see shortly a perfect consolidation to effect which, nothing shall be spared on my part, short of the abandonment of the principles of our revolution. A just and solid republican government maintained

---

[1]As a member of the Continental Congress, and as an important participant in the affairs culminating in the formation of the United States of America, John Dickinson, lawyer and statesman, had much in common with Thomas Jefferson.

here, will be a standing monument and example for the aim and imitation of the people of other countries; and I join with you in the hope and belief that they will see, from our example, that a free government is of all others the most energetic; that the inquiry which has been excited among the mass of mankind by our revolution and its consequences, will ameliorate the condition of man over a great portion of the globe. What a satisfaction have we in the contemplation of the benevolent effects of our efforts, compared with those of the leaders on the other side, who have discountenanced all advances in science as dangerous innovations, have endeavored to render philosophy and republicanism terms of reproach, to persuade that man cannot be governed but by the rod, etc. I shall have the happiness of living and dying in the contrary hope. Accept assurances of my constant and sincere respect and attachment, and my affectionate salutations.

TO DR. JOSEPH PRIESTLEY

Washington, March 21, 1801

DEAR SIR,—I learned some time ago that you were in Philadelphia, but that it was only for a fortnight; and I supposed you were gone. It was not till yesterday I received information that you were still there, had been very ill, but were on the recovery. I sincerely rejoice that you are so. Yours is one of the few lives precious to mankind, and for the continuance of which every thinking man is solicitous. Bigots may be an exception. What an effort, my dear Sir, of bigotry in politics and religion have we gone through! The barbarians really flattered themselves they should be able to bring back the times of Vandalism, when ignorance put everything into the hands of power and priestcraft. All advances in science were proscribed as innovations. They pretended to praise and encourage education, but it was to be the education of our ancestors. We were to look backwards, not forwards, for improvement; the President himself declaring, in one of his answers to addresses, that we were never to expect to go beyond them in real science. This was the real ground of all the attacks on you. Those who live by mystery and *charlatanerie*, fearing you would render them useless by simplifying the Christian philosophy,—the most sublime and benevolent, but most perverted system that ever shone on man,—endeavored to crush your well-earned and well-deserved fame. But it was the Lilliputians upon Gulliver. Our countrymen have recovered from the alarm into which art and industry had thrown them; science and honesty are replaced on their high ground; and you, my dear Sir, as their great apostle, are on its pinnacle. It is with heartfelt satisfaction that, in the first moments of my public action, I can hail you with welcome to our land, tender to you the homage of its respect and esteem, cover you under the protection of those laws which were made for the wise and good like you, and disdain the legitimacy of that libel on legislation, which, under the form of a law, was for some time placed among them.

As the storm is now subsiding, and the horizon becoming serene, it is pleasant to consider the phenomenon with attention. We can no longer say there is nothing new under the sun. For this whole chapter in the history of man is new. The great extent of our republic is new. Its sparse habitation is new. The mighty wave of public opinion which has rolled over it is new. But the most pleasing novelty is, its so quietly subsiding over such an extent of surface to its true level again. The order and good sense displayed in this recovery from delusion, and in the momentous crisis which lately arose, really bespeaks a strength of character in our nation which augurs well for the duration of our republic; and I am much better satisfied now of its stability than I was before it was tried. I have been, above all things, solaced by the prospect which opened on us, in the event of a non-election of a President; in which case, the federal government would have been in the situation of a clock or watch run down. There was no idea of force, nor of any occasion for it. A convention, invited by the republican members of Congress, with the virtual President and Vice-President, would have been on the ground in eight weeks, would have repaired the Constitution where it was defective, and wound it up again. This peaceable and legitimate resource, to which we are in the habit of implicit obedience, superseding all appeal to force, and being always within our reach, shows a precious principle of self-preservation in our composition, till a change of circumstances shall take place, which is not within prospect at any definite period. . . .

TO SAMUEL ADAMS

Washington, March 29, 1801

I addressed a letter to you, my very dear and ancient friend, on the 4th of March: not indeed to you by name, but through the medium of some of my fellow-citizens, whom occasion called on me to address. In meditating the matter of that address, I often asked myself, is this exactly in the spirit of the patriarch, Samuel Adams? Is it as he would express it? Will he approve of it? I have felt a great deal for our country in the times we have seen. But individually for no one so much as yourself. When I have been told that you were avoided, insulted, frowned on, I could but ejaculate, "Father, forgive them, for they know not what they do." I confess I felt an indignation for you, which for myself I have been able, under every trial, to keep entirely passive. However, the storm is over, and we are in port. The ship was not rigged for the service she was put on. We will show the smoothness of her motions on her republican tack. I hope we shall once more see harmony restored among our citizens, and an entire oblivion of past feuds. Some of the leaders who have most committed themselves cannot come into this. But I hope the great body of our fellow-citizens will do it. I will sacrifice everything but principle to procure it. A few examples of justice on officers who have perverted their functions to the oppression of their fellow-citizens, must, in justice to those citizens, be made. But opinion, and the just maintenance of it, shall never be a crime in my view: nor bring injury on the individual. Those whose misconduct in office ought to have produced their removal even by my predecessor, must not be protected by the delicacy due only to honest men. How much I lament that time has deprived me of your aid! It would have been a day of glory which should have called you to the first office of the administration. But give us your counsel, my friend, and give us your blessing; and be assured that there exists not in the heart of man a more faithful esteem than mine to you, and that I shall ever bear you the most affectionate veneration and respect.

TO ROBERT R. LIVINGSTON[1]

Monticello, September 9, 1801

. . . . On an element which nature has not subjected to the jurisdiction of any particular nation, but has made common to all for the purposes to which it is fitted, it would seem that the particular portion of it which happens to be occupied by the vessel of any nation, in the course of its voyage, is for the moment, the exclusive property of that nation, and, with the vessel, is exempt from intrusion by any other, and from its jurisdiction, as much as if it were lying in the harbor of its sovereign. In no country, we believe, is the rule otherwise, as to the subjects of property common to all. Thus the place occupied by an individual in a highway, a church, a theatre, or other public assembly, cannot be intruded on, while its occupant holds it for the purposes of its institution. The persons on board a vessel traversing the ocean, carrying with them the laws of their nation, have among themselves a jurisdiction, a police, not established by their individual will, but by the authority of their nation, of whose territory their vessel still seems to compose a part, so long as it does not enter the exclusive territory of another. No nation ever pretended a right to govern by their laws the ship of another nation navigating the ocean. By what law then can it enter that ship while in peaceable and orderly use of the common element? We recognize no natural precept for submission to such a right; and perceive no distinction between the movable and immovable jurisdiction of a friend, which would authorize the entering the one and not the other, to seize the property of an enemy.

It may be objected that this proves too much, as it proves you cannot enter the ship of a friend to search for contraband of war. But this is not proving too much. We believe the practice of seizing what is called contraband of war, is an abusive practice, not founded in natural right. War between two nations cannot diminish the rights of the rest of the world remaining at peace. The doctrine that the rights of nations remaining quietly in the exercise of moral and social duties, are to give

[1]As Minister to France during Jefferson's administration, the negotiations of Robert Livingston, statesman, diplomat, and scientific experimenter, resulted in the Louisiana Purchase.

way to the convenience of those who prefer plundering and murdering one another, is a monstrous doctrine; and ought to yield to the more rational law, that "the wrong which two nations endeavor to inflict on each other, must not infringe on the rights or conveniences of those remaining at peace." And what is *contraband*, by the law of nature? Either everything which may aid or comfort an enemy, or nothing. Either all commerce which would accommodate him is unlawful, or none is. The difference between articles of one or another description, is a difference in degree only. No line between them can be drawn. Either all intercourse must cease between neutrals and belligerents, or all be permitted. Can the world hesitate to say which shall be the rule? Shall two nations turning tigers, break up in one instant the peaceable relations of the whole world? Reason and nature clearly pronounce that the neutral is to go on in the enjoyment of all its rights, that its commerce remains free, not subject to the jurisdiction of another, nor consequently its vessels to search, or to enquiries whether their contents are the property of an enemy, or are of those which have been called contraband of war. . . . .

TO THE SECRETARY OF THE TREASURY (ALBERT GALLATIN)

Washington, April 1, 1802

. . . , we might hope to see the finances of the Union as clear and intelligible as a merchant's books, so that every member of Congress, and every man of any mind in the Union, should be able to comprehend them to investigate abuses, and consequently to control them. Our predecessors have endeavored by intricacies of system, and shuffling the investigator over from one officer to another, to cover everything from detection. I hope we shall go in the contrary direction, and that by our honest and judicious reformations, we may be able, within the limits of our time, to bring things back to that simple and intelligible system on which they should have been organized at first. . . .

TO DOCTOR BENJAMIN RUSH

Washington, April 21, 1803

DEAR SIR,—In some of the delightful conversations with you, in the evenings of 1798–99, and which served as an anodyne to the afflictions of the crisis through which our country was then laboring, the Christian religion was sometimes our topic; and I then promised you, that one day or other, I would give you my views of it. They are the result of a life of inquiry and reflection, and very different from that anti-Christian system imputed to me by those who know nothing of my opinions. To the corruptions of Christianity I am, indeed, opposed; but not to the genuine precepts of Jesus himself. I am a Christian, in the only sense in which he wished any one to be; sincerely attached to his doctrines, in preference to all others; ascribing to himself every *human* excellence; and believing he never claimed any other. At the short interval since these conversations, when I could justifiably abstract my mind from public affairs, the subject has been under my contemplation. But the more I considered it, the more it expanded beyond the measure of either my time or information. In the moment of my late departure from Monticello, I received from Dr. Priestley, his little treatise of "Socrates and Jesus Compared." This being a section of the general view I had taken of the field, it became a subject of reflection while on the road, and unoccupied otherwise. The result was, to arrange in my mind a syllabus, or outline of such an estimate of the comparative merits of Christianity, as I wished to see executed by some one of more leisure and information for the task, than myself. This I now send you, as the only discharge of my promise I can probably ever execute. And in confiding it to you, I know it will not be exposed to the malignant perversions of those who make every word from me a text for new misrepresentations and calumnies. I am moreover averse to the communication of my religious tenets to the public; because it would countenance the presumption of those who have endeavored to draw them before that tribunal, and to seduce public opinion to erect itself into that inquisition over the rights of conscience, which the laws have so justly proscribed. It behooves every man who values liberty of conscience for himself, to resist invasions of it in the case of others;

or their case may, by change of circumstances, become his own. It behooves him, too, in his own case, to give no example of concession, betraying the common right of independent opinion, by answering questions of faith, which the laws have left between God and himself. Accept my affectionate salutations.

Syllabus of an Estimate of the Merit of the Doctrines of Jesus, compared with those of others

In a comparative view of the Ethics of the enlightened nations of antiquity, of the Jews and of Jesus, no notice should be taken of the corruptions of reason among the ancients, to wit, the idolatry and superstition of the vulgar, nor of the corruptions of Christianity by the learned among its professors.

Let a just view be taken of the moral principles inculcated by the most esteemed of the sects of ancient philosophy, or of their individuals; particularly Pythagoras, Socrates, Epicurus, Cicero, Epictetus, Seneca, Antoninus.

I. Philosophers. 1. Their precepts related chiefly to ourselves, and the government of those passions which, unrestrained, would disturb our tranquillity of mind.[1] In this branch of philosophy they were really great.

2. In developing our duties to others, they were short and defective. They embraced, indeed, the circle of kindred and friends, and inculcated patriotism, or the love of our country in the aggregate, as a primary obligation: towards our neighbors and countrymen they taught justice, but scarcely viewed them as within the circle of benevolence.

---

[1]To explain, I will exhibit the heads of Seneca's and Cicero's philosophical works, the most extensive of any we have received from the ancients. Of ten heads in Seneca, seven relate to ourselves, viz. *de ira, consolatio, de tranquilitate, de constantia sapientis, de otio sapientis, de vita beata, de brevitate vitae;* two relate to others, *de clementia, de beneficiis;* and one relates to the government of the world, *de providentia.* Of eleven tracts of Cicero, five respect ourselves, viz. *de finibus, Tusculana, academica, paradoxa, de Senectute;* one, *de officiis,* relates partly to ourselves, partly to others; one, *de amicitia,* relates to others; and four are on different subjects, to wit, *de natura deorum, de divinatione, de fato, and somnium Scipionis.* [Jefferson's footnote.]

Still less have they inculcated peace, charity and love to our fellow men, or embraced with benevolence the whole family of mankind.

II. Jews. 1. Their system was Deism; that is, the belief in one only God. But their ideas of him and of his attributes were degrading and injurious.

2. Their Ethics were not only imperfect, but often irreconcilable with the sound dictates of reason and morality, as they respect intercourse with those around us; and repulsive and anti-social, as respecting other nations. They needed reformation, therefore, in an eminent degree.

III. Jesus. In this state of things among the Jews, Jesus appeared. His parentage was obscure; his condition poor; his education null; his natural endowments great; his life correct and innocent: he was meek, benevolent, patient, firm, disinterested, and of the sublimest eloquence.

The disadvantages under which his doctrines appear are remarkable.

1. Like Socrates and Epictetus, he wrote nothing himself.

2. But he had not, like them, a Xenophon or an Arrian to write for him. I name not Plato, who only used the name of Socrates to cover the whimsies of his own brain. On the contrary, all the learned of his country, entrenched in its power and riches, were opposed to him, lest his labors should undermine their advantages; and the committing to writing his life and doctrines fell on unlettered and ignorant men; who wrote, too, from memory, and not till long after the transactions had passed.

3. According to the ordinary fate of those who attempt to enlighten and reform mankind, he fell an early victim to the jealousy and combination of the altar and the throne, at about thirty-three years of age, his reason having not yet attained the *maximum* of its energy, nor the course of his preaching, which was but of three years at most, presented occasions for developing a complete system of morals.

4. Hence the doctrines which he really delivered were defective as a whole, and fragments only of what he did deliver have come to us mutilated, misstated, and often unintelligible.

5. They have been still more disfigured by the corruptions of schismatizing followers, who have found an interest in sophisticating and perverting the simple doctrines he taught, by engrafting on them the mysticisms of a Grecian sophist, frittering them into subtleties, and

obscuring them with jargon, until they have caused good men to reject the whole in disgust, and to view Jesus himself as an impostor.

Notwithstanding these disadvantages, a system of morals is presented to us, which, if filled up in the style and spirit of the rich fragments he left us, would be the most perfect and sublime that has ever been taught by man.

The question of his being a member of the Godhead, or in direct communication with it, claimed for him by some of his followers, and denied by others, is foreign to the present view, which is merely an estimate of the intrinsic merits of his doctrines.

1. He corrected the Deism of the Jews, confirming them in their belief of one only God, and giving them juster notions of his attributes and government.

2. His moral doctrines, relating to kindred and friends, were more pure and perfect than those of the most correct of the philosophers, and greatly more so than those of the Jews; and they went far beyond both in inculcating universal philanthropy, not only to kindred and friends, to neighbors and countrymen, but to all mankind, gathering all into one family, under the bonds of love, charity, peace, common wants and common aids. A development of this head will evince the peculiar superiority of the system of Jesus over all others.

3. The precepts of philosophy, and of the Hebrew code, laid hold of actions only. He pushed his scrutinies into the heart of man; erected his tribunal in the region of his thoughts, and purified the waters at the fountain head.

4. He taught, emphatically, the doctrines of a future state, which was either doubted, or disbelieved by the Jews; and wielded it with efficacy, as an important incentive, supplementary to the other motives to moral conduct.

TO GENERAL HORATIO GATES[1]

Washington, July 11, 1803

DEAR GENERAL,—I accept with pleasure, and with pleasure reciprocate your congratulations on the acquisition of Louisiana; for it is a
subject of mutual congratulation, as it interests every man of the nation.
The territory acquired, as it includes all the waters of the Missouri and
Mississippi, has more than doubled the area of the United States, and
the new parts is not inferior to the old in soil, climate, productions
and important communications. If our Legislature dispose of it with
the wisdom we have a right to expect, they may make it the means of
tempting all our Indians on the east side of the Mississippi to remove to
the west, and of condensing instead of scattering our population. I find
our opposition is very willing to pluck feathers from Monroe, although
not fond of sticking them into Livingston's coat. The truth is, both have
a just portion of merit; and were it necessary or proper, it would be
shown that each has rendered peculiar services, and of important value.
These grumblers, too, are very uneasy lest the administration should
share some little credit for the acquisition, the whole of which they
ascribe to the accident of war. They would be cruelly mortified could
they see our files from May, 1801, the first organization of the administration, but more especially from April, 1802. They would see, that
though we could not say when war would arise, yet we said with energy
what would take place when it should arise. We did not, by our
intrigues, produce the war; but we availed ourselves of it when it happened. The other party saw the case now existing, on which our representations were predicated, and the wisdom of timely sacrifice. But
when these people make the war give us everything, they authorize us
to ask what the war gave us in their day? They had a war; what did
they make it bring us? Instead of making our neutrality the ground of
gain to their country, they were for plunging into the war. And if they
were now in place, they would now be at war against the atheists and
disorganizers of France. They were for making their country an

[1]General Horatio Gates, although British born, espoused the patriot cause and served
with distinction in the American Army during the Revolution.

appendage to England. We are friendly, cordially and conscientiously friendly to England. We are not hostile to France. We will be rigorously just and sincerely friendly to both. I do not believe we shall have as much to swallow from them as our predecessors had. . . . .

TO MONSIEUR CABANIS[1]

Washington, July 12, 1803

DEAR SIR,—I lately received your friendly letter . . . with the two volumes on the relations between the physical and moral faculties of man. This has ever been a subject of great interest to the inquisitive mind, and it could not have got into better hands for discussion than yours. That thought may be a faculty of our material organization, has been believed in the gross; and though the "modus operandi" of nature, in this, as in most other cases, can never be developed and demonstrated to beings limited as we are, yet I feel confident you will have conducted us as far on the road as we can go, and have lodged us within reconnoitering distance of the citadel itself. . . . .

TO WILSON C. NICHOLAS[2]

Monticello, September 7, 1803

. . . . I am aware of the force of the observations you make on the power given by the Constitution to Congress, to admit new States into the Union, without restraining the subject to the territory then constituting the United States. But when I consider that the limits of the United States are precisely fixed by the treaty of 1783, that the Constitution expressly declares itself to be made for the United States, I cannot help believing the intention was not to permit Congress to admit into the Union new States, which should be formed out of the

[1]Pierre Jean George Cabanis, doctor and Ideologic philosopher, was a pioneer in the field of experimental physiology.

[2]As United States Senator and Representative, and as Governor of Virginia, Wilson Cary Nicholas was a vigorous supporter of his long-time friend Thomas Jefferson.

territory for which, and under whose authority alone, they were then acting. I do not believe it was meant that they might receive England, Ireland, Holland, etc. into it, which would be the case on your construction. When an instrument admits two constructions, the one safe, the other dangerous, the one precise, the other indefinite, I prefer that which is safe and precise. I had rather ask an enlargement of power from the nation, where it is found necessary, than to assume it by a construction which would make our powers boundless. Our peculiar security is in the possession of a written Constitution. Let us not make it a blank paper by construction. I say the same as to the opinion of those who consider the grant of the treaty making power as boundless. If it is, then we have no Constitution. If it has bounds, they can be no others than the definitions of the powers which that instrument gives. It specifies and delineates the operations permitted to the federal government, and gives all the powers necessary to carry these into execution. Whatever of these enumerated objects is proper for a law, Congress may make the law; whatever is proper to be executed by way of a treaty, the President and Senate may enter into the treaty; whatever is to be done by a judicial sentence, the judges may pass the sentence. Nothing is more likely than that their enumeration of powers is defective. This is the ordinary case of all human works. Let us go on then perfecting it, by adding, by way of amendment to the Constitution, those powers which time and trial show are still wanting. But it has been taken too much for granted, that by this rigorous construction the treaty power would be reduced to nothing. I had occasion once to examine its effect on the French treaty, made by the old Congress, and found that out of thirty odd articles which that contained, there were one, two, or three only which could not now be stipulated under our present Constitution. I confess, then, I think it important, in the present case, to set an example against broad construction, by appealing for new power to the people. If, however, our friends shall think differently, certainly I shall acquiesce with satisfaction; confiding, that the good sense of our country will correct the evil of construction when it shall produce ill effects. . . . . .

TO JEAN BAPTISTE SAY[1]

Washington, February 1, 1804

DEAR SIR,—I have to acknowledge the receipt of your obliging letter, and with it, of two very interesting volumes on Political Economy. These found me engaged in giving the leisure moments I rarely find, to the perusal of Malthus' work on population, a work of sound logic, in which some of the opinions of Adam Smith, as well as of the economists, are ably examined. I was pleased, on turning to some chapters where you treat the same questions, to find his opinions corroborated by yours. I shall proceed to the reading of your work with great pleasure. In the meantime, the present conveyance, by a gentleman of my family going to Paris, is too safe to hazard a delay in making my acknowledgments for this mark of attention, and for having afforded to me a satisfaction, which the ordinary course of literary communications could not have given me for a considerable time.

The differences of circumstance between this and the old countries of Europe, furnish differences of fact whereon to reason, in questions of political economy, and will consequently produce sometimes a difference of result. There, for instance, the quantity of food is fixed, or increasing in a slow and only arithmetical ratio, and the proportion is limited by the same ratio. Supernumerary births consequently add only to your mortality. Here the immense extent of uncultivated and fertile lands enables every one who will labor, to marry young, and to raise a family of any size. Our food, then, may increase geometrically with our laborers, and our births, however multiplied, become effective. Again, there the best distribution of labor is supposed to be that which places the manufacturing hands alongside the agricultural; so that the one part shall feed both, and the other part furnish both with clothes and other comforts. Would that be best here? Egoism and first appearances say yes. Or would it be better that all our laborers should be employed in agriculture? In this case a double or treble portion of fertile lands would be brought into culture; a double or treble creation

---

[1]Jean Baptiste Say, philosopher of scientific economics, modified and developed the work of Adam Smith. He was founder and editor of the *Décade philosphique*, organ of the French Ideologists.

of food be produced, and its surplus go to nourish the now perishing births of Europe, who in return would manufacture and send us in exchange our clothes and other comforts. Morality listens to this, and so invariably do the laws of nature create our duties and interests, that when they seem to be at variance, we ought to suspect some fallacy in our reasonings. In solving this question, too, we should allow its just weight to the moral and physical preference of the agricultural, over the manufacturing, man. My occupations permit me only to ask questions. They deny me the time, if I had the information, to answer them. Perhaps, as worthy the attention of the author of the *Traité d'Economie Politique*, I shall find them answered in that work. If they are not, the reason will have been that you wrote for Europe; while I shall have asked them because I think for America. Accept, Sir, my respectful salutations, and assurances of great consideration.

TO JUDGE JOHN TYLER[1]

Washington, June 28, 1804

. . . . No experiment can be more interesting than that we are now trying, and which we trust will end in establishing the fact, that man may be governed by reason and truth. Our first object should therefore be, to leave open to him all the avenues to truth. The most effectual hitherto found, is the freedom of the press. It is, therefore, the first shut up by those who fear the investigation of their actions. The firmness with which the people have withstood the late abuses of the press, the discernment they have manifested between truth and falsehood, show that they may safely be trusted to hear everything true and false, and to form a correct judgment between them. As little is it necessary to impose on their senses, or dazzle their minds by pomp, splendor, or forms. Instead of this artificial, how much surer is that real respect, which results from the use of their reason, and the habit of bringing everything to the test of common sense.

[1]Judge John Tyler, Revolutionary patriot, Governor of Virginia, and father of President John Tyler, had met Jefferson when Jefferson was studying law in Williamsburg. The two men continued to be friends until Tyler's death in 1813.

I hold it, therefore, certain, that to open the doors of truth, and to fortify the habit of testing everything by reason, are the most effectual manacles we can rivet on the hands of our successors to prevent their manacling the people with their own consent. The panic into which they were artfully thrown in 1798, the frenzy which was excited in them by their enemies against their apparent readiness to abandon all the principles established for their own protection, seemed for awhile to countenance the opinions of those who say they cannot be trusted with their own government. But I never doubted their rallying; and they did rally much sooner than I expected. On the whole, that experiment on their credulity has confirmed my confidence in their ultimate good sense and virtue. . . . .

TO C. F. C. DE VOLNEY[1]

Washington, February 8, 1805

. . . . In no case, perhaps, does habit attach our choice or judgment more than in climate. The Canadian glows with delight in his sleigh and snow; the very idea of which gives me the shivers. The comparison of climate between Europe and North America, taking together its corresponding parts, hangs chiefly on three great points. 1. The changes between heat and cold in America are greater and more frequent, and the extremes comprehend a greater scale on the thermometer in America than in Europe. Habit, however, prevents these from affecting us more than the smaller changes of Europe affect the European. But he is greatly affected by ours. 2. Our sky is always clear; that of Europe always cloudy. Hence a greater accumulation of heat here than there, in the same parallel. 3. The changes between wet and dry are much more frequent and sudden in Europe than in America. Though we have double the rain, it falls in half the time. Taking all these together, I prefer much the climate of the United States to that of Europe. I think it a more cheerful one. It is our cloudless sky which

[1]Constantin François Chasseboeuf Volney, French *savant* and author of *Les Ruines*, which Jefferson translated into English, was a close friend of Jefferson's during his stay in America.

has eradicated from our constitutions all disposition to hang ourselves, which we might otherwise have inherited from our English ancestors. During a residence of between six and seven years in Paris, I never, but once, saw the sun shine through a whole day, without being obscured by a cloud in any part of it; and I never saw the moment, in which, viewing the sky through its whole hemisphere, I could say there was not the smallest speck of a cloud in it. I arrived at Monticello, on my return from France, in January; and during only two months' stay there, I observed to my daughters, who had been with me to France, that, twenty odd times within that term, there was not a speck of a cloud in the whole hemisphere. Still I do not wonder that an European should prefer his gray to our azure sky. Habit decides our taste in this, as in most other cases. . . . .

TO THE CHIEFS OF THE CHEROKEE NATION

Washington, January 10, 1806

MY FRIENDS AND CHILDREN, CHIEFLY OF THE CHEROKEE NATION,— Having now finished our business and finished it I hope to mutual satisfaction, I cannot take leave of you without expressing the satisfaction I have received from your visit. I see with my own eyes that the endeavors we have been making to encourage and lead you in the way of improving your situation have not been unsuccessful; it has been like grains sown in good ground, producing abundantly. You are becoming farmers, learning the use of the plough and the hoe, enclosing your grounds and employing that labor in their cultivation which you formerly employed in hunting and in war; and I see handsome specimens of cotton cloth raised, spun and wove by yourselves. You are also raising cattle and hogs for your food, and horses to assist your labors. Go on, my children, in the same way and be assured the further you advance in it the happier and more respectable you will be.

Our brethren, whom you have happened to meet here from the West and Northwest, have enabled you to compare your situation now with what it was formerly. They also make the comparison, and they see how far you are ahead of them, and seeing what you are they are encouraged to do as you have done. You will find your next want to be mills to grind your corn, which by relieving your women from the loss of time in beating it into meal, will enable them to spin and weave more. When a man has enclosed and improved his farm, builds a good house on it and raised plentiful stocks of animals, he will wish when he dies that these things shall go to his wife and children, whom he loves more than he does his other relations, and for whom he will work with pleasure during his life. You will, therefore, find it necessary to establish laws for this. When a man has property, earned by his own labor, he will not like to see another come and take it from him because he happens to be stronger, or else to defend it by spilling blood. You will find it necessary then to appoint good men, as judges, to decide contests between man and man, according to reason and to the rules you shall establish. If you wish to be aided by our counsel and experience in these things we shall always be ready to assist you with our advice.

My children, it is unnecessary for me to advise you against spending all your time and labor in warring with and destroying your fellow-men, and wasting your own members. You already see the folly and iniquity of it. Your young men, however, are not yet sufficiently sensible of it. Some of them cross the Mississippi to go and destroy people who have never done them an injury. My children, this is wrong and must not be; if we permit them to cross the Mississippi to war with the Indians on the other side of that river, we must let those Indians cross the river to take revenge on you. I say again, this must not be. The Mississippi now belongs to us. It must not be a river of blood. It is now the water-path along which all our people of Natchez, St. Louis, Indiana, Ohio, Tennessee, Kentucky and the western parts of Pennsylvania and Virginia are constantly passing with their property, to and from New Orleans. Young men going to war are not easily restrained. Finding our people on the river they will rob them, perhaps kill them. This would bring on a war between us and you. It is better to stop this in time by forbidding your young men to go across the river to make war. If they go to visit or to live with the Cherokees on the other side of the river we shall not object to that. That country is ours. We will permit them to live in it.

My children, this is what I wished to say to you. To go on in learning to cultivate the earth and to avoid war. If any of your neighbors injure you, our beloved men whom we place with you will endeavor to obtain justice for you and we will support them in it. If any of your bad people injure your neighbors, be ready to acknowledge it and to do them justice. It is more honorable to repair a wrong than to persist in it. Tell all your chiefs, your men, women and children, that I take them by the hand and hold it fast. That I am their father, wish their happiness and well-being, and am always ready to promote their good.

My children, I thank you for your visit and pray to the Great Spirit who made us all and planted us all in this land to live together like brothers that He will conduct you safely to your homes, and grant you to find your families and your friends in good health.

TO THE REVEREND DOCTOR G. C. JENNER[1]

Monticello, May 14, 1806

SIR,—I have received a copy of the evidence at large respecting the discovery of the vaccine inoculation which you have been pleased to send me, and for which I return you my thanks. Having been among the early converts, in this part of the globe, to its efficiency, I took an early part in recommending it to my countrymen. I avail myself of this occasion of rendering you a portion of the tribute of gratitude due to you from the whole human family. Medicine has never before produced any single improvement of such utility. Harvey's discovery of the circulation of the blood was a beautiful addition to our knowledge of the animal economy, but on a review of the practice of medicine before and since that epoch, I do not see any great amelioration which has been derived from that discovery. You have erased from the calendar of human afflictions one of its greatest. Yours is the comfortable reflection that mankind can never forget that you have lived. Future nations will know by history only that the loathsome smallpox has existed and by you has been extirpated.

Accept my fervent wishes for your health and happiness and assurances of the greatest respect and consideration.

---

[1]This is undoubtedly Dr. Edward Jenner, the famous English physician, who discovered vaccination.

TO JOHN NORVELL[1]

Washington, June 11, 1807

. . . . To your request of my opinion of the manner in which a newspaper should be conducted, so as to be most useful, I should answer, "by restraining it to true facts and sound principles only." Yet I fear such a paper would find few subscribers. It is a melancholy truth, that a suppression of the press could not more completely deprive the nation of its benefits, than is done by its abandoned prostitution to falsehood. Nothing can now be believed which is seen in a newspaper. Truth itself becomes suspicious by being put into that polluted vehicle. The real extent of this state of misinformation is known only to those who are in situations to confront facts within their knowledge with the lies of the day. I really look with commiseration over the great body of my fellow citizens, who, reading newspapers, live and die in the belief, that they have known something of what has been passing in the world in their time; whereas the accounts they have read in newspapers are just as true a history of any other period of the world as of the present, except that the real names of the day are affixed to their fables. General facts may indeed be collected from them, such as that Europe is now at war, that Bonaparte has been a successful warrior, that he has subjected a great portion of Europe to his will, etc., etc.; but no details can be relied on. I will add, that the man who never looks into a newspaper is better informed than he who reads them; inasmuch as he who knows nothing is nearer to truth than he whose mind is filled with falsehoods and errors. He who reads nothing will still learn the great facts, and the details are all false.

Perhaps an editor might begin a reformation in some such way as this. Divide his paper into four chapters, heading the 1st, Truths. 2d, Probabilities. 3d, Possibilities. 4th, Lies. The first chapter would be very short, as it would contain little more than authentic papers, and information from such sources, as the editor would be willing to risk his own reputation for their truth. The second would contain what,

[1]Norvell, a resident of Danville, Virginia, had written Jefferson concerning starting a newspaper.

from a mature consideration of all circumstances, his judgment should conclude to be probably true. This, however, should rather contain too little than too much. The third and fourth should be professedly for those readers who would rather have lies for their money than the blank paper they would occupy

Such an editor too, would have to set his face against the demoralizing practice of feeding the public mind habitually on slander, and the depravity of taste which this nauseous aliment induces. Defamation is becoming a necessary of life; insomuch, that a dish of tea in the morning or evening cannot be digested without this stimulant. Even those who do not believe these abominations, still read them with complaisance to their auditors, and instead of the abhorrence and indignation which should fill a virtuous mind, betray a secret pleasure in the possibility that some may believe them, though they do not themselves. It seems to escape them, that it is not he who prints, but he who pays for printing a slander, who is its real author. . . . .

TO GOVERNOR JAMES SULLIVAN[1]

Washington, June 19, 1807

. . . . With respect to the tour my friends of the north have proposed that I should make in that quarter, I have not made up a final opinion. The course of life which General Washington had run, civil and military, the services he had rendered, and the space he, therefore, occupied in the affections of his fellow citizens, take from his examples the weight of precedent for others, because no others can arrogate to themselves the claims which he had on the public homage. To myself, therefore, it comes as a new question, to be viewed under all the phases it may present. I confess that I am not reconciled to the idea of a chief magistrate parading himself through the several States, as an object of public gaze, and in quest of an applause which, to be valuable, should be purely voluntary. I had rather acquire silent goodwill by a faithful discharge of my duties, than owe expressions of it to my putting myself in the way of receiving them. Were I to make such

[1]Governor of Massachusetts.

a tour to Portsmouth or Portland, I must do it to Savannah, perhaps to Orleans and Frankfort. As I have never yet seen the time when the public business would have permitted me to be so long in a situation in which I could not carry it on, so I have no reason to expect that such a time will come while I remain in office. A journey to Boston or Portsmouth, after I shall be a private citizen, would much better harmonize with my feelings, as well as duties; and, founded in curiosity, would give no claims to an extension of it. I should see my friends too, more at our mutual ease, and be left more exclusively to their society. However, I end as I began, by declaring I have made up no opinion on the subject, and that I reserve it as a question for future consideration and advice. . . . .

TO DOCTOR CASPER WISTAR[1]

Washington, June 21, 1807

. . . the disorders of the animal body, and the symptoms indicating them, are as various as the elements of which the body is composed. The combinations, too, of these symptoms are so infinitely diversified, that many associations of them appear too rarely to establish a definite disease; and to an unknown disease, there cannot be a known remedy. Here then, the judicious, the moral, the humane physician should stop. Having been so often a witness to the salutary efforts which nature makes to re-establish the disordered functions, he should rather trust to their action, than hazard the interruption of that, and a greater derangement of the system, by conjectural experiments on a machine so complicated and so unknown as the human body, and a subject so sacred as human life. Or, if the appearance of doing something be necessary to keep alive the hope and spirits of the patient, it should be of the most innocent character. One of the most successful physicians I have ever known, has assured me, that he used more bread pills, drops of colored water, and powders of hickory ashes, than of all other medicines put together. It was certainly a pious fraud. But the adventur-

[1]Casper Wistar was professor of anatomy and surgery at the University of Pennsylvania and, succeeding Jefferson in 1815, was president of the American Philosophical Society.

ous physician goes on, and substitutes presumption for knowledge. From the scanty field of what is known, he launches into the boundless region of what is unknown. He establishes for his guide some fanciful theory of corpuscular attraction, of chemical agency, of mechanical powers, of stimuli, of irritability accumulated or exhausted, of depletion by the lancet and repletion by mercury, or some other ingenious dream, which lets him into all nature's secrets at short hand. On the principle which he thus assumes, he forms his table of nosology, arrays his diseases into families, and extends his curative treatment, by analogy, to all the cases he has thus arbitrarily marshalled together. I have lived myself to see the disciples of Hoffman, Boerhaave, Stahl, Cullen, Brown, succeed one another like the shifting figures of a magic lantern, and their fancies, like the dresses of the annual doll-babies from Paris, becoming, from their novelty, the vogue of the day, and yielding to the next novelty their ephemeral favor. The patient, treated on the fashionable theory, sometimes gets well in spite of the medicine. The medicine, therefore, restored him, and the young doctor receives new courage to proceed in his bold experiments on the lives of his fellow-creatures. I believe we may safely affirm, that the inexperienced and presumptuous band of medical tyros let loose upon the world, destroys more of human life in one year, than all the Robinhoods, Cartouches, and Macheaths do in a century. It is in this part of medicine that I wish to see a reform, an abandonment of hypothesis for sober facts, the first degree of value set on clinical observation, and the lowest on visionary theories. I would wish the young practitioner, especially, to have deeply impressed on his mind, the real limits of his art, and that when the state of his patient gets beyond these, his office is to be a watchful, but quiet spectator of the operations of nature, giving them fair play by a well-regulated regimen, and by all the aid they can derive from the excitement of good spirits and hope in the patient. . . . .

TO MONSIEUR DUPONT DE NEMOURS[1]

Washington, July 14, 1807

. . . . Burr's conspiracy has been one of the most flagitious of which history will ever furnish an example. He had combined the objects of separating the western States from us, of adding Mexico to them, and of placing himself at their head. But he who could expect to effect such objects by the aid of American citizens, must be perfectly ripe for Bedlam. Yet although there is not a man in the United States who is not satisfied of the depth of his guilt, such are the jealous provisions of our laws in favor of the accused, and against the accuser, that I question if he can be convicted. Out of the forty-eight jurors who are to be summoned, he has a right to choose the twelve who are to try him, and if any one of the twelve refuses to concur in finding him guilty, he escapes. This affair has been a great confirmation in my mind of the innate strength of the form of our government. He had probably induced near a thousand men to engage with him, by making them believe the government connived at it. A proclamation alone, by undeceiving them, so completely disarmed him, that he had not above thirty men left, ready to go all lengths with him. The first enterprise was to have been the seizure of New Orleans, which he supposed would powerfully bridle the country above, and place him at the door of Mexico. It has given me infinite satisfaction that not a single native Creole of Louisiana, and but one American, settled there before the delivery of the country to us, were in his interest. His partisans there were made up of fugitives from justice, or from their debts, who had flocked there from other parts of the United States, after the delivery of the country, and of adventurers and speculators of all descriptions. . . . . .

---

[1]Jefferson first met Pierre Samuel DuPont de Nemours, celebrated liberal and educator, in Paris. Their friendship, solidified in 1800 when the noted physiocrat established residence in America, continued until the latter's death in 1817.

TO CHARLES PINCKNEY[1]

Washington, March 30, 1808

. . . . With France we are in no *immediate* danger of war. Her future views it is impossible to estimate. The immediate danger we are in of a rupture with England, is postponed for this year. This is effected by the embargo, as the question was simply between that and war. That may go on a certain time, perhaps through the year, without the loss of their property to our citizens, but only its remaining unemployed on their hands. A time would come, however, when war would be preferable to a continuance of the embargo. Of this Congress may have to decide at their next meeting. In the meantime, we have good information, that a negotiation for peace between France and England is commencing through the medium of Austria. The way for it has been smoothed by a determination expressed by France (through the Moniteur, which is their government paper) that herself and her allies will demand from Great Britain no renunciation of her maritime principles; nor will they renounce theirs. Nothing shall be said about them in the treaty, and both sides will be left in the next war to act on their own. No doubt the meaning of this is, that all the *Continental* powers of Europe will form themselves into an armed neutrality, to enforce their own principles. Should peace be made, we shall have safely rode out the storm in peace and prosperity. If we have anything to fear, it will be after that. Nothing should be spared from this moment in putting our militia in the best condition possible, and procuring arms. I hope, that this summer, we shall get our whole seaports put into that state of defence, which Congress has thought proportioned to our circumstances and situation; that is to say, put *hors d'insulte* from a maritime attack, by a moderate squadron. If armies are combined with their fleets, then no resource can be provided, but to meet them in the field. We propose to raise seven regiments only for the present year, depending always on our militia for the operations of the first year of war.

[1]Charles Cotesworth Pinckney of South Carolina, Revolutionary soldier, statesman, and diplomat, had opposed Jefferson, as Federalist candidate, in the Presidential election of 1804.

On any other plan, we should be obliged always to keep a large standing army. . . . .

TO THE PRINCE REGENT OF PORTUGAL

Washington, May 5, 1808

GREAT AND GOOD FRIEND,—Having learnt the safe arrival of your Royal Highness at the city of Rio Janeiro, I perform with pleasure the duty of offering you my sincere congratulations by Mr. Hill, a respected citizen of the United States, who is specially charged with the delivery of this letter.

I trust that this event will be as propitious to the prosperity of your faithful subjects as to the happiness of your Royal Highness, in which the United States of America have ever taken a lively interest. Inhabitants now of the same land, of that great continent which the genius of Columbus has given to the world, the United States feel sensibly that they stand in new and closer relations with your Royal Highness, and that the motives which heretofore nourished the friendly relations which have so happily prevailed, have acquired increased strength on the transfer of your residence to their own shores. They see in prospect, a system of intercourse between the different regions of this hemisphere of which the peace and happiness of mankind may be the essential principle. To this principle your long-tried adherence, for the benefit of those you governed, in the midst of warring powers, is a pledge to the new world that its peace, its free and friendly intercourse, will be your chief concern. On the part of the United States I assure you, that these which have hitherto been their ruling objects, will be most particularly cultivated with your Royal Highness and your subjects at Brazil, and they hope that that country so favored by the gifts of nature, now advanced to a station under your immediate auspices, will find, in the interchange of mutual wants and supplies, the true aliment of an unchanging friendship with the United States of America.

TO MONSIEUR LASTEYRIE[1]

Washington, July 15, 1808

SIR,—I have duly received your favor of March 28th, and with it your treatises on the culture of the sugar cane and cotton plant in France. The introduction of new cultures, and especially of objects of leading importance to our comfort, is certainly worthy the attention of every government, and nothing short of the actual experiment should discourage an essay of which any hope can be entertained. Till that is made, the result is open to conjecture; and I should certainly conjecture that the sugar cane could never become an article of profitable culture in France. We have within the ancient limits of the United States, a great extent of country which brings the orange to advantage, but not a foot in which the sugar cane can be matured. France, within its former limits, has but two small spots, (Olivreles and Hieres) which brings the orange in open air, and *a fortiori*, therefore, none proper for the cane. I should think the maple-sugar more worthy of experiment. There is no part of France of which the climate would not admit this tree. I have never seen a reason why every farmer should not have a sugar orchard, as well as an apple orchard. The supply of sugar for his family would require as little ground, and the process of making it as easy as that of cider. Mr. Micheaux, your botanist here, could send you plants as well as seeds, in any quantity from the United States. I have no doubt the cotton plant will succeed in some of the southern parts of France. Whether its culture will be as advantageous as those they are now engaged in, remains to be tried. We could, in the United States, make as great a variety of wines as are made in Europe, not exactly of the same kinds, but doubtless as good. Yet I have ever observed to my countrymen, who think its introduction important, that a laborer cultivating wheat, rice, tobacco, or cotton here, will be able with the proceeds, to purchase double the quantity of the wine he could make. Possibly the same quantity of land and labor in France employed on the rich produce of your Southern

[1]Lasteyrie du Saillant was an outstanding French agronomist and a sponsor of progressive agricultural and industrial societies.

counties, would purchase double the quantity of the cotton they would yield there. This however may prove otherwise on trial, and therefore it is worthy the trial. In general, it is a truth that if every nation will employ itself in what it is fittest to produce, a greater quantity will be raised of the things contributing to human happiness, than if every nation attempts to raise everything it wants within itself. . . . .

TO THOMAS JEFFERSON RANDOLPH[1]

Washington, November 24, 1808

MY DEAR JEFFERSON, ... Your situation, thrown at such a distance from us, and alone, cannot but give us all great anxieties for you. As much has been secured for you, by your particular position and the acquaintance to which you have been recommended, as could be done towards shielding you from the dangers which surround you. But thrown on a wide world, among entire strangers, without a friend or guardian to advise, so young too, and with so little experience of mankind, your dangers are great, and still your safety must rest on yourself. A determination never to do what is wrong, prudence and good humor, will go far towards securing to you the estimation of the world. When I recollect that at fourteen years of age, the whole care and direction of myself was thrown on myself entirely, without a relation or friend qualified to advise or guide me, and recollect the various sorts of bad company with which I associated from time to time, I am astonished I did not turn off with some of them, and become as worthless to society as they were. I had the good fortune to become acquainted very early with some characters of very high standing, and to feel the incessant wish that I could ever become what they were. Under temptations and difficulties, I would ask myself what would Dr. Small, Mr. Wythe, Peyton Randolph do in this situation? What course in it will insure me their approbation? I am certain that this mode of deciding on my conduct, tended more to correctness than any reasoning powers I possessed. Knowing the even and dignified line they pur-

[1]Thomas Jefferson Randolph, Jefferson's oldest and favorite grandson was the son of Thomas Mann Randolph and Martha Jefferson.

sued, I could never doubt for a moment which of two courses would be in character for them. Whereas, seeking the same object through a process of moral reasoning, and with the jaundiced eye of youth, I should often have erred. From the circumstances of my position, I was often thrown into the society of horse racers, card players, fox hunters, scientific and professional men, and of dignified men; and many a time have I asked myself, in the enthusiastic moment of the death of a fox, the victory of a favorite horse, the issue of a question eloquently argued at the bar, or in the great council of the nation, well, which of these kinds of reputation should I prefer? That of a horse jockey? a fox hunter? an orator? or the honest advocate of my country's rights? Be assured, my dear Jefferson, that these little returns into ourselves, this self-catechising habit, is not trifling nor useless, but leads to the prudent selection and steady pursuit of what is right.

I have mentioned good humor as one of the preservatives of our peace and tranquillity. It is among the most effectual, and its effect is so well imitated and aided, artificially, by politeness, that this also becomes an acquisition of first rate value. In truth, politeness is artificial good humor, it covers the natural want of it, and ends by rendering habitual a substitute nearly equivalent to the real virtue. It is the practice of sacrificing to those whom we meet in society, all the little conveniences and preferences which will gratify them, and deprive us of nothing worth a moment's consideration; it is the giving a pleasing and flattering turn to our expressions, which will conciliate others, and make them pleased with us as well as themselves. How cheap a price for the good will of another! When this is in return for a rude thing said by another, it brings him to his senses, it mortifies and corrects him in the most salutary way, and places him at the feet of your good nature, in the eyes of the company. But in stating prudential rules for our government in society, I must not omit the important one of never entering into dispute or argument with another. I never saw an instance of one of two disputants convincing the other by argument. I have seen many, on their getting warm, becoming rude, and shooting one another. Conviction is the effect of our own dispassionate reasoning, either in solitude, or weighing within ourselves, dispassionately, what we hear from others, standing uncommitted in argument ourselves. It was one of the rules which, above all others, made Doctor Franklin the most amiable of men in society, "never to contradict anybody." If he was urged to announce an opinion, he did it rather by asking questions, as if for information, or by suggesting doubts. When I hear another express an opinion which is not mine, I say to myself, he has a right to his opinion, as I to mine; why should I question it? His error does me no injury, and shall I become a Don Quixote, to bring all men by force of argument to one opinion? If a fact be misstated, it is probable he is gratified by a belief of it, and I have no right to deprive him of the gratification. If he wants information, he will ask it, and then I will give it in measured terms; but if he still believes his own story, and shows a desire to dispute the fact with me, I hear him and say nothing. It is his affair, not mine, if he prefers error. There are two classes of disputants most frequently to be met with among us. The first is of young students, just entered the threshold of science, with a first view of its outlines, not yet filled up with the details and modifications which a further progress would bring to their knowledge. The other consists of the ill-tempered and rude men in society, who have taken up a passion for politics. (Good humor and politeness never introduce into mixed society, a question on which they foresee there will be a difference of opinion.) From both of these classes of disputants, my dear Jefferson, keep aloof, as you would from the infected subjects of yellow fever or pestilence. Consider yourself, when with them, as among the patients of Bedlam, needing medical more than moral counsel. Be a listener only, keep within yourself, and endeavor to establish with yourself the habit of silence, especially on politics. In the fevered state of our country, no good can ever result from any attempt to set one of these fiery zealots to rights, either in fact or principle. They are determined as to the facts they will believe, and the opinions on which they will act. Get by them, therefore, as you would by an angry bull; it is not for a man of sense to dispute the road with such an animal. You will be more exposed than others to have these animals shaking their horns at you, because of the relation in which you stand with me. Full of political venom, and willing to see me and to hate me as a chief in the antagonist party, your presence will be to them what the vomit grass is to the sick dog, a nostrum for producing ejaculation. Look upon them exactly with that eye, and pity them as objects to whom you can administer only occasional ease. My character is not within their power. It is in the hands of my fellow citizens at large, and will be consigned to honor or infamy by the verdict of the republican mass of our country, according to what themselves will have seen, not what their enemies and mine shall have said. Never, therefore, consider these puppies in politics as requiring any notice from you, and always show that you are not afraid to leave my character to the umpirage of public opinion. Look steadily to the pursuits which have carried you to Philadelphia, be very select in the society you attach yourself to, avoid taverns, drinkers, smokers, idlers, and dissipated persons generally; for it is with such that broils and contentions arise; and you will find your path more easy and tranquil. The limits of my paper warn me that it is time for me to close with my affectionate adieu.

TO THOMAS LEIPER[1]

Washington, January 21, 1809

. . . . I have lately inculcated the encouragement of manufactures to the extent of our own consumption at least, in all articles of which we raise the raw material. On this the federal papers and meetings have sounded the alarm of Chinese policy, destruction of commerce, etc.; that is to say, the iron which we make must not be wrought here into ploughs, axes hoes, etc., in order that the ship-owner may have the profit of carrying it to Europe, and bringing it back in a manufactured form, as if after manufacturing our own raw materials for our own use, there would not be a surplus produce sufficient to employ a due proportion of navigation in carrying it to market and exchanging it for those articles of which we have not the raw material. Yet this absurd hue and cry has contributed much to federalize New England, their doctrine goes to the sacrificing agriculture and manufactures to commerce; to the calling all our people from the interior country to the sea-shore to turn merchants, and to convert this great agricultural country into a city of Amsterdam. But I trust the good sense of our country will see that its greatest prosperity depends on a due balance between

[1]Thomas Leiper was a Scottish born merchant who served in the Revolution against England and who later became a staunch Jeffersonian.

agriculture, manufactures and commerce, and not in this protuberant navigation which has kept us in hot water from the commencement of our government, and is now engaging us in war. That this may be avoided, if it can be done without a surrender of rights, is my sincere prayer. Accept the assurances of my constant esteem and respect

TO JOHN HOLLINS

Washington, February 19, 1809

. . . . General Washington, in his time, received from the same Society[1] the seed of the perennial succory, which Arthur Young had carried over from France to England, and I have since received from a member of it the seed of the famous turnip of Sweden, now so well known here. I mention these things, to show the nature of the correspondence which is carried on between societies instituted for the benevolent purpose of communicating to all parts of the world whatever useful is discovered in any one of them. These societies are always in peace, however their nations may be at war. Like the republic of letters, they form a great fraternity spreading over the whole earth, and their correspondence is never interrupted by any civilized nation. . . . .

TO M. HENRI GRÉGOIRE, ÉVÊQUE ET SÉNATEUR À PARIS

Washington, February 25, 1809

SIR,—I have received the favor of your letter of August 17th, and with it the volume you were so kind as to send me on the "Literature of Negroes." Be assured that no person living wishes more sincerely than I do, to see a complete refutation of the doubts I have myself entertained and expressed on the grade of understanding allotted to them by nature, and to find that in this respect they are on a par with ourselves. My doubts were the result of personal observation on the

[1]The Board of Agriculture of London.

limited sphere of my own State, where the opportunities for the development of their genius were not favorable, and those of exercising it still less so. I expressed them therefore with great hesitation; but whatever be their degree of talent it is no measure of their rights. Because Sir Isaac Newton was superior to others in understanding, he was not therefore lord of the person or property of others. On this subject they are gaining daily in the opinions of nations, and hopeful advances are making towards their re-establishment on an equal footing with the other colors of the human family. I pray you therefore to accept my thanks for the many instances you have enabled me to observe of respectable intelligence in that race of men, which cannot fail to have effect in hastening the day of their relief; and to be assured of the sentiments of high and just esteem and consideration which I tender to yourself with all sincerity.

TO MONSIEUR DUPONT DE NEMOURS

Washington, March 2, 1809

. . . . Within a few days I retire to my family, my books and farms; and having gained the harbor myself, I shall look on my friends still buffeting the storm with anxiety indeed, but not with envy. Never did a prisoner, released from his chains, feel such relief as I shall on shaking off the shackles of power. Nature intended me for the tranquil pursuits of science, by rendering them my supreme delight. But the enormities of the times in which I have lived, have forced me to take a part in resisting them, and to commit myself on the boisterous ocean of political passions. I thank God for the opportunity of retiring from them without censure, and carrying with me the most consoling proofs of public approbation. I leave everything in the hands of men so able to take care of them, that if we are destined to meet misfortunes, it will be because no human wisdom could avert them. Should you return to the United States, perhaps your curiosity may lead you to visit the hermit of Monticello. He will receive you with affection and delight; hailing you in the meantime with his affectionate salutations and assurances of constant esteem and respect.

P. S. If you return to us, bring a couple of pair of true-bred shepherd's dogs. You will add a valuable possession to a country now beginning to pay great attention to the raising sheep.

TO THE INHABITANTS OF ALBEMARLE COUNTY,[1] IN VIRGINIA

Monticello, April 3, 1809

Returning to the scenes of my birth and early life, to the society of those with whom I was raised, and who have been ever dear to me, I receive, fellow citizens and neighbors, with inexpressible pleasure, the cordial welcome you are so good as to give me. Long absent on duties which the history of a wonderful era made incumbent on those called to them, the pomp, the turmoil, the bustle and splendor of office, have drawn but deeper sighs for the tranquil and irresponsible occupations of private life, for the enjoyment of an affectionate intercourse with you, my neighbors and friends, and the endearments of family love, which nature has given us all, as the sweetener of every hour. For these I gladly lay down the distressing burden of power, and seek, with my fellow citizens, repose and safety under the watchful cares, the labors and perplexities of younger and abler minds. The anxieties you express to administer to my happiness, do, of themselves, confer that happiness; and the measure will be complete, if my endeavors to fulfil my duties in the several public stations to which I have been called, I have obtained for me the approbation of my country. The part which I have acted on the theatre of public life, has been before them; and to their sentence I submit it; but the testimony of my native county, of the individuals who have known me in private life, to my conduct in its various duties and relations, is the more grateful, as proceeding from eye witnesses and observers, from triers of the vicinage. Of you, then, my neighbors, I may ask, in the face of the world, "whose ox have I taken, or whom have I defrauded? Whom have I oppressed, or of whose hand have I received a bribe to blind mine eyes therewith?" On your verdict I rest with conscious security. Your wishes for my hap-

[1]This is one of the very first letters Jefferson wrote after his final retirement from public office.

piness are received with just sensibility, and I offer sincere prayers for your own welfare and prosperity.

TO JOHN WYCHE

Monticello, May 19, 1809

SIR,—Your favor of March 19th came to hand but a few days ago, and informs me of the establishment of the Westward Mill Library Society, of its general views and progress. I always hear with pleasure of institutions for the promotion of knowledge among my country-men. The people of every country are the only safe guardians of their own rights, and are the only instruments which can be used for their destruction. And certainly they would never consent to be so used were they not deceived. To avoid this, they should be instructed to a cer-tain degree. I have often thought that nothing would do more extensive good at small expense than the establishment of a small circulating library in every county, to consist of a few well-chosen books, to be lent to the people of the country, under such regulations as would secure their safe return in due time. These should be such as would give them a general view of other history, and particular view of that of their own country, a tolerable knowledge of Geography, the elements of Natural Philosophy, of Agriculture and Mechanics. Should your example lead to this, it will do great good. Having had more favorable opportunities than fall to every man's lot of becoming acquainted with the best books on such subjects as might be selected, I do not know that I can be otherwise useful to your society than by offering them any information respecting these which they might wish. My services in this way are freely at their command, and I beg leave to tender to yourself my salutations and assurances of respect.

TO DOCTOR B. S. BARTON[1]

Monticello, September 21, 1809

DEAR SIR,—I received last night your favor of the 14th, and would with all possible pleasure have communicated to you any part or the whole of the Indian vocabularies which I had collected, but an irreparable misfortune has deprived me of them. I have now been thirty years availing myself of every possible opportunity of procuring Indian vocabularies to the same set of words; my opportunities were probably better than will ever occur again to any person having the same desire. I had collected about fifty, and had digested most of them in collateral columns, and meant to have printed them the last of my stay in Washington. But not having yet digested Captain Lewis' collection, nor having leisure then to do it, I put it off till I should return home. The whole, as well digest as originals, were packed in a trunk of stationery, and sent round by water with about thirty other packages of my effects from Washington, and while ascending James river, this package on account of its weight and presumed precious contents, was singled out and stolen. The thief being disappointed on opening it, threw into the river all its contents, of which he thought he could make no use. Among them were the whole of the vocabularies. Some leaves floated ashore and were found in the mud; but these were very few, and so defaced by the mud and water that no general use can be made of them. On the receipt of your letter I turned to them, and was very happy to find, that the only morsel of an original vocabulary among them, was Captain Lewis' of the Pani language, of which you say you have not one word. I therefore enclose it to you as it is, and a little fragment of some other, which I see is in his handwriting, but no indication remains on it of what language it is. It is a specimen of the condition of the little which was recovered. I am the more concerned at this accident, as of the two hundred and fifty words of my vocabularies, and the one hundred and thirty words of the great Russian vocabularies of the languages of the other quarters of the globe, seventy-three

[1]Benjamin Smith Barton, a nephew of David Rittenhouse the astronomer, was a well-known physician and naturalist.

were common to both, and would have furnished materials for a comparison from which something might have resulted. Although I believe no general use can ever be made of the wrecks of my loss, yet I will ask the return of the Pani vocabulary when you are done with it. Perhaps I may make another attempt to collect, although I am too old to expect to make much progress in it. . . . .

TO REV. SAMUEL KNOX[1]

Monticello, February 12, 1810

. . . . The boys of the rising generation are to be the men of the next, and the sole guardians of the principles we deliver over to them. That I have acted through life of those on sincere republicanism I feel in every fibre of my constitution. And when men who feel like myself, bear witness in my favor, my satisfaction is complete . . . The times which brought us within mutual observation were awfully trying. But truth and reason are eternal. They have prevailed. And they will eternally prevail, however in times and places they may be overborne for a while by violence, military, civil, or ecclesiastical. The preservation of the holy fire is confided to us by the world, and the sparks which will emanate from it will ever serve to rekindle it in other quarters of the globe, *numinibus secundis.*[2] . . . .

---

[1]Samuel Knox, a Scottish-born Presbyterian minister and educator, at one time was considered for the professorship of languages and belles-lettres at the proposed University of Virginia.

[2]With the help of the gods.

TO GENERAL THADDEUS KOSCIUSKO[1]

Monticello, February 26, 1810

MY DEAR GENERAL AND FRIEND,—I have rarely written to you; never but by safe conveyances; and avoiding everything political, lest coming from one in the station I then held, it might be imputed injuriously to our country, or perhaps even excite jealousy of you. Hence my letters were necessarily dry. Retired now from public concerns, totally unconnected with them, and avoiding all curiosity about what is done or intended, what I say is from myself only, the workings of my own mind, imputable to nobody else.

The anxieties which I know you have felt, on being exposed to the jostlings of a warring world, a country to which, in early life, you devoted your sword and services when oppressed by foreign dominion, were worthy of your philanthropy and disinterested attachment to the freedom and happiness of man. Although we have not made all the provisions which might be necessary for a war in the field of Europe, yet we have not been inattentive to such as would be necessary here. From the moment that the affair of the Chesapeake rendered the prospect of war imminent, every faculty was exerted to be prepared for it, and I think I may venture to solace you with the assurance, that we are, in a good degree, prepared. Military stores for many campaigns are on hand, all the necessary articles (sulphur excepted), and the art of preparing them among ourselves, abundantly; arms in our magazines for more men than will ever be required in the field, and forty thousand new stand yearly added, of our own fabrication, superior to any we have ever seen from Europe; heavy artillery much beyond our need; an increasing stock of field pieces, several foundries casting one every other day each; a military school of about fifty students, which has been in operation a dozen years; and the manufacture of men constantly going on, and adding forty thousand young soldiers to our force every year that the war is deferred; at all our seaport towns of the least

[1]Thaddeus Kosciusko, the Polish soldier and statesman who had served the American forces during the Revolution, was, in most essentials, a Jeffersonian democrat. He and Jefferson exchanged letters until Kosciusko's death.

consequence we have erected works of defence, and assigned them gunboats, carrying one or two heavy pieces, either eighteen, twenty-four, or thirty-two pounders, sufficient in the smaller harbors to repel the predatory attacks of privateers or single armed ships, and proportioned in the larger harbors to such more serious attacks as they may probably be exposed to. All these were nearly completed, and their gunboats in readiness, when I retired from the government. The works of New York and New Orleans alone, being on a much larger scale, are not yet completed. The former will be finished this summer, mounting four hundred and thirty-eight guns, and, with the aid of from fifty to one hundred gunboats, will be adequate to the resistance of any fleet which will ever be trusted across the Atlantic. The works for New Orleans are less advanced. These are our preparations. They are very different from what you will be told by newspapers, and travellers, even Americans. But it is not to them the government communicates the public condition. Ask one of them if he knows the exact state of any particular harbor, and you will find probably that he does not know even that of the one he comes from. You will ask, perhaps, where are the proofs of these preparations for one who cannot go and see them. I answer, in the acts of Congress, authorizing such preparations, and in your knowledge of me, that, if authorized, they would be executed.

Two measures have not been adopted, which I pressed on Congress repeatedly at their meetings. The one, to settle the whole ungranted territory of Orleans, by donations of land to able-bodied young men, to be engaged and carried there at the public expense, who would constitute a force always ready on the spot to defend New Orleans. The other was, to class the militia according to the years of their birth, and make all those from twenty to twenty-five liable to be trained and called into service at a moment's warning. This would have given us a force of three hundred thousand young men, prepared by proper training, for service in any part of the United States; while those who had passed through that period would remain at home, liable to be used in their own or adjacent States. These two measures would have completed what I deemed necessary for the entire security of our country. They would have given me, on my retirement from the government of the nation, the consolatory reflection, that having found, when I was called to it, not a single seaport town in a condition to repel a levy of contribution by a single privateer or pirate, I had left every harbor so prepared by works and gunboats, as to be in a reasonable state of security against any probable attack; the territory of Orleans acquired, and planted with an internal force sufficient for its protection; and the whole territory of the United States organized by such a classification of its male force, as would give it the benefit of all its young population for active service, and that of a middle and advanced age for stationary defence. But these measures will, I hope, be completed by my successor, who, to the purest principles of republican patriotism, adds a wisdom and foresight second to no man on earth.

So much as to my country. Now a word as to myself. I am retired to Monticello, where, in the bosom of my family, and surrounded by my books, I enjoy a repose to which I have been long a stranger. My mornings are devoted to correspondence. From breakfast to dinner, I am in my shops, my garden, or on horseback among my farms; from dinner to dark, I give to society and recreation with my neighbors and friends; and from candle light to early bed-time, I read. My health is perfect; and my strength considerably reinforced by the activity of the course I pursue; perhaps it is as great as usually falls to the lot of near sixty-seven years of age. I talk of ploughs and harrows, of seeding and harvesting, with my neighbors, and of politics too, if they choose, with as little reserve as the rest of my fellow citizens, and feel, at length, the blessing of being free to say and do what I please, without being responsible for it to any mortal. A part of my occupation, and by no means the least pleasing, is the direction of the studies of such young men as ask it. They place themselves in the neighboring village, and have the use of my library and counsel, and make a part of my society. In advising the course of their reading, I endeavor to keep their attention fixed on the main objects of all science, the freedom and happiness of man. So that coming to bear a share in the councils and government of their country, they will keep ever in view the so]e objects of all legitimate government. . . . .

TO GOVERNOR JOHN LANGDON[1]

Monticello, March 5, 1810

. . . . The practice of Kings marrying only in the families of Kings, has been that of Europe for some centuries. Now, take any race of animals, confine them in idleness and inaction, whether in a stye, a stable or a state-room, pamper them with high diet, gratify all their sexual appetites, immerse them in sensualities, nourish their passions, let everything bend before them, and banish whatever might lead them to think, and in a few generations they become all body and no mind; and this, too, by a law of nature, by that very law by which we are in the constant practice of changing the characters and propensities of the animals we raise for our own purposes. Such is the regimen in raising Kings, and in this way they have gone on for centuries. While in Europe, I often amused myself with contemplating the characters of the then reigning sovereigns of Europe. Louis the XVI. was a fool, of my own knowledge, and in despite of the answers made for him at his trial. The King of Spain was a fool, and of Naples the same. They passed their lives in hunting, and despatched two couriers a week, one thousand miles, to let each other know what game they had killed the preceding days. The King of Sardinia was a fool. All these were Bourbons. The Queen of Portugal, a Braganza, was an idiot by nature. And so was the King of Denmark. Their sons, as regents, exercised the powers of government. The King of Prussia, successor to the great Frederick, was a mere hog in body as well as in mind. Gustavus of Sweden, and Joseph of Austria, were really crazy, and George of England, you know, was in a straight waistcoat. There remained, then, none but old Catharine, who had been too lately picked up to have lost her common sense. In this state Bonaparte found Europe; and it was this state of its rulers which lost it with scarce a struggle. These animals had become without mind and powerless; and so will every hereditary monarch be after a few generations. Alexander, the grandson of Catharine, is as yet an exception. He is able to hold his own. But he is only of the third generation. His race is not yet worn out. And so endeth the book of Kings,

[1]Governor of New Hampshire.

from all of whom the Lord deliver us, and have you, my friend, and all such good men and true, in His holy keeping.

TO GOVERNOR JOHN TYLER

Monticello, May 26, 1810

. . . . I have indeed two great measures at heart, without which no republic can maintain itself in strength. 1. That of general education, to enable every man to judge for himself what will secure or endanger his freedom. 2. To divide every county into hundreds, of such size that all the children of each will be within reach of a central school in it. But this division looks to many other fundamental provisions. Every hundred, besides a school, should have a justice of the peace, a constable and a captain of militia. These officers, or some others within the hundred, should be a corporation to manage all its concerns, to take care of its roads, its poor, and its police by patrols, etc. (as the selectment of the eastern townships). Every hundred should elect one or two jurors to serve where requisite, and all other elections should be made in the hundreds separately, and the votes of all the hundreds be brought together. Our present captaincies might be declared hundreds for the present, with a power to the courts to alter them occasionally. These little republics would be the main strength of the great one. We owe to them the vigor given to our revolution in its commencement in the Eastern States, and by them the Eastern States were enabled to repeal the embargo in opposition to the Middle, Southern and Western States, and their large and lubberly division into counties which can never be assembled. General orders are given out from a centre to the foreman of every hundred, as to the sergeants of an army, and the whole nation is thrown into energetic action, in the same direction in one instant and as one man, and becomes absolutely irresistible. Could I once see this I should consider it as the dawn of the salvation of the republic, and say with old Simeon, "nunc dimittis Domine." But our children will be as wise as we are, and will establish in the fullness of time those things not yet ripe for establishment. So be it, and to yourself health, happiness and long life.

TO COLONEL WILLIAM DUANE[1]

Monticello, August 12, 1810

. . . . Our laws, language, religion, politics and manners are so deeply laid in English foundations, that we shall never cease to consider their history as a part of ours, and to study ours in that as its origin. Every one knows that judicious matter and charms of style have rendered Hume's history the manual of every student. I remember well the enthusiasm with which I devoured it when young, and the length of time, the research and reflection which were necessary to eradicate the poison it had instilled into my mind. It was unfortunate that he first took up the history of the Stuarts, became their apologist, and advocated all their enormities. To support his work, when done, he went back to the Tudors, and so selected and arranged the materials of their history as to present their arbitrary acts only, as the genuine samples of the constitutional power of the crown, and, still writing backwards, he then reverted to the early history, and wrote the Saxon and Norman periods with the same perverted view. Although all this is known, he still continues to be put into the hands of all our young people, and to infect them with the poison of his own principles of government. It is this book which has undermined the free principles of the English government, has persuaded readers of all classes that these were usurpations on the legitimate and salutary rights of the crown, and has spread universal toryism over the land. And the book will still continue to be read here as well as there. . . . .

---

[1] William Duane, journalist and politician, was an acquaintance of Jefferson of many years standing. As editor of the *Aurora*, the most powerful mouthpiece of the Jeffersonians, he had exerted considerable influence during the formative years of the Union.

TO J. B. COLVIN[1]

Monticello, September 20, 1810

. . . . A strict observance of the written laws is doubtless *one* of the high duties of a good citizen, but it is not *the highest*. The laws of necessity, of self-preservation, of saving our country when in danger, are of higher obligation. To lose our country by a scrupulous adherence to written law, would be to lose the law itself, with life, liberty, property and all those who are enjoying them with us; thus absurdly sacrificing the end to the means. When, in the battle of Germantown, General Washington's army was annoyed from Chew's house, he did not hesitate to plant his cannon against it, although the property of a citizen. When he besieged Yorktown, he leveled the suburbs, feeling that the laws of property must be postponed to the safety of the nation. While the army was before York, the Governor of Virginia took horses, carriages, provisions and even men by force, to enable that army to stay together till it could master the public enemy; and he was justified. A ship at sea in distress for provisions, meets another having abundance, yet refusing a supply; the law of self-preservation authorizes the distressed to take a supply by force. In all these cases, the unwritten laws of necessity, of self-preservation, and of the public safety, control the written laws of *meum* and *tuum*. . . . .

TO DR. BENJAMIN RUSH

Monticello, January 16, 1811

. . . . My present course of life admits less reading than I wish. From breakfast, or noon at latest, to dinner, I am mostly on horseback, attending to my farm or other concerns, which I find healthful to my body, mind and affairs; and the few hours I can pass in my cabinet, are devoured by correspondences; not those with my intimate friends, with whom I delight to interchange sentiments, but with others, who, writ-

[1]John Colvin was the editor of the *Republican Advocate* in Fredericktown, Maryland.

ing to me on concerns of their own in which I have had an agency, or from motives of mere respect and approbation, are entitled to be answered with respect and a return of good will. My hope is that this obstacle to the delights of retirement, will wear away with the oblivion which follows that, and that I may at length be indulged in those studious pursuits, from which nothing but revolutionary duties would ever have called me.

I shall receive your proposed publication and read it with the pleasure which everything gives me from your pen. Although much of a sceptic in the practice of medicine, I read with pleasure its ingenious theories.

I receive with sensibility your observations on the discontinuance of friendly correspondence between Mr. Adams and myself, and the concern you take in its restoration. This discontinuance has not proceeded from me, nor from the want of sincere desire and of effort on my part, to renew our intercourse. You know the perfect coincidence of principle and of action, in the early part of the Revolution, which produced a high degree of mutual respect and esteem between Mr. Adams and myself. Certainly no man was ever truer than he was, in that day, to those principles of rational republicanism which, after the necessity of throwing off our monarchy, dictated all our efforts in the establishment of a new government. And although he swerved, afterwards, towards the principles of the English constitution, our friendship did not abate on that account. While he was Vice-President, and I Secretary of State, I received a letter from President Washington, then at Mount Vernon, desiring me to call together the Heads of departments, and to invite Mr. Adams to join us (which, by-the-bye, was the only instance of that being done) in order to determine on some measure which required despatch; and he desired me to act on it, as decided, without again recurring to him. I invited them to dine with me, and after dinner, sitting at our wine, having settled our question, other conversation came on, in which a collision of opinion arose between Mr. Adams and Colonel Hamilton, on the merits of the British constitution, Mr. Adams giving it as his opinion, that, if some of its defects and abuses were corrected, it would be the most perfect constitution of government ever devised by man. Hamilton, on the contrary, asserted, that with its existing vices, it was the most perfect model of government that could be formed; and that the correction of its vices would render it an impracticable government. And this you may be assured was the real line of difference between the political principles of these two gentlemen. Another incident took place on the same occasion, which will further delineate Mr. Hamilton's political principles. The room being hung around with a collection of the portraits of remarkable men, among them were those of Bacon, Newton and Locke, Hamilton asked me who they were. I told him they were my trinity of the three greatest men the world had ever produced, naming them. He paused for some time: "the greatest man," said he, "that ever lived, was Julius Caesar." Mr. Adams was honest as a politician, as well as a man; Hamilton honest as a man, but, as a politician, believing in the necessity of either force or corruption to govern men.

You remember the machinery which the federalists played off, about that time, to beat down the friends to the real principles of our Constitution, to silence by terror every expression in their favor, to bring us into war with France and alliance with England, and finally to homologize our Constitution with that of England. Mr. Adams, you know, was overwhelmed with feverish addresses, dictated by the fear, and often by the pen, of the *bloody buoy*, and was seduced by them into some open indications of his new principles of government, and in fact, was so elated as to mix with his kindness a little superciliousness towards me. Even Mrs. Adams, with all her good sense and prudence, was sensibly flushed. And you recollect the short suspension of our intercourse, and the circumstance which gave rise to it, which you were so good as to bring to an early explanation, and have set to rights, to the cordial satisfaction of us all. The nation at length passed condemnation on the political principles of the federalists, by refusing to continue Mr. Adams in the Presidency. On the day on which we learned in Philadelphia the vote of the city of New York, which it was well known would decide the vote of the State and that, again, the vote of the Union, I called on Mr. Adams on some official business. He was very sensibly affected, and accosted me with these words: "Well, I understand that you are to beat me in this contest, and I will only say that I will be as faithful a subject as any you will have." "Mr. Adams," said I, "this is no personal contest between you and me. Two systems of principles on the subject of government divide our fellow citizens into two parties. With one of these you concur, and I with the other. As we have been longer on the public stage than most of those now living, our names happen to be more generally known. One of these parties, therefore, has put your name at its head, the other mine. Were we both to die to-day, to-morrow two other names would be in the place of ours, without any change in the motion of the machinery. Its motion is from its principle, not from you or myself." "I believe you are right," said he, "that we are but passive instruments, and should not suffer this matter to affect our personal dispositions." But he did not long retain this just view of the subject. I have always believed that the thousand calumnies which the federalists, in bitterness of heart, and mortification at their ejection, daily invented against me, were carried to him by their busy intriguers, and made some impression. When the election between Burr and myself was kept in suspense by the federalists, and they were meditating to place the President of the Senate at the head of the government, I called on Mr. Adams with a view to have this desperate measure prevented by his negative. He grew warm in an instant, and said with a vehemence he had not used towards me before, "Sir, the event of the election is within your own power. You have only to say you will do justice to the public creditors, maintain the navy, and not disturb those holding offices, and the government will instantly be put into your hands. We know it is the wish of the people it should be so." "Mr. Adams," said I, "I know not what part of my conduct, in either public or private life, can have authorized a doubt of my fidelity to the public engagements. I say, however, I will not come into the government by capitulation. I will not enter on it, but in perfect freedom to follow the dictates of my own judgment." I had before given the same answer to the same intimation from Gouverneur Morris. "Then," said he, "things must take their course." I turned the conversation to something else, and soon took my leave. It was the first time in our lives we had ever parted with anything like dissatisfaction. And then followed those scenes of midnight appointment, which have been condemned by all men. The last day of his political power, the last hours, and even beyond the midnight, were employed in filling all offices, and especially permanent ones, with the bitterest federalists, and providing for me the alternative, either to execute the government by my enemies, whose study it would be to thwart and defeat all my measures, or to incur the odium of such numerous removals from office, as might bear me down. A little time and reflection effaced in my mind this temporary dissatisfaction with Mr. Adams, and restored me to that just estimate of his virtues and passions, which a long acquaintance had enabled me to fix. And my first wish became that of making his retirement easy by any means in my power; for it was understood he was not rich. I suggested to some republican members of the delegation from his State, the giving him, either directly or indirectly, an office, the most lucrative in that State, and then offered to be resigned, if they thought he would not deem it affrontive. They were of opinion he would take great offence at the offer; and moreover, that the body of republicans would consider such a step in the outset as auguring very ill of the course I meant to pursue. I dropped the idea, therefore, but did not cease to wish for some opportunity of renewing our friendly understanding.

Two or three years after, having had the misfortune to lose a daughter, between whom and Mrs. Adams there had been a considerable attachment, she made it the occasion of writing me a letter, in which, with the tenderest expressions of concern at this event, she carefully avoided a single one of friendship towards myself, and even concluded it with the wishes "of her who *once* took pleasure in subscribing herself your friend, Abigail Adams." Unpromising as was the complexion of this letter, I determined to make an effort towards removing the cloud from between us. This brought on a correspondence which I now enclose for your perusal, after which be so good as to return it to me, as I have never communicated it to any mortal breathing, before. I send it to you, to convince you I have not been wanting either in the desire, or the endeavor to remove this misunderstanding. Indeed, I thought it highly disgraceful to us both, as indicating minds not sufficiently elevated to prevent a public competition from affecting our personal friendship. I soon found from the correspondence that conciliation was desperate, and yielding to an intimation in her last letter, I ceased from further explanation. I have the same good opinion of Mr. Adams which I ever had. I know him to be an honest man, an able one with his pen, and he was a powerful advocate on the floor of Congress. He has been alienated from me, by belief in the lying suggestions contrived for electioneering purposes, that I perhaps mixed in the activity and intrigues of the occasion. My most intimate friends can testify that I was perfectly passive. They would sometimes, indeed, tell me what was going on; but no man ever heard me take part in such conversations; and none ever misrepresented Mr. Adams in my presence, without my asserting his just character. With very confidential persons I have doubtless disapproved of the principles and practices of his administration. This was unavoidable. But never with those with whom it could do him any injury. Decency would have required this conduct from me, if disposition had not; and I am satisfied Mr. Adams' conduct was equally honorable towards me. But I think it part of his character to suspect foul play in those of whom he is jealous, and not easily to relinquish his suspicions.

I have gone, my dear friend, into these details, that you might know everything which had passed between us, might be fully possessed of the state of facts and dispositions, and judge for yourself whether they admit a revival of that friendly intercourse for which you are so kindly solicitous. I shall certainly not be wanting in anything on my part which may second your efforts, which will be the easier with me, inasmuch as I do not entertain a sentiment of Mr. Adams, the expression of which could give him reasonable offence. And I submit the whole to yourself, with the assurance, that whatever be the issue, my friendship and respect for yourself will remain unaltered and unalterable.

TO COLONEL WILLIAM DUANE

Monticello, March 28, 1811

. . . . The last hope of human liberty in this world rests on us. We ought, for so dear a state, to sacrifice every attachment and every enmity. Leave the President free to choose his own coadjutors, to pursue his own measures, and support him and them, even if we think we are wiser than they, honester than they are, or possessing more enlarged information of the state of things. If we move in mass, be it ever so circuitously, we shall attain our object; but if we break into squads, every one pursuing the path he thinks most direct, we become an easy conquest to those who can now barely hold us in check. I repeat again, that we ought not to schismatize on either men or measures. Principles alone can justify that. If we find our government in all its branches rushing headlong, like our predecessors, into the arms of monarchy, if we find them violating our dearest rights, the trial by jury, the freedom of the press, the freedom of opinion, civil or religious, or opening on our peace of mind or personal safety the sluices of terrorism, if we see them raising standing armies, when the absence of all other danger points to these as the sole objects on which they are to be employed, then indeed let us withdraw and call the nation to its tents. But while our functionaries are wise, and honest, and vigilant, let us move compactly under their guidance, and we have nothing to fear. Things may here and there go a little wrong. It is not in their power to prevent it. But all will be right in the end, though not perhaps by the shortest means.

TO DR. BENJAMIN RUSH

Poplar Forest, August 17, 1811

DEAR SIR,—I write to you from a place ninety miles from Monticello, near the New London of this State, which I visit three or four times a year, and stay from a fortnight to a month at a time. I have fixed myself comfortably, keep some books here, bring others occasionally, am in the solitude of a hermit, and quite at leisure to attend to my absent friends. I note this to show that I am not in a situation to examine the dates of our letters, whether I have overgone the annual period of asking how you do? I know that within that time I have received one or more letters from you, accompanied by a volume of your introductory lectures, for which accept my thanks. I have read them with pleasure and edification, for I acknowledge facts in medicine as far as they go, distrusting only their extension by theory. Having to conduct my grandson through his course of mathematics, I have resumed that study with great avidity. It was ever my favorite one. We have no theories there, no uncertainties remain on the mind; all is demonstration and satisfaction. I have forgotten much, and recover it with more difficulty than when in the vigor of my mind I originally acquired it. It is wonderful to me that old men should not be sensible that their minds keep pace with their bodies in the progress of decay.

Our old revolutionary friend Clinton, for example, who was a hero, but never a man of mind, is wonderfully jealous on this head. He tells eternally the stories of his younger days to prove his memory, as if memory and reason were the same faculty. Nothing betrays imbecility so much as the being insensible of it. Had not a conviction of the danger to which an unlimited occupation of the executive chair would expose the republican constitution of our government, made it conscientiously a duty to retire when I did, the fear of becoming a dotard and of being insensible of it, would of itself have resisted all solicitations to remain. I have had a long attack of rheumatism, without fever and without pain while I keep myself still. A total prostration of the muscles of the back, hips and thighs, deprived me of the power of walking, and leaves it still in a very impaired state. A pain when I walk, seems to have fixed itself in the hip, and to threaten permanence. I take moderate rides, without much fatigue; but my journey to this place, in a hard-going gig, gave me great sufferings which I expect will be renewed on my return as soon as I am able. The loss of the power of taking exercise would be a sore affliction to me. It has been the delight of my retirement to be in constant bodily activity, looking after my affairs. It was never damped as the pleasures of reading are, by the question of *cui bono?* for what object? I hope your health of body continues firm. Your works show that of your mind. The habits of exercise which your calling has given to both, will tend long to preserve them. The sedentary character of my public occupations sapped a constitution naturally sound and vigorous, and draws it to an earlier close. But it will still last quite as long as I wish it. There is a fulness of time when men should go, and not occupy too long the ground to which others have a right to advance. We must continue while here to exchange occasionally our mutual good wishes. I find friendship to be like wine, raw when new, ripened with age, the true old man's milk and restorative cordial. God bless you and preserve you through a long and healthy old age.

TO JOHN ADAMS

Monticello, January 21, 1812

DEAR SIR,—I thank you beforehand (for they are not yet arrived) for the specimens of homespun you have been so kind as to forward me by post. I doubt not their excellence, knowing how far you are advanced in these things in your quarter. Here we do little in the fine way, but in coarse and middling goods a great deal. Every family in the country is a manufactory within itself, and is very generally able to make within itself all the stouter and middling stuffs for its own clothing and household use. We consider a sheep for every person in the family as sufficient to clothe it, in addition to the cotton, hemp and flax which we raise ourselves. For fine stuff we shall depend on your northern manufactories. Of these, that is to say, of company establishments, we have none. We use little machinery. The spinning jenny, and loom with the flying shuttle, can be managed in a family; but nothing more complicated. The economy and thriftiness resulting from our household manufactures are such that they will never again be laid aside; and nothing more salutary for us has ever happened than the British obstructions to our demands for their manufactures. Restore free intercourse when they will, their commerce with us will have totally changed its form, and the articles we shall in future want from them will not exceed their own consumption of our produce.

A letter from you[1] calls up recollections very dear to my mind. It carries me back to the times when, beset with difficulties and dangers, we were fellow laborers in the same cause, struggling for what is most valuable to man, his right of self-government. Laboring always at the same oar, with some wave ever ahead, threatening to overwhelm us, and yet passing harmless under our bark, we knew not how we rode through the storm with heart and hand, and made a happy port. Still we did not expect to be without rubs and difficulties; and we have had them. First, the detention of the western ports, then the coalition of

[1]Through Benjamin Rush, the friendship between Jefferson and Adams, interrupted because of political misunderstandings, was renewed, and grew even stronger until the day of their deaths.

Pilnitz, outlawing our commerce with France, and the British enforcement of the outlawry. In your day, French depredations; in mine, English, and the Berlin and Milan decrees; now, the English orders of council, and the piracies they authorize. When these shall be over, it will be the impressment of our seamen or something else; and so we have gone on, and so we shall go on, puzzled and prospering beyond example in the history of man. And I do believe we shall continue to grow, to multiply and prosper until we exhibit an association, powerful, wise and happy, beyond what has yet been seen by men. As for France and England, with all their preëminence in science, the one is a den of robbers, and the other of pirates. And if science produces no better fruits than tyranny, murder, rapine and destitution of national morality, I would rather wish our country to be ignorant, honest and estimable, as our neighboring savages are. But whither is senile garrulity leading me? Into politics, of which I have taken final leave. I think little of them and say less. I have given up newspapers in exchange for Tacitus and Thucydides, for Newton and Euclid, and I find myself much the happier. Sometimes, indeed, I look back to former occurrences, in remembrance of our old friends and fellow laborers, who have fallen before us. Of the signers of the Declaration of Independence, I see now living not more than half a dozen on your side of the Potomac, and on this side, myself alone. You and I have been wonderfully spared, and myself with remarkable health, and a considerable activity of body and mind. I am on horseback three or four hours of every day; visit three or four times a year a possession I have ninety miles distant, performing the winter journey on horseback. I walk little, however, a single mile being too much for me, and I live in the midst of my grandchildren, one of whom has lately promoted me to be a great-grandfather. I have heard with pleasure that you also retain good health, and a greater power of exercise in walking than I do. But I would rather have heard this from yourself, and that, writing a letter like mine, full of egotisms, and of details of your health, your habits, occupations and enjoyments, I should have the pleasure of knowing that in the race of life, you do not keep, in its physical decline, the same distance ahead of me which you have done in political honors and achievements. No circumstances have lessened the interest I feel in these particulars respecting yourself; none have suspended for one moment my sincere esteem for you, and I now salute you with unchanged affection and respect.

TO F. A. VAN DER KEMP[1]

Monticello, March 22, 1812

. . . . The only orthodox object of the institution of government is to secure the greatest degree of happiness possible to the general mass of those associated under it. The events which this work proposes to embrace will establish the fact that unless the mass retains sufficient control over those intrusted with the powers of their government, these will be perverted to their own oppression, and to the perpetuation of wealth and power in the individuals and their families selected for the trust. Whether our Constitution has hit on the exact degree of control necessary, is yet under experiment; and it is a most encouraging reflection that distance and other difficulties securing us against the brigand governments of Europe, in the safe enjoyment of our farms and firesides, the experiment stands a better chance of being satisfactorily made here than on any occasion yet presented by history. To promote, therefore, unanimity and perseverance in this great enterprise, to disdain despair, encourage trial, and nourish hope, and the worthiest objects of every political and philanthropic work; and that this would be the necessary result of that which you have delineated, the facts it will review, and the just reflections arising out of them, will sufficiently answer. I hope, therefore, that it is not *in petto* merely, but already completed; and that my fellow citizens, warned in it of the rocks and shoals on which other political associations have been wrecked, will be able to direct theirs with a better knowledge of the dangers in its way. . . . . .

[1]Van der Kemp was a Dutch minister, writer and exiled patriot who became a naturalized American citizen. Intellectual confidant of Jefferson and Adams, he wrote a pamphlet on Jefferson's theory of natural history.

TO JAMES MAURY[1]

Monticello, April 25, 1812

. . . . Our two countries are to be at war, but not you and I. And why should our two countries be at war, when by peace we can be so much more useful to one another? Surely the world will acquit our government from having sought it. Never before has there been an instance of a nation's bearing so much as we have borne. Two items alone in our catalogue of wrongs will forever acquit us of being the aggressors: the impressment of our seamen, and the excluding us from the ocean. The first foundations of the social compact would be broken up, were we definitively to refuse to its members the protection of their persons and property, while in their lawful pursuits. I think the war will not be short, because the object of England, long obvious, is to claim the ocean as her domain, and to exact transit duties from every vessel traversing it. This is the sum of her orders of council, which were only a step in this bold experiment, never meant to be retracted if it could be permanently maintained. And this object must continue her in war with all the world. To this I see no termination, until her exaggerated efforts, so much beyond her natural strength and resources, shall have exhausted her to bankruptcy. The approach of this crisis is, I think, visible in the departure of her precious metals, and depreciation of her paper medium. We, who have gone through that operation, know its symptoms, its course, and consequences. In England they will be more serious than elsewhere, because half the wealth of her people is now in that medium, the private revenue of her money-holders, or rather of her paper-holders, being, I believe, greater than that of her land-holders. Such a proportion of property, imaginary and baseless as it is, cannot be reduced to vapor but with great explosion. She will rise out of its ruins, however, because her lands, her houses, her arts will remain, and the greater part of her men. And these will give her again that place among nations which is proportioned to her natural means, and which we all wish her to hold. We believe that the just standing of all nations is the

---

[1]James Maury, an old schoolmate of Jefferson, had been, for years, a citizen of England.

health and security of all. We consider the overwhelming power of England on the ocean, and of France on the land, as destructive of the prosperity and happiness of the world, and wish both to be reduced only to the necessity of observing moral duties. We believe no more in Bonaparte's fighting merely for the liberty of the seas, than in Great Britain's fighting for the liberties of mankind. The object of both is the same, to draw to themselves the power, the wealth and the resources of other nations. We resist the enterprises of England first, because they first come vitally home to us. And our feelings repel the logic of bearing the lash of George the III. for fear of that of Bonaparte at some future day. When the wrongs of France shall reach us with equal effect, we shall resist them also. But one at a time is enough; and having offered a choice to the champions, England first takes up the gauntlet.

The English newspapers suppose me the personal enemy of their nation. I am not so. I am an enemy to its injuries, as I am to those of France. If I could permit myself to have national partialities, and if the conduct of England would have permitted them to be directed towards her, they would have been so. . . . .

TO JOHN MELISH[1]

Monticello, January 13, 1813

. . . . I had no conception that manufactures had made such progress there [the Western States], and particularly of the number of carding and spinning machines dispersed through the whole country. We are but beginning here to have them in our private families. Small spinning jennies of from half a dozen to twenty spindles, will soon, however, make their way into the humblest cottages, as well as the richest houses; and nothing is more certain, than that the coarse and middling clothing for our families, will forever hereafter continue to be made within ourselves. I have hitherto myself depended entirely on foreign manufactures; but I have now thirty-five spindles agoing, a hand card-

---

[1]John Melish, Scottish geographer, traveler, and merchant, had lived many years in the United States. His *Travels in the United States of America* . . ., presented a very favorable picture of life in this country.

ing machine, and looms with the flying shuttle, for the supply of my own farms, which will never be relinquished in my time. The continuance of the war will fix the habit generally, and out of the evils of impressment and of the orders of council a great blessing for us will grow. I have not formerly been an advocate for great manufactories. I doubted whether our labor, employed in agriculture, and aided by the spontaneous energies of the earth, would not procure us more than we could make ourselves of other necessaries. But other considerations entering into the question, have settled my doubts.

The candor with which you have viewed the manners and condition of our citizens, is so unlike the narrow prejudices of the French and English travellers preceding you, who, considering each the manners and habits of their own people as the only orthodox, have viewed everything differing from that test as boorish and barbarous, that your work will be read here extensively, and operate great good.

Amidst this mass of approbation which is given to every other part of the work, there is a single sentiment which I cannot help wishing to bring to what I think the correct one; and, on a point so interesting, I value your opinion too highly not to ambition its concurrence with my own. Stating in volume one, page sixty-three, the principle of difference between the two great political parties here, you conclude it to be, "whether the controlling power shall be vested in this or that set of men." That each party endeavors to get into the administration of the government, and exclude the other from power, is true, and may be stated as a motive of action: but this is only secondary; the primary motive being a real and radical difference of political principle. I sincerely wish our differences were but personally who should govern, and that the principles of our constitution were those of both parties. Unfortunately, it is otherwise; and the question of preference between monarchy and republicanism, which has so long divided mankind elsewhere, threatens a permanent division here.

Among that section of our citizens called federalists, there are three shades of opinion. Distinguishing between the *leaders* and *people* who compose it, the *leaders* consider the English constitution as a model of perfection, some, with a correction of its vices, others, with all its corruptions and abuses. This last was Alexander Hamilton's opinion, which others, as well as myself, have often heard him declare, and that a correction of what are called its vices, would render the English an impracticable government. This government they wished to have established here, and only accepted and held fast, *at first,* to the present constitution, as a steppingstone to the final establishment of their favorite model. This party has therefore always clung to England as their prototype, and great auxiliary in promoting and effecting this change. A weighty MINORITY, however, of these *leaders*, considering the voluntary conversion of our government into a monarchy as too distant, if not desperate, wish to break off from our Union its eastern fragment, as being, in truth, the hot-bed of American monarchism, with a view to a commencement of their favorite government, from whence the other States may gangrene by degrees, and the whole be thus brought finally to the desired point. For Massachusetts, the prime mover in this enterprise, is the last State in the Union to mean a *final* separation, as being of all the most dependent on the others. Not raising bread for the sustenance of her own inhabitants, not having a stick of timber for the construction of vessels, her principal occupation, nor an article to export in them, where would she be, excluded from the ports of the other States, and thrown into dependence on England, her direct, and natural, but now insidious rival? At the head of this MINORITY is what is called the Essex Junto of Massachusetts. But the MAJORITY of these *leaders* do not aim at separation. In this, they adhere to the known principle of General Hamilton, never, under any views, to break the Union. Anglomany, monarchy, and separation, then, are the principles of the Essex federalists. Anglomany and monarchy, those of the Hamiltonians, and Anglomany alone, that of the portion among the *people* who call themselves federalists. These last are as good republicans as the brethren whom they oppose, and differ from them only in their devotion to England and hatred of France which they have imbibed from their leaders. The moment that these leaders should avowedly propose a separation of the Union, or the establishment of regal government, their popular adherents would quit them to a man, and join the republican standard; and the partisans of this change, even in Massachusetts, would thus find themselves an army of officers without a soldier.

The party called republican is steadily for the support of the present constitution. They obtained at its commencement, all the amendments to it they desired. These reconciled them to it perfectly, and if they have any ulterior view, it is only, perhaps, to popularize it further, by shortening the Senatorial term, and devising a process for the responsibility of judges, more practicable than that of impeachment. They esteem the people of England and France equally, and equally detest the governing powers of both.

This I verily believe, after an intimacy of forty years with the public councils and characters, is a true statement of the grounds on which they are at present divided, and that it is not merely an ambition for power. An honest man can feel no pleasure in the exercise of power over his fellow citizens. And considering as the only offices of power those conferred by the people directly, that is to say, the executive and legislative functions of the General and State governments, the common refusal of these, and multiplied resignations, are proofs sufficient that power is not alluring to pure minds, and is not, with them, the primary principle of contest. This is my belief of it; it is that on which I have acted; and had it been a mere contest who should be permitted to administer the government according to its genuine republican principles, there has never been a moment of my life in which I should have relinquished for it the enjoyments of my family, my farm, my friends and books.

You expected to discover the difference of our party principles in General Washington's valedictory, and my inaugural address. Not at all. General Washington did not harbor one principle of federalism. He was neither an Angloman, a monarchist, nor a separatist. He sincerely wished the people to have as much self-government as they were competent to exercise themselves. The only point on which he and I ever differed in opinion, was, that I had more confidence than he had in the natural integrity and discretion of the people, and in the safety and extent to which they might trust themselves with a control over their government. He has asseverated to me a thousand times his determination that the existing government should have a fair trial, and that in support of it he would spend the last drop of his blood. He did this the more repeatedly, because he knew General Hamilton's political bias, and my apprehensions from it. It is a mere calumny, therefore, in the monarchists, to associate General Washington with their principles. But that may have happened in this case which has been often seen in ordinary cases, that, by oft repeating an untruth, men come to believe it themselves. It is a mere artifice in this party to bolster themselves up on the revered name of that first of our worthies. If I have dwelt longer on this subject than was necessary, it proves the estimation in which I hold your ultimate opinions, and my desire of placing the subject truly before them. In so doing, I am certain I risk no use of the communication which may draw me into contention before the public. Tranquillity is the *summum bonum* of a Septagenaire. . . . .

TO COLONEL WILLIAM DUANE

Monticello, January 22, 1813

DEAR SIR,—I do not know how the publication of the Review turned out in point of profit, whether gainfully or not. I know it ought to have been a book of great sale. I gave a copy to a student of William and Mary college, and recommended it to Bishop Madison, then President of the college, who was so pleased with it that he established it as a school-book, and as the young gentleman informed me, every copy which could be had was immediately bought up, and there was a considerable demand for more. You probably know best whether new calls for it have been made. President Madison was a good whig. . . . Your experiment on that work will enable you to decide whether you ought to undertake another, not of greater but of equal merit. I have received from France a MS. work on Political Economy, written by De Tutt Tracy, the most conspicuous writer of the present day in the metaphysical line. He has written a work entitled Ideology, which has given him a high reputation in France. He considers that as having laid a solid foundation for the present volume on Political Economy, and will follow it by one on Moral Duties. The present volume is a work of great ability. It may be considered as a review of the principles of the Economists, of Smith and of Say, or rather an elementary book on the same subject. As Smith had corrected some principles of the Economists, and Say some of Smith's, so Tracy has done as to the whole. He has, in my opinion, corrected fundamental errors in all of them, and by simplifying principles, has brought the subject within a narrow compass. I think the volume would be of about the size of the

Review of Montesquieu. Although he puts his name to the work, he is afraid to publish it in France, lest its freedom should bring him into trouble. If translated and published here, he could disavow it, if necessary. In order to enable you to form a better judgment of the work, I will subjoin a list of the chapters or heads, and if you think proper to undertake the translation and publication, I will send the work itself. You will certainly find it one of the very first order. . . . . .

TO COLONEL WILLIAM DUANE

Monticello, April 4, 1813

. . . . It is true that I am tired of practical politics, and happier while reading the history of ancient than of modern times. The total banishment of all moral principle from the code which governs the intercourse of nations, the melancholy reflection that after the mean, wicked and cowardly cunning of the cabinets of the age of Machiavelli had given place to the integrity and good faith which dignified the succeeding one of a Chatham and Turgot, that this is to be swept away again by the daring profligacy and avowed destitution of all moral principle of a Cartouche and a Blackbeard, sickens my soul unto death. I turn from the contemplation with loathing, and take refuge in the histories of other times, where, if they also furnish their Tarquins, their Catilines and Caligulas, their stories are handed to us under the brand of a Livy, a Sallust and a Tacitus, and we are comforted with the reflection that the condemnation of all succeeding generations has confirmed the censures of the historian, and consigned their memories to everlasting infamy, a solace we cannot have with the Georges and Napoleons but by anticipation. . . . . .

TO JOHN ADAMS

Monticello, May 27, 1813

. . . . I sincerely congratulate you on the successes of our little navy; which must be more gratifying to you than to most men, as having been the early and constant advocate of wooden walls. If I have differed with you on this ground, it was not on the principle, but the time; supposing that we cannot build or maintain a navy which will not immediately fall into the same gulf which has swallowed not only the minor navies, but even those of the great second-rate powers of the sea. Whenever these can be resuscitated, and brought so near to a balance with England that we can turn the scale, then is my epoch for aiming at a navy. In the meantime, one competent to keep the Barbary States in order, is necessary; these being the only smaller powers disposed to quarrel with us. . . . .

TO JOHN ADAMS

Monticello, June 27, 1813

. . . . Men have differed in opinion, and been divided into parties by these opinions, from the first origin of societies, and in all governments where they have been permitted freely to think and to speak. The same political parties which now agitate the United States, have existed through all time. Whether the power of the people or that of the aristoi[1] should prevail, were questions which kept the States of Greece and Rome in eternal convulsions, as they now schismatize every people whose minds and mouths are not shut up by the gag of a despot. And in fact, the terms of whig and tory belong to natural as well as to civil history. They denote the temper and constitution of mind of different individuals. To come to our own country, and to the times when you and I became first acquainted, we well remember the violent parties which agitated the old Congress, and their bitter contests. There you and I were together, and the Jays, and the Dickinsons, and other anti-independents, were arrayed against us. They cherished the monarchy of England, and we the rights of our countrymen. When our present government was in the mew, passing from Confederation to Union, how bitter was the schism between the Feds and Antis! Here you and I were together again. For although, for a moment, separated by the Atlantic from the scene of action, I favored the opinion that nine States should confirm the constitution, in order to secure it, and the others

[1]In Jefferson's letter this appears in Greek.

hold off until certain amendments, deemed favorable to freedom, should be made. I rallied in the first instant to the wiser proposition of Massachusetts, that all should confirm, and then all instruct their delegates to urge those amendments. The amendments were made, and all were reconciled to the government. But as soon as it was put into motion, the line of division was again drawn. We broke into two parties, each wishing to give the government a different direction; the one to strengthen the most popular branch, the other the more permanent branches, and to extend their permanence. Here you and I separated for the first time, and as we had been longer than most others on the public theatre, and our names therefore were more familiar to our countrymen, the party which considered you as thinking with them, placed your name at their head; the other, for the same reason, selected mine. But neither decency nor inclination permitted us to become the advocates of ourselves, or to take part personally in the violent contests which followed. We suffered ourselves, as you so well expressed it, to be passive subjects of public discussion. . . .

TO DR. SAMUEL BROWN[1]

Monticello, July 14, 1813

DEAR SIR,—Your favors of May 25th and June 13th have been duly received, as also the first supply of Capsicum, and the second of the same article with other seeds. I shall set great store by the Capsicum, if it is hardy enough for our climate, the species we have heretofore tried being too tender. The Galvance too, will be particularly attended to, as it appears very different from what we cultivate by that name. I have so many grandchildren and others who might be endangered by the poison plant, that I think the risk overbalances the curiosity of trying it. The most elegant thing of that kind known is a preparation of the Jamestown weed, Datura-Stramonium, invented by the French in the time of Robespierre. Every man of firmness carried it constantly in his pocket to anticipate the guillotine. It brings on the sleep of death

---

[1]Dr. Samuel Brown held the chair of theory and practice of medicine at the University (later Washington and Lee University) in Lexington, Virginia.

as quietly as fatigue does the ordinary sleep, without the least struggle or motion. Condorcet, who had recourse to it, was found lifeless on his bed a few minutes after his landlady had left him there, and even the slipper which she had observed half suspended on his foot, was not shaken off. It seems far preferable to the Venesection of the Romans, the Hemlock of the Greeks, and the Opium of the Turks. I have never been able to learn what the preparation is, other than a strong concentration of its lethiferous principle. Could such a medicament be restrained to self-administration, it ought not to be kept secret. There are ills in life as desperate as intolerable, to which it would be the rational relief, *e.g.*, the inveterate cancer. As a relief from tyranny indeed, for which the Romans recurred to it in the times of the emperors, it has been a wonder to me that they did not consider a poignard in the breast of the tyrant as a better remedy. . . . .

TO ISAAC MCPHERSON[1]

Monticello, August 13, 1813

. . . . It has been pretended by some, (and in England especially,) that inventors have a natural and exclusive right to their inventions, and not merely for their own lives, but inheritable to their heirs. But while it is a moot question whether the origin of any kind of property is derived from nature at all, it would be singular to admit a natural and even an hereditary right to inventors. It is agreed by those who have seriously considered the subject, that no individual has, of natural right, a separate property in an acre of land, for instance. By an universal law, indeed, whatever, whether fixed or movable, belongs to all men equally and in common, is the property for the moment of him who occupies it, but when he relinquishes the occupation, the property goes with it. Stable ownership is the gift of social law, and is given late in the progress of society. It would be curious then, if an idea, the fugitive fermentation of an individual brain, could, of natural right, be claimed in exclusive and stable property. If nature has made any

---

[1]McPherson was a Baltimore inventor who had written Jefferson concerning scientific matters.

one thing less susceptible than all others of exclusive property, it is the action of the thinking power called an idea, which an individual may exclusively possess as long as he keeps it to himself; but the moment it is divulged, it forces itself into the possession of every one, and the receiver cannot dispossess himself of it. Its peculiar character, too, is that no one possesses the less, because every other possesses the whole of it. He who receives an idea from me, receives instruction himself without lessening mine; as he who lights his taper at mine, receives light without darkening me. That ideas should freely spread from one to another over the globe, for the moral and mutual instruction of man, and improvement of his condition, seems to have been peculiarly and benevolently designed by nature, when she made them, like fire, expansible over all space, without lessening their density in any point, and like the air in which we breathe, move, and have our physical being, incapable of confinement or exclusive appropriation. Inventions then cannot, in nature, be a subject of property. Society may give an exclusive right to the profits arising from them, as an encouragement to men to pursue ideas which may produce utility, but this may or may not be done, according to the will and convenience of the society, without claim or complaint from anybody. . . . .

TO JOHN ADAMS

Monticello, October 13, 1813

. . . . To compare the morals of the Old, with those of the New Testament, would require an attentive study of the former, a search through all its books for its precepts, and through all its history for its practices, and the principles they prove. As commentaries, too, on these, the philosophy of the Hebrews must be inquired into, their Mishna, their Gemara, Cabbala, Jezirah, Sohar, Cosri, and their Talmud, must be examined and understood, in order to do them full justice. Brucker, it would seem, has gone deeply into these repositories of their ethics, and Enfield, his epitomizer, concludes in these words: "Ethics were so little understood among the Jews, that in their whole compilation called the Talmud, there is only one treatise on moral subjects. Their books of morals chiefly consisted in a minute enumeration of duties. From the law of Moses were deduced six hundred and thirteen precepts, which were divided into two classes, affirmative and negative, two hundred and forty-eight in the former, and three hundred and sixty-five in the latter. It may serve to give the reader some idea of the low state of moral philosophy among the Jews in the middle age, to add that of the two hundred and forty-eight affirmative precepts, only three were considered as obligatory upon women, and that in order to obtain salvation, it was judged sufficient to fulfill any one single law in the hour of death; the observance of the rest being deemed necessary, only to increase the felicity of the future life. What a wretched depravity of sentiment and manners must have prevailed, before such corrupt maxims could have obtained credit! It is impossible to collect from these writings a consistent series of moral doctrine." Enfield, B. 4, chapter 3. It was the reformation of this "wretched depravity" of morals which Jesus undertook. In extracting the pure principles which he taught, we should have to strip off the artificial vestments in which they have been muffled by priests, who have travestied them into various forms, as instruments of riches and power to themselves. We must dismiss the Platonists and Plotinists, the Stagyrites, and Gamalielites, the Eclectics, the Gnostics and Scholastics, their essences and emanations, their Logos and Demiurgos, Æons and Dæmons, male and female, with a long train of etc., etc., etc., or, shall I say at once, of nonsense. We must reduce our volume to the simple evangelists, select, even from them, the very words only of Jesus, paring off the amphiboligisms into which they have been led, by forgetting often, or not understanding, what had fallen from him, by giving their own misconceptions as his dicta, and expressing unintelligibly for others what they had not understood themselves. There will be found remaining the most sublime and benevolent code of morals which has ever been offered to man. I have performed this operation for my own use, by cutting verse by verse out of the printed book, and arranging the matter which is evidently his, and which is as easily distinguishable as diamonds in a dunghill. The result is an octavo of forty-six pages, of pure and unsophisticated doctrines, such as were professed and acted on by the *unlettered* Apostles, the Apostolic Fathers, and the Christians of the first century. Their Platonizing successors, indeed, in after times, in order to legitimate the corruptions which they had incorporated into the doctrines of Jesus, found it necessary to disavow the primitive Christians, who had taken their principles from the mouth of Jesus himself, of his Apostles, and the Fathers cotemporary with them. They excommunicated their followers as heretics, branding them with the opprobrious name of Ebionites or Beggars. . . . .

TO JOHN ADAMS

Monticello, October 28, 1813

. . . . I agree with you that there is a natural aristocracy among men. The grounds of this are virtue and talents. Formerly, bodily powers gave place among the aristoi. But since the invention of gunpowder has armed the weak as well as the strong with missile death, bodily strength, like beauty, good humor, politeness and other accomplishments, has become but an auxiliary ground of distinction. There is also an artificial aristocracy, founded on wealth and birth, without either virtue or talents; for with these it would belong to the first class. The natural aristocracy I consider as the most precious gift of nature, for the instruction, the trusts, and government of society. And indeed, it would have been inconsistent in creation to have formed man for the social state, and not to have provided virtue and wisdom enough to manage the concerns of the society. May we not even say, that that form of government is the best, which provides the most effectually for a pure selection of these natural aristoi into the offices of government? The artificial aristocracy is a mischievous ingredient in government, and provision should be made to prevent its ascendency. . . . .

With respect to aristocracy, we should further consider, that before the establishment of the American States, nothing was known to history but the man of the old world, crowded within limits either small or overcharged, and steeped in the vices which that situation generates. A government adapted to such men would be one thing; but a very different one, that for the man of these States. Here every one may have land to labor for himself, if he chooses; or, preferring the exercise of any other industry, may exact for it such compensation as not only to afford a comfortable subsistence, but wherewith to provide for a cessation from labor in old age. Every one, by his property, or by his satisfactory situation, is interested in the support of law and order. And such men may safely and advantageously reserve to themselves a wholesome control over their public affairs, and a degree of freedom, which, in the hands of the *canaille* of the cities of Europe, would be instantly perverted to the demolition and destruction of everything public and private. The history of the last twenty-five years of France, and of the last forty years in America, nay of its last two hundred years, proves the truth of both parts of this observation.

But even in Europe a change has sensibly taken place in the mind of man. Science had liberated the ideas of those who read and reflect, and the American example had kindled feelings of right in the people. An insurrection has consequently begun, of science, talents, and courage, against rank and birth, which have fallen into contempt. It has failed in its first effort, because the mobs of the cities, the instrument used for its accomplishment, debased by ignorance, poverty, and vice, could not be restrained to rational action. But the world will recover from the panic of this first catastrophe. Science is progressive, and talents and enterprise on the alert. Resort may be had to the people of the country, a more governable power from their principles and subordination; and rank, and birth, and tinsel-aristocracy will finally shrink into insignificance, even there. This, however, we have no right to meddle with. It suffices for us, if the moral and physical condition of our own citizens qualifies them to select the able and good for the direction of their government, with a recurrence of elections at such short periods as will enable them to displace an unfaithful servant, before the mischief he meditates may be irremediable. . . . .

TO DR. THOMAS COOPER[1]

Monticello, January 16, 1814

. . . . You ask if it is a secret who wrote the commentary on Montesquieu? It must be a secret during the author's life. I may only say at present that it was written by a Frenchman, that the original MS.

---

[1]Dr. Thomas Cooper, famous English scientist, educator, and free-thinker, like his friend and fellow expatriate Dr. Joseph Priestley, was a close friend of Thomas Jefferson.

in French is now in my possession, that it was translated and edited by
General Duane, and that I should rejoice to see it printed in its original tongue, if any one would undertake it. No book can suffer more
by translation, because of the severe correctness of the original in the
choice of its terms. I have taken measures for securing to the author his
justly-earned fame, whenever his death or other circumstances may
render it safe for him. Like you, I do not agree with him in everything,
and have had some correspondence with him on particular points. But
on the whole, it is a most valuable work, one which I think will form
an epoch in the science of government, and which I wish to see in the
hands of every American student, as the elementary and fundamental
institute of that important branch of human science. . . .

TO MONSIEUR N. G. DUFIEF[1]

Monticello, April 19, 1814

DEAR SIR,—Your favor of the 6th instant is just received, and I shall
with equal willingness and truth, state the degree of agency you had,
respecting the copy of M. de Becourt's book, which came to my hands.
That gentleman informed me, by letter, that he was about to publish a
volume in French, "Sur la Création du Monde, un Système d'Organi-
sation Primitive," which, its title promised to be, either a geological or
astronomical work. I subscribed; and, when published, he sent me a
copy; and as you were my correspondent in the book line in Philadelphia, I took the liberty of desiring him to call on you for the price,
which, he afterwards informed me, you were so kind as to pay him for
me, being, I believe, two dollars. But the sole copy which came to me
was from himself directly, and, as far as I know, was never seen by you.

I am really mortified to be told that, *in the United States of of America,* a fact like this can become a subject of inquiry, and of criminal
inquiry too, as an offence against religion; that a question about the
sale of a book can be carried before the civil magistrate. Is this then our

[1]Nicholas Gouin Dufief was a bookseller in Philadelphia and the author of *Nature
Displayed.* He was, over a period of many years, one of Jefferson's principal book
agents.

freedom of religion? and are we to have a censor whose imprimatur shall say what books may be sold, and what we may buy? And who is thus to dogmatize religious opinions for our citizens? Whose foot is to be the measure to which ours are all to be cut or stretched? Is a priest to be our inquisitor, or shall a layman, simple as ourselves, set up his reason as the rule for what we are to read, and what we must believe? It is an insult to our citizens to question whether they are rational beings or not, and blasphemy against religion to suppose it cannot stand the test of truth and reason. If M. de Becourt's book be false in its facts, disprove them; if false in its reasoning, refute it. But, for God's sake, let us freely hear both sides, if we choose. . . . .

TO THOMAS LAW, ESQ.[1]

Poplar Forest, June 13, 1814

DEAR SIR,—The copy of your Second Thoughts on Instinctive Impulses, with the letter accompanying it, was received just as I was setting out on a journey to this place, two or three days distant from Monticello. I brought it with me and read it with great satisfaction, and with the more as it contained exactly my own creed on the foundation of morality in man. It is really curious that on a question so fundamental, such a variety of opinions should have prevailed among men, and those, too, of the most exemplary virtue and first order of understanding. It shows how necessary was the care of the Creator in making the moral principle so much a part of our constitution as that no errors of reasoning or of speculation might lead us astray from its observation in practice. Of all the theories on this question, the most whimsical seems to have been that of Wollaston, who considers *truth* as the foundation of morality. The thief who steals your guinea does wrong only inasmuch as he acts a lie in using your guinea as if it were his own. Truth is certainly a branch of morality, and a very important one to society. But presented as its foundation, it is as if a tree taken up by the roots, had its stem reversed in the air, and one of its

[1]Thomas Law, former British civil servant in India, settled in the United States out of preference for American institutions. He wrote on moral philosophy and financial theory, and helped develop the city of Washington.

branches planted in the ground. Some have made the love of God the foundation of morality. This, too, is but a branch of our moral duties, which are generally divided into duties to God and duties to man. If we did a good act merely from the love of God and a belief that it is pleasing to Him, whence arises the morality of the Atheist? It is idle to say, as some do, that no such being exists. We have the same evidence of the fact as of most of those we act on, to wit: their own affirmations, and their reasonings in support of them. I have observed, indeed, generally, that while in Protestant countries the defections from the Platonic Christianity of the priests is to Deism, in Catholic countries they are to Atheism. Diderot, D'Alembert, D'Holbach, Condorcet, are known to have been among the most virtuous of men. Their virtue, then, must have had some other foundation than the love of God.

The καλον[1] of others is founded in a different faculty, that of taste, which is not even a branch of morality. We have indeed an innate sense of what we call beautiful, but that is exercised chiefly on subjects addressed to the fancy, whether through the eye in visible forms, as landscape, animal figure, dress, drapery, architecture, the composition of colors, etc., or to the imagination directly, as imagery, style, or measure in prose or poetry, or whatever else constitutes the domain of criticism or taste, a faculty entirely distinct from the moral one. Self-interest, or rather self-love, or *egoism*, has been more plausibly substituted as the basis of morality. But I consider our relations with others as constituting the boundaries of morality. With ourselves we stand on the ground of identity, not of relation, which last, requiring two subjects, excludes self-love confined to a single one. To ourselves, in strict language, we can owe no duties, obligation requiring also two parties. Self-love, therefore, is no part of morality. Indeed it is exactly its counterpart. It is the sole antagonist of virtue, leading us constantly by our propensities to self-gratification in violation of our moral duties to others. Accordingly, it is against this enemy that are erected the batteries of moralists and religionists, as the only obstacle to the practice of morality. Take from man his selfish propensities, and he can have nothing to seduce him from the practice of virtue. Or subdue those propensities by education, instruction or restraint, and virtue remains

[1]The beautiful.

without a competitor. Egoism, in a broader sense, has been thus presented as the source of moral action. It has been said that we feed the hungry, clothe the naked, bind up the wounds of the man beaten by thieves, pour oil and wine into them, set him on our own beast and bring him to the inn, because we receive ourselves pleasure from these acts. So Helvetius, one of the best men on earth, and the most ingenious advocate of this principle, after defining "interest" to mean not merely that which is pecuniary, but whatever may procure us pleasure or withdraw us from pain, [*de l'esprit*, 2, I,] says, [ib. 2, 2,] "the humane man is he to whom the sight of misfortune is insupportable, and who to rescue himself from this spectacle, is forced to succor the unfortunate object." This indeed is true. But it is one step short of the ultimate question. These good acts give us pleasure, but how happens it that they give us pleasure? Because nature hath implanted in our breasts a love of others, a sense of duty to them, a moral instinct, in short, which prompts us irresistibly to feel and to succor their distresses, and protests against the language of Helvetius, [ib. 2, 5,] "what other motive than self-interest could determine a man to generous actions? It is as impossible for him to love what is good for the sake of good, as to love evil for the sake of evil." The Creator would indeed have been a bungling artist, had he intended man for a social animal, without planting in him social dispositions. It is true they are not planted in every man, because there is no rule without exceptions; but it is false reasoning which converts exceptions into the general rule. Some men are born without the organs of sight, or of hearing, or without hands. Yet it would be wrong to say that man is born without these faculties, and sight, hearing, and hands may with truth enter into the general definition of man.

The want or imperfection of the moral sense in some men, like the want or imperfection of the senses of sight and hearing in others, is no proof that it is a general characteristic of the species. When it is wanting, we endeavor to supply the defect by education, by appeals to reason and calculation, by presenting to the being so unhappily conformed, other motives to do good and to eschew evil, such as the love, or the hatred, or rejection of those among whom he lives, and whose society is necessary to his happiness and even existence; demonstrations by sound calculation that honesty promotes interest in the long run; the rewards and penalties established by the laws; and ultimately the prospects of a future state of retribution for the evil as well as the good done while here. These are the correctives which are supplied by education, and which exercise the functions of the moralist, the preacher, and legislator; and they lead into a course of correct action all those whose disparity is not too profound to be eradicated. Some have argued against the existence of a moral sense, by saying that if nature had given us such a sense, impelling us to virtuous actions, and warning us against those which are vicious, then nature would also have designated, by some particular ear-marks, the two sets of actions which are, in themselves, the one virtuous and the other vicious. Whereas, we find, in fact, that the same actions are deemed virtuous in one country and vicious in another. The answer is, that nature has constituted *utility* to man, the standard and test of virtue. Men living in different countries, under different circumstances, different habits and regimens, may have different utilities; the same act, therefore, may be useful, and consequently virtuous in one country which is injurious and vicious in another differently circumstanced. I sincerely, then, believe with you in the general existence of a moral instinct. I think it the brightest gem with which the human character is studded, and the want of it as more degrading than the most hideous of the bodily deformities. I am happy in reviewing the roll of associates in this principle which you present in your second letter, some of which I had not before met with. To these might be added Lord Kaims, one of the ablest of our advocates, who goes so far as to say, in his Principles of Natural Religion, that a man owes no duty to which he is not urged by some impulsive feeling. This is correct, if referred to the standard of general feeling in the given case, and not to the feeling of a single individual. Perhaps I may misquote him, it being fifty years since I read his book.

The leisure and solitude of my situation here has led me to the indiscretion of taxing you with a long letter on a subject whereon nothing new can be offered you. I will indulge myself no farther than to repeat the assurances of my continued esteem and respect.

TO JOHN ADAMS

Monticello, July 5, 1814

. . . . Shall you and I last to see the course the sevenfold wonders of the times will take? The Attila of the age dethroned, the ruthless destroyer of ten millions of the human race, whose thirst for blood appeared unquenchable, the great oppressor of the rights and liberties of the world, shut up within the circle of a little island of the Mediterranean, and dwindled to the condition of an humble and degraded pensioner on the bounty of those he had most injured. How miserably, how meanly, has he closed his inflated career! What a sample of the bathos will his history present! He should have perished on the swords of his enemies, under the walls of Paris. . . . .

But Bonaparte was a lion in the field only. In civil life, a cold-blooded, calculating, unprincipled usurper, without a virtue; no statesman, knowing nothing of commerce, political economy, or civil government, and supplying ignorance by bold presumption. . . . .

TO EDWARD COLES[1]

Monticello, August 25th, '14

DEAR SIR,—Your favour of July 31, was duly received, and was read with peculiar pleasure. The sentiments breathed through the whole do honor to both the head and heart of the writer. Mine on the subject of slavery of negroes have long since been in possession of the public, and time has only served to give them stronger root. The love of justice and the love of country plead equally the cause of these people, and it is a moral reproach to us that they should have pleaded it so long in vain, and should have produced not a single effort, nay I fear not much serious willingness to relieve them & ourselves from our present condition of moral & political reprobation. From those of the

[1]Edward Coles, Jefferson's neighbor in Albemarle County, was at this time President Madison's private secretary. Later Governor of Illinois, to which state he and his freed slaves had removed, he devoted the greater part of his life to the cause of Abolition. [Ford.]

former generation who were in the fulness of age when I came into public life, which was while our controversy with England was on paper only, I soon saw that nothing was to be hoped. Nursed and educated in the daily habit of seeing the degraded condition, both bodily and mental, of those unfortunate beings, not reflecting that that degradation was very much the work of themselves & their fathers, few minds have yet doubted but that they were as legitimate subjects of property as their horses and cattle. The quiet and monotonous course of colonial life has been disturbed by no alarm, and little reflection on the value of liberty. And when alarm was taken at an enterprize on their own, it was not easy to carry them to the whole length of the principles which they invoked for themselves. In the first or second session of the Legislature after I became a member, I drew to this subject the attention of Col. Bland, one of the oldest, ablest, & most respected members, and he undertook to move for certain moderate extensions of the protection of the laws to these people. I seconded his motion, and, as a younger member, was more spared in the debate; but he was denounced as an enemy of his country, & was treated with the grossest indecorum. From an early stage of our revolution other & more distant duties were assigned to me, so that from that time till my return from Europe in 1789, and I may say till I returned to reside at home in 1809, I had little opportunity of knowing the progress of public sentiment here on this subject. I had always hoped that the younger generation receiving their early impressions after the flame of liberty had been kindled in every breast, & had become as it were the vital spirit of every American, that the generous temperament of youth, analogous to the motion of their blood, and above the suggestions of avarice, would have sympathized with oppression wherever found, and proved their love of liberty beyond their own share of it. But my intercourse with them, since my return has not been sufficient to ascertain that they had made towards this point the progress I had hoped. Your solitary but welcome voice is the first which has brought this sound to my ear; and I have considered the general silence which prevails on this subject as indicating an apathy unfavorable to every hope. Yet the hour of emancipation is advancing, in the march of time. . . . .

TO PETER CARR

Monticello, September 7, 1814

DEAR SIR,—On the subject of the academy or college proposed to be established in our neighborhood, I promised the trustees that I would prepare for them a plan, adapted, in the first instance, to our slender funds, but susceptible of being enlarged, either by their own growth or by accession from other quarters.

I have long entertained the hope that this, our native State, would take up the subject of education, and make an establishment, either with or without incorporation into that of William and Mary, where every branch of science, deemed useful at this day, should be taught in its highest degree. With this view, I have lost no occasion of making myself acquainted with the organization of the best seminaries in other countries, and with the opinions of the most enlightened individuals, on the subject of the sciences worthy of a place in such an institution. In order to prepare what I have promised our trustees, I have lately revised these several plans with attention; and I am struck with the diversity of arrangement observable in them—no two alike. Yet, I have no doubt that these several arrangements have been the subject of mature reflection, by wise and learned men, who, contemplating local circumstances, have adapted them to the conditions of the section of society for which they have been framed. I am strengthened in this conclusion by an examination of each separately, and a conviction that no one of them, if adopted without change, would be suited to the circumstances and pursuit of our country. The example they set, then, is authority for us to select from their different institutions the materials which are good for us, and, with them, to erect a structure, whose arrangement shall correspond with our own social condition, and shall admit of enlargement in proportion to the encouragement it may merit and receive. As I may not be able to attend the meetings of the trustees, I will make you the depository of my ideas on the subject, which may be corrected, as you proceed, by the better view of others, and adapted, from time to time, to the prospects which open upon us, and which cannot be specifically seen and provided for.

In the first place, we must ascertain with precision the object of our institution, by taking a survey of the general field of science, and marking out the portion we mean to occupy at first, and the ultimate extension of our views beyond that, should we be enabled to render it, in the end, as comprehensive as we would wish.

1. Elementary schools.

It is highly interesting to our country, and it is the duty of its functionaries, to provide that every citizen in it should receive an education proportioned to the condition and pursuits of his life. The mass of our citizens may be divided into two classes—the laboring and the learned. The laboring will need the first grade of education to qualify them for their pursuits and duties; the learned will need it as a foundation for further acquirements. A plan was formerly proposed to the legislature of this State for laying off every county into hundreds or wards of five or six miles square, within each of which should be a school for the education of the children of the ward, wherein they should receive three years' instruction gratis, in reading, writing, arithmetic as far as fractions, the roots and ratios, and geography. The Legislature at one time tried an ineffectual expedient for introducing this plan, which having failed, it is hoped they will some day resume it in a more promising form.

2. General schools.

At the discharging of the pupils from the elementary schools, the two classes separate—those destined for labor will engage in the business of agriculture, or enter into apprenticeships to such handicraft art as may be their choice; their companions, destined to the pursuits of science, will proceed to the college, which will consist, 1st of general schools; and, 2d, of professional schools. The general schools will constitute the second grade of education.

The learned class may still be subdivided into two sections: 1, Those who are destined for learned professions, as means of livelihood; and, 2, The wealthy, who, possessing independent fortunes, may aspire to share in conducting the affairs of the nation, or to live with usefulness and respect in the private ranks of life. Both of these sections will require instruction in all the higher branches of science; the wealthy to qualify them for either public or private life; the professional section will need those branches, especially, which are the basis of their future profession, and a general knowledge of the others, as auxiliary to that, and necessary to their standing and association with the scientific class. All the branches, then, of useful science, ought to be taught in the general schools, to a competent degree, in the first instance. These sciences may be arranged into three departments, not rigorously scientific, indeed, but sufficiently so for our purposes. These are, I. Language; II. Mathematics; III. Philosophy.

I. Language. In the first department, I would arrange a distinct science. 1, Languages and History, ancient and modern; 2, Grammar; 3, Belles Lettres; 4, Rhetoric and Oratory; 5, A school for the deaf, dumb and blind. History is here associated with languages, not as a kindred subject, but on the principle of economy, because both may be attained by the same course of reading, if books are selected with that view.

II. Mathematics. In the department of Mathematics, I should give place distinctly: 1, Mathematics pure; 2, Physico-Mathematics; 3, Physics; 4, Chemistry; 5, Natural History, to wit: Mineralogy; 6, Botany; and 7, Zoology; 8, Anatomy; 9, the Theory of Medicine.

III. Philosophy. In the Philosophical department, I should distinguish: 1, Ideology; 2, Ethics; 3, the Law of Nature and Nations; 4, Government; 5, Political Economy.

But, some of these terms being used by different writers, in different degrees of extension, I shall define exactly what I mean to comprehend in each of them.

I. 3. Within the term of Belles Lettres I include poetry and composition generally, and criticism.

II. 1. I consider pure mathematics as the science of, I, Numbers, and 2, Measure in the abstract; that of numbers comprehending Arithmetic, Algebra and Fluxions; that of Measure (under the general appellation of Geometry), comprehending Trigonometry, plane and spherical, conic sections, and transcendental curves.

II. 2. Physico-Mathematics treat of physical subjects by the aid of mathematical calculation. These are Mechanics, Statics, Hydrostatics, Hydrodynamics, Navigation, Astronomy, Geography, Optics, Pneumatics, Acoustics.

II. 3. Physics, or Natural Philosophy (not entering the limits of Chemistry) treat of natural substances, their properties, mutual relations and action. They particularly examine the subjects of motion, action, magnetism, electricity, galvanism, light, meteorology, with an etc. not easily enumerated. These definitions and specifications render immaterial the question whether I use the generic terms in the exact degree of comprehension in which others use them; to be understood is all that is necessary to the present object.

3. Professional Schools.

At the close of this course the students separate; the wealthy retiring, with a sufficient stock of knowledge, to improve themselves to any degree to which their views may lead them, and the professional section to the professional schools, constituting the third grade of education, and teaching the particular sciences which the individuals of this section mean to pursue, with more minuteness and detail than was within the scope of the general schools for the second grade of instruction. In these professional schools each science is to be taught in the highest degree it has yet attained. They are to be the

1st Department, the fine arts, to wit: Civil Architecture, Gardening, Painting, Sculpture, and the Theory of Music; the

2d Department, Architecture, Military and Naval; Projectiles, Rural Economy (comprehending Agriculture, Horticulture and Veterinary), Technical Philosophy, the Practice of Medicine, Materia Medica, Pharmacy and Surgery. In the

3d Department, Theology and Ecclesiastical History; Law, Municipal and Foreign.

To these professional schools will come those who separated at the close of their first elementary course, to wit:

The lawyer to the law school.

The ecclesiastic to that of theology and ecclesiastical history.

The physician to those of medicine, materia medica, pharmacy and surgery.

The military man to that of military and naval architecture and projectiles.

The agricultor to that of rural economy.

The gentleman, the architect, the pleasure gardener, painter and musician to the school of fine arts.

And to that of technical philosophy will come the mariner, carpenter, shipwright, pumpmaker, clockmaker, machinist, optician, metallurgist, founder, cutler, druggist, brewer, vintner, distiller, dyer, painter, bleacher, soapmaker, tanner, powdermaker, saltmaker, glassmaker, to learn as much as shall be necessary to pursue their art understandingly, of the sciences of geometry, mechanics, statics, hydrostatics, hydraulics, hydrodynamics, navigation, astronomy, geography, optics, pneumatics, physics, chemistry, natural history, botany, mineralogy and pharmacy.

The school of technical philosophy will differ essentially in its functions from the other professional schools. The others are instituted to ramify and dilate the particular sciences taught in the schools of the second grade on a general scale only. The technical school is to abridge those which were taught there too much *in extenso* for the limited wants of the artificer or practical man. These artificers must be grouped together, according to the particular branch of science in which they need elementary and practical instruction; and a special lecture or lectures should be prepared for each group. And these lectures should be given in the evening, so as not to interrupt the labors of the day. The school, particularly, should be maintained wholly at the public expense, on the same principles with that of the ward schools. Through the whole of the collegiate course, at the hours of recreation on certain days, all the students should be taught the manual exercise; military evaluations and manœuvers should be under a standing organization as a military corps, and with proper officers to train and command them.

A tabular statement of this distribution of the sciences will place the system of instruction more particularly in view:

1st or Elementary Grade in the Ward Schools.

Reading, Writing, Arithmetic, Geography.

2d, or General Grade.

1. Language and History, ancient and modern.
2. Mathematics, viz: Mathematics pure, Physico-Mathematics, Physics, Chemistry, Anatomy, Theory of Medicine, Zoology, Botany and Mineralogy.
3. Philosophy, viz: Ideology, and Ethics, Law of Nature and Nations, Government, Political Economy.

3d, or Professional Grades.

Theology and Ecclesiastical History; Law, Municipal and Foreign;

Practice of Medicine; Materia Medica and Pharmacy; Surgery; Architecture, Military and Naval, and Projectiles; Technical Philosophy; Rural Economy; Fine Arts.

On this survey of the field of science, I recur to the question, what portion of it we mark out for the occupation of our institution? With the first grade of education we shall have nothing to do. The sciences of the second grade are our first object; and, to adapt them to our slender beginnings, we must separate them into groups, comprehending many sciences each, and greatly more, in the first instance, than ought to be imposed on, or can be competently conducted by a single professor permanently. They must be subdivided from time to time, as our means increase, until each professor shall have no more under his care than he can attend to with advantage to his pupils and ease to himself. For the present, we may group the sciences into professorships, as follows, subject, however, to be changed, according to the qualifications of the persons we may be able to engage.

I. Professorship.

Languages and History, ancient and modern.
Belles-Lettres, Rhetoric and Oratory.

II. Professorship.

Mathematics pure, Physico-Mathematics.
Physics, Anatomy, Medicine, Theory.

III. Professorship.

Chemistry, Zoology, Botany, Mineralogy.

IV. Professorship.

Philosophy.

The organization of the branch of the institution which respects its government, police and economy, depending on principles which have no affinity with those of its institution, may be the subject of separate and subsequent consideration.

With this tribute of duty to the board of trustees, accept assurances of my great esteem and consideration.

TO DR. THOMAS COOPER

Monticello, September 10, 1814

. . . . And, first, we have no paupers, the old and crippled among us, who possess nothing and have no families to take care of them, being too few to merit notice as a separate section of society, or to affect a general estimate. The great mass of our population is of laborers; our rich, who can live without labor, either manual or professional, being few, and of moderate wealth. Most of the laboring class possess property, cultivate their own lands, have families, and from the demand for their labor are enabled to exact from the rich and the competent such prices as enable them to be fed abundantly, clothed above mere decency, to labor moderately and raise their families. They are not driven to the ultimate resources of dexterity and skill, because their wares will sell although not quite so nice as those of England. The wealthy, on the other hand, and those at their ease, know nothing of what the Europeans call luxury. They have only somewhat more of the comforts and decencies of life than those who furnish them. Can any condition of society be more desirable than this? . . . .

TO SAMUEL H. SMITH, ESQ.[1]

Monticello, September 21, 1814

DEAR SIR,—I learn from the newspapers that the vandalism of our enemy has triumphed at Washington over science as well as the arts, by the destruction of the public library with the noble edifice in which it was deposited.[2] Of this transaction, as of that of Copenhagen, the world will entertain but one sentiment. They will see a nation suddenly

[1]Samuel Harrison Smith, a long-time friend of Jefferson, was editor of the *National Intelligencer and Washington Advertiser*, which had been the official organ of the Jefferson administration. At the time of this letter, he was chairman of the Library Committee for the Library of Congress.

[2]When the British attacked Washington in the autumn of 1814 the Library of Congress was destroyed.

withdrawn from a great war, full armed and full handed, taking advantage of another whom they had recently forced into it, unarmed, and unprepared, to indulge themselves in acts of barbarism which do not belong to a civilized age. When Van Ghent destroyed their shipping at Chatham, and De Ruyter rode triumphantly up the Thames, he might in like manner, by the acknowledgment of their own historians, have forced all their ships up to London bridge, and there have burnt them, the Tower, and city, had these examples been then set. London, when thus menaced, was near a thousand years old; Washington is but in its teens.

I presume it will be among the early objects of Congress to re-commence their collection. This will be difficult while the war continues, and intercourse with Europe is attended with so much risk. You know my collection, its condition and extent. I have been fifty years making it, and have spared no pains, opportunity or expense, to make it what it is. While residing in Paris, I devoted every afternoon I was disengaged, for a summer or two, in examining all the principal bookstores, turning over every book with my own hand, and putting by everything which related to America, and indeed whatever was rare and valuable in every science. Besides this, I had standing orders during the whole time I was in Europe, on its principal book-marts, particularly Amsterdam, Frankfort, Madrid and London, for such works relating to America as could not be found in Paris. So that in that department particularly, such a collection was made as probably can never again be effected, because it is hardly probable that the same opportunities, the same time, industry, perseverance and expense, with some knowledge of the bibliography of the subject, would again happen to be in concurrence. During the same period, and after my return to America, I was led to procure, also, whatever related to the duties of those in the high concerns of the nation. So that the collection, which I suppose is of between nine and ten thousand volumes, while it includes what is chiefly valuable in science and literature generally, extends more particularly to whatever belongs to the American statesman. In the diplomatic and parliamentary branches, it is particularly full. It is long since I have been sensible it ought not to continue private property, and had provided that at my death, Congress should have the refusal of it at their own price. But the loss they have now incurred, makes the present the proper moment for their accommodation, without regard to the small remnant of time and the barren use of my enjoying it. I ask of your friendship, therefore, to make for me the tender of it to the library committee of Congress, not knowing myself of whom the committee consists. I enclose you the catalogue, which will enable them to judge of its contents. Nearly the whole are well bound, abundance of them elegantly, and of the choicest editions existing. They may be valued by persons named by themselves, and the payment made convenient to the public. It may be, for instance, in such annual instalments as the law of Congress has left at their disposal, or in stock of any of their late loans, or of any loan they may institute at this session, so as to spare the present calls of our country, and await its days of peace and prosperity. They may enter, nevertheless, into immediate use of it, as eighteen or twenty wagons would place it in Washington in a single trip of a fortnight. I should be willing indeed, to retain a few of the books, to amuse the time I have yet to pass, which might be valued with the rest, but not included in the sum of valuation until they should be restored at my death, which I would carefully provide for, so that the whole library as it stands in the catalogue at this moment should be theirs without any garbling. Those I should like to retain would be chiefly classical and mathematical. Some few in other branches, and particularly one of the five encyclopedias in the catalogue. . . . .

TO WILLIAM SHORT, ESQ.

Monticello, November 28, 1814

. . . . Although withdrawn from all anxious attention to political concerns, yet I will state my impressions as to the present war, because your letter leads to the subject. The essential grounds of the war were, 1st, the orders of council; and 2d, the impressment of our citizens; (for I put out of sight from the love of peace the multiplied insults on our government and aggressions on our commerce, with which our pouch, like the Indian's, had long been filled to the mouth.) What immediately produced the declaration was, Ist, the proclamation of the Prince Regent that he would never repeal the orders of council as to us, until Bonaparte should have revoked his decrees as to all other nations as well as ours; and 2d, the declaration of his minister to ours that no arrangement whatever could be devised, admissible in lieu of impressment. It was certainly a misfortune that *they* did not know themselves at the date of this silly and insolent proclamation, that within one month they would repeal the orders, and that *we*, at the date of our declaration, could not know of the repeal which was then going on one thousand leagues distant. Their determinations, as declared by themselves, could alone guide us, and they shut the door on all further negotiation, throwing down to us the gauntlet of war or submission as the only alternatives. We cannot blame the government for choosing that of war, because certainly the great majority of the nation thought it ought to be chosen, not that they were to gain by it in dollars and cents; all men know that war is a losing game to both parties. But they know also that if they do not resist encroachment at some point, all will be taken from them, and that more would then be lost even in dollars and cents by submission than resistance. It is the case of giving a part to save the whole, a limb to save life. It is the melancholy law of human societies to be compelled sometimes to choose a great evil in order to ward off a greater; to deter their neighbors from rapine by making it cost them more than honest gains. The enemy are accordingly now disgorging what they had so ravenously swallowed. The orders of council had taken from us near one thousand vessels. Our list of captures from them is now one thousand three hundred, and, just become sensible that it is small and not large ships which gall them most, we shall probably add one thousand prizes a year to their past losses. Again, supposing that, according to the confession of their own minister in Parliament, the Americans they had impressed were something short of two thousand, the war against us alone cannot cost them less than twenty millions of dollars a year, so that each American impressed has already cost them ten thousand dollars, and every year will add five thousand dollars more to his price. We, I suppose, expend more; but had we adopted the other alternative of submission, no mortal can tell what the cost would have been. I consider the war then as entirely justifiable on our part, although I am still sensible it is a deplorable misfortune to us. It has arrested the course of the most remarkable tide of prosperity any nation ever experienced, and has closed such prospects of future improvement as were never before in the view of any people. Farewell all hopes of extinguishing public debt! farewell all visions of applying surpluses of revenue to the improvements of peace rather than the ravages of war. Our enemy has indeed the consolation of Satan on removing our first parents from Paradise: from a peaceable and agricultural nation, he makes us a military and manufacturing one. We shall indeed survive the conflict. Breeders enough will remain to carry on population. We shall retain our country, and rapid advances in the art of war will soon enable us to beat our enemy, and probably drive him from the continent. . . . .

TO THE MARQUIS DE LAFAYETTE

Monticello, February 14, 1815

. . . . Possibly you may remember, at the date of the *jeu de paume*, how earnestly I urged yourself and the patriots of my acquaintance, to enter then into a compact with the king, securing freedom of religion, freedom of the press, trial by jury, *habeas corpus*, and a national legislature, all of which it was known he would then yield, to go home, and let these work on the amelioration of the condition of the people, until they should have rendered them capable of more, when occasions would not fail to arise for communicating to them more. This was as much as I then thought them able to bear, soberly and usefully for themselves. You thought otherwise, and that the dose might still be larger. And I found you were right; for subsequent events proved they were equal to the Constitution of 1791. Unfortunately, some of the most honest and enlightened of our patriotic friends, (but closet politicians merely, unpractised in the knowledge of man,) thought more could still be obtained and borne. They did not weigh the hazards of a transition from one form of government to another, the value of what they had already rescued from those hazards, and might hold in security if they pleased, nor the imprudence of giving up the certainty of such a degree of liberty, under a limited monarch, for the uncertainty of a little more under the form of a republic. You differed from them. You were for stopping there, and for securing the Constitution which the National Assembly had obtained. Here, too, you were right; and from this fatal error of the republicans, from their separation from yourself and the constitutionalists, in their councils, flowed all the subsequent sufferings and crimes of the French nation. The hazards of a second change fell upon them by the way. The foreigner gained time to anarchise by gold the government he could not overthrow by arms, to crush in their own councils the genuine republicans, by the fraternal embraces of exaggerated and hired pretenders, and to turn the machine of Jacobinism from the change to the destruction of order; and, in the end, the limited monarchy they had secured was exchanged for the unprincipled and bloody tyranny of Robespierre, and the equally unprincipled and maniac tyranny of Bonaparte. You are now rid of him, and I sincerely wish you may continue so. But this may depend on the wisdom and moderation of the restored dynasty. It is for them now to read a lesson in the fatal errors of the republicans; to be contented with a certain portion of power, secured by formal compact with the nation, rather than, grasping at more, hazard all upon uncertainty, and risk meeting the fate of their predecessor, or a renewal of their own exile. . . . .

TO JAMES MAURY

Monticello, June 15, 1815

I congratulate you, my dear and ancient friend, on the return of peace, and the restoration of intercourse between our two countries. What has passed may be a lesson to both of the injury which either can do the other, and the peace now opened may show what would be the value of a cordial friendship; and I hope the first moments of it will be employed to remove the stumbling block which must otherwise keep us eternal enemies. I mean the impressment of our citizens. This was the sole object of the continuance of the late war, which the repeal of the orders of council would otherwise have ended at its beginning. If according to our estimates, England impressed into her navy 6,000 of our citizens, let her count the cost of the war, and a greater number of men lost in it, and she will find this resource for manning her navy the most expensive she can adopt, each of these men having cost her £30,000 sterling, and a man of her own besides. On that point we have thrown away the scabbard, and the moment an European war brings her back to this practice, adds us again to her enemies. But I hope an arrangement is already made on this subject. Have you no statesmen who can look forward two or three score years? It is but forty years since the battle of Lexington. One-third of those now living saw that day, when we were about two millions of people, and have lived to see this, when we are ten millions. One-third of those now living, who see us at ten millions, will live another forty years, and see us forty millions; and looking forward only through such a portion of time as has passed since you and I were scanning Virgil together, (which I believe is near three score years,) we shall be seen to have a population of eighty millions, and of not more than double the average density of the present. What may not such a people be worth to England as customers and friends? and what might she not apprehend from such a nation as enemies? Now, what is the price we ask for our friendship? Justice, and the comity usually observed between nation and nation. . . . .

TO ALBERT GALLATIN

Monticello, October 16, 1815

. . . . I grieve for France; although it cannot be denied that by the afflictions with which she wantonly and wickedly overwhelmed other nations, she has merited severe reprisals. For it is no excuse to lay the enormities to the wretch who led to them, and who has been the author of more misery and suffering to the world, than any being who ever lived before him. After destroying the liberties of his country, he has exhausted all its resources, physical and moral, to indulge his own maniac ambition, his own tyrannical and overbearing spirit. His sufferings cannot be too great. But theirs I sincerely deplore, and what is to be their term? The will of the allies? There is no more moderation, forbearance, or even honesty in theirs, than in that of Bonaparte. They have proved that their object, like his, is plunder. They, like him, are shuffling nations together, or into their own hands, as if all were right which they feel a power to do. In the exhausted state in which Bonaparte has left France, I see no period to her sufferings, until this combination of robbers fall together by the ears. The French may then rise up and choose their side. And I trust they will finally establish for themselves a government of rational and well-tempered liberty. So much science cannot be lost; so much light shed over them can never fail to produce to them some good, in the end. . . . .

TO COLONEL CHARLES YANCEY[1]

Monticello, January 6, 1816

. . . . Like a dropsical man calling out for water, water, our deluded citizens are clamoring for more banks, more banks. The American mind is now in that state of fever which the world has so often seen in the history of other nations. We are under the bank bubble, as England was under the South Sea bubble, France under the Mississippi bubble, and as every nation is liable to be, under whatever bubble, design, or delusion may puff up in moments when off their guard. We are now taught to believe that legerdemain tricks upon paper can produce as solid wealth as hard labor in the earth. It is vain for common sense to urge that *nothing* can produce but *nothing;* that it is an idle dream to believe in a philosopher's stone which is to turn everything into gold, and to redeem man from the original sentence of his Maker, "in the sweat of his brow shall he eat his bread." Not Quixote enough, however, to attempt to reason Bedlam to rights, my anxieties are turned to the most practicable means of withdrawing us from the ruin into which we have run. Two hundred millions of paper in the hands of the people, (and less cannot be from the employment of a banking capital known to exceed one hundred millions,) is a fearful tax to fall at haphazard on their heads. The debt which purchased our independence was but of eighty millions, of which twenty years of taxation had in 1809 paid but the one half. And what have we purchased with this tax of two hundred millions which we are to pay by wholesale but usury, swindling, and new forms of demoralization. Revolutionary history has warned us of the probable moment when this baseless trash is to receive its fiat. Whenever so much of the precious metals shall have returned into the circulation as that every one can get some in exchange for his produce,

[1]Yancey was a prominent member of the Virginia legislature in 1820. He was the son of Robert Yancey, Rector of Trinity Parish, Virginia.

paper, as in the Revolutionary war, will experience at once an universal rejection. When public opinion changes, it is with the rapidity of thought. Confidence is already on the totter, and every one now handles this paper as if playing at Robin's alive. That in the present state of the circulation the banks should resume payments in specie, would require their vaults to be like the widow's cruse. The thing to be aimed at is, that the excesses of their emissions should be withdrawn as gradually, but as speedily, too, as is practicable, without so much alarm as to bring on the crisis dreaded. Some banks are said to be calling in their paper. But ought we to let this depend on their discretion? Is it not the duty of the legislature to endeavor to avert from their constituents such a catastrophe as the extinguishment of two hundred millions of paper in their hands? The difficulty is indeed great; and the greater, because the patient revolts against all medicine. I am far from presuming to say that any plan can be relied on with certainty, because the bubble may burst from one moment to another; but if it fails, we shall be but where we should have been without any effort to save ourselves. Different persons, doubtless, will devise different schemes of relief. One would be to suppress instantly the currency of all paper not issued under the authority of our own State or of the General Government; to interdict after a few months the circulation of all bills of five dollars and under; after a few months more, all of ten dollars and under; after other terms, those of twenty, fifty, and so on to one hundred dollars, which last, if any must be left in circulation, should be the lowest denomination. These might be a convenience in mercantile transactions and transmissions, and would be excluded by their size from ordinary circulation. But the disease may be too pressing to await such a remedy. With the legislature I cheerfully leave it to apply this medicine, or no medicine at all. I am sure their intentions are faithful; and embarked in the same bottom, I am willing to swim or sink with my fellow citizens. If the latter is their choice, I will go down with them without a murmur. But my exhortation would rather be "not to give up the ship." . . . .

TO CHARLES THOMSON[1]

Monticello, January 9, 1816

. . . . I retain good health, am rather feeble to walk much, but ride with ease, passing two or three hours a day on horseback, and every three or four months taking in a carriage a journey of ninety miles to a distant possession, where I pass a good deal of my time. My eyes need the aid of glasses by night, and with small print in the day also; my hearing is not quite so sensible as it used to be; no tooth shaking yet, but shivering and shrinking in body from the cold we now experience, my thermometer having been as low as 12° this morning. My greatest oppression is a correspondence afflictingly laborious, the extent of which I have been long endeavoring to curtail. This keeps me at the drudgery of the writing-table all the prime hours of the day, leaving for the gratification of my appetite for reading, only what I can steal from the hours of sleep. Could I reduce this epistolary corvée within the limits of my friends and affairs, and give the time redeemed from it to reading and reflection, to history, ethics, mathematics, my life would be as happy as the infirmities of age would admit, and I should look on its consummation with the composure of one *"qui summum nec me tuit diem nec optat."*[2] . . . .

TO JOSEPH C. CABELL[3]

Monticello, February 2, 1816

. . . . No, my friend, the way to have good and safe government, is not to trust it all to one, but to divide it among the many, distributing to every one exactly the functions he is competent to. Let the national government be entrusted with the defence of the nation, and

[1]Misspelled Thompson in Memorial Edition. Charles Thomson, Irish born Secretary of the Continental Congress, was an old, esteemed friend of Jefferson.

[2]"Who neither fear nor desire my last day."

[3]Joseph Carrington Cabell was Jefferson's principal co-worker in establishing the University of Virginia.

its foreign and federal relations; the State governments with the civil rights, laws, police, and administration of what concerns the State generally; the counties with the local concerns of the counties, and each ward direct the interests within itself. It is by dividing and subdividing these republics from the great national one down through all its subordinations, until it ends in the administration of every man's farm by himself; by placing under every one what his own eye may superintend, that all will be done for the best. What has destroyed liberty and the rights of man in every government which has ever existed under the sun? The generalizing and concentrating all cares and powers into one body, no matter whether of the autocrats of Russia or France, or of the aristocrats of a Venetian senate. And I do believe that if the Almighty has not decreed that man shall never be free, (and it is a blasphemy to believe it,) that the secret will be found to be in the making himself the depository of the powers respecting himself, so far as he is competent to them, and delegating only what is beyond his competence by a synthetical process, to higher and higher orders of functionaries, so as to trust fewer and fewer powers in proportion as the trustees become more and more oligarchical. The elementary republics of the wards, the county republics, the State republics, and the republic of the Union, would form a gradation of authorities, standing each on the basis of law, holding every one its delegated share of powers, and constituting truly a system of fundamental balances and checks for the government. Where every man is a sharer in the direction of his ward-republic, or of some of the higher ones, and feels that he is a participator in the government of affairs, not merely at an election one day in the year, but every day; when there shall not be a man in the State who will not be a member of some one of its councils, great or small, he will let the heart be torn out of his body sooner than his power be wrested from him by a Cæsar or a Bonaparte. How powerfully did we feel the energy of this organization in the case of embargo? I felt the foundations of the government shaken under my feet by the New England townships. There was not an individual in their States whose body was not thrown with all its momentum into action; and although the whole of the other States were known to be in favor of the measure, yet the organization of this little selfish minority enabled it to overrule the Union. What would the unwieldy counties of the Middle, the

South, and the West do? Call a county meeting, and the drunken loungers at and about the court-houses would have collected, the distances being too great for the good people and the industrious generally to attend. The character of those who really met would have been the measure of the weight they would have had in the scale of public opinion. As Cato, then, concluded every speech with the words, "*Carthago delenda est*," so do I every opinion, with the injuction, "divide the counties into wards." Begin them only for a single purpose; they will soon show for what others they are the best instruments. God bless you, and all our rulers, and give them the wisdom, as I am sure they have the will, to fortify us against the degeneracy of our government, and the concentration of all its powers in the hands of the one, the few, the well-born or the many.

TO MR. JOSEPH MILLIGAN[1]

Monticello, April 6, 1816

SIR,—Your favor of March 6th did not come to hand until the 15th. I then expected I should finish revising the translation of Tracy's book within a week, and could send the whole together. I got through it, but, on further consideration, thought I ought to read it over again, lest any errors should have been left in it. It was fortunate I did so, for I found several little errors. The whole is now done and forwarded by this mail, with a title, and something I have written which may serve for a Prospectus, and indeed for a Preface also, with a little alteration. . . .

My name must in nowise appear connected with the work. I have no objection to your naming me *in conversation,* but not in print, as the person to whom the original was communicated. Although the author puts his name to the work, yet, if called to account for it by his government, he means to disavow it, which its publication at such a distance will enable him to do. But he would not think himself at liberty to do this if avowedly sanctioned by me here. The best open mark of approbation I can give is to subscribe for a dozen copies; or

[1]Joseph Milligan was a well-known Georgetown bookdealer whom Jefferson had known and respected for years.

if you would prefer it, you may place on your subscription paper a letter in these words: "Sir, I subscribe with pleasure for a dozen copies of the invaluable book you are about to publish on Political Economy. I should be happy to see it in the hands of every American citizen." . . . .

TITLE.—"A Treatise on Political Economy by the Count Destutt Tracy, member of the Senate and Institute of France, and of the American Philosophical Society, to which is prefixed a supplement to a preceding work on the Understanding or Elements of Ideology, by the same author, with an analytical table, and an introduction on the faculty of the will, translated from the unpublished French original."

Prospectus.—Political Economy in modern times assumed the form of a regular science first in the hands of the political sect in France, called the Economists. They made it a branch only of a comprehensive system on the natural order of societies. Quesnai first, Gournay, Le Frosne, Turgot and Dupont de Nemours, the enlightened, philanthropic, and venerable citizen, now of the United States, led the way in these developments, and gave to our inquiries the direction they have since observed. Many sound and valuable principles established by them, have received the sanction of general approbation. Some, as in the infancy of a science might be expected, have been brought into question, and have furnished occasion for much discussion. Their opinions on production, and on the proper subjections of taxation, have been particularly controverted; and whatever may be the merit of their principles of taxation, it is not wonderful they have not prevailed; not on the questioned score of correctness, but because not acceptable to the people, whose will must be the supreme law. Taxation is in fact the most difficult function of government—and that against which their citizens are most apt to be refractory. The general aim is therefore to adopt the mode most consonant with the circumstances and sentiments of the country.

Adam Smith, first in England, published a rational and systematic work on Political Economy, adopting generally the ground of the Economists, but differing on the subjects before specified. The system being novel, much argument and detail seemed then necessary to establish principles which now are assented to as soon as proposed. Hence his book, admitted to be able, and of the first degree of merit, has yet been considered as prolix and tedious.

In France, John Baptist Say has the merit of producing a very superior work on the subject of Political Economy. His arrangement is luminous, ideas clear, style perspicuous, and the whole subject brought within half the volume of Smith's work. Add to this considerable advances in correctness and extension of principles.

The work of Senator Tracy, now announced, comes forward with all the lights of his predecessors in the science, and with the advantages of further experience, more discussion, and greater maturity of subjects. It is certainly distinguished by important traits; a cogency of logic which has never been exceeded in any work, a rigorous enchainment of ideas, and constant recurrence to it to keep it in the reader's view, a fearless pursuit of truth whithersoever it leads, and a diction so correct that not a word can be changed but for the worse; and, as happens in other cases, that the more a subject is understood, the more briefly it may be explained, he has reduced, not indeed all the details, but all the elements and the system of principles within the compass of an 8vo, of about 400 pages. Indeed we might say within two-thirds of that space, the one-third being taken up with some preliminary pieces now to be noticed.

Mr. Tracy is the author of a treatise on the Elements of Ideology, justly considered as a production of the first order in the science of our thinking faculty, or of the understanding. Considering the present work but as a second section to those Elements under the titles of Analytical Table, Supplement, and Introduction, he gives in these preliminary pieces a supplement to the Elements, shows how the present work stands on that as its basis, presents a summary view of it, and, before entering on the formation, distribution, and employment of property and personality, a question not new indeed, yet one which has not hitherto been satisfactorily settled. These investigations are very metaphysical, profound, and demonstrative, and will give satisfaction to minds in the habit of abstract speculation. Readers, however, not disposed to enter into them, after reading the summary view, entitled, "on our actions," will probably pass on at once to the commencement of the main subject of the work, which is treated of under the following heads:

Of Society.

Of Production, or the formation of our riches.

Of Value, or the measure of utility.

Of change of form, or fabrication.

Of change of place, or commerce.

Of Money.

Of the distribution of our riches.

Of Population.

Of the employment of our riches, or consumption.

Of public revenue, expenses and debts.

Although the work now offered is but a translation, it may be considered in some degree as the original, that having never been published in the country in which it was written. The author would there have been submitted to the unpleasant alternative either of mutilating his sentiments, where they were either free or doubtful, or of risking himself under the unsettled regimen of the press. A manuscript copy communicated to a friend here has enabled him to give it to a country which is afraid to read nothing, and which may be trusted with anything, so long as its reason remains unfettered by law.

In the translation, fidelity has been chiefly consulted. A more correct style would sometimes have given a shade of sentiment which was not the author's, and which, in a work standing in the place of the original, would have been unjust towards him. Some Gallicisms have, therefore, been admitted, where a single word gives an idea which would require a whole phrase of dictionary English. Indeed, the horrors of Neologism, which startle the purist, have given no alarm to the translator. Where brevity, perspecuity, and even euphony can be promoted by the introduction of a new word, it is an improvement to the language. It is thus the English language has been brought to what it is; one-half of it having been innovations, made at different times, from the Greek, Latin, French, and other languages. And is it the worse for these? Had the proposterous idea of fixing the language been adopted by our Saxon ancestors, of Pierce Plowman, of Chaucer, of Spenser, the progress of ideas must have stopped with that of the language. On the contrary, nothing is more evident than that as we advance in the knowledge of new things, and of new combinations of old ones, we must have new words to express them. Were Van Helmont, Stane, Scheele, to rise from the dead at this time, they would scarcely understand one word of their own science. Would it have been better, then, to have abanboned the science of Chemistry, rather than admit innovations in its terms? What a wonderful accession of copiousness and force has the French language attained, by the innovations of the last thirty years! And what do we not owe to Shakespeare for the enrichment of the language, by his free and magical creation of words? In giving a loose to Neologism, indeed, uncouth words will sometimes be offered; but the public will judge them, and receive or reject, as sense or sound shall suggest, and authors will be approved or condemned according to the use they make of this license, as they now are from their use of the present vocabulary. The claim of the present translation, however, is limited to its duties of fidelity and justice to the sense of its original; adopting the author's own word only where no term of our own language would convey his meaning.

TO JOHN ADAMS

Monticello, April 8, 1816

. . . . You ask, if I would agree to live my seventy or rather seventy-three years over again? To which I say, yea. I think with you, that it is a good world on the whole; that it has been framed on a principle of benevolence, and more pleasure than pain dealt out to us. There are, indeed, (who might say nay) gloomy and hypochondriac minds, inhabitants of diseased bodies, disgusted with the present, and despairing of the future; always counting that the worst will happen, because it may happen. To these I say, how much pain have cost us the evils which have never happened! My temperament is sanguine. I steer my bark with Hope in the head, leaving Fear astern. My hopes, indeed, sometimes fail; but not oftener than the forebodings of the gloomy. There are, I acknowledge, even in the happiest life, some terrible convulsions, heavy set-offs against the opposite page of the account. I have often wondered for what good end the sensations of grief could be intended. All our other passions, within proper bounds, have an useful object. And the perfection of the moral character is, not in a stoical apathy, so hypocritically vaunted, and so untruly too, because impossible, but in a just equilibrium of all the passions. I wish the pathologists then would tell us what is the use of grief in the economy, and of what good it is the cause, proximate or remote.

Did I know Baron Grimm while at Paris? Yes, most intimately. He was the pleasantest and most conversable member of the diplomatic corps while I was there; a man of good fancy, acuteness, irony, cunning and egoism. No heart, not much of any science, yet enough of every one to speak its language; his forte was belles-lettres, painting and sculpture. In these he was the oracle of society, and as such, was the Empress Catharine's private correspondent and factor, in all things not diplomatic. . . . . Although I never heard Grimm express the opinion directly, yet I always supposed him to be of the school of Diderot, D'Alembert, D'Holbach; the first of whom committed his system of atheism to writing in *"Le bon sens,"* and the last in his *"Systeme de la Nature."* It was a numerous school in the Catholic countries, while the infidelity of the Protestant took generally the form of theism. The former always insisted that it was a mere question of definition between them, the hypostasis of which, on both sides, was *"Nature,"* or *"the Universe;"* that both agreed in the order of the existing system, but the one supposed it from eternity, the other as having begun in time. And when the atheist descanted on the unceasing motion and circulation of matter through the animal, vegetable and mineral kingdoms, never resting, never annihilated, always changing form, and under all forms gifted with the power of reproduction; the theist pointing "to the heavens above, and to the earth beneath, and to the waters under the earth," asked, if these did not proclaim a first cause, possessing intelligence and power; power in the production, and intelligence in the design and constant preservation of the system; urged the palpable existence of final causes; that the eye was made to see, and the ear to hear, and not that we see because we have eyes and hear because we have ears; an answer obvious to the senses, as that of walking across the room, was to the philosopher demonstrating the non-existence of motion. It was in D'Holbach's conventicles that Rousseau imagined all the machinations against him were contrived; and he left, in his Confessions, the most biting anecdotes of Grimm. . . . .

TO JOHN TAYLOR[1]

Monticello, May 28, 1816

DEAR SIR,—On my return from a long journey and considerable absence from home, I found here the copy of your "Enquiry into the Principles of our Government," which you had been so kind as to send me; and for which I pray you to accept my thanks. The difficulties of getting new works in our situation, inland and without a single book-store, are such as had prevented my obtaining a copy before; and letters which had accumulated during my absence, and were calling for answers, have not yet permitted me to give to the whole a thorough reading; yet certain that you and I could not think differently on the fundamentals of rightful government, I was impatient, and availed myself of the intervals of repose from the writing-table, to obtain a cursory idea of the body of the work.

I see in it much matter for profound reflection; much which should confirm our adhesion, in practice, to the good principles of our Constitution, and fix our attention on what is yet to be made good. The sixth section on the good moral principles of our government, I found so interesting and replete with sound principles, as to postpone my letter-writing to its thorough perusal and consideration. Besides much other good matter, it settles unanswerably the right of instructing representatives, and their duty to obey. The system of banking we have both equally and ever reprobated. I contemplate it as a blot left in all our Constitutions, which, if not covered, will end in their destruction, which is already hit by the gamblers in corruption, and is sweeping away in its progress the fortunes and morals of our citizens. Funding I consider as limited, rightfully, to a redemption of the debt within the lives of a majority of the generation contracting it; every generation coming equally, by the laws of the Creator of the world to the free possession of the earth He made for their subsistence, unincumbered by their predecessors, who, like them, were but tenants for life. You have

---

[1]John Taylor of Caroline [Virginia], political writer, agriculturist, and philosopher of agrarian liberalism, was the author of *An Inquiry into the Principles and Policy of the Government of the United States.*

successfully and completely pulverized Mr. Adams' system of orders, and his opening the mantle of republicanism to every government of laws, whether consistent or not with natural right. Indeed, it must be acknowledged, that the term *republic* is of very vague application in every language Witness the self-styled republics of Holland, Switzerland, Genoa, Venice, Poland. Were I to assign to this term a precise and definite idea, I would say, purely and simply, it means a government by its citizens in mass, acting directly and personally, according to rules established by the majority; and that every other government is more or less republican, in proportion as it has in its composition more or less of this ingredient of the direct action of the citizens. Such a government is evidently restrained to very narrow limits of space and population. I doubt if it would be practicable beyond the extent of a New England township. The first shade from this pure element, which, like that of pure vital air, cannot sustain life of itself, would be where the powers of the government, being divided, should be exercised each by representatives chosen either *pro hac vice*,[1] or for such short terms as should render secure the duty of expressing the will of their constituents. This I should consider as the nearest approach to a pure republic, which is practicable on a large scale of country or population. And we have examples of it in some of our State Constitutions, which, if not poisoned by priest-craft, would prove its excellence over all mixtures with other elements; and, with only equal doses of poison, would still be the best. Other shades of republicanism may be found in other forms of government, where the executive, judiciary and legislative functions, and the different branches of the latter, are chosen by the people more or less directly, for longer terms of years, or for life, or made hereditary; or where there are mixtures of authorities, some dependent on, and others independent of the people. The further the departure from direct and constant control by the citizens, the less has the government of the ingredient of republicanism; evidently none where the authorities are hereditary, as in France, Venice, etc., or self-chosen, as in Holland; and little, where for life, in proportion as the life continues in being after the act of election.

The purest republican feature in the government of our own State,

[1]For the occasion.

is the House of Representatives. The Senate is equally so the first year, less the second, and so on. The Executive still less, because not chosen by the people directly. The Judiciary seriously anti-republican, because for life; and the national arm wielded, as you observe, by military leaders, irresponsible but to themselves. Add to this the vicious constitution of our county courts (to whom the justice, the executive administration, the taxation, police, the military appointments of the county, and nearly all our daily concerns are confided), self-appointed, self-continued, holding their authorities for life, and with an impossibility of breaking in on the perpetual succession of any faction once possessed of the bench They are in truth, the executive, the judiciary, and the military of their respective counties, and the sum of the counties makes the State. And add, also, that one-half of our brethren who fight and pay taxes, are excluded, like Helots, from the rights of representation, as if society were instituted for the soil, and not for the men inhabiting it; or one-half of these could dispose of the rights and the will of the other half, without their consent.

> "What constitutes a State?
> Not high-raised battlements, or labor'd mound,
> Thick wall, or moated gate;
> Not cities proud, with spires and turrets crown'd;
> No: men, high-minded men;
> Men, who their duties know;
> But know their rights; and knowing, dare maintain.
> These constitute a State."

In the General Government, the House of Representatives is mainly republican; the Senate scarcely so at all, as not elected by the people directly, and so long secured even against those who do elect them; the Executive more republican than the Senate, from its shorter term, its election by the people, in *practice*, (for they vote for A only on an assurance that he will vote for B,) and because, *in practice also*, a principle of rotation seems to be in a course of establishment; the judiciary independent of the nation, their coercion by impeachment being found nugatory.

If, then, the control of the people over the organs of their government be the measure of its republicanism, and I confess I know no other measure, it must be agreed that our governments have much less of republicanism than ought to have been expected; in other words, that the people have less regular control over their agents, than their rights and their interests require. And this I ascribe, not to any want of republican dispositions in those who formed these Constitutions, but to a submission of true principle to European authorities, to speculators on government, whose fears of the people have been inspired by the populace of their own great cities, and were unjustly entertained against the independent, the happy, and therefore orderly citizens of the United States. Much I apprehend that the golden moment is past for reforming these heresies. The functionaries of public power rarely strengthen in their dispositions to abridge it, and an unorganized call for timely amendment is not likely to prevail against an organized opposition to it. We are always told that things are going on well; why change them? *"Chista bene, non si muove,"* said the Italian, "let him who stands well, stand still." This is true; and I verily believe they would go on well with us under an absolute monarch, while our present character remains, of order, industry and love of peace, and restrained, as he would be, by the proper spirit of the people. But it is while it remains such, we should provide against the consequences of its deterioration. And let us rest in the hope that it will yet be done, and spare ourselves the pain of evils which may never happen.

On this view of the import of the term *republic*, instead of saying, as has been said, "that it may mean anything or nothing," we may say with truth and meaning, that governments are more or less republican, as they have more or less of the element of popular election and control in their composition; and believing, as I do, that the mass of the citizens is the safest depository of their own rights and especially, that the evils flowing from the duperies of the people, are less injurious than those from the egoism of their agents, I am a friend to that composition of government which has in it the most of this ingredient. And I sincerely believe, with you, that banking establishments are more dangerous than standing armies; and that the principle of spending money to be paid by posterity, under the name of funding, is but swindling futurity on a large scale.

I salute you with constant friendship and respect.

TO SAMUEL KERCHEVAL[1]

Monticello, July 12, 1816

. . . . I am not among those who fear the people. They, and not the rich, are our dependence for continued freedom. And to preserve their independence, we must not let our rulers load us with perpetual debt. We must make our election between *economy and liberty,* or *profusion and servitude.* If we run into such debts, as that we must be taxed in our meat and in our drink, in our necessaries and our comforts, in our labors and our amusements, for our callings and our creeds, as the people of England are, our people, like them, must come to labor sixteen hours in the twenty-four, give the earnings of fifteen of these to the government for their debts and daily expenses; and the sixteenth being insufficient to afford us bread, we must live, as they now do, on oatmeal and potatoes; have no time to think, no means of calling the mismanagers to account; but be glad to obtain subsistence by hiring ourselves to rivet their chains on the necks of our fellow suffers. Our land-holders, too, like theirs, retaining indeed the title and stewardship of estates called theirs, but held really in trust for the treasury, must wander, like theirs, in foreign countries, and be contented with penury, obscurity, exile, and the glory of the nation. This example reads to us the salutary lesson, that private fortunes are destroyed by public as well as by private extravagance. And this is the tendency of all human governments. A departure from principle in one instance becomes a precedent for a second; that second for a third; and so on, till the bulk of the society is reduced to be mere automatons of misery, to have no sensibilities left but for sinning and suffering. Then begins, indeed, the *bellum omnium in omnia,* which some philosophers observing to be so general in this world, have mistaken it for the natural, instead of the abusive state of man. And the fore horse of this frightful team is public debt. Taxation follows that, and in its train wretchedness and oppression.

Some men look at constitutions with sanctimonious reverence, and

---

[1]Samuel Kercheval had written Jefferson concerning a revision of the first Constitution of Virginia.

deem them like the ark of the covenant, too sacred to be touched. They
ascribe to the men of the preceding age a wisdom more than human,
and suppose what they did to be beyond amendment. I knew that age
well; I belonged to it, and labored with it. It deserved well of its country. It was very like the present, but without the experience of the present; and forty years of experience in government is worth a century of
book-reading; and this they would say themselves, were they to rise
from the dead. I am certainly not an advocate for frequent and untried
changes in laws and constitutions. I think moderate imperfections had
better be borne with; because, when once known, we accommodate
ourselves to them, and find practical means of correcting their ill
effects. But I know also, that laws and institutions must go hand in
hand with the progress of the human mind. As that becomes more
developed, more enlightened, as new discoveries are made, new truths
disclosed, and manners and opinions change with the change of circumstances, institutions must advance also, and keep pace with the
times. We might as well require a man to wear still the coat which fitted him when a boy, as civilized society to remain ever under the regimen of their barbarous ancestors. It is this preposterous idea which
has lately deluged Europe in blood. Their monarchs, instead of wisely
yielding to the gradual change of circumstances, of favoring progressive
accommodation to progressive improvement, have clung to old abuses,
entrenched themselves behind steady habits, and obliged their subjects to seek through blood and violence rash and ruinous innovations,
which, had they been referred to the peaceful deliberations and collected wisdom of the nation, would have been put into acceptable and
salutary forms. Let us follow no such examples, nor weakly believe that
one generation is not as capable as another of taking care of itself, and
of ordering its own affairs. Let us, as our sister States have done, avail
ourselves of our reason and experience, to correct the crude essays of
our first and unexperienced, although wise, virtuous, and well-meaning
councils. Ana lastly, let us provide in our Constitution for its revision
at stated periods. What these periods should be, nature herself indi-
cates. By the European tables of mortality, of the adults living at any
one moment of time, a majority will be dead in about nineteen years.
At the end of that period then, a new majority is come into place; or,
in other words, a new generation. Each generation is as independent

of the one preceding, as that was of all which had gone before. It has then, like them, a right to choose for itself the form of government it believes most promotive of its own happiness; consequently, to accommodate to the circumstances in which it finds itself, that received from its predecessors; and it is for the peace and good of mankind, that a solemn opportunity of doing this every nineteen or twenty years, should be provided by the Constitution; so that it may be handed on, with periodical repairs, from generation to generation, to the end of time, if anything human can so long endure. It is now forty years since the constitution of Virginia was formed. The same tables inform us, that, within that period, two-thirds of the adults then living are now dead. Have then the remaining third, even if they had the wish, the right to hold in obedience to their will, and to laws heretofore made by them, the other two-thirds, who, with themselves, compose the present mass of adults? If they have not, who has? The dead? But the dead have no rights. They are nothing; and nothing cannot own something. Where there is no substance, there can be no accident. This corporeal globe, and everything upon it, belong to its present corporeal inhabitants, during their generation. They alone have a right to direct what is the concern of themselves alone, and to declare the law of that direction; and this declaration can only be made by their majority. That majority, then, has a right to depute representatives to a convention, and to make the Constitution what they think will be the best for themselves. But how collect their voice? This is the real difficulty. If invited by private authority, or county or district meetings, these divisions are so large that few will attend; and their voice will be imperfectly, or falsely, pronounced. Here, then, would be one of the advantages of the ward divisions I have proposed. The mayor of every ward, on a question like the present, would call his ward together, take the simple yea or nay of its members, convey these to the county court, who would hand on those of all its wards to be the proper general authority; and the voice of the whole people would be thus fairly, fully, and peaceably expressed, discussed, and decided by the common reason of the society. If this avenue be shut to the call of sufferance, it will make itself heard through that of force, and we shall go on, as other nations are doing, in the endless circle of oppression, rebellion, reformation; and oppression, rebellion, reformation, again; and so on forever. . . . .

TO JOHN ADAMS

Monticello, August 1, 1816

. . . . We shall have our follies without doubt. Some one or more of them will always be afloat. But ours will be the follies of enthusiasm, not of bigotry, not of Jesuitism. Bigotry is the disease of ignorance, of morbid minds; enthusiasm of the free and buoyant. Education and free discussion are the antidotes of both. We are destined to be a barrier against the returns of ignorance and barbarism. Old Europe will have to lean on our shoulders, and to hobble along by our side, under the monkish trammels of priests and kings, as she can. What a colossus shall we be when the southern continent comes up to our mark! What a stand will it secure as a ralliance for the reason and freedom of the globe! I like the dreams of the future better than the history of the past,—so good night! I will dream on, always fancying that Mrs. Adams and yourself are by my side marking the progress and the obliquities of ages and countries.

TO MRS. ABIGAIL ADAMS[1]

Monticello, January 11, 1817

I owe you, dear Madam, a thousand thanks for the letters communicated in your favor of December 15th, and now returned. They give me more information than I possessed before, of the family of Mr. Tracy. But what is infinitely interesting, is the scene of the exchange of Louis XVIII. for Bonaparte. What lessons of wisdom Mr. Adams must have read in that short space of time! More than fall to the lot of others in the course of a long life. Man, and the man of Paris, under those circumstances, must have been a subject of profound speculation! It would be a singular addition to that spectacle, to see the same beast in the cage of St. Helena, like a lion in the tower. That is probably the closing verse of the chapter of his crimes. But not so with Louis. He has other vicissitudes to go through.

[1]Abigail Adams was the wife of John Adams.

I communicated the letters, according to your permission, to my grand-daughter, Ellen Randolph, who read them with pleasure and edification. She is justly sensible of, and flattered by your kind notice of her; and additionally so, by the favorable recollections of our northern visiting friends. If Monticello has anything which has merited their remembrance, it gives it a value the more in our estimation; and could I, in the spirit of your wish, count backwards a score of years, it would not be long before Ellen and myself would pay our homage personally to Quincy. But those twenty years! Alas! where are they? With those beyond the flood. Our next meeting must then be in the country to which they have flown,—a country for us not now very distant. For this journey we shall need neither gold nor silver in our purse, nor scrip, nor coats, nor staves. Nor is the provision for it more easy than the preparation has been kind. Nothing proves more than this that the Being who presides over the world is essentially benevolent. Stealing from us, one by one, the faculties of enjoyment, searing our sensibilities, leading us, like the horse in his mill, round and round the same beaten circle,

> —To see what we have seen,
> To taste the tasted, and at each return
> Less tasteful; o'er our palates to decant
> Another vintage—

Until satiated and fatigued with this leaden iteration, we ask our own *congé.* I heard once a very old friend, who had troubled himself with neither poets nor philosophers, say the same thing in plain prose, that he was tired of pulling off his shoes and stockings at night, and putting them on again in the morning. The wish to stay here is thus gradually extinguished; but not so easily that of returning once, in awhile, to see how things have gone on. Perhaps, however, one of the elements of future felicity is to be a constant and unimpassioned view of what is passing here. If so, this may well supply the wish of occasional visits. Mercier has given us a vision of the year 2440; but prophecy is one thing, and history another. On the whole, however, perhaps it is wise and well to be contented with the good things which the master of the feast places before us, and to be thankful for what we have, rather than thoughtful about what we have not. You and I, dear Madam, have already had more than an ordinary portion of life, and more, too, of health than the general measure. On this score I owe boundless thankfulness. Your health was, some time ago, not so good as it has been; and I perceive in the letters communicated some complaints still. I hope it is restored; and that life and health may be continued to you as many years as yourself shall wish, is the sincere prayer of your affectionate and respectful friend.

TO CHARLES THOMSON

Monticello, Janry. 29, 1817[1]

.... It is a singular anxiety which some people have that we should all think alike. Would the world be more beautiful were all our faces alike? were our tempers, our talents, our tastes, our forms, our wishes, aversions and pursuits cast exactly in the same mould? If no varieties existed in the animal, vegetable or mineral creation, but all move strictly uniform, catholic & orthodox, what a world of physical and moral monotony it would be! These are the absurdities into which those run who usurp the throne of God and dictate to Him what He should have done. May they with all their metaphysical riddles appear before that tribunal with as clean hands and hearts as you and I shall. There, suspended in the scales of eternal justice, faith and works will show their worth by their weight. God bless you and preserve you long in life & health.

TO JOSEPH DELAPLAINE[2]

Monticello, April 12, 1817

DEAR SIR,—My repugnance is so invincible to be saying anything of my own history as if worthy to occupy the public attention that I

---

[1][Ford.]

[2]Jefferson and Joseph Delaplaine, contemporary historian, occasionally corresponded concerning matters of historical interest.

have suffered your letter of March 17, but not received till March 28, to lie thus long without resolution enough to take it up. I indulged myself at some length on a former occasion because it was to repel a calumny still sometimes repeated after the death of its numerous brethren, by which a party at one time thought they could vote me down, deeming even science itself as well as my affection for it a fit object of ridicule and a disqualification for the affairs of government. I still think that many of the objects of our inquiry are too minute for public notice. The number of names and ages of my children, grand-children, great-grandchildren, etc., would produce fatigue and disgust to your readers of which I would be an unwilling instrument, it will certainly be enough to say that from one daughter living and another deceased, I have numerous family of grandchildren and an increasing one of great-grandchildren.

I was married on New Year's day of 1772, and Mrs. J. died in the autumn of 1782. I was educated at William and Mary College, in Williamsburg. I read Greek, Latin, French, Italian, Spanish and English of course, with something of its radics, the Anglo-Saxon. I became a member of the legislature of Virginia in 1769 at the accession of Lord Botetourt to our government. I could not readily make a statement of the literary societies of which I am a member, they are many and would be long to enumerate and would savor too much of vanity and pedantry. Would it not be better to say merely that I am a member of many literary societies in Europe and America.

Your statements of the corrections of the Declaration of Independence by Dr. Franklin and Mr. Adams are neither of them at all exact. I should think it better to say generally that the rough draft was communicated to those two gentleman, who each of them made two or three short and verbal alterations only, but even this is laying more stress on mere composition than it merits, for that alone was mine. The sentiments were of all America. . . .

TO BARON ALEXANDER VON HUMBOLDT[1]

Monticello, June 13, 1817

. . . . The physical information you have given us of a country [Spain] hitherto so shamefully unknown, has come exactly in time to guide our understandings in the great political revolution now bringing it into prominence on the stage of the world. The issue of its struggles, as they respect Spain, is no longer matter of doubt. As it respects their own liberty, peace and happiness, we cannot be quite so certain. Whether the blinds of bigotry, the shackles of the priesthood, and the fascinating glare of rank and wealth, give fair play to the common sense of the mass of their people, so far as to qualify them for self-government, is what we do not know. Perhaps our wishes may be stronger than our hopes. The first principle of republicanism is, that the *lex majoris partis*[2] is the fundamental law of every society of individuals of equal rights; to consider the will of the society enounced by the majority of a single vote, as sacred as if unanimous, is the first of all lessons in importance, yet the last which is thoroughly learnt. This law once disregarded, no other remains but that of force, which ends necessarily in military despotism. This has been the history of the French Revolution, and I wish the understanding of our Southern brethren may be sufficiently enlarged and firm to see that their fate depends on its sacred observance. . . . .

TO MONSIEUR BARBÉ DE MARBOIS[3]

Monticello, June 14, 1817

. . . . When I left France at the close of '89, your revolution was, as I thought, under the direction of able and honest men. But the mad-

[1]Jefferson frequently corresponded with Friedrich Heinrich Alexander (Baron von) Humboldt, the famous German naturalist and traveler.

[2]Law of the majority.

[3]M. Barbé de Marbois had been Secretary of the French Legation in Philadelphia. His inquiries had prompted Jefferson to write the Notes on *Virginia*.

ness of some of their successors, the vices of others, the malicious intrigues of an envious and corrupting neighbor, the tracasserie of the Directory, the usurpations, the havoc, and devastations of your Attila, and the equal usurpations, depredations and oppressions of your hypocritical deliverers, will form a mournful period in the history of man, a period of which the last chapter will not be seen in your day or mine, and one which I still fear is to be written in characters of blood. Had Bonaparte reflected that such is the moral construction of the world, that no national crime passes unpunished in the long run, he would not now be in the cage of St. Helena; and were your present oppressors to reflect on the same truth, they would spare to their own countries the penalties on their present wrongs which will be inflicted on them on future times. The seeds of hatred and revenge which they are now sowing with a large hand, will not fail to produce their fruits in time. Like their brother robbers on the highway, they suppose the escape of the moment a final escape, and deem infamy and future risk countervailed by present gain. Our lot has been happier. When you witnessed our first struggles in the War of Independence, you little calculated, more than we did, on the rapid growth and prosperity of this country; on the practical demonstration it was about to exhibit, of the happy truth that man is capable of self-government, and only rendered otherwise by the moral degradation designedly superinduced on him by the wicked acts of his tyrants.

I have much confidence that we shall proceed successfully for ages to come, and that, contrary to the principle of Montesquieu, it will be seen that the larger the extent of country, the more firm its republican structure, if founded, not on conquest, but in principles of compact and equality. My hope of its duration is built much on the enlargement of the resources of life going hand in hand with the enlargement of territory, and the belief that men are disposed to live honestly, if the means of doing so are open to them. With the consolation of this belief in the future result of our labors, I have that of other prophets who foretell distant events, that I shall not live to see it falsified. My theory has always been, that if we are to dream, the flatteries of hope are as cheap, and pleasanter than the gloom of despair. I wish to yourself a long life of honors, health and happiness.

TO GEORGE TICKNOR[1]

Poplar Forest near Lynchburg, Nov. 25, 1817

. . . . I had before heard of the military ingredients which Bonaparte had infused into all the schools of France, but have never so well understood them as from your letter. The penance he is now doing for all his atrocities must be soothing to every virtuous heart. It proves that we have a god in heaven. That he is just, and not careless of what passes in this world. And we cannot but wish to this inhuman wretch, a long, long life, that time as well as intensity may fill up his sufferings to the measure of his enormities. But indeed what sufferings can atone for his crimes against the liberties & happiness of the human race; for the miseries he has already inflicted on his own generation, & on those yet to come, on whom he has rivetted the chains of despotism! . . . .

TO JOHN TRUMBULL[2]

Monticello, Jan. 8, 1818

DEAR SIR,—I can have no hesitation in placing my name on the roll of subscribers to the print of your Declaration of Independence, & I desire to do it for two copies. the advance of price from 18.66 to 20. D. cannot be objected to by anyone because of the disproportionate decrease in the value of the money. what discourages our citizens in the purchase of prints is the tawdry taste prevailing for gew-gaw gilt frames. these flaring things injure greatly the effect of the print. a narrow fillet of gilt on the inner & outer edge, merely to relieve the black of the main breadth, permits the eye to rest in composure on the field of the print, undisturbed by the glare of a massive, refulgent border.

---

[1]George Ticknor, later to become a distinguished author and educator, was at this time studying in Europe. He had visited Jefferson at Monticello prior to going abroad, and the older man's paternal interest in Ticknor was exceeded only by his respect and admiration for Jefferson. [Ford.]

[2]John Trumbull, the painter of the American Revolution, is still the most famous interpreter of this period. [MS. Franklin Collection, Yale University.]

frames of the prevailing style cost as much, & often more than the print itself. while it is right to indulge the luxury of the rich with copies of exquisite & perfect execution would it not be worth your while to have one of mere outline engraved which could be sold for a dollar apiece? were such to be had, scarcely a hovel in the U. S. would be without one, and 50. of them would be sold for one of the superior. however you understand the public taste better than I do, and will do what is for your own best interest, which I sincerely wish to see prompted, because you possess my sincere and affectionate esteem. . . . .

TO COUNT DUGNANI[1]
(PAPAL NUNCIO)

Monticello, February 14, 1818

. . . . During the terrible revolutions of Europe I felt great anxiety for you, and have never yet learnt with certainty how far they affected you. Your letter to the Archbishop being from Rome and so late as September makes me hope that all is well, and thanks be to God the tiger who revelled so long in the blood and spoils of Europe is at length, like another Prometheus, chained to his rock, where the vulture of remorse for his crimes will be preying on his vitals and in like manner without consuming them. Having been, like him, intrusted with the happiness of my country, I feel the blessing of resembling him in no other point. I have not caused the death of five or ten millions of human beings, the devastation of other countries, the depopulation of my own, the exhaustion of all its resources, the destruction of its liberties, nor its foreign subjugation. All this he has done to render more illustrious the atrocities perpetrated for illustrating himself and his family with plundered diadems and sceptres. On the contrary, I have the consolation to reflect that during the period of my administration not a drop of the blood of a single fellow citizen was shed by the sword of war or of the law, and that after cherishing for eight years their peace and prosperity I laid down their trust of my own accord and in the midst of their bless-

[1]Count Antonio Dugnani was the foreign ambassador sent by Pope Pius VI to the Court of France in 1789.

ings and importunities to continue in it. But, beginning to be sensible of the effect of age, I feared that its infirmities might injure their interests and believed the example would be salutary against inveteration in office, and I now enjoy in retirement the comfort of their good will and of a conscience calm and without reproach. . . . .

TO DR. BENJAMIN WATERHOUSE

Monticello, March 3, 1818

DEAR SIR,—I have just received your favor of February 20th, in which you observe that Mr. Wirt, on page 47 of his Life of Patrick Henry, quotes me as saying that "Mr. Henry certainly gave the first impulse to the ball of revolution." I well recollect to have used some such expression in a letter to him, and am tolerably certain that our own State being the subject under contemplation, I must have used it with respect to that only. Whether he has given it a more general aspect I cannot say, as the passage is not in the page you quote, nor, after thumbing over much of the book, have I been able to find it. In page 417 there is something like it, but not the exact expression, and even there it may be doubted whether Mr. Wirt had his eye on Virginia alone, or on all the colonies. But the question, who commenced the Revolution? is as difficult as that of the first inventors of a thousand good things. For example, who first discovered the principle of gravity? Not Newton; for Galileo, who died the year that Newton was born, had measured its force in the descent of gravid bodies. Who invented the Lavoiserian chemistry? The English say Dr. Black, by the preparatory discovery of latent heat. Who invented the steamboat? Was it Gerbert, the Marquis of Worcester, Newcomen, Savary, Papin, Fitch, Fulton? The fact is, that one new idea leads to another, that to a third, and so on through a course of time until some one, with whom no one of these ideas was original, combines all together, and produces what is justly called a new invention. I suppose it would be as difficult to trace our Revolution to its first embryo. We do not know how long it was hatching in the British Cabinet before they ventured to make the first of the experiments which were to develop it in the end and to produce complete parliamentary supremacy. Those you mention in Massachusetts as preceding the stamp act, might be the first visible symptoms of that design. The proposition of that act in 1764, was the first here. Your opposition, therefore, preceded ours, as occasion was sooner given there than here, and the truth, I suppose, is, that the opposition in every colony began whenever the encroachment was presented to it. This question of priority is as the inquiry would be who first, of the three hundred Spartans, offered his name to Leonidas? I shall be happy to see justice done to the merits of all, by the unexceptionable umpirage of date and facts, and especially from the pen which is proposed to be employed in it.

I rejoice, indeed, to learn from you that Mr. Adams retains the strength of his memory, his faculties, his cheerfulness, and even his epistolary industry. This last is gone from me. The aversion has been growing on me for a considerable time, and now, near the close of seventy-five, is become almost insuperable. I am much debilitated in body, and my memory sensibly on the wane. Still, however, I enjoy good health and spirits, and am as industrious a reader as when a student at college Not of newspapers. These I have discarded. I relinquish, as I ought to do, all intermeddling with public affairs, committing myself cheerfully to the watch and care of those for whom, in my turn, I have watched and cared. When I contemplate the immense advances in science and discoveries in the arts which have been made within the period of my life, I look forward with confidence to equal advances by the present generation, and have no doubt they will consequently be as much wiser than we have been as we than our fathers were, and they than the burners of witches. Even the metaphysical contest, which you so pleasantly described to me in a former letter, will probably end in improvement, by clearing the mind of Platonic mysticism and unintelligible jargon. Although age is taking from me the power of communicating by letter with my friends as industriously as heretofore, I shall still claim with them the same place they will ever hold in my affections, and on this ground I, with sincerity and pleasure, assure you of my great esteem and respect.

TO NATHANIEL BURWELL, ESQ.[1]

Monticello, March 14, 1818

DEAR SIR,—Your letter of February 17th found me suffering under an attack of rheumatism, which has but now left me at sufficient ease to attend to the letters I have received. A plan of female education has never been a subject of systematic contemplation with me. It has occupied my attention so far only as the education of my own daughters occasionally required. Considering that they would be placed in a country situation, where little aid could be obtained from abroad, I thought it essential to give them a solid education, which might enable them, when become mothers, to educate their own daughters, and even to direct the course for sons, should their fathers be lost, or incapable, or inattentive. My surviving daughter accordingly, the mother of many daughters as well as sons, has made their education the object of her life, and being a better judge of the practical part than myself, it is with her aid and that of one of her élèves, that I shall subjoin a catalogue of the books for such a course of reading as we have practiced.

A great obstacle to good education is the inordinate passion prevalent for novels, and the time lost in that reading which should be instructively employed. When this poison infects the mind, it destroys its tone and revolts it against wholesome reading. Reason and fact, plain and unadorned, are rejected. Nothing can engage attention unless dressed in all the figments of fancy, and nothing so bedecked comes amiss. The result is a bloated imagination, sickly judgment, and disgust towards all the real businesses of life. This mass of trash, however, is not without some distinction; some few modelling their narratives, although fictitious, on the incidents of real life, have been able to make them interesting and useful vehicles of a sound morality. Such, I think, are Marmontel's new moral tales, but not his old ones, which are really immoral. Such are the writings of Miss Edgeworth, and some of those of Madame Genlis. For a like reason, too, much poetry should not be indulged. Some is useful for forming style

---

[1]Nathaniel Burwell was a member of a distinguished Virginia family.

and taste. Pope, Dryden, Thompson, Shakespeare, and of the French, Molière, Racine, the Corneilles, may be read with pleasure and improvement.

The French language, become that of the general intercourse of nations, and from their extraordinary advances, now the depository of all science, is an indispensable part of education for both sexes. In the subjoined catalogue, therefore, I have placed the books of both languages indifferently, according as the one or the other offers what is best.

The ornaments too, and the amusements of life, are entitled to their portion of attention. These, for a female, are dancing, drawing, and music. The first is a healthy exercise, elegant and very attractive for young people. Every affectionate parent would be pleased to see his daughter qualified to participate with her companions, and without awkwardness at least, in the circles of festivity, of which she occasionally becomes a part. It is a necessary accomplishment, therefore, although of short use; for the French rule is wise, that no lady dances after marriage. This is founded in solid physical reasons, gestation and nursing leaving little time to a married lady when this exercise can be either safe or innocent. Drawing is thought less of in this country than in Europe. It is an innocent and engaging amusement, often useful, and a qualification not to be neglected in one who is to become a mother and an instructor. Music is invaluable where a person has an ear. Where they have not, it should not be attempted. It furnishes a delightful recreation for the hours of respite from the cares of the day, and lasts us through life. The taste of this country, too, calls for this accomplishment more strongly than for either of the others.

I need say nothing of household economy, in which the mothers of our country are generally skilled, and generally careful to instruct their daughters. We all know its value, and that diligence and dexterity in all its processes are inestimable treasures. The order and economy of a house are as honorable to the mistress as those of the farm to the master, and if either be neglected, ruin follows, and children destitute of the means of living.

This, Sir, is offered as a summary sketch on a subject on which I have not thought much. It probably contains nothing but what has

already occurred to yourself, and claims your acceptance on no other
ground than as a testimony of my respect for your wishes, and of my
great esteem and respect.

TO JOHN ADAMS

Monticello, November 13, 1818

The public papers, my dear friend, announce the fatal event[1] of
which your letter of October the 20th had given me ominous foreboding.
Tried myself in the school of affliction, by the loss of every form
of connection which can rive the human heart, I know well, and feel
what you have lost, what you have suffered, are suffering, and have yet
to endure. The same trials have taught me that for ills so immeasurable,
time and silence are the only medicine. I will not, therefore, by
useless condolences, open afresh the sluices of your grief, nor, although
mingling sincerely my tears with yours, will I say a word more where
words are vain, but that it is of some comfort to us both, that the term
is not very distant, at which we are to deposit in the same cerement,
our sorrows and suffering bodies, and to ascend in essence to an ecstatic
meeting with the friends we have loved and lost, and whom we shall
still love and never lose again. God bless you and support you under
your heavy affliction.

TO DOCTOR VINE UTLEY

Monticello, March 21, 1819

SIR,—Your letter of February the 18th came to hand on the 1st
instant; and the request of the history of my physical habits would have
puzzled me not a little, had it not been for the model with which you
accompanied it, of Doctor Rush's answer to a similar inquiry. I live so
much like other people, that I might refer to ordinary life as the history
of my own. Like my friend the Doctor, I have lived temperately,

[1]The death of Adams's wife, Abigail.

eating little animal food, and that not as an aliment, so much as a condiment for the vegetables, which constitute my principal diet. I double however, the Doctor's glass and a half of wine. and even treble it with a friend; but halve its effects by drinking the weak wines only. The ardent wines I cannot drink, nor do I use ardent spirits in any form. Malt liquors and cider are my table drinks, and my breakfast, like that also of my friend, is of tea and coffee. I have been blest with organs of digestion which accept and concoct, without ever murmuring, whatever the palate chooses to consign to them, and I have not yet lost a tooth by age. I was a hard student until I entered on the business of life, the duties of which leave no idle time to those disposed to fulfil them; and now, retired, and at the age of seventy-six, I am again a hard student. Indeed, my fondness for reading and study revolts me from the drudgery of letter-writing. And a stiff wrist, the consequence of an early dislocation, makes writing both slow and painful. I am not so regular in my sleep as the Doctor says he was, devoting to it from five to eight hours, according as my company or the book I am reading interests me; and I never go to bed without an hour, or half hour's previous reading of something moral, whereon to ruminate in the intervals of sleep. But whether I retire to bed early or late, I rise with the sun. I use spectacles at night, but not necessarily in the day, unless in reading small print. My hearing is distinct in particular conversation, but confused when several voices cross each other, which unfits me for the society of the table. I have been more fortunate than my friend in the article of health. So free from catarrhs that I have not had one, (in the breast, I mean) on an average of eight or ten years through life. I ascribe this exemption partly to the habit of bathing my feet in cold water every morning, for sixty years past. A fever of more than twenty-four hours I have not had above two or three times in my life. A periodical headache has afflicted me occasionally, once, perhaps, in six or eight years, for two or three weeks at a time, which seems now to have left me; and except on a late occasion of indisposition, I enjoy good health; too feeble, indeed, to walk much, but riding without fatigue six or eight miles a day, and sometimes thirty or forty. I may end these egotisms, therefore, as I began, by saying that my life has been so much like that of other people, that I might say with Horace, to every one "*nomine mutato, narratur fabula de te.*"[1] I must not end, however, without due thanks for the kind sentiments of regard you are so good as to express towards myself; and with my acknowledgments for these, be pleased to accept the assurances of my respect and esteem.

TO MR. LAPORTE[2]

Monticello, June 4, 1819

SIR,—In answer to your request to be informed of the particular style of dieting the students which would be approved by the visitors of the University, I can only say that, the University not being yet in action, nor the Hotels for boarding houses in readiness which will be at their disposal, no style of dieting has been agreed on: but if I may form a judgment from the conversations we have had on the subject I think something like the following course will meet their approbation.

for breakfast. wheat or cornbread, at the choice of each particular, with butter, and milk, or Coffee-au-lait, at the choice of each. no meat.

for dinner. a soup, a dish of salt meat, a dish of fresh meat, & as great a variety of vegetables well cooked as you please.

for supper, corn or wheat bread at their choice, & milk, or Coffee-au lait, also at their choice, but no meat.

their drink at all times water, a young stomach needing no stimulating drinks, and the habit of using them being dangerous.

and I should recommend as late a dinner as the rules of their school will permit.

no game of chance to be permitted in the house.

[1]"With a change of name, the tale can be told of you."

[2]Mr. Laporte was in charge of one of the Hotels (students' rooming and boarding house) for the proposed University of Virginia. [MS., University of Virginia.]

TO WILLIAM SHORT

Monticello, October 31, 1819

DEAR SIR,—Your favor of the 21st is received. My late illness, in which you are so kind as to feel an interest, was produced by a spasmodic stricture of the ileum, which came upon me on the 7th inst. The crisis was short, passed over favorably on the fourth day, and I should soon have been well but that a dose of calomel and jalap, in which were only eight or nine grains of the former, brought on a salivation. Of this, however, nothing now remains but a little soreness of the mouth. I have been able to get on horseback for three or four days past.

As you say of yourself, I too am an Epicurian. I consider the genuine (not the imputed) doctrines of Epicurus as containing everything rational in moral philosophy which Greece and Rome have left us. Epictetus indeed, has given us what was good of the Stoics; all beyond, of their dogmas, being hypocrisy and grimace. Their great crime was in their calumnies of Epicurus and misrepresentations of his doctrines; in which we lament to see the candid character of Cicero engaging as an accomplice. Diffuse, vapid, rhetorical, but enchanting. His prototype Plato, eloquent as himself, dealing out mysticisms incomprehensible to the human mind, has been deified by certain sects usurping the name of Christians; because, in his foggy conceptions, they found a basis of impenetrable darkness whereon to rear fabrications as delirious, of their own invention. These they fathered blasphemously on Him whom they claimed as their Founder, but who would disclaim them with the indignation which their caricatures of His religion so justly excite. Of Socrates we have nothing genuine but in the Memorabilia of Xenophon; for Plato makes him one of his Collocutors merely to cover his own whimsies under the mantle of his name; a liberty of which we are told Socrates himself complained. Seneca is indeed a fine moralist, disfiguring his work at times with some Stoicisms, and affecting too much of antithesis and point, yet giving us on the whole a great deal of sound and practical morality. But the greatest of all the reformers of the depraved religion of His own country, was Jesus of Nazareth. Abstracting what is really His from the rubbish in which it is buried, easily distinguished by its lustre from the dross of His biographers, and as separable from that as the diamond from the dunghill, we have the outlines of a system of the most sublime morality which has ever fallen from the lips of man; outlines which it is lamentable He did not live to fill up. Epictetus and Epicurus give laws for governing ourselves, Jesus a supplement of the duties and charities we owe to others. The establishment of the innocent and genuine character of this benevolent Moralist, and the rescuing it from the imputation of imposture, which has resulted from artificial systems,[1] invented by ultra-Christian sects, unauthorized by a single word ever uttered by Him, is a most desirable object, and one to which Priestley has successfully devoted his labors and learning. It would in time, it is to be hoped, effect a quiet euthanasia of the heresies of bigotry and fanaticism which have so long triumphed over human reason, and so generally and deeply afflicted mankind; but this work is to be begun by winnowing the grain from the chaff of the historians of His life. I have sometimes thought of translating Epictetus (for he has never been tolerably translated into English) by adding the genuine doctrines of Epicurus from the Syntagma of Gassendi, and an abstract from the Evangelists of whatever has the stamp of the eloquence and fine imagination of Jesus. The last I attempted too hastily some twelve or fifteen years ago. It was the work of two or three nights only, at Washington, after getting through the evening task of reading the letters and papers of the day. But with one foot in the grave, these are now idle projects for me. My business is to beguile the wearisomeness of declining life, as I endeavor to do, by the delights of classical reading and of mathematical truths, and by the consolations of a sound philosophy, equally indifferent to hope and fear.

I take the liberty of observing that you are not a true disciple of our master Epicurus, in indulging the indolence to which you say you are yielding. One of his canons, you know, was that "that indulgence which presents a greater pleasure, or produces a greater pain, is to be avoided." Your love of repose will lead, in its progress, to a suspension of healthy exercise, a relaxation of mind, an indifference to everything around you, and finally to a debility of body, and hebetude of

---

[1]*E.g.* The immaculate conception of Jesus, His deification, the creation of the world by Him, His miraculous powers, His resurrection and visible ascension, His corporeal presence in the Eucharist, the Trinity, original sin, atonement, regeneration, election, orders of Hierarchy, etc. [Jefferson's note.]

mind, the farthest of all things from the happiness which the well-regulated indulgences of Epicurus ensure; fortitude, you know, is one of his four cardinal virtues. That teaches us to meet and surmount difficulties; not to fly from them, like cowards; and to fly, too, in vain, for they will meet and arrest us at every turn of our road. Weigh this matter well; brace yourself up; take a seat with Correa, and come and see the finest portion of your country, which, if you have not forgotten, you still do not know, because it is no longer the same as when you knew it. It will add much to the happiness of my recovery to be able to receive Correa and yourself, and prove the estimation in which I hold you both. Come, too, and see our incipient University, which has advanced with great activity this year. By the end of the next, we shall have elegant accommodations for seven professors, and the year following the professors themselves. No secondary character will be received among them. Either the ablest which America or Europe can furnish, or none at all. They will give us the selected society of a great city separated from the dissipations and levities of its ephemeral insects.

I am glad the bust of Condorcet has been saved and so well placed. His genius should be before us; while the lamentable, but singular act of ingratitude which tarnished his latter days, may be thrown behind us.

I will place under this a syllabus of the doctrines of Epicurus, somewhat in the lapidary style, which I wrote some twenty years ago; a like one of the philosophy of Jesus, of nearly the same age, is too long to be copied. Vale, *et tibi persuade carissimum te esse mihi.*

Syllabus of the doctrines of Epicurus

Physical.—The Universe eternal.

Its parts, great and small, interchangeable.

Matter and Void alone.

Motion inherent in matter which is weighty and declining.

Eternal circulation of the elements of bodies.

Gods, an order of beings next superior to man, enjoying in their sphere, their own felicities; but not meddling with the concerns of the scale of beings below them.

Moral.—Happiness the aim of life.

Virtue the foundation of happiness.

Utility the test of virtue.

Pleasure active and In-do-lent.

In-do-lence is the absence of pain, the true felicity.

Active, consists in agreeable motion; it is not happiness, but the means to produce it.

Thus the absence of hunger is an article of felicity; eating the means to obtain it.

The *summum bonum* is to be not pained in body, nor troubled in mind.

i.e. In-do-lence of body, tranquillity of mind.

To procure tranquillity of mind we must avoid desire and fear, the two principal diseases of the mind.

Man is a free agent.

Virtue consists in 1. Prudence. 2. Temperance. 3. Fortitude. 4. Justice.

To which are opposed, 1. Folly. 2. Desire. 3. Fear. 4. Deceit.

TO DR. THOMAS COOPER[1]

Monticello, March 13, 1820

. . . . I must explain to you the state of religious parties with us. about ⅓ of our state is Baptist, ⅓ Methodist, and of the remaining third two parts may be Presbyterian and one part Anglican. The Baptists are sound republicans and zealous supporters of their government. The Methodists are republican mostly, satisfied with their governmt. medling with nothing but the concerns of their own calling and opposing nothing. these two sects are entirely friendly to our university. the anglicans are the same. the Presbyterian *clergy* alone (not their followers) remain bitterly federal and malcontent with their government. they are violent, ambitious of power, and intolerant in politics as in religion and want nothing but license from the laws to kindle again the fires of their leader John Knox, and to give us a 2d blast from his trumpet. Having a little more monkish learning than the clergy of the other sects, they are jealous of the general diffusion of science, and therefore hostile to our Seminary lest it should qualify their antagonists

[1][MS., University of Virginia.]

of the other sects to meet them in equal combat. Not daring to attack the institution with the avowal of their real motives, they peck at you, at me, and every feather they can spy out. but in this they have no weight, even with their own followers. excepting a few old men among them who may still be federal & Anglomen, their main body are good citizens, friends to their government, anxious for reputation, and therefore friendly to the University. . . . .

TO JOHN HOLMES[1]

Monticello, April 22, 1820

I thank you, dear Sir, for the copy you have been so kind as to send me of the letter to your constituents on the Missouri question. It is a perfect justification to them. I had for a long time ceased to read newspapers, or pay any attention to public affairs, confident they were in good hands, and content to be a passenger in our bark to the shore from which I am not distant. But this momentous question, like a fire-bell in the night, awakened and filled me with terror. I considered it at once as the knell of the Union. It is hushed, indeed, for the moment. But this is a reprieve only, not a final sentence. A geographical line, coinciding with a marked principle, moral and political, once conceived and held up to the angry passions of men, will never be obliterated; and every new irritation will mark it deeper and deeper. I can say, with conscious truth, that there is not a man on earth who would sacrifice more than I would to relieve us from this heavy reproach, in any *practicable* way. The cession of that kind of property, for so it is misnamed, is a bagatelle which would not cost me a second thought, if, in that way, a general emancipation and *expatriation* could be effected; and, gradually, and with due sacrifices, I think it might be. But as it is, we have the wolf by the ears, and we can neither hold him, nor safely let him go. Justice is in one scale, and self preservation in the other. Of one thing I am certain, that as the passage of slaves from one State to

[1]A member of the Massachusetts Senate, Holmes led the protest against the Hartford Convention and broke with the Federalists. The denunciations of his former party form a series of brilliant political speeches.

another, would not make a slave of a single human being who would not be so without it, so their diffusion over a greater surface would make them individually happier, and proportionally facilitate the accomplishment of their emancipation, by dividing the burden on a greater number of coadjutors. An abstinence too, from this act of power, would remove the jealousy excited by the undertaking of Congress to regulate the condition of the different descriptions of men composing a State. This certainly is the exclusive right of every State, which nothing in the Constitution has taken from them and given to the General Government. Could Congress, for example, say, that the non-freemen of Connecticut shall be freemen, or that they shall not emigrate into any other State?

I regret that I am now to die in the belief, that the useless sacrifice of themselves by the generation of 1776, to acquire self-government and happiness to their country, is to be thrown away by the unwise and unworthy passions of their sons, and that my only consolation is to be, that I live not to weep over it. If they would but dispassionately weigh the blessings they will throw away, against an abstract principle more likely to be effected by union than by scission, they would pause before they would perpetrate this act of suicide on themselves, and of treason against the hopes of the world. To yourself, as the faithful advocate of the Union, I tender the offering of my high esteem and respect.

TO WILLIAM SHORT

Monticello, August 4, 1820

. . . . The day is not distant, when we may formally require a meridian of partition through the ocean which separates the two hemispheres, on the hither side of which no European gun shall ever be heard, nor an American on the other; and when, during the rage of the eternal wars of Europe, the lion and the lamb, within our regions, shall lie down together in peace. The excess of population in Europe, and want of room, render war, in their opinion, necessary to keep down that excess of numbers. Here, room is abundant, population scanty, and peace the necessary means for producing men, to whom the redundant soil is offering the means of life and happiness. The principles of society there and here, then, are radically different, and I hope no American patriot will ever lose sight of the essential policy of interdicting in the seas and territories of both Americas, the ferocious and sanguinary contests of Europe. I wish to see this coalition begun. I am earnest for an agreement with the maritime powers of Europe, assigning them the task of keeping down the piracies of their seas and the cannibalisms of the African coasts, and to us, the suppression of the same enormities within our seas; and for this purpose, I should rejoice to see the fleets of Brazil and the United States riding together as brethren of the same family, and pursuing the same object. And indeed it would be of happy augury to begin at once this concert of action here, on the invitation of either to the other government, while the way might be preparing for withdrawing our cruisers from Europe, and preventing naval collisions there which daily endanger our peace. . . . .

TO JOHN ADAMS

Monticello, August 15, 1820

. . . . But enough of criticism: let me turn to your puzzling letter of May the 12th, on matter, spirit, motion, etc. Its crowd of scepticisms kept me from sleep. I read it, and laid it down; read it, and laid it down, again and again; and to give rest to my mind, I was obliged to recur ultimately to my habitual anodyne, "I feel, therefore I exist." I feel bodies which are not myself: there are other existences then. I call them *matter*. I feel them changing place. This gives me *motion*. Where there is an absence of matter, I call it *void*, or *nothing*, or *immaterial space*. On the basis of sensation, of matter and motion, we may erect the fabric of all the certainties we can have or need. I can conceive *thought* to be an action of a particular organization of matter, formed for that purpose by its Creator, as well as that *attraction* is an action of matter, or *magnetism* of loadstone. When he who denies to the Creator the power of endowing matter with the mode of action called *thinking*, shall show how He could endow the sun with the mode of action called *attraction*, which reins the planets in the track of their orbits, or how an absence of matter can have a will, and by that will put matter into motion, then the Materialist may be lawfully required to explain the process by which matter exercises the faculty of think-ing. When once we quit the basis of sensation, all is in the wind. To talk of *immaterial* existences, is to talk of *nothings*. To say that the human soul, angels, God, are immaterial, is to say, they are *nothings*, or that there is no God, no angels, no soul. I cannot reason otherwise: but I believe I am supported in my creed of materialism by the Lockes, the Tracys and the Stewarts. At what age[1] of the Christian Church this heresy of *immaterialism*, or masked atheism, crept in, I do not exactly know. But a heresy it certainly is. Jesus taught nothing of it. He told us, indeed, that "God is a Spirit," but He has not defined what a spirit is, nor said that it is not *matter*. And the ancient fathers generally, of the three first centuries, held it to be matter, light and thin indeed, an etherial gas; but still matter. . . . .

Rejecting all organs of information, therefore, but my senses, I rid myself of the pyrrhonisms with which an indulgence in speculations hyperphysical and antiphysical, so uselessly occupy and disquiet the mind. A single sense may indeed be sometimes deceived, but rarely; and never all our senses together, with their faculty of reasoning. They evidence realities, and there are enough of these for all the purposes of life, without plunging into the fathomless abyss of dreams and phantasms. I am satisfied, and sufficiently occupied with the things which are, without tormenting or troubling myself about those which may indeed be, but of which I have no evidence. I am sure that I really know many, many things, and none more surely than that I love you with all my heart, and pray for the continuance of your life until you shall be tired of it yourself.

TO WILLIAM ROSCOE[2]

Monticello, December 27, 1820

. . . . Your Liverpool institution will also aid us in the organization of our new University, an establishment now in progress in this State, and to which my remaining days and faculties will be devoted. When

---

[1]That of Athanasius and the Council of Nicæa, anno 324. [Jefferson's note.]

[2]Roscoe was an English historian, pamphleteer, verse writer, and liberal.

ready for its professors, we shall apply for them chiefly to your island. Were we content to remain stationary in science, we should take them from among ourselves; but, desirous of advancing, we must seek them in countries already in advance; and identity of language points to our best resource. To furnish inducements, we provide for the professors separate buildings, in which themselves and their families may be handsomely and comfortably lodged, and to liberal salaries will be added lucrative perquisites. This institution will be based on the illimitable freedom of the human mind. For here we are not afraid to follow truth wherever it may lead, nor to tolerate any error so long as reason is left free to combat it. . . . .

TO JOHN ADAMS

Monticello, September 12, 1821

. . . . Yet I will not believe our labors are lost. I shall not die without a hope that light and liberty are on steady advance. We have seen, indeed, once within the records of history, a complete eclipse of the human mind continuing for centuries. And this, too, by swarms of the same northern barbarians, conquering and taking possession of the countries and governments of the civilized world. Should this be again attempted, should the same northern hordes, allured again by the corn, wine, and oil of the south, be able again to settle their swarms in the countries of their growth, the art of printing alone, and the vast dissemination of books, will maintain the mind where it is, and raise the conquering ruffians to the level of the conquered, instead of degrading these to that of their conquerors. And even should the cloud of barbarism and despotism again obscure the science and liberties of Europe, this country remains to preserve and restore light and liberty to them. In short, the flames kindled on the 4th of July, 1776, have spread over too much of the globe to be extinguished by the feeble engines of despotism; on the contrary, they will consume these engines and all who work them. . . . .

TO JAMES SMITH[1]

Monticello, December 8, 1822

SIR,—I have to thank you for your pamphlets on the subject of Unitarianism, and to express my gratification with your efforts for the revival of primitive Christianity in your quarter. No historical fact is better established, than that the doctrine of one God, pure and uncompounded, was that of the early ages of Christianity; and was among the efficacious doctrines which gave it triumph over the polytheism of the ancients, sickened with the absurdities of their own theology. Nor was the unity of the Supreme Being ousted from the Christian creed by the force of reason, but by the sword of civil government, wielded at the will of the fanatic Athanasius. The hocus-pocus phantasm of a God like another Cerberus, with one body and three heads, had its birth and growth in the blood of thousands and thousands of martyrs. And a strong proof of the solidity of the primitive faith, is its restoration, as soon as a nation arises which vindicates to itself the freedom of religious opinion, and its external divorce from the civil authority. The pure and simple unity of the Creator of the universe, is now all but ascendant in the Eastern States; it is dawning in the West, and advancing towards the South; and I confidently expect that the present generation will see Unitarianism become the general religion of the United States. The Eastern presses are giving us many excellent pieces on the subject, and Priestley's learned writings on it are, or should be, in every hand. In fact, the Athanasian paradox that one is three, and three but one, is so incomprehensible to the human mind, that no candid man can say he has any idea of it, and how can he believe what presents no idea? He who thinks he does, only deceives himself. He proves, also, that man, once surrendering his reason, has no remaining guard against absurdities the most monstrous, and like a ship without rudder, is the sport of every wind. With such persons, gullibility which they call faith, takes the helm from the hand of reason, and the mind becomes a wreck.

I write with freedom, because while I claim a right to believe in one

---

[1]James Smith, resident of Ohio, was a theological writer.

God, if so my reason tells me, I yield as freely to others that of believing in three. Both religions, I find, make honest men, and that is the only point society has any right to look to. Although this mutual freedom should produce mutual indulgence, yet I wish not to be brought in question before the public on this or any other subject, and I pray you to consider me as writing under that trust. I take no part in controversies, religious or political. At the age of eighty, tranquillity is the greatest good of life, and the strongest of our desires that of dying in the good will of all mankind. And with the assurance of all my good will to Unitarian and Trinitarian, to Whig and Tory, accept for yourself that of my entire respect.

TO ROBERT WALSH[1]

Monticello, April 5, 1823

DEAR SIR,—Your favor of Mar. 18 has been duly recieved [sic]. I have had several applications, within a few years past, from different persons, to furnish them with materials for writing my life, and have uniformly declined it on the ground of the decay of my memory, the decline of the powers of body & mind, the heaviness of age, and the crippled state of both my hands, which renders writing the most painful labor I can undertake. these causes are becoming every day stronger; and I assure you, dear Sir, that they should not be urged in answer to a request from you but from their unwelcome and absolute reality. I am greatly changed since I had the pleasure of seeing you here; and am going down hill so rapidly as to be sensible of it from month to month. were my biography worth the desire of the public, there is certainly no pen by which I could be more flattered to have it given them than your's. with these uncontroulable [sic] obstacles, I must moreover question an opinion stated in your prospectus. I do not think a biography should be written, or at least not published, during the life of the person the subject of it. it is impossible that the writer's delicacy should permit him to speak as freely of the faults or

[1]Robert Walsh, journalist and writer, was the founder of the first American quarterly, the *American Review of History and Politics*. [MS. University of Virginia.]

errors of a living, as of a dead character. there is still however a better reason. the letters of a person, especially of one whose business has been chiefly transacted by letters, form the only full and genuine journal of his life; and few can let them go out of their own hands while they live. a life written after these hoards become opened to investigation must supercede any previous one. it may be observed too that before you will have got through with the dead, the living will be dying off and furnishing fresh matter. however I do not pretend but to suggest these considerations to you, nor to urge more than my regrets at my own disability. . . . .

TO JOHN ADAMS

Monticello, April 11, 1823

. . . . I can never join Calvin in addressing *his God*. He was indeed an atheist, which I can never be or rather his religion was dæmonism. If ever man worshiped a false God, he did. The Being described in his five points, is not the God whom you and I acknowledge and adore, the Creator and benevolent Governor of the world; but a dæmon of malignant spirit. It would be more pardonable to believe in no God at all, than to blaspheme Him by the atrocious attributes of Calvin. Indeed, I think that every Christian sect gives a great handle to atheism by their general dogma, that, without a revelation, there would not be sufficient proof of the being of a God. Now one-sixth of mankind only are supposed to be Christians; the other five-sixths then, who do not believe in the Jewish and Christian revelation, are without a knowledge of the existence of a God! This gives completely a *gain de cause* to the disciples of Ocellus, Timæus, Spinosa, Diderot and D'Holbach. The argument which they rest on as triumphant and unanswerable is, that in every hypothesis of cosmogony, you must admit an eternal pre-existence of something; and according to the rule of sound philosophy, you are never to employ two principles to solve a difficulty when one will suffice. They say then, that it is more simple to believe at once in the eternal pre-existence of the world, as it is now going on, and may forever go on by the principle of reproduction which we see and witness, than to believe in the eternal pre-existence of an ulterior cause, or Creator of the world, a Being whom we see not and know not, of whose form, substance and mode, or place of existence, or of action, no sense informs us, no power of the mind enables us to delineate or comprehend. On the contrary, I hold, (without appeal to revelation) that when we take a view of the universe, in its parts, general or particular, it is impossible for the human mind not to perceive and feel a conviction of design, consummate skill, and indefinite power in every atom of its composition. The movements of the heavenly bodies, so exactly held in their course by the balance of centrifugal and centripetal forces; the structure of our earth itself, with its distribution of lands, waters and atmosphere; animal and vegetable bodies, examined in all their minutest particles; insects, mere atoms of life, yet as perfectly organized as man or mammoth; the mineral substances, their generation and uses; it is impossible, I say, for the human mind not to believe, that there is in all this, design, cause and effect, up to an ultimate cause, a Fabricator of all things from matter and motion, their Preserver and Regulator while permitted to exist in their present forms, and their regeneration into new and other forms. We see, too, evident proofs of the necessity of a superintending power, to maintain the universe in its course and order. Stars, well known, have disappeared, new ones have come into view; comets, in their incalculable courses, may run foul of suns and planets, and require renovation under other laws; certain races of animals are become extinct; and were there no restoring power, all existences might extinguish successively, one by one, until all should be reduced to a shapeless chaos. So irresistible are these evidences of an intelligent and powerful Agent, that, of the infinite numbers of men who have existed through all time, they have believed, in the proportion of a million at least to unit, in the hypothesis of an eternal pre-existence of a Creator, rather than in that of a self-existent universe. Surely this unanimous sentiment renders this more probable, than that of the few in the other hypothesis. Some early Christians, indeed, have believed in the co-eternal pre-existence of both the Creator and the world, without changing their relation of cause and effect. . . . .

TO GENERAL SAMUEL SMITH[1]

Monticello, May 3, 1823

. . . . A tax on whiskey is to discourage its consumption; a tax on foreign spirits encourages whiskey by removing its rival from competition. The price and present duty throw foreign spirits already out of competition with whiskey, and accordingly they are used but to a salutary extent. You see no persons besotting themselves with imported spirits, wines, liquors, cordials, etc. Whiskey claims to itself alone the exclusive office of sot-making. Foreign spirits, wines, teas, coffee, segars, salt, are articles of as innocent consumption as broadcloths and silks; and ought, like them, to pay but the average *ad velorem* duty of other imported comforts. All of them are ingredients in our happiness, and the government which steps out of the ranks of the ordinary articles of consumption to select and lay under disproportionate burdens a particular one, because it is a comfort, pleasing to the taste, or necessary to health, and will therefore be bought, is, in that particular, a tyranny. . . . .

TO THE PRESIDENT OF THE UNITED STATES (JAMES MONROE)

Monticello, October 24, 1823

DEAR SIR,—The question presented by the letters you have sent me, is the most momentous which has ever been offered to my contemplation since that of Independence. That made us a nation, this sets our compass and points the course which we are to steer through the ocean of time opening on us. And never could we embark on it under circumstances more auspicious. Our first and fundamental maxim should be, never to entangle ourselves in the broils of Europe. Our second, never to suffer Europe to intermeddle with cis-Atlantic affairs. America, North and South, has a set of interests distinct from those of Europe, and peculiarly her own. She should therefore have a sys-

[1]Smith had temporarily accepted direction of the Navy Department under Jefferson, but had declined permanent appointment in order to manage his commercial and shipping affairs.

tem of her own, separate and apart from that of Europe. While the last is laboring to become the domicile of despotism, our endeavors should surely be, to make our hemisphere that of freedom. One nation, most of all, could disturb us in this pursuit; she now offers to lead, aid, and accompany us in it. By acceding to her proposition, we detach her from the bands, bring her mighty weight into the scale of free government, and emancipate a continent at one stroke, which might otherwise linger long in doubt and difficulty. Great Britain is the nation which can do us the most harm of any one, or all on earth; and with her on our side we need not fear the whole world. With her then, we should most sedulously cherish a cordial friendship; and nothing would tend more to knit our affections than to be fighting once more, side by side, in the same cause. Not that I would purchase even her amity at the price of taking part in her wars. But the war in which the present proposition might engage us, should that be its consequence, is not her war, but ours. Its object is to introduce and establish the American system, of keeping out of our land all foreign powers, of never permitting those of Europe to intermeddle with the affairs of our nations. It is to maintain our own principle, not to depart from it. And if, to facilitate this, we can effect a division in the body of the European powers, and draw over to our side its most powerful member, surely we should do it. But I am clearly of Mr. Canning's opinion, that it will prevent instead of provoking war. With Great Britain withdrawn from their scale and shifted into that of our two continents, all Europe combined would not undertake such a war. For how would they propose to get at either enemy without superior fleets? Nor is the occasion to be slighted which this proposition offers, of declaring our protest against the atrocious violations of the rights of nations, by the interference of any one in the internal affairs of another, so flagitiously begun by Bonaparte, and now continued by the equally lawless Alliance, calling itself Holy.

But we have first to ask ourselves a question. Do we wish to acquire to our own confederacy any one or more of the Spanish provinces? I candidly confess, that I have ever looked on Cuba as the most interesting addition which could ever be made to our system of States. The control which, with Florida Point, this island would give us over the Gulf of Mexico, and the countries and isthmus bordering on it, as well as all those whose waters flow into it, would fill up the measure of our political well-being. Yet, as I am sensible that this can never be obtained, even with her own consent, but by war; and its independence, which is our second interest, (and especially its independence of England,) can be secured without it, I have no hesitation in abandoning my first wish to future chances, and accepting its independence, with peace and the friendship of England, rather than its association, at the expense of war and her enmity.

I could honestly, therefore, join in the declaration proposed, that we aim not at the acquisition of any of those possessions, that we will not stand in the way of any amicable arrangement between them and the Mother country; but that we will oppose, with all our means, the forcible interposition of any other power, as auxiliary, stipendiary, or under any other form or pretext, and most especially, their transfer to any power by conquest, cession, or acquisition in any other way. I should think it, therefore, advisable, that the Executive should encourage the British government to a continuance in the dispositions expressed in these letters, by an assurance of his concurrence with them as far as his authority goes; and that as it may lead to war, the declaration of which requires an act of Congress, the case shall be laid before them for consideration at their first meeting, and under the reasonable aspect in which it is seen by himself.

I have been so long weaned from political subjects, and have so long ceased to take any interest in them, that I am sensible I am not qualified to offer opinions on them worthy of any attention. But the question now proposed involves consequences so lasting, and effects so decisive of our future destinies, as to rekindle all the interest I have heretofore felt on such occasions, and to induce me to the hazard of opinions, which will prove only my wish to contribute still my mite towards anything which may be useful to our country. And praying you to accept it at only what it is worth, I add the assurance of my constant and affectionate friendship and respect.

TO MONSIEUR A. CORAY[1]

Monticello, October 31, 1823

. . . . The government of Athens, for example, was that of the people of one city making laws for the whole country subjected to them. That of Lacedæmon was the rule of military monks over the laboring class of the people, reduced to abject slavery. These are not the doctrines of the present age. The equal rights of man, and the happiness of every individual, are now acknowledged to be the only legitimate objects of government. Modern times have the signal advantage, too, of having discovered the only device by which these rights can be secured, to wit: government by the people, acting not in person, but by representatives chosen by themselves, that is to say, by every man of ripe years and sane mind, who either contributes by his purse or person to the support of his country. The small and imperfect mixture of representative government in England, impeded as it is by other branches, aristocratical and hereditary, shows yet the power of the representative principle towards improving the condition of man. With us, all the branches of the government are elected by the people themselves, except the judiciary, of whose science and qualifications they are not competent judges. Yet, even in that department, we call in a jury of the people to decide all controverted matters of fact, because to that investigation they are entirely competent, leaving thus as little as possible, merely the law of the case, to the decision of the judges. And true it is that the people, especially when moderately instructed, are the only safe, because the only honest, depositories of the public rights, and should therefore be introduced into the administration of them in every function to which they are sufficient; they will err sometimes and accidentally, but never designedly, and with a systematic and persevering purpose of overthrowing the free principles of the government. Hereditary bodies, on the contrary, always existing, always on the watch for their own aggrandizement, profit of every opportunity of

[1]Greek doctor, philologist and translator of the ancient Greeks, Coray lived in Paris. There he promoted the cause of Greek liberty, and was unofficial messenger of good will for his people in Europe.

advancing the privileges of their order, and encroaching on the rights of the people. . . . .

TO THE MARQUIS DE LAFAYETTE

Monticello, November 4, 1823

. . . . For in truth, the parties of Whig and Tory, are those of nature. They exist in all countries, whether called by these names, or by those of Aristocrats and Democrats, Coté Droite and Coté Gauche, Ultras and Radicals, Serviles and Liberals. The sickly, weakly, timid man, fears the people, and is a Tory by nature. The healthy, strong and bold, cherishes them, and is formed a Whig by nature. On the eclipse of federalism with us, although not its extinction, its leaders got up the Missouri question, under the false front of lessening the measure of slavery, but with the real view of producing a geographical division of parties, which might insure them the next President. The people of the North went blindfold into the snare, followed their leaders for awhile with a zeal truly moral and laudable, until they became sensible that they were injuring instead of aiding the real interests of the slaves, that they had been used merely as tools for electioneering purposes; and that trick of hypocrisy then fell as quickly as it had been got up. To that is now succeeding a distinction, which, like that of Republican and Federal, or Whig and Tory, being equally intermixed through every State, threatens none of those geographical schisms which go immediately to a separation. The line of division now, is the preservation of State rights, as reserved in the Constitution, or by strained constructions of that instrument, to merge all into a consolidated government. The Tories are for strengthening the Executive and General Government; the Whigs cherish the representative branch, and the rights reserved by the States, as the bulwark against consolidation, which must immediately generate monarchy. And although this division excites, as yet, no warmth, yet it exists, is well understood, and will be a principle of voting at the ensuing election, with the reflecting men of both parties. . . . .

TO MR. DAVID HARDING, PRESIDENT OF THE JEFFERSON
DEBATING SOCIETY OF HINGHAM

Monticello, April 20, 1824

SIR,—I have duly received your favor of the 6th instant, informing me of the institution of a debating society in Hingham, composed of adherents to the republican principles of the Revolution; and I am justly sensible of the honor done my name by associating it with the title of the society. The object of the society is laudable, and in a republican nation, whose citizens are to be led by reason and persuasion, and not by force, the art of reasoning becomes of first importance. In this line antiquity has left us the finest models for imitation; and he who studies and imitates them most nearly, will nearest approach the perfection of the art. Among these I should consider the speeches of Livy, Sallust, and Tacitus, as pre-eminent specimens of logic, taste, and that sententious brevity which, using not a word to spare, leaves not a moment for inattention to the hearer. Amplification is the vice of modern oratory. It is an insult to an assembly of reasonable men, disgusting and revolting instead of persuading. Speeches measured by the hour, die with the hour. I will not, however, further indulge the disposition of the age to sermonize, and especially to those surrounded by so much better advice. . . . .

TO MAJOR JOHN CARTWRIGHT[1]

Monticello, June 5, 1824

. . . . Can one generation bind another, and all others, in succession forever? I think not. The Creator has made the earth for the living, not the dead. Rights and powers can only belong to persons, not to things, not to mere matter, unendowed with will. The dead are not even things. The particles of matter which composed their bodies, make part now of the bodies of other animals, vegetables, or minerals,

[1]Major John Cartwright was a political reformer and author of *The English Constitution Produced and Illustrated.*

of a thousand forms. To what then are attached the rights and powers they held while in the form of men? A generation may bind itself as long as its majority continues in life; when that has disappeared, another majority is in place, holds all the rights and powers their predecessors once held, and may change their laws and institutions to suit themselves. Nothing then is unchangeable but the inherent and unalienable rights of man. . . . .

TO HENRY LEE[1]

Monticello, August 10, 1824

. . . . As to myself, it is many years since I have ceased to read but a single paper. I am no longer, therefore, a general subscriber for any other. Yet, to encourage the hopeful in the outset, I have sometimes subscribed for the first year on condition of being discontinued at the end of it, without further warning. I do the same now with pleasure for yours; and unwilling to have outstanding accounts, which I am liable to forget, I now enclose the price of the tri-weekly paper. I am no believer in the amalgamation of parties, nor do I consider it as either desirable or useful for the public; but only that, like religious differences, a difference in politics should never be permitted to enter into social intercourse, or to disturb its friendships, its charities, or justice. In that form, they are censors of the conduct of each other, and useful watchmen for the public. Men by their constitutions are naturally divided into two parties: 1. Those who fear and distrust the people, and wish to draw all powers from them into the hands of the higher classes. 2. Those who identify themselves with the people, have confidence in them, cherish and consider them as the most honest and safe, although not the most wise depository of the public interests. In every country these two parties exist, and in every one where they are free to think, speak, and write, they will declare themselves. Call them, therefore, Liberals and Serviles, Jacobins and Ultras, Whigs and

[1]Henry Lee was the son of General Henry Lee who was a bitter critic and political enemy of Jefferson. When editing his father's *Memoirs*, Lee developed a correspondence with Jefferson, and tried to make amends for his father's unmerited censure.

Tories, Republicans and Federalists, Aristocrats and Democrats, or by whatever name you please, they are the same parties still, and pursue the same object. The last appellation of Aristocrats and Democrats is the true one expressing the essence of all. A paper which shall be governed by the spirit of Mr. Madison's celebrated report, of which you express in your prospectus so just and high an approbation, cannot be false to the rights of all classes. The grandfathers of the present generation of your family I knew well. They were friends and fellow laborers with me in the same cause and principle. Their descendants cannot follow better guides. Accept the assurance of my best wishes and respectful consideration.

TO CHARLES SIGOURNEY[1]

Monticello, August 15, 1824

. . . . in April last we were enabled to send an Agent to Great Britain to procure some professors, those of the first order not being to be had in this country. for had it been in our power to seduce from their present situations some of the eminent characters established in our American seminaries, it was forbidden by every honorable principle; and a resort to secondary and unemployed characters would not have fulfilled the object of our institution. we considered too that a country which is willing that it's [sic] science should be stationary where it is, may employ it's own eléves [sic]; but if it wishes to advance, it must seek instructors from countries already in advance of them. I know that our pride & prejudices bristle up at the employment of foreigners, but it is science we want, and to this we must sacrifice our pride and prejudices. some difficulties will arise in accommodating to our habits the ideas, methods and manners of those we employ. this too is a part of the price we are to pay for their aid. we must meet the difficulty, compromise with it, and make up our minds, with the honey, to swallow the few dregs we can not separate from it. no good in life can be obtained pure and unmixed we must take it as it is

[1]Charles Sigourney, English-trained educator, had corresponded with Jefferson concerning the plans for the University of Virginia. [MS., Library of Congress.]

offered, alloyed always with some evil. and at what other price have we obtained all our arts and sciences? . . . .

. . . . I have lately been reading the most extraordinary of all books, and at the same time the most demonstrative by numerous and unequivocal facts. It is Flourend's experiments on the functions of the nervous system, in vertebrated animals. He takes out the cerebrum completely, leaving the cerebellum and other parts of the system uninjured. The animal loses all its senses of hearing, seeing, feeling, smelling, tasting, is totally deprived of will, intelligence, memory, perception, etc., yet lives for months in perfect health, with all its powers of motion, but without moving but on external excitement, starving even on a pile of grain, unless crammed down its throat; in short, in a state of the most absolute stupidity. He takes the cerebellum out of others, leaving the cerebrum untouched. The animal retains all its senses, faculties, and understanding, but loses the power of regulated motion, and exhibits all the symptoms of drunkenness. While he makes incisions in the cerebrum and cerebellum, lengthwise and crosswise, which heal and get well, a puncture in the medulla elongata is instant death; and many other most interesting things too long for a letter. Cabanis had proved by the anatomical structure of certain portions of the human frame, that they might be capable of receiving from the hand of the Creator the faculty of thinking; Flourend proves that they have received it; that the cerebrum is the thinking organ; and that life and health may continue, and the animal be entirely without thought, if deprived of that organ. I wish to see what the spiritualists will say to this. Whether in this state the soul remains in the body, deprived of its essence of thought? or whether it leaves it, as in death, and where it goes? His memoirs and experiments have been reported on with approbation by a committee of the Institute, composed of Cuvier, Bertholet, Dumaril, Portal and Pinel. But all this, you and I shall know better when we meet again, in another place, and at no distant period. In the meantime, that the revived powers of your frame, and the anodyne of philosophy may preserve you from all suffering, is my sincere and affectionate prayer.

TO THOMAS JEFFERSON SMITH[1]

Monticello, February 21, 1825

This letter will, to you, be as one from the dead. The writer will be in the grave before you can weigh its counsels. Your affectionate and excellent father has requested that I would address to you something which might possibly have a favorable influence on the course of life you have to run, and I too, as a namesake, feel an interest in that course. Few words will be necessary, with good dispositions on your part. Adore God. Reverence and cherish your parents. Love your neighbor as yourself, and your country more than yourself. Be just. Be true. Murmur not at the ways of Providence. So shall the life into which you have entered, be the portal to one of eternal and ineffable bliss. And if to the dead it is permitted to care for the things of this world, every action of your life will be under my regard. Farewell.

The portrait of a good man by the most sublime of poets, for your imitation.

Lord, who's the happy man that may to Thy blest courts repair,
Not stranger-like to visit them, but to inhabit there?
'Tis he whose every thought and deed by rules of virtue moves,
Whose generous tongue disdains to speak the thing his heart disproves.
Who never did a slander forge, his neighbor's fame to wound,
Nor hearken to a false report, by malice whispered round.
Who vice, in all its pomp and power, can treat with just neglect;
And piety, though clothed in rags, religiously respect.
Who to his plighted vows and trust has ever firmly stood,
And though he promise to his loss, he makes his promise good.
Whose soul in usury disdains his treasure to employ,

[1]Thomas Jefferson Smith was the son of Jefferson's old friend Samuel Harrison Smith, one-time editor of the *National Intelligencer*.

Whom no rewards can ever bribe the guiltless to destroy.
The man who, by this steady course, has happiness insur'd,
When earth's foundations shake, shall stand, by Providence secur'd.

A Decalogue of Canons for observation in practical life

1. Never put off till to-morrow what you can do to-day.
2. Never trouble another for what you can do yourself.
3. Never spend your money before you have it.
4. Never buy what you do not want, because it is cheap; it will be dear to you.
5. Pride costs us more than hunger, thirst, and cold.
6. We never repent of having eaten too little.
7. Nothing is troublesome that we do willingly.
8. How much pain have cost us the evils which have never happened.
9. Take things always by their smooth handle.
10. When angry, count ten, before you speak; if very angry, an hundred.

TO HENRY LEE

Monticello, May 8, 1825

. . . . But with respect to our rights, and the acts of the British government contravening those rights, there was but one opinion on this side of the water. All American Whigs thought alike on these subjects. When forced, therefore, to resort to arms for redress, an appeal to the tribunal of the world was deemed proper for our justification. This was the object of the Declaration of Independence. Not to find out new principles, or new arguments, never before thought of, not merely to say things which had never been said before; but to place before mankind the common sense of the subject, in terms so plain and firm as to command their assent, and to justify ourselves in the independent stand we are compelled to take. Neither aiming at originality of principle or sentiment, nor yet copied from any particular and previous writing, it was intended to be an expression of the American mind, and to give to that expression the proper tone and spirit called for by the occasion. All its authority rests then on the harmonizing sentiments of the day, whether expressed in conversation, in letters, printed essays, or in the elementary books of public right, as Aristotle, Cicero, Locke, Sidney, etc. The historical documents which you mention as in your possession, ought all to be found, and I am persuaded you will find, to be corroborative of the facts and principles advanced in that Declaration. . . . .

TO ELLEN W. COOLIDGE[1]

Monticello, August 27, 1825

Your affectionate letter, my dear Ellen, of the 1st inst. came to hand in due time. The assurances of your love, so feelingly expressed, were truly soothing to my soul, and none were ever met with warmer sympathies. We did not know until you left us what a void it would make in our family. Imagination had illy sketched its full measure to us; and, at this moment, everything around serves but to remind us of our past happiness, only consoled by the addition it has made to yours. Of this we are abundantly assured by the most excellent and amiable character to which we have committed your future well-being, and by the kindness with which you have been received by the worthy family into which you are now engrafted. We have no fear but that their affections will grow with their growing knowledge of you, and the assiduous cultivation of these becomes the first object in importance to you. I have no doubt you will find also the state of society there more congenial with your mind than the rustic scenes you have left although these do not want their points of endearment. Nay, one single circumstance changed, and their scale would hardly be the lightest. One fatal stain deforms what nature had bestowed on us of her fairest gifts.

I am glad you took the delightful tour which you describe in your letter. It is almost exactly that which Mr. Madison and myself pursued in May and June, 1791. Setting out from Philadelphia, our course was

---

[1]Ellen Wayles Coolidge was the second surviving daughter of Thomas Mann and Martha (Jefferson) Randolph. She married Joseph Coolidge, Jr., of Boston, in May, 1825.

to New York, up the Hudson to Albany, Troy, Saratoga, Fort Edward, Fort George. Lake George, Ticonderoga, Crown Point, penetrated into Lake Champlain, returned the same way to Saratoga, thence crossed the mountains to Bennington, Northampton, along Connecticut River to its mouth, crossed the Sound into Long Island, and along its northern margin to Brooklyn, re-crossed to New York, and returned. But from Saratoga till we got back to Northampton was then mostly desert. Now it is what thirty-four years of free and good government have made it. It shows how soon the labor of men would make a paradise of the whole earth, were it not for misgovernment, and a diversion of all his energies from their proper object—the happiness of man,—to the selfish interests of kings, nobles, and priests.

Our University goes on well. We have passed the limit of 100 students some time since. As yet it has been a model of order and good behavior, having never yet had occasion for the exercise of a single act of authority. We studiously avoid too much government. We treat them as men and gentlemen, under the guidance mainly of their own discretion. They so consider themselves, and make it their pride to acquire that character for their institution. In short, we are as quiet on that head as the experience of six months only can justify. Our professors, too, continue to be what we wish them. Mr. Gilmer accepts the Law chair, and all is well.

My own health is what it was when you left me. I have not been out of the house since, except to take the turn of the Roundabout twice; nor have I any definite prospect when it will be otherwise.

I shall not venture into the region of small news, of which your other correspondents of the family are so much better informed. I am expecting to hear from Mr. Coolidge on the subject of the clock for the Rotunda. Assure him of my warmest affections and respect, and pray him to give you ten thousand kisses for me, and they will still fall short of the measure of my love to you. If his parents and family can set any store by the esteem and respect of a stranger, mine are devoted to them.

TO DR. JAMES MEASE[1]

Monticello, September 26, 1825

DEAR SIR,—It is not for me to estimate the importance of the circumstances concerning which your letter of the 8th makes inquiry. They prove, even in their minuteness, the sacred attachments of our fellow citizens to the event of which the paper of July 4th, 1776, was but the Declaration, the genuine effusion of the soul of our country at that time. Small things may, perhaps, like the relics of saints, help to nourish our devotion to this holy bond of our Union, and keep it longer alive and warm in our affections. This effect may give importance to circumstances, however small. At the time of writing that instrument, I lodged in the house of a Mr. Graaf, a new brick house, three stories high, of which I rented the second floor, consisting of a parlor and bed-room, ready furnished. In that parlor I wrote habitually, and in it wrote this paper, particularly. So far I state from written proofs in my possession. The proprietor, Graaf, was a young man, son of a German, and then newly married. I think he was a bricklayer, and that his house was on the south side of Market street, probably between Seventh and Eighth streets, and if not the only house on that part of the street, I am sure there were few others near it. I have some idea that it was a corner house, but no other recollections throwing light on the question, or worth communication. I am ill, therefore only add assurance of my great respect and esteem.

[1]Dr. James Mease, one time a student of Benjamin Rush, was a writer and scientist as well as a physician. He was curator of the American Philosophical Society at the time of this letter.

TO [GEORGE WASHINGTON LEWIS?[1]]

Monticello, October 25, 1825

DEAR SIR,—I know not whether the professors to whom ancient and modern history are assigned in the University, have yet decided on the course of historical reading which they will recommend to their schools. If they have, I wish this letter to be considered as not written, as their course, the result of mature consideration, will be preferable to anything I could recommend. Under this uncertainty, and the rather as you are of neither of these schools, I may hazard some general ideas, to be corrected by what they may recommend hereafter.

In all cases I prefer original authors to compilers. For a course of ancient history, therefore, of Greece and Rome especially, I should advise the usual suite of Heredotus, Thucydides, Xenophon, Diodorus, Livy, Cæsar, Suetonius, Tacitus, and Dion, in their originals if understood, and in translations if not For its continuation to the final destruction of the empire we must then be content with Gibbon, a compiler, and with Segur, for a judicious recapitulation of the whole. After this general course, there are a number of particular histories filling up the chasms, which may be read at leisure in the progress of life. Such is Arrian, 2 Curtius, Polybius, Sallust, Plutarch, Dionysius, Halicarnassus, Micasi, etc. The ancient universal history should be on our shelves as a book of general reference, the most learned and most faithful perhaps that ever was written. Its style is very plain but perspicuous.

In modern history, there are but two nations with whose course it is interesting to us to be intimately acquainted, to wit: France and England. For the former, Millot's General History of France may be sufficient to the period when I Davila commences. He should be followed by Perefixe, Sully, Voltaire's Louis XIV and XV, la Cretelles XVIIIme siècle, Marmontel's Regence, Foulongion's French Revolution, and Madame de Stael's, making up by a succession of particular history, the general one which they want.

Of England there is as yet no general history so faithful as Rapin's.

[1]George Washington Lewis, member of a distinguished Virginia family, was one of the first students at the University of Virginia.

He may be followed by Ludlow, Fox, Belsham, Hume and Brodie. Hume's, were it faithful, would be the finest piece of history which has ever been written by man. Its unfortunate bias may be partly ascribed to the accident of his having written backwards. His maiden work was the History of the Stuarts. It was a first essay to try his strength before the public. And whether as a Scotchman he had really a partiality for that family, or thought that the lower their degradation, the more fame he should acquire by raising them up to some favor, the object of his work was an apology for them. He spared nothing, therefore, to wash them white, and to palliate their misgovernment. For this purpose he suppressed truths, advanced falsehoods, forged authorities, and falsified records. All this is proved on him unanswerably by Brodie. But so bewitching was his style and manner, that his readers were unwilling to doubt anything, swallowed everything, and all England became Tories by the magic of his art. His pen revolutionized the public sentiment of that country more completely than the standing armies could ever have done, which were so much dreaded and deprecated by the patriots of that day.

Having succeeded so eminently in the acquisition of fortune and fame by this work, he undertook the history of the two preceding dynasties, the Plantagenets and Tudors. It was all-important in this second work, to maintain the thesis of the first, that "it was the people who encroached on the sovereign, not the sovereign who usurped on the rights of the people." And, again, chapter 53d, "the grievances under which the English labored [to wit: whipping, pillorying, cropping, imprisoning, fining, etc.,] when considered in themselves, without regard to the Constitution, scarcely deserve the name, nor were they either burdensome on the people's properties, or anywise shocking to the natural humanity of mankind." During the constant wars, civil and foreign, which prevailed while these two families occupied the throne, it was not difficult to find abundant instances of practices the most despotic, as are wont to occur in times of violence. To make this second epoch support the third, therefore, required but a little garbling of authorities. And it then remained, by a third work, to make of the whole a complete history of England, on the principles on which he had advocated that of the Stuarts. This would comprehend the Saxon and Norman conquests, the former exhibiting the genuine form and

political principles of the people constituting the nation and founded in
the rights of man; the latter built on conquest and physical force, not
at all affecting moral rights, nor even assented to by the free will of
the vanquished. The battle of Hastings, indeed, was lost, but the natural rights of the nation were not staked on the event of a single battle. Their will to recover the Saxon constitution continued unabated,
and was at the bottom of all the unsuccessful insurrections which succeeded in subsequent times. The victors and vanquished continued in
a state of living hostility, and the nation may still say, after losing the
battle of Hastings,

> "What though the field is lost?
> All is not lost; the unconquerable will
> And study of revenge, immortal hate
> And courage never to submit or yield."

The government of a nation may be usurped by the forcible intrusion of an individual into the throne. But to conquer its will, so as to
rest the right on that, the only legitimate basis, requires long acquiescence and cessation of all opposition. The Whig historians of England,
therefore, have always gone back to the Saxon period for the true principles of their constitution, while the Tories and Hume, their
Coryphæus, date it from the Norman conquest, and hence conclude
that the continual claim by the nation of the good old Saxon laws, and
the struggles to recover them, were "encroachments of the people on
the crown, and not usurpations of the crown on the people." Hume,
with Brodie, should be the last histories of England to be read. If first
read, Hume makes an English Tory, from whence it is an easy step to
American Toryism. But there is a history, by Baxter, in which, abridg-
ing somewhat by leaving out some entire incidents as less interesting
now than when Hume wrote, he has given the rest in the identical
words of Hume, except that when he comes to a fact falsified, he states
it truly, and when to a suppression of truth, he supplies it, never otherwise changing a word. It is, in fact, an editic expurgation of Hume.
Those who shrink from the volume of Rapin, may read this first, and
from this lay a first foundation in a basis of truth.

For modern continental history, a very general idea may be first aimed at, leaving for future and occasional reading the particular histories of such countries as may excite curiosity at the time. This may be obtained from Mollet's Northern Antiquities, Vol. Esprit et Mœurs des Nations, Millot's Modern History, Russel's Modern Europe, Hallam's Middle Ages, and Robertson's Charles V. . . . .

TO JAMES MADISON

Monticello, February 17, 1826

. . . . In the selection of our Law Professor,[1] we must be rigorously attentive to his political principles. You will recollect that before the Revolution, Coke Littleton was the universal elementary book of law students, and a sounder Whig never wrote, nor of profounder learning in the orthodox doctrines of the British constitution, or in what were called English liberties. You remember also that our lawyers were then all Whigs. But when his black-letter text, and uncouth but cunning learning got out of fashion, and the honeyed Mansfieldism of Blackstone became the students' hornbook, from that moment, that profession (the nursery of our Congress) began to slide into toryism, and nearly all the young brood of lawyers now are of that hue. They suppose themselves, indeed, to be Whigs, because they no longer know what Whigism or republicanism means. It is in our seminary that that vestal flame is to be kept alive; it is thence it is to spread anew over our own and the sister States. If we are true and vigilant in our trust, within a dozen or twenty years a majority of our own legislature will be from one school, and many disciples will have carried its doctrines home with them to their several States, and will have leavened thus the whole mass. New York has taken strong ground in vindication of the Constitution; South Carolina had already done the same. Although I was against our leading, I am equally against omitting to follow in the same line, and backing them firmly; and I hope that yourself or some other will mark out the track to be pursued by us.

You will have seen in the newspapers some proceedings in the legislature, which have cost me much mortification. My own debts had

[1]For the University of Virginia.

become considerable, but not beyond the effect of some lopping of property, which would have been little felt, when our friend Nicholas[1] gave me the *coup de grace*. Ever since that I have been paying twelve hundred dollars a year interest on his debt, which, with my own, was absorbing so much of my annual income, as that the maintenance of my family was making deep and rapid inroads on my capital, and had already done it. Still, sales at a fair price would leave me completely provided. Had crops and prices for several years been such as to maintain a steady competition of substantial bidders at market, all would have been safe. But the long succession of years of stunted crops, of reduced prices, the general prostration of the farming business, under levies for the support of manufacturers, etc., with the calamitous fluctuations of value in our paper medium, have kept agriculture in a state of abject depression, which has peopled the Western States by silently breaking up those on the Atlantic, and glutted the land market, while it drew off its bidders. In such a state of things, property has lost its character of being a resource for debts. High land in Bedford, which, in the days of our plethory, sold readily for from fifty to one hundred dollars the acre, (and such sales were many then,) would not now sell for more than from ten to twenty dollars, or one-quarter or one-fifth of its former price. Reflecting on these things, the practice occurred to me, of selling, on fair valuation, and by way of lottery, often resorted to before the Revolution to effect large sales, and still in constant usage in every State for individual as well as corporation purposes. If it is permitted in my case, my lands here alone, with the mills, etc., will pay everything, and leave me Monticello and a farm free. If refused, I must sell everything here, perhaps considerably in Bedford, move thither with my family, where I have not even a log hut to put my head into, and whether ground for burial, will depend on the depredations which, under the form of sales, shall have been committed on my property. The question then with me was *ultrum horum?* But why afflict you with these details? Indeed, I cannot tell, unless pains are lessened by communication with a friend. The friendship which has subsisted between

---

[1]Name deleted in Memorial Edition. Jefferson had endorsed a $20,000 note for his friend and fellow-statesman Wilson Cary Nicholas. Nicholas's default of this note caused Jefferson acute financial distress.

us, now half a century, and the harmony of our political principles and pursuits, have been sources of constant happiness to me through that long period. And if I remove beyond the reach of attentions to the University, or beyond the bourne of life itself, as I soon must, it is a comfort to leave that institution under your care, and an assurance that it will not be wanting. It has also been a great solace to me, to believe that you are engaged in vindicating to posterity the course we have pursued for preserving to them, in all their purity, the blessings of self-government, which we had assisted too in acquiring for them. If ever the earth has beheld a system of administration conducted with a single and steadfast eye to the general interest and happiness of those committed to it, one which, protected by truth, can never know reproach, it is that to which our lives have been devoted. To myself you have been a pillar of support through life. Take care of me when dead, and be assured that I shall leave with you my last affections.

TO ROGER C. WEIGHTMAN[1]

Monticello, June 24, 1826

RESPECTED SIR,—The kind invitation I receive from you, on the part of the citizens of the city of Washington, to be present with them at their celebration on the fiftieth anniversary of American Independence, as one of the surviving signers of an instrument pregnant with our own, and the fate of the world, is most flattering to myself, and heightened by the honorable accompaniment proposed for the comfort of such a journey. It adds sensibly to the sufferings of sickness, to be deprived by it of a personal participation in the rejoicings of that day. But acquiescence is a duty, under circumstances not placed among those we are permitted to control. I should, indeed, with peculiar delight, have met and exchanged there congratulations personally with the small band, the remnant of that host of worthies, who joined with us on that day, in the bold and doubtful election we were to make for

---

[1]Roger C. Weightman, as chairman of a proposed Independence Day celebration in Washington, had written Jefferson asking him to be present at the ceremonies. Jefferson's reply, written less than two weeks before his death, is his last extant letter.

our country, between submission or the sword; and to have enjoyed with them the consolatory fact, that our fellow citizens, after half a century of experience and prosperity, continue to approve the choice we made. May it be to the world, what I believe it will be (to some parts sooner, to others later, but finally to all), the signal of arousing men to burst the chains under which monkish ignorance and superstition had persuaded them to bind themselves, and to assume the blessings and security of self-government. That form which we have substituted, restores the free right to the unbounded exercise of reason and freedom of opinion. All eyes are opened, or opening, to the rights of man. The general spread of the light of science has already laid open to every view the palpable truth, that the mass of mankind has not been born with saddles on their backs, nor a favored few booted and spurred, ready to ride them legitimately, by the grace of God. These are grounds of hope for others. For ourselves, let the annual return of this day forever refresh our recollections of these rights, and an undiminished devotion to them.

I will ask permission here to express the pleasure with which I should have met my ancient neighbors of the city of Washington and its vicinities, with whom I passed so many years of a pleasing social intercourse; an intercourse which so much relieved the anxieties of the public cares, and left impressions so deeply engraved in my affections, as never to be forgotten. With my regret that ill health forbids me the gratification of an acceptance, be pleased to receive for yourself and those for whom you write, the assurance of my highest respect and friendly attachments.

Index

Abolition of slavery, 586–587
Aborigines, American, 211–212
"Academical village," xl
Academy of Sciences, French, 467
Acoustics, 590
Act of Virginia for establishing religious freedom, text, 289–291
Acts, Great Britain, for securing His Majesty's Dockyards, Magazines, etc., 282
Adams, Abigail (Smith), 79, 484, 558, 560, 630n; letters to, 618–620
—John, xxi, xxxi–xxxiii, 14, 16, 19, 22, 30, 51, 59–62, 79–80, 117–118, 120, 271, 464, 494–496, 509n, 566n, 612, 621, 627; TJ's relations with, 557–561; letters to, 401–403, 465–466, 483–484, 493, 564–566, 573–575, 577–580, 586, 609–610, 618, 630, 639–640, 641, 644–645, 654–655
—John Quincy, xxxviii
—Samuel, 14; letters to, 509–510, 516
Adriatic Sea, 134
Agde, 70
Agrarianism, 259, 526–527, 611n
Agriculture, xxvii, 138, 259–261, 305, 358, 456, 506, 526–527, 529–530, 539–540, 543–544, 547, 564, 569, 591, 593, 611n; encouragement of, 300; European, 389–390; French, 127–131, 134–136, 138; Italian, 131–134; restrictions on, 297; Virginia, 187–200, 249
Aix-en-Provence, 70
Aix-la-Chapelle, 384
Albany, N.Y., 658
Albemarle County, Va., xviii, 13, 457, 459, 586n; TJ's address to inhabitants of, 546–547; TJ's resolves for, xx
Albemarle Sound, 213
Albenga, 70, 134–135
Alberti, Francis see Fabroni, John
Alembert, Jean le Rond d', 583, 610
Alexander I of Russia, 553
Alexandria, Va., 213
Algebra, 590

Algiers, 59, 65
Alien act, 503
Alien and sedition acts, xxxii, xxxiv, 502
Aliens, 237, 252, see also naturalization
Allen, Mr. 511
—Ethan, 337
Allegheny Mountains, 177, 182, 183, 212
Allegheny River, 181n
Almanacs, 467
Alps, 130, 131, 390
Alvensleben, Philip Charles, count von, 74
Amendments, constitutional, 575
America, climate of, 528–529; exploration of, 211
"American," pseudonym of Alexander Hamilton, 478
American Philosophical Society, 510n, 534n, 606, 659n
American Review of History and Politics, 643n
American Revolution, xxii–xxiii, 165, 170, 419, 461, 554, 556, 587, 600, 601–602, 626–627, 651; effect on France, 67; finances of, 113; in Boston, 334–335
American state papers, TJ's, 267
Americans, character of, 387
Amsterdam, 73, 74, 80–81, 294, 462
Anacreon, 349
Anarchy, 371
Anas, TJ's, 109–121
Anatomy, 50, 247, 393, 506, 534n, 590, 592, 593, 654
Ancenis, 135
Andes mountains, 187
Angers, 135
Anglo-Saxon, 621; TJ's essay on, 145–158
Anglomaniacs, 71
Animals, degeneracy of, 168
Annapolis, 52, 55, 59, 110, 111
Anne, Queen, 37
Annual message, 1802, text of, 308–309; 1803, text of, 309–312; 1804, text of, 313; 1808, text of, 320–321
Anthropology, xxxix
Antibes, 70

Antoninus, 349, 520
Antwerp, 80, 294
Apalachies Indians, 181
Apollo Room, xx, 10, 12
Appenines, 134
Appiani, architect, 132
Appomattox River, 179, 213
Archbishop of France, 83
Architecture, 46–47, 138, 365, 368–369,
    384, 385, 462–463, 591, 592–593; Vir-
    ginia capital, 353–354; Virginia, TJ's
    criticism of, 248–251
Arenas, 384
Argiles, 135
Argyle, Duke of, 167
Aristocracies, xxix, 49, 139, 358, 359, 604,
    652–653; French, 83–84, 88, 94, 98, 99,
    446–447; hereditary, 110–111; natural,
    579–580
Arithmetic, 590, 592
Arkansas River, 180
Armies, 304–305; foreign, 287; standing,
    25, 264, 404, 416, 499, 502, 537–538,
    562
Arnold, Benedict, 335, 337–338
Arrian, 521, 660
Articles of Confederation, 166–167, 220,
    391–392, 404; drafting of, 22, 29–37;
    failure of, 75–79, 110; territorial gov-
    ernment under, 291–293
Artists, slave, 242
Artois, Charles Philippe, comte d', 84, 88,
    90, 94, 95, 402, 435–436, 439, 447
Arts, xl, 333, 354, 506, 567; fine, 248, 506,
    591, 593, 624–625; handicraft, 259;
    mechanical, 138, 365, 430–431; plastic,
    201; progress in, 627; technical,
    591–592
Assemblages, unlawful, 287
Assembly of Notables, French, 68–69,
    81–82, 91, 379, 385, 397, 419–421,
    429
Astronomy, 201, 506, 581, 590, 592
Atheism, xxxv, 418, 523, 583, 610
Auckland, William Eden, Lord, 73, 74
Aurora, 555n
Austria, 59, 73, 74, 537
Autobiographies, Franklin's, 102, 103–104;
    TJ's, 271, 620–621; text of, 7–104
Autocracies, 604
Auvergne, 431

Avignon, 70

Bache, William, 102; letter to, 509
Bacon, Francis, 163, 558
"Bagatelle," 369
Bailly, Jean Sylvain, 94, 95, 446, 447
Baker, Polly, 169
Balbec, architecture of, 354
Baltimore, George Calvert, Lord, 216
Baltimore, Md., xli, 51–52, 213
Banishment, 68
Banister, John, Jr., letter to, 358–360
Banjoes, 240n
Bank of U.S., xxix, 116, 503
Bankers, 79–81
Banks, 601–602, 611
Banneker, Benjamin, letter to, 467
Baptists, 636; text of address to, 307
Barbary pirates, 63–66
Barbary states, 574; war with, xxxiv,
    302–303
Barbé de Marbois, François, marquis de,
    letter to, 622–623
Barentin, Charles Paul Nicholas, vicomte
    de Montchat, 443
Bareti, Guiseppe, 350
Bar-le-duc, 81
Barnave, Joseph, 98
Barton, Dr. Benjamin S., letter to, 548–549
Basle, 97
Bassoons, 339
Bastille, 68, 367; fall of, 93–95, 445–447
Battlefields, Revolutionary, 463
Bauvau, Prince of, 97
Baxter, 662
Bayard, James, 512
Beaujolais, 70, 129–130, 384
Beaune, 129
Beauty, theory of, 583–584
Becarria, Giovanni Battista, 46
Beckley, John, 464, 465
Bedford County, Va., 664
Beggars, 127, 233
"Belinda," see Burwell, Rebecca
Bellini, Charles, letter to, 355–356
—Luisa, 356
Belsham, 661
Bennett, Richard, 219
Bennington, 463, 658
Bercourt, 581–582
Berlin, 72

Berthelot, Pierre Eugene Marcelin, 654
Bézieres, 70, 135
Bezout, Etienne, 350
Bible, 399–400; morality of, 577–579
Big-bone Lick, 190
Bigotry, 514, 618
Bill of attainder against TJ, 14
Bill of rights, U. S., xxviii, 339, 404, 405,
    408–409, 412–413, 416–417, 418, 425,
    426–428; Virginia, 253
Bingham, William, 481
Biography, of TJ, 643–644
Birds, 431
Black, Dr. Joseph, 626
"Blackbeard," pirate, 573
Blackstone, William, 663
Blacon, 98
Blair, John, 426
Bland, Richard, 170, 266, 587
Blind, education of, 590
Blockades, xxxvi–xxxvii
Blowing Cave, 185–186
Blue Ridge Mountains, 8, 179, 182–184,
    186, 206, 212, 371
Board of Agriculture, London, 544n
Boerhaave, Herman, 535
Bois le duc, 80
Bonaparte, Napoleon see Napoleon I
Bonne, 81
Book of common prayer, 218
Books, xxv, 166, 355–356, 397, 398, 424,
    460, 552, 562, 611, 641, 657; catalog
    of, 628–629; TJ's collection of,
    594–596; law, 663; list of recom-
    mended, 457–459; selection of,
    348–350; translated, 581; value of, 547
Bordeaux, 136, 462; archbishop of, 97
Boston, 59, 163, 534; closing of port of, xx,
    12, 279–280; port of 281; Revolution-
    ary war in, 334–336; "tea party," 280
Botany, 393, 431, 463, 506, 590, 592, 593
Botetourt, Norborne Berkeley, baron de,
    10, 621
Bouchain, 80
Boundaries, U.S., xxxvi, 309–311, 524–525
Bourbon, duchess of, 167; family, 553
Boxing, 359
Boyle, Sir Robert, 247
Brabant, 396
Bracton, Henry de, 43
Brafferton Indian School, 247–248

Braganza family, 553
Brain, experiments on, 654
Brandy, 345
Brazil, 538, 639
Breckenridge, John, xxxv
Brehan, marquise de, 377
Breteuil, Louis Auguste, baron de, 84, 92
Bricks, 354
Bridges, 369, 430
Brienne, comte de, 70
Brittany, 364; riots in, 428
Brodie, George, 661, 662
Broglie, Victor François de, 84, 91, 92,
    443–444
Brooklyn, 658
Brown, Dr. John, 535
—Dr. Samuel, letter to, 575–576
Brucker, Johann Jakob, 577
Brunswick, Charles William, duke of,
    72–74
Brussels, 91
Bruxelles, 80
Buchanan, James, 353
Buffalo, 190
Buffon, George Louis Leclerc, comte de,
    188n, 190, 193n, 197, 200, 202, 363
Burgh, Ulick de, 456
Burgoyne, Gen. John, 463
Burgundy, 70, 127–128; soil of, 389; wine
    of, 129
Burial customs, Indian, 208–210
Burke, Edmund, 14, 95, 464
—John Daly, 50
Burr, Aaron, xxxiii, xxxvii, 512, 536, 559
Burwell, Lewis, 329n, 332
—Nathaniel, letter to, 628–630
—Rebecca ("Belinda"), xviii–xix, 329n, 332
Bute, John Stuart, Earl of, 167

Cabala, 577
Cabals, 475–477, 478
Cabanis, Pierre Jean George, 654
Cabell, Joseph C., letter to, 603–605
Cabinet makers, 338
Caesar, 349n, 385, 604, 660
Caius Caesar, 354
Calfpasture River, 185
California, 211
Caligula, 573
Calonne, Charles Alexandre, 68–69,
    419–420

Calvin, John 644
Cameos, 132
Cambray, 80
Camoens, Luis, 201
Canada, 184; American campaign in, 335–338
Canals, 314, 372
Cancer, 576
Canning, George, 647
Capital, U.S., location of, 115–116, 293
Capitol, U.S., 463; Virginia, 46, 353–354; Williamsburg, 249
Capsicum seeds, 575–576
Carcassonne, 70
Card playing, 541
Carlsruhe, 81, 462
Carmarthen, Francis Godolphin, marquis of, 62
Carmichael, William, 73, 169; letter to, 411–412
Carr, Dabney, 10–11, 347n
—Martha (Jefferson), 347n
—Peter, 459; letters to, 347–350, 397–401, 588–593
Carrington, Edward, letters to, 381–382, 395–396, 408, 412–413
Carroll, Daniel, 120
Carrying trade, 305, 365, 543–544
Cartouche, Louis Dominique, 573
Cartwright, John, letter to, 651–652
Casa Belgioisa, 132
Casa Candiani, 132
Casa Roma, 132
Cascades, Virginia, 184–186
Casino, TJ on, 132–133
Castelnaudary, 70
Castries, Charles Eugene Gabriel de la, marquis de, 70
Catalogs, library, 596
Catherine II, Empress of Russia, 553, 610
Catholics, 610
Catiline, 573
Cato, 241, 605
Cattle, 127
Caverns, Virginia, 184–186
Cedar Creek, 186
Censorship, 82
Census, U.S., 303
Ceres (ship), 59
Cette, 70
Chalons sur Marne, 81

Chamber of Deputies, French, 385
Chambertin, 129
Champagne, France, 70, 389; wine of, 127
Chancery courts, 39, 50
Chanteloup, 137
Charity, 584
Charles I, 216, 276
Charlotte, Queen, 62
Charlottesville, Va., xl
Charters, of College of William and Mary, 247
Chase, Jeremiah, 55
—Samuel, 29–30, 33
Chastellux, François Jean, marquis de, 135–136; letter to, 340
Chateau de Grillemont, 135–136
Chateau de Laye-Epinaye, 129–130, 384
Chateau de Sevigny, 128
Chateau Thierry, 81
Chatham, William Pitt, Earl of, 334, 573
Chaucer, Geoffrey, 608
Chaudière River, 335
Cheese, xxvii, 132, 133
Chemistry, 50, 358, 393, 506, 590, 592, 593
Cherokee Indians, text of address to, 529–531
Chesapeake (ship), xxxviii, 550
Chesapeake Bay, 170, 213
Chesterfield, Va., 7, 101
Chew, Mr., 556
Chickasaw Indians, 180
Chickahominy River, 178–179, 375
Children, labor of, 127
Chivasco, TJ on, 131–132
Chowanoc Indians, 208
Christianity, xxxvi, 46, 234, 248, 510–511, 514, 519–522, 633–634, 640, 642–643, 644–645; Platonic, 583
Christmas, 327–328
Church of England, 39–41, 48, 212, 252–254
Churches, established, 40, 48, 256, 307, 511
Ciandola, 131
Cicero, 349, 350, 520, 633, 657
Ciliano, 131–132
Cincinnati, Society of, 110–111, 485–486
Cinquac, 177
Citeaux, monks of, 129
Citizenship, 41, 292; laws on, 306; right to, 204

City planning, 462–463
Civil power, 25, 434
Claiborne, William, 219
Clarinets, 338–339
Clark, Mr., 53
Clarmont, marquis de, 129
Classics, 8, 358
Claudius, 241
Clergy, French, 82, 83, 86, 87, 89, 90, 420, 421, 429, 435, 437–440, 446; U.S. 511
Clerissault, Charles Louis, 46
Clermont (ship), 101
Cleves, 81
Climate, 192–194, 528–529, 539
Clinton, De Witt, 563
Clothing, 341
Coblentz, 81
Cohoes, Ohio, 180
Coinage, TJ's report on, 52–53
Coke, Sir Edward, 329, 663
Col de Tende, 70
Coles, Edward, letter to, 586–587
College of William and Mary see William and Mary College
Colleges, 48–49, 486
Colley, Capt. Nathaniel, 101
Cologne, 81
Columbian Order, text of address to, 319–320
Columbus, 538
Colvin, John B., letter to, 556
Commerce, 13, 300, 302, 308, 351, 365, 383, 586; freedom of, 69, 288; restraint of, 82, 321; study of, 506; U.S., xxx, 305, 356–357, 466, 492–493, 496–498, 543–544; U.S. report on, 296–297; Virginia, 258–260
Commercial treaties, U.S., xxiv
Committees of correspondence, xx, 11
Common law see Law, common
Common sense, 67, 381, 398, 423, 601
Common Sense, Paine's, 87, 223, 430
Conchology, 135–136
Condé, Louis Joseph, prince de, 447
Condorcet, M.A.J.N.C., 376, 467, 576, 635
Congress, xxiv, 165, 180; TJ in, 271; powers of, 75–79, 395–396
Coni, 70, 131
Connecticut, 59, 66, 658

Constitutional Conventions, 42–43, 75–79, 395–396
Constitutions, 25, 27, 291; British, 117, 165, 204, 282, 470, 474, 557, 661, 663; comparison of, 393; French, 86–89, 98–100, 422, 435, 441–442, 479, 509; right to change, 615–617; state, 77–78; territorial, 291; theories of, 611–614; U.S., xxviii, 57, 121, 165, 204, 298, 313, 402–403, 408–409, 410, 412–413, 418, 424–428, 429–430, 454, 485, 499–500, 511–512, 524–525, 566, 638, 663; U.S., amendments to, 76–77, 314, 412–413; U.S. attacks on, 558; U.S. construction of, xxxv, 472; U.S. discussion of, 403–407; U.S., implied powers, 503–505; U.S., power to amend, 408–409, 430, 515; U.S., ratification of, 416, 574–575; U.S., reform of, 395; U.S., threats to, 476–478, 650. *See also* Bill of Rights, U.S., Virginia constitution
Consular conventions, 81
Continental Congress, xxi, xxiv, 14–15, 52, 165, 166, 271, 334, 574, 603n, 663; debates in, 29–37, 57–58; disagreements in, 54; TJ in, 271, 391; proposed, 12–13; resolutions, 17–23
Conventions, treaty, 294–295
Cook, Capt. James, 66, 211
Cookery, 455, 460
Coolidge, Ellen Wayles (Randolph), letter to, 657–658
—Joseph, Jr., 657n
Cooper, Dr. Thomas, xxxix; letters to, 580–581, 594, 636–637
Copenhagen, 96
Coray, Daimant, letters to, 649–650
Corbin, Alice, 330
Cordilleras, 371
Corinthian columns, 384
Corneille, Pierre, 629
—Thomas, 629
Cornwallis, Charles, Lord, xxii
Corny, Louis Dominque Ethis de, 93, 445
Correa da Serra, Jose, 635
Corruption in government, 116–117
Corvées, 69, 82
Cosri, 577
Cosway, Maria Louisa Catherine Cecelia

(Hadfield), xxvi–xxvii; letter to, 367–377
—Richard, xxvi, 367, 377
Côte, 129
Cotton, 539–540
Cotton gin, Whitney's, 483
Counties, 48–49
Courts of chancery, 39
Cowes, xxvii, 59–60, 101
Cowpasture river, 185
Coxe, Tench, letter to, 484–485
Craney Island, Virginia, 178
Craven, John, 511
Creve-Coeur, Hector St. Jean de, letter to, 379–380
Crimes, 171
Criminal law, 44, 130
Croft, Herbert, letter to, 145–146
Cromwell, Oliver, 217, 510
Crown Point, 337, 463, 658
Cuba, 647
Cullen, William, 535
Cumberland River, 181n
Currency, 567; TJ's report on, 52–53; speculation in, 470–471; U.S., xxiv, 112–115; Virginia, 262–263
Currie, James, 364
Curtis, Edmond, 219
Curtuis, 660
Cussy les forges, 128
Customs, French, 379
Cutting, John B., letter to, 415–416
Cuvier, G.L.C.F.D., baron, 654

Dagout, 98
Danbury Baptist Association, text of address to, 307
D'Ancarville see Hancarville
Dancing, 629
D'Anville, duchess de la Rochefoucauld, 369
Dares Phrygius, 507
Datura-stramonium, 575–576
D'Aubenton, 191n, 196
Dauphin, 440
Davila, Enrico Caterino, 118, 333, 660
Deaf, education of, 590
Deane, Silas, 51, 169, 497
Dearborn, Henry, 506
Death, 630
Debt assumption, xxix, 113–116

Debtors, laws on, 232
Debts, British, 251–252, 392; hereditary, 448–453; French national, 432, 434; of American colonists, 277; public, 79–81, 112–115, 308, 311, 460, 598; U.S., 357, 362–363, 469–473
Décade philosophique, 562n
Declaration of Independence, xxi, xli–xlii, 167, 171, 266, 271, 504, 621, 641, 656–657, 659; drafting of, xxi, 17–22; engraving of, 624–625; 50th anniversary of, 665–666; signers of, 565; text of, 23–29
Declaration of rights, 17, 408–409; French, 91, 97, 421–422, 432–434, 441–442, 443, 598–599; U.S., 76, 426–428, 429–430; Virginia, 253
Declaration of the causes and necessity of taking up arms, TJ's, 15–16
Defense, national, 320–321, 537–538, 550–552
Deism, 510, 583; of Jews, 521–522
De La Lande, Pierre Antoine, 350
Delaplaine, Joseph, letter to, 620–621
de la Tour, 129
Delaware, 57, 493
De Lorne, 456
Democracy, xxxiv, xli–xlii; American, xvii; principles of, 272
Democratic societies, 485
Democrats, 653
Demonism, 418
Denmark, 59, 61, 62, 65
Descartes, René, 255
Despotisms, 92, 300, 414–415, 444, 492, 624, 641; elective, 222
Destutt de Tracy, Alexandre César Victor Charles, 572–573, 580–581, 618, 640; discussion of work of, 605–609
"Dialogue between my head & my heart," TJ's, xxvi, 367–377
Diana, sculpture of, 130, 384
Dickinson, John, 13, 15–17, 23, 574; letter to, 513–514
Dictators, xxiii, 229–230
Diderot, Denis, 583, 610, 644
Diet, 630–631
Dieuze, 81
Dijon, 129
Dinwiddie, Robert, 266
Diodorus Siculus, 349, 660

Dion, 660
Diplomacy, 63
Discourses on Davila, Adams', 118
Disease, theory of, 534–535
d'Ivernois, François, letter to, 486–488
Dodge, Nehemiah, 307
Dogs, shepherd, 461, 546
Don Quixote, 455
Donald, Alexander, letter to, 408–410
Dorset, Duke of, 74
Douglass, Rev. William, 8
Dramatists, xviii
Drawing, 386, 629
Dress, advice on, 341
Drunkenness, 356, 359
Dryden, John, 629
Duane, William, 581; letters to, 555,
    561–562, 572–573
Dufief, Nicholas Gouin, letter to, 581–582
Dugnani, Antonia, count, 625–626
Dumaril, 654
Dumb, education of, 590
"Dungeness," Va., 7
Dunmore, John Murray, Earl of, xx, 11,
    12, 15, 335
Dupont de Nemours, Pierre Samuel, 508,
    606; letters to, 536, 545–546
Duport, Adrien, 98
Dusseldorf, 81
Duties, import, 296–297
Duty, 520–521
Dutch, treaty with Great Britain, 56–57
Duysberg, 81

"Earth belongs to the living," 449–453,
    483–484, 500, 549, 616–617, 651–652
East India Co., 280
Eclectics, 578
Economists, political, 526
Economy, government, xxxiv, 314, 615;
    household, 629
Eden, Lord *see* Auckland
Eddystone lighthouse, 54
Edgeworth, Maria, 628
Edinburgh Review, on TJ, xxvii–xxviii
Education, 170, 314, 383, 407, 584, 585,
    618, 640–641; advice on, 347–350,
    358–360, 386–388, 393–395, 397–401,
    455–459, 540–543, 552, 562, 588–593,
    660–663; general, 554; TJ's, 327,
    540–541, 600, 621, 631; military, 624;

of George IV, 423; of Indians *see* Indi-
    ans; of Jesus, 521; of women, 455, 460,
    628–629; philosophy of, xxxix–xl; pub-
    lic, 48–49; scheme of, 506–509; theory
    of, 489–490; Virginia, xl, 50, 486–488;
    Virginia plan for, 243–248
Egypt, 63
Electricity, 590–591
Elephants, 191–192
Elizabeth, Queen, 213–214
Elizabeth City, Va., 169–170
Elizabeth River, 178
Elk, for Buffon, 363
Ellery, Christopher, 56
Embargo, xxxvii–xxxviii, 537, 554, 564,
Emancipation, 586–587, 604, 637–638, 650
Encyclopédie, 378, 424
*Encyclopédie methodique et dictionnaire
    d'Economie Politique*, 111
Encyclopedists, 202
Endymion, sculpture of, 130
Enfield, William, 577–578
England, xxxvi–xxxviii, 167; history of,
    660–662; TJ in, xxvii; TJ's impressions
    of, 364–365
*The English Constitution produced and illus-
    trated*, 651*n*
Enlightenment, age of, xvii
Entails, abolition of, xxi–xxii, 49–50, 237
Entangling alliances, 408
Enterprise (schooner), 303
Epictetus, 242, 349, 520, 521, 633, 634
Epicurus, 520, 633
Episcopalians, 636
Eppes, Elizabeth (Wayles), 338
—Francis, 101; letter to, 336–338
—Maria (Jefferson), xxxvi, 59–60, 70, 387,
    388, 424; death of, 560; letters to, 455,
    459–460, 502–503
"Eppington," Va., 103
Equality, 341; of representation, 34–35
*Essay towards facilitating instruction in the
    Anglo-Saxon* . . . TJ's, 145–158
Ethics, 8, 506, 590, 592, 603; parative,
    577–579; Jewish, 521, 522; of Jesus,
    520, 522
Etiquette, American, 410
Euripides, 349
Europe, climate of, 528–529; education in,
    358–360; inequalities in, 381–382;
    opinions on U.S., 362–363; politics in,

396–397; society in, 341–342, 355–356; U.S. relations with, 408, 646–648; wars in, 413–414, 566

Euthanasia, 576

Evans, Lewis, 181

Executive power, 69, 75, 98, 116, 378, 391, 395–396, 424–425, 429–430, 492, 613, 650; constitutional limits on, 319

Exercise, 349–350, 386, 394, 398–399, 563, 634

Exile, 82

Exports, 343–345, 351

Extravagance, 365

Fabroni, John [correction for Francis Alberti], letter to, 338–339

Fairfax, Thomas, Lord, 216

Falling Spring, Va., 184, 371

Fame, 347

Farmers, 127, 379–380, 493; "chosen people of God," 259; value of, 351

Farmers-general, 63, 344–345

Farming, 483–484, 489, 556, 664

Faubourg St. Antoine, 85

Fauquier, Francis, xix, 8–9

Federal government, powers of, 377–378

Federalist Papers, 417–418, 456

Federalist Party, xxx

Federalists, xxviii, xxxi, xxxii–xxxiii, xxxvii, 119, 272, 299, 424, 474, 484n, 511–513, 543, 558–559, 569–572, 574–575, 636–637, 650, 653

Fenestrange, 81

Fenno, John, xxix

Ferries, Va. 248

Fertilizing, 389–390

Feudalism, 97, 130, 285–286

Feuillants, 478

Fiction, 332–333

Fier Rodrigue (ship), 178

Finances, French, 419–421; TJ's, xl–xli; U.S., 518

Fisheries, 308

Fisher's Bar, 179

Fitch, John, 626

Fitzherbert, Mary Anne, 423

Flag of truce, 337

Fleschelles, Jacques de, 93–94, 445

Florida, xxxvi, 647

Flourend, Pierre Jean Marie, 654

Fluvanna River, 179

Fontainebleau, 360–361, 377

Food, at University of Virginia, 632

Force, 287, 300, 467

Foreign affairs, 303, 473

Fort Edwards, 658

Fort George, 463, 658

Fort Henry, 463

Fort William, 463

Fossils, Virginia, 187–189

Foster, Capt., 337

Fothergill, John, 166

Foulow, Joseph François, 84, 92, 444

Fourth of July, xli–xlii

Fox, 661

—Charles James, 423

France, xxxiv–xxxviii, 18, 52, 65, 71; agriculture in, 539–540; charter of rights for, 432–434; contrast to America, 341–342; education in, 393–394; government of, 392; history of, 660; imports U.S. flour, 85; inequalities in, 366–367; influence of American Revolution on, 67; TJ in, xxvi–xxvii, 112, 271; TJ's tour of , 70, 127–131, 135–139, 384–385, 389–391, 396–397; TJ's love for, 101, 345–347, 352–353, 500; manners in, 355–356; national debt of, 450–453; politics in, 381–382, 396–397, 401–402, 410–411, 414–416, 418–422, 428–429, 434–438, 440–448, 478–479, 484–485, 509, 598–599; relations with Great Britain, 383; relations with U. S., xxx, 343–345, 476–477, 481, 496–497, 501–502, 523–524, 537, 565, 568; riots in, 85; treaties with, 59, 73, 294–296

Frankfort, Ky., 534

Frankfort-on-Main, 81, 462

Franklin, Benjamin, xxi, xxiv, xxv, xxviii, 16, 22, 33, 51, 54, 58, 59–61, 62, 79, 81, 102–104, 201, 202, 379–380, 541–542, 621; TJ's anecdotes of, 166–169

—William Temple, 103–104

Franks, Col., 59

Fraser, 74

Frederick the Great, 61, 71, 72, 362, 553

Frederick William II, 73, 74, 553

Fredericksburg, Va., 502

Fredericktown, Md., 183

Free trade, 357, 540

Freedom, xli–xlii, 319, 366–367, 431, 479, 486, 489, 665–666; defense of, 320–321; in France, 67; moral, xli–xlii; of commerce, 296–298; of conscience, 89; of discussion, 316–317; of person, 76, 82, 89, 429, 433–434; of navigation, 293–294, 302–303; of opinion, 298, 562; of the press, xxxii, 76, 82, 84, 89, 121, 317, 404, 409, 416, 417, 421, 425, 429, 434, 511, 532, 562, 581–582, 598; of the seas, xxxvi–xxxviii, 61, 302–303, 313, 320, 321, 517–518, 567–568, 597, 599–600; of thought, 272, 429, 641; of trade, 274–277; religious, xxii, 9, 45–46, 76, 171, 298, 307, 315, 404, 409, 416, 425, 499, 562, 581–582, 598, 642–643; religious, in France, 379; religious, Virginia act for, xxii, 45–46, 271–272, 289–291, 378
Freemen, 30–32
Frejus, 70
French Directory, xxxii, 54, 623
French horns, 338–339
French language, 358, 393–394, 398, 423, 621, 629
French Revolution, xxv–xxvi, 67–69, 112, 428–429, 478–479, 598–599, 622–623, 660; effect on U.S., 118–120; Franklin on, 102–103; TJ on, 84–101; outbreak of, 442–448
Freneau, Philip, xxix, 121
Friendship, 373–374, 409, 465–466, 475, 480, 493, 498, 546, 563, 599, 630
Frontignan, 70
Fry, Joshua, 7–8, 181
Fulton, Robert, 626
Fur trade, 66

Gabelles, 69, 82, 379
Galerie du Loire, 463
Galileo, 255, 626
Gallatin, Albert, xxxiv; letters to, 518, 600–601
Galvance, 575
Gamaliel, 578
Gambling, 632
Gardener, 119
Gardeners, 338
Gardens, 138; King's, 369; pleasure, 365, 591
Gardes meubles, 463

Garland, John, 457
Garonne River, 70
Gaspee (revenue cutter), xx
Gates, Gen. Horatio, letters to, 523–524
—Sir Thomas, 214
Geismer, Baron, letter to, 352–353
Generations, rights of, 448–449, 484, 549, 616–617, 651–652
Genet, Edmund, xxx, 481
Geneva, 358, 486
Genius, 199–202, 243–244, 431, 489, 635
Genlis, Stéphanie Félicité, 628
Genoa, 59, 70, 133–134
Gentil, Mons., 135
Geography, 244, 431, 508, 547
Geology, 581
Geometry, 290
George III, xx, 12, 24–27, 62, 121, 167, 219, 271, 273, 281–289, 335–336, 365, 414, 568, 573
George IV, 573, 596; character of, 422–423
Georgetown, D.C., 115, 605n
Georgia, 260
Gerbert, Martin, Baron von Honau, 626
Germantown, Pa., 556
Germany, TJ in, xxvii, 81
Gerry, Elbridge, xxxii, 56, 501; letters to, 495–500
Gibbon, Edward, 349n, 660
Gibraltar, 302
Gilmer, Francis Walker, 658
Gimson weed, 575
Girardin, Louis Hue, 50
Givet, 73
Gnostics, 578
God, existence of , 399–400
Godfrey, Thomas, 201n
Goldsmith, Oliver, 349
Goochland County, Va., 7
Gouffier, Choiseul, 47
Gournay, Pierre Mathias, 80, 606
Government, xix, 139, 352, 500, 665; British, 555; by corruption and force, 557–558; changing of, 598–599; civil, 204, 304; comparisons of, 34–37, 504, 612, 638–639, 649–650; division of powers of, 395–396; economy in, 499, 615; federal and state, 377–378; free, xxx, x–xl; French, 98; good, 299–300; hereditary, 118; importance of knowledge of history in, 246; Indian, 207;

interest in agriculture, 539–540; legitimate powers of, 254–255; monarchical, 111–112; objects of, 24, 441–442, 566; principles of, 418; reform of, 67–68; religious interference in, 636–637; republican, 49–50, 111, 119, 228–230, 453, 487; right to change, 414; Roman, 230, 255; science of, 581; state, 220; strength of, 536; study of, 590, 592; theory of, 603–605; U.S. territorial, xxiv, 291–293, 524–525

Governor's Palace, Williamsburg, xix, 249

Graaf, Mr., 659

Grain, 63

Grammar, 350, 458, 590

Grammar schools, 50

Grand, Ferdinand, 79

Great Britain, xxx, 52, 61, 66; navy, 574; Orders in Council, 596–597; politics, 396–397, 414; relations with France, 352–353; Parliament, 280, 284–285, 334; interference in colonial affairs, 216–217; relations with U.S., 484, 492–493, 496–497, 501, 523–524, 537, 564–565, 567–568, 647–648; treaties, 55–56, 57, 58–59; U.S. heritage from, 555; War with Netherlands, 70–75

Great Kanahway River, 177, 179, 181n, 203

Great Miami River, 181n

Great Sandy River, 181n

Greece, 349; architecture of, 354; government of, 649; history of, 660

Greek language, 8, 170, 244, 245, 247, 327, 507, 621

Green River, 181n

Greene, Nathaniel, xxiii

Grimm, Frederic Melchoir, Baron, 66, 610

Grist mills, 365

Grotius, Hugo, 296

Guiandot River, 181n

Guiche, Madame de, 94, 447

Guillotine, 96

Guitars, 240n

Gulf of Mexico, xxxvi, 181, 183, 647

Gustavus IV Adolphus, 553

Habeas corpus, right of, 76, 89, 404, 416–417, 421, 425, 433–434, 598

Hadley, John, 201n

Hague, 61, 71, 79, 80

Halicarnassus, 660

Hallam, Henry, 663

Halle aux Bleds, 368, 369

Hamburg, 59, 121

Hamilton, Alexander, xxix–xxx, xxxi–xxxiii, xxxvii, 111–113, 114–117, 120, 121, 165, 475–478, 493, 495, 512, 557–558, 569–570

Hamiltonians, 495–496

Hampton Roads, 179

Hanau, 81

Hancarville, Pierre François Hugues d', 367

Hancock, John, 14

Happiness, 89, 346, 366, 372–374, 382, 386, 394–395, 480, 484, 514, 566, 609, 623, 625, 658, 665; morals essential for, 374

Harding, David, letter to, 651

Harmer, Col. Josiah, 59, 169

Harpsichords, 338

Harrison, Benjamin, 15, 16

Harrison's Bar, 179

Hartford convention, 119

Hartley, David, 61

Harvard University, 430n

Harvey, Dr. William, 531

Harvie, John, 271–272; letter to, 327

Havre, 60, 101

Hay, William, 353

Hazard, Ebenezer, letter to, 461–462

Health, 349–350, 386, 388, 394, 401, 534–535, 565, 620, 627, 630–632, 666; TJ's, 552, 562–563, 603

Heidelberg, 81

Helvetius, Claude Adrien, 456, 584

Hemlock, 576

Henriade, 201n

Henry IV, 333

Henry, Patrick, xx, 10–12, 13–14, 38, 42, 170; life of, 626

Heretics, 253–254, 579

Herodotus, 349, 350, 660

Hieres, 70, 130

Hill, Mr., 538

Hingham Debating Society, 651

Histoire des deux Indes, Raynal's, 169

Historians, 660–663

Histories, of Virginia, 265–267

History, 76, 244–245, 506, 547, 555, 573, 590, 591, 592, 593, 603, 619, 641, 657;

as moral exercise, 333; knowledge of, important in government, 246; sources of, 461–462; study of, 348–349, 393

History of Virginia, Burke's, 50

Hocheim, 81

Hockhocking River, 181*n*

Hoffman, Friedrich, 535

Hogendorp, Charles von, letter to, 356–357

Holbach, Paul Thierry d', 583, 610, 644

Holland, 72, 73, 294; invasion of, 73–74; TJ in, xxvii, 79–81; politics in, 396

Hollins, John, letter to, 544

Holmes, John, letter to, 637–638

Holy Alliance, 96–97

Home, Henry, Lord Kames, 585

Homer, 201*n*, 242, 349, 380, 507

Honesty, 490, 515, 516, 518

Hopkins, Mr., 36

Hopkinson, Francis, letter to, 424–426

Horace, 349, 631–632

Horrocks, Rev. James, 332

Horse racing, 359, 541

Horses, 349

Hospital for insane, Williamsburg, 249

Hospitality, Virginia, 327

Hotel de Salm, 384, 463

Hotel de Ville, 93–94, 445

Hotel des Invalides, 93, 95, 445

Howe, Lord and Lady, 103

—Admiral Richards, 336

—Gen. William, 336

Howell, David, 56

Hudson River, 336–337, 658

Humanism, xxv

Humanity, 315

Humboldt, Friedrich Heinrich Alexander, Baron von, letter to, 622

Hume, David, 456, 555, 661–662

Humphreys, David, 120–121, 169; letter to, 428–430

Hunter, William, letter to, 453

Hunting, 360, 541

Hurt, Rev. Mr., 14

Hydrodynamics, 590, 592

Hydrostatics, 590–592

Hypocrisy, 289

Ideologists, French, 526*n*

Ignorance, 366–367

Illinois River, 180, 181*n*, 190, 311

Imagination, 332

Immigrants, 488–489

Impeachment, 284

Imports, duties on, 314, 345, 646

Impressment of seamen, xxxvii, 556, 597, 599

Inaugural address, TJ's, xxxiv; 1801, 272; text of, 297–301; 1805, text, 313–318

Independence, 319; American, 223–224, 335–336

Indian languages, 207

Indians, 26, 180, 181, 190, 272, 381, 382, 523; arts of, 239–240; burial customs, 208–210; conversion and education, 247–248; education of, 198, 302, 308, 311, 315–316, 529–531; lands of, 235–236, 291; missionaries to, 247–248; North American, 197–200; rights of, 310–311, 315–316; societies of, 378; text of address to, 308, 529–531; Virginia, 206–212; vocabularies of, xxxvi, 548–549; wars of, 202

Individualism, 339–340

Inquiry into the Principles and Politics of the Government of the United States, Taylor's, 611*n*

Inquiry into the Rights of the British Colonies, 1766, 266

Insurrections, 26

Intemperance, 442–423

Intolerance, 618

Inventions, 133, 379–380, 430–431, 467, 576–577, 626

Iron works, 235

Isolationists, xxvii

Italian language, 358, 394, 398, 621

Italy, TJ in, xxvi, xxvii, 70, 131–134, 389–391, 396

Izard, Ralph, letter to, 413–414

Jackson River, 179

Jacobins, 119, 478–479, 599, 652–653

James I of England, 214, 216; Statutes of, 44

James II, 19

James River, 8, 178, 179, 182, 186, 206–207, 213, 235

Jamestown, Va., 41, 179, 207, 214, 217

Jamestown weed, 575

Jay, John, 15–16, 51, 72, 100, 412, 574; letters to, 351–352, 379, 422–423, 434–440, 442–448

Jay's Treaty, xxxii, 119–120, 490
Jefferson, Field, 7
—George, 457n
—Jane (Randolph), 7, 8
—John Garland, letter to, 457–459
—Lucy Elizabeth, 59, 70
—Maria see Eppes, Maria (Jefferson)
—Martha see Randolph, Martha (Jefferson)
—Martha, TJ's sister, 347n
—Martha (Wayles) Skelton, xix–xx, xxiv, 9; death of, 51, 340, 621
—Peter, xvii–xviii, 7–8, 327n
—Thomas, autobiography of, 7–104; birth of, xvii; breaks wrist, 70; financial straits of, 663–665; Public Papers, texts of, 273–321
—Thomas, TJ's grandfather, 3
Jenner, Dr. Edward, letter to, 531
Jesuits, 618
Jesus, 399–400, 519–522; doctrines of, 520–522; morals of, 578–579; philosophy of, 640
Jews, religion of, 520–522, 633–635
Jezirah, 577
Johansberg, 81
Johnson, Mr., 10
Jones, Dr. Walter, letters to, 163n
—Wat, 332
Joseph II of Austria, 553
Journals, travel, TJ's, 127–139
Judicial systems, 77–78
Judiciary, U.S., 305; Virginia, 38
Judiciary powers see Powers
Julius Caesar, 558
Juries, trial by, 25, 39, 50, 76, 89, 306, 334, 404–405, 416, 422, 425, 442, 562, 598
Justice, 317–318, 423, 520–521, 600, 624
Justin, 349; code of, 43

Kames, Lord see Home, Henry, Lord Kames
Kamchatka, 66, 67, 211
Kaskaskia Indians, protection of, 310–311
Kaskaskia River, 180, 181n
Keith, Sir Walter, 266
Kelh, 81
Kennebec River, 335
Kentucky, 187; secession in, 363
Kentucky Resolution, TJ's, xxxii–xxxiii
Kentucky River, 181n

Kercheval, Samuel, letter to, 615–617
Kings, 405–406; rights of, 441; TJ on, 96, 553
Knowledge, xxxviii, 355–356, 506; applied, 391; diffusion of, 243–246
Knox, Henry, 110
—John, 636
—Samuel, letter to, 549
Kosciusko, Thaddeus, xxxix; letter to, 550–552
Krumpholz, Johann Baptiste, 369

Labor, xxvii, 579; rights of, 299–300; of children, 127; of women, 127, 132, 135
Laborers, 139, 589, 594; status of, 30–32
Lacretelle, Pierre Louis, 376, 660
Lafayette, Marie Adrienne Françoise, marquise de, 455
—Marie Joseph Paul Yves Gilbert Motier, marquis de, xxiv, xxv–xxvi, 63, 68, 91, 94, 95, 98, 100, 383, 431–433, 437, 443, 446, 447, 467; letters to, 389–391, 454–455, 598–599, 650; Virginia lands for, 364
Lake Champlain, 658
Lake George, 463, 658
Lameth, Alexandre, 98
Lamoignon, 86
Land, laws on 234–236; taxes on, 32, 35
Land tenure, 285–286, 579; British, 364; European, 389–390
Lands, public, 357; sale of, 664; uncultivated, 361–362
Langdon, John, letter to, 553–554
Langon, 70
Languages, 350, 358, 398, 508, 555, 590, 592, 593, 608–609, 629; Indian, 248; TJ on, 145–158; TJ's knowledge of, 621; modern, 50; study of, 507, 508; teaching of, 244–245; theories of, 608–609
Languedoc, canal of, 70, 135
La Pérouse, Jean François de, 431
La Porte, Jean Baptiste de, 92;
—P., letters to, 632
La Rochefoucauld, Cardinal de, 439
La Rochelle, 70
Lasteyrie du Saillant, letter to, 539–540
Latin, 8, 170, 244, 245, 247, 327, 358, 394, 423, 507, 621
Latrobe, Benjamin H., 47

La Tude, Jean Henry de, 377
Launay, Bernard René, 93, 94, 445, 446
Laurens, Henry, 51
La Vaugayon, Paul François de Q. de S., duc de, 84, 92
Lavoisier, Antoine Laurent, 626
Law, Thomas, letter to, 582–585
Law, 170, 207; books on, 457–458; common, 45, 226, 236, 503; constitutional, xxxii; criminal, 44, 69; English, 232, 285–286; international, 313; TJ's practice of, 9; majority, 622; moral, 295; Mosiac, 578; natural, 226, 293, 395; of descents, 44; of nations, 293–296, 517–518; of nature, 288, 318; of Nature and Nations, 590, 592; parliamentary, 171; professors of, 50, 247, 248, 658; study of, xix, xx, 359, 393–394, 459, 506, 591, 592
Laws, 34, 555, 604; evils of unstable, 407; for public good, 24; French, 81–83, 91, 433; mild, 371; object of, 441; observation of, 556; property, 242; reform of, 372; U.S., 341; wholesome, 316; Virginia *see* Virginia, laws
Lawyers, 58
Laye, M. de, 130
Lear, Tobias, 120
Ledyard, John, 66, 67
Lee; peace commissioner, 51
—Dr. Arthur, 55, 266
—Francis Lightfoot, 10–12, 13
—Henry, letters to, 652–653, 656–657
—Richard Henry, 10–12, 15–16, 19, 115
—Thomas Lightfoot, 43, 44
Le Frosne, 606
Legislation, commercial, 296–297
Legislative powers *see* Powers
Legislatures, colonial, 285–286
Legrand, Jacques Guillaume, 368, 369
Leiper, Thomas, letter to, 543–544
L'Enfant, Pierre Charles, letter to, 462–463
Leonidas, 627
Le Saumal, 135
Letter writing, 603
Letters, 643–644; TJ's, 327–666
Letters of an American Farmer, 379n
Lettres de cachet, 82, 83, 429
Levant, 63
Levees, 120, 165, 360
Lewis, George W., letters to, 660–663

Lewis, John, 170–171
—Meriwether, 548
—Nicholas, 457
—Warner, 332
Lex talionis, 44
Lexington, Mass., battle of, 600
Leyden, 80
Libel, 317, 417, 434, 527
Liberties, decay of, 36
Liberty, xxxix, 26, 27, 165, 201, 204, 287, 298, 315, 319, 321, 339, 341, 351, 413, 414–415, 479, 487, 492, 556, 561, 568, 587, 598, 600, 601, 604, 622, 624, 625, 641; individual, xxxii; of conscience, 519; of person, 433; people only source of, 407; personal, 139; public, 222, 381–382, 403; right to, 24
Libraries, 48
Library; TJ's, 457–458; 552; TJ's offered to Library of Congress, 594–596; value of, 547; Virginia, xl
Library of Congress, xxxv, 594–596
Life, liberty and property, 556; philosophy of *see* Philosophy; right to, 24
Ligny, 81
Lilly, Gabriel, 511
Limone, TJ on, 131
Liston, Robert, 73
Literature, 590, 593; classical, 507; TJ on, 332–333; morality in, 628; Negro, 544–545; study of, 349, 350
Little Miami River, 181n
Livingston, Robert R., 17, 22, 517–518, 523
—William, 15
Livy, 349n, 387, 399, 573, 651, 660
Locke, John, 163, 456, 558, 640, 657
Loménie de Brienne, Etienne Charles, 69
London, xxvi, xxvii, 62–63, 72, 79, 81, 352; description of, 365
Long Island, N. Y., 658
L'Orient, 70
Lottery, TJ's, xli
Louis XIV, 450
Louis XVI, xxv, 68–69, 71, 82, 83, 87–100, 294, 345, 346, 360, 379, 383, 385, 392, 397, 402, 411, 415–416, 419–420, 421, 429, 432, 434–437, 439–440, 442–444, 446–447, 553–554; letter of, 439
Louis XVIII, 618

Louisiana, 536
Louisiana Purchase, xxxiv–xxxv, xxxvi, 309–311, 517n, 523, 551–552
Louvre, 80
Loyalists, American, xxviii
Loyalty, TJ on, xxvii
Lucius, Caesar, 354
"Lucienne," 369
Ludlow, Edmund, 661
Luxembourg, duc de, letter to, 439
Luxuries, tax on, 314
Luxury, 359, 363
Luzerne, Ann Cézar, marquis de la, 72, 84, 91, 92
—Cesar Henri, comte de, 70, 97, 443, 444
Lynchburg, Va., xxxiv
Lyons, Peter, 512
Lyons, 70, 384, 462; TJ on, 130

McClurg, James, 332
Machiavelli, 573
McPherson, Isaac, letter to, 576–577
Madison, James, xxviii, xxix, xxxi, 42, 76, 120, 350, 376, 463, 586n, 653, 657–658; letters to, 353–354, 364, 377–378, 382–383, 391–392, 403–407, 416–418, 426–428, 448–453, 479–482, 494–495, 663–665; President, xxxviii; Secretary of State, xxxiv
—James, Bishop, 572; letter to, 360–362
Madison's Cave, 184
Madrid, 73
Magna Charta, 45
Maison Quarrée, 46, 354, 384
Maison neuve, 128
Majority will, 120, 293, 298, 430, 509, 622
Malesherbes, Chrétien Guillaume de Lamoignon, 69, 392
Malines, 80
Malmesburg, Charles Harris, Lord, 72
Malta, 65
Malthus, Thomas Robert, 526
Mammoths, 190–194, 196
Manheim, 81
Mannahoac Indian, 206–207
Manners, 423, 541–542, 555, 578, 653; American, 360, 569; French, 347, 355–356
Manufactures, 138, 305, 314, 664; American, 276–277; domestic, 297, 483, 489, 543–544, 564, 568–569; evils of,

258–260, 352–353; protection of, 308; Virginia, 258–260
Maps, American, xxxvi; of Virginia, 8, 181
Marble, 132
Marbois, François de Barbé, marquis de, xxiii, 60
Maria Theresa of Austria, 396
Marie Antoinette, 68, 82, 84, 90, 95–96, 392, 402, 436, 439–440, 447
Marly, 87, 88, 369; Council at, 434–435
Marmontel, Jean François, 333, 628, 660
Marriage, 359; laws on, 234
Marseilles, 70, 388, 462
Marshall, John, xxx, xxxii, xxxiii, xxxvii, 11, 110, 501
Martin, 132
Martinique, 481
Maryland, 57, 177–178, 260; boundaries, 220; Constitutional Convention, 413; slavery in, 342
Mason, George, 42–44
Massachusetts, 169; Committee of Correspondence, 11–12; debt of, 113–114; government of, 229; opposes Stamp Acts, 10; plan for U.S. Constitution, 412–413, 425, 575; politics in, 570; rebellion in, 406; Revolution in, 626–627;
Materialism, 639–640
Mathematics, 7–8, 50, 170, 200–202, 247, 248, 327, 350, 358, 393, 423, 506, 508, 590, 592, 593, 603
Maubourg, 98
Maury, Rev. James, xviii, 8
—James, letters to, 567–568, 599–600
Mayence, 81
Mazzei, Phillip, letter to, 492–493
Mease, Dr. James, letter to, 659
Meaux, 81
Mechanical arts, 138
Mechanics, 547
Medical students, 411–412
Medicine, 50, 247, 506, 531, 534–535, 575n, 590, 591, 592, 593; study of, 359; theory of, 557, 562–563; veterinary, 591, 593
Mediterranean, 63–66, 134, 305; pirates in, 302–303
Meherrin Indians, 208
Meherrin River, 208
Melish, John, letter to, 568–572

Mennonites, 234
Mercer, James, 15, 504
Mercier, Louis Sébastien, 619
Mersault,128–129
Message, 1st annual, text of, 301–307
Metaphysics, 572, 627
Meteorology, 590
Methodists, 636
Meusnier, Jean Baptiste Marie, 111, 488–489
Mexico, xxxvii, 536
Miami Indians, text of address to, 308
Micasi, 660
"Midnight appointments," xxxiii, 559–560
Milan, 70, 462; TJ on, 132
Military, education, 383; power *see* Power; preparedness and freedom, 320–321; stores, 305
Militia, 205–206, 499, 551
Milligan, Joseph, letter to, 605–609
Millot, 660, 663
Mills, 235, 365
Milton, John, 201n, 349
Milton, Va., 50
Mineralogy, 431, 590, 592, 593
Mines, Virginia, 187–202
Minister plenipotentiary, TJ as, 59, 271
Minorities, duties of, 509; power of, 604; rights of, 298
Minuets, 328
Mirabeau, Victor Riqueti, marquis de, 89, 443
Miracles, 634n
Mishna, 577
Mississippi bubble, 601
Mississippi River, 177, 179–180, 181, 182, 183, 260, 523, 530; navigation of, xxxiv–xxxv, 293–294, 309–311, 363, 378
Missouri question, 637–638, 650
Missouri River, 180–181, 371, 523
Mobs, 412; Dutch, 72; European, 580; French, 402, 437, 444–445
Molière, Jean Baptiste Poquelin, 629
Molinos, Jacques, 368, 369
Monacan Indians, 206–207
Monaco, 70
Monarchies, xxix, 109–110, 111–112, 117–118, 121, 165, 204, 227–229, 405–406, 428, 441–442, 472, 492, 499, 510, 553–554, 562, 569–572, 650

Monarchists, 116
Monarchy, French, 98; principles of, 91
Money, paper, 113–115; public, 214
Moniteur (newspaper), 537
Monitor's Letters, 1769, 266
Monocrats, 485
Monongahela River, 181n
Monopolies, 82; restriction of, 404, 409, 417, 425
Monrachet, 129
Monroe, James, xxxix, 56, 523; letters to, 339–340, 396–397, 646–648; President, xl
Monroe Doctrine, xl, 646–648
Mons, 80
Montague, Charles, 14
Montaigne, Michel de, 490
Montesquieu, Charles Louis de Secondat, baron de la Brede et de, 407, 415, 456, 487, 573; commentary on, 580–581
Montesson, M. de, 94, 447
Montgomery, Gen. Richard, 335
"Monticello," xx, xxi, xxviii, xxxviii–xli, 347, 353, 468, 502, 512, 519, 529, 545, 552, 562; description of, 371
Montmorin-St-Herem, Armond Marc, comte de, xxvi, 63, 69, 74, 81, 85, 88, 92, 97, 99, 392, 436, 440, 448
Montpellier, France, 70, 462
Montreal, 335
Monuments, Indian, 208
Moral: character, 609–610; duties, 295, 572; faculties, 524; philosophy see Philosophy; reasoning, 540–541; rules, 318; sense, 242, 398–399
Moralists, classical, xviii
Morality, xxxvi, 347–348, 360, 374–375, 401, 423, 500, 580, 623, 655–656; in history, 332–333; in literature, 628; Indian, 207; natural, 207, 582–585; of Bible, 577–579; of Jesus, 520–522, 633–636; study of, 349
Morocco, 59
Morris, Gouverneur, 52, 504, 559
—Lewis, 512
—Robert, 52–53, 55, 115, 481
"Most favored nation," 62
Mounier, Jean Joseph, 98
"Mount Vernon,"117
Moustier, Elénore François Elie, comte de, 377; letter to, 410–411, 460

Moyenvie, 81
Murder, 44, 333
Music, xxxi, 328, 338–339, 356, 386, 424, 455, 591, 629; of Negroes, 240
Musicians, domestic band of, 338–339
Muskingum River, 181n
Mussenbroek, Peter van, 350

Napoleon I, xxxii, xxxv, xxxvi, 58, 96, 509, 510, 532, 568, 573, 586, 596–597, 599, 604, 618, 623, 624, 625
Napoleonic wars, 600
Nassau, 81
Nassau-Siegen, Charles Henri Nicolas Othon, Prince, 70–75
Nassau-Orange, Princess of, 71, 72, 73
National Assembly of France, xxvi, 94–95, 440
National Gazette, xxix, 121n
National Intelligencer, 594n
Nations, laws of, 294–296, 351–352, 517–518; U.S. relations with, 300
Natural Bridge, 183, 371; description of, 186
Natural history, 50, 187–202, 350, 358, 393, 431, 566n, 590, 592
Natural philosophy see Philosophy
Natural reason, 204
Natural rights see Rights
Naturalization, 25, 234, 237, 306; see also Aliens
Nature, philosophy of, 524
Nature Displayed, 581n
Navigation, 308, 351, 356–357, 590, 592; freedom of, 293–294, 296–297, 302–303, 309–310; steam, 430–431; U.S., 305, 477, 543–544
Navy, 264–265, 304–305, 499, 502, 537, 639; British, 599; French, 68; U.S., 573–574
Necker, Jacques, 83, 86, 88, 90, 94, 97, 420, 434, 435–438, 442, 443
Negroes, 237–242, 586–587; abilities of, 467; as property, 30–32; first importation of, 39; literature of, 544–545
Nelson, Stephen S., 307
—Thomas, Jr., 51
Neologism, 608–609
Neutrality, 72–73, 312, 320–321, 485, 496, 498, 518
New England, xxxviii; commerce of, 280

New Hampshire, 59; constitutional convention, 413
New Jersey, 229
New Orleans, La., xxxiv–xxxv, 309, 534; defense of, 551, 552
New Testament, 399–400
New York, xli, 77, 256, 658, 663; capital in, 120; colonial legislature suspended, 279; Congress in, 104; constitutional convention, 413; defense of, 551; government of, 229; TJ in, xxviii; Revolution in, 336–337; riots in, 411–412
Newcastle, Va., 213
Newcomen, Thomas, 626
Newspapers, xxix, 352, 381, 426, 438, 448, 493, 495, 497, 652; London, 371–372; methods of conducting, 532–533; republican, 501
Newton, Isaac, 163, 255, 545, 558, 626
Niagara Falls, 184, 371
Nice, 70, 130–131
Nicholas, Robert Carter, 12, 15, 40, 170, 266
—Wilson Cary, xxxv, 524–525, 664
Nimegeuen, 81
Nismes, 46, 354, 384–385
Nivernois, Louis Jules Mancini, duc de, 69
Noailles, Louis, vicomte de, 97
Nobility, French, 83, 86–90, 97, 385, 420–421, 429, 434, 435, 439, 440, 446–447
Noli, 70, 134
Non–importation, 10, 166
Non–intercourse, xxxvi–xxxviii, 320, 485
Nootka Sound, 66
Norfolk, Va., 101, 178, 213
North, Frederick, Lord, 103; proposals, 15–16
North Carolina, xxii, 57, 77, 178; boundaries, 8, 220; General Assembly, text of TJ's address to, 318–319; rice culture in, 70
North Holston River, 191, 192
North Mountain, 185
Northampton, Mass., 658
Northwest territory, government of, xxiv
Norvell, John, letter to, 532–533
"Notes on the Establishment of a Money Unit," TJ's, xxiv
Notes on Virginia, TJ's, xxiii; text of, 177–267; writing of, 60–61

Nottoway Indians, 207
Nottoway River, 207
Novara, 70
Novels, criticism of, 628–629
Novi, 70
Noyons, 91
Nuys, 129

Oboes, 338–339
Ocellus, 644
Odometers, 53, 132
Ohio River, 177, 179–181, 190, 311
Oils, 345
Okisko, Indian king, 213
Old Point Comfort, 214
Oligarchies, 227, 228
Olioules, 130
Olive culture, 132
Oneglia, 70
Opinion, 574; difference of, 255–256; freedom of, 298–299
Opium, 576
Oppenheim, 81
Optics, 590, 591, 592
Optimism, 609–610, 623
Orange, 384; Prince of, *see* Nassau-Siegen
Oranges, 130, 539
Oratory, 590, 593, 651
Orcai, Mons. d', 136
Ordinance of the Northwest Territory, xxiv
Orleans, Louis Philippe, duc de, 82, 437
Orleans, 462
Osborne's, Va., 7
Ossian, 349, 502

Pagan Creek, 178
Page, John, xviii; letters to, 327–332, 364–365
—Mann, letter to, 489–490
Paine, Thomas, xxxv, 87, 430, 464, 465; letters to, 440–442, 474
Painting, 138–139, 356, 371, 591, 593
Palazza Marcello Durazzo, 133
Palmyra, arch of, 354
Pani Indians, 548–549
Panther Gap, 185
Paper currency, 602, 664; speculation in, 469–473
Papin, Denis, 626
Paris, 60, 62–63, 74, 81, 87, 101, 462; climate of, 529; revolution in, 92–94; riots in, 83
Passy, 60, 168–169
Patapsco River, 213
Patents, 430–431, 483, 576–577
Patriot Party, Dutch, 71, 74
Patriot (Reform) Party, French, xxvi, 67–68, 98–100, 420, 421, 598
Patriotism, 316, 319, 353, 403, 433, 500, 552, 556, 586, 639
Pavia, 70
Payne, Elisha, 32
Peace, xli, 300, 302, 308, 312–314, 485
Peace mission, U.S., xxxii, 51, 52
Peaks of Otter, 183
Pedigrees, 7
Pendleton, Edmund, xxii, 13, 38, 40, 43, 45, 48, 170, 236n, 426; letter to, 501–502
Penitentiary, 47
Penn, William, 178
Pennsylvania, 57, 177, 178, 256, 493; boundaries, 220, 266; government of, 229; University of, 534n
Penobscot, Me., 114
People, 569; faith in, 613–615, 650, 652–653; only safe repository of rights, 649–650; source of government, 527–528; tyranny of, 661; understanding of, 501–502; wisdom of, 381–382
Perefixe, Hardouin de Beaumont de, 660
Peronne, 80
Pessimism, 609–610
Petersburg, Va., 179, 213
Phaedrus, 242
Phalsbourg, 81
Pharmacy, 591, 592
Philadelphia, xxi, xxix, xxxi, xli, 13, 14–15, 102, 365, 369, 375, 659; capital in, 115–116; Congress, 111; TJ in, 51–52
Phillips, William, 206
Philology, 548–549
Philosophy, xviii, 167, 201, 202, 350, 374, 500, 514, 590, 591, 592, 593, 655; ancient, 520; Christian, 514; Hebrew, 577–578; moral, 50, 170, 248, 398, 423, 578, 582–585; natural, 50, 170, 248, 350, 358, 393, 423, 506, 547; of education, xxxix; of life, 609–610, 619–620, 633–636, 639–640, 653–654, 655–656

Physics, 289–290, 350, 359, 590, 592, 593

Physiocrats, 526–527, 536n, 572

Physiology, 524n

Pickering, Judge, 78n

Piedmont, 63, 70

Pierrelatte, 390

Piers Plowman, 608

Pilnits, coalition of, 564–565

Pinckney, Charles C., xxxii; letter to, 537–538

Pinel, Philippe, 654

Pinto de Souza Coutinho, Luiz, chevalier, 63

Pirates, xxxiv, 63–66, 302–303

Plans, of cities, 462

Plantagenet, house of, 661

Plato, 349, 521, 578, 583, 627, 633

Pleasure, 584

Plotinus, 578

Plows, 482; TJ's design for, xxxi

Plutarch, 660

Pneumatics, 590, 592

Poetry, 240, 459, 590, 593

Poets, xviii, 200–201, 349, 350

Poland, 67

Polignac, Yolande, duchesse de, 94, 402, 447

Politeness, 496

Political economy, 456, 572, 586, 590, 592, 606–608

Politics, xxxix, xl, 139, 634–635, 426, 514, 542–543, 555, 565, 573; party, xxviii–xxix, 112, 119, 558–560, 569–572, 574–575, 650–653; study of, 393, 394, 506; U.S., 492–493, 514–516

Polybius, 660

Pommard, 129

Pompadour, Jeanne Antoinette Poisson le Normant D'Etoiles, marquise de, 377

Pont D'Ainay, 130

Pont St. Maxence, 80

Poor, laws on, 232–233

Pope, Alexander, 349, 507, 629

"Poplar Forest," xxxix, 562

Population, problem of, 203–204, 526–527

Port de Neuilly, 369

Portal, 654

Porte, 59

Portland, 534

Portsmouth, 233, 534

Portugal, 59, 63, 65; Prince Regent, letter to, 538; Queen of, 553

Potomac River, 115, 177, 182, 206–207, 371

Potter, Susan, 330

Poverty, 127, 361, 375, 594

Power, 571; abuse of, 82; limits on, 69, 76–79, 89, 91; vs freedom, 316–317; vs right, 318; vs virtue, 579; veto, 43, 75, 391

Powers, 651–652; balance of, 75; civil, 25, 287; concentration of, 303–304; constitutional, 309; division of, 377–378, 404, 424–425, 429–430, 504, 603–605; executive, 69, 220, 228; federal, 78–79; implied, 395, 503–505; judiciary, 25, 75, 98, 220, 391, 404, 410, 424, 426, 430, 492, 504, 613; legislative, 24–25, 75, 98, 116, 220, 395, 404, 424, 429–430, 475, 492, 504, 613, 650; military, 25, 287, 300, 434; taxing, 69

Powhatan Indians, 206–207

Powtewatamie Indians, text of address to, 308

Praetorian Palace, 384

Prejudice, 366–367

Presbyterians, 40, 636–637

President, John Adams as, 493–498, 558–561; TJ as, xxxi, xxxiii–xxxviii, 271, 512–513, 545–547, 550, 625–626; eligibility of, 76–77, 319, 402–403, 405–406, 409, 413, 418, 425, 430, 499, 533, 563; Washington as, 472–473

President's House, 463

Press, abuses of, 527; curbing of, xxxiii; freedom of, 317, 381; French, 419; influences on, 497

Price, Richard, letters to, 342–343, 418–422

Priestley, Joseph, xxxvi, xxxix, 519, 580n, 634, 642; letters to, 506–509, 514–515

Primogeniture, abolition of, xxi–xxii, 38, 44, 49–50, 237

Principles, 272, 288

Principles of Natural Religion, 585

Pringle, Sir John, 166

Prisons, 46, 47

Privateers, 61, 551

Privileges, special, 434

Property, 556; distribution of, 361–362, 594; laws on, 517; right Negroes as,

30–32; right to, 576–577, *see also* Rights
Protestants, 610
Prussia, 59, 61, 396
Psalms, 655–656
Public good, 112, 317
Public mind, 469
Public office, 359, 387, 457, 472–473, 479–482, 483, 486, 545–546, 550
Public opinion, 77, 316, 429, 515, 605
Public papers, TJ's, 273–321
Public records, 490–492
Public service, 339–340, 571, 589
"Publicola," *pseud.* of John Adams, 464, 465
Puffendorf, Samuel, baron, 296
Punishment, 44–48, 171, 289
Puritans, 12
Pursuit of happiness, 24
Puy Ségur, Jacques François, 92, 444
Pythagorus, 520

Quadruple Alliance, 73
Quakers, 40, 234, 252–253
Quesnay, François, 606
Qu'est ce que le Tier État, 86–87
Quintus Curtius, 349

Racine, 200, 629
Raleigh, Sir Walter, 39, 213–214, 265, 266
Raleigh Tavern, xviii, xx, 10
Randolph, Ann Cary, 468
—Cornelia, 511
—Edmund, 120; letter to, 503–505
—Ellen, 512, 619
—Isham, 7
—Jane, xvii
—John, letter to, 335–336
—John of Roanoke, xxxvii, 335n
—Martha (Jefferson), xxxviii, 59–60, 102, 424, 540, 628, 657n; letters to, 341, 386–389, 461, 468, 511–512
—Peyton, 11, 13–14, 170, 327, 540
—Thomas Jefferson, letter to, 540–543
—Thomas Mann, letters to, 393–395, 456, 461, 463–465, 512–513
—Virginia Jefferson, 346n
Rapin de Thoyras, Paul de, 660–661
Rappahannock River, 187
Rastadt, 81
Ravaillac, François, 333

Raynal, Guillaume, abbé de, 168, 200, 202
Read, Jacob, 55, 57
Reading, 556
Reason, 86, 255, 507, 527–528, 549; in religion, 399; natural, 204, power of, 299
Rebellions, 103, 230; U.S., 381–383; value of, 383, 403, 406–407
Recueil de Dissertations, Sauvagière's, 136
Redress of grievances, 68
Reign of Terror, 96, 118–119, 623
Religion, xxxix, 127, 423, 426, 500, 508, 510–511, 519–522, 555, 583, 610, 633–637, 639–640, 642–643, 655; advice on, 399–400; bigotry in, 514–515; comparative, 418; established, 39–40, 298; freedom of, *see* Freedom; in Virginia, 252–257; TJ's early, 331; natural, 585; Negroes, 240; sects in, 234
Rennes, 70
Representation, equality of, 34–35
Republic of letters, 544
Republican Advocate, 556n
Republicanism, 109, 453, 474, 494, 513–514, 516, 549
Republicans, xxxi, xxxiii, xxxiv, 299, 428, 470–471, 474, 501, 512–513, 569–572, 574–575, 636, 650, 651, 653, 663; democratic, xxix
Republics, 111, 165, 612, 622; education needed in, 554
Retirement, TJ's, 562–563
Reveillon, Mons., 85
Revolution, American see American Revolution; French, *see* French Revolution
Revolutions, xxiv, 300; Dutch, 20–21; South American, 363, 622
Rhetoric, 8, 393, 394, 458, 590, 593, 651
Rhine River, 81
Rhode Island, 10, 57, 454; constitutional convention, 413; government of, 229
Rhone River, 70
Rice, 63, 70, 132–133, 345, 539–540
Richard II, 284
Richmond, Va., xxiii, 46, 179, 213, 353n, 483, 502; market, 369
Right, 86; common, 226; of emigration, 273–274; of expatriation, 41–42; of self-government, 293, 564; to employment, 361–362

Rights, 429–430, 649–650; American, 277–280; chartered, 217–219; civil, 289–290, 300, 604; common, 67; constitutional, xxxv, 486; conventional, 219; inalienable, xxi, 24; individual, 339–340, 449; minority, 298; natural, 38, 50, 112, 219, 271, 288, 291, 293, 307, 449, 486, 576–577; of British America, 656; of citizens, 91; of conscience, 307; of deposit, 309; of Kings, 91; of man, 91, 100, 272, 423, 441, 453, 604, 652, 666; of nations, 91, 313, 647–648; of thinking, 429; property, 317, 351, 441, 579–580; religious, 253–254; States, 33–34, 300, 503–505; to inventions, 576–577; to trial by jury, 76

Rights of Man, Paine's, 464, 465, 474

Rio de Janeiro, 538

Riots, 420, 428; suppression of, 281, 287

Rittenhouse, David, 201, 376, 548n

Rivanna River, 179

Rivers, navigable, 293–294, 308, 309, 310; Virginia, 178–181

"Road to glory," 28

Roads, 314, 372, 502; Virginia, 248

Roanoke River, 7, 178

Robbins, Ephraim, 307

Robespierre, Maximilien François Marie Isidore, 509, 575, 599

Robertson, William, 663

Rochefort, 70

Rochefoucauld family, 490

Rochefoucauld de Liancourt, duc de la, 94, 446

Rock Creek, 462

Rockingham County, Va., 184

Roland de Platière, Jean Marie, 481

Romanie, 129

Rome, 59, 354, 358, 384, 385; history of, 660; slaves of, 241–242

Roscoe, William, letter to, 640–641

Rotterdam, 80

Rotunda, University of Virginia, 658

Rousseau, Jean Jacques, 610

Roye, 80

Rozzano, 133

Rudesheim, 81

Ruggieri Brothers, 369

Rumsey, James, 430–431

Rush, Benjamin, xxxvi, 36, 564n, 630–631,
659n; letters to, 510–511, 519–522, 556–561, 562–563

Rushworth, John, 12

Russia, 59, 66, 73, 74, 413

Russell, John, first Earl of Bedford, 663

Rutledge, Edward, 15, 17, 22; letters to, 414–415, 498–499

—John, Jr., 137

St. Andrew Club, 121

St. Cloud, 369

St. Denis, 367

St. Diziers, 81

St. Etienne Rabaud de, letter to, 432–434

St. Feriole, 70

St. Germains, 369–370

St. Lawrence River, 182

St. Lazare prison, 93, 445

St. Ouen, 91

St. Petersburg, 66, 67, 74

St. Priest, François Emmanuel Guignard, chevalier, 92, 97, 444, 448

Sallust, 573, 651, 660

Salm, Rhingrave of, 74

Salt Lick, 190

Salt River, 181n

Sancho, Ignatius, 240

San Domingo, 481

Saratoga, 463, 658

Sardinia, 59

Sarsnet, marquis de, 129

Saunderson, John, 169n

Sauvagiere, Mons. de la, 135–136

Savannah, 233, 534

Savery, Thomas, 626

Saxony, 59

Say, Jean Baptiste, 607; letter to, 526–527

Sceaux, gardes de, 86, 91, 97

Scheele, Carl Wilhelm, 609

Scholastics, 578

Schools, elementary, 48; grammar, 244; night, 592; public, 508; Virginia, plan for, 589–593

Schuylkill River, 369

Science, xl, xlii, 8, 166, 201–202, 347, 374, 376, 394, 397, 398, 431, 487, 500, 506, 514, 515, 565, 580, 589–591, 601, 609, 627, 653–655; advance of, 514

Scotland, 167

Sculpture, 130, 356, 384, 591

Seamen, impressment of, 26

Seas, freedom of, *see* Freedom

Search, right of, 517–518

Secession, 114, 119, 570

Second Thoughts on Instinctive Impulses, 582

Secretary of State, TJ as, xxviii, xxx, 165, 271, 454; TJ offered, 101–102; TJ resigns, 482; TJ's opinions as, 109–121

Sedition act, 503

Ségur, Louis Philippe, comte de, 70

Seine River, 70

Self-interest, 583–584

Self–preservation, 556

Sémoulin, 66

Senate, term of office, 499

Seneca, 349, 520

Senlis, 80

Sens, 127

Settimo, 131

Seutonius, 349*n*, 660

Sewall's Point, 178

Shadwell, Va., xvii, 7, 331

Shakespeare, 333, 349

Shay's rebellion, 406

Sheep, 546, 564

Shells, fossil, 187–189

Shenandoah County, 184

Sherman, Roger, 22

Shipbuildings, 570

Shippen, William, 137

Short, William, xxxix, 432, 448; letters to, 466–467, 478–479, 596–597, 633–636, 638–639

Sicily, 65

Sidney, Algernon, 657

Sieyès, Emmanuel Joseph, abbé, 87, 97

Sigourney, Charles, letter to, 653–654

Simeon, 554

Sioto River, 181*n*

Skelton, Bathurst, 9

—Martha (Wayles) *see* Jefferson, Martha (Wayles) Skelton

Skipwith, Robert, letter to, 332–333

Slavery, xx, 23, 26, 30–32, 39, 44, 167, 339, 342–343, 479, 486, 586–587, 650; evil effects in Virginia, 257–258; TJ's opposition to, 237–243; prohibited in territories, 291–293

Slaves, emancipation of, 9, 49, 205, 237, 637–638; laws governing, 231, 234; Roman, 241–242

Sleepy Hole, 178

Slodtz, Michael Angelo, 130, 384

Small, Dr. William, xix, 334–335, 540

Smallpox, 531

Smith, Mr., 121

—Adam, 456, 526, 572, 606–607

—James, letter to, 642–643

—Capt. John, 8, 207, 265

—Jonathan B., 464, 465

—Samuel, letter to, 646

—Samuel Harrison , 655*n*; letter, 594–596

—Thomas, 214

—Thomas Jefferson, letter to, 655–656

—William, 114

—William Stephens, 62; letter to, 403

"Snowden," 7, 8

Societies, Indian, 381, 382; learned, 544; literary, 621; political, 319–320; religious, 315

Society, 204, 398, 584–585, 594, 652, 657; duties, 307; European, 341–342, 355–356, 358–360; free, xvii; French, xxv; Indian, 378; people source of authority in, 294–296; rights of, 577

Socrates, 468, 520, 521, 633

Socrates and Jesus Compared, Priestley's, 519

Socratic dialogues, 349

Sohar, 577

Soissons, 91

Sophocles, 349

South America, 187, 363, 647–648; revolutions in, 622

South Carolina, xxii, 59, 114, 178, 663; boundaries, 220; constitutional convention, 413; rice culture in, 70

South Sea Bubble, 601

Spain, xxxiv–xxxv, xxxvi, xxxvii, 18, 59, 214, 294, 398; aggressions of, 363; colonies of, 647; King of, 553; quadruple alliance, 73; revolts against, 622; treaties, 65

Spanish language, 350, 358, 394, 398, 621

Speculation, 113–116, 120, 470–473

Spencer, Edmund, 608

Spinning jennies, 564, 568–569

Spinosa, 644

Spirit of Laws, 456

Stael, Madame de, 660

Stafford (ship), 178

Stagyrites, 578

Stahl, George Ernest, 535

Stamp Acts, 170, 278–279, 502, 503, 627; resolutions on, xx, 10, 266

Stane, 608–609

Stanley, 190

States, constitutions of, 612; debts of, xxix, 113–116; powers of, 75, 377–378, 395, 403–405, 603–605; western, 536

States General, France, 71, 72, 82–83, 86, 411, 415–416, 419–421, 428–429, 433–437, 438–440, 442–443

States' rights, 33–34, 110, 638, 650

Steam engines, 365

Steam navigation, 430–431, 626

Sterne, Laurence, 333, 398

Sterrett, Andrew, 303

Steuben, Frederick William A. H. F., baron von, 110, 412

Stewart, Dugald, 640

Stillwater battlefield, 463

Stith, William, 265–266

Strasburg, 81, 462

Stuart, Archibald, letter to, 362–364

—House of, 555, 661–662

Suffolk, 178

Suffrage, 221, 246

Suffren, Pierre André, bailli de, 73

Sugar, 539

Sullivan, James, letter to, 533–534

Sully, 660

Summary View of the Rights of British America, TJ's, xx, 14, 271; text of, 273–289

Sur la Creation du Monde, 581–582

Surgery, 506, 534n, 591, 592

Sweden, 65, 413

Swift, Jonathan, 349

Tacitus, 349n, 399, 573, 651, 660

Tailles, 82

Taliaferro, Richard, 171

Talleyrand-Perigord, Charles Maurice de, xxxii

Talmud, 577

Tammany Society, text of address to, 319–320

Tarleton, Banastre, xxii

Tarquin, 573

Tasso, 201n

Taxation, xxx, xxxiv, 29–32, 218, 219, 362; right of, 89, 100, 288–289; theories of, 606–607

Taxes, 68, 311, 404, 502, 601, 613, 615,

646; French, 82, 83, 397, 433, 434; land, 32, 35; limit on, 69; power to collect, 460; reduction of, 314; tea, 100, 278, 280; U.S., 469–473

Taylor, John, letter to, 611–614

Temperance, 356, 359, 632, 646

Temple, William, 56

Tende, 131

Tennessee River, 181n, 190, 191

"Tennis court oath," 435, 598

Terence, 242, 349

Territory, western, government for, 291–293

Tessé, comtesse de, letter to, 384–385

Texas, xxxvi

Theism, 610

Theology, 591, 592

Thompson, Mr., 332, 629

—General, 337

Thomson, Charles, letters to, 603, 620

Threshing machines, 482

Thucydides, 349, 350, 660

Thulemeyer, Baron, 61

Tiber Creek, 462

Ticknor, George, letter to, 624

Ticonderoga, 463, 658

Tiers–Etat, 84, 86, 87, 89, 90, 421, 429, 436, 437, 438, 439, 440, 471

Timaeus, 644

Tithes, 82, 97

Tobacco, 247, 357, 539; evils of culture of, 260–262; French monopoly of, 63, 343–345

Tories, 121, 251, 252, 365, 574, 643, 650, 653, 662

Torture, 69, 82

Toul, 81

Toulon, 70

Toulouse, 70, 419

Tour du Pin, 97

Touraine, 136

Tours, 135–136

Tracy, Nathaniel, 59

Trade, 219; free, 19, 273–277, 344–345

Traite d'Economie Politique, Say's, 527

Travel, disadvantages of, 400–401

Travel journals, TJ's, 127–139

Travels in United States of America, Melish's, 568n

Treason, 44

Treaties, xxxiv, 52, 55–57, 59, 61–63, 96,

178, 180, 296–297, 345; right to renounce, 294–296; U.S., xxx, 59, 63–66, 73–74, 119–120, 165, 309, 504, 525

Treatise on Political Economy, Destutt de Tracy's, 605–609

"Tree of liberty," 403

Trenton, 52

Tresilian, Sir Robert, 284

Tripoli, 59, 302

Trist, Elizabeth, letter to, 346–347
—Nicholas P., 346n, 509n
—Virginia Jefferson (Randolph), 346n, 509n

Troy, 658

Trumbull, John, 368; letter to, 624–625

Truth, xl, xlii, 333, 348, 527, 532–533, 549, 582–583, 641

"Tuckahoe," Va., xvii, 102

Tudor, House of, 555, 661

Tuileries, 384

Tull, Jethro, 482

Tunis, 59

Turgot, Anne Robert Jacques, 456, 573

Tuscany, 59, 61–62

Tuteloe Indians, 208

Tyler, John, letters to, 527–528, 554

Tyranny, 89, 100, 223, 229, 230, 276, 289, 428, 453, 511, 565, 576, 599, 623, 646

Union, 119, 288; division of, 472; right to dissolve, 299, threats to, 557–558

Unitarianism, 642–643

United Netherlands, 59, 70–72

United States credit, xxvii; foreign relations, 646–648; ships flour to France, 85; Treasury, 79–81, 115

United States Gazette, xxix

Universities, 48, 245; plan for, 506–509

University of Virginia, xl, 549n, 603n, 636–637; essay on Anglo-Saxon for, TJ's, 145–158; plans for, 588–593; progress of, 635, 638; professors for, 653, 663, 665; student diet at, 632; teaching of history in, 660–663

Utilitarianism, 332–333, 390–391

Utley, Dr. Vine, letter to, 630–632

Utrecht, 72, 74, 81

Vaccination, smallpox, 531

Valenciennes, 8

Van der Kemp, Francis Adrien, letter to, 566

Van Helmont, Francis M., 608–609

Vattel, Emrich von, 296

Vaudreuil-Cavagnal, Pierre François, marquis de, 94, 184, 447

Veaune, 129

Venesection, 576

Venetian blinds, 133

Venice, 59, 65

Verac, Charles Oliver de St. Georges, marquis de, 71

Vercelli, 70

Vergennes, Charles Gravier, comte de, 61, 63, 65–66, 69, 343–346, 383

Verget, Mons. de, 136

Vermanton, 127

Vermi, comte de, 132

Vermont, abbé de, 94, 447

Vermont, 463

Versailles, 61, 65, 74, 87, 92, 95

Veterinary medicine, 591, 593

Veto power, 43, 75, 391

Vienna, 396

Villedeuil, 69, 91, 443

Vineyards, French, 128–129

Virgil, 200, 201n, 349, 600

Virginia, 57, 77, 112; administration of justice in, 231–246; boundaries of, 8, 177–178, 214–215; cities, 212–213; colonial charters, 177, 213–230; colony, articles for surrender to commonwealth, 1651, 217–219; committee for revisal of laws of, 37–42, 43–50, 171, 236–237; constitution, 213–230; constitutional convention, 223, 271; convention of delegates, xx, 14–15; council of state, 42; counties, 212–213, 283–284; education in, 486–488; exports, 260–262; Fry & Jefferson map of, 8; General Assembly, xx, xxiv, 16, 58, 165, 271, TJ in, 271; General Court, 9, 170; House of Burgesses, xvii, 10, 12, 14, 170–171, TJ in, xx; House of Delegates, xxi, 171, TJ in, 9, 41–50; imports, 260–262; invasion of, 50–51; TJ governor of, xxii–xxiii, 50–51, 271; TJ's *Notes on,* xxiii, 60–61, 177–267; lands for Lafayette, 364; laws, 231–246, 504–505; TJ's collection of, 490–492; reform of, xxi–xxii, revised by TJ, 37–42, 43–50, 171; militia of,

205–206; mountains, 181–183; public income, 263–265; population of, 202–205; Revolution in, xxii–xxiii, 335–336, 352n, 375, 626–627; settlement of, 206; soil of, 127; state government criticized, 612–613; Statute for Religious Freedom, xxii, 45–46, 271–272, 289–291, 378

Virginia Company of London, 7, 214–217

Virginia Resolution, Madison's, xxxii

Virtue, 431; foundation of, 582–583; in literature, 332–333

Vitry, 81

Vitteaux, 128

Volcanoes, 183

Volney, Constantin Chassebouef, letter to, 528–529

Voltaire, François Marie Arouet, 135, 188–189, 200, 202, 355, 660

Vougeau, 129

Voulenay, 128, 129

Wabash River, 181n, 190

Wages, 132

Wales, 7

Walker, John, 332

Walsh, Robert, letters to, 166n, 643–644

War, 70–75, 89, 96, 304, 308, 314, 351–352, 409, 415, 453, 484–485, 497–498, 502, 518, 523, 544, 646–648; atrocities of, 594–595; civil, 33; danger of, 537–538; evils of, 263–265

War Department, 475

War of 1812, 564–568, 573–575, 594–600

Wars, European, 301–302, 311–313, 320, 396–397, 498, 532, 550, 566, 625, 638–639, 661–662; Indian, 530–531

Warwick, Va., 179, 221

Washington, George, xxii, xxiii, xxviii, xxx, 58, 76, 101–102, 109, 110, 112, 116, 118, 201, 202, 336–337, 454, 462, 465, 481, 485, 504, 510, 533, 544, 556, 557, 571; TJ's conversations with, 120–121; TJ's sketch of, 163–166; letters to, 431–432, 468–478, 482–483

Washington, D. C., xxix, xxxiv, 78, 665–666; burned by British, 594–595; capital in, 116, plan of, 462–463

Washington Advertiser, 594n

Waterhouse, Dr. Benjamin, xxxix; letter to, 626–627

Watkin's Point, 177

Wayles, John, 9

Wealth, distribution of, 594; measures of, 30–32

Wealth of Nations, 456

Weavers, 338

Weeauk Indians, text of address to, 308

Weightman, Roger, letter to, 665–666

Weights and measures, 262–263

Wells, Samuel Adams, 11, 29

Weopomeioc Indians, 213

West Indies, 73, 85, 466

Westward Mill Library Society, letter to, 547

Whale oil, 63

Wheat, 539

Wheatley, Phyllis, 240

Wheels, invention of, 379–380

Whigs, 77, 574, 643, 650, 652–653, 656, 662, 663

Whiskey, 646

White, Alexander, 115

Whitney, Eli, letter to, 483

Will, 382; Divine, 331; of nations, 307

Willard, Dr. Joseph, letter to, 430–431

William the Norman, 285–286

William III, 284

William and Mary College, xviii, xix, 7, 8, 48, 244, 265, 327n, 343, 506, 508, 572, 588; disturbance at, 332; history of, 247–248; TJ at, 8–9, 621; TJ visitor of, 50; professors, 50, 247–248

Williamsburg, Va., xviii, xx, 10, 12–13, 41, 45, 50, 171, 213, 271, 329, 330, 394, 621

Williamson, 55

Wilson, Mr., 404

—James, 17, 31, 36

Wine, xxvii, 335, 345, 539, 646; French, 128–129; Italian, 131; TJ on, 138

Wirt, William, 10, 11, 626

Wistar, Dr. Caspar, letter to, 534–535

Witherspoon, John, 32, 34

Wolf, Johann Christian, 296

Wollaston, William, 582

Women, education of, 386–389, 628–630; European, 359; French, 361; Indian, 198–199; labor of, 127, 132, 135; qualities of, 370

Worcester, Edward Somerset, marquis of, 626

Worms, 81
Wyche, John, letter to, 547
Wythe, Elizabeth (Taliaferro), 171
—George, xix, xxii, 8–9, 13, 19, 42–45,
    236n, 343, 359, 394, 397, 426, 540;
    TJ's biography of, 161–172; letters to,
    366–367, 490–492

"X. Y. Z." affair, xxxii, 118–119, 501, 511
Xenophon, 521, 633, 660

Xenophontis Anabasis, 349–350

Yancey, Charles, letter to, 601–602
—Robert, 601n
Yorktown, 163; siege of, 556
Young, Arthur, 544

Zane, Isaac, 185
Zoology, xxxix, 431, 506, 590, 592, 593

A NOTE ON THE TYPE

The principal text of this Modern Library edition
was composed in a digitized version of
Horley Old Style, a typeface issued by
the English type foundry Monotype in 1925.
It has such distinctive features
as lightly cupped serifs and an oblique horizontal bar
on the lowercase "e."